NONPROFIT LAW

ASPEN SELECT SERIES

NONPROFIT LAW: THE LIFE CYCLE OF A CHARITABLE ORGANIZATION

SECOND EDITION

Elizabeth Schmidt
Professor of Practice, School of Public Policy
University of Massachusetts, Amherst
Fellow, Center for Legal Innovation
Vermont Law School

Wolters Kluwer

To contact Customer Service, e-mail customer.service@wolterskluwer.com, call 1-800-234-1660, fax 1-800-901-9075, or mail correspondence to:

Wolters Kluwer
Attn: Order Department
PO Box 990
Frederick, MD 21705

Printed in the United States of America.

1 2 3 4 5 6 7 8 9 0

ISBN 978-1-4548-7996-1

About Wolters Kluwer Legal & Regulatory US

Wolters Kluwer Legal & Regulatory US delivers expert content and solutions in the areas of law, corporate compliance, health compliance, reimbursement, and legal education. Its practical solutions help customers successfully navigate the demands of a changing environment to drive their daily activities, enhance decision quality and inspire confident outcomes.

Serving customers worldwide, its legal and regulatory solutions portfolio includes products under the Aspen Publishers, CCH Incorporated, Kluwer Law International, ftwilliam.com and MediRegs names. They are regarded as exceptional and trusted resources for general legal and practice-specific knowledge, compliance and risk management, dynamic workflow solutions, and expert commentary.

To grandchildren, mine and others,
for whose future the nonprofit sector works so tirelessly.

SUMMARY OF CONTENTS

CONTENTS

PREFACE TO THE SECOND EDITION

In faith and hope the world will disagree, but all mankind's
concern is charity.

Alexander the Great

The law of charitable organizations is important. It is also complex. If you are a law student, you are likely to come into contact with charitable organizations at some point in your legal career. Whether you specialize in tax-exempt transactions, work or volunteer for a nonprofit, or serve on a nonprofit board, an understanding of the practical legal issues confronting these organizations will serve you (and your community) well. If you are a public policy or business student who plans to work or volunteer for a nonprofit organization, these laws may be even more important to understand. Few nonprofits can afford to hire lawyers, and yet it is impossible to manage or govern well in this sector without an understanding of the rules that guide the sector.

This casebook covers the unique legal issues that charitable organizations face. It uses the traditional casebook format to cover abstract legal principles, but it also has a practical bent. The book is organized around the life cycle of a §501(c)(3) organization, the type of tax-exempt organization that is often called a "charitable" organization. This book will introduce you to the legal issues that arise when the organization is formed, when it raises funds, while it is operational, and when it either winds down its affairs or transforms into a different organization.

You will be asked to apply the legal principles you learn in a practical setting. Most of the hypothetical questions will put you in the position of an attorney, a judge, or an executive director of a §501(c)(3) organization. The book is also designed so that, if the instructor chooses, students can create, operate, and dissolve a virtual §501(c)(3) charitable organization over the course of the semester. Additionally, this practical approach offers a helpful perspective for clinical courses.

The book is organized into four units. The first, Starting the Nonprofit Organization, introduces the book, explains state law requirements for starting a nonprofit corporation, explores the fiduciary duties for boards of directors, and examines the requirements for obtaining recognition as a §501(c)(3) organization. The second unit focuses on legal issues that arise when the §501(c)(3) organization raises money: charitable contributions, charitable solicitations, foundations and alternatives to foundations, and the law relating to nonprofits' commercial activity. The third unit, dealing with topics that arise once the organization is fully functional, presents the subjects of inurement and intermediate sanctions, joint ventures and subsidiaries, lobbying and political activity, and accountability. The final unit covers the topics of merger, conversion to for-profit status, and dissolution. Real-world legal issues do not always appear in this order, of course, but this organization offers a cohesive approach to understanding the legal issues. By the time you complete the four units, you should have a solid foundation to understand, reconcile, and act upon the complex issues that will confront you as you work with any of the hundreds of thousands of nonprofit organizations that inhabit our vibrant civil society.

NEW FOR THE SECOND EDITION

This second edition of *Nonprofit Law: The Life Cycle of a Charitable Organization* reflects the legal changes that have taken place at the state and federal level in the past five years, adds some new cases, updates statistics from the first edition, shortens cases and notes whenever possible, and improves on the organization and style of some of the passages. It also brings in new examples of actual situations that have occurred over the last five years, which illustrate both the complexities of this area of the law and the difficulties in enforcing it. Finally, the book delves into more public policy questions surrounding the charitable sector in an effort to encourage students to consider ways in which the legal framework can help the nonprofit sector work more effectively.

The political and economic landscape for charities has changed considerably since the first edition of this book was published in 2011. This second edition reflects these changes by updating statistics and noting trends in the sector. It discusses changes in the number of organizations in the sector, the varying rates of recovery since the Great Recession, and the escalating discussions about salaries in the sector at both the lower and higher ends of the scale. The book also discusses the growing trends in social enterprises, which some see as a boon and others see as a competitor to the sector. These contextual notes should help students place the legal challenges that nonprofits face in perspective.

Perhaps the most striking political occurrence in the United States in the past five years has been the paralysis of the federal government. Nowhere is this more obvious than in the nonprofit sector. In 2010 the Internal Revenue Service (IRS) began scrutinizing applications for exemption that it thought had the potential for being overly political. This scrutiny slowed the process down so much that all applications for exemption, however innocuous, were placed in long queues. Matters worsened when allegations emerged that the IRS had targeted conservative-leaning organizations and was acting in a political manner itself. Investigations began, top officials lost their jobs, and the IRS grew even more paralyzed. Since then the backlog of applications for exemption has disappeared, largely due to the new Form 1023-EZ for small organizations, but areas of confusion remain, particularly with regard to political activity.

Chapter 11 of the second edition covers this paralysis in detail, even though the situation mainly concerned exempt organizations that are not the focus of this book—§501(c)(4) organizations, and to a lesser extent §501(c)(5)s and §501(c)(6)s. The book veers from a focus on §501(c)(3)s for the last part of the chapter because this situation has had a profound effect on the entire nonprofit sector, including §501(c)(3)s.

Neither the IRS, Congress, nor the federal courts have been entirely silent, however, and this book reflects their actions during the last five years. Once the IRS introduced Form 1023-EZ, it began automatic revocation of tax-exempt organizations that had not completed a tax information form in three years. It also completed compliance checks on colleges and universities, studied the efficacy of the new version of Form 990, which was introduced in 2008, and both studied and finalized rules concerning supporting organizations and donor-advised funds. These changes are reflected in this second edition.

The federal courts have also continued to respond to litigation, and the notes reflect numerous appellate cases decided in the last five years. The book also introduces a handful of edited cases for students to read, both to replace older cases and to clarify issues.

State legislatures, state charity officials, and state courts have been much more active than their federal counterparts in the past five years, and this edition reflects those changes as well. Chapters 2, 3, 6, 12, and 13 of the first edition were already largely, if not entirely, devoted to state law issues. In the second edition, Chapter 2 has been reorganized to emphasize the decisions that start-up nonprofits must make and to de-emphasize the older cases on nonprofit purposes. Chapter 3 has also been reorganized to include the topic of bylaws, which were initially covered in Chapter 2, and to consider policies that nonprofits should adopt in order to follow current "best practices" in nonprofit governance. Both Chapters 2 and 3 reflect changes in California and New York nonprofit laws, which are especially important in the case of New York, because New York completely overhauled its nonprofit laws in 2013.

Chapter 4 discusses state law pressures on educational and health care organizations and includes an expanded discussion of state property tax issues. Chapter 6 expands on cause-related marketing and asks questions about the constitutionality of fundraising statutes passed in several states over the past five years. It also delves into issues surrounding fundraising through social media and crowd-funding platforms like Kickstarter. Chapter 8 discusses state cases concerning overly commercial nonprofits, and Chapter 9 discusses state discussions on inurement.

Both Chapter 2 and Chapter 10 discuss state law developments in the area of social enterprise. Chapter 2 does so in the context of decisions made at the beginning of a nonprofit, specifically whether to incorporate as a nonprofit or a for-profit social enterprise. Chapter 10 does so in order to compare the efficacy of achieving a mission through traditional hybrid organizations in the forms of parent-subsidiary relationships or joint ventures with the choice of one of the new hybrid forms that state legislatures have authorized in the past several years.

As mentioned above, this second edition also expands several policy discussions, most notably discussions about nonprofit governance, tax-exempt hospitals, the charitable deduction, private foundations, supporting organizations and donor-advised funds, and political activity in charitable and other tax-exempt organizations. These are all areas in which there may well be change in the next few years, and the students using this book should be prepared to be part of that change.

Finally, the book is interspersed with examples of challenges that nonprofit organizations have faced in the past few years.[1] It includes case studies of Hull House, Central Asia Institute, the Detroit bankruptcy, the Catholic Diocese, and the August Wilson Center. It also covers the thwarted closure of Sweet Briar College as well as the successful closure of the Corcoran Art Museum. Similarly, it discusses the successful effort to rename Avery Fisher Hall at the Lincoln Center and the unsuccessful attempt to rename Paul Smith's College. It puts students in the role of nonprofit managers and directors who have to decide whether to accept gifts from Bill Cosby, the Washington Redskins Foundation, or the former NAVY Seal who violated military protocol to write a book about capturing Osama Bin-Laden, all of which have been embroiled in controversy over the last few years. The book also raises questions about the actions of both the Donald J. Trump Foundation and the Clinton Foundation.

Among the occurrences covered in this second edition is the Chan-Zuckerberg Initiative, the plan by Facebook founder Mark Zuckerberg and his wife to deploy 90% of their assets to improving world conditions without using a §501(c)(3) as the giving vehicle. The Chan-Zuckerberg Initiative has been called an "end to philanthropy as we have known it."[2] I disagree. Philanthropy is alive and well, and a generation of students is eager to improve conditions around the world. It is with great hope that this book can help those students attain some of the skills needed to turn that eagerness into effectiveness that I complete the second edition to this book.

Elizabeth Schmidt

June 2016

---

[1] Professors who are using this book can find a more detailed list of the changes from the first to the second edition on the book's website, http://aspenlawschool.com/books/non_profit.

[2] Leslie Lankowski, *Ending Philanthropy as We Know It*, WALL ST. JOURNAL (Dec. 2, 2015).

ACKNOWLEDGMENTS

As with all work, this book could not have been completed without enormous help from others.

This second edition benefited enormously from the help of those who adopted the book, and I would like to thank each of you who took the time to correspond with me about your experiences using the first edition. In particular, I would like to thank Marion Galston and Carrie Garber Siegrest, both of whom provided invaluable input into this edition. The second edition also benefited from colleagues and students at five schools where I have taught. Particular thanks go to Jackie Bishop, Katherine Colon, Susan Newton, Satu Zoller, Nalyn Yim, Brenda Bushouse, and Obed Pasha at the University of Massachusetts Amherst; Oliver Goodenough, Jeannie Eicks, and Niko Malkovich at the Center for Legal Innovation at Vermont Law School; Lisa Gring-Pemble and Aaron Scott Miller at George Mason University; Rebecca Green and Austin Graham at William and Mary Law School; and Kate Jellema from Marlboro College's MBA for Sustainability and MA in Mission Driven Organizations programs. I would also like to thank the team at Wolters Kluwer that turned this second edition into reality—Susan McClung, Sarah Hains, Angela Dooley, Lisa Brunner, Katherine Russell, and John Devins.

Of course, the second edition depends entirely on the first, and therefore the acknowledgments from the first edition still stand. They stated:

I would like to thank Professors Jayne Barnard, Ingrid Hillinger, Linda Smiddy, Stephanie Willbanks, Marion Fremont-Smith, and Mark Sidel for providing intellectual and moral support. Cathy Livingston and Steve Halliday helped teach from early versions of specific chapters of the book, and students at the College of William and Mary and Vermont Law School provided feedback on those earlier drafts. Wallace Tapia, Gerry Treacy, and Tavian Mayer helped work through some practical implications of the legal principles. Laura Gillen provided administrative support, and Wendy Smith obtained copyright permissions. Their smiling faces and encouragement did more toward getting this work finished than they can imagine. Thanks, too, to research assistants Abel Russ, Patricia Melochik, Steven Campbell, Dana May Christensen, Jason Hart, Scott Sakowski, Megan Sigur, Emily Slagle, and Lisa Stevens, as well as to Cynthia Lewis for supervising most of the assistants. I am also appreciative of the time Carol McGeehan, John Devins, Doug Gallaher, and Dave Mason spent walking me through the steps of editing the book and getting it published. My friends and family deserve special kudos for being good sports when I could talk only about excise taxes and Forms 990—especially my husband Buzz, whose intellectual brilliance and loving support infuses every paragraph of this book.

The following materials are reprinted with permission from the author or the publisher:

1. Jeffrey Berry, "The Lobbying Law Is More Charitable Than They Think," *Washington Post* (Nov. 30, 2003), B01.
2. Arthur C. Brooks, "Charitable Explanation," *Wall Street Journal* (Nov. 27, 2006), A12.
3. Alan Cantor, "Strings on Donor-Advised Funds Are Making Charity Supporters Angry," *Chronicle of Philanthropy* (Aug. 12, 2015).
4. Rick Cohen, "Time to Stop Excusing the Inexcusable: Foundation Trustees Who Play by Their Own Rules," Nonprofit Quarterly (Dec. 21, 2003).
5. John Colombo, "The Marketing of Philanthropy and the Charitable Contributions Deduction: Integrating Theories for the Deduction and Tax Exemption," *Wake Forest Law Review* 36 (2001), 657, 682-685.
6. Robert E. Cooper, Jr., "Why Taking Legal Action Against Charity Fraud Is so Hard," *Chronicle of Philanthropy* (July 23, 2015)
7. Marilyn Dickey, "Research, Money, Personal Support Are Key to Successful Charity Start-ups," *Chronicle of Philanthropy* (July 12, 2002).
8. Daniel Flynn and Yunhe (Evelyn) Tian, "The Death of Hull House," Nonprofit Quarterly (Feb. 10, 2015)
9. Marion Fremont-Smith, "Attorney General Oversight of Charities," Hauser Center for Nonprofit Organizations, Working Paper 41 (2007).
10. Peter Frumkin, *On Being Nonprofit: A Conceptual and Policy Primer* (Cambridge, Mass., Harvard University Press, 2002). Copyright © 2002 by the President and Fellows of Harvard College.
11. Giving USA, "Contributions by Source Contribution" and "2015 Contributions by Type of Recipient," Giving USA 2015 (2015)
12. Arianna Huffington, "Not All Charity Is Created Equal," in *Fanatics and Fools: The Game Plan for Winning Back America* (Hyperion, 2004), p. 293.
13. Stanley Katz, "Should We Kill the Goose That Laid the Golden Egg? Do We Need a Functional Definition of Charity in the United States? (2015).
14. Mark Kramer, "The Future of Philanthropy," Remarks for Panel (Skoll World Forum, March 29, 2007).
15. La Piana Associates, Inc., "Mergers: David La Piana's First Merger" and "Partnership Matrix," http://www.lapiana.org/resources/cases/mergers/09_1998.html; http://www.lapiana.org/defined/matrix.html.
16. Tanya Marsh, "A Dubious Distinction: Rethinking Tax Treatment of Private Foundations and Public Charities," *Virginia Tax Review* 22 (2002), 137, 138-139, 142-144, 148-152.
17. Ruth McCambridge, "Is Accountability the Same as Regulation? Not Exactly," *Nonprofit Quarterly* (Autumn 2005), 3-8.
18. Brice S. McKeever, "The Nonprofit Sector in Brief 2015: Public Charities, Giving, and Volunteering 2015" (Urban Institute, 2015).
19. Marcus S. Owens, *Federal Oversight: The Role of the IRS* (National Center on Philanthropy and the Law, 2007).

20. Lester Salamon, *The Resilient Sector: The State of Nonprofit America* (Brookings Institution Press, 2003), pp. 11-14.
21. Peter Swords, "Nonprofit Accountability: The Sector's Response to Government Regulation," Case Western Reserve University (March 16, 1999), http://www.qual990.org/np_account.html.
22. Thomson and Thomson, PC, "Subsidiaries of Tax-Exempt Organizations," http://www.t-tlaw.com/bus-04.htm.
23. Burton Weisbrod, "The Pitfalls of Profits," *Stanford Social Innovation Review* (Winter 2004), 40-47.

STARTING THE NONPROFIT ORGANIZATION

CHAPTER 1

INTRODUCTION TO THE LAW OF CHARITABLE ORGANIZATIONS

Purpose of this chapter:

- Introduce terminology of and theory about the nonprofit sector
- Consider differences and similarities among the sectors
- Discuss rationales for the sector
- Introduce students to skepticism about the sector

To think about as you read:

Is there a nonprofit organization you would like to start or one with which you are familiar? Does it fit within the definition of a nonprofit presented in this chapter? Is the terminology you are learning helpful to understanding this organization? Do any of the rationales for the nonprofit sector explain its presence as a nonprofit? Do any of the criticisms of the sector apply to the organization you are considering?

I. WHAT IS THE NONPROFIT SECTOR?

Approximately two million organizations in the United States consider themselves "nonprofit." Some are so large that they rival *Fortune* 500 companies in terms of payroll and impact on the economy. Others are so small that all the work is performed by one part-time volunteer. Some are incorporated; others are not. Some take care of the poor; others, such as the PGA, could arguably be said to take care of the rich.

What defines a nonprofit organization? Is there a single concept that ties all nonprofits together? The Peter Frumkin article that follows attempts to answer this question. The two pieces following the Frumkin article introduce you to the terminology used in this book, and the final piece in this section outlines the life cycle of the type of nonprofit that is the focus of this book—the 501(c)(3) organization.

As you read this chapter, think about a nonprofit organization that you would like to create or with which you are familiar. Does it fit Frumkin's definition of a nonprofit organization? Is the terminology helpful? How would you classify the organization? Do any of the theories presented in section III explain why this organization is nonprofit instead of for profit? Would any of the criticisms in section IV be applicable to your organization?

PETER FRUMKIN, ON BEING NONPROFIT: THE BIGGER PICTURE

Working Knowledge (Harvard University Press, Sept. 2, 2002)

Three Features of Nonprofit and Voluntary Organizations

Attempting to define the fundamental features of the disparate entities that constitute the nonprofit and voluntary sector is a complex and daunting task. Yet there are at least three features that connect these widely divergent entities: (1) they do not coerce participation; (2) they operate without distributing profits to stakeholders; and (3) they exist without simple and clear lines of ownership and accountability. Taken together, these three features might make nonprofit and voluntary organizations appear weak, inefficient, and directionless, but nothing could be further from the truth. In reality, these structural features give these entities a set of unique advantages that position them to perform important societal functions neither government nor the market is able to match.

Perhaps the most fundamental of the three features is the sector's noncoercive nature. Citizens cannot be compelled by nonprofit organizations to give their time or money in support of any collective goal. This means that, in principle at least, nonprofits must draw on a large reservoir of good will. This noncoercive character is also what most starkly differentiates the sector from government, which can levy taxes, imprison violators of the law, and regulate behavior in myriad ways. The power of coercion that the public sector possesses is a powerful tool for moving collectivities toward common ends, but it is also a source of strife and contention. Trust in government is now low, making the effective use of state power more and more difficult as its legitimacy fades. For nonprofit and voluntary organizations, these issues do not arise. Free choice is the coin of the realm: Donors give because they choose to do so. Volunteers work of their own volition. Staff actively seek employment in these organizations, often at lower wages than they might secure elsewhere. Clients make up their own minds that these organizations have something valuable to offer. Though they stand ready to receive, nonprofit and voluntary organizations *demand* nothing. As a consequence, nonprofits occupy a moral high ground of sorts when compared to public sector organizations that have the ability to compel action and coerce those who resist.

In some ways, the noncoercive character of the nonprofit and voluntary sector situates it closer to the market than to government. Business depends on the free choice of consumers in a competitive market where alternatives are often plentiful and where no firm has the capacity to compel anyone to purchase its goods or services. Similarly, nonprofit organizations cannot coerce participation or consumption of their services. The sector makes choices available, rather than deciding for others. When it comes to the mobilization of funds, the parallel between business and nonprofits is equally clear. Just as no one forces anyone to buy shares or invest in enterprises, no one forces anyone to give or volunteer in the nonprofit world. The flow of resources to a nonprofit depends entirely on the quality and relevance of its mission and its capacity to deliver value. To the extent that a business firm or a nonprofit organization is performing well, investors and donors will be attracted to it. Should things take a turn for the worse, investment funds and philanthropic funds usually seek out other options quickly.

The second feature of nonprofit and voluntary organizations sharply differentiates them from business firms, however. While corporations are able to distribute earnings to shareholders, nonprofit and voluntary organizations cannot make such distributions to outside parties. Rather, they must use all residual funds for the advancement of the organization's mission. By retaining residuals rather than passing them on to investors, nonprofit organizations seek to reassure clients and donors that their mission takes precedence over the financial remuneration of any interested parties. The nondistribution constraint has been seen as a tool that nonprofits can use to capitalize on failures in the market. Since there are certain services, such as child care and health care, that some consumers feel uncomfortable receiving if the provider is profit driven, nonprofits are able to step in and meet this demand by promising that no investors will benefit by cutting corners or by delivering unnecessary services.

While the noncoercive feature of nonprofits brings nonprofits closer to business and separates them from government, the nondistribution constraint pushes nonprofits closer to the public sector and away from the private sector. Government's inability to pay out profits from the sale of goods or services is related to its need to be perceived as impartial and equitable. With nonprofits, the nondistribution constraint also builds legitimacy and public confidence, though this does not mean that special powers are vested in these organizations. In both sectors, the nondistribution constraint strongly reinforces the perception that these entities are acting for the good of the public.

The third feature of nonprofit and voluntary organizations is that they have unclear lines of ownership and accountability. This trait separates these entities from both business and government. Businesses must meet the expectations of shareholders or they risk financial ruin. The ownership question in the business sector is clear and unambiguous: Shareholders own larger or smaller amounts of equity in companies depending on the number of shares held. Similarly, government is tethered to a well-identified group of individuals, namely voters. Executive and legislative bodies—and the public agencies they supervise at the federal, state, and local levels—must heed the will of the electorate if they are to pursue public purposes effectively and retain the support and legitimacy needed to govern. There is also a long tradition in the United States of conceiving government as "belonging" to citizens, though the ways in which this ownership claim can be exercised are severely limited. In the nonprofit sector, clear lines of ownership and accountability are absent.

Nonprofit and voluntary organizations must serve many masters, none of which is ultimately able to exert complete control over these organizations. Donors, clients, board members, workers, and local communities all have stakes, claims, or interests in nonprofit and voluntary organizations. Yet none of these parties can be clearly identified as the key ownership group. The relative strength of these ownership claims depends on how an organization is funded and on its chosen mission. Nonprofit organizations that depend heavily on charitable contributions are often held closely accountable by their donors, some of whom believe that as social investors they have a real stake in the organizations to which they contribute. Nonprofits that are largely driven by service fees or commercial revenues are in a different position. While these more commercial organizations do not have donors asserting claims over them, social entrepreneurs and professional staff may view themselves as the key stakeholders in these more businesslike organizations.

Often, however, the lines of ownership and accountability are rendered more complex by the fact that many nonprofit organizations combine funding from multiple sources—foundations, corporations, and government—with earned income, making it hard to point to any particular party as the key stakeholder to whom these special institutions must answer. One might be tempted to point out that nonprofit and voluntary organizations are almost always governed by boards, and to propose this as a solution to the ownership and accountability issue. Unfortunately, board members are not owners. They are stewards who are held responsible for the actions of their organization. In the end, nonprofit and voluntary organizations are authorized to act in the public interest by the communities in which they operate, though the lines of accountability are weaker than those in the public sector and the lines of ownership far more obscure than in the business sector.

A. PLACING NONPROFITS IN CONTEXT: AN INTRODUCTION TO THE TERMINOLOGY

One of the hallmarks of the nonprofit sector is its terminology—it can be confusing, and laymen often use one term to mean another. The term "tax-exempt," for example, is not always interchangeable with "nonprofit," but you will sometimes hear the terms used interchangeably. As budding lawyers, you will need to know the correct terminology and understand how the various components of the nonprofit sector fit together. Following is an introduction to these concepts. They will become more familiar as you progress through the chapters of the book.

As suggested in the Frumkin article, the U.S. economy is traditionally divided into three sectors: the government, the for-profit sector, and the nonprofit sector. The nonprofit sector is also sometimes called "the not-for-profit sector," "civil society," "the voluntary sector," "the third sector," "the independent sector," and "the nongovernmental sector." Although all these terms are technically and legally correct, we will use the term "nonprofit sector" in this book, unless the author of an article or a statute we are discussing has used another term.

"Nonprofit" does not mean that the organization cannot make a profit. Rather, it means that the profit is not distributed to shareholders. That is the "nondistribution constraint" that Frumkin described above. State statutes dealing with nonprofits have language that codifies this constraint. Not surprisingly, the state statutes have their own terms for nonprofit organizations. The Virginia Statute, for example, calls them "nonstock" corporations; New York speaks of "not-for-profit" corporations, and California regulates "public benefit," "mutual benefit," and "religious" organizations.

Within the nonprofit sector are many types of organizations. Not all of these organizations are corporations. They can also be unincorporated associations and even trusts. For reasons discussed in Chapter 2, most nonprofit organizations are corporations, however, and most nonprofit corporations are also tax-exempt (i.e., exempt from federal income tax). This does not mean they never pay taxes. They may pay state income taxes, employment taxes, sales taxes, and even unrelated business income taxes, a concept we will cover later in this book.

The two largest categories of tax-exempt organizations are §501(c) organizations and political organizations, such as the Democratic and Republican parties. There are 29 types of §501(c) tax-exempt organizations (sometimes called TEOs). The most common is the §501(c)(3) organization, which will be the main focus of this book. Other important §501(c) categories include §501(c)(4) social welfare organizations, §501(c)(5) labor and agricultural organizations, §501(c)(6) business leagues, §501(c)(7) social and recreational clubs, and §501(c)(8) fraternal benefit organizations.

Section 501(c)(3) organizations have another tax benefit that is not generally available to the other §501(c) organizations:[1] donations to §501(c)(3) organizations are tax deductible to the donor. We will spend a good deal of time later in this book discussing which organizations should be accorded this special status, but one shorthand that is sometimes used is that these are "public benefit" organizations. Other types of tax-exempt organizations, such as fraternities, labor unions, and business associations, are created for the "mutual benefit" of their members, and are often called "mutual benefit organizations." Like public benefit organizations, mutual benefit organizations are allowed tax-exempt status because they are not designed to make a profit for shareholders. Because they are created for the mutual benefit of their members, however, the tax code does not allow those who provide funding for these organizations to take a charitable tax deduction for their contributions.

---

[1] A non-501(c) organization with a program that acts like a §501(c)(3) organization, such as a scholarship fund for orphans of firefighters that is part of a firefighters' organization, may be able to accept tax-deductible donations for that program.

Section 501(c)(3) organizations can also be divided into two types of organizations—public charities and private foundations. In general, public charities obtain funding from public support—donations, government support, and by charging for their services. Most of the organizations that come to mind when one thinks of nonprofit organizations are public charities—museums, homeless shelters, nonprofit hospitals, and private schools, among others. Private foundations, on the other hand, obtain their funding from a single or a small number of sources. They are often grant-making institutions, such as the Gates Foundation, the Ford Foundation, and the Rockefeller Foundation. Chapter 7 discusses in detail the distinction between these organizations and the different legal rules they must follow.

Figure 1-1
The Nonprofit Organization Universe

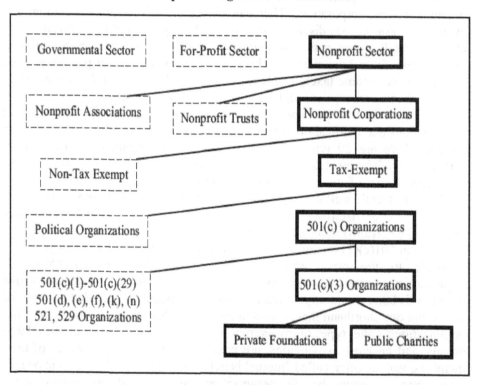

Figure 1-1 depicts the relationships among the organizations defined above.[2] The testimony of Professor John Colombo before the House Ways and Means

---

[2] This book will concentrate on nonprofit corporations that are recognized as §501(c)(3) public charities, as depicted in Figure 1-1. For an explanation of each of the tax exempt entities mentioned in Figure 1-1, see IRS Publication 527, available at https://www.irs.gov/pub/irs-pdf/p557.pdf, accessed May 12, 2016.

Committee reinforces the definitions and introduces the policies behind the tax treatment of these organizations.

JOHN COLOMBO, TESTIMONY BEFORE THE HOUSE COMMITTEE ON WAYS AND MEANS

Serial No. 109-6 (April 20, 2005)

Mr. Chairman, Members of the Committee:

My name is John Colombo. I am a professor of law at the University of Illinois College of Law in Urbana-Champaign, and I have taught about and written on issues of tax-exempt organizations for the past 18 years. I think my job today is to give you some background and context regarding tax exemption rules, particularly as they apply to private foundations and trade associations.

Charitable Exemption vs. Other Exemption

Let me start with two very basic and very useful distinctions to keep in mind when assessing policies regarding nonprofits and tax exemption. The first distinction is that when it comes to tax exemption, there are charities exempt under Code Section 501(c)(3) and then there is everything else. Section 501(c) grants exemption to 28 different kinds of organizations,[3] but the "charities vs. everything else" distinction is a very useful way to think about this for several reasons. First, in general only charities exempt under 501(c)(3) are eligible to receive additional major tax benefits like tax-deductible contributions. Other exempt entities, like trade associations (which are exempt under §501(c)(6), rather than §501(c)(3)), get exemption from having to pay the corporate income tax on their earnings, but are *not* permitted to receive deductible contributions.

Second, the underlying rationales for exemption vary between charitable organizations and everything else. Although we academics carry on a lively debate about the rationale for charitable tax exemption, all of us would agree, I think, that at some level exemption for charities is tied to a concept that they are improving general public welfare in some way. For noncharitable entities, however, the rationale tends to be much more entity-specific.

For example, trade associations are exempt if they carry on activities designed to promote a common business interest of its members; such organizations must not "engage in a regular business of a kind ordinarily carried on for profit." These organizations are exempt because they represent simply a pooling of resources by people with a common interest to conduct activities that, if conducted by the members themselves, would not be profit-making businesses. Hence we believe that creating an "association" for members to pool their resources in this manner should not result in taxation of those pooled resources.

---

[3] [The Patient Protection and Affordable Care Act of 2010 created a type of 501(c) tax-exempt entity that did not exist at the time of Professor Colombo's testimony: §501(c)(29), CO-OP Health Insurance Issuers. 42 U.S.C. §18001 (2010).—*Ed.*]

But if a trade association does conduct regular business activities or provides specific services for members, then the organization should not be exempt because it no longer represents this nontaxable collective pooling of resources, but rather is now engaging in a for-profit business.

Third, charities constitute the bulk of exempt organizations under 501(c). Data compiled in 2002 indicated that there were in excess of 900,000 exempt charitable organizations in the IRS's master file, constituting well over half the total number of all exempt organizations. Trade associations under 501(c)(6) were the next most numerous category, with approximately 84,000 organizations, but still less than a tenth of the number of charitable organizations.

Public Charities vs. Private Foundations

The second major distinction in tax-exemption law occurs within the charitable sector itself. This distinction is between public charities and private foundations. People often get confused about the tax-exempt status of private foundations; so the first thing to remember is that private foundations are charitable organizations eligible for exemption under Section 501(c)(3) just as much as a church or a private school. The IRS has long recognized that making monetary grants to other charities is itself a charitable activity, and that's largely what private foundations do—make grants to other charitable organizations. Historically, in fact, private foundations preceded the income tax. The wealthy industrialists of the 19th century, such as Andrew Carnegie, for example, created trusts to benefit charitable organizations long before we had a functioning income tax. As a result, prior to 1969, private foundations and public charities were treated pretty much the same for tax purposes.

In the 1969 Tax Reform Act, however, Congress decided to subject private foundations to more specific regulation designed to prevent abuses of the private foundation form. The best way to understand why we have this heightened regulation of private foundations is to focus on two main differences between private foundations and public charities: accountability and continuing control.

Public charities are organizations that are accountable to the general public because they get their money in one way or another from a broad cross-section of the public. Private foundations, however, generally receive their funding from a single individual or family, and therefore are accountable to and controlled by that primary donor.

These two distinctions are the basis for our different regulation of public charities and private foundations. When you have true public accountability and "public control" over assets, then you have some reason to believe that the managers of the charity will be careful about their mission and the execution of that mission, because a publicized misstep will have significant adverse effects on the public funding of that organization. Think back to the adverse publicity for the United Way a couple of years ago when its CEO's salary and perks were disclosed in the national media, or the outcry that happened when the Red Cross decided to divert some money donated for 9/11 victims to other needs—I believe, in fact, that this Committee held hearings about the Red Cross's decision and was instrumental in bringing the weight of public accountability to bear on that.

When you do not have this public accountability, however, and you have significant continuing control by one person or family over donated wealth, then there is enormous room for abuse, which is why we have the much tighter regulatory scheme for private foundations.

B. THE LIFE CYCLE OF A §501(c)(3) ORGANIZATION

This book is organized according to the life cycle of a §501(c)(3) organization, specifically a §501(c)(3) public charity. It will cover §501(c)(3) private foundations in Chapter 7 and touch on some other types of tax-exempt organizations, but its emphasis is on public charities because most nonprofit organizations are public charities, and most of the legal and policy discussions about the nonprofit sector concern these organizations. Many of the concepts covered in this book are applicable to other nonprofit organizations, however, and if you later come across other types of nonprofit organizations, many of the concepts covered in this book will be applicable.

The life cycle of the §501(c)(3) organization is covered in four units that cover the issues raised when one begins a §501(c)(3) organization, when one is raising money for that organization, when one is running the organization, and when the organization is dissolving, merging into another organization or becoming a for-profit organization. Table 1-1 is adapted from charts on the life cycle of public charities and private foundations that the Internal Revenue Service (IRS) has produced.[4]

Table 1-1

PUBLIC CHARITY	PRIVATE FOUNDATION

□ **Starting Out**
  ➤ Organizing Documents:
    Articles, Trust, or Charter
    □ Required provisions
    □ Governance and related topics
  ➤ By-laws
    □ State law requirements
  ➤ EIN
  ➤ Charitable Solicitation
    □ Initial state registration
    □ Periodic state reporting
    □ State charity offices
	□ **Starting Out**
	  ➤ Types of Foundations
	    □ Private operating
	    □ Exempt operating
	    □ Grant-making foundations
	  ➤ Organizing documents
	    □ Required provisions
	  ➤ By-laws
	    □ Required provisions
	    □ Annual accounting period
	    □ State law requirements
	  ➤ EIN

---

[4] The IRS charts are found at http://www.irs.gov/charities/charitable/article/0,,id=122670,00.html and http://www.irs.gov/charities/foundations/article/0,,id=127912,00.html.

Table 1-1 (*Cont'd*)

PUBLIC CHARITY	PRIVATE FOUNDATION

□ **Applying to the IRS**
➢ Requirements for exemption
➢ Application forms
➢ IRS processing
□ **Ongoing Compliance**
➢ Jeopardizing exemption
  □ Inurement/private benefit
  □ Intermediate sanctions
  □ Lobbying/political activity
  □ Not filing annual return or notice
➢ Employment taxes
➢ Retirement plan compliance
➢ Substantiation and disclosure
  □ Charitable contributions
  □ Noncash contributions
➢ Public disclosure requirements
	□ **Applying to the IRS**
	➢ Requirements for exemption
	➢ Application forms
	➢ IRS processing
	□ **Ongoing Compliance**
	➢ Jeopardizing exemption
	  □ Inurement/private benefit
	  □ Lobbying/political activity
	  □ Not filing annual return
	➢ Private foundation excise taxes
	  □ Net investment income tax
	  □ Self-dealing
	  □ Failure to distribute income
	  □ Excess business holdings
	  □ Jeopardizing investments
	  □ Taxable expenditures
	➢ Substantiation and disclosure
	  □ Charitable contributions
	  □ Noncash contributions
	➢ Public disclosure requirements

□ **Significant Events**
➢ Reporting changes to IRS
➢ Private letter rulings and determination letters
➢ Audits of exempt organizations
  □ Potential consequences of examination
  □ Examination procedures
  □ Power of attorney
➢ Termination—notifying IRS
	□ **Significant Events**
	➢ Reporting changes to IRS
	➢ Private letter rulings and determination letters
	➢ IRS audits
	  □ Potential consequences
	  □ Examination procedures
	  □ Power of attorney
	➢ Termination of private foundation and procedures

II. HISTORICAL AND DESCRIPTIVE OVERVIEW

Today's nonprofit laws, like all other laws, have their origins in earlier times. Tax-exempt nonprofits were in existence in some form long before for-profit corporations or a federal income tax. (Sometimes the legal rationale for a nonprofit law seems to be "It's always been that way.") Instead of a comprehensive history of nonprofit law, which would require an understanding of current law, this section of Chapter 1 provides some historical tidbits, provides statistics on the sector today, and then explores the future of the philanthropic sector. The historical tidbits are drawn from James Fishman, *The Development of Nonprofit Corporation Law and an Agenda for Reform*, 34 EMORY L.J. 617 (1985); Henry Hansmann, *The Evolving Law of Nonprofit Organizations: Do Current Trends Make Good Policy?* 39 CASE W. RES. L. REV. 807, 810-818 (1988); Thomas Kelley, *Rediscovering Vulgar Charity, A Historical Analysis of America's Tangled Nonprofit Law* 73 FORDHAM L. REV. 2437 (2005); Mamoun Abuarqub and Isabel Phillips, A BRIEF HISTORY OF HUMANITARIANISM IN THE MUSLIM WORLD (Secours Islamique 2009); and Roger Colinvaux, *Charity in the 21st Century: Trending Toward Decay*, 11 FLORIDA TAX. J. 1 (2011).

A. HISTORICAL TIDBITS

- Ancient Egyptians were buried with records of the "blessed givings" that they had shared with the poor during their lifetimes.
- Buddhism, founded in 400 B.C., taught that love and charity were important virtues.
- Hindu scriptures stressed the duty to give to the needy.
- Early Jewish doctrine also taught that humans have a moral obligation to aid those in need.
- Early Christianity taught that people should love their enemies, practice good deeds, and offer alms generously. By the sixth century, Catholic monasteries were centers for relieving poverty, tending the sick, and providing education.
- In the seventh century, the Prophet Mohammed recommended setting aside a piece of land and using its revenues to aid the poor. This practice, called the *waqf*, is the Islamic equivalent of the charitable foundation, and it helped create early hospitals, orphanages, schools, and religious institutions. The use of the *waqf* remains prevalent in the Islamic world.
- As the Middle Ages arrived, landed nobles began to take responsibility for caring for their needy subjects in exchange for loyalty, labor, and a willingness to fight for them. Cities, towns, and guilds also began to take care of the poor, but monasteries remained primary vehicles for charity.
- In the thirteenth century, papal decrees encouraged individuals to donate to charitable or religious purposes. The price for failure to follow this norm was eternal damnation.
- The Statute of Charitable Uses Act from 1601 is generally considered the first written charitable law in England and the basis of all subsequent Anglo-American charity law. It attempted to define the concept of charity as a way to encourage private charitable efforts. It includes:

    [S]ome for relief of aged, impotent, and poor people, some for maintenance of sick and maimed soldiers and mariners, schools of learning, free schools and scholars in universities, some for repair of bridges, ports, havens, causeways, churches, sea-banks, and highways, some for education and preferment of orphans, some for or towards relief, stock or maintenance for houses of correction, some for marriages of poor maids, some for supportation, aid and help of young tradesmen, handicraftsmen, and persons decayed; and others for relief or redemption of prisoners or captives, and for aid or ease of any poor inhabitants concerning payments of fifteens, setting out of soldiers and other taxes.

- Although the British settlers of the New World brought their charitable instincts across the Atlantic (and, according to Pilgrim lore, received charity from Native Americans), such instincts grew in a land in which communities came into existence before strong governments. The only way many public needs could be addressed was through individuals, and/or the community, who could take care of them. As the frontier opened up, this tradition of self-help and caring for one's own increased.

- British charitable law is based on charitable trusts. U.S. charitable law, although it has some parallels to trust law, is less reliant on this body of law. After the American Revolution, many states repealed all British statutes; consequently, several states refused to uphold the validity of the charitable trusts. As a result, American nonprofits are more likely to be in corporate than in trust form, but trusts are still formed, and trust law continues to influence some aspects of nonprofit corporate law.

- Alexis de Tocqueville, a French political thinker who traveled extensively in the United States, noted the American tendency to create associations in *Democracy in America:* [5]

  Americans of all ages, all conditions, and all dispositions constantly form associations.... Wherever at the head of some new undertaking you see the government in France, or a man of rank in England, in the United States you will be sure to find an association.... As soon as several of the inhabitants of the United States have taken up an opinion or a feeling which they wish to promote in the world, they look out for mutual assistance; and as soon as they have found one another out, they combine. From that moment they are no longer isolated men, but a power seen from afar, whose actions serve for an example and whose language is listened to. . . . These associations, virtually all of which are nonprofit organizations, are far more prevalent in the United States than in the rest of the world.

- Before the nineteenth century, there was no real distinction between nonprofit, for-profit, cooperative, or governmental organizations, because corporate charters were granted individually by the legislature and tailored to the particular organization in question. By the middle of the nineteenth century, though, legislatures began to allow corporations to form without a specific legislative act. Most states eventually categorized these corporations as for-profit, nonprofit, or cooperative.

---

[5] Alexis de Toqueville, Democracy in America (1840), Book II, Ch. 5; translation reprinted online at University of Virginia, American Studies, http://xroads.virginia.edu/~HYPER/DETOC/ch2_05.htm, accessed April 15, 2016.

- In the late nineteenth century, Andrew Carnegie, John D. Rockefeller, and others amassed great fortunes and gave much of their money away to charitable organizations. They created grant-making foundations, which were designed to solve society's intractable problems rather than simply hand out charity.
- Congress enacted the first federal income tax in 1913. Charitable institutions were exempt. It built on the Tariff Acts of 1894 and 1909, both of which also exempted charitable corporations.
- During the Depression, the idea that charitable organizations could and should work with the government to solve social problems took hold. Since that time, the government has often used private charities to carry out its social goals.
- By 1950, many nonprofit organizations competed directly with for-profit organizations. NYU Law School, for example, ran a large macaroni company and owned Limoges China, neither of which paid income taxes. Congress introduced the Unrelated Business Income Tax in 1950 in order to equalize the tax consequences for such organizations. This law began what Professor Henry Hansmann has called "a broad retreat from the consistently favorable treatment that nonprofits had come to enjoy."[6]
- In 1969, Congress created the distinction between public charity and private foundations in order to prevent abuses created when one person (or a small group of people) can place a large sum of money in one nonprofit corporation and maintain control over how that money is spent over time. Private foundations are regulated more carefully than public charities.
- Federal enactments in the late 1990s and early 2000s drew on the stricter rules that private foundations follow to create complicated rules for most charities. These regulations, and their predecessors, have been cast in the form of negative requirements—listing what the organizations may not do— instead of listing positive requirements that they must fulfill if they want to obtain and retain their tax exemption.
- Laws passed in the first decade of the 21st century, however, offered a patchwork of affirmative requirements for credit counseling organizations and hospitals. Professor Colvinaux hopes that these laws could be the start of a trend toward creating affirmative requirements that specific types of charities must fulfill in order to obtain tax-exempt status and in order to accept tax-deductible contributions. As you read this book, you will see that, for the most part, the current law of public charities involves negative prescriptions rather than affirmative requirements. If Professor Colvinaux is right, that may be changing.

---

[6] Henry Hansmann, *The Evolving Law of Nonprofit Organizations: Do Current Trends Make Good Policy?* 39 CASE W. RES. L. REV. 807, 814 (1988).

B. SCOPE OF THE SECTOR TODAY: A FEW STATISTICS

The nonprofit sector is larger than many imagine it to be. In 2012 public charities reported $1.74 trillion in revenue, $1.63 trillion in expenses, and over $3 trillion in assets. The nonprofit sector pays out almost 10% of the wages and salaries paid in the United States, and it is responsible for 5.3% of the U.S. gross domestic product (GDP).[7] The following statistics and charts can give you an idea of the scope of the sector.

1. Number of Tax-Exempt Organizations

The IRS publicizes the number of exempt organizations in the IRS Data Book, Table 25. In 2015, the IRS recognized 1,702,267 tax-exempt organizations. Of those, 91% (1,548,948) are §501(c) organizations, and 76% of the §501(c) organizations (1,184,547) are classified as §501(c)(3). Figure 1-2 shows the remarkable growth of the sector over the past 20 years. Despite a downturn that occurred when the IRS began revoking the exemption of §501(c)(3)s that did not file annual tax returns, the number of §501(c)(3)s has almost doubled in that time.[8] Most of these organizations are small, however. In 2012, three-fourths of public charities had annual expenses of less than $500,000, and only 4% of charitable organizations had annual expenses above $10 million.[9]

Figure 1-2
Number of IRS Recognized 501(c)(3) Organizations, 1995–2015

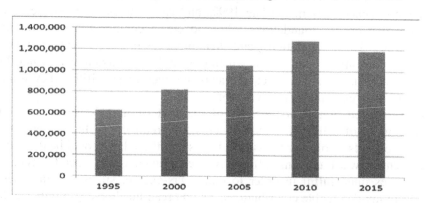

---

[7] National Center for Charitable Statistics, *Quick Facts About Nonprofits*, http://nccs.urban.org /statistics/quickfacts.cfm, accessed April 4, 2016.

[8] The 2015 data in the paragraph and the chart are from IRS DATA BOOK 2015, Table 25, http://www.irs.gov/pub/irs-soi/15databk.pdf. The numbers in the chart from earlier years are from earlier IRS Data Books. These numbers do not include certain §501(c)(3) organizations that need not apply for recognition of exemption, such as churches, integrated auxiliaries of churches, and organizations with normal gross receipts in each taxable year of $5,000 or less. In 2010, the IRS revoked the exemptions of more than 300,000 §501(c)(3)s for failure to file annual tax returns. That change was reflected in the 2011 statistics and explains the downturn after 2010.

[9] Independent Sector, *The Sector's Economic Impact*, https://www.independentsector.org /economic_role, accessed June 26, 2015.

2. Information Forms Filed and Examined

Following are the numbers of information forms filed by tax-exempt entities and examined by the IRS in 2014 and 2015.[10]

Tax-exempt organization returns processed calendar year 2014:   787,339
Tax-exempt returns examined fiscal year 2015:   19,024
Forms 990 and 990-EZ examined fiscal year 2014:   2,712
Percentage of EO returns examined fiscal year 2015:   2.0%

3. Classification of Tax-Exempt Organizations

To capture the diversity of nonprofit organizations in the United States, the National Taxonomy of Exempt Entities includes over 630 categories that group organizations under eight major headings.[11] Figure 1-3 shows the number of §501(c)(3) public charities classified within each of these major categories in May 2015.[12]

Figure 1-3
Registered Public Charities by Major Purpose or Activity, May 2015

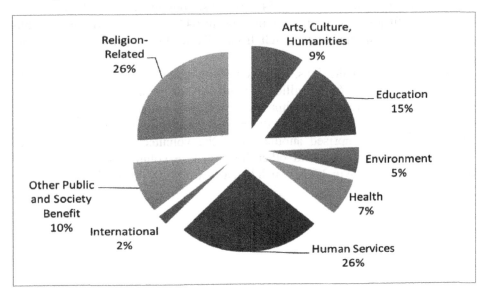

---

[10] These statistics are from the IRS DATA BOOK 2015, Table 13. The number of tax information returns that were processed in 2014 includes Forms 990 and 990-EZ, which are tax information forms filed by §501(c)(3) public charities that normally have more than $50,000 in gross receipts. That number does *not* include almost 500,000 Forms 990-N, the electronic postcard that §501(c)(3)s with gross receipts below $50,000 a year must file. Forms 990 are discussed in detail in Chapter 12.

[11] Statement of Elizabeth Boris, Ph.D., Director, Center on Nonprofits and Philanthropy, the Urban Institute, Testimony before the Subcommittee on Oversight of the House Committee on Ways and Means, Serial 110-60, Sept. 25, 2007.

[12] The statistics for the figure are from http://nccs.urban.org/tools/DataWeb.cfm.

4. Employment in the Nonprofit Sector

In 2012, the nonprofit sector in the United States employed 11.4 million workers and paid out $532 billion in wages.[13] The nonprofit sector accounted for 10.3% of the workforce, with almost as many employed in this sector as in the manufacturing sector.

Employment in the nonprofit sector has proven to be quite resilient. Between 2000 and 2010, employment in the sector grew at an annual rate of 2.1%. During that same time, the for-profit sector lost jobs at an average annual rate of minus 0.6%. Despite two recessions in that decade, the nonprofit sector gained employment every year, even as overall employment dropped significantly. Moreover, job growth was found in every field of the nonprofit sector and in every region of the country. This growth occurred because nonprofit jobs tend to be in service industries, such as health care and education, which are growing areas of the economy. Jobs in areas that are declining, such as manufacturing, are rarely found in the nonprofit sector. One area of concern, however, is that for-profit companies are moving into the service industries and are capturing some of the market share. For example, nonprofits held 62% of the jobs in the social assistance field in 2000, but only 54% of those jobs in 2010. In the education field, nonprofit jobs fell from 68% in 2000 to 64% in 2010, and the nonprofit share of jobs in the health field fell from 45% to 43% during the same time period.[14]

In addition to paid jobs, the nonprofit sector "employs" millions of volunteers. In 2013, 62.8 million Americans, or approximately ¼ of the population, volunteered. Approximately 1/3 of those volunteers helped religious organizations, and ¼ worked with educational organizations. Social services and health volunteers comprised another ¼ of the volunteers, and the rest were involved with sports, arts, and other fields. These volunteers contributed 7.9 billion hours of service in 2013, which had an estimated value of $184 billion.[15]

---

[13] BLS Commissioner, *Announcing New Research Data on Jobs and Pay in the Nonprofit Sector*. BUREAU OF LABOR STATISTICS, October 17, 2014. For more on these statistics and interesting breakdowns and charts of this data, see Erik Friesenhahn, *Nonprofits in America: New Research Data on Employment, Wages, and Establishments*, NONPROFIT QUARTERLY (March 10, 2016).

[14] Lester M. Salamon, S. Wojcech Sokolowski, and Stephanie L. Geller, HOLDING DOWN THE FORT: NONPROFIT EMPLOYMENT DURING A DECADE OF TURMOIL, NONPROFIT DATA ECONOMIC BULLETIN #39 (Johns Hopkins Center for Civil Society Studies 2012).

[15] Corporation for National & Community Service, Volunteering and Civic Engagement in America, http://www.volunteeringinamerica.gov/national, accessed April 3, 2016.

5. Charitable Contributions

Charitable giving in the United States usually hovers around 2 percentage points of GDP. In 2014, for example, charitable giving amounted to $358.38 billion, which was 2.1% of GDP. That was an increase of 7.1% over 2013, and it was the first time donations topped the record that was set in 2007, just before a major recession. The sector had actually experienced a 14% drop in giving between 2007 and 2009. That was the most serious decline in 60 years of statistics on charitable giving. Figures 1-4 and 1-5 shed more light on charitable contributions made in 2014 by illuminating by sources of gifts and the recipients of these gifts.[16] Figure 1-6 reveals the sources of all revenues, including charitable gifts, as reported by public charities for 2014.[17]

Figure 1-4
2014 Contributions by Source

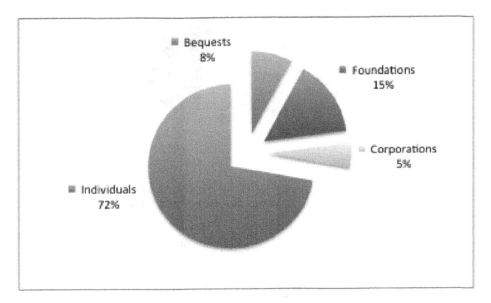

---

[16] The information for Figures 1-4 and 1-5 is from GIVING USA, 2015, GIVING USA FOUNDATION.™

[17] Brice S. McKeever, THE NONPROFIT SECTOR IN BRIEF 2015: PUBLIC CHARITIES, GIVING, AND VOLUNTEERING (Urban Institute, 2015).

Figure 1-5
2014 Contributions by Type of Recipient

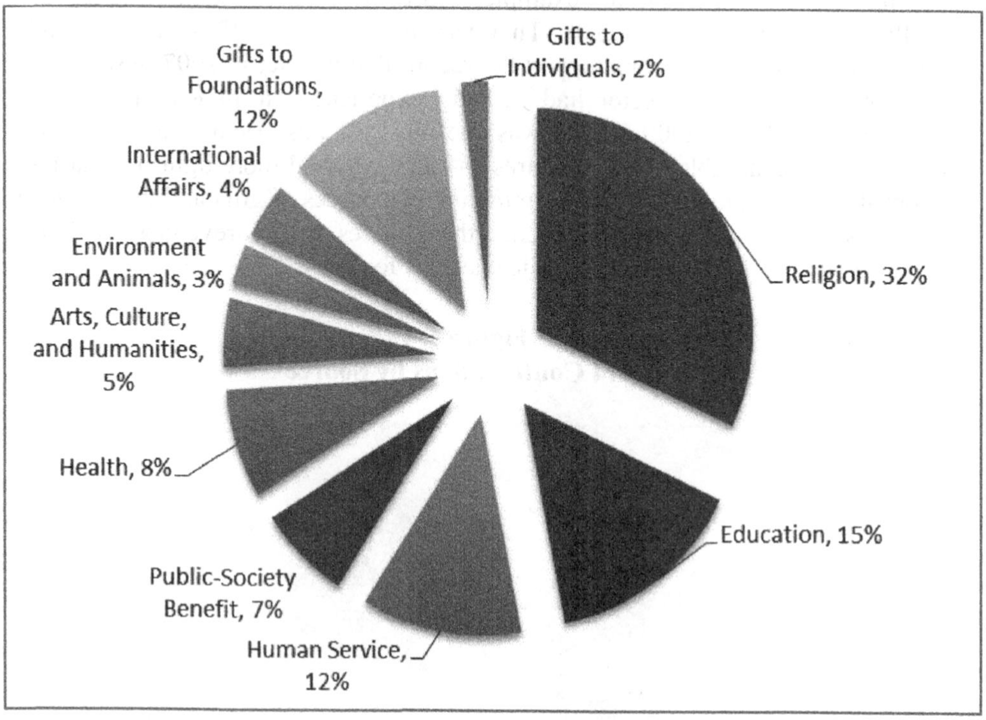

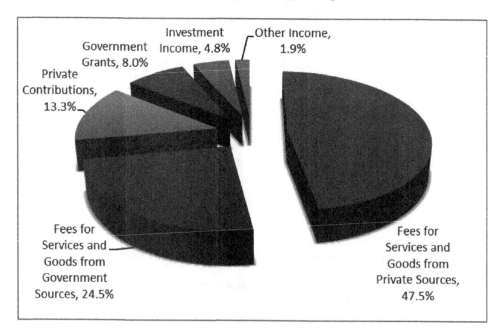

Figure 1-6
2013 Sources of Revenue for Reporting Charities

C. THE NONPROFIT OF THE FUTURE

MARK KRAMER, THE FUTURE OF PHILANTHROPY,
REMARKS FOR PANEL

2007 Skoll World Forum (March 29, 2007)

I want to suggest that we are on the cusp of a generational divide—that the following generation will not see a separate nonprofit sector and a separate for-profit sector. We grew up thinking about a division. On the one hand, there is a for-profit business. You make money and you don't really care about social issues to the extent you can get away with it. On the other hand, there's the nonprofit sector and civil society, whose job it is to solve social problems. That division is very hard for us to let go of, but we are going through a transition to a generation that will not see it that way.... In the future people will not see philanthropy as the primary means of solving social problems....

(First, let me be clear. I am not saying philanthropy will disappear. Harvard University is too good at fundraising for that to happen. There are many rewards that come from the status, the prestige, and the association with many major institutions that are phenomenally effective at fundraising. Harvard spends about $60 million a year on its fundraising alone. But I think you would probably agree with me that adding to Harvard or the Metropolitan Museum of Art's endowment is not a major step toward solving social problems.)

... Five different strands lead me to this conclusion. First, the current system is not working.... We have a phenomenal nonprofit sector in America. Its revenue is almost $1 trillion a year. It employs about 7% of the work force. It has grown at a very healthy rate over the last 50 years. And every problem you would care to look at, whether it's environmental, educational, or social welfare, is the same or worse over this period of phenomenal growth in the nonprofit sector. Also, ... social and environmental issues are long-term issues, and you can coast for many decades without feeling the effects [of apathy and poor choices]. I think that our generation and the next two generations are the ones who will not have the luxury of avoiding the effects of our past choices.

The system is not working in terms of the philanthropic sector; it's also not working in terms of the corporate sector. You look at the auto industry ... or the health care industry in the United States, both of which are self-destructing because they found it easier to spend money lobbying to prevent legislation that would bring them into line with concerns of much of the population and much of the world. As a result, they are paying the price ... as they are finding their economic model falling apart.

It's also not working in terms of government. The United States spends more on public education than the GDP of all but sixteen countries in the world, and our students consistently rank toward the bottom of the list of developed countries. So I suggest that the problems are becoming inescapable, and the way we have been doing it isn't working. Social entrepreneurship is an interim step, in many ways, that has emerged as we ... grapple with ... how to find more effective ways of addressing social problems.

The second strand ... is the shifts in behavior that we see by both sectors.... The social value proposition of a business is [now] the key competitive advantage. Businesses need to consider social issues, not just to be good neighbors or good citizens, not just in response to activists, but because that is the only way they will succeed. We see this happening with companies of all sizes. We see GE announcing that green technology is the growth industry they are going to focus on. Microsoft will soon announce an initiative to focus on the five billion people that can't afford computers and define ways to give people computers for free and a kind of time-sharing arrangement for the software....

We also have found that companies can be tremendously powerful agents for social change. One of my favorite examples is the Equator Principle where nine major global banks got together to set social, safety and environmental standards for major construction projects like dams and pipelines around the world. It took about a year for them to negotiate the standards, but as soon as they put them in place, 75% of all major project financing in the world was under those standards, and it became impossible to build something without meeting them. I challenge you to think of how a nonprofit organization could in one year have changed the safety and environmental standards for construction projects around the world.

We also see a shift in behavior in the nonprofit sector. Foundations are taking a much more instrumental approach. They are defining clear goals, and they are looking at their progress toward the goal. They are actually holding themselves accountable for the change happening in the world, looking less at what was the outcome of a particular grant and looking at whether the needle is moving on the issue that they are taking responsibility for addressing.

[There are also more] partnerships between the nonprofit and for-profit sectors, as well as government.... [C]orporations bring capabilities to solving social problems that you can't imagine solving without engaging companies. Issues like health care involve corporations. Issues like economic development involve corporations. We can't think of these as social problems that can be addressed without business.

The third strand is social investment.... [L]ooking at trends in what we call mission investing by foundations,[18] we have found that the number of foundations that are doing social investment has doubled in recent years; the amount of new money going into mission investing has tripled.... To give you a sense of the momentum, mission investments grew at about 3% a year over the thirty-two years up to 2000. In the next five years, they grew at 16% a year.

... [T]hese investments are not as risky as people might have thought. Seventy-five per cent of the foundations making these investments had a zero default rate. Of those that kept adequate records ... 90% received an internal rate

---

[18] [FN1]The term "investment" is used in the traditional sense of investing in something that is going to give you your money back and hopefully a financial return on top of it. ["Mission investing" refers to investments of a foundation's endowment assets that seek a social return consistent with the foundation's mission, as well as a financial return. —*Ed.*]

of return that was equal to or higher than the expected return they had when they went into the investment.

People are also beginning to accept the idea of a blended return, the idea of trading off some financial return for social benefit. Ashoka[] and ... Deutsche Bank are putting together a $20 million social investment fund that will invest in eye care in India. We are working with UBS and a large foundation to put together what will be a $75 to $100 million fund that will invest in health care businesses in Africa, in the belief again that you can't create an infrastructure without private enterprise. The cost of capital in Africa now is 30%,[19] given the risk. We think ... a considerable number of philanthropically inclined high net worth individuals would be happy to get 6 or 8 % return and accept as the difference the social benefit that they are achieving in Africa. Again and again we see examples of people accepting this trade-off.

Fourth, ... a flood of talent is coming in [to work on social issues].... People are achieving great wealth more quickly and at greater magnitude than ever before, and many of those people are looking for the next challenge.... What can they do once the challenge of earning money and the need to earn money is no longer particularly satisfying? How can they get involved in the nonprofit sector?

We see it at another level of MBA students graduating and choosing to come to nonprofit consulting firms, ... taking lesser compensation but being able to work on social issues. We also see it in the traditional business context as businesses want to tout their volunteering and social investment and contributions as a way of attracting talent.[20] But it's a tremendous amount of talent, ... and these people are very comfortable using the for-profit tools to achieve social ends.

Lastly I wanted to touch on this idea of what makes effective donors. [The] Gates Foundation asked us to interview a couple dozen people who give away at least $1 million a year and are perceived as highly effective donors by their peers or other experts in philanthropy. We wanted to know what made them that way, and frankly these were a very diverse group. They made their money in different ways, lived in different regions of the country, were men and women, young and older. We didn't expect to find anything much in common.

We actually did find a common thread that ran through all the interviews. These donors started out in philanthropy very skeptical that philanthropy would actually make a real difference in the world. They gave out of a sense of obligation, because people approached them, or they participated on boards, but they didn't really think that philanthropy was going to make much of a difference. Every one of them went through what we began to call a "first hand stretch experience." At some point, they came across an issue of great personal significance to them. It could be a son with a brain disease, a beautiful historic theater that was going to be torn down, or a nature preserve that someone had

---

[19] [This means that enterprises in Africa find they need to promise a 30% return in order to attract investment capital, given the risks of investing in Africa. —Ed.]

[20] [FN 2] The nonprofit sector so far has not been very good at utilizing this talent. I think the common response has been, "Give us your money and go enjoy the south of France."

hiked on as a child that was going to be developed. In every case, it was an issue that really mattered and there was a sense of urgency. They decided to take action, and they shifted away from thinking about giving away money to thinking about how I can solve a problem.

That was a very fundamental shift. They began to roll up their sleeves and got involved. Many of these people ended up spending half or all of their time on their philanthropic projects. Many of them created new organizations, actively brought in others as collaborators, and became world authorities on the issue that they were trying to solve. They began to see some impact from their efforts.... They didn't always solve the problem, but they saw that their efforts were making progress. It changed how they thought about philanthropy.... [I]n philanthropy, people can stay at the same place on the learning curve their whole life, and yet every now and then you run into people who really are making a difference in the world. [I]t was this first hand stretch experience that really changed people's approach....

So when you put it together, people in the nonprofit sector are increasingly using for-profit tools; serious businesses in the for-profit sector are increasingly trying to solve social issues; people are accepting the idea of a financial and social return together; and there is this tremendous upwelling of talent that wants to use what they have learned and the money they have earned to be able to achieve social change. It is very hard for us to let go of the idea of two separate sectors.... It's a generational shift that is coming from a number of different directions, and more importantly, if we are going to address the problems that we have let slide too long, we need to merge these two sectors.

NOTES AND QUESTIONS

1. Additional information on the history of philanthropy can be found in Olivier Kunz, HISTORY OF PHILANTHROPY IN AMERICA (Princeton University Press 2012). *See also* HistPhil, a blog dedicated to the history of philanthropy, which helps bring into context many of today's nonprofit issues. http://histphil.org, last accessed Aug. 2, 2015.

2. A more qualitative picture of the current nonprofit sector can be found in the report published by the association for nonprofits, Independent Sector: THREADS: INSIGHTS FROM THE CHARITABLE COMMUNITY (2015), found at https://philanthropynewyork.org/sites/default/files/resources/ThreadsReport. pdf. Building on community conversations with over 2,000 individuals in 13 cities, this report examines current trends that can affect the nonprofit sector and translates those trends into challenges and opportunities for the sector.

3. For further reading on the future of the sector, see Helmut Anheier, *The Nonprofit of 2025*, STANFORD SOCIAL INNOVATION REVIEW (Spring 2013); John Brothers, *Is a Renewed Economy Based on the Nonprofit Model in our Future?* NONPROFIT QUARTERLY (June 27, 2013). Additionally, Katherine Fulton presented a 2007 TED Talk, *You Are the Future of Philanthropy*, which sets forth several trends that are continuing today. http://www.ted.com/talks/katherine_fulton_you_are_the_future_of_philanthr

opy. *See also* Jeremy Rifkinmarch, *The Rise of Anti-Capitalism*, NY TIMES (Nov. 14, 2014), which argues that the sharing economy and the Internet of Things are creating a postmarket society, which will, by necessity, function much as civil society does today.

4. Compare the number of organizations in each subsector of the nonprofit sector with the amount of resources that each subsector receives. Should the legal system do anything to encourage a reallocation of those resources?

5. Did it surprise you that private foundations and corporations provide such a small percentage of contributions or that contributions provide such a small percentage of nonprofits' revenues? Would you prefer that either of these facts be different? If so, would you suggest that we have laws that encourage a change or that we allow the free market to determine how nonprofits receive their resources?

6. If Professor Hansmann is correct in his assertion that the history of nonprofit law in the last 60 years reflects "a broad retreat from the consistently favorable treatment that nonprofits had come to enjoy," why have so many new nonprofits been created? Wouldn't one expect that more restrictive laws would discourage people from starting nonprofit organizations?

III. RATIONALES FOR THE NONPROFIT SECTOR

Why do we have a nonprofit sector? How is a nonprofit organization different from a for-profit or governmental organization? Following are descriptions of economic, political, and social theories that try to answer these questions. As we will see, these theories overlap, and yet none completely explains the existence of the nonprofit sector. We will encounter similar difficulties when we look for theories to explain tax exemption and the charitable tax deduction. Does this difficulty mean that we have defined the sector incorrectly? Should we accept one theory in some circumstances and another in other circumstances? As you learn about and discuss the laws surrounding the nonprofit sector, you will have the opportunity to consider whether the lack of a single coherent theory creates a somewhat inconsistent legal framework. You will also be able to see that most, if not all, laws have their roots in at least one of these theories.

A. ECONOMIC THEORY

Economic theories posit that nonprofit organizations emerge when a "market failure" exists. In general, markets work well to help us determine how much to produce and distribute of "private goods," those items that we ordinarily buy and sell in the for-profit marketplace, such as consumer items. Markets do not work, however, for "public goods"—goods that cost the same to produce for one person as for many people and for which no easy mechanism exists to prevent others from accessing these goods once one person has access to them. Public goods include military protection and clean air. It is difficult to set a price for such items because, once one person has access to them, others will gain access without payment. They become "free riders."

The government can avoid this "free rider" problem if it produces and distributes these public goods because it can coerce the payment of taxes. The government does provide many of these public goods, such as military protection and roads. But the government is constrained by the voters, and it can provide only as much in the form of public goods as the majority of American voters support.

Inevitably, a minority of Americans see more merit in these public goods than the average voter, and they are willing to fund more of whatever public good is not being produced by the government. For example, citizens of a neighborhood for whom the city cannot afford to pave the streets may be willing to pave the neighborhood roads themselves. And citizens who suffer from a rare disease will undoubtedly see more of a need to fund medical research into that disease than the average voter. They, their friends, and those they can convince of the importance of medical research for this particular disease may well join forces to create a nonprofit devoted to studying this disease. Thus, the nonprofit sector becomes a private response to instances of "market failure" and "government failure."

Henry Hansmann has refined this "public goods" theory with the "contract failure" theory. He maintains that nonprofits typically arise in situations in which the consumers do not have adequate information to judge whether they are receiving the quantity and quality of the service they are purchasing. For example, donors sending funds abroad in order to advance international development cannot ordinarily judge whether these funds actually reach their destination. Donors to listener-supported radio cannot determine whether the other listeners are paying as much for the broadcasts as they are. And children in daycare or hospital patients may be unable to explain whether they are receiving quality services. In such situations of asymmetrical information, a for-profit firm has both the incentive and the opportunity to provide inadequate service. Nonprofit organizations do not face these temptations, due to the nondistribution constraint, which disallows distributions of the nonprofit's profits. Thus, those paying for these services may well prefer to engage with a nonprofit organization because they trust nonprofit organizations to provide the services that they say they will provide.

These "failure" theories look at the demand side of the equation by examining the needs that nonprofits address. Other theorists have looked at the supply side and have developed what are called "entrepreneurship" theories. These theorists suggest that nonprofits do not always simply fill in the gaps left behind by businesses and governments. Instead, these are institutions infused with the moral and philosophical values of their founders. These founders are primarily motivated by abstract, values-based concerns, such as faith or social justice. The nondistribution constraint, and even the provision of services, are secondary to these values. Thus, instead of filling in gaps left by businesses and the governments, nonprofits serve to maximize the values of the founders and their followers.

B. POLITICAL THEORY

Political scientists look at nonprofit organizations from the point of view of their relationship with the government and their role in supporting democracy. According to political scientists, both governments and nonprofits produce public goods, but the private groups do not face the same constraints that the government does. Most obviously, nonprofits have no need to please the majority of voters, and this freedom from the average voter allows nonprofits to carry on different functions from the government.

For example, nonprofits can accommodate the diversity of values, beliefs, and practices that exist within a democracy. The nonprofit sector can accommodate right-leaning and left-leaning groups, denominational schools, and groups that celebrate a specific ethnic minority group. As such, they help encourage a pluralistic society and allow people who might otherwise feel marginalized to feel part of the democracy. Nonprofits' ability to move more quickly than the government can also make them seem warmer and more humane.

Nonprofits can also engage in experimentation and incur much greater risk than a government can afford to take with public funds. It is sometimes said that the nonprofit sector provides the research and development for society. A program that works well may eventually be adopted by the market sector if it can be monetized, and by the governmental sector if it produces a public good for a majority of the population.

Finally, nonprofits provide freedom from the bureaucracy that necessarily accompanies governmental efforts. Governments must ensure that they treat all their citizens equally, and they create policies and procedures in order to document this equal treatment. Nonprofits do not treat their stakeholders unfairly, of course, but they are generally smaller and less in need of bureaucratic protection. Additionally, nonprofit supporters voluntarily contribute their time and money and can withdraw their support if they witness unfair treatment of themselves or of other nonprofit stakeholders. This watchdog function can take the place of bureaucratic policies and procedures and allow the nonprofit to address the issue more efficiently.

C. SOCIOLOGICAL THEORY

Sociological theorists, who examine the relationships of people between and among groups, consider nonprofits as "mediating institutions" that provide a buffer between individuals and larger bureaucracies, such as the government. Nonprofits help build community and allow communities to solve their own problems.

One way individuals deal with the larger society is to create their own associations or community. When individuals see a social need, they simply band together to fill that gap, as deToqueville noted. We see this in political advocacy groups, nonprofits that care for others such as daycare centers and nursing homes, and in mutual interest groups, such as book clubs and groups supporting a particular ethnic or cultural group.

Nonprofits can also serve a role in socializing individuals, reinforcing values and creating bonds of trust. Following is an excerpt from a book by Lester Salamon that outlines some of the social roles that nonprofits play.

LESTER SALAMON, THE RESILIENT SECTOR: THE STATE OF NONPROFIT AMERICA

(Brookings Institution Press, 2003), pp. 11–14

Quite apart from their economic importance, nonprofit organizations make crucial contributions to national and community life.

The Service Role

In the first place, nonprofit organizations are *service providers:* they deliver much of the hospital care, higher education, social services, cultural entertainment, employment and training, how-income housing, community development, and emergency aid services available in the United States. More concretely, this set of organizations constitutes:

- half of the nation's hospitals;
- one-third of its health clinics;
- over a quarter of its nursing homes;
- nearly half (46 percent) of its higher education institutions;
- four-fifths (80 percent) of its individual and family service agencies;
- 70 percent of its vocational rehabilitation facilities;
- 30 percent of its day care centers;
- over 90 percent of its orchestras and operas; and
- the delivery vehicles for 70 percent of its foreign disaster assistance.

While disagreements exist over how "distinctive" nonprofit services are compared to those provided by businesses or governments, nonprofits are well known for identifying and responding to unmet needs, for innovating, and for delivering services of exceptional quality. Nonprofit organizations thus pioneered assistance to AIDS victims, hospice care, emergency shelter for the homeless, food pantries for the hungry, drug abuse treatment efforts, and dozens more, too numerous to mention. Similarly, many of the nation's premier cultural and educational institutions are private, nonprofit organizations—institutions like Harvard, Princeton, Yale, Stanford, the University of Chicago, Johns Hopkins University, the Metropolitan Museum of Art, and the Cleveland Symphony, to name just a few. While public and for-profit organizations also provide crucial services, there is no denying the extra dimension added by the country's thousands of private, non-profit groups in meeting public needs that neither the market can, or will, adequately address.

The Advocacy Role

In addition to delivering services, nonprofit organizations also contribute to national life by identifying unaddressed problems and bringing them to public attention, by protecting basic human rights, and by giving voice to a wide assortment of social, political, environmental, ethnic, and community interests and concerns. Most of the social movements that have animated American life over the past century or more operated in and through the nonprofit sector. Included here are the antislavery, women's suffrage, populist, progressive, civil rights, environmental, antiwar, women's, gay rights, and conservative movements. The nonprofit sector has thus helped make the constitutional protections of free speech operational by permitting individuals to join their voices with others to effect social and political change. As such, it has operated as a critical social safety valve, permitting aggrieved groups to bring their concerns to broader public attention and to rally support to improve their circumstances. This advocacy role may, in fact[,] be more important to the nation's social health than are the service functions this sector also performs.

The Expressive Role

Political and policy concerns are not the only ones to which the nonprofit sector gives expression. Rather, this set of institutions provides the vehicles through which an enormous variety of other sentiments and impulses—artistic, religious, cultural, ethnic, social, recreational—also find expression. Opera companies, symphonies, soccer clubs, churches, synagogues, fraternal societies, book clubs, and girl scouts are just some of the manifestations of this expressive function. Through them, nonprofit organizations enrich human existence and contribute to the social and cultural vitality of national and community life.

The Community-Building Role

Nonprofit organizations are also important in building what scholars are increasingly coming to call "social capital," those bonds of trust and reciprocity that seem to be crucial for a democratic policy and a market economy to function effectively. Alexis de Tocqueville understood this point well when he wrote in *Democracy in America* that

> Feelings and opinions are recruited, the heart is enlarged, and the human mind is developed, only by the reciprocal influence of men upon one another ... these influences are almost null in democratic countries; they must therefore be artificially created and this can only be accomplished by associations.

By establishing connections among individuals, involvement in associations teaches norms of cooperation that carry over into political and economic life, enlarging that nation's pool of social capital.

The Value Guardian Role

Finally, nonprofit organizations embody, and therefore help to nurture and sustain, a crucial national value emphasizing individual initiative in the public good. They thus give institutional expression to two seemingly contradictory principles that are both important parts of the American national character—the principle of individualism, the notion that people should have the freedom to act on matters that concern them; and the principle of solidarity, the notion that people have responsibilities not only to themselves, but to their fellow human beings and to the communities of which they are part. By fusing these two principles, nonprofit organizations reinforce both, establishing an arena of action through which individuals can take the initiative not simply to promote their own well-being but also to advance the well-being of others. In short, nonprofit America is not only a sizable part of the American economy. It remains, as well, a crucial contributor to the quality of American life.

NOTES

1. The description of the theoretical basis for the nonprofit sector above is drawn from Henry Hansmann, *Economic Theories of Nonprofit Organizations*, in THE NONPROFIT SECTOR: A RESEARCH HANDBOOK, ed. W. Powell (Yale Univ. Press 1987), pp. 28–31; James Douglas, *Political Theories of Nonprofit Organizations*, in *id.*, p. 44; Steven Rathgeb Smith and Michael Lipsky, *Nonprofit Organizations and Community*, in THE NATURE OF THE NONPROFIT SECTOR, ed. J. Steven Ott (Westview Press, 2001), pp. 253–255; Michael Worth, UNDERSTANDING NONPROFIT MANAGEMENT, 4TH ED. (Sage Publications 2016), pp. 50–56; Helmut K. Anheier, NONPROFIT ORGANIZATIONS: THEORY, MANAGEMENT, POLICY, 2nd Ed. (Routledge 2014).

2. Lester Salamon has developed a "voluntary failure" theory that contrasts with the market and governmental failure theories described above. Instead of seeing the nonprofit sector as a residual response to failures in other sectors, he argues that the nonprofit sector is the preferred method for providing collective goods. The government is actually the residual sector that compensates for the shortcomings and failures of the nonprofit sector, such as when it cannot raise sufficient funds to fulfill a social need. Lester M. Salamon, PARTNERS IN PUBLIC SERVICE: GOVERNMENT-NONPROFIT RELATIONS IN THE MODERN WELFARE STATE (Johns Hopkins Univ. Press, 1995), pp. 44–49.

IV. CHALLENGING ASSUMPTIONS ABOUT THE SECTOR

Before exploring the substantive legal framework for the nonprofit sector, we will examine some assumptions about the nonprofit sector that you may or may not hold. Although these questions have no correct answers, your responses to them will inform your opinions on how the sector should be regulated. Assumptions about the sector, which are often unexpressed and even unacknowledged, also inform the decisions of legislators, regulators, and judges. Although we have already discussed the first question from a theoretical point of view and we will address the others at various other points in this book, they are placed here to make you think and to ask you to test your assumptions.

A. WHAT IS THE ROLE OF THE NONPROFIT SECTOR?

Politicians watch polls. Businesses watch profits. Academics just watch. That leaves charities to look out for the most vulnerable among us, and find ways to mend and change what is wrong.

Todd Cohen, Charity Can Fuel Change, PHILANTHROPY J. (Sept. 2, 2003).

I think we all ... appreciate the special contribution the tax-exempt sector makes to the country. It is a vitally important sector that enjoys a privileged place not only in the tax code, but in our national psyche. We want the sector to do well. We need the sector to do well. We expect much of it. We want it to be populated by those who believe in, who are driven by, the concept of service. This is a concept that, of course, can be expressed in many ways. Those who aid the poor and the distressed, those who educate, who perform scientific research, who enliven our arts and our cultural life, who cure the sick, who provide religious leadership in our churches, synagogues and mosques—all are serving others. And all are an essential part of our national fabric and collectively reflect our diverse and creative nation.

Sarah Ingram Hall, *Nonprofit Governance—The View from the IRS*, Georgetown University Law Center Continuing Legal Education (June 23, 2009).

[C]harity has become something of a lifestyle, with large donations buying you entrance into concerts, gala dinners, special exhibits, networking events (see Global Initiative, Clinton), and much else. In such cases, charitable donations are closer to purchasing tickets than selflessly and anonymously giving up private wealth for public ends.

Ezra Klein, *How Charity Subsidizes the Rich*, AM. PROSPECT (Oct. 1, 2007), http://www.prospect.org/csnc/blogs/ezraklein_archive?month=10&year=2007& base_name=how_charity_subsidizes_the_ric.

B. ARE THERE TOO MANY NONPROFITS?

The proliferation of charities has attracted attention in powerful quarters, including the U.S. Senate.... While the Senate is considering whether new charity laws are needed, some nonprofit and legal experts are urging the IRS to deny charity status to organizations that are duplicating efforts already under way.... Some nonprofit observers also want foundations to reduce the number of charities they support and provide financial incentives for charities to merge or collaborate.

Ben Gose, *America's Charity Explosion: Are 800,000 Charities Too Many to Serve Society, or Not Enough?* CHRON. PHILANTHROPY, (Jan. 6, 2005), http://www.philanthropy. com/premium/articles/v17/i06/06000601.htm#growth.

Not everyone agrees that there are too many charities. "Who's to say when we have too many?" asks Robert Ottenhoff, chief executive of GuideStar, an organization that tracks nonprofits. "The number is a sign of vitality and creativity and that people want to do something about a problem."

Jeremiah Hall, *Too Many Ways to Divide Donations?* CHRISTIAN SCIENCE MONITOR, June 20, 2005.

C. ARE HIGH SALARIES A SYMBOL OF ABUSE IN THE SECTOR?

Shocked and appalled at ... exorbitant executive salaries, some critics believe the IRS should put a cap on the salary a nonprofit CEO can earn. As of right now, the IRS simply states that nonprofit CEOs should receive "reasonable compensation.".... While some organizations believe $150,000 is perfectly sensible, others apparently think their noble CEOs deserve millions. After all, there's nothing quite like driving your Ferrari home to your 6,000-square-foot mansion after a long, hard day of fighting for the cause.

Amy Bell, *Nonprofit Millionaires*, Forbes.com (Dec. 17, 2009)

Even if the nonprofits aren't supposed to turn a profit,[21] that doesn't mean that those who work for them are not entitled to profit from their labors. Like Fortune 500 executives, nonprofit executives have student loans, kids to put through college, retirements to save for, and mortgage payments. And just maybe, these folks would like to take a vacation or pursue a hobby. We see no reason that just because nonprofit executives work for charities that they must sacrifice lifestyle. All we ask is that they be paid no more than market rate for their services.... So why shouldn't the head of ... a large and complex organization be well compensated?

Jack Siegel, *Senators Tom Coburn and Charles Grassley Shouldn't Be Criticizing Anybody over Financial Management*, Charity Governance Blog (Aug. 9, 2010), http://www.charitygovernance.com/charity_governance/ 2010/08/senators-tom-coburn-and-charles-grassley-shouldnt-be-criticizing-anybody-over-financial-management.html

D. IS THE NONPROFIT SECTOR HAMPERED BY IRRATIONAL REGULATIONS?

Ironically, by denying charity the tools of capitalism while allowing the for-profit sector to feast on them, we place charity at a severe disadvantage to the for-profit sector, on every front and at every level. The hands of charity are tied, while the for-profit sector scoops every penny off the economic table.... It is a further irony that we prohibit charity from using the tools of capitalism to rectify

---

[21] [Siegel does recognize that nonprofit organizations can earn a profit, or "surplus," as long as they follow the nondistribution constraint.—*Ed.*]

the very disparities some would claim capitalism creates. We allow people to make huge profits doing any number of things that harm the poor, but prohibit anyone from making a profit doing anything that will help them.

Dan Pallotta, UNCHARITABLE: HOW RESTRAINTS ON NONPROFITS UNDERMINE THEIR POTENTIAL (Tufts University Press 2009), 9, 41, 43

E. DOES THE NONPROFIT SECTOR DO MORE HARM THAN GOOD?

Ultimately there would be nothing wrong with having hundreds of thousands of nonprofit organizations if such a social organization did not preclude a more equitable system of social welfare. The most salient issues include: the high financial cost of having a ... nonprofit sector ... [that] removes funds which in other nations would be available for public spending; the structural bias of the nonprofit sector, like the YMCA, which tends to favor the middle class; and the social policy favoring the proliferation of private organizations, which leads to a fragmented service system and causes considerable confusion and lack of quality service to the many needy groups in our society.

David Wagner, WHAT'S LOVE GOT TO DO WITH IT? A CRITICAL LOOK AT AMERICAN CHARITY (New Press 2000), 128–129.

Sometimes I wonder . . . whether these various forms of giving back have become to our era what the papal indulgence was to the Middle Ages: a relatively inexpensive way of getting oneself seemingly on the right side of justice, without having to alter the fundamentals of one's life.

Anand Giridharadas, quoted in David Brooks, *Two Cheers for Capitalism*, NY Times (July 31, 2015).

Model Ts made millions of businesses and workers more productive and created that "public welfare" that the Ford Foundation struggles to achieve. Ford Motor created wealth for society, as well as for Henry Ford, and you can't do the latter without the former. . . . The Ford Foundation plans to focus on six areas of inequality. . . . But none are productive, none drive profits, and none will achieve the huge leaps in public welfare that Henry Ford pulled off so long ago. . . . Government spending is by definition not productive, as you realize every time you step into a DMV. Same goes for charitable giving—no profit means no measure of value or productivity.

Andy Kessler, *The Capitalist as the Ultimate Philanthropist, The Ford Foundation Vows to Fight Inequality but Will Have a Hard Time Beating Henry's Example*, WALL ST. J. (June 24, 2015).

F. OR IS THE NONPROFIT SECTOR WHAT DRIVES OUR ECONOMY AND SAVES DEMOCRACY?

Most people think that Americans are generous because we are rich. The truth is that we are rich, in significant part, because we are generous.... Just imagine, for instance, how your city ... would look if every building funded by individual generosity were suddenly to disappear. The hospitals, museums, universities, theaters—gone. Imagine the workday the rest of us would experience if all the people educated thanks to privately donated, needs based scholarships were suddenly to stay home for a week.... . Over the decades, and in fact centuries, private donors in America have typically made their gifts far earlier and far more quickly than other funders and investors, such as business or government, usually even before the market or our legislators have realized that there is a critical need. This is generally true because generous citizens are individually prepared to take higher risks and invest in more experimental efforts than businesses or government....

Claire Gaudiani, THE GREATER GOOD: HOW PHILANTHROPY DRIVES THE AMERICAN ECONOMY AND CAN SAVE CAPITALISM (2004), 9-10, 14-15.

PROBLEM

Imagine that your community has been devastated by a natural disaster. There is no electricity and people are trapped in their homes. What will be needed to help your fellow citizens, and which sector should provide for which needs? What does your response say about your assumptions concerning the role of the nonprofit sector? Which rationale for the existence of the nonprofit sector best explains your response?

CHAPTER 2

STARTING THE ORGANIZATION AT THE STATE LEVEL

Purpose of this chapter:

- Consider the complexities of starting a nonprofit
- Understand the legal structure options available to those who want to engage in charitable activities
- Explore the legal purposes and powers of nonprofit organizations
- Expose students to articles of incorporation, their functions, and the types of provisions that belong in them

To think about as you read:

Consider an organization that you would like to start that would confer social benefit on the community. Alternatively, think about a collection that you would like to display to the public in a museum setting. Do you need to start an organization, or can you accomplish your goals without one? Can you think of any reasons you might want to start the organization as a for-profit instead of a nonprofit organization? Assuming that you choose a nonprofit form, would it be better as a corporation, an unincorporated organization, or a trust? Assuming that you choose to incorporate, should the state refuse to allow incorporation if several existing organizations share your mission? What if your organization is overtly commercial or distasteful to modern sensitivities? Why did you come to these conclusions? If you have no problems with incorporation, what provisions should you put in your articles of incorporation that will help your new nonprofit corporation run smoothly?

I. INTRODUCTION

Anyone who wants to start a nonprofit organization has a number of decisions to make, beginning with whether to start the organization at all, and if so, whether it should be a traditional for-profit, a nonprofit, or a social enterprise. If the organizer decides on a nonprofit organization, he or she must determine whether to set it up as a trust, an unincorporated organization, or a corporation. He or she must also decide whether the organization should be a membership organization. This chapter begins with a discussion of the factors that influence these decisions.

After this initial discussion, the remainder of the chapter assumes that the decision has been made to use the nonprofit corporate form. The chapter explores which purposes should be considered legitimate for nonprofit corporations and then considers the articles of incorporation, which, when filed, start the clock on the nonprofit's existence.

II. IS A NEW ORGANIZATION ADVISABLE?

Any lawyer who works with nonprofits will acknowledge that a large percentage of the people who begin nonprofit organizations are unaware of the legal, financial, and time commitments that the organization will require for effective management and legal compliance. A lawyer's first service for such a client should be to point out the decisions and potential pitfalls that may lie ahead. Among the decisions are whether to start an organization at all. The following article and essays discuss this question and provide some alternatives to creating a new organization.

MARILYN DICKEY, RESEARCH, MONEY, PERSONAL SUPPORT ARE KEY TO SUCCESSFUL CHARITY START-UPS

Chronicle of Philanthropy (July 12, 2002)

Starting a nonprofit organization can be an exhilarating, rewarding experience, say charity founders, provided that founders have the right ingredients: time and financial resources, in-depth knowledge of the issue at hand, reasonable goals, a workable strategy to achieve them, support from people who can help with the legwork, and the backing of family and friends. And clearly many individuals believe they have what it takes to make a nonprofit group run: The Internal Revenue Service awarded charity status to 865,096 organizations last year. But for some would-be founders, the excitement of creation overshadows the signs that the charity's basic premise won't work: The group doesn't have the capacity to do the job, or its organizers aren't up to the task. Or maybe its finances are too shaky to sustain it, or it duplicates the work of an existing organization. …

Even if all signs point toward starting a new organization, Mr. Berns [executive director of the Maryland Association of Nonprofits] urges prospective charity founders to consider whether the organization would more likely succeed as a for-profit business. With a nonprofit group, he says, "you don't have the same control over your destiny as in a for-profit. With a for-profit business, you own it. If you found a nonprofit, you don't own it. You have founded something that takes on a life of its own. You hire a board of directors that can get rid of you."

The nuts and bolts of starting a nonprofit group are the easy part, says Mr. Pratt, who is ... executive director of the [Minnesota Council of Nonprofits], which works to strengthen the state's nonprofit groups. But long before charity founders reach the point of writing bylaws and applying for tax-exempt status, he says, they need to conduct research. "That's an important stage, the walking-around stage, which is establishing the bona fides for the organizer as well as for the organization," he says. "You have this honeymoon, when you can just tell people, 'Here's what I'm thinking about doing. What do you think?' "

Some otherwise viable nonprofit organizations never begin for a very simple reason: The potential founder can't give up a paycheck long enough to do the groundwork. "The whole process takes time, so if you have nothing to live on, it's very hard to start an organization," says Stephanie Roth, editor of the *Grassroots Fundraising Journal.*

Usually when people start a charity, the seed money comes from their own sources, Ms. Roth says. They may have wealth of their own, they may be married to someone who is bringing in enough money to support their whole family, or they may have friends and relatives willing to chip in. But some people do manage to keep their jobs and work on their nonprofit effort in their spare time. "One scenario is that someone is really excited about an idea or is upset about a need that no one's addressing, and usually they don't get paid for it initially," says Ms. Roth. "They're working around the kitchen table and trying to do whatever their job is at the same time."

It is possible to get some support from foundations, even before a fledgling organization attains nonprofit status, says Mr. Pratt. A foundation may be willing to give enough money to allow someone to spend six months exploring an idea, he says. Or a founder could get a fiscal agent—a charity that will accept donations to an organization until it receives charity status from the IRS. The donor then gets the tax deduction, and the new charity gets the money. That's what Mr. Ero-Phillips did when he started the African American Relief and Development Initiative. His employer at the time, an umbrella group for Twin Cities charities that is now called Pillsbury United Community, helped jump-start the new charity by paying him a salary, in the form of a loan, during his group's start-up period. Pillsbury also provided office space and computers.

"It helps when you have somebody providing initial support," Mr. Ero-Phillips says. "Many new organizations try to use their own money to do their work—to have an office, to pay the utility bills—and at the end of the day if they do not get funded, then they will be down in a hole."

Charity founders have another important piece of advice: Don't go it alone. The job and time commitment are huge, and working with other volunteers or with co-founders can ease some of the burden, says Aspen Baker, co-founder and director of Exhale, an Oakland, Calif., hot line that provides post-abortion counseling. The organization was started by four people and a network of volunteers. "We have one person building relationships with the abortion clinics, another person who had fund-raising experience working with us on grants, and a huge network of other volunteers picking up other pieces," she says.

For Frankie Blackburn, founding Impact Silver Spring, in Maryland, which trains minorities to take on leadership roles, was a labor of love but also a huge undertaking. "What many people miss is what impact it has on your life and your family's life. It is impossible to really achieve this without support at home," she says. "And if you're single, you have to have some other support network. It feeds into every part of your life."

During the planning stages, Ms. Blackburn put in anywhere from 20 to 40 hours a week of work. Now that the organization is up and running, she works about 55 hours a week as the organization's executive director. But, she says, a founder should be prepared to wear many hats. "You have to be open to doing everything," she says. "The first year or two, up till recently, I spent hours in Costco buying supplies. I must have spent half my time packing and unpacking my car. You spend so much time doing nonprofessional work."

Ms. Blackburn, like many charity founders, says she didn't start out primarily to found an organization. "I started out to help people do something," she says. "But I love it, because I have freedom and a place to put so much of my creative energy."

A. COMMON PITFALLS

Good intentions are not enough to guarantee successful nonprofits. As with any new venture, the founders must identify their clients or customers, their market niche, and their financing sources. Unlike other ventures, nonprofits must also plan for and be able to measure their social impact.

Insufficient planning is a major reason that nonprofit organizations fail. Founders need not spend months and years writing a complex business plan, but they should at least be able to develop a "social business model canvas" and apply the "lean startup" methods to their venture. The social business model canvas forces the founders to concentrate on the issues described above. Lean startup principles allow entrepreneurs to test their ideas without spending much money and to adjust them before they make major mistakes.[1] Part of the planning involves establishing a well-defined and coherent mission and setting up a strong board of directors.

Ignorance of the complexities of running a nonprofit is a second common pitfall, and a failure to understand financial information a close third. Not only are the legal rules complex enough that law students spend an entire semester learning them, but financing nonprofits is difficult, and nonprofits have multiple

---

[1] *See* Steve Blank, *Why the Lean Startup Changes Everything*, Harv. Bus. Rev. (May 2013); The Young Foundation, *Introducing the Social Business Model Canvas*, (2013), http://youngfoundation.org/ventures/introducing-the-social-business-model-canvas-2/, last accessed May 8, 2016.

stakeholders whose interests must be addressed. Founders need to understand budgets and basic accounting principles, even if they have the funds to hire an accountant. They need to know where and how to seek funding, whether their services will be free, and how to set up a financial records system. They also need to recognize that it is expensive to start a nonprofit. Insufficient initial funding makes it less likely that the organization will last long enough for a strong fundraising program to get underway.

Nonprofits are also complex because they need to please their clients and customers, the board of directors, their funders, the IRS, the state charity regulators, and even the general public. Those constituencies may have differing interests, and running the organization can be quite a balancing act. Only those nonprofit leaders who use the mission statement as a guide, who pay close attention to financial and other details, and who exhibit strong personal skills will be prepared to handle this balancing act.

B. ALTERNATIVES TO STARTING A NEW ORGANIZATION

Starting a new organization is not always the answer. Sometimes volunteering, either as an individual or with an existing nonprofit, is the way to create the social good that one is trying to create. With 1.2 million existing §501(c)(3) organizations in the United States, a founder needs to ask whether working with an established organization will better serve society's needs. Would duplicating someone else's efforts simply weaken both organizations? Wouldn't it be better to combine forces with the other organization?[2]

One alternative to creating a separate §501(c)(3) is to enter a fiscal sponsorship with an existing §501(c)(3). In essence, the founders create a charitable program within another §501(c)(3). So long as this program furthers the tax-exempt purpose of the fiscal sponsor, the founders can carry on their activities without incorporating or applying to be recognized as a §501(c)(3). The fiscal sponsor accepts tax-deductible contributions from donors seeking to further this program, and it generally disburses the funds to pay for the program's expenses. The fiscal sponsor must retain control and discretion as to the use of the funds and ensure that the distributions are to projects that further its own tax-exempt purpose. It must also maintain records to prove that the funds have been used appropriately. The sponsored program pays a fee to the fiscal agent, which is usually either a percentage of the funds raised or a percentage of funds spent. In return, the program receives back office support, which leaves time and energy to further the mission of the program. The program can become its own §501(c)(3) at a later date.

---

[2] *See* David Callahan, *There Are Way Too Many Nonprofits: What Are Funders Going to Do About It?* INSIDE PHILANTHROPY (Jan. 14, 2015). A comment to this article by Jim Schafer provides a thoughtful alternative argument. http://www.insidephilanthropy.com/home/2015/1/14/there-are-way-too-many-nonprofits-what-are-funders-going-to.html, accessed May 8, 2016.

III. CONSIDERATIONS OF FORM DURING THE STARTUP PHASE

Founders who have the knowledge, tenacity, and resources to start a nonprofit, and who clearly see both the need for a new organization and a way forward, have many legal decisions to make as they begin their organization. Although the vast majority of this book assumes that the founders have created a nonprofit, tax-exempt corporation, that option is not the only one. Founders must determine whether to set up business as a nonprofit entity, whether to incorporate, and, if they choose the nonprofit corporation, which type of nonprofit works best for their organization. Following is Figure 2-1, a chart that outlines the decisions that must be made when founding the organization at the state level, as well as a discussion of those options.

FIGURE 2-1

Decision Tree When Starting an Organization That Seeks to "Do Good."

1. IS A NEW ORGANIZATION NECESSARY?

If yes, then ask:

1. Incorporate or not?

If yes, continue reading this book	If no, choose among: 1. Unincorporated association 2. Trust 3. LLC

If no, then choose among:

1. Individual or group action
2. Work with another group
3. Use a fiscal sponsorship

2. Nonprofit?

If yes, continue reading this book	If no, choose among: 1. Sole proprietorship, partnership 2. LLC 3. C-corp 4. S-corp 5. Benefit corporation 6. L^3C 7. Public benefit, social purpose, benefit LLC

FIGURE 2-1 (*Cont'd*)

2. IF "YES" TO 1 AND 2 ABOVE AND A NONPROFIT CORPORATION IS CHOSEN, ADDITIONAL CHOICES INCLUDE:

1. *Mutual or public benefit?*
2. *Membership or nonmembership?*
3. *National Taxonomy of Exempt Entities (NTEE) code*
4. *Which state?*

A. NONPROFIT OR FOR-PROFIT SOCIAL ENTERPRISE?

As mentioned in the Marilyn Dickey article, the nonprofit form is not always the best form for a new organization, even if the purpose is truly charitable. How should the person who wants to start a new organization make the decision as to which form to use? One approach is to look at the functions of the nonprofit sector (discussed in Chapter 1) and ask whether the organization fills any or all of those functions. A second approach is to look at practical considerations. What financial, tax, marketing, public relations, and control-of-the-organization implications would there be if the organization were created as a for-profit as opposed to a nonprofit?[3] Could it ever make sense to have a for-profit soup kitchen or a nonprofit oil-drilling operation?

In the past, it was almost always clear whether an organization should organize as a nonprofit or a for-profit, but the lines between the sectors are blurring, making the decision more difficult. Increasingly, for-profit organizations recognize that promoting positive social change helps their financial bottom line, and nonprofits need to commercialize some of their offerings in order to stay afloat financially. In today's parlance, many of these organizations would be called "social enterprises." Although the term has multiple definitions, this book defines a social enterprise as an enterprise that generates earned income in support of social purposes. A social enterprise measures its success through a double bottom line—evaluating both its social and financial returns on investment. Most nonprofit organizations fit this definition, but social enterprises are not restricted to the nonprofit world.[4]

---

[3] A discussion of the privileges offered nonprofit organizations can be found in Bazil Facchina, Evan Showell, and Jan Stone, *Privileges and Exemptions Enjoyed by Nonprofit Organizations: A Catalog and Some Thought on Nonprofit Policymaking*, in Topics in Philanthropy, NYU PROG. PHILANTHROPY & THE LAW (1993).

[4] Some commentators would not include nonprofits as social enterprises unless the commercial activity lies at the core of the organization's mission. Thus, an art museum that charges admission to finance its operations would not be a social enterprise, but a bakery with a mission to provide job training for the unemployed would qualify. Others insist on a triple bottom line—one that adds environmental consciousness and perhaps strong labor relations to the double bottom line. Still others require that the enterprise be sufficiently innovative as to transform the situation that has created a social problem.

A social enterprise that is not organized as a nonprofit can be set up using traditional for-profit forms or one of the newer hybrid business forms. The traditional for-profit choices include C-corporations, S-corporations, and limited liability companies (LLCs). The presumption for these forms is that their primary purpose will be to make money for the shareholders or members. (Owners of corporations are called "shareholders" and owners of LLCs are called "members"). Some legal scholars question the truth of this presumption, and certainly if the shareholders and members agree that a social purpose is paramount, it can be. Nevertheless, the social purpose will not be legally required, and these forms cannot gain the "halo effect" that nonprofit organizations often have. Further, the profits that the business makes are taxed, and they cannot accept tax-deductible gifts, which are two of the most important benefits of §501(c)(3) organizations.

These for-profit forms do offer something that the nonprofit corporation cannot offer, however—the possibility that the owners can partake in the business's profits. Additionally, the people running these businesses are not required to follow the rules and restrictions that tax-exempt organizations must follow. Thus, some entrepreneurs decide it is worth foregoing the tax-exempt status of the nonprofit in order to gain these advantages.

Which of the three traditional for-profit forms will an entrepreneur choose? Each situation is different, of course, but the law surrounding the C-corporation is quite well settled, which makes many investors more comfortable with businesses organized this way. Thus, a business that is likely to make a good deal of money with the help of outside investment, such as a firm that will sell an inexpensive renewable energy source, may choose a C-corporation form in order to attract investors.

C-corporations face what is called "double taxation," however. That means that the corporation pays an income tax on its net earnings, and the shareholders pay tax again on any distributions of profit that the corporation has distributed to the shareholders. S-corporations and LLCs[5] are not taxed at the entity level. Instead, the owners pay a personal income tax on those profits. As between LLCs and S-corps, the LLC offers more flexibility and is less expensive to start. LLCs are also less expensive and more flexible than C-corporations, and most new for-profit businesses are set up as LLCs. All three of these for-profit forms have been in existence for at least 40 years and have a track record that might encourage an entrepreneur to choose one of these forms instead of one of the new hybrid forms.

On the other hand, the traditional for-profit forms are not set up to acknowledge a social purpose. Despite disagreement as to whether these business entities permit a social purpose, there is wide agreement they do not require one. And yet, increasingly, entrepreneurs seek a business form that allows and even requires the pursuit of a social mission while pursuing profits. As a result, most

---

[5] LLCs can elect whether to be taxed as a corporation or not, but most choose the pass-through option, described here.

states have passed legislation since 2008 that recognizes at least one hybrid business form that formally has both a social purpose and a profit-making one. The two main types of social enterprises are the L³C and the benefit corporation.[6] Benefit corporation are taxed as if they were C-corporations, and L³C are taxed as LLCs.

The L³C, which stands for "low-profit limited liability company," is a for-profit organization designed to retain the flexibility of an LLC, but with a primary motivation to achieve a charitable goal. The organization cannot have the profit motive as its primary motive, although it can realize a profit and distribute the profit to the members if the organization is profitable. The L³C cannot engage in lobbying or political campaign activity. If the organization's charitable purpose ceases to be its primary one, it simply becomes an LLC. In 2016, the L³C was recognized in 8 states and three Indian nations, and approximately 1,326 companies had registered as L³Cs.[7]

The L³C has not grown as fast as the benefit corporation and its derivatives, the public benefit corporation and the social purpose corporation. The first benefit corporation legislation was passed in 2010 and by 2016, benefit corporation legislation had passed in 31 states, with legislation pending in an additional 7 states.[8]

The benefit corporation requires that the organization have a general public benefit (i.e. a material positive impact on society and the environment), and it allows the organization to seek a specific benefit purpose as well. Directors must take social and environmental considerations into account when making corporate decisions, and in most states, they must appoint a "benefit director," who has a special obligation to consider the public benefit when decisions are made. Most states' benefit corporation statutes also require these organizations to measure their progress against a third-party standard and publish their annual "benefit reports." Members of the board of directors and those who own at least 2% of the corporation can bring a benefit enforcement proceeding to require the corporation to pursue the public benefit, but neither the board nor the corporation faces monetary damages for failure to pursue the benefit, and the corporate status does not change if that benefit is not pursued. In essence, benefit corporations depend on transparency—reporting by the organizations—to influence investors and customers and thereby enforce the statutory provisions. In 2016, there were

---

[6] Other hybrid forms also exist. For example, Delaware, which is generally recognized as the most important state for corporate law, recognizes the public benefit corporation, as does Colorado. Washington, California, Florida, and Texas recognize the social purpose corporation, and Maryland and Oregon recognize the benefit LLC. *See* Cassaday Brewer, Social Enterprise Entity Comparison Chart, (May 17, 2015). Available at http://ssrn.com/abstract=2304892; *See also* Carter Bishop, Fifty State Series: L³C & B Corporation Legislation Table (2014). Suffolk University Law School Research Paper No. 10-11, available at http://ssrn.com/abstract=1561783.

[7] Intersector L³C Tally, http://www.intersectorl3c.com/l3c_tally.html, last accessed May 8, 2016.

[8] State by State Status of Legislation, http://www.benefitcorp.net, last accessed May 15, 2016.

more almost 4,000 benefit corporations in the United States, among them Patagonia, Seventh Generation, Plum Organics, and King Arthur Flour.[9]

The hybrid forms discussed above and the certification system are quite new, and significant variations exist among the state statutes. Organizations are not bound by the choices in their states, however, because an organization that forms in one state can do business in another. For example, if the founders and their attorneys agree that an organization doing business in North Carolina would best be served as a benefit corporation, which is not currently recognized in North Carolina, it can incorporate as a benefit corporation in a state like Virginia, which recognizes this business form, and then do business in North Carolina, as long as it also completes the proper paperwork in North Carolina.

And yet the recent adoption of these statutes, combined with the patchwork nature of their adoption across the country have made some founders wary of using them for their social enterprises. In contrast, the nonprofit corporation is well established, and the rules within each state and with the Internal Revenue Service (IRS) are known. There is no question that the social purpose is paramount, particularly with the §501(c)(3) organizations discussed in this book. The annual reports are mandatory, and there are distinct legal consequences at both the state and federal levels if the nondistribution constraint is violated. The organization itself can make a profit, but the profits cannot be distributed, which is one of the hallmarks of the new hybrid entities. Thus, an entrepreneur with a business idea that should bring in significant revenue has a number of factors to consider.

Examples of Organizations That Made This Nonprofit/ For-Profit Social Enterprise Choice

Newman's Own, the organization that actor Paul Newman began in 1982 to market his salad dressing, is a for-profit organization that gives 100% of its after-tax profits to charity. As of the end of 2015, the organization had given away $460 million.[10] Why do you think Paul Newman started the organization as a for-profit? Could he have set it up as a nonprofit organization, given the definitions you learned in the last chapter? Remember that setting up a nonprofit corporation is different from obtaining federal tax exemption, which will be covered in Chapter 4. The Green Bay Packers football team, for example, is organized as a nonprofit business that is not tax exempt.

Greyston Bakery and Together We Bake have similar missions, but one is organized as a for-profit and one as a nonprofit. Greyston Bakery's slogan is: "We don't hire people to bake brownies; we bake brownies to hire people." Greyston Bakery has an open hiring policy. It hires its entry-level employees without screening or interviews on a first-come, first-serve basis. All employees receive training and services while baking brownies for others, including the

---

[9] Find a Benefit Corporation, Benefit Corporation, http://benefitcorp.org/businesses/find-a-benefit-corp, accessed May 8, 2016.

[10] http://newmansownfoundation.org/about-us/total-giving/, accessed May 8, 2016.

brownies for Ben and Jerry's Chocolate Fudge Brownie ice cream. Greyston Bakery is a for-profit benefit corporation that is owned by a nonprofit, the Greyston Foundation.

Together We Bake (TWB) is a comprehensive workforce training and personal development program for women in need of a second chance. Women attend 10 weeks of classes and then set out to find their own jobs. TWB's cookies and granola are sold in Whole Foods and other retailers in northern Virginia. TWB is a nonprofit organization that has no intention of becoming for-profit, despite Greyston's success as a benefit corporation. Its founders believe that it can better fulfill its mission using this form.

Priscilla Chan and her husband, Mark Zuckerberg, the founder of Facebook, have announced they will use 99% of their Facebook fortune to help solve global problems, using the for-profit LLC, the Chan Zuckerberg Initiative, as the legal vehicle for their philanthropy. People with wealth on their scale, including John D. Rockefeller and Bill Gates, have traditionally used private foundations for this purpose, but this couple chose the LLC instead. Can you begin to see why they made this decision?[11]

Such decisions are not new ones. Hospitals and colleges, for example, can ordinarily be organized as either nonprofit or for-profit entities. Few would call them social enterprises, possibly because they are not usually considered innovative enough to disrupt a current model, but their donors, managers, and boards of directors are aware of the different rules for each type of organization, and from time to time they switch from one form to the other for financial or public relations reasons. It is widely thought, for example, that the decision of the National Football League (NFL) to give up its tax-exempt status, was motivated in part because it would no longer have to reveal executive salaries.[12]

B. TO INCORPORATE OR NOT?

Although this book focuses on nonprofit corporations, the nonprofit organization need not be established as a corporation. A nonprofit organization can also be organized as an unincorporated association, a trust, or an LLC. The nonprofit organization cannot, however, be organized as a sole proprietorship or a partnership. Why?

---

[11] For more information on these enterprises, see http://www.newmansownfoundation.org; http://greyston.com; http://togetherwebake.org; http://omidyarnetwork.com; https://www.facebook.com/chanzuckerberginitiative/; and Letter to Our Daughter (https://www.facebook.com/notes/mark-zuckerberg/a-letter-to-our-daughter/10153375081581634). The Omidyar Network (http://omidyar.com) is another large organization that has chosen to forego the tax benefits of a §501(c)(3) private foundation in order to invest in both nonprofit and for-profit entities that can help bring about positive social change.

[12] *See e.g.* Chris Isidor, *NFL Gives Up Tax Exempt Status, CNN Money,* April 28, 2015. Chapter 13 deals with conversions to for-profit tax status.

Following is a discussion of the pros and cons of creating each of these types of organizations. Note that tax consequences generally are *not* factors in this decision. Tax-exempt I.R.C. Section 501(c)(3) organizations, for example, which we will spend much of this book discussing, can be in the form of unincorporated associations, trusts, LLCs, or nonprofit corporations.

Nonprofit Corporation

Most nonprofit organizations in the United States are nonprofit corporations. The state nonprofit corporation statutes are quite thorough with regard to corporate powers and governance. They provide that a corporation is an entity that can sue and be sued, contract, and hold property. The corporation is governed by a board of directors who have defined terms of service and whose potential liability is not as high as trustees of a trust. Because the legal consequences of so many situations are spelled out in the nonprofit statute, the nonprofit corporation offers more certainty for those situations than an unincorporated association or a trust. Despite the thorough description of corporate powers and governance, the nonprofit statutes also allow for flexibility with regard to changing directors and amending the organizational documents. In addition, corporations provide protection against individual liability. Once the organization is properly incorporated, the corporation will be liable for its actions, and its funders, board, employees, and volunteers will be protected against individual liability.

Unincorporated Associations

An unincorporated association is a group of two or more people working together for a common purpose, who have not formalized the organization as a corporation or a trust. These organizations are generally quite informal and flexible, and they do not need any formal organizing documents, unless they are seeking exempt status under §501. (If they are seeking exempt status, they will need organizational documents that provide the same basic information found in a corporate charter or trust instrument.) An unincorporated association is not a separate legal entity. Therefore, unless state statutory law declares otherwise, the organization cannot hold property or contract in its own name, and its members can be held personally liable for the acts of the association.

Many small nonprofit organizations are unincorporated associations. Those running smaller operations may be unaware of alternative forms of organization, or they could have decided incorporation is unnecessary because they have no real property, do not need to raise funds, and would probably fail to comply with all of the paperwork requirements necessary to remain incorporated, if they did so in the first place.

Occasionally, sophisticated organizations remain unincorporated for business or philosophical reasons. The PGA provides one such example. If those unincorporated associations exist in a state that offers limited liability to the members of an unincorporated association, the risk of liability is not as high as it would be in states without such protection.[13]

Limited Liability Company (LLC)

As we noted above, an LLC is a specific type of unincorporated association that receives protection against the liability that it would otherwise face as an unincorporated association. Its members have more leeway to choose how they are organized and governed than they would in a corporation, and they can choose to be taxed as a partnership or as a corporation.

Some states allow LLCs to be set up for nonprofit purposes, and the IRS recognizes that an LLC can be tax exempt if its members are all tax-exempt entities and all the other requirements for tax exemption are met.[14] The LLC organizational structure is useful for nonprofit joint ventures and subsidiaries in states that recognize nonprofit LLCs, but it is not ordinarily considered the best organizational structure for a new nonprofit.

Trust

The charitable trust is the oldest formal nonprofit entity, and it is still the most predominant nonprofit form in England. It is created through a trust instrument that irrevocably dedicates specific property to the benefit of the community, rather than to the benefit of an individual. It is quite difficult to change the purpose of a trust, which is governed by one or more trustees. These trustees are generally held to a higher fiduciary standard than directors of a nonprofit corporation. The trustees make and implement decisions regarding the trust property, and they serve indefinite terms. Nonprofit organizations that manage funds and grant money often find this form useful, but operating organizations that may need to amend their organizational documents are more likely to incorporate. Those who govern the organization may also prefer the corporate form, as their risk of liability is somewhat less. On the other hand, a trust does not need the approval of the state, so it can be formed easily and quickly.

For further reading on decisions about whether to incorporate and whether to be a nonprofit or a for-profit social enterprise, see Nancy Melman and Lisa

---

[13] The Uniform Unincorporated Associations Act and its successor, the Revised Uniform Unincorporated Associations Act, both recognize unincorporated associations as legal entities that can sue, be sued, and hold real property. Revised Uniform Unincorporated Associations Act (2008). A total of 12 states adopted the original act, *Id.,* and at least Kentucky, Nevada, and Iowa have adopted the revised act. KRS §§273A.005-273A.165 (2015); NRS §§81.700-81.890 (2009); Iowa Code §§501B.1-501B.32 (2010).

[14] *See* Richard McCrary and Ward Thomas, B. Limited Liability Companies as Exempt Organizations—Update (2001 CPE Text), updatingTopic B, *Limited Liability Companies as Exempt Organizations—Update,* 2000 (for 2001). Exempt Organizations CPE Technical Instruction Program Textbook. *See also* David Walker, *A Consideration of an LLC for a 501(C)(3) Nonprofit Organization,* 38 Wm. Mitchell L. Rev. 627 (2012).

Watts, *Nonprofit Organizations: A Guide to Choosing Form* (New York University School of Law, National Center on Philanthropy and the Law 2007); Robert Wexler, *Effective Social Enterprise—A Menu of Legal Structures*, 63 EXEMPT ORG. TAX REV. 565 (2009); Elizabeth Searing, *Judging a Book by Its Cover: The Role of Corporate Form in Social Enterprise Start-Ups* (September 30, 2014), available at http://ssrn.com/abstract=2534782; Eden S. Blair and Tanya Marcum, *Heed Our Advice: Exploring How Professionals Guide Small Business Owners in Start-Up Entity Choice*, 53 J. SMALL BUS. MGMT. 249 (2015).

C. PUBLIC BENEFIT OR MUTUAL BENEFIT?

Chapter 1 introduced the concept of public benefit and mutual benefit organizations. Some state statutes use this classification system as an organizing device, but even if a state statute does not do so, all nonprofit organizations can fit into one of these two categories. The purpose or mission of an organization will determine which classification applies. If the organization serves the interests of its members, it will be a mutual benefit organization. Clubs, fraternities, and labor unions are examples of mutual benefit organizations. Only if the organization serves the interests of others—that is, of the public—will it be a public benefit organization.

This distinction is important in those states that have adopted this classification as part of their nonprofit corporation laws. It is also important in terms of the federal tax exemption classification. Although the Internal Revenue Code does not use this language, only public benefit organizations can become §501(c)(3) tax-exempt organizations that are exempt from federal income tax and are eligible to receive tax-deductible contributions from donors. Mutual benefit organizations are likely to be recognized as tax-exempt organizations, but they cannot accept tax-deductible contributions. Because this book concentrates on §501(c)(3) public charities, mutual benefit organizations will be covered only incidentally. Nonetheless, you should be aware that both types of organizations are nonprofit organizations that can receive tax exemption, and a founder of a nonprofit has the option of starting the organization as either type.

D. MEMBERSHIP OR NONMEMBERSHIP ORGANIZATION?

Assuming that the founders of the nonprofit organization have chosen the nonprofit corporate form, they will need to decide whether the organization should have members before they draw up articles of incorporation and bylaws. This decision will determine how the corporation is governed and controlled. Nonmembership organizations are governed by a board of directors, which makes its own decisions and elects its own board members. Membership organizations, on the other hand, have members that elect the directors, approve bylaw amendments, and vote on major decisions, such as mergers and dissolution.

Members in a membership organization are analogous to shareholders in a for-profit corporation, except that they cannot accept distributions of profits. The members' powers are enumerated in an organization's bylaws, which should include provisions dealing with the election and removal of members, requirements for meetings, and the percentage of votes needed to approve a measure. In addition, member consent is usually needed before the provisions relating to the members' powers can be changed.

Membership organizations can get a large number of people interested in and willing to work for an organization. As a result, advocacy groups, mutual benefit organizations, and churches are often membership organizations. A drawback to membership organizations, however, is that they have an additional layer of governance that can make decision making more bureaucratic and increase the chance that the organization will fail to follow all the requirements. Most public charities decide that this bureaucracy is unnecessary. They choose not to have members, and they rely solely on their board of directors for governance.

This book will concentrate on nonmembership corporations unless otherwise specified. For an example of a case in which the bylaws stated that members should elect the board, but in fact the board acted as a self-perpetuating (nonmembership) board until a policy dispute arose, see *Matter of Veniglia v. Nori*, 892 N.E.2d 850; 862 N.Y.S.2d 457 (2008) (court reversed lower-court decision invalidating board decisions that failed to follow the original bylaws, by finding that the original bylaws had long since been abandoned, and, in any case, were invalid under the Religious Corporations Law).

Note that the term "member" can be confusing because nonprofit corporations sometimes call their donors "members." These nonprofits may provide discounts or special privileges to their "members," but they do not accord them any corporate powers. Unless an organization specifically spells out the existence and function of members in its bylaws, it is a nonmembership organization. To be safe, however, a nonmembership organization may wish to explain in its bylaws that its use of the term "member" does not confer any corporate powers or responsibilities.

E. VARIATIONS AMONG STATE NONPROFIT CORPORATIONS STATUTES

Most nonprofit organizations are set up as nonprofit corporations. Those who create nonprofit corporations must follow the laws of their state's nonprofit corporation act. The nondistribution constraint, discussed in Chapter 1, is a major component of all state noncorporation acts. These statutes also set forth the powers and allowable purposes of nonprofit organizations, describe the state's rules about articles of incorporation and bylaws, define the fiduciary duties of the board of directors (Chapter 3), regulate fundraising (Chapter 6), and set forth requirements for dissolving the corporation (Chapter 13).

Unfortunately, the states' laws are not uniform. The American Bar Association adopted the Model Nonprofit Corporation Act, Third Edition

(MNCA, 3d Ed.), in August 2008. Since that date, at least New York, Michigan, Tennessee, and Iowa, and Washington, D.C., have changed their nonprofit corporation acts, and none of them has adopted the MNCA 3d Ed. in its entirety. Thus, nonprofits and their lawyers must pay close attention to the laws of their particular jurisdiction. It is unclear how many jurisdictions have adopted variations of this new business form.[15]

This chapter includes provisions from the nonprofit laws in New York and California, as well as some provisions from the MNCA, 3d Ed. Each statute has a slightly different approach to nonprofit law. One of the major differences is the way they classify their nonprofit organizations. California divides nonprofits into public benefit, mutual benefit, and religious organizations. New York classifies them as "charitable" or "noncharitable," which roughly correlates to public benefit and mutual benefit. Other states have different classifications. Virginia, for example, distinguishes the way that the organization is governed—whether it is a membership organization in which members elect the board of directors, or whether it is governed directly by the board. The MNCA, 3d Ed., eliminates the distinctions among the different types of nonprofit corporations.

NOTE

Organizations that want to be recognized as social enterprises have another option, in addition to pursuing one of the legal forms described above—a certification system. All for-profit businesses, whatever their legal form, can qualify as certified B corporations if they meet certain social and environmental standards. This certification system helps companies to keep their social and environmental objectives in the forefront and to signal their social credentials to others. As of 2016, there were 1,674 certified B corporations in 41 countries.[16] Among the more well known brands that are certified B corporations are Ben and Jerry's, Etsy, and Dansko Shoes. The benefit corporations mentioned above also have the B corporation certification. This book will revisit the concept of social enterprises in Chapter 10.

IV. LEGITIMATE PURPOSES OF NONPROFIT CORPORATIONS

Should states automatically confer nonprofit status on organizations that pay the statutory fee and draft articles of incorporation and bylaws, or should there be some "nonprofit" purpose behind these organizations? Following are the parts of

---

[15] In 2008, the nonprofit corporation act of 12 states was based on the Model Nonprofit Act of 1952, and 26 were loosely based on the Revised Model Nonprofit Act of 1988. Another 5 made no distinction between for-profit and nonprofit corporations. Michael E. Malamut, *Summary of Sources of State Nonprofit Corporation Laws*, NAT'L PARLIAMENTARIAN, April 2008, at 8.

[16] Certified B Corporations, http://bcorporation.net, accessed May 8, 2016.

the New York Not-for-Profit Law, the California Corporations Code, and the MNCA, 3d Ed., that relate to the powers and purposes of nonprofit organizations, as well as an essay that describes the way that decisions were made in the past. Today's provisions are quite broad, and they have the effect of allowing almost every organization to become nonprofit. Can you think of any organizations that would not qualify under these statutes? Is it good to be this permissive or should the law be more restrictive?

NEW YORK NOT-FOR-PROFIT CORPORATION LAW, §§201, 204, 501, 508, AND 515

§201. Purposes

(a) A corporation, as defined in paragraph (a) of sec. 102 (Definitions), may be formed under this chapter as a charitable corporation or a non-charitable corporation unless it may be formed under any other corporate law of this state in which event it may not be formed under this chapter unless such other corporate law expressly so provides.

(b) A corporation formed under this chapter on or after July First, Two Thousand Fourteen shall either be a charitable corporation or a non-charitable corporation. Any corporation formed for both charitable purposes and non-charitable purposes shall be deemed a charitable corporation for purposes of this chapter. . . .

§204. Limitation on activities

Notwithstanding any other provision of this chapter or any other general law, a corporation of any kind to which this chapter applies shall conduct no activities for pecuniary profit or financial gain, whether or not in furtherance of its corporate purposes, except to the extent that such activity supports its other lawful activities then being conducted.

§501. Stock and shares prohibited; membership certificates authorized

A corporation shall not have stock or shares or certificates for stock or for shares, but may issue non-transferable membership certificates or cards to evidence membership. ...

§508. Income from corporate activities

A corporation whose lawful activities involve among other things the charging of fees or prices for its services or products shall have the right to receive such income and, in so doing, may make an incidental profit. All such incidental profits shall be applied to the maintenance, expansion or operation of the lawful activities of the corporation, and in no case shall be divided or distributed in any manner whatsoever among the members, directors, or officers of the corporation.

§515. Dividends prohibited; certain distributions of cash or property authorized

(a) A corporation shall not pay dividends or distribute any part of its income or profit to its members, directors, or officers.

CALIFORNIA CORPORATIONS CODE, §§5111, 5410, AND 5420

---

§5111. Formation of corporation; Purpose

Subject to any other provisions of law of this state applying to the particular class of corporation or line of activity, a corporation may be formed under this part for any public or charitable purposes.

§5410. Distributions prohibited

No corporation shall make any distribution. ...

§5420. Liability of person receiving distributions; Actions

(a) Any person who receives any distribution is liable to the corporation for the amount so received by such person with interest thereon at the legal rate on judgments until paid.

MODEL NONPROFIT CORPORATION ACT, 3D ED. (2008), §§3.01, 6.40, AND 6.41

---

§3.01. Purposes

(a) Every nonprofit corporation has the purpose of engaging in any lawful activity unless a more limited purpose is set forth in the articles of incorporation.

§6.40. Distributions Prohibited

(a) Except as permitted under Section 6.22 or 6.41, a nonprofit corporation shall not pay dividends or make distributions of any part of its assets, income, or profits to its members, directors, members of a designated body, or officers.

§6.41. Compensation and Other Permitted Payments

(a) A nonprofit corporation may pay reasonable compensation or reimburse reasonable expenses to members, directors, members of a designated body, or officers for services rendered.

NOTE ON PURPOSES OF NONPROFIT CORPORATIONS

In the early years of the United States, a distinction between for-profit and nonprofit corporations did not exist. All corporations were chartered to do business through legislative action, and they needed a public purpose, even if that purpose would be profitable. By the mid-19th century, this process seemed cumbersome, and general incorporation statutes came into being for certain purposes.

Eventually, for-profit and nonprofit corporations received different designations. For-profit charters were liberalized so that businesses could be chartered "for any lawful purpose." Nonprofit statutes remained somewhat more restrictive. A nonprofit charter would be granted for organizations that agreed to pursue certain permissible purposes and not to distribute profits. A government employee or judge would determine if the organization met these goals.

This process left a good deal of discretion in the hands of individuals and led to some decisions that denied nonprofit incorporation to entities that would receive a nonprofit charter today. In the mid-20th century, cases denying corporate status to organizations seeking to change the law, to groups trying to educate others about homosexuality, and to groups trying to address the same issue as another nonprofit were not uncommon. Organizations that seemed too commercial in the eyes of the decision maker or that didn't pass the "smell test" were also likely to be turned down.

Since that time, the restrictions have relaxed considerably. Most states allow nonprofit corporate status for "any lawful purpose" and state that the corporation's existence begins once its governing documents are filed with the state. What are the ramifications of liberalizing the acceptable purposes for incorporating as a nonprofit corporation? Are they all positive? *See* Norman Silber, A CORPORATE LAW OF FREEDOM: THE EMERGENCE OF THE MODERN NONPROFIT SECTOR (2001); James Fishman, *The Development Of Nonprofit Corporation Law And An Agenda For Reform*, 34 Emory L.J. 617.

QUESTIONS

1. In *State v. Brown*, 133 N.E. 2d (Ohio 1956), the court decided not to overrule the state's decision to refuse to accept the articles of incorporation for an organization that planned to run a nudist facility and enlighten the public on the benefits of nudism. The court found that such a facility would violate Ohio's law against the practice of nudism. As mentioned above, nonprofit incorporation statutes have been liberalized since the mid-20th century. Would this case be decided differently today, assuming that Ohio's law had not changed?

2. Many nonprofit practitioners and commentators believe that there are too many nonprofits. Should a state be authorized to refuse to accept the articles of incorporation for a nonprofit that duplicates the work of another nonprofit? In 1959, a New York court did just that [*In re Sidney Gelb*

Chapter for Cancer Research, 187 N.Y.S. 2s 184 (1959)]. How would that case be decided under the current New York statute?

3. Some nonprofit charters violate current public policy. Would a nonprofit that promotes "freedom of association" and studies "problems of intergroup relations, in areas of ethnic characteristics and patterns" (in other words, a white supremacist group) be allowed to incorporate under current statutes? *See Association for the Preservation of Freedom of Choice, Inc. v Shapiro*, 174 N.E. 3d 487 (NY 1961). *See also* Michael Kimmelman, *What D'Ya Call a House of Sex? A Museum. Oh.* N.Y. Times (Jan. 18, 2000) (founder of the "Smithsonian of sex" explaining that the organization is a for-profit because it was denied nonprofit status on the grounds that "the term 'Museum of Sex' made a mockery of the institution of a museum.")

4. Who should determine whether an organization should be able to incorporate as a nonprofit corporation? Should it be the incorporators? Someone in the government? A judge? What standard should that decision maker use when making the determination?

V. ARTICLES OF INCORPORATION

Articles of incorporation provide the general legal framework for a nonprofit corporation. Typically, the articles set forth the name of the organization, its purpose, whether it is a membership organization, and the registered agent. Each state has its own requirements, however, and the incorporators may choose to add other provisions, so long as they are consistent with the state statute. Articles are more difficult to change than bylaws, so incorporators usually include provisions that are unlikely to change during the organization's existence. Following are statutory provisions that relate to articles of incorporation in a nonprofit corporation, a case that turned on the language of an organization's articles of incorporation, and sample articles of incorporation.

NEW YORK NOT-FOR-PROFIT CORPORATION LAW,
§§401, 402, AND 403

---

§401 Incorporators

One or more natural persons at least eighteen years of age may act as incorporators of a corporation to be formed under this chapter.

§402 Certificate of incorporation; contents

(a) A certificate, entitled "Certificate of Incorporation of (name of corporation), under section 402 of the Not-for-Profit Corporation Law," shall be signed by each incorporator with his name and address included in such certificate and delivered to the department of state. It shall set forth:

(1) The name of the corporation.

(2) That the corporation is a corporation as defined in subparagraph (a)(5) of section 102 (Definitions);

(2-a) The purpose or purposes for which it is formed, it being sufficient to state that the purpose of the corporation is for any purpose for which corporations may be organized under this chapter as a charitable or non-charitable corporation, and whether it is a charitable corporation or a noncharitable corporation under section 201 (Purposes); any corporation may also set forth any activities that it intends to carry out in furtherance of such purpose or purposes; provided that this subparagraph shall not be interpreted to require that the certificate of incorporation set forth such activities or otherwise state how the corporation's purposes will be achieved. . . .

(3) The county within the state in which the office of the corporation is to be located. It may also set forth the post office address of an office without the state, at which, pursuant to section 621 (Books and records; right of inspection; prima facie evidence), the books and records of account of the corporation shall be kept.

(4) The names and addresses of the initial directors.

(5) The duration of the corporation if other than perpetual.

(6) A designation of the secretary of state as agent of the corporation upon whom process against it may be served and the post office address within or without this state to which the secretary of state shall mail a copy of any process against it served upon him.

(7) If the corporation is to have a registered agent, his name and address within this state and a statement that the registered agent is to be the agent of the corporation upon whom process against it may be served.

§403. Certificate of incorporation; effect

Upon the filing of the certificate of incorporation by the department of state, the corporate existence shall begin, and such certificate shall be conclusive evidence that all conditions precedent have been fulfilled and that the corporation has been formed under this chapter, except in an action or special proceeding brought by the attorney-general. ...

CALIFORNIA CORPORATIONS CODE, §§5120, 5130, 5131, 5132, AND 5134

§5120. Formation

(a) One or more persons may form a corporation under this part by executing and filing articles of incorporation.

(b) If initial directors are named in the articles, each director named in the articles shall sign and acknowledge the articles; if initial directors are not named in the articles, the articles shall be signed by one or more persons who thereupon are the incorporators of the corporation.

(c) The corporate existence begins upon the filing of the articles and continues perpetually, unless otherwise expressly provided by law or in the articles.

(d) At the time of filing pursuant to this section, the Secretary of State shall forward a copy of the filed araticles of incorporation to the Attorney General.

§5130. Articles of incorporation; Contents

The articles of incorporation of a corporation formed under this part shall set forth:

(a) The name of the corporation.

(b) The following statement: "This corporation is a nonprofit public benefit corporation and is not organized for the private gain of any person. It is organized under the Nonprofit Public Benefit Corporation Law for (public or charitable [insert one or both]) purposes." [If the purposes include "public" purposes, the articles shall, and in all other cases the articles may, include a further description of the corporation's purposes.]

(c) The name and street address in this state of the corporation's initial agent for service of process in accordance with subdivision (b) of Section 6210.

(d) The initial street address of the corporation.

(e) The initial mailing address of the corporation, if different from the initial street address.

§5131. Statement limiting purposes or powers of corporation

The articles of incorporation may set forth a further statement limiting the purposes or powers of the corporation.

§5132. Additional provisions specified

(a) The articles of incorporation may set forth any or all of the following provisions, which shall not be effective unless expressly provided in the articles:

(1) A provision limiting the duration of the corporation's existence to a specified date....

(b) Nothing contained in subdivision (a) shall affect the enforceability, as between the parties thereto, of any lawful agreement not otherwise contrary to public policy.

(c) The articles of incorporation may set forth any or all of the following provisions:

(1) The names and addresses of the persons appointed to act as initial directors....

(4) A provision that requires an amendment to the articles, as provided in subdivision (a) of Section 5812, or to the bylaws, and any amendment or repeal of that amendment, to be approved in writing by a specified person or persons other than the board or the members....

(5) Any other provision, not in conflict with law, for the management of the activities and for the conduct of the affairs of the corporation, including any provision that is required or permitted by this part to be stated in the bylaws.

§5134. Powers of incorporator to perfect organization

If initial directors have not been named in the articles, the incorporator or incorporators, until the directors are elected, may do whatever is necessary and proper to perfect the organization of the corporation, including the adoption and amendment of bylaws of the corporation and the election of directors and officers.

MODEL NONPROFIT CORPORATION ACT, 3D ED. (2008), §§2.01, 2.02, 2.03, AND 10.01

§2.01. Incorporators

One or more persons may act as the incorporators of a nonprofit corporation by delivering articles of incorporation to the secretary of state for filing.

§2.02. Articles of Incorporation

(a) The articles of incorporation must set forth:

(1) a name for the nonprofit corporation that satisfies the requirements of Section 4.01;
(2) the street address of the corporation's initial registered office and the name of its initial registered agent at that office;
(3) that the corporation is incorporated under this [act]; and
(4) the name of each incorporator.

(b) The articles of incorporation may set forth:

(1) the names of the individuals who are to serve as the initial directors;
(2) provisions creating one or more designated bodies;
(3) the names of the initial members of a designated body;
(4) whether the corporation will have members;
(5) the names of the initial members, if any;
(6) provisions not inconsistent with law regarding:
(i) the purpose or purposes for which the nonprofit corporation is organized;

(ii) managing the business and regulating the affairs of the corporation;

(iii) defining, limiting, and regulating the powers of the corporation, its board of directors, any designated body, and the members, if any;

(iv) the characteristics, qualifications, rights, limitations, and obligations attaching to each or any class of members; or

(v) the distribution of assets on dissolution;

(7) any provision that this [act] requires or permits to be set forth in the articles or bylaws;

(8) a provision permitting or making obligatory indemnification of a director for liability (as defined in Section 8.50(5)) to any person for any action taken, or any failure to take any action, as a director, except liability for:

(i) receipt of a financial benefit to which the director is not entitled;

(ii) an intentional infliction of harm;

(iii) a violation of Section 8.33; or

(iv) an intentional violation of criminal law; and

(9) provisions required if the corporation is to be exempt from taxation under federal, state, or local law....

(d) The articles of incorporation need not set forth any of the corporate powers enumerated in this [act]....

§2.03. Incorporation

(a) Unless a delayed effective date is specified, the corporate existence begins when the articles of incorporation are filed.

(b) The filing of the articles of incorporation by the secretary of state is conclusive proof that the incorporators satisfied all conditions precedent to incorporation except in a proceeding by the state to cancel or revoke the incorporation or involuntarily dissolve the nonprofit corporation.

§10.01. Authority to Amend

A nonprofit corporation may amend its articles of incorporation at any time to add or change a provision that is required or permitted in the articles as of the effective date of the amendment or to delete a provision that is not required to be contained in the articles.

QUEEN OF ANGELS HOSPITAL V. YOUNGER

---

66 Cal. App. 3d 359; 136 Cal. Rptr. 36; 1977 Cal. App. (1977)

[*Editor's Note:* The Franciscan Sisters of the Sacred Heart founded Queen of Angels Hospital (hereinafter Queen) in 1927. The Sisters raised the $600,000 needed to build the hospital by soliciting financial backing from others, at times even begging on the street and going hungry to save funds. The hospital grew steadily through the 1930s and 1940s, and at one point, most of the residents of Los Angeles had been born there. By the 1970s, Queen decided to lease the hospital building to a for-profit corporation, W.D.C., and use the proceeds from the lease to operate clinics. Queen, a corporation, and the Franciscan Sisters of the Sacred Heart, an unincorporated association, filed a declaratory relief action against the attorney general to determine the validity of this lease agreement. The attorney general challenged the fees, and the trial court ruled in favor of the plaintiffs. Both sides appealed. As you read this case, think about why this case is even before the court. Why didn't the hospital simply amend its articles of incorporation? Why did the attorney general oppose an idea that had the potential of helping more residents of Los Angeles receive medical attention? We will reconsider this case in Chapter 13, where you will learn more about what has happened to this hospital since 1977. For now, you might find it interesting to learn that the Queen of Angels Hospital building, which can be seen from the Hollywood Freeway, has been shown in several movies, including *Patriot Games, Ghost, Nixon, Apollo 13, Halloween 6, The Usual Suspects, Reality Bites,* and *Naked Gun 33⅓*][17]

Facts

The facts are not disputed; the materiality of some of the facts is. Plaintiff Queen of Angels Hospital is a nonprofit corporation, first incorporated in 1927....

... In April 1971 ... Queen's board of directors approved a lease to be effective May 1, 1971, between Queen as lessor and W.D.C. Services, Inc., hospital entrepreneurs, as lessee. Queen leased the hospital, excepting the outpatient clinic and a convent house, to W.D.C. for 25 years with 2 options for 10 additional years each. The minimum annual rental guaranteed Queen was $800,000 for the first two years and $1 million a year thereafter.

Queen intends to use a substantial portion of the lease proceeds to establish and operate additional medical clinics in east and south central Los Angeles, which clinics will dispense free medical care, aid and advice to the poor and needy. It is not disputed that an outpatient clinic is not functionally equivalent to a hospital....

Discussion

1. The Hospital

The Attorney General contends that under its articles of incorporation, Queen held its assets in trust primarily for the purpose of operating a hospital, and the use of those assets exclusively for outpatient clinics would constitute an

---

[17] [The information about funding the initial hospital and the movies filmed there is from http://wikimapia.org/7707048/The-Dream-Center-Formerly-The-Queen-of-Angels-Hospital-1926-1989, accessed May 8, 2016. The information about the lawsuit is from the case itself. —*Ed.*]

abandonment of Queen's primary charitable purpose and a diversion of charitable trust assets. As noted, it is not disputed that a "hospital" is not the functional equivalent of an "outpatient clinic."

The rules governing the use of the assets of a nonprofit charitable organization are well established: "[All] the assets of a corporation organized solely for charitable purposes must be deemed to be impressed with a charitable trust by virtue of the express declaration of the corporation's purposes, and notwithstanding the absence of any express declaration by those who contribute such assets as to the purpose for which the contributions are made.... It follows that ... [a nonprofit corporation cannot] legally divert its assets to any purpose other than charitable purposes, and said property [is] therefore 'irrevocably dedicated' to exempt purposes within the meaning of the welfare exemption." (*Pacific Home v. County of Los Angeles*, 41 Cal. 2d 844, 852 [264 P.2d 539].)

"Since there is usually no one willing to assume the burdens of a legal action, or who could properly represent the interests of the trust or the public, the Attorney General has been empowered to oversee charities as the representative of the public...." (*Holt v. College of Osteopathic Physicians & Surgeons*, 61 Cal. 2d 750, 754.)

The Attorney General asserts—and plaintiffs insist—that the articles "determine the uses to which trust funds may be put." The Attorney General also asserts, and plaintiffs are equally adamant, that the character of an institution is to be determined not alone by the powers of the corporation as defined in its charter, but also by the manner of conducting its activities.... Indeed, plaintiffs assert that such a "practical construction is virtually controlling."

With this apparent agreement in principle we turn to an examination of the articles of incorporation and the relevant undisputed facts.

The articles of incorporation, ... amended in 1941, provides in relevant part as follows:

> Second: That the purposes for which said corporation is formed are:
>
> (1) To establish, ... own, ... maintain, ... and operate a hospital in the City of Los Angeles, ... to furnish, ... hospital care, ... and medical and surgical treatment of every kind and character, and to receive, treat and care for patients, invalids, the aged and infirm, and generally to conduct and carry on, and to do all things necessary or advisable in conducting and carrying on a hospital;
>
> (2) To perform and to foster and support acts of Christian charity particularly among the sick and ailing; to practice, foster and encourage religious beliefs and activities, particularly those of the Holy Roman Catholic Church; to house and care for unprotected and indigent sick, aged and infirm persons regardless of race, creed, sex or age;
>
> (3) To educate, ... nurses and medical students, and to provide facilities for the same;
>
> (4) That it is a corporation which is not formed for pecuniary gain ... and any revenue received ... from the operation and carrying on of said hospital shall be used in improving the same ... or shall be used in enlarging and improving said hospital and in enlarging the field and scope of its charitable, religious and educational activities;

(5) To lease or purchase any real estate, ... which may be necessary, proper or useful in carrying out the purposes or for the benefit of the hospital, or as may be deemed to be conducive to the welfare of this corporation;[18]

(6) To ... receive and hold ... such ... property as may be necessary, useful or advantageous in the carrying out of the general purposes or for the benefit of the hospital or as may be deemed to be conducive to the welfare of this corporation;...

First, what is most apparent in the articles of incorporation is that the name of the corporation, Queen of Angels Hospital, describes a "hospital." Second, although—as plaintiffs point out—the articles refer to a plural "purposes," the framework of those multiple purposes is the operation of a hospital. Clinics are not even mentioned. Thus, subclause 1 begins and ends with the operation of a hospital. Subclause 2, which begins with the performance of "acts of Christian charity particularly among the sick and ailing," concludes with the conjunctive purpose, "to house and care" for persons, suggesting a hospital facility. Subclause 3, which refers to the education of nurses and medical students, intimates a reference back to the hospital. Most important, subclause 4 provides that "any revenue received ... from the operation and carrying on of said hospital" shall be used either to improve the hospital or in other charitable religious and educational activities, indicating that the "hospital" would continue, although other activities might be added or expanded.

The articles of incorporation alone—without resort to additional evidence—compel the inference that although Queen is entitled to do many things besides operating a hospital, essential to all those other activities is the continued operation of a hospital.

This conclusion is made inescapable by the undisputed additional evidence that, from 1927 when Queen was first incorporated, until 1971, when the lease agreement was entered into, Queen of Angels Hospital Corporation did in fact continuously operate a hospital.

Queen also represented to the public that it was a hospital.... Such acts further bind Queen to its primary purpose of operating a hospital.

In brief, whatever else Queen of Angels Hospital Corporation may do under its articles of incorporation, it was intended to and did operate a hospital and cannot, consistent with the trust imposed upon it, abandon the operation of the hospital business in favor of clinics.

Queen's argument in response does not meet the issue. Plaintiffs point out, as we have noted, that the corporation has multiple "purposes"; that the purpose "to

---

[18] [FN 2] The articles also contain a "parity clause," which provides that the corporation may generally "do all acts and things which may be necessary, proper, useful, or advantageous to the full carrying out of the purposes of this corporation, ... and all objects, purposes, and powers specified in each of the clauses ... shall be regarded but not abridged by any of the objects, powers, and purposes." Although Queen places much emphasis on this clause, under the usual rules (Civ. Code, §3534), this clause must be read in light of the specific enumeration of powers that precedes it.

furnish, ... medical and surgical treatment" is broad enough to authorize the operation of a clinic or clinics and that acts of "Christian charity" encompass all forms of medical aid, care, and advice to the poor and needy. None of the foregoing is disputed. The question is not whether Queen can use some of its assets or the proceeds from the operation of the hospital for purposes other than running a hospital; it certainly can and has. The question is whether it can cease to perform the primary purpose for which it was organized. That, we believe, it cannot do.

Moreover, the issue is not, as plaintiffs contend, whether the operation of clinics serving the poor in the areas in which they live is as worthy a use of charitable funds. We can assume that such operation would be a desirable purpose for a nonprofit corporation. This corporation is, however, bound by its articles of incorporation. Queen may maintain a hospital and retain control over its assets or it may abandon the operation of a hospital and lose those assets to the successor distributees, but it cannot do both.

That the issue is not the desirability of the new use to which Queen wishes to put the trust assets is illustrated by *Holt v. College of Osteopathic Physicians & Surgeons, supra*, 61 Cal. 2d 750. In *Holt* the purposes stated in the articles of incorporation were to establish and conduct an osteopathic medical and surgical college. The college operated as an osteopathic school from 1914 until about May 1961, when the trustees decided to delete the word "osteopathic" and to become an allopathic medical school.

Although it was not suggested that the teaching of allopathic medicine was in any way a less desirable use of charitable funds than the teaching of osteopathic medicine, the court held: "We have concluded that the complaint states a cause of action for enjoining a threatened breach of a charitable trust. If the allegations of the complaint are true, the charitable purpose of COPS is primarily to conduct a college of osteopathy," and there is "a distinction between osteopathic and allopathic medicine."

We think the principle of *Holt* is controlling; here, as in *Holt*, the issue is not whether the new and different purpose is equal to or better than the original purpose, but whether that purpose is authorized by the articles....

The judgment is reversed.

SAMPLE ARTICLES OF INCORPORATION

Articles of Incorporation of the undersigned, a majority of whom are citizens of the United States, desiring to form a Non-Profit Corporation under the Non-Profit Corporation Law of _____, do hereby certify:

First: The name of the Corporation shall be _____.

Second: The place in this state where the principal office of the Corporation is to be located is the City of _____, _____ County.

Third: Said corporation is organized exclusively for charitable, religious, educational, and scientific purposes, specifically _____ .

Fourth: The names and addresses of the persons who are the initial trustees of the corporation are as follows: Name _____ Address _____ .

Fifth: No part of the net earnings of the corporation shall inure to the benefit of, or be distributable to its members, trustees, officers, or other private persons, except that the corporation shall be authorized and empowered to pay reasonable compensation for services rendered and to make payments and distributions in furtherance of the purposes set forth in Article Third hereof. No substantial part of the activities of the corporation shall be the carrying on of propaganda, or otherwise attempting to influence legislation, and the corporation shall not participate in, or intervene in (including the publishing or distribution of statements) any political campaign on behalf of or in opposition to any candidate for public office. Notwithstanding any other provision of these articles, the corporation shall not carry on any other activities not permitted to be carried on (a) by a corporation exempt from federal income tax under section 501(c)(3) of the Internal Revenue Code, or the corresponding section of any future federal tax code, or (b) by a corporation, contributions to which are deductible under section 170(c)(2) of the Internal Revenue Code, or the corresponding section of any future federal tax code.

[*Editor's Note:* The language in the previous paragraph and the next is not required to incorporate at the state level in most states. Most articles of incorporation include such language, however, because, as you will learn in Chapter 4, the IRS will require this or similar language in the articles of incorporation before it will grant tax exemption. The IRS also offers an alternative statement to the last sentence in the previous paragraph if the reference to federal law would make the limitation invalid in the domicile of the organization. That sentence is: "Notwithstanding any other provision of these articles, this corporation shall not, except to an insubstantial degree, engage in any activities or exercise any powers that are not in furtherance of the purposes of this corporation."]

Sixth: Upon the dissolution of the corporation, assets shall be distributed for one or more exempt purposes within the meaning of section 501(c)(3) of the Internal Revenue Code, or the corresponding section of any future federal tax code, or shall be distributed to the federal government, or to a state or local government, for a public purpose. Any such assets not so disposed of shall be disposed of by a Court of Competent Jurisdiction of the county in which the principal office of the corporation is then located, exclusively for such purposes or to such organization or organizations, as said Court shall determine, which are organized and operated exclusively for such purposes.

In witness whereof, we have hereunto subscribed our names this _____ day of 20 _____ .

[Adapted from IRS Publication 557, *Tax-Exempt Status for Your Organization*.]

NOTE

As mentioned above, nonprofits can incorporate in one state and then qualify to do business in another. Relatively few nonprofits take advantage of this option. *See* Garry Jenkins, *Incorporation Choice, Uniformity, and the Reform of Nonprofit State Law*, 41 GA. L. REV. 1113 (2007). For an interesting case in which a trust tried to move from Tennessee to Mississippi, see *Working v. Costa*, 216 S.W.3d 758 (Tenn. App. 2006) (Dispute arose over whether the trustees followed the correct procedures before moving this large charitable trust to Mississippi from Tennessee. The Tennessee court found that the transfer was invalid because the trustees had not obtained court approval before the move, so domicile remained in Tennessee.)

VI. ADDITIONAL CONSIDERATIONS IN STARTING A NONPROFIT

Filing articles of incorporation is just one of the legal steps involved in starting a nonprofit organization. One also needs to check local zoning requirements to be certain that the chosen location is acceptable, apply for a local business license, and file a local personal property tax return on the business assets. The founder will need to draft the bylaws (Chapter 3) and apply for state as well as federal tax exemption (Chapter 4). The organization must also need to pay state property or sales taxes, even if it is exempt from state income tax. The organization will definitely need to pay payroll taxes if it has employees, and it will also need to pay attention to employment, contract, and intellectual property laws. Finally, it will be required to file annual reports with both the state and the IRS.

Once the articles of incorporation have been filed (and the accompanying fee paid), the organization will hold its initial meeting of the board of directors. It will elect the board, authorize the board to begin operating the business, and authorize the creation of a bank account. At that and all subsequent meetings, careful minutes should be taken. *See* Don Griesman, *Agenda and Minutes of First Board Meeting*, DON GRIESMAN'S NONPROFIT BLOG (July 22, 2008), http://dongriesmannsnonprofitblog.blogspot.com/2008/07/agenda-and-minutes-of-first-board.html. Chapter 3 covers the bylaws and the initial meeting in more detail.

These are the legal requirements. Operational requirements include developing an annual budget with fundraising goals, creating and implementing an operating plan, evaluating staff, and paying bills. As you can see, starting a nonprofit is not for the faint of heart. So let's begin.

PROBLEM

Madeline Hopkins has come up with an idea for an organization that provides breast milk to infants who cannot obtain breast milk from their biological mothers. She will need to find mothers willing to donate or sell their milk, test the milk for contamination, find a way to store it safely, and determine how to deliver it to infants who need it. Her organization will also provide education on the importance of breast milk for babies.

Madeline's research has revealed that no such organization exists within 500 miles of her home, and hundreds of babies within that geographic region could use the milk. She has also found that similar organizations are organized as both nonprofits and as for-profits. Madeline lives in a state that recognizes traditional nonprofit and for-profit business forms, as well as L^3Cs and benefit corporations. She has come to you for advice on which form would be best. What are the pros and cons of each of the options? What is your recommendation? You will undoubtedly have to make some assumptions in order to make the recommendation.

DRAFTING PROBLEM: FORMING THE NONPROFIT CORPORATION

Assume that you are forming either a nonprofit corporation. Its mission could be a traditional art museum, a nonprofit that supplies breast milk to babies without access to it, or a nonprofit with a mission of your choice. Your job is to adapt the sample articles of incorporation that are included in this chapter to the interests of your particular organization. You should also ensure that your articles comport with the law of the state in which your organization is located. For the purposes of this exercise, your organization is located in California, New York, or a state that has adopted the Model Nonprofit Act, 3d Ed. The cases and statutes in this chapter are relevant. Also, find articles of incorporation of a similar nonprofit from the same state and compare the two forms. If the two are different, would your organization be better off adopting one or the other? Be prepared to explain your decision. *Please do not do any other research for this assignment.*

A few items to note for this exercise:

- Your professor will be the secretary of state, commissioner, attorney general, or whatever term is used in your state for the person who will determine whether the corporation has been formed.
- One caveat: Even if your state does not require a clause in the articles of incorporation that specifies that the charity has charitable purposes or that it cannot distribute its assets upon dissolution, leave those provisions in, as they will be needed for the IRS when you seek tax exemption.

CHAPTER 3

THE BOARD OF DIRECTORS AND THE GOVERANANCE ROLE

Purpose of this chapter:

- Understand the concept of governance and why it is important
- Examine several state statutes on governance and understand their similarities and differences
- Consider the importance of and ways to draft bylaws and governance policies
- Understand fiduciary duties and consider policy issues surrounding those duties
- Contemplate the complexities of protecting the organization's financial assets through UPMIFA and case law
- Consider the lawyer's role when fiduciary duties appear to be breached
- Examine issues surrounding the enforcement of fiduciary duties

To think about as you read:

Assume that you are the outside attorney for either the organization that you have created for this course or for your local art museum. You have assembled an initial board of directors, all of whom are very knowledgeable about the substantive issues your organization will face, and most of whom are excellent fundraisers. None of them has any idea that any legal issues may arise, however. You have been asked to educate them at their initial meeting about their legal responsibilities and any legal liability they may face. What will you say?[1]

---

[1] You will learn more throughout this book about the duties and potential liabilities of boards of directors, so your presentation will necessarily be somewhat incomplete. Although all legal issues are relevant to board members because they are responsible for ensuring that the organization follows the law, Chapter 9, which discusses laws that relate to those who benefit illegally from a nonprofit organization, will be particularly relevant.

I. INTRODUCTION

Once incorporators have determined the purpose of a nonprofit corporation, they must choose a governance structure. This chapter introduces the legal requirements for a nonprofit corporation's board of directors. It begins with a description of board governance and the bylaws and policies that, along with the articles of incorporation, make up the board's governing documents. The chapter then examines the board's fiduciary duties—the duties of care and loyalty, and, depending on the jurisdiction, the duty of obedience. When and how should these duties be recognized and what constitutes a breach of one or more of these duties? These questions lead to a discussion of enforcement of fiduciary duties.

Anyone who is setting up a nonprofit corporation, either as an incorporator, a drafter of the organizing documents, or a member of the initial board of directors, needs to understand these laws. Once the organization is operational, the board will need to follow its governance structure and uphold its fiduciary duties throughout the lifetime of the organization. A well-run nonprofit organization almost always has strong governance. Those that get into trouble almost always have governance shortcomings.

II. GENERAL CONCEPTS OF GOVERNANCE

A. WHAT IS NONPROFIT GOVERNANCE?

Those who govern nonprofit organizations must follow rules ensuring that the organization conducts its activities in ways that respect the nondistribution constraint and further the mission of the organization. They have a fiduciary duty to the organization that varies somewhat depending on the form of the nonprofit organization. Members of unincorporated associations are governed according to the organization's articles of association, constitution, or bylaws, if they exist. Charitable trusts are governed by trustees, and nonprofit corporations have boards of directors that govern the organization and oversee its operations.

Most nonprofits are corporations, and state laws require nonprofit corporations to have a board of directors that govern the organizations and oversee their operations. These statutes do not tell the board how to respond to every situation. Instead, they provide broad parameters for decisions and leave most of the specifics about how the board is elected and how it makes its decisions to the drafters of the bylaws. For the most part, the default provisions of the statute come into play only if the bylaws are not specific about a situation that arises during the lifetime of the nonprofit corporation. Some states also require nonprofits to have certain policies. The bylaws, articles, and policies are called the organization's "governance documents."

Generally, the board of directors makes policy decisions, supervises the senior staff, ensures that the organization remains fiscally and legally healthy and that the organization's activities advance its purpose. Directors[2] act as a single body; they do not make individual decisions.

Boards of directors can look quite different from one organization to another. Boards can be large or small. They can be all-volunteer or paid. Some boards do the day-to-day tasks as well as the governing, while others are only governing bodies. Some boards appoint board members as officers of the organization; others designate staff for those positions. In addition, some boards do all the work as a board, while others designate some of the work to committees of the board. Each of these decisions must be made before the organization comes into existence, although the bylaws that determine such decisions can be amended.

As discussed in Chapter 2, in a membership organization, members share the governance of the organization with the board of directors. Although this book does not focus on membership organizations, an attorney should always be aware of the ways in which this extra level of governance could change the governance and everyday activities of the corporation in determining whether to set up a corporation as a membership organization.

B. BYLAWS

Bylaws are the internal rules that govern the nonprofit corporation. They fill in the details of the framework that the articles of incorporation have established. Bylaws contain rules and procedures for holding meetings, voting on issues, electing directors and officers, and other provisions that will help the nonprofit run smoothly. If a situation is not covered in the bylaws, the law of the state of incorporation will provide a default provision.[3] Because that provision may not lead to the result that the organization desires, the drafter of the bylaws needs to exercise special care in determining what would be best for the organization that is being created. Following are several statutory provisions that relate to bylaws, a case that emphasizes the importance of well-drafted bylaws; some sample bylaws; and a drafting exercise.

---

[2] Some nonprofit corporations call their directors "trustees." Although trustees of charitable trusts are held to a different standard than directors of nonprofit corporations, the words are often used interchangeably. The structure of the nonprofit organization, rather than the term used, determines the legal status of the governing board. In other words, whether the board members of a nonprofit corporation are called "trustees" or "directors," they must follow the nonprofit corporation law of their state.

[3] Occasionally, as when it specifies a minimum number of directors, the state law preempts the board's decision-making powers, but for the most part, the state law provides default provisions.

NEW YORK NOT-FOR-PROFIT CORPORATION CODE, §§602, 701, 702, 703, 706, 707, 708, 710, 711, 713, AND 715

---

§602. By-laws

(a) The initial by-laws of a corporation may be adopted by its incorporators at the organization meeting and, if not so adopted by the incorporators, by its board. Any reference in this chapter to a "by-law adopted by the members" includes a by-law adopted by the incorporators....

(f) The by-laws may contain any provision relating to the business of the corporation, the conduct of its affairs, its rights or powers or the rights or powers of its members, directors or officers, not inconsistent with this chapter or any other statute of this state or the certificate of incorporation.

§701. Board of Directors

(a) Except as otherwise provided in the certificate of incorporation, a corporation shall be managed by its board of directors. Each director shall be at least eighteen years of age.

(b) If the certificate of incorporation vests the management of the corporation, in whole or in part, in one or more persons other than the board, individually or collectively, such other person or persons shall be subject to the same obligations and the same liabilities for managerial acts or omissions as are imposed upon directors by this chapter.

§702. Number of Directors

(a) The number of directors constituting the entire board shall be not less than three. Subject to such limitation, such number may be fixed by the by-laws.... or by any number within a range set forth in the by-laws. If not otherwise fixed under this paragraph, the number shall be three.

(b) The number of directors may be increased or decreased by amendment of the by-laws....

§703. Election and Term of Office of Directors

...

(b) Directors shall be elected or appointed in the manner and for the term of office provided in the certificate of incorporation or the by-laws. The term of office of directors ... shall not exceed five years.... In the absence of a provision fixing the term, it shall be one year.

(c) Each director shall hold office until the expiration of the term for which he is elected or appointed, and until his successor has been elected or appointed and qualified.

§706. Removal of Directors

(a) ... [A]ny or all of the directors may be removed for cause by vote of the members, or by vote of the directors provided there is a quorum of not less than a majority present at the meeting of directors at which such action is taken.

(b) ... [I]f the certificate of incorporation or the by-laws so provide, any or all of the directors may be removed without cause by vote of the members....

(d) An action to procure a judgment removing a director for cause may be brought by the attorney-general or by ten percent of the members whether or not entitled to vote. The court may bar from re-election any director so removed for a period fixed by the court.

§707. Quorum of Directors

Unless a greater proportion is required by this chapter or by the certificate of incorporation or by a by-law adopted by the members, a majority of the entire board shall constitute a quorum for the transaction of business or of any specified item of business, except that the certificate of incorporation or the by-laws may fix the quorum at less than a majority of the entire board, provided that in the case of a board of fifteen members or less the quorum shall be at least one-third of the entire number of members and in the case of a board of more than fifteen members the quorum shall be at least five members plus one additional member for every ten members (or fraction thereof) in excess of fifteen.

§ 708. Action by the Board

(b) Unless otherwise restricted by the certificate of incorporation or the by-laws, any action required or permitted to be taken by the board or any committee thereof may be taken without a meeting if all members of the board or the committee consent to the adoption of a resolution authorizing the action. Such consent may be written or electronic. . . . The resolution and the written consents thereto by the members of the board or committee shall be filed with the minutes of the proceedings of the board or committee.

(c) Unless otherwise restricted by the certificate of incorporation or the by-laws, any one or more members of the board or of any committee thereof who is not physically present at a meeting of the board or a committee may participate by means of a conference telephone or similar communications equipment or by electronic video screen communication. Participation by such means shall constitute presence in person at a meeting as long as all persons participating in the meeting can hear each other at the same time and each director can participate in all matters before the board, including, without limitation, the ability to propose, object to, and vote upon a specific action to be taken by the board or committee.

§710. Place and Time of Meetings of the Board

(a) Meetings of the board, annual, regular, or special, may be held at any place within or without this state, unless otherwise provided by the certificate of incorporation or the by-laws.

(b) The time and place for holding annual or regular meetings of the board shall be fixed by or under the by-laws, or, if not so fixed, by the board.

(c) A special meeting may be called at any time by the president or other corporate officer as provided in the by-laws or as determined by the board; and, in the case of a corporation without members, by any director upon written demand of not less than one-fifth of the entire board.

§711. Notice of Meetings of the Board

(a) Unless otherwise provided by the by-laws, regular meetings of the board may be held without notice if the time and place of such meetings are fixed by the by-laws or the board. Special meetings of the board shall be held upon notice to the directors.

(b) The by-laws may prescribe what shall constitute notice of meeting of the board. A notice, or waiver of notice, need not specify the purpose of any regular or special meeting of the board, unless required by the by-laws.

(c) Notice of a meeting need not be given to any alternate director, nor to any director who submits a signed waiver of notice whether before or after the meeting, or who attends the meeting without protesting, prior thereto or at its commencement, the lack of notice to him.

(d) A majority of the directors present, whether or not a quorum is present, may adjourn any meeting to another time and place. If the by-laws so provide, notice of any adjournment of a meeting of the board to another time or place shall be given to the directors who were not present at the time of the adjournment and, unless such time and place are announced at the meeting, to the other directors.

§ 713 (f)

No employee of the corporation shall serve as chair of the board or hold any other title with similar responsibilities.

§ 715 Related Party Transactions

(a) No corporation shall enter into any related party transaction unless the transaction is determined by the board to be fair, reasonable, and in the corporation's best interest at the time of such determination. Any director, officer, or key employee who has an interest in a related party transaction shall disclose in good faith to the board, or an authorized committee thereof, the material facts concerning such interest.

(b) With respect to any related party transaction involving a charitable corporation and in which a related party has a substantial financial interest, the board of such corporation, or an authorized committee thereof, shall:

(1) Prior to entering into the transaction, consider alternative transactions to the extent available

(2) Approve the transaction by not less than a majority vote of the directors or committee members present at the meeting; and

(3) Contemporaneously document in writing the basis for the board authorized committee's approval, including its consideration of any alternative transactions. . . .

(g) No related party may participate in deliberations or voting relating to matters set forth in this section; provided that nothing in this section shall prohibit the board or authorized committee from requesting that a related party present information concerning a related party transaction at a board or committee meeting prior to the commencement of deliberations or voting relating thereto.

CALIFORNIA CORPORATIONS CODE (NONPROFIT PUBLIC BENEFIT CORPORATIONS LAW), §§5150, 5151, 5210, 5220, 5221, 5222, 5224, AND 5227

§5150

(a) Except as provided in subdivision (c), and Sections 5151, 5220, 5224, 5512, 5613, and 5616, bylaws may be adopted, amended or repealed by the board unless the action would materially and adversely affect the rights of members as to voting or transfer. . . .

(c) The articles or bylaws may restrict or eliminate the power of the board to adopt, amend or repeal any or all bylaws, subject to subdivision (e) of Section 5151.

(d) Bylaws may also provide that repeal or amendment of those bylaws, or the repeal or amendment of specified portions of those bylaws, may occur only with the approval in writing of a specified person or persons other than the board or members....

§5151

(a) The bylaws shall set forth (unless that provision is contained in the articles, in which case it may only be changed by an amendment of the articles) the number of directors of the corporation, or ... that the number of directors shall be not less than a stated minimum nor more than a stated maximum with the exact number of directors to be fixed, within the limits specified, by approval of the board or the members (Section 5034), in the manner provided in the bylaws, subject to subdivision (e). The number or minimum number of directors may be one or more.

(c) The bylaws may contain any provision, not in conflict with law or the articles, for the management of the activities and for the conduct of the affairs of the corporation, including but not limited to:

(1) Any provision referred to in subdivision (c) of Section 5132.

(2) The time, place and manner of calling, conducting and giving notice of members', directors' and committee meetings, or of conducting mail ballots.

(3) The qualifications, duties, and compensation of directors; the time of their election; and the requirements of a quorum of directors' and committee meetings.

(4) The appointment and authority of committees.

(5) The appointment, duties, compensation, and tenure of officers.

(6) The mode of determination of members of record.

(7) The making of reports and financial statements to members.

(8) Setting, imposing, and collecting dues, assessments, and admission fees.

§5210

Each corporation shall have a board of directors. Subject to the provisions of this part..., the activities and affairs of a corporation shall be conducted and all corporate powers shall be exercised by or under the direction of the board. The board may delegate the management of the activities of the corporation to any person or persons, management company, or committee however composed, provided that the activities and affairs of the corporation shall be managed and all corporate powers shall be exercised under the ultimate direction of the board.

§5220

(a) ... [T]he terms of directors of a corporation without members may be up to six years. In the absence of any provision in the articles or bylaws, the term shall be one year. The articles or bylaws may provide for staggering the terms of directors by dividing the total number of directors into groups of one or more directors. The terms of office of the several groups and the number of directors in each group need not be uniform....

§5221

(a) The board may declare vacant the office of a director who has been declared of unsound mind by a final order of court, or convicted of a felony, or been found by a final order or judgment of any court to have breached any duty under Article 3 (commencing with Section 5230), or, if at the time a director is elected, the bylaws provide that a director may be removed for missing a specified number of board meetings, fails to attend the specified number of meetings.

(b) As provided in paragraph (3) of subdivision (c) of Section 5151, the articles or bylaws may prescribe the qualifications of directors. The board, by a majority vote of the directors who meet all of the required qualifications to be a director, may declare vacant the office of any director who fails or ceases to meet any required qualification that was in effect at the beginning of that director's current term of office.

§5222

(a) Subject to subdivisions (b) and (f), any or all directors may be removed without cause if:...

(3) In a corporation with no members, the removal is approved by a majority of the directors then in office.

§5224

(a) Unless otherwise provided in the articles or bylaws and except for a vacancy created by the removal of a director, vacancies on the board may be filled by approval of the board..., if the number of directors then in office is less than a quorum, by (1) the unanimous written consent of the directors then in office, (2) the affirmative vote of a majority of the directors then in office at a meeting held pursuant to notice or waivers of notice complying with Section 5211, or (3) a sole remaining director.

§5227

(a) Any other provision of this part notwithstanding, not more than 49 percent of the persons serving on the board of any corporation may be interested persons.

(b) For the purpose of this section, "interested persons" means either:

(1) Any person currently being compensated by the corporation for services rendered to it within the previous 12 months, whether as a full- or part-time employee, independent contractor, or otherwise, excluding any reasonable compensation paid to a director as director; or

(2) Any brother, sister, ancestor, descendant, spouse, brother-in-law, sister-in-law, son-in-law, daughter-in-law, mother-in-law, or father-in-law of any such person.

(c) A person with standing under Section 5142 may bring an action to correct any violation of this section. The court may enter any order which shall provide an equitable and fair remedy to the corporation, including, but not limited to, an order for the election of additional directors, an order to enlarge the size of the board, or an order for the removal of directors.

(d) The provisions of this section shall not affect the validity or enforceability of any transaction entered into by a corporation.

MODEL NONPROFIT CORPORATION ACT, 3D ED.
(2008), §§2.06, 10.20, 8.01-8.12, AND 8.20-8.24

§2.06. Bylaws

(a) The incorporators or the board of directors of a nonprofit corporation may adopt initial bylaws for the corporation.

(b) The bylaws of a nonprofit corporation may contain any provision for managing the activities and regulating the affairs of the corporation that is not inconsistent with law or the articles of incorporation.

§10.20. Amendment by Board of Directors or Members

(a) Except as provided in the articles of incorporation or bylaws, the members of a membership corporation may amend or repeal the corporation's bylaws.

(b) The board of directors of a membership corporation or nonmembership corporation may amend or repeal the corporation's bylaws, unless the articles of incorporation or bylaws or Sections 10.21 or 10.22 reserve that power exclusively to the members or a designated body in whole or part.

§8.01. Requirement for and Functions of Board of Directors

(a) A nonprofit corporation must have a board of directors.

(b) Except as provided in Section 8.12, all corporate powers must be exercised by or under the authority of the board of directors of the nonprofit corporation, and the activities and affairs of the corporation must be managed by or under the direction, and subject to the oversight, of its board of directors.

§8.02. Qualifications of Directors

A director of a nonprofit corporation must be an individual. The articles of incorporation or bylaws may prescribe other qualifications for directors. A director need not be a resident of this state or a member of the corporation unless the articles or bylaws so prescribe.

§8.03. Number of Directors

(a) A board of directors must consist of three or more directors, with the number specified in or fixed in accordance with the articles of incorporation or bylaws.

(b) The number of directors may be increased or decreased (but to no fewer than three) from time to time by amendment to, or in the manner provided in, the articles of incorporation or bylaws.

§8.04. Selection of Directors

...

(b) The directors of a nonmembership corporation (other than any initial directors named in the articles of incorporation or elected by the incorporators) shall be elected, appointed, or designated as provided in the articles or bylaws. If no method of designation or appointment is set forth in the articles or bylaws, the directors (other than any initial directors) shall be elected by the board.

§8.05. Terms of Directors Generally

(a) The articles of incorporation or bylaws may specify the terms of directors. If a term is not specified in the articles or bylaws, the term of a director is one year. Except for directors who are appointed by persons who are not members or who are designated in a manner other than by election or appointment, the term of a director may not exceed five years....

(c) Except as provided in the articles of incorporation or bylaws, the term of a director elected to fill a vacancy expires at the end of the unexpired term that the director is filling....

§8.06. Staggered Terms for Directors

The articles of incorporation or bylaws may provide for staggering the terms of directors by dividing the total number of directors into groups of one or more directors. The terms of office and number of directors in each group do not need to be uniform.

§8.07. Resignation of Directors

(a) A director may resign at any time by delivering a signed notice in the form of a record to the chair of the board of directors or to an executive officer or the secretary of the corporation.

(b) A resignation is effective when the notice is delivered unless the notice specifies a later effective time.

§8.08. Removal of Directors by Members or Other Persons

...

(b) The board of directors may remove a director of a nonmembership corporation:

(1) With or without cause, unless the articles of incorporation or bylaws provide that directors may be removed only for cause. The articles or bylaws may specify what constitutes cause for removal.

(2) As provided in subsection (c).

(c) The board of directors of a membership corporation or nonmembership corporation may remove a director who:

(1) has been declared of unsound mind by a final order of court;

(2) has been convicted of a felony;

(3) has been found by a final order of court to have breached a duty as a director under [Subchapter] 8C;

(4) has missed the number of board meetings specified in the articles of incorporation or bylaws, if the articles or bylaws at the beginning of the director's current term provided that a director may be removed for missing the specified number of board meetings; or

(5) does not satisfy at the time any of the qualifications for directors set forth in the articles of incorporation or bylaws at the beginning of the director's current term, if the decision that the director fails to satisfy a qualification is made by the vote of a majority of the directors who meet all of the required qualifications.

(d) A director who is designated in the articles of incorporation or bylaws may be removed by an amendment to the articles or bylaws deleting or changing the designation....

§8.10. Vacancy on Board

(a) Except as otherwise provided in subsection (b), the articles of incorporation, or the bylaws, if a vacancy occurs on the board of directors, including a vacancy resulting from an increase in the number of directors, the vacancy may be filled by a majority of the directors remaining in office even if they constitute less than a quorum....

§8.11. Compensation of Directors

Unless the articles of incorporation or bylaws provide otherwise, the board of directors may fix the compensation of directors.

§8.12. Designated Body

(a) Some, but less than all, of the powers, authority or functions of the board of directors of a nonprofit corporation under this [act] may be vested by the articles of incorporation or bylaws in a designated body. If such a designated body is created:

(1) The provisions of this [chapter] and other provisions of law on the rights, duties, and liabilities of the board of directors or directors individually also apply to the designated body and to the members of the designated body individually. The provisions of this [chapter] and other provisions of law on meetings, notice, and the manner of acting of the board of directors also apply to the designated body in the absence of an applicable rule in the articles of incorporation, bylaws or internal operating rules of the designated body.

(2) To the extent the powers, authority, or functions of the board of directors have been vested in the designated body, the directors are relieved from their duties and liabilities with respect to those powers, authority, and functions.

(3) A provision of the articles of incorporation regarding indemnification of directors or limiting the liability of directors adopted pursuant to Section 2.02(b)(8) or (c) applies to members of the designated body, except as otherwise provided in the articles....

(c) The articles of incorporation or bylaws may prescribe qualifications for members of a designated body. Except as otherwise provided by the articles or bylaws, a member of a designated body does not need to be:

(1) an individual,

(2) a director, officer, or member of the nonprofit corporation, or

(3) a resident of this state.

§8.20. Meetings

(a) The board of directors may hold regular or special meetings in or out of this state.

(b) Unless the articles of incorporation or bylaws provide otherwise, the board of directors may permit any or all directors to participate in a regular or special meeting by, or conduct the meeting through the use of, any means of communication by which all directors participating may simultaneously hear each other during the meeting. A director participating in a meeting by this means is considered to be present in person at the meeting.

§8.21. Action without Meeting

(a) Except to the extent that the articles of incorporation or bylaws require that action by the board of directors be taken at a meeting, action required or permitted by this [act] to be taken by the board of directors may be taken without a meeting if each director signs a consent in the form of a record describing the action to be taken and delivers it to the nonprofit corporation.

(b) Action taken under this section is the act of the board of directors when one or more consents signed by all the directors are delivered to the nonprofit corporation. The consent may specify the time at which the action taken in the consent is to be effective. A director's consent may be withdrawn by a revocation in the form of a record signed by the director and delivered to the corporation prior to delivery to the corporation of unrevoked consents signed by all the directors.

(c) A consent signed under this section has the effect of action taken at a meeting of the board of directors and may be described as such in any document.

§8.22. Call and Notice of Meeting

(a) Unless the articles of incorporation or bylaws provide otherwise, regular meetings of the board of directors may be held without notice of the date, time, place, or purpose of the meeting.

(b) Unless the articles of incorporation or bylaws provide for a longer or shorter period, special meetings of the board of directors must be preceded by at least two days' notice of the date, time, and place of the meeting. The notice need not describe the purpose of the special meeting unless required by the articles of incorporation or bylaws.

(c) Unless the articles of incorporation or bylaws provide otherwise, the chair of the board, the highest-ranking officer of the corporation, or 20% of the directors then in office may call and give notice of a meeting of the board of directors.

(d) The articles of incorporation or bylaws may authorize oral notice of meetings of the board of directors.

§8.23. Waiver of Notice

(a) A director may waive any notice required by this [act], the articles of incorporation, or the bylaws before or after the date and time stated in the notice. Except as provided by subsection (b), the waiver must be in the form of a record, signed by the director entitled to the notice, and filed with the minutes or corporate records.

(b) A director's attendance at or participation in a meeting waives any required notice to the director of the meeting, unless the director at the beginning of the meeting (or promptly upon arrival) objects to holding the meeting or transacting business at the meeting and does not thereafter vote for or assent to action taken at the meeting.

§8.24. Quorum and Voting

(a) Except as provided in subsection (b), the articles of incorporation, or the bylaws, a quorum of the board of directors consists of a majority of the directors in office before a meeting begins.

(b) The articles of incorporation or bylaws may authorize a quorum of the board of directors to consist of no fewer than the greater of one-third of the number of directors in office or two directors.

(c) If a quorum is present when a vote is taken, the affirmative vote of a majority of directors present is the act of the board of directors unless a greater vote is required by the articles of incorporation or bylaws.

(d) A director who is present at a meeting of the board of directors when corporate action is taken is considered to have assented to the action taken unless one of the following applies:

(1) The director objects at the beginning of the meeting (or promptly upon arrival) to holding it or transacting business at the meeting.

(2) The director dissents or abstains from the action and:

(i) the dissent or abstention is entered in the minutes of the meeting; or

(ii) the director delivers notice in the form of a record of the director's dissent or abstention to the presiding officer of the meeting before its adjournment or to the corporation promptly after adjournment of the meeting.

(e) The right of dissent or abstention is not available to a director who votes in favor of the action taken.

AMERICAN CENTER FOR EDUCATION, INC. V. CAVNAR

80 Ca. App. 3d 476, 145 Cal. Rptr. 736 (1978)

ACE is a nonmembership, nonprofit, conservative and patriotic tax-exempt corporation which was organized under the laws of the District of Columbia on January 17, 1969, but which has always had its principal place of business in Los Angeles. Plaintiff, Hurst B. Amyx, was the founding president of ACE. From January 21, 1969, until May 15, 1970, Amyx was president, Cavnar vice president and treasurer, and Todt vice president and secretary of ACE. From January 21, 1969, until April 20, 1970, the board of directors and the executive committee of ACE consisted of these three individuals and another individual (Cartlidge), who resigned on the last-mentioned date and was not replaced.

Strong differences over the program being pursued by ACE arose between Amyx, on the one hand, and Cavnar and Todt on the other. Acting on the advice of a District of Columbia attorney (Manuel), the attorney who had incorporated ACE, Cavnar and Todt went to Amyx's office on May 15, 1970, to convene a meeting of ACE's executive committee. The purpose of this meeting was to oust Amyx as an officer, director and member of the executive committee. Under the articles of incorporation of ACE, the minimum number of directors was three, and under the bylaws of ACE, three members of the board of directors and three members of the executive committee likewise constituted quorums of these bodies. As soon as Cavnar pronounced the word "meeting," Amyx left the room. Thereupon, while in Amyx's office, while going from there to a Hollywood branch of UCB (where ACE's funds were located), and at this branch (where they again encountered Amyx) Cavnar and Todt attempted to function as the executive committee of ACE. In so doing, they purportedly ousted Amyx from all of his offices, replaced him as president with Cavnar, and elected Davies a director.

At this time, ACE had a checking account with a balance of $149,536.58 at this branch. The agreement between UCB and ACE required that all checks on this account be signed by Amyx and either Cavnar or Todt.

Amyx, Cavnar, and Todt had a confrontation at the bank in the presence of the branch manager (Benecke). Cavnar and Todt told Benecke that Amyx was being removed from his various offices with ACE. Amyx informed the manager that this purported removal was invalid and that he would hold UCB liable for any funds of ACE that the bank dispensed without his signature.

Later that afternoon, Benecke, without examining the bylaws of ACE, which Amyx offered to him, and without consulting with UCB's legal department, transferred by means of a memorandum charge $137,793.22 of ACE's funds from its checking account to a savings account which had been opened in ACE's name by Cavnar and Todt. Subsequently, these funds were transferred to a checking account bearing ACE's name, but on which the only authorized signers were Cavnar and Todt.

At 6 p.m. on the same day, May 15, 1970, the purported new board of directors of ACE, namely Cavnar, Todt, and Davies, met. Cavnar resigned as president and Todt as secretary. Todt was then elected president, Cavnar treasurer, and Davies secretary. Following this, Todt, Cavnar, and Davies noticed a board meeting for May 25, 1970, for ratification of the purported actions of the executive committee and the board of directors on May 15, 1970, and for the election of new officers and directors.

Following the events of May 15, 1970, Todt and Cavnar caused Amyx to be locked out of his offices at ACE by means of barriers and armed guards, and discharged those staff members of ACE whom he had employed.

Amyx was served with a copy of the notice of the May 25 meeting, but he did not attend. The meeting took place, and the purported actions of May 15 were ratified by Cavnar and Todt with Davies abstaining. Another division of this court, however, in the already cited prior appeal in this litigation, indicated that on the record in that appeal, the special board meeting of May 25, 1970, *may* not have been called in accordance with ACE's bylaws.... The trial court herein went further. It concluded that the board of directors meeting of May 25, 1970, was invalid for want of a quorum.

On June 24, 1970, Amyx filed the instant action on behalf of himself and ACE. In it he challenged the legality of his purported ouster and the obtaining of control by Cavnar and Todt of ACE's funds on deposit with UCB.

The trial court found that in the attempted ouster of Amyx and in the transfer of the control of the funds of ACE on deposit at UCB, Cavnar and Todt abused their authority and discretion as directors and of ACE and apparently also acted negligently and wrongfully. The trial court and the advisory jury found as well that UCB negligently and wrongfully paid out ACE's monies on deposit with UCB upon instruments not signed by Amyx and that the sum of $80,000 represented the damages ACE suffered by reason of misconduct on the part of UCB, Cavnar and Todt in connection with the takeover and subsequent thereto....

II. Merits

A. Validity of the Executive Committee Meeting at the Bank and of the Actions Taken ... on May 15, 1970

Many of the complex issues which are raised in this case must ultimately turn upon the answers to the questions of whether the ouster of Amyx as president and as a member of the executive committee and the election of Davies as a director at the executive committee meeting of May 15, 1970, at the bank were valid corporate acts. The trial court found variously as a matter of fact and concluded as a matter of law that they were not. Our examination of the elements of valid corporate action leads us to a contrary conclusion.

1. Procedural Requisites

a. Notice

The jury found by special interrogatory that Amyx was given sufficient legal notice of a purported meeting of the executive committee held on May 15, 1970, and the court adopted this finding. This finding correctly based upon another finding of the trial court that the custom and practice of the executive committee had been to meet informally without prior notice and wherever convenient to its members.

Meetings of boards of directors are valid where it has become customary for the board to convene such meetings without notice but with a quorum present. More should not be required of an executive committee, especially where the membership of the executive committee and the board of directors is identical.

The jury's finding in the instant case does not specify which of the purported executive committee meetings on May 15 Amyx received valid notice of; but this ambiguity presents no difficulty because our analysis is based on the meeting of which he manifestly had the most notice—the meeting at the bank.

b. Quorum

Even if we regard Amyx's hasty retreats as successfully frustrating Cavnar and Todt's attempt to assemble a quorum, thus invalidating the attempted meetings of the executive committee in Amyx's office and on the street, the meeting which occurred a few minutes later at the bank does not share this defect.

With valid notice of an executive committee meeting, Amyx went to the bank with the intention of preventing Cavnar and Todt from wresting control over the corporate funds from him.... [H]e certainly must have expected to encounter Cavnar and Todt at the bank. Furthermore, from the prior events of that afternoon, he knew that these adversaries of his were attempting to convene a corporate meeting.

Amyx, nevertheless, entered the bank and saw them standing with Benecke about 25 feet away. Rather than prevent a quorum from assembling, Amyx walked over to the group and injected himself into the conversation.... The confrontation lasted for about 10 minutes.

While ... a director cannot be trapped into attendance at a directors' meeting, this rule does not apply where a director remains at and participates in the meeting. Again, we see no reason why the rule should be any different for meetings of an executive committee.

It follows that if the gathering at the bank was a meeting of the executive committee, Amyx's presence and participation waive any objections which he otherwise might have had as to both notice and to his being counted for a quorum.

c. *Procedural Informality*

The trial court found that Cavnar and Todt attempted to function as the executive committee while at the bank and stated that the evidence was clear that Amyx was present at that time. Amyx's refusal to characterize the gathering as a meeting is, under the circumstances, irrelevant because neither want of unanimity nor lack of formality will invalidate action taken where all of the members of an executive committee come together and consider a question....

Cavnar and Todt experienced no more difficulty than would reasonably be expected where two directors are required to obtain the attendance of a third at a meeting in order to remove him over his own objection. This necessarily is an arduous task, but it should not be impossible. Continuation of the corporate deadlock inherent in this situation is contrary to wise public policy.

A meeting which proceeds smoothly and without disruption is not a prerequisite to valid corporate action. Amyx voluntarily joined the group standing in the lobby of the bank. He knew of Cavnar and Todt's intention to call a meeting, and he was accustomed to conducting ACE's business informally with them. He remained in their company for 10 minutes during which time, as the court found, they attempted to act as the executive committee. He vigorously participated with them in a debate of the very issues which he went to the bank to resolve. And when that debate was over, the majority had prevailed. We find no procedural defect in these events.

d. *Location*

That the meeting was held in a bank lobby is not fatal to its validity. Valid corporate meetings have been held on a street corner, in a hallway, and in a laboratory. Moreover, as already stated, the trial court in the instant case found that "the custom and practice of the Executive Committee of the Center was to meet informally *wherever* convenient to the Executive Committee members...." (Italics added.)...

2. Their Validity Otherwise

Having established that the May 15, 1970, meeting of ACE's executive committee at the bank met all procedural requisites, we now focus on the validity otherwise of the actions taken at that meeting: specifically, the removal of Amyx as president of ACE and as member of the executive committee and the election of Davies to the board of directors. The trial court found that Cavnar and Todt each "committed gross abuse of their authority and discretion as directors and officers of the Center [ACE]" in, among other things, "holding a purported board of directors meeting of the Center [ACE] on said date, May 15, 1970...."

As we will discuss below, Cavnar's and Todt's actions during the May 15 meeting at the bank were within their grant of authority and discretion. Consequently, the election of Davies to the board and the removal of Amyx as an officer and member of the executive committee were valid.

a. Power of the Executive Committee to Remove an Officer without Cause

... In order to establish the validity of the executive committee's removal of Amyx as president of ACE, two questions must be answered: First, did the executive committee have the authority to remove an officer? Second, could the committee do so without establishing cause?

The bylaws of ACE vest the power to elect officers in the board of directors. The bylaws further provide that the officers of ACE "serve at the will of the board of directors." Thus, the power to remove was inferentially granted. Moreover, neither the articles of incorporation nor the bylaws of ACE suggest that these powers of appointment and removal are granted exclusively to the board of directors. We therefore conclude that they are included in the general delegation of power to the executive committee contained in the bylaws of ACE.

This general grant of authority was consistent with the provisions of the California Corporations Code then in effect regarding the power of an executive committee. Section 822 stated that the board of directors may delegate to the executive committee any of the powers of the board in the management of the corporation except the power to declare dividends or adopt, amend, or repeal the bylaws of the corporation.

While it is evident that the members of ACE's executive committee were thus empowered generally to remove its officers, the question remains whether cause for their removal had to be first established. As we have previously noted, the bylaws of ACE provide that officers "serve at the will of the board of directors." This and similar language has been consistently held to obviate the necessity for establishing cause for the removal of a corporate officer by the board of directors. We conclude that the board of directors of ACE possessed the power to remove Amyx from his office as president without cause. As we have already indicated, the bylaws of ACE delegated a general power to discharge the duties of the board of directors to the executive committee. We believe this general delegation of power included the board's power to remove an officer without cause. Thus, Cavnar and Todt, as the majority of the executive committee, acted within their authority in removing Amyx as president of ACE.

b. Power of the Executive Committee to Remove a Fellow Member without Cause

There are no provisions in either the bylaws or articles of incorporation of ACE regarding the removal of members of the executive committee. As we have noted earlier, however, the power to appoint carries with it the power to remove, and such power is granted in the bylaws of ACE to the board of directors. There is no reason to believe that this power regarding appointment and removal of members of the executive committee is not included in the general delegation of power to the executive committee contained in the bylaws of ACE.

Similarly, there is nothing in either the articles of incorporation or the bylaws of ACE that would lead us to believe that members of the executive committee cannot be removed without cause. Under both the articles of incorporation and the bylaws of ACE directors may be removed without cause. As previously indicated, officers of ACE are also subject to removal without cause. Absent any provision to the contrary, there is no reason to assume that the members of the executive committee are safeguarded from removal to a greater extent than either the officers or directors of the corporation.

We therefore conclude that Amyx was properly removed as a member of the executive committee at the May 15, 1970, meeting at the bank.

c. Power of the Executive Committee to Elect a Director

We can see nothing negligent or wrongful in the election of Davies as a director of ACE by Cavnar and Todt. The bylaws of ACE state that the power to fill vacancies in the board of directors may be delegated to the executive committee. One of the duties of the board of directors under ACE's articles of incorporation is the "appointment" of directors. As already noted, the bylaws of ACE directly empower the executive committee to exercise the powers of the board of directors in the interim between board meetings. Consequently, the majority of ACE's executive committee, namely Cavnar and Todt, was empowered to elect Davies as director.

B. Validity of the May 25, 1970, Board of Directors Meeting and the Actions Taken Thereat

1. Validity of the Meeting

Since ACE's executive committee lacked the power to remove a director under the law of this case, Amyx was not removed as director on May 15. The jury was appropriately so instructed. Removing Amyx as director required a valid meeting of the board of directors. The jury was, however, erroneously instructed that they should regard as having been conclusively determined that the May 25 meeting of the board of directors was not called in compliance with ACE's bylaws.

This error flowed from a misinterpretation of the following statement made in the earlier opinion of this court in this case: "It therefore does not follow from the facts disclosed by the record that the May 25 board meeting was called in accordance with ACE's bylaws."

The statement is both conditional and negative, and, standing alone, it does not support the trial court's interpretation. Taken in context, its meaning becomes clear. Having determined that there were triable issues of fact as to whether any of the May 15 executive committee meetings were valid and whether Davies had been validly elected a director on that date, another division of this court turned its attention to the question of whether the partial summary judgment before it could be upheld solely on the basis of the purported May 25 meeting of ACE's board of directors.... Since Amyx did not attend and since the bylaws required the presence of three directors to constitute a quorum, the validity of the actions taken on the latter date depended on the then unresolved question of the validity of Davies' election ten days before. It therefore did not follow from that record that the May 25 meeting was valid.

Since we have held that Davies was validly elected a director on May 15, it is now apparent that the May 25 meeting was a valid corporate act. We need not give the same exhaustive analysis to the question of the validity of this meeting as we did to the meeting of the executive committee at the bank. Suffice it to say that Amyx testified that he received notice and that he did not attend. Uncontradicted evidence indicates that the meeting was attended by Cavnar, Todt, Davies, and an attorney. The trial court's finding that the meeting lacked a quorum is incorrect in light of Davies' attendance.

2. Validity of the Removal of Amyx as a Director

It has been held that a board of directors has no inherent power to remove a fellow director since all directors are elected by the shareholders.... In this case, however, the removal of Amyx as a director of ACE by his fellow directors was proper. Since ACE, a nonprofit corporation, had neither shareholders nor members, its directors held this power to remove directors normally reserved to shareholders.... And the bylaws of ACE make explicit the power of the board to appoint and remove directors. As directors of such a corporation Cavnar, Todt, and Davies were entitled to remove Amyx at any time.

There was no necessity to establish cause for the removal of Amyx as director. The bylaws of ACE specify that removal without cause is proper. Even without such a provision, cause is apparently not required under California law for the removal of elected directors....

SAMPLE BYLAWS

Below is a sample set of bylaws for a nonprofit corporation. As you can see from the brackets that indicate a need for a decision, there is plenty of room for variation in an organization's bylaws. For more information on bylaws, see Ellis Carter, Bylaws: What to Include and What to Leave Out (June 7, 2010), available at http://charitylawyerblog.com/2010/06/07/nonprofit-bylaws-what-to-include-and-what-to-leave-out-2/. Mr. Carter suggests a provision discussing conflicts of interest, which is missing from the sample bylaws. Do you think such a provision should be added to the sample?

ARTICLE I: Name

The name of the corporation shall be _____.

ARTICLE II: Members

The corporation [shall have/shall not have] members.

ARTICLE III: Board of Directors

Section 1. Powers and Qualifications. The Board of Directors shall have general power to control and manage the business affairs and property of the corporation, subject to any limitations and in accordance with the purposes set forth in the Articles of Incorporation. Each member shall have the following qualifications: [List the qualifications, if any, the incorporators think are necessary for the organization to succeed. The incorporators may want to list state law requirements here as well, although the law will prevail over a silent or contradictory bylaws provision.].

Section 2. Number. The number of Directors constituting the entire Board after the first annual meeting of the Board of Directors shall be _____ [Alternative: no fewer than _____ or more than _____.].

Section 3. Appointment and Election. The initial Directors shall be appointed by the incorporator[s]. Thereafter, the Board of Directors shall elect directors by an affirmative vote of a majority of the members present and voting at a meeting duly called for the purpose.

Section 4: Term. Directors shall serve for a term of _____ years, provided that each Director shall continue in office until a successor has been elected or until he or she dies, resigns, or is removed. Directors [may/may not] be elected to _____ consecutive terms. In the case of a Trustee originally elected to a term of less than _____ years, such term [shall/shall not] be counted in applying the rule regarding limitation of consecutive terms stated in the preceding sentence.

Section 5: Resignation and Removal. A Director may resign at any time by giving written notice to the Chair or Co-Chair, the President or the Secretary. Unless otherwise specified in the notice the resignation shall take effect upon receipt of such resignation, and acceptance of the resignation shall not be necessary to make it effective. Any Director may be removed [at any time/at a meeting called only for that purpose] [for cause/with or without cause], provided that there is a quorum of [not less than a majority/a fraction] of the entire Board of Directors present at the meeting of Directors at which such action is taken.

Section 6: Vacancies and Newly Created Directorships. Any newly created directorships and any vacancies on the Board of Directors arising at any time and from any cause may be filled at any meeting of the Board of Directors by [a majority/a fraction] of the Directors then in office.

Section 7: Meetings. Meetings of the Board may be held at any place within or without the State of _____ as the Board may from time to time fix, or as shall be specified in the notice or waivers of notice thereof. The annual meeting shall be held in _____ of each year at a time and place fixed by the Board. Other regular meetings of the Board shall be held no less than _____ times during the year. Special meetings of the Board shall be held whenever called by [a fraction] of the Board of Directors, [the Chair, or the Executive Director].

Section 8: Notice of Meetings. Notice of the time, place and purpose of every meeting of the Board of Directors shall be given by the Secretary or other officer to each Director at least _____ days before such meeting by mailing, telegraphing, delivering, telephoning, faxing or emailing the notice to the Director's residence or business address or such place as the Director has indicated in writing.

Section 9: Waiver of Notice. A Director may waive notice of any meeting by submitting a signed waiver of notice before or after the meeting, or attending the meeting without protesting the lack of notice, prior thereto or at its commencement.

Section 10: Quorum and Voting. Unless otherwise provided by law or these bylaws, the presence of [fraction] of the entire Board of Directors shall constitute a quorum for the transaction of business at a meeting of the Directors. Members of the Board of Directors who participate in person or by means of equipment that allows all persons participating in any meeting of the Board of Directors or any committee to hear each other simultaneously shall be deemed to be present at such meeting. The vote of [fraction] of the Directors present at the time of the vote, if a quorum [is present at such time/was present at any point of the meeting] shall be the act of the Board of Directors.

Section 11: Informal Action by the Board. Any action required or permitted to be taken by the Board or by any committee thereof may be taken without a meeting if all members of the Board or the committee consent in writing to the adoption of a resolution authorizing the action. Such action and written consents shall be filed with the minutes of proceedings of the Board of Directors or the committee.

Section 12: Compensation. [Any Director of the Corporation may receive a reasonable salary or other reasonable compensation for services rendered to the Corporation when authorized by [fraction] of the Board of Directors. No compensation shall be paid to Directors.]

ARTICLE IV: Committees

Section 1: Executive Committee. The Board of Directors may, from time to time, by resolution adopted by a majority of the entire Board of Directors, create an Executive Committee, consisting of the Chair or Co-Chair, the Vice Chair, the President and such other Directors as the Board may determine, provided that the Executive Committee shall have no fewer than _____ members. The Executive Committee shall have all of the powers of the Directors when the Board of Directors is not in session except the Executive Committee may not amend the bylaws or elect Directors, Officers, or members of committees.

Section 2: Other Committees. The Board of Directors may, from time to time, create such other committees as the activities of the Corporation may require, and delegate such authority to such committees as the Board of Directors may deem appropriate, provided that any committee which is authorized by the Board of Directors to exercise any of the powers of the Board of Directors shall consist of at least three Directors and the only voting members of any such committee shall be Directors.

Section 3: Appointment and Procedure of Committees. Unless otherwise provided by the Board of Directors, members of committees shall be elected by the Board of Directors and shall serve for a term of _____ year(s). [Fraction] of the members of each committee shall constitute a quorum for the transaction of any business. Except as otherwise provided by these bylaws or by the Board of Directors, each committee shall determine its own rules of procedure and the Chair or Co-Chair shall designate the chair of each committee. Each committee shall keep records of its proceedings. Copies of the minutes of each meeting shall be filed with the corporate records and supplied to each member of the Board of Trustees.

ARTICLE V: Officers, Employees, and Agents

Section 1: Officers. The Officers of the Corporation shall be a Chairperson, a Secretary, a Treasurer, and such other Officers, including one or more Vice Chairpersons, as the Board of Directors may from time to time appoint. One person [may/may not] hold more than one office in the Corporation [except that no one person may hold the offices of _____]. The Chairperson shall be a member of the Board of Directors. The other officers [shall be/may, but need not, be] members of the Board of Directors. No instruments required to be signed by more than one officer may be signed by one person in more than one capacity.

Section 2: Election, Term of Office, and Removal. The officers of the Corporation shall be elected for a _____-year term at the annual meeting of the Board of Directors. Any officer of the Corporation may be removed by a vote of [fraction] of the entire Board. A vacancy in any office shall be filled by the Board of Trustees for the balance of the term of office, provided that any vacancy in the office of Chairperson shall be filled by the Vice Chair, if one has been appointed by the Board, for the balance of the term of office.

Section 3: Other Agents and Employees. The Board of Directors may appoint agents and employees who shall have such authority and perform such duties as may be prescribed by the Board. No other Officer or agent need be a Director of the Corporation.

Section 4: Compensation of Officers, Agents, and Employees. The Corporation may pay its officers, employees, and agents compensation commensurate with their services and reimbursement for expenses incurred in the performance of their duties. The amount of compensation shall be fixed by the Board or, if the Board delegates power to any officer or officers, then by such officer or officers.

ARTICLE VI: Office, Books, and Annual Reports

Section 1: Office. The office of the Corporation shall be located at such place as the Board of Directors may from time to time determine.

Section 2: Books. The Corporation shall keep correct books of account of its activities and transactions at the office of the Corporation, including a minute book, which shall contain a copy of the articles of incorporation, these bylaws, and all minutes of meetings of the Board of Directors.

Section 3: Annual Report. At each annual meeting, the President and the Treasurer shall present to the Board of Directors a report in such form and with such contents as may be required from time to time by law and by the Board of Directors, and a copy of such reports shall be filed with the minutes of the meeting.

Section 4: Fiscal Year. The fiscal year shall be determined in the discretion of the Board of Directors, but in the absence of such determination, it shall be the calendar year.

ARTICLE VII: Indemnification

The Corporation shall indemnify any Director or Officer against any threatened, pending, or completed action, suit, or proceeding relating to or arising out of the performance of his or her duties in the manner and to the full extent provided by law.

ARTICLE VIII: Amendments

These Bylaws may be altered, amended, restated, or repealed, in whole or in part, and new Bylaws may be adopted by the affirmative vote of [fraction] of the entire Board at any meeting of the Board of Directors. Notice of the proposed alteration, amendment, restatement, repeal, or new Bylaw provision, including the proposed text thereof, shall be included in the notice of the meeting at which such action is considered.

These Bylaws were approved at a meeting of the Board of Directors on _____.

DRAFTING PROBLEM

Using the sample bylaws above as your guide, please add bylaws to the articles of incorporation that you drafted in Chapter 2. You should ensure that the bylaws are consistent with the articles and that they comport with the laws of the state in which your organization is located.

This exercise is not as simple as filling in the blanks. The *ACE* case and the subsequent notes illustrate the problems with sloppy drafting. In fact, it can be quite difficult to draft consistent and unambiguous provisions that help an organization fulfill its mission. Even though many of the decisions are initially managerial decisions, they become legally binding on the organization once they are formalized. Thus, bylaws drafters must make careful and thoughtful decisions and include provisions for amending the bylaws in case the organization determines at a later date to change one or more provisions.

This assignment asks you to assume that your organization is not a membership organization, but you should be aware of the additional complexities that a membership organization creates for the drafter of the bylaws. Decisions about classes of members, procedures for their election and removal, their qualifications, and the decisions they must approve should all be included in the bylaws. Failure to abide by any of them can wreak havoc on the organization. A guide to creating effective bylaws is Benson Tesdahl, *Better Bylaws: Creating Effective Rules for Your Nonprofit Board*, 2d ed. (Board Source 2010).

A few items to note for this exercise:

- Make sure that your articles and bylaws are consistent. Also, make sure that the articles and bylaws are consistent with the statutes in your state.
- The state statutes leave a good deal of discretion to you. Feel free to add to or change the provisions of both the articles of incorporation and bylaws. If you think that it would be better to specify committees or compensation rather than include the vague provision of the sample bylaws, feel free to do so. Conversely, you can take specific provisions from the sample documents, such as the number of Directors on the Board of Directors, and make them more vague (e.g., "the number of directors will be no less than 3 or more than 25").

C. POLICIES

Before 2000, nonprofit governance received relatively scant attention, but a series of scandals in both the for-profit and nonprofit corporate worlds in the early 2000s led to more scrutiny. Several states passed new laws, most notably the California Nonprofit Integrity Act in 2004 and the New York Nonprofit Revitalization Act in 2013. The Sarbanes-Oxley Act in 2002 applied mainly to large for-profit corporations, but it set standards for good governance for all corporate entities, and two of its provisions, those dealing with whistleblowing protection and document destruction, apply to nonprofits as well as for-profits. In addition, Independent Sector developed a prescription for good nonprofit governance called *The Principles for Good Governance and Ethical Practice,* which it updated in 2015, and the Internal Revenue Service (IRS) now asks questions about nonprofit governance on its exemption application and on tax information forms.

Nonprofit organizations have responded to these governance changes by adding policies that the organization must follow. The most common policies are discussed below.

Conflict of Interest Policies

Perhaps the most important policy for a nonprofit is a conflict of interest policy. New York requires such a policy, NY CSL §715-a, and IRS Form 1023, which an organization seeking § 501(c)(3) tax exemption must file, asks whether the organization has a conflict of interest policy that conforms with the example provided in the appendix to its instructions. If the answer is "yes," applicants must include a copy of the policy. If the answer is "no," applicants must explain how they will assure that conflicts will be handled appropriately. Form 1023 does not require such a policy before the organization is recognized for exemption, but it obviously recommends one. Form 990, the tax information form that larger §501(c)(3) organizations file on an annual basis with the IRS, also asks about this policy and how the organization ensures it is followed. *The Principles for Good Governance and Ethical Practice* also recommend such a policy.

The IRS sample policy requires officers, directors, and members of committees to acknowledge in writing on an annual basis that they have received, read and understood their organization's policy and that they plan to comply with its provisions. It also requires each organization to review its operations and decisions periodically to ensure that the policies are followed.

The sample requires "interested persons," which it defines as anyone with a direct or indirect financial interest in the organization, to disclose all conflicts of interest, along with the facts that are relevant to the conflict. The organization is not prohibited from engaging in a transaction with the person who has a conflict, but it must explore other possibilities to see if it can negotiate a better arrangement with an individual or organization that does not have a conflict. Further, the conflicted person cannot vote on a transaction with which he or she has an interest.

One way to think about these policies is that they require disclosure, discussion, decision by disinterested directors, and documentation.[4]

Whistleblower Policies

One of the two provisions of the Sarbanes-Oxley Act that applies to nonprofit as well as for-profit corporations is the one that protects whistleblowers and provides criminal penalties for those who retaliate against them. Although New York is the only state that requires whistleblower policies (for larger nonprofits), NY CSL NFPCA § 715 (b), all nonprofits will be better served by having such policies. *The Principles of Good Governance and Ethical Behavior* recommends adopting whistleblower policies,[5] and IRS Form 990 asks whether the reporting organizations have done so.

A strong whistleblower policy will affirm the nonprofit's commitment to following the law and provide a procedure through which employees can report any action or policy that they reasonably believe violates the law. The policy should stress the importance of such reports and provide an alternative procedure in case the whistleblower feels uncomfortable following the primary procedure. The policy should also explain which actions the nonprofit will take upon receiving such information and state that no retaliatory action will be taken against the person who makes such a report. Ultimately, all volunteers and employees should sign this document.

Document Retention and Destruction Policies

A second Sarbanes-Oxley provision that applies to nonprofit corporations makes it a crime to alter, cover up, falsify, or destroy a document in order to prevent its use in an official proceeding. It is also a crime to persuade someone else to do this. All nonprofits need to maintain appropriate records, and they need

---

[4] Council on Foundation, *Conflicts of Interest and Form 1023.* http://www.cof.org /content/conflicts-interest-and-form-1023, last accessed May 8, 2016.

[5] Independent Sector, *The Principles of Good Governance and Ethical Behavior* (2007; updated 2015).

to have systems in place to keep them as long as necessary and to remove them when they are no longer needed. The policy should cover paper and electronic documents, as well as backup and archiving systems and voice mails. If an official investigation is underway, or even just suspected, all document destruction must stop, even if it coincides with the time that the documents would ordinarily be purged, pursuant to the policy. Although document retention and destruction policies are not required by law, they can protect nonprofits—and individuals—from criminal sanctions.

Compensation Policies

Many larger organizations also create policies for compensation of officers, directors, and key employees. These are the positions whose salaries are most likely to violate the nondistribution constraint at the state level and the excess benefit transaction rules at the federal level.[6] These policies generally provide the nonprofit with the guidance that will afford them the most protection under the federal laws, which are covered in Chapter 9.

Other Policies and Practical Considerations

Conflict of interest and compensation policies help to ensure that nonprofit organizations observe the nondistribution constraint. Some nonprofits also adopt gift acceptance policies, reimbursement of expenses policies, or both in order to reinforce the importance of this constraint. *The Principles for Good Governance and Ethical Practice* suggest that charitable organizations adopt both these policies. They also recommend that charitable organizations institute investment policies.

Nonprofit organizations could have other policies relating to their finances, such as financial reserves policies. They might also have personnel policies about hiring and firing volunteers and employees, as well as sexual harassment and nondiscrimination policies. Adopting policies about board training and self-evaluation could also be a wise decision, and confidentiality and data protection policies could be important for some organizations.

Once the policies are adopted, the board needs to ensure that they are followed. Failing to follow a policy could be worse than not having one at all. The board should also review the policies every few years to determine whether they should be amended to reflect changes within the organization or in the law.

NOTES AND QUESTIONS

1. Could the court in the *ACE* case have come to the opposite conclusion? What would have happened to the organization if Amyx had won? What should the drafters of the bylaws have done to avoid this type of situation in the first place? Would the court have been able to come to the conclusion that it did if ACE had used the sample bylaws reproduced above?

---

[6] Chapter 9 covers these excess benefit transaction rules.

2. Unfortunately, power struggles and disputes over bylaws are not unusual. *See e.g., Swain v. Wiley College,* 74 S.W.3d 143 (Tex. App. 2002) (decision not to renew the contract of the president of the college was valid even though the notice for the meeting at which the decision was made was improper, because a quorum was present and no one with standing to question the results of the meeting raised the issue); *Herning v. Eason,* 739 P.2d 167 (Alaska 1987) (court found that proxy votes for removing the pastor could be counted because the state law authorized proxy voting and the bylaws did not explicitly prohibit proxy voting); *Tackney v. U.S. Naval Academy Alumni Assn.,* 971 A.2d 309 (Md. 2009) (interplay between two bylaws allowed for conflicting interpretations about whether board chair could stay on the board a year after his term ended, so court deferred to board's interpretation).

3. Not all power struggles on boards are played out in courts. Sometimes, of course, they are played out in private. Other times, they find expression in the newspapers. *See* Greg Winter, *School Learns Cost of a Gift-Giver's Anger,* N.Y. TIMES (Nov. 14, 2002, p. A-1 (after Case Western University ran up huge cost overruns in its new business school, Peter Lewis, who had pledged $25 million to the school, threatened to withhold donations to Case Western and every other Cleveland nonprofit until the entire board of Case Western resigned). *See also* Evan Perez and Corey Dad, *Foundation Devoted to Dr. King's Dream Has Real-World Woes,* WALL ST. J., Jan. 14, 2006, p. A-1 (power struggle among family members of the Reverend Martin Luther King, Jr. over the way that the foundation should be run).

4. Most of the provisions in state nonprofit corporation laws are default provisions that allow the board to make decisions and come into play only if the board is silent on a particular matter. Some, however, are prescriptive. For example, New York requires board members to be 18 years old,[7] and most states require boards to have at least three board members. Several states, including California, require that a majority of the board be independent. Approximately half the states require large nonprofits to have audit committees and to provide an audited financial statement to the state.[8]

5. In 2014, 99% of medium-sized nonprofits and 96% of large organization had conflict of interest policies. More than 90% of these organizations also had whistleblower and document retention policies. Board Source, LEADING WITH INTENT: A NATIONAL INDEX OF NONPROFIT BOARD PRACTICES (2015). These percentages have undoubtedly increased in recent years, because IRS Form 990, the tax information form that medium and large charities file on an annual basis, now asks questions about conflict of interest, whistleblower, and document-retention and destruction policies. That document is available to the public, and if nothing else, it is designed to pressure public charities

---

[7] NY CSL N-CPL §7.01. The New York statute provides for limited exceptions for youth-oriented activities. That part of §7.01 was not included above.

[8] Amy Blackwood, Nathan Dietz, and Tom Pollock, *The State of Nonprofit Governance* (2014).

into adopting and enforcing better governance policies. Form 990 is covered in Chapter 12.

6. Is there a correlation between good governance and the absence of fraud? The IRS believes so, which is why it has added governance questions to the tax information form that §501(c)(3)s file annually, Form 990.[9] Scholarly research has confirmed this belief. Erica Harris, Christine Petrovitz, and Michelle Yetman, *Why Bad Things Happen to Good Organizations: The Link Between Governance and Asset Diversions in Public Charities* (2015), available at http://ssrn.com/abstract=2604372.

III. FIDUCIARY DUTIES OF THE BOARD OF DIRECTORS

The members of the board of directors of a nonprofit organization have specific legal duties that are spelled out in most state nonprofit codes. Most codes, courts, and commentators agree that a board has two fiduciary duties with regard to the nonprofit corporation: care and loyalty. Some have found a third duty as well: obedience.

Generally speaking, the duty of care is the duty to pay attention to the organization—to monitor its activities, see that its mission is being accomplished, and guard its financial resources. Phrases such as "good faith," "ordinarily prudent person," and "reasonably believes to be in the best interests of the corporation" describe this duty in broad terms so that it can be adapted to the particular situation. The duty of loyalty, also called the "duty of fair dealing," reminds board members to keep the interests of the corporation paramount and avoid benefiting unfairly from their relationship with the corporation. The duty of obedience, which emphasizes the importance of a nonprofit's mission, is not recognized by all jurisdictions or commentators. Its supporters see it as a way to emphasize the difference between for-profit and nonprofit governance, but its detractors see it as unnecessary.

The following statutes and cases spell out and illustrate these duties. As you read them, consider the different ways that the duties are characterized and whether this difference in language could make a difference in a particular case. Also note that, because the duties overlap somewhat, most cases dealing with fiduciary duties of board members will involve more than one fiduciary duty. You should be able to identify several duties that are at issue in each case. Nevertheless, the *Stern* and *Lemington* cases illustrate issues concerning the duties of care and loyalty, and the *MEETH* case demonstrates the duty of obedience. Following these three cases is an excerpt from the Uniform Prudent Management of Investment Funds Act (UPMIFA), which spells out the fiduciary duties when a nonprofit has significant sums of money. The UPMIFA excerpt is

---

[9] Internal Revenue Service, *2015 Instructions for Form 990 Return of Organization Exempt from Income Tax.*

followed by a case that arose when the Hershey School Trust, a $7 billion charity, attempted to diversify its portfolio.

A. FIDUCIARY DUTIES OF CARE AND LOYALTY

MODEL NONPROFIT CORPORATION ACT, 3D ED. (2008),
§§8.30, 8.32, 8.60, AND 8.70

§8.30. Standards of Conduct for Directors

(a) Each member of the board of directors, when discharging the duties of a director, shall act:

(1) in good faith, and

(2) in a manner the director reasonably believes to be in the best interests of the nonprofit corporation.

(b) The members of the board of directors or a committee of the board, when becoming informed in connection with their decision-making function or devoting attention to their oversight function, must discharge their duties with the care that a person in a like position would reasonably believe appropriate under similar circumstances.

(c) In discharging board or committee duties a director must disclose, or cause to be disclosed, to the other board or committee members information not already known by them but known by the director to be material to the discharge of their decision-making or oversight functions, except that disclosure is not required to the extent that the director reasonably believes that doing so would violate a duty imposed by law, a legally enforceable obligation of confidentiality, or a professional ethics rule.

(d) In discharging board or committee duties a director who does not have knowledge that makes reliance unwarranted may rely on the performance by any of the persons specified in subsection (f)(1), (3), or (4) to whom the board may have delegated, formally or informally by course of conduct, the authority or duty to perform one or more of the board's functions that are delegable under applicable law.

(e) In discharging board or committee duties a director who does not have knowledge that makes reliance unwarranted may rely on information, opinions, reports, or statements, including financial statements and other financial data, prepared or presented by any of the persons specified in subsection (f).

(f) A director may rely, in accordance with subsection (d) or (e), on:

(1) one or more officers or employees of the nonprofit corporation whom the director reasonably believes to be reliable and competent in the functions performed or the information, opinions, reports, or statements provided;

(2) legal counsel, public accountants, or other persons retained by the corporation as to matters involving skills or expertise the director reasonably believes are matters:

(i) within the particular person's professional or expert competence, or

(ii) as to which the particular person merits confidence;

(3) a committee of the board of directors of which the director is not a member if the director reasonably believes the committee merits confidence; or

(4) in the case of a corporation engaged in religious activity, religious authorities and ministers, priests, rabbis, imams, or other persons whose positions or duties the director reasonably believes justify reliance and confidence and whom the director believes to be reliable and competent in the matters presented.

(g) A director is not a trustee with respect to the nonprofit corporation with respect to any property held or administered by the corporation, including property that may be subject to restrictions imposed by the donor or transferor of the property.

§8.32. Loans to or Guarantees for Directors and Officers (Optional)

(a) A nonprofit corporation may not lend money to or guarantee the obligation of a director or officer of the corporation....

(c) The fact that a loan or guarantee is made in violation of this section does not affect the borrower's liability on the loan.

§8.60. Conflicting Interest Transactions; Voidability

(a) A contract or transaction between a nonprofit corporation and one or more of its members, directors, members of a designated body, or officers or between a nonprofit corporation and any other corporation, partnership, association, or other entity in which one or more of its directors, members of a designated body, or officers are directors or officers, hold a similar position, or have a financial interest, is not void or voidable solely for that reason, or solely because the member, director, member of a designated body, or officer is present at or participates in the meeting of the board of directors that authorizes the contract or transaction, or solely because his or their votes are counted for that purpose, if:

(1) the material facts as to the relationship or interest and as to the contract or transaction are disclosed or are known to the board of directors and the board in good faith authorizes the contract or transaction by the affirmative votes of a majority of the disinterested directors even though the disinterested directors are less than a quorum;

(2) the material facts as to the relationship or interest of the member, director, or officer and as to the contract or transaction are disclosed or are known to the members entitled to vote thereon, if any, and the contract or transaction is specifically approved in good faith by vote of those members; or

(3) the contract or transaction is fair as to the corporation as of the time it is authorized, approved, or ratified by the board of directors or the members.

(b) Common or interested directors may be counted in determining the presence of a quorum at a meeting of the board that authorizes a contract or transaction specified in subsection (a).

(c) This section is applicable except as otherwise restricted in the articles of incorporation or bylaws.

§8.70. Business Opportunities

(a) The taking advantage, directly or indirectly, by a director of a business opportunity may not be the subject of equitable relief, or give rise to an award of damages or other sanctions against the director, in a proceeding by or in the right of the nonprofit corporation on the ground that the opportunity should have first been offered to the corporation, if before becoming legally obligated or entitled respecting the opportunity the director brings it to the attention of the corporation and action by the members or the directors disclaiming the corporation's interest in the opportunity is taken in compliance with the procedures set forth in section 8.60, as if the decision being made concerned a conflicting interest transaction.

(b) In any proceeding seeking equitable relief or other remedies, based upon an alleged improper taking advantage of a business opportunity by a director, the fact that the director did not employ the procedure described in subsection (a) before taking advantage of the opportunity does not support an inference that the opportunity should have been first presented to the nonprofit corporation or alter the burden of proof otherwise applicable to establish that the director breached a duty to the corporation in the circumstances.

(c) As used in this section, "director" includes a member of a designated body.

STERN V. LUCY WEBB HAYES NATIONAL TRAINING SCHOOL FOR DEACONESSES[10]

---

381 F. Supp. 1003 (D.D.C. 1974)

GESELL, District Judge.

This is a class action which was tried to the Court without a jury. Plaintiffs were certified as a class under Rule 23(b)(2) of the Federal Rules of Civil Procedure and represent patients of Sibley Memorial Hospital, a District of Columbia non-profit charitable corporation organized under D.C. Code §29-1001 et seq. They challenge various aspects of the Hospital's fiscal management. The

---

[10] [This case is usually referred to as the *Sibley Hospital* case. This book will use that name when referring to this case in notes, questions, and other commentary.—*Ed.*]

amended complaint named as defendants nine members of the Hospital's Board of Trustees,[11] six financial institutions, and the Hospital itself....

The two principal contentions in the complaint are that the defendant trustees conspired to enrich themselves and certain financial institutions with which they were affiliated by favoring those institutions in financial dealings with the Hospital, and that they breached their fiduciary duties of care and loyalty in the management of Sibley's funds.

I. Corporate History

In 1960, ... the Sibley Board of Trustees revised the corporate by-laws, ... [T]he Board was to consist of from 25 to 35 trustees, who were to meet at least twice each year. Between such meetings, an Executive Committee was to represent the Board, and was authorized . . . to open checking and savings accounts, approve the Hospital budget, renew mortgages, and enter into contracts. A Finance Committee was created to review the budget and to report regularly on the amount of cash available for investment. Management of those investments was to be supervised by an Investment Committee, which was to work closely with the Finance Committee in such matters.

In fact, management of the Hospital from the early 1950's until 1968 was handled almost exclusively by two trustee officers: Dr. Orem, the Hospital Administrator, and Mr. Ernst, the Treasurer.... They dominated the Board and its Executive Committee, which routinely accepted their recommendations and ratified their actions. Even more significantly, neither the Finance Committee nor the Investment Committee ever met or conducted business from the date of their creation until 1971, three years after the death of Dr. Orem. As a result, budgetary and investment decisions during this period, like most other management decisions affecting the Hospital's finances, were handled by Orem and Ernst, receiving only cursory supervision from the Executive Committee and the full Board.

Dr. Orem's death on April 5, 1968, obliged some of the other trustees to play a more active role in running the Hospital.... Mr. Ernst still made most of the financial and investment decisions for Sibley, but his actions and failures to act came slowly under increasing scrutiny by several of the other trustees, particularly after a series of disagreements between Ernst and the Hospital Comptroller which led to the discharge of the latter early in 1971.

[Additionally, the Court found that every defendant trustee held stock in one or more of the banks and investment companies with which the hospital did business. The hospital held more than $1 million of investible assets in noninterest-bearing checking accounts at banks with ties to the board, and it held some interest-bearing certificates of deposit that offered lower interest rates than those available at other institutions. Sibley also obtained a loan from a

---

[11] [FN1] The directors of the Hospital are termed "trustees" under the by-laws. However, the use of the term by the Court does not imply a legal conclusion as to the duty they owe the Hospital and its patients.

consortium of banks with ties to directors, which was renewed when it could have been repaid. Finally, one board member probably voted in favor of Sibley's hiring a firm that he owned for investment advice, and another member personally negotiated a deal between the hospital and his bank.]

III. Breach of Duty

Plaintiffs [contend] that the facts reveal serious breaches of duty on the part of the defendant trustees and the knowing acceptance of benefits from those breaches by the defendant banks and savings and loan associations.

A. The Trustees

Basically, the trustees are charged with mismanagement, nonmanagement, and self-dealing. The applicable law is unsettled. The charitable corporation is a relatively new legal entity which does not fit neatly into the established common law categories of corporation and trust. As the discussion below indicates, however, the modern trend is to apply corporate rather than trust principles in determining the liability of the directors of charitable corporations, because their functions are virtually indistinguishable from those of their "pure" corporate counterparts.

1. Mismanagement

Both trustees and corporate directors are liable for losses occasioned by their negligent mismanagement of investments. However, the degree of care required appears to differ in many jurisdictions. A trustee is uniformly held to a high standard of care and will be held liable for simple negligence, while a director must often have committed "gross negligence" or otherwise be guilty of more than mere mistakes of judgment....

This distinction may amount to little more than a recognition of the fact that corporate directors have many areas of responsibility, while the traditional trustee is often charged only with the management of the trust funds and can therefore be expected to devote more time and expertise to that task. Since the board members of most large charitable corporations fall within the corporate rather than the trust model, being charged with the operation of ongoing businesses, it has been said that they should only be held to the less stringent corporate standard of care. More specifically, directors of charitable corporations are required to exercise ordinary and reasonable care in the performance of their duties, exhibiting honesty and good faith.

2. Nonmanagement

Plaintiffs allege that the individual defendants failed to supervise the management of Hospital investments or even to attend meetings of the committees charged with such supervision. Trustees . . . not only have an affirmative duty to "maximize the trust income by prudent investment," *Blankenship v. Boyle*, 329 F. Supp. 1089, 1096 (D.D.C. 1971), but they may not delegate that duty, even to a committee of their fellow trustees. A corporate director, on the other hand, may delegate his investment responsibility . . ., but he must continue to exercise general supervision over the activities of his delegates. Once again, the rule for charitable corporations is closer to the traditional corporate rule: directors should at least be permitted to delegate investment decisions to a committee of board members, so long as all directors assume the responsibility for supervising such committees by periodically scrutinizing their work.

Total abdication of the supervisory role, however, is improper even under traditional corporate principles. A director who fails to acquire the information necessary to supervise investment policy or consistently fails even to attend the meetings at which such policies are considered has violated his fiduciary duty to the corporation. While a director is, of course, permitted to rely upon the expertise of those to whom he has delegated investment responsibility, such reliance is a tool for interpreting the delegate's reports, not an excuse for dispensing with or ignoring such reports. A director whose failure to supervise permits negligent mismanagement by others to go unchecked has committed an independent wrong against the corporation. . . .

3. Self-dealing

Under District of Columbia Law, neither trustees nor corporate directors are absolutely barred from placing funds under their control into a bank having an interlocking directorship with their own institution. In both cases, however, such transactions will be subjected to the closest scrutiny to determine whether or not the duty of loyalty has been violated.... In the absence of clear evidence of wrongdoing, ... the courts appear to have used different standards to determine whether or not relief is appropriate, depending again on the legal relationship involved. Trustees may be found guilty of a breach of trust even for mere negligence in the maintenance of accounts in banks with which they are associated, ... while corporate directors are generally only required to show "entire fairness" to the corporation and "full disclosure" of the potential conflict of interest to the Board....

Most courts apply the less stringent corporate rule to charitable corporations in this area.... It is, however, occasionally added that a director should not only disclose his interlocking responsibilities but also refrain from voting on or otherwise influencing a corporate decision to transact business with a company in which he has a significant interest or control....

Although defendants have argued against the imposition of even these limitations on self-dealing by the Sibley trustees, the Hospital Board recently adopted a new by-law, based upon guidelines issued by the American Hospital Association, which essentially imposes the modified corporate rule described above....

[T]he Court holds that a director or so-called trustee of a charitable hospital organized under the Non-Profit Corporation Act of the District of Columbia (D.C. Code §29-1001 et seq.) is in default of his fiduciary duty to manage the fiscal and investment affairs of the hospital if it has been shown by a preponderance of the evidence that:

(1) while assigned to a particular committee of the Board having general financial or investment responsibility under the by-laws of the corporation, he has failed to use due diligence in supervising the actions of those officers, employees or outside experts to whom the responsibility for making day-to-day financial or investment decisions has been delegated; or

(2) he knowingly permitted the hospital to enter into a business transaction with himself or with any corporation, partnership or association in which he then had a substantial interest or held a position as trustee, director, general manager or principal officer without having previously informed the persons charged with approving that transaction of his interest or position and of any significant reasons, unknown to or not fully appreciated by such persons, why the transaction might not be in the best interests of the hospital; or

(3) except as required by the preceding paragraph, he actively participated in or voted in favor of a decision by the Board or any committee or subcommittee thereof to transact business with himself or with any corporation, partnership or association in which he then had a substantial interest or held a position as trustee, director, general manager, or principal officer; or

(4) he otherwise failed to perform his duties honestly, in good faith, and with a reasonable amount of diligence and care.

Applying these standards to the facts in the record, the Court finds that each of the defendant trustees has breached his fiduciary duty to supervise the management of Sibley's investments. [Neither the Investment nor the Finance Committee met for 10 years, and the Executive Committee did not even acquire] enough information to vote intelligently on the opening of new bank accounts. . . . [A]ll of the individual defendants ignored the investment sections of the yearly audits. . . . In short, these men have in the past failed to exercise even the most cursory supervision over the handling of Hospital funds and failed to establish and carry out a defined policy.

The record is unclear on the degree to which full disclosure preceded the frequent self-dealing which occurred during the period under consideration. It is reasonable to assume that the Board was generally aware of the various bank affiliations of the defendant trustees, but there is no indication that these conflicting interests were brought home to the relevant committees when they voted to approve particular transactions. Similarly, while plaintiffs have shown no active misrepresentation on defendants' part, they have established instances in which an interested trustee failed to alert the responsible officials to better terms known to be available elsewhere.

It is clear that all of the defendant trustees have, at one time or another, affirmatively approved self-dealing transactions. Most of these incidents were of relatively minor significance. . . . Others cannot be so easily disregarded. Defendant Ferris' advice and vote in the relatively small Investment Committee to recommend approval of the investment contract with Ferris & Co. may have been crucial to that transaction. . . . And defendant Smith, in his capacity as President of Jefferson Federal, personally negotiated the interest rates on a $230,000 certificate account with the Hospital.

That the Hospital has suffered no measurable injury from many of these transactions—including the mortgage and the investment contract—and that the excessive deposits which were the real source of harm were caused primarily by the uniform failure to supervise rather than the occasional self-dealing vote are both facts that the Court must take into account in fashioning relief, but they do not alter the principle that the trustee of a charitable hospital should always avoid active participation in a transaction in which he or a corporation with which he is associated has a significant interest.

IN RE LEMINGTON HOME FOR THE AGED

---

777 F.3d 620 (3d Cir. 2015)

[*Editor's Note:* Prior to this opinion, this case had come before the Third Circuit two other times. The second was a procedural decision, but the first was an appeal from a summary judgment on the same issues that appear in this case— breach of fiduciary duties and deepening insolvency. The district court initially ordered summary judgment because it said that the directors were protected by the "business judgment rule," in that they had relied on counsel, held several meetings, and considered several alternatives before filing for bankruptcy. The Third Circuit overruled this decision because it found that factual issues remained that precluded the application of the business judgment rule as a matter of law. It explained the rule as follows: "The business judgment rule should insulate officers and directors from judicial intervention in the absence of fraud or self-dealing, if challenged decisions were within the scope of the directors' authority, if they exercised reasonable diligence, and if they honestly and rationally believed their decisions were in the best interests of the company." *In re Lemington Home for the Aged*, 659 F.3d 282 (2011), citing *Cuker v. Mikalauskas*, 547 Pa. 600, 692 A.2d 1042, 1048 (Pa. 1997). The following opinion does not explicitly mention the business judgment rule, but it obviously does not apply it. As you read this opinion, consider why this doctrine did not apply, at least for the members of the board of directors, for whom there was no evidence of self-dealing.]

In the present appeal, the Defendants, two former Officers and fourteen former Directors of the nursing home, present several challenges to the jury's verdict, which found them liable for breach of fiduciary duties and deepening insolvency. . .

The Lemington Home for the Aged ("the Home"), established in 1883, "was the oldest, non-profit, unaffiliated nursing home in the United States dedicated to the care of African-America[n] seniors." As part of its mission statement, the Home sought to "[e]stablish, support, maintain and operate an institution that is able to extend nursing home care for persons who are infirm due to age and other reasons, without regard to age, sex, race, religion, and to do so regardless of whether such persons themselves have the ability to pay for such care."

Defendant Mel Lee Causey was hired to serve as the Home's Administrator and Chief Executive Officer in September 1997. Defendant James Shealey became the Home's Chief Financial Officer in December 2002 and reported to Causey. . . . The "Director Defendants" . . . had "direct supervisory control, authority and responsibility" over Causey.

The Home had been "beset with financial troubles" for decades, but had remained afloat with help from the City of Pittsburgh, Allegheny County, and donations from several private foundations. The Home's financial difficulties became particularly acute during the early 2000s, under the management of the Officer Defendants. . . .

On January 6, 2005, the Board convened and voted to close the Home. However, its Chapter 11 petition was not filed until April 13 of that year. . . .

In November 2005, the Bankruptcy Court granted the request made by the Committee of Unsecured Creditors ("the Committee") to bring this adversary proceeding against Causey, Shealey, and the Director Defendants claiming breach of fiduciary duty, breach of the duty of loyalty, and deepening insolvency. The District Court granted summary judgment in favor of Defendants on all claims.

On appeal, we vacated the District Court's grant of summary judgment in its entirety, concluding that "our independent review of the record discloses genuine disputes of material facts on all claims." . . .

[After more procedural wrangling which brought this case to the appeals court a second time], the case proceeded to a six-day jury trial, which began on February 19, 2013. At the close of the Committee's case, the Defendants moved for judgment as a matter of law, which the District Court granted with respect to the breach of the duty of loyalty claim against the Director Defendants and denied in all other respects. Following the close of trial, the jury deliberated for three days before returning a compensatory damages verdict against fifteen of the seventeen Defendants, jointly and severally, in the amount of $2,250,000.[12] . . .

Following the verdict, the Defendants filed a motion for judgment as a matter of law, a new trial, or remittitur. The District Court denied that motion in its entirety. This appeal followed. . . .

The Defendants first argue that the Committee introduced insufficient evidence at trial to establish that the Director and Officer Defendants had breached their duty of care and that the Officer Defendants had additionally breached their duty of loyalty. We disagree. The Committee presented evidence to the jury that was sufficient to support a rational finding that the Defendants had breached their fiduciary duties by failing to exercise reasonable diligence and prudence in their oversight and management of the Home.

---

[12] [The jury also awarded punitive damages, which the appeals court affirmed with regard to Causey and Sheahey but rejected for the other defendants. That decision is not part of the discussion in this book.—Ed.]

Pennsylvania law provides:

[A]n officer shall perform his duties as an officer in good faith, in a manner he reasonably believes to be in the best interests of the corporation and with such care, including reasonable inquiry, skill and diligence, as a person of ordinary prudence would use under similar circumstances. 15 Pa. Cons. Stat. Ann § 5712(c).

The duty of loyalty under Pennsylvania law "requires that corporate officers devote themselves to the corporate affairs with a view to promote the common interests and not their own." *Tyler v. O'Neill*, 994 F. Supp. 603, 612 (E.D. Pa. 1998). . . .

Evidence presented at trial demonstrated that Causey fell far short of fulfilling [her] responsibilities. Throughout Causey's tenure, the Home was not in compliance with federal and state regulations. Causey began her role as Administrator in 1997. "[T]here were significant problems identified by the Pennsylvania Department of Health, the inspectors of the nursing home from 1998 through 2004 . . . ." The Home was cited repeatedly for failing to keep proper documentation of residents' clinical records. In 2004, the Department of Health launched an investigation following the death of patient Elaine Carrington. The review concluded that "Causey lacks the qualifications, the knowledge of the PC regulations and the ability to direct staff to perform personal care services as required." This evaluation, citing Causey's inexperience and lack of qualifications, came after Causey had already been in the role of Administrator for more than six years.

The jury also heard testimony that, at the time of Ms. Carrington's death, Causey was not working at the Home full-time, despite holding the title of Administrator and collecting her full salary. Pennsylvania law requires all facilities of the Home's size to employ a full-time Administrator. But in an application for long-term disability benefits she filed with the state, Causey represented that she was working only "20 to 24 hours per week at Lemington" for more than eight months in 2004. When confronted at trial with this portion of her benefits application, Causey avoided giving a precise figure for how many hours she worked during this period, although she eventually admitted, "I was working part-time."

We are satisfied that the jury was presented with more than sufficient evidence to conclude that Causey breached her duty of care. Additionally, testimony regarding Causey's self-interested decision to stay on as an Administrator despite being unable to serve full-time as required under state law supported the jury's verdict that she breached her duty of loyalty by collecting her full salary while not in fact fulfilling the duties of the role for which she was being compensated.

The jury also heard sufficient evidence to support its determination that defendant Shealey breached his duties of care and loyalty as Chief Financial Officer. The Committee presented testimony from William Terrence Brown, a nursing home consultant who had conducted an assessment of the Home on behalf of a major creditor in May 2005. Brown testified that he repeatedly asked Shealey for [financial] information, but it was not provided to him.

Brown also testified that, towards the end of his review of the Home, Shealey, in an attempt to avoid Brown's persistent requests for basic financial information, locked himself in his office. Brown responded by "camp[ing] outside" of Shealey's office, waiting for him to leave in order to speak with him about the Home's finances. Brown testified that when he finally managed to speak with Shealey:

> I said, Mr. Shealey, there really aren't any books; are there? And he said no.
>
> So I said, well, Mr. Shealey, you got to have something that you keep an idea of what kind of cash is in the bank. So what do you use for that?
>
> And he said, well, I've got, you know, a little Excel spread sheet I use, only I try to keep a bank balance.

When pressed by Brown as to how long he had operated without a general ledger that recorded the Home's finances in detail, Shealey admitted that "June 30, 2004, was the last time they kept any books." Brown testified that Shealey never provided him with the Excel spreadsheet he allegedly used in lieu of a general ledger. Despite Shealey's failure to provide these documents to Brown, minutes from a Board meeting following Brown's visit state that Shealey informed the Board that Brown had "received everything he requested." Brown also testified that, under Shealey, the Home had failed to bill for Medicare since August 2004. Brown calculated that this resulted in the Home failing to collect at least $500,000 it was due for services rendered.

The Committee also introduced into evidence an email that Shealey sent to a representative of Mount Ararat Baptist Church ("Mt. Ararat") in April 2005, before the Home had filed for bankruptcy. The proposal suggested that Mt. Ararat purchase Lemington "to create a revitalized faith-based retirement community" named Mount Ararat Retirement Community ("MARC"). The proposal indicated that Shealey would "assume the position of MARC President and Chief Executive Officer." Director Baldwin testified that he believed Shealey's involvement in this potential sale was inappropriate, as Shealey would receive a benefit if the Home was merged with Mt. Ararat.

The jury therefore heard sufficient evidence to find that Shealey fell far short of fulfilling his duty to act "with such care, including reasonable inquiry, skill and diligence, as a person of ordinary prudence would use under similar circumstances." 15 Pa. Cons. Stat. Ann. § 5712(c). A person serving as Chief Financial Officer with reasonable skill and diligence would not fail to maintain a general ledger for over nine months, refuse to meet with a consultant hired by a major creditor of the Home, and forgo collection of upwards of $500,000 due to the Home in Medicare payments. Shealey's decision to stay on as CFO despite his inability to competently fulfill the duties with which he was charged, combined with his proposal that Mt. Ararat purchase the Home and elevate him to the position of President and CEO, also gave the jury a sufficient basis for concluding that Shealey acted in self-interest, breaching his duty of loyalty to the Home . . .

The evidence also supported a finding that the Director Defendants breached their duty of care by failing to take action to remove Causey and Shealey once the results of their mismanagement became apparent . . .

Pennsylvania law provides:

(a) *Directors.*—A director of a nonprofit corporation shall stand in a fiduciary relation to the corporation and shall perform his duties as a director . . . in good faith, in a manner he reasonably believes to be in the best interests of the corporation and with such care, including reasonable inquiry, skill and diligence, as a person of ordinary prudence would use under similar circumstances. In performing his duties, a director shall be entitled to rely in good faith on information, opinions, reports or statements, including financial statements and other financial data, in each case prepared or presented by any of the following: (1) One or more officers or employees of the corporation whom the director reasonably believes to be reliable and competent in the matters presented. (2) Counsel, public accountants or other persons as to matters which the director reasonably believes to be within the professional or expert competence of such person . . . .

(b) *Effect of actual knowledge.*—A director shall not be considered to be acting in good faith if he has knowledge concerning the matter in question that would cause his reliance to be unwarranted. 15 Pa. Cons. Stat. Ann. § 5712.

The jury heard testimony that the Board was "responsible for the oversight of the nursing home Administrator and for the hiring and firing" of the Home's management staff. The Directors were aware that the Home had "three times the deficiencies" of the average nursing home operating in the state during Causey's tenure as Administrator. The jury heard testimony that an independent review of the Home in 2001 recommended that, due to the Home's continued citations for health violations, Causey should be replaced with a "seasoned nursing home administrator." The report further urged that "[t]he facility cannot improve overall patient care without a competent administrator on staff . . . ."Although the Board sought and obtained a grant of $178,000 from the Pittsburgh Foundation to fund the search for a new Administrator, the funds were never used to find a replacement for Causey, who remained at the Home despite increasing evidence that her "performance as the nursing home administrator was poor." . . .

This evidence supported the jury's finding that the Director Defendants did not exercise reasonable prudence and care in continuing to employ Causey and Shealey. The Director Defendants kept Causey in the role of Administrator and CEO for six years in the face of abnormally high deficiency findings. Even after she ceased working at the Home full-time, in violation of state law, the Director Defendants allowed Causey to continue in her role as Administrator. This is not a case where directors, acting in good-faith reliance "on information, opinions, reports or statements" prepared by employees or experts, made a business decision to continue to employ an Administrator whose performance was arguably less than ideal. 15 Pa. Cons. Stat. Ann. § 5712(a). The jury heard testimony that the Director Defendants received several independent reports documenting Causey's shortcomings and urging that she be replaced. The Director Defendants therefore had actual knowledge of her mismanagement, yet stuck their heads in the sand in the face of repeated signs that residents were receiving care that was severely deficient. This is enough to support the jury's verdict that the Director Defendants breached their duty of care to the Home.

The Defendants next argue that the Committee introduced insufficient evidence to support the jury's verdict that the Defendants had deepened the Home's insolvency. . . . [T]he tort of deepening insolvency. . . [is] "an injury to the Debtors' corporate property from the fraudulent expansion of corporate debt and prolongation of corporate life." We are satisfied that the Committee introduced sufficient evidence to support the jury's deepening insolvency verdict.

The Committee presented evidence that the Director Defendants concealed for over three months the Board's January 2005 decision to close the Home and deplete the patient census, [which the jury found caused] further deterioration of the Home's finances to the detriment of its creditors. . . . [T]he Board's decision to deplete the patient census before it filed for bankruptcy resulted in a "slow death" of the Home's ability to generate revenue. . . [D]uring the bankruptcy process, the Board failed to disclose in its monthly operating reports that the Home had received a $1.4 million Nursing Home Assessment Tax payment in May 2005, which could have increased the Home's chances of finding a buyer. An email from the Board's bankruptcy attorney to the Board summed up the mismanagement of the bankruptcy process, warning that "we have not established a sale process in a manner that is customarily done in Chapter 11 cases. Nobody has had the opportunity to bid and we have no meaningful financial records."

As to the Officer Defendants, the Committee presented evidence that Causey and Shealey's mismanagement of the Home's finances, inattention to recordkeeping and patient billing, and failure to conduct a proper bankruptcy process damaged the already insolvent Home's value . . . Thus, the jury's verdict on the deepening insolvency claim had ample evidentiary support.

B. FIDUCIARY DUTY OF OBEDIENCE

MANHATTAN EYE, EAR, AND THROAT HOSPITAL V. SPITZER

186 Misc. 2d 126, 715 N.Y.S.2d 575 (1999)

[*Editor's Note:* Manhattan Eye, Ear, and Throat Hospital is an acute-care specialty hospital in ophthalmology, otolaryngology, and plastic surgery. After receiving a bid for the hospital from Memorial Sloan Kettering Cancer Center

(MSKCC) and a real estate developer (Downtown), the board decided to sell the hospital and invest the proceeds in free-standing diagnostic and treatment centers (D & T Centers) in underserved areas of the city. The hospital sought authorization from the state Supreme Court to do so under §511 of the New York Not-for-Profit Corporation Act. The attorney general opposed MEETH's petition.]

...

Conclusions of Law

At issue is whether, as required under section 511(d) of the Not-For-Profit Corporation Law, MEETH has shown "to the satisfaction of the court," both that the "consideration and the terms of the transaction are fair and reasonable" and that "the purposes of the corporation ... will be promoted" by the sale of all or substantially all of the hospital's assets to Downtown and MSKCC.... Given my findings of fact, I conclude that MEETH has not satisfied either prong of section 511. Therefore I deny MEETH's petition to approve the proposed sale.

Before turning to section 511, there are several areas that warrant brief discussion. Not-for-profit corporations operate under legal regimes designed for traditional for-profit corporations. However, fundamental structural differences between not-for-profit corporations and for-profit corporations render this approach incapable of providing effective internal mechanisms to guard against directors' improvident use of charitable assets. For example, in the for-profit context, shareholder power ensures that boards make provident decisions, while in the not-for-profit context, this internal check does not exist.... This distinction is even more significant in the case of charitable corporations, such as MEETH, where there are no members, because the Board is essentially self-perpetuating.

The Not-For-Profit Corporation Law addresses this lack of accountability by requiring court approval of fundamental changes in the life of a type B charitable corporation, [13] such as a disposition of all or substantially all assets, since there are no shareholders whose approval can be sought. The Attorney General is made a statutory party to such petitions, and his "active participation" is presumed. This is to ensure that the interests of the ultimate beneficiaries of the corporation, the public, are adequately represented and protected from improvident transactions. It is pursuant to this mandate that this court is called upon to review the sale of substantially all of MEETH's assets to MSKCC and Downtown.

A charitable board is essentially a caretaker of the not-for-profit corporation and its assets. As caretaker, the board "ha[s] the fiduciary obligation to act on behalf of the corporation ... and advance its interests" in "good faith and with that degree of diligence, care and skill which ordinarily prudent men would exercise under similar circumstances in like positions." (N-PCL 717[a].) This formulation of the board's duty of care is an "expansion" of the comparable section of the Business Corporation Law which does not contain the words

---

[13] [In 1999, the New York Not-for-Profit Corporation Law had four categories of nonprofit corporations. Those that would now be called "charitable" were usually categorized as "Type B" at that time.—*Ed.*]

"care" and "skill," and firmly establishes the appropriate standard of care for directors of a not-for-profit corporation.

It is axiomatic that the board of directors is charged with the duty to ensure that the mission of the charitable corporation is carried out. This duty has been referred to as the "duty of obedience." It requires the director of a not-for-profit corporation to "be faithful to the purposes and goals of the organization," since "[u]nlike business corporations, whose ultimate objective is to make money, nonprofit corporations are defined by their specific objectives: perpetuation of particular activities are central to the *raison d'etre* of the organization." (Bjorklund, *op. cit.*, §11-4[a], at 414.)... But the duty of obedience, perforce, must inform the question of whether a proposed transaction to sell all or substantially all of a charity's assets promotes the purposes of the charitable corporation when analyzed under section 511....

[*Editor's Note:* After determining that the terms of the sale were not fair and reasonable, the Court wrote:] Under the second prong of section 511, which requires that "the purposes of the corporation ... will be promoted" (N-PCL 511[d]), MEETH's petition fares no better.... While MEETH has argued that the proposal to abandon the acute care, teaching and research hospital component of its mission and to pursue the D&T Centers does not require an amendment, this argument is belied by the Board's own action on April 29th, authorizing submission of an amendment to its certificate of incorporation (although never submitted) expressly providing for the D&T Centers. This is behavioral evidence that the Board knew that it was proposing a fundamental change in the corporation's mission, which indeed it was doing. For generations MEETH's mission, as stated in its certificate of incorporation, was understood to be the operation of an acute care, specialty teaching and research hospital dedicated to "plastic surgery" and to the treatment of "persons suffering from diseases of the eye, ear, nose, or throat." While it is certainly correct that the definition of "hospital" contained in section 2801(1) of the Public Health Law includes a diagnostic and treatment center, as MEETH now argues ... [t]he conclusion is inescapable that the proposed use of the assets involves a new and fundamentally different corporate purpose.

... [I]t may be appropriate, in certain cases, to solve financial difficulties by eliminating the organization's mission by selling its assets and then undertaking a new mission, [but one should focus] attention upon the duty of obedience, which mandates that a board, in the first instance, seek to preserve its original mission. Embarkation upon a course of conduct which turns it away from the charity's central and well-understood mission should be a carefully chosen option of last resort. Otherwise, a board facing difficult financial straits might find sale of its assets, and "reprioritization" of its mission, to be an attractive option, rather than taking all reasonable efforts to preserve the mission, which has been the object of its stewardship.

As has been documented in the findings of fact, the record is clear that this case is not a situation where the Board first made a reasoned and studied determination that there was a lack of need for MEETH as a hospital, or that the financial difficulties made it impossible to ensure the survival of MEETH. Rather, the credible evidence is that MEETH's decision to sell was impelled by MSKCC's offer, which caused the Board to recognize the value of the underlying real estate; then its realization that it could "monetize" this asset drove subsequent events.

The MSKCC offer initially drove the decision to retain a strategic advisor, Shattuck Hammond, which had a direct and substantial interest in a sale of the real estate, i.e., the 1% transaction fee. This arrangement, regardless of whether it was traditional in investment banking, as Mr. Hammond testified, resulted in a situation where the Board put its reliance upon a strategic advisor which had an actual interest in the recommendations of its strategic study. It is not necessary for me to conclude that this conflict of interest compromised the result; the fee arrangement certainly gives the appearance that the integrity of the process was flawed and that the Board had not obtained the assistance of a truly independent expert. Moreover, there does not appear to have been full disclosure to the Board of the potential for a conflict of interest in the expert. The evidence showed that two Board members were unaware of the percentage fee which was a part of Shattuck Hammond's retention. Additionally, there was no discussion or deliberation by the Board over the fact that its strategic advisor had a direct, and perhaps disabling, financial interest in the outcome of the strategic option it was recommending. Nor was there a decision by the Board to retain and rely upon Shattuck Hammond, notwithstanding this issue. The issue simply was never raised.

This decision to "monetize" drove the need to change the corporate purposes, and these new or reprioritized purposes then became the basis for the argument that "purposes of the corporation ... will be promoted." A careful evaluation of whether there was a basis for changing the corporate purposes should have determined the need to sell, not vice versa. The total absence of any study beforehand, . . . and the retention of health care experts . . . only to prepare a business plan "for fulfillment" or in "support" of the D&T proposal, not to independently evaluate the plan's feasibility, buttresses the conclusion that the sale drove the change in purpose. Indeed, the report submitted by Dr. Cicero and Mr. Kachmarick states that "[t]he following business plan describes how MEETH will achieve [its] goal, in keeping with its expanded mission statement." To argue that MEETH was returning to its original purposes without an iota of evidence that it made this fundamental determination prior to the decision to sell and close, cannot obscure the fact that this decision, of necessity, eliminated MEETH's historic mission, its historic raison d'etre.

Moreover, the record also demonstrates that the Board failed to properly consider the various alternatives submitted which would have preserved MEETH's mission. The Board had concluded that these alternatives were the equivalent of "giving the keys away," and summarily rejected them....

In sum, it is evident that this petition fails to meet the two-pronged test of section 511.... I conclude ... this sales transaction should be disapproved.

C. UNIFORM PRUDENT MANAGEMENT OF INVESTMENT FUNDS ACT (UPMIFA)

At one level, even when a great deal of money is at stake, the fiduciary duties of care, loyalty, and possibly obedience should be enough to guide boards in their investment decisions. At another level, however, the complexity of the financial markets makes it difficult for even the most trained money managers to make investment decisions. Questions inevitably arise as to whether the board should invest conservatively, follow modern portfolio theory, or engage in risky but lucrative investments. To help guide board members in their investment decisions, the National Conference of Commissioners on Uniform State Laws approved UPMIFA in 2006. In 2015, UPMIFA had been adopted in 49 states (all but Pennsylvania), the District of Columbia, and the U.S. Virgin Islands.[14] UPMIFA applies to unincorporated and incorporated charitable institutions. It applies to trusts managed by a charity, but not to funds of charitable trusts that are managed by a corporate or individual trustee. Section 3, reproduced below, sets out the standard of care in managing and investing funds.

Sect. 3. Standard of Conduct in Managing and Investing Institutional Fund.

(a) Subject to the intent of a donor expressed in a gift instrument, an institution, in managing and investing an institutional fund, shall consider the charitable purposes of the institution and the purposes of the institutional fund.

(b) In addition to complying with the duty of loyalty imposed by law other than this [act], each person responsible for managing and investing an institutional fund shall manage and invest the fund in good faith and with the care an ordinarily prudent person in a like position would exercise under similar circumstances.

(c) In managing and investing an institutional fund, an institution:

(1) may incur only costs that are appropriate and reasonable in relation to the assets, the purposes of the institution, and the skills available to the institution; and

(2) shall make a reasonable effort to verify facts relevant to the management and investment of the fund.

(d) An institution may pool two or more institutional funds for purposes of management and investment.

(e) Except as otherwise provided by a gift instrument, the following rules apply:

---

[14] Uniform Law Commission, Uniform Prudent Management of Funds Act, http://uniformlaws.org/Act.aspx?title=Prudent%20Management%20of%20Institutional%20Funds %20Act, last accessed May 8, 2016. UPMIFA updated the Uniform Management of Institutional Funds Act (UMIFA) and incorporated some of the provisions of the Uniform Prudent Investor Act (UPIA).

(1) In managing and investing an institutional fund, the following factors, if relevant, must be considered:

(A) general economic conditions;

(B) the possible effect of inflation or deflation;

(C) the expected tax consequences, if any, of investment decisions or strategies;

(D) the role that each investment or course of action plays within the overall investment portfolio of the fund;

(E) the expected total return from income and the appreciation of investments;

(F) other resources of the institution;

(G) the needs of the institution and the fund to make distributions and to preserve capital; and

(H) an asset's special relationship or special value, if any, to the charitable purposes of the institution.

(2) Management and investment decisions about an individual asset must be made not in isolation but rather in the context of the institutional fund's portfolio of investments as a whole and as a part of an overall investment strategy having risk and return objectives reasonably suited to the fund and to the institution.

(3) Except as otherwise provided by law other than this [act], an institution may invest in any kind of property or type of investment consistent with this section.

(4) An institution shall diversify the investments of an institutional fund unless the institution reasonably determines that, because of special circumstances, the purposes of the fund are better served without diversification.

(5) Within a reasonable time after receiving property, an institution shall make and carry out decisions concerning the retention or disposition of the property or to rebalance a portfolio, in order to bring the institutional fund into compliance with the purposes, terms, and distribution requirements of the institution as necessary to meet other circumstances of the institution and the requirements of this [act].

(6) A person that has special skills or expertise, or is selected in reliance upon the person's representation that the person has special skills or expertise, has a duty to use those skills or that expertise in managing and investing institutional funds.

D. FIDUCIARY DUTIES TO OTHERS

IN RE MILTON HERSHEY SCH. TRUST (APPEAL OF MILTON HERSHEY SCHOOL)

807 A.2d 324 (Pa. Commw. Ct. 2002)

Opinion by President Judge COLINS.

[*Editor's Note:* In 1909, Milton and Catherine Hershey established the Milton Hershey School Trust to provide for the health, education, and welfare of orphaned boys at the Hershey School. They initially endowed the school with 486 acres of farmland and later added $60 million, mostly in Hershey Chocolate Company (now Hershey Foods) stock. By 2002, the corpus of the trust had grown to $5 billion, approximately half of which was held in Hershey Foods stock. The trustees, with the encouragement of the attorney general's office, began to consider diversifying their assets. The Hershey School Trust held voting control over the candy company and needed to sell substantially all of the company in order to diversify. Once the Trust made its intentions known, a firestorm of protest ensued, and the attorney general then intervened to stop the sale. The lower court issued a special injunction, prohibiting the Trust from entering into any agreement or understanding that could commit the Trust to a sale. The Trust appealed.]

In 1909, Milton S. Hershey and Catherine, his wife, by deed of trust endowed for the benefit of orphan children an institution now known as the Milton Hershey School. In 1918, after Catherine's death, Mr. Hershey added to the trust (hereafter referred to as the School Trust) most of his fortune including the controlling shares of stock of the Hershey Chocolate Company (now Hershey Foods Corporation). The Hershey Trust Company, then owned by Mr. Hershey, was and still is the trustee of the School Trust and, as directed in the trust deed, the members of the Board of Directors of the Hershey Trust Company also serve as the Board of Managers of the School.

The Deed of Trust directs that the Milton Hershey School shall be located in Derry Township, Pennsylvania, and gives preference to children born in the Pennsylvania counties of Dauphin (where Derry Township is located) and Lebanon and Lancaster which adjoin Dauphin County. In 1935, Mr. Hershey established the M. S. Hershey Foundation providing for vocational, cultural, or professional training of any resident of Derry Township and subsequently established the Derry Township School Trust which subsidizes the Derry Township School District. These Trusts are also administered by the Hershey Trust Company. Moreover, in the area in close proximity to his chocolate factory he created a community, now known as Hershey, including banks, a department store, community center, hotel, sports facilities, theatre, hospital, utility companies, transportation, and homes for himself and for many of his employees. Milton Hershey's charitable interests were narrowly restricted. He was concerned for children and for his community.

Shares of Hershey Foods Corporation amounting to a controlling interest in the Corporation have comprised the corpus of the School Trust from 1918 until the present date. At the request of the present Directors/Managers, the Hershey Foods Corporation is soliciting bids for the acquisition of the Corporation which would include purchase of the shares of stock held in the School Trust representing 77% of the voting power of all outstanding shares of the Hershey Foods Corporation.

The only purpose asserted by the Hershey Trust Company and the Board of Managers for the current proposal to sell Hershey Foods Corporation is to diversify its portfolio of assets in the School Trust.

The Attorney General has sufficiently carried his burden of proving the potential harm that he seeks to prevent, namely, the adverse economic and social impact against the public interest if a sale of Hershey Foods Corporation takes place, particularly in its effect on employees of the Corporation and the community of Derry Township. The persuasive thrust of the testimony of Richard A. Zimmerman, a former CEO and Chairman of the Board of Hershey Foods Corporation with years of experience in mergers and acquisitions, was that a sale of the controlling interest in Hershey Foods Corporation creates a likelihood that there will be reduction in the work force and that relocations of plant operations and closing of duplicate facilities will be matters of probable immediate consideration by the acquiring company. We would add that this Court is not required to be blind and deaf to that which has been commonplace information to the public during the recent past period of numerous mergers and acquisitions of public companies.

Granted, the deed of trust gives the trustee discretionary powers of investment and a court will not ordinarily interfere with what appears to be an act within that discretion. The rule is, however, a general rule, not an absolute.

Mr. Hershey maintained the controlling interest in his chocolate business as essentially the sole asset of the corpus of the School Trust from 1918 when he made the gift until he died in 1945.... The symbiotic relationship among the School, the community, and the Company is common knowledge. The business was not, during Mr. Hershey's life, is not now, nor foreseeably in financial difficulty, and the School, according to statements by officers of the Directors/Managers has ample funds in its accumulated income to carry out its purposes. The proposal by the Directors/Managers is for the sale of all of the shares of Hershey Foods Corporation. There is no suggestion of a sale of such number of shares as would still reserve control of the Corporation nor explanation why, if any need for funds exists for which a sale is necessary, it could not be met while still keeping control. The question certainly occurs as to whether an immediate premium share price obtained in losing control is a reasonable trade-off for permanently retaining it.

The foregoing circumstances, we conclude, sufficiently raise, for fuller investigation in connection with the Citation, the issue of whether the sale proposal comports with Mr. Hershey's intent as indicated in his scheme for trust management, as well as an issue whether under all relevant circumstances, the act of these respondents, the Directors/Managers, is so unreasonable as it relates to their duty to the School Trust that it amounts to a capriciousness that is an abuse of their discretion.

The only explanation given by the Director/Managers for the proposed sale is that they have a duty to diversify their investment portfolio. Their consultant who recommends this divesting of the asset that has sustained the School for most of its years was unaware that the law of Pennsylvania for long years, until 1999, was that a trustee had no obligation to diversify the trust corpus.... Nor did he know that in 1999 when the Legislature enacted a modified version of the Uniform Prudent Investor Act, 20 Pa. C.S. §7201 et seq. (1999), the section (§7204) requiring trustees to reasonably diversify investments was not made applicable to existing trusts. The official comment to §7204 reads in relevant part: "... This section is not made applicable to existing trusts because Pennsylvania had not required diversification.... Retroactivity would have required drafters of old trusts to have been clairvoyant to have negated a non-existent duty to diversify."

It is also significant that this same consultant, having stated that his investment objective is to make enough money to support the School's current and prospective educational program in perpetuity at a reasonable level of risk, admitted on cross-examination that he had never known the Milton Hershey School not to have enough money to do what it needs to do....

Next, the Directors/Managers argue that the law of Pennsylvania establishes that the duty of a trustee is to administer the trust solely for the benefit of the beneficiaries of the trust, quoting in support the statement under Comment p. of §1701(1) of the Restatement, Trusts which reads, "The trustee is under a duty to the beneficiary in administering the trust not to be guided by the interest of any third person." We are familiar with these rules but do not construe them to mean that as long as the act of a trustee is an exercise of a power given in the trust instrument and purports to serve the trust, the trustee can act with impunity and without regard for adverse effects on others. We know of no case that employs the rules advanced by the Directors/Managers in the context of an Attorney General asserting his duty to see that the public interest is not harmed by an act of a trustee that may otherwise be lawful and purports to be in furtherance of the trust. Few such issues are likely to arise and rarely one with the aspects of the case before us. How many trusts enjoy holding a controlling interest in one of this nation's largest, historically profitable, and best-known corporations? The duties of a trustee and the Attorney General are concomitant in so far as assuring that the benefits of a charitable trust are delivered in accordance with the Settlor's intent; but because the socio-economic benefits of a charitable trust extend beyond the designated beneficiaries to the public itself; although ordinarily compatible with each other, the Attorney General has an added responsibility of assuring that compatibility.

In sum, we are satisfied that the Attorney General, under the facts of this case, notably the circumstance that the threatened action by the Directors/Managers of the School Trust appears to be excessive and unnecessary for any foreseeable needs of the Trust, has the duty and the power to investigate its consequences and to take such actions as the consequences may warrant.

Accordingly, our conclusion of law is that the Attorney General is entitled to the relief requested.

Dissenting Opinion by Judge PELLEGRINI.

I respectfully dissent from the majority's opinion because I disagree that the Attorney General has authority to become fully involved under a *parens patriae* theory to protect the "public" regarding the proposed sale by the Milton Hershey School Deed of Trust (Deed of Trust) of trust assets that constitute a controlling interest in the Hershey Foods Corporation prior to the Trustees making any decision under the trust laws of Pennsylvania to actually sell trust assets. If that were the case, then the Attorney General could become fully involved in the decision-making process of every charitable trust or, for that matter, in every charity in Pennsylvania....

The majority affirms the trial court's order, dismisses the Trust's application for a stay and directs the trial court to rule on the merits of the controversy. It does so disregarding the Trust's argument that the Attorney General has no authority to participate in the decision-making process of the Trust under the guise of protecting the public. Instead, it states that while this is an important issue, it is not the focus of review because all that must be determined is whether the trial court had "apparently reasonable grounds" to support its decision to grant the preliminary injunction. . . .

While I do not disagree with the majority that the trial court decision is reasonable, before we can sustain a preliminary injunction, not only do we have to find that the decree was reasonable, but we must also determine that the grant of the injunction was in accordance with the law; in this case, the Probate, Estate and Fiduciaries Code (PEFC).

The decree is not accordance with law because nowhere in the PEFC is there any authority for the Attorney General to essentially act as co-trustee or comanager of the Trust and be part of the process leading up to a decision by the Trustees to take a certain action. Nonetheless, the trial court determined that the Attorney General had standing to proceed and authority to inquire as to whether the Trust's exercise of its power was inimical to the public interest because "responsibility for the public supervision of charitable trusts traditionally has been delegated to the Attorney General to be performed as an exercise of his *parens patriae* powers." However, for the Attorney General to properly exercise *parens patriae* powers, his concern must be on behalf of the public *and* tied to the express desires of the Trust settler. The Deed of Trust specifically gives the Trust Company, with approval by the School, sole and exclusive authority over the management of investments, including the sale of stock.

Absent a showing that the Trustee's actions are against the terms of the Trust or that the Trust provisions themselves are against public interest, the *parens patriae* powers of the Attorney General do not apply.

Additionally, Section 7141 of the PEFC gives the Trust the power to sell any property of the Trust, and Section 3355 of the PEFC, expressly limits the authority of a court to restrain a sale of a trust asset that is authorized under the governing Deed of Trust. That section provides:

> The court, on its own motion or upon application of any party in interest, in its discretion, *may restrain* a personal representative from making any sale under an authority *not given by the governing instrument* or from carrying out any contract of sale made by him under an authority not so given. (Emphasis added.)

Under this provision, the only power the court is given is to restrain a sale, not to foreclose the Trustees from reaching an agreement to be approved, let alone what the trial court did here by foreclosing any meaningful negotiation that will lead to an *understanding* that can be brought to the court for approval. Moreover, there is no basis in the law, either statutory or case, giving the Attorney General a right to become "fully involved" in the decision-making of the Trust; he is neither a co-manager nor co-Trustee of the Trust. Once the Trustees exercise the discretion given to them and reach an agreement, only then can the Attorney General take action to challenge the agreement by arguing it violates the terms of the Trust. Until an agreement is negotiated, terms made final, and covenants known, it is impossible to know what or if there would be negative effects from any sale. If that is not the law, then the Attorney General, under his understanding of his *parens patriae* powers, can become fully involved in the decision-making of any charitable institution in this Commonwealth.

Accordingly, for the foregoing reasons, I dissent and would reverse the trial court's grant of a preliminary injunction.

NOTES AND QUESTIONS

1. As the *Sibley Hospital* case suggests, the fiduciary standard for trustees has traditionally been different from the standard for boards of directors. Is that a distinction without a difference? Didn't the *Sibley Hospital* directors violate their fiduciary duties under either standard?

2. If the board acts as a single body, what is the role of the individual? How can an individual be sued if the board made the deliberation? Why do you think only 15 of the 17 directors in the *Lemington* case were found to have breached the duty of care? What is the responsibility of the board member who has been outvoted on an issue?

3. Is the duty of loyalty encompassed in the duty of care? *See* American Law Institute, PRINCIPLES OF THE LAW OF NONPROFIT ORGANIZATIONS, TENTATIVE DRAFT NO. 1 (2008).

4. Should the duty of obedience exist, or is it encompassed within the other duties? For a discussion of this issue, see Linda Sugin, *Resisting the Corporatization of Governance: Turning Obedience into Fidelity*, 76 FORDHAM L. REV (2007); Jeremy Benjamin, *Reinvigorating Nonprofit Directors' Duty of Obedience*, 30 CARDOZO L. REV. 1677 (2009); Johnny R.

Buckles, *How Deep Are the Springs of Obedience Norms That Bind the Overseers of Charities?* 62 CATH. U. L. REV. 920 (2014).

5. Should the business judgment rule have protected any of the defendants in these cases?

6. What role should the board have with regard to finances? Should everyone on the board have the same duty to understand and watch the organization's bottom line?

7. Should attorneys, who have specialized knowledge, have a stronger fiduciary duty when they serve on boards of nonprofit corporations than those who do not have a law degree? Is it a breach of the duty of loyalty for an attorney to do legal work for the organization? Does your answer to this question differ if the services are offered pro bono?

8. To whom or what do the directors/trustees owe their fiduciary duties? If it is to the organization, weren't the *Hershey* trustees obeying this duty? Part of the duty of care is to ensure that the organization remains fiscally solvent. Even if the corporation was not in immediate jeopardy, were the trustees not being prudent in their attempt to diversify? Or do the directors also owe a duty to the community? *See* Jennifer Komorowski, *The Hershey Trust's Quest to Diversify: Redefining the State Attorney General's Role When Charitable Trusts Wish to Diversify*, 45 WM. & MARY L. REV. 1769 (2004); Mark Sidel, *The Struggle for Hershey: Community Accountability and the Law in Modern American Philanthropy*, 65 U. PITT. L. REV. 1 (2003); and Jonathon Klick and Robert Sitkoff, *Agency Costs, Charitable Trusts, and Corporate Control: Evidence from Hershey's Kiss-off*, 108 COLUM. L. REV. 749 (2008).

9. How does the provision in the Model Nonprofit Corporation Act, Third Edition (MNCA 3d Ed.) for handling conflicts of interest compare to the sample IRS conflict of interest form? If the state law already has a procedure in place for handling conflicts of interest, why should an organization adopt a conflict of interest policy?

IV. CASE STUDIES

Whenever a nonprofit organization runs into difficulty, the board's actions—and inactions—are examined. Recent problems at prominent nonprofits have provided examples that can illustrate these difficulties and show how complicated some of the issues are.

A. THE SMITHSONIAN INSTITUTION

INDEPENDENT REVIEW COMMITTEE, A REPORT TO THE BOARD OF REGENTS OF THE SMITHSONIAN INSTITUTION (June 18, 2007)

[*Editor's note*. In 2007, an Inspector General report disclosed that the Secretary of the Smithsonian,[15] William Small, received almost $1 million in salary and was reimbursed for first-class travel, lavish gifts, and the use of his home for official functions (to the tune of another $1 million). The Senate reacted to this news by freezing a proposed $17 million increase in the Smithsonian's budget, and Mr. Small resigned. An independent committee then made recommendations to the Board of Regents. This report found that the board had never learned of Mr. Small's compensation, nor did it review his expenses or time away from the Smithsonian. It also found the Smithsonian's internal financial controls and audit function were inadequate, in part because Mr. Small marginalized the general counsel and outside auditors who might have pointed out lapses or wrongdoing. Finally, the board failed to provide sufficient oversight to the Smithsonian Business Ventures, the for-profit arm of the Smithsonian. Despite these problems, the Report found that the Smithsonian appeared to remain a strongly ethical institution. Following are excerpts from that report.]

The root cause of the Smithsonian's current problems can be found in failures of governance and management. The governance structure of the Institution is antiquated and in need of reform. . . . Mr. Small created an imperialistic and insular culture in the Office of the Secretary in which the Secretary, rather than the Board, dominated the setting of policy and strategic direction for the Smithsonian.

The Board of Regents allowed this culture to prevail by failing to provide badly needed oversight of Mr. Small and the operations of the Smithsonian. The Board did not look behind the tightly controlled data provided by Mr. Small. Nor did it engage in the active inquiry of Mr. Small and Smithsonian management that would have alerted the Board to problems....

... [T]he Regents are fiduciaries of the Smithsonian. First, the Regents are trustees charged with managing the original Smithson trust for the benefit of the American people. Second, the Regents are analogous to directors of a nonprofit organization and therefore must fulfill the fiduciary duties of directors. . . .

The duties required of one in such a fiduciary capacity are well established in the law. The duty of care generally describes the level of attention required of a director in all matters related to the organization.... A director will fulfill the duty of care if, prior to making a decision, he or she seeks out and considers all material information reasonably available to him or her. To fulfill the duty of

---

[15] The top administrator of the Smithsonian Institution is called the Secretary, and the board is called the Board of Regents. It is a quasi-governmental institution, in that Congress has some authority over it, but it must also abide by the rules of a nonprofit organization.

care, the directors should follow deliberate procedures and consult with appropriate committees, officers or employees of the organization or other outside experts in making corporate decisions. This often means going beyond what is provided to the board by in-house staff, including consulting with outside experts, talking directly to, and questioning, employees with knowledge of the facts and, above all, asking thoughtful and probing questions. Board members may not simply rely on the word of senior management without further inquiry.

The duty of loyalty requires a director to act in the interest of the entity rather than in the personal interest of the director or some other person or organization.... There have been no allegations, nor is the IRC aware of any evidence whatsoever, that any Regent violated this duty of loyalty....

Recommendations

The Committee recommends that, wherever possible, the Board of Regents should implement the following recommendations by reorganizing its internal governance structures and procedures.

1. The Regents Must Act Quickly to Address the Governance Crisis

The current crisis of governance at the Smithsonian and the resulting loss of public confidence necessitate urgent action by the Regents. To restore public and Congressional confidence, the Regents must devote substantial time and resources over the next several months to considering and then implementing the chosen governance recommendations from the IRC and the Smithsonian's Committee on Governance.

[*Editor's Note:* Recommendations 2 and 3 discuss Mr. Small's expenses and the salary of the Secretary. Recommendation 4 proposes changes in the Smithsonian's policies.]

5. The Smithsonian Should Have an Active Governing Board with a Chairman Who Can Provide the Time and Proper Oversight

The Board of a nonprofit organization must "oversee the operations of the organization in such manner as will assure effective and ethical management.".. . This relationship between the Board and the Secretary is a "constructive partnership" in which the Board sets strategic plans and then delegates operations to the Secretary....

The time commitment necessary to fulfill the fiduciary responsibility placed on the directors of an organization as large and complex as the Smithsonian is significant....

The IRC believes the Smithsonian could preserve its unique historical structure [which includes the Chief Justice, the Vice President of the United States, and members of Congress], yet at the same time address the pressing need for active oversight, through the establishment of a Governing Board that would take on the fiduciary responsibility for overseeing the operations and management of Smithsonian. The IRC recommends that the Governing Board meet no less frequently than every other month. The Governing Board should, as the current Board does, also govern through active committees, particularly through the Audit and Review, Human Resources and Compensation and Nominating and Governance Committees. The Governing Board would consist of all Regents except the Chief Justice and Vice President. Service as a Regent must require that all members of the Governing Board, including members of Congress, be willing and able to assume a role with clear fiduciary responsibilities and to devote the time necessary to carry out those duties personally....

The Governing Board should reserve, at every meeting, time for an executive session where issues involving management, including the Secretary's performance, can be freely and openly discussed without the presence of employees. The IRC also recommends that the Executive Committee be enlarged to five members, and its activity limited in practice to handling routine affairs of the Board between meetings and when special meetings, either in person or telephonically, cannot be arranged. All actions of the Executive Committee should be presented to the Governing Board for review.

6. The Role of the Chief Justice and Vice President Should Be Clarified

The Committee believes that it is not feasible to expect the Chief Justice to devote the hours necessary to service as a fiduciary Regent. The Committee also questions if it is appropriate and necessary for the Chief Justice to have fiduciary obligations to a separate entity, even if that entity is closely linked to the government, and to assume the legal and reputational risks associated with being a fiduciary. The same situation applies to the Vice President.... If the Smithsonian desires to have positions for individuals that honor them for their contributions to the arts and sciences, including their financial generosity, it should establish nonfiduciary advisory boards for the Institution in general as well as for its various museums and divisions....

7. Congressional Regents Should Accept Fiduciary Responsibilities

A clear understanding needs to be reached regarding the role of the Congressional Regents. Service as a Regent must require that all members of the Governing Board be willing and able to assume a role with clear fiduciary responsibilities and to devote the time necessary to carry out those duties personally. So that there will be neither an actual nor an appearance of conflict of interest, the IRC believes that any Congressional Regent who serves on one of the Congressional authorizing or appropriations committees with authority over the Smithsonian should recuse himself or herself from votes in Congress involving Smithsonian financial matters.

8. The Board Should Be Expanded or Reorganized to Allow for the Addition of Regents with Needed Expertise

The Board must expand the level of expertise among the Regents on key issues, especially financial controls and facilities and museum management, and ensure that the Regents who are appointed have sufficient time and attention to dedicate to the Smithsonian. . . . To achieve this expansion of current expertise and ensure that Regents are active and engaged, the Committee recommends the Regents consider the following: (1) if current Regents have sufficient time and interest in continuing to serve; (2) adding to Board Committees—such as Audit and Review, Governance and Compensation and Human Resources—non-Regent members with special expertise; (3) employing outside experts to advise the Board and its Committees in specific subject areas; and (4) increasing the total number of citizen Regents from 9 to 11 by either adding two additional citizen Regents or reducing the number of Congressional Regents from six to four—two from the House and two from the Senate.

To make sure that the Smithsonian Board is made up of individuals capable of providing the necessary expertise, the Regents should move to a nominating process that allows for a broader field of candidates. . . . Contributions to the Smithsonian should not be the determining factor for service on the Board, but only one of many factors considered in the selection of Regents. Care should be taken to avoid appointing Regents who have clear personal and professional ties to the Secretary that may compromise the Board's independence.

9. Internal Financial Controls, Audit Functions and the Role of the General Counsel and Inspector General Must Be Strengthened

The Smithsonian's system of internal controls and audit needs to be strengthened through additional resources, adoption of best practices and retention of personnel with substantial experience in the financial and audit area. . . . The Committee understands that the Smithsonian is in the process of selecting an outside auditor, and the Committee recommends that the Smithsonian expeditiously implement the recommendations of this auditor, as well as those recommendations contained in prior management letters.

Corporate governance principles require that the general counsel of an organization be the gatekeeper of information for the Board and a guardian of the Board's independence. The General Counsel of the Smithsonian has been hindered from playing this role due to lack of regular, direct access to the Board. The Committee recommends that (1) the Smithsonian provide the General Counsel's office and Office of the Inspector General with the necessary tools and resources to perform their gatekeeper and guardian functions, (2) the General Counsel serve as the Smithsonian's corporate secretary and (3) the Smithsonian ensure vigorous compliance with the Inspector General Act.

10. Smithsonian Executives Should Be Permitted to Participate in Only Nonprofit Board Activities Subject to Prior Approval

Generally, the Smithsonian has been careful in monitoring the outside work of its employees. The exceptions have been Mr. Small and the Deputy Secretary, both of whom have been allowed to collect significant compensation for service on the boards of for-profit corporations. As discussed above, these outside commitments have taken these individuals away from the Smithsonian during working hours for significant periods of time. The Board must develop a uniform policy on outside work. . . .

[T]he IRC recommends that the Board prohibit its executives from serving on the boards of for-profit corporations. With respect to nonprofit boards, the Regents should control and require prior approval of any outside activities, including service on any other nonprofit or professional service boards and teaching and lecturing obligations, weighing carefully the time commitments needed and the benefits to the Smithsonian. Any compensation received by any Smithsonian employee for service on any outside board or organization should not be kept by the individual, but should be turned over to the Smithsonian for the benefit of the Institution.

QUESTIONS

1. Eight years after this report, the Smithsonian Institution's website indicates that the Chief Justice of the Supreme Court and the Vice President of the United States are ex officio members of the board, but the board structure has not changed.[16] There are still 17 members, 6 from Congress and 9 from the general public. Many of the members of the board from 2007 are still serving. Is this the substantive change that the Independent Review Committee (IRC) was seeking? If so, how would it affect the governance? If not, was the report you read a waste of time, effort, and money?

2. For several years, the Smithsonian's Executive Committee approved the Secretary's compensation. The IRC found that the entire board should have made this determination. If you have drafted bylaws for your organization, look at them again. Would the executive committee be allowed to approve the executive director's compensation? If so, should you amend your bylaws? Which duties of the entire board should not be able to be delegated to the executive committee?

3. What is the role of the general counsel in a nonprofit organization? Whom does he or she represent? The IRC found that Mr. Small had isolated the general counsel so that he could not discover the improprieties. What should the Smithsonian's general counsel have done in this situation? What should he have done if he had found improprieties?

4. Did the Smithsonian regents violate any fiduciary duties? If so, what were they and what should be the remedy? What could they have done to avoid these lapses? Is it possible that some or all of these lapses constitute a failure to follow "best practices" but not a violation of fiduciary duties?

5. The IRC recommended that the secretary be forbidden from sitting on for-profit boards. Do you agree with this recommendation? Why would it be all right, if approved by the regents, to sit on a nonprofit board, but not to sit on a for-profit board?

---

[16] http://www.si.edu/about/regents/members.htm, accessed Aug. 13, 2015.

B. HULL HOUSE

DANIEL FLYNN AND YUNHE (EVELYN) TIAN, *THE DEATH OF HULL HOUSE*, NONPROFIT QUARTERLY (FEB. 10, 2015)[17]

Hull House opened on September 18, 1889, . . . Jane Addams and Ellen Gates Starr founded this settlement house—one of the first in the United States, and eventually the country's most famous—on the premise that "the dependence of classes on each other is reciprocal; and that as the social relation is essentially a reciprocal relation, it gives a form of expression that has peculiar value.". . . From its early days, Hull House exhibited a strong dual-pronged mission: assist the impoverished and vulnerable of society with basic needs and cultural competencies, and advocate for the rights and dignity of each citizen.

Jane Addams remained at Hull House until her death, in 1935. . . . By the time of her passing, Hull House had grown from one settlement home into thirteen houses that comprised the Hull House community. Hull House had also become a hotbed of political activity. . . In the 1960s, Hull House was displaced by expansion of the University of Illinois and lost its original settlement house structure, becoming instead a system of community and neighborhood centers around Chicago. And in the 1990s, the economic growth of the period encouraged the organization to reshape its operations to focus on foster care, child care, domestic violence counseling, and job training. The financial boom allowed Hull House to quadruple its budget and confidently enter the twenty-first century.

Unfortunately, the twenty-first century did not bring continued prosperity for Hull House. In mid-January of 2012, Hull House announced that it would be forced to close in March. In fact, it closed just one week after that announcement, on Friday, January 25. Nearly three hundred employees and upward of sixty thousand yearly clients received less than one week's notice.

The death of such a well-established, iconic nonprofit organization inevitably raises many questions about mismanagement, especially given its extensive executive team and the many accomplished professionals—including at least five financial advisers, five attorneys, and several CEOs—who served on its board of trustees. The management failures at Hull House can be organized into two primary categories: financial negligence and poor governance.

Financial Negligence

The only financial documents available for Hull House span 1998 to 2010, but they show significant signs of economic distress over that thirteen-year period. By 2010, Hull House had entered the "'zone of insolvency,' a period of

---

[17] [This article was submitted as part of the graduate course "The Nonprofit Sector: Concepts and Theories," at the Penn School of Social Policy and Practice at the University of Pennsylvania.—*Ed.*]

financial distress where […] the legal responsibilities of board members change from […] safeguarding their organization's mission and assets, to safeguarding the interests of all of its stakeholders." ith better financial management, Hull House could have avoided this crisis, and simple financial analysis supports this claim.

First, basic financial analysis reveals revenue drops of nearly 19 percent between 2001 and 2002 ($40,567,863 to $32,932,988), as well as a continuous decrease in total revenue from 2007 to 2010, totaling 27.3 percent ($32,011,227 to $23,286,579) In addition, when looking at the various revenue sources and expense categories, one finds that almost 90 percent of Hull House's revenue came directly from government payments, and this percentage peaked at 95.2 percent of total revenue in 2001. On average, less than 10 percent of revenue came from public contributions, and only about 1.5 percent of total expenses each year were spent on fundraising. The lack of diversified revenue, overreliance on government contracts, and poor fundraising performance were all substantial indicators of poor financial planning.

Second, there were also clear warnings of Hull House's high level of financial unsustainability from the financial vulnerability measurement. This tool takes program service expenses divided by total revenue, and indicates whether or not an organization generates enough revenue to support its program functions (not even taking into account administration or fundraising expenses). Hull House consistently had vulnerability measurements near 90 percent, and, after 2005, yearly rates exceeded 100 percent. By the late 2000s, Hull House was unable to financially support its programs, and it never took drastic enough measures to overcome those deficits.

Third, ratio analysis comparing Hull House with other similar settlement houses and industry benchmarks further paints the picture of an organization in financial crisis The savings indicator, calculated by dividing net income by total expenses, measures what percentage of revenue an organization saves each year. The common industry benchmark for large human needs organizations is .015, and Hull House not only never reached this threshold during the 2000s but also was consistently outperformed financially by two other well-known settlement houses: Henry Street Settlement and University Settlement.

Likewise, the debt ratio also reveals Hull House's poor financial performance. This indicator, calculated by dividing total liabilities by total assets, measures the riskiness of an organization's debt structure. A lower result signals a healthier organization with less financial risk; Hull House's industry benchmark is slightly below .5. Hull House again performs poorly, with debt ratios doubling, tripling, and even quadrupling this industry standard.

Nonetheless, despite poor debt ratios, this measurement only tells part of Hull House's story. First, accounts receivables consistently made up as high as 40 percent of total assets, and these were mostly from government contracts that were often paid late. Therefore, there were deep cash- flow issues that the ratio does not reveal. More significantly, however, US GAAP principles do not require property to be listed at fair market value, and Hull House's properties—many of which were bought decades prior and had been greatly depreciated—were listed at low values or had been removed completely from the balance sheet. For instance, despite owning numerous community centers around Chicago, Hull House's 2010 Form 990 lists only $930,049 in land, buildings, and equipment, meaning that the organization had significantly more assets than were listed. Given the growing organizational debt, one must ask why Hull House did not choose to sell some of these valuable properties to cover its increasing liabilities.

A final indicator of Hull House's financial distress was its exceedingly high leverage, both in terms of current and long-term liabilities. This is especially evident upon examining Hull House's "other liabilities" presented in its 990s. This broad category of debt included loans from the Hull House Foundation, unfunded pension payments, checks drawn in excess of deposits, and government contract advances. Of special concern were the cash advances Hull House received on its government contracts for over $2 million on an annual basis, from 1998 to 2005, and for over $1 million from 2006 to 2010. Ultimately, these "other liabilities" reveal that Hull House remedied its cash flow and fundraising issues by "spending tomorrow's funding to pay for yesterday's expenses." This irresponsible cycle could not last forever, and it contributed to organizational death.

Poor Governance

One of the three legally required duties for nonprofit boards is the "duty of care," a responsibility that requires board members to "participate in well-informed decisions on behalf of the nonprofit." With such overt signs of financial distress in Hull House's yearly financial statements, serious questions remain as to whether or not the Hull House board fulfilled this responsibility. One can posit that a board comprised of successful business people—a number of whom worked in the financial sector—would be able to accurately interpret basic financial documents. If this is the case, board members either did not take the time to carefully review these documents—which would mean they violated their duty of care—or failed to take sufficiently aggressive measures to improve the organization's financial situation and correct bad financial practices. If, somehow, the board was financially illiterate, it had a responsibility to recognize and address this deficiency. The financial woes at Hull House ran deep, but with strong, active governance, these problems could have been identified and rectified before organizational death.

As suggested above, there is evidence that the Hull House board suffered from poor internal and external communication. . . .

Externally, stakeholders criticized Hull House for not publicizing their financial problems earlier or louder and instead presenting a sugarcoated image of the organization. . . . The board's reluctance to be transparent about Hull House's true condition (or inability to recognize its precarious situation) exemplifies both a failure in its obligation to organizational stakeholders and a failure in strategic governance.

Mission Drift

Despite evidence of severe financial negligence and poor governance, one must consider the possibility that these woes were symptomatic of a different cause of Hull House's death: mission drift. Any casual observer could note that the Hull House of 2012—in revenue sources, mission, operations, and physical structure—looked starkly different from Jane Addams's original settlement house, and these divergences from the founding structure require further exploration.

In the early days, Hull House survived (in an era before tax deductions) through in-kind gifts and financial donations sought out by Addams. . . . Fundraising from individuals was, for many years past Addams, the primary source of money for Hull House, yet by January 2012, 85 percent of Hull House's revenues were from government contracts. Moreover, the organization struggled desperately to attract private contributions. Not only does this altered fundraising model significantly hinder the opportunity to bring together different social classes for mutual benefit—an original intent of the organization—but it also makes the key collaborative partnership not with the public but with an entity Addams viewed with suspicion: government. . . .

Furthermore, and perhaps most notably, the mission and operations of Hull House had changed drastically since the early days.. . . . Hull House's original approach to helping people meet their basic needs or gain life skills only faintly resembled current notions of social services. Furthermore, these "services" offered by Hull House were never central to the settlement's mission; [which was to be] a basis for wider social action." Hull House was instrumental in advocating for reforms ranging from the creation of public spaces and organizations to new labor protection laws to better sanitation services for poor neighborhoods. Eventually, the organization became not a political challenger seeking social change but instead a political instrument implementing government programs. . .

A final significant difference in the modern Hull House and its founding version was its physical structure. . . . [R]ather than retain a similar model with various properties in the same neighborhood [when it was forced to sell its properties in the 1960s,] Hull House opted to decentralize, and instead became an expansive, often disjointed network of neighborhood centers around Chicago. This signaled the end not only of a single community focus but also of the cohabitation of different social classes. The Hull House Association, as it was renamed after this shift, resembled a traditional nonprofit organization more than a settlement house.

This restructuring, however, was not unique to Hull House,. . . . Many comparable organizations underwent similar transitions:. . .. If anything, this restructuring was the norm for settlement houses, and though many organizations founded in the original settlement model have closed, many others . . . continue to thrive today. . . .

[T]hese developments did not [automatically] bring about financial distress or ineffective board leadership. Moreover, nonprofit missions *should* evolve as the organization and times demand, and Hull House thrived for many years after its mission had deviated from Addams's original settlement-house model. Ultimately, the cause of death for Hull House was a three-pronged attack—financial mismanagement, poor governance, and mission drift—that ravaged all facets of the organization. If Hull House had managed one or two of these areas more effectively, perhaps it could have staved off death and even paved the path to recovery. Sadly, it succumbed to all three conditions.

NOTES AND QUESTIONS

1. Compare Hull House's Form 990 to one from another large organization. Using the analysis of this article, do you conclude that the other nonprofit is in better financial shape?

2. Why do the authors think that Hull House's board violated the duty of care? Do you agree? The authors suggest that the directors were either financially illiterate or not paying attention, but they also mention how difficult it was to raise money from individuals, which suggests that the board was aware of the difficulties. Was it a violation of the duty of care not to be more transparent about the difficulties, or to be miscommunicating with the staff?

3. Do you agree with the mission drift analysis? Did the board breach the duty of obedience?

4. Another storied organization that announced it would close in 2015 was Sweet Briar College, which had been in existence for 114 years. The school had faced financial and enrollment difficulties for years, and the board announced in March that it could no longer sustain operations, despite an $84 million endowment. Lawrence Biemiller, *Is Sweet Briar's Closing a Warning Sign for Other Small Colleges?* CHRONICLE OF HIGHER EDUCATION (March 3, 2015). Committed students, alumni, and supporters rallied to save the school. A new nonprofit, Saving Sweet Briar, quickly raised millions of dollars, and several lawsuits ensued. One, brought by students, parents, and alumni succeeded in obtaining a six-month injunction that prevented the school from using funds to shut down. The second, brought by Amherst County Attorney Ellen Bowyer, sought to enjoin the school's closing because that decision would violate the terms of the will that established the school in 1901. Although a lower court refused the injunction, the Virginia Supreme Court allowed it, pending the resolution of the issues raised in the suit. *Commonwealth ex rel. Bowyer*, 2015 Va. Unpub. LEXIS. In June 2015, the parties announced a settlement, keeping the school open for at least one more year. The agreement provided that Saving Sweet Briar would provide $12 million for the school's operation in 2015–2016 and that the school could use another $16 million from its endowment. (The attorney general allowed this unusual step.) Most of the board would also resign. Susan Svriuga, *Sweet Briar Survives: Judge Approves Settlement Deal to Keep the College Open*, WASHINGTON POST (June 22, 2015). Ultimately, all the board members and the president were replaced. Ruth McCambridge, *Sweet Briar Names New Board, New President, and New Chair—Teresa Tomlinson*, NONPROFIT

QUARTERLY (July 7, 2015). As with all such situations like this, the board's competence was called into question, and, like Hull House, it was criticized for not being more transparent with its other stakeholders. *See* Ruth McCambridge, *Sweet Briar: One More Stakeholder Revolt Against an Out-of-Touch Board?* NONPROFIT QUARTERLY (March 13, 2015); Susan Sviuga, *Sweet Briar's Leadership Was a Short-Sighted Mess, Former Board Member Says*, WASHINGTON POST (June 8, 2015).

C. CENTRAL ASIA INSTITUTE

OFFICE OF CONSUMER PROTECTION, MONTANA ATTORNEY GENERAL'S INVESTIGATIVE REPORT OF GREG MORTENSON (APRIL 5, 2012)

[*Editor's Note:* In 2011, a segment of *60-Minutes* episode and an exposé by Jon Krakauer, *Three Cups of Deceit,* suggested that the Central Asia Institute (CAI), a nonprofit that built schools in Africa and Afghanistan, had serious financial and governance issues. Greg Mortenson, CAI's founder and chief executive, and a member of the board, had written two best-sellers about his work, which helped raise millions of dollars for CAI. The organization's financial controls were weak, however, and the board never fixed the deficiencies that an early CFO, several early board members, and outside auditors had brought to its attention. In addition, even though CAI paid all the expenses dealing with his books—production costs, travel expenses for speaking engagements, and advertising—Mortenson kept the royalties. CAI had an employment contract with Mortenson and some policies to ensure some reimbursement, but Mortenson had not repaid anything at the time of the exposes. The Montana Attorney General Steve Bullock then investigated and focused on governance issues at CAI (specifically a lack of financial controls and violations of the nondistribution constraint). Excerpts from the Attorney General's report follow. It includes a rebuttal from Mortenson and the Central Asia Institute.]

The board's history and testimony from certain members, however, supports a conclusion that there was a deliberate effort to put people who are loyal to Mortenson on the board. The three board members who resigned in 2002 were effectively ousted, based on tensions and conflict that had developed with Mortenson. Meeting minutes show Hornbein, the board chair, and Wiltsie, the board treasurer, repeatedly asked for documentation to prove that CAI was getting a positive return on the money Mortenson was spending. Hornbein in particular requested itemized lists of Mortenson's travel expenses, of the money coming in, and of contacts being made. He also advocated for phasing out Mortenson's role in overseeing daily operations. In short, the board members who resigned were essentially trying to perform the kinds of oversight functions expected of boards of directors for organizations such as CAI.

Despite being made aware of ongoing problems relating to accountability for expenditures and other financial issues, the CAI board never adequately addressed those problems. Specifically, the board did not exercise sufficient control and direction over Mortenson. Any efforts to do so were complicated by his dual role as executive director and a voting member of the board. . . .

The small size of the board also contributed to a lack of effective oversight. [Although] the structure and size of CAI's board complies with the corporate law requirements However, the board, as constituted for the past several years, lacked sufficient independence and size to manage the affairs of a charity with financial resources and programs as large as CAI's. . . .

As the executive director of CAI, Mortenson was ultimately responsible for the management of the charity and overseeing execution of the organization's internal policies and procedures adopted by the board.

[The Attorney General found that the board violated its duty of care for allowing financial improprieties and for not following its own procedures. He also found that Mortenson violated both the duties of care and loyalty, but he found no evidence of criminal wrongdoing. Mortenson agreed to pay $1 million back to the nonprofit; the existing board members agreed to resign within a year; and CAI would increase its board to at least seven members. Mortenson was allowed to remain with the organization, but he could not be responsible for managerial or financial oversight.]

Central Asia Institute (CAI) and Greg Mortenson Joint Statement In Connection with Montana Attorney General Narrative Report

We . . . respectfully disagree with some of the analysis, as well as the legal conclusions in the report. It is also important to us to provide greater context to the perceived deficiencies that are the subject of the report.

Montana law sets forth specifically that the "duty of care" requires directors and officers to discharge their duties in good faith; with the care an ordinarily prudent person would exercise under similar circumstances; and in a manner the director or officer reasonably believes to be in the best interests of the corporation. Through this language, Montana has specifically codified the legal standard commonly known as the "business judgment rule;" Under the business judgment rule, the judgment of directors of corporations enjoys the benefit of a presumption of good faith and promotion of the best interests of the corporation they serve.

The Parties believe that the Board is entitled to exercise—and, in fact, did exercise—its best business judgment. That business judgment is a subjective determination and, as just noted, it enjoys the benefit of a presumption of good faith that will not be disturbed if any rational business purpose can be attributed to its decision. Historically, the Board of CAI has had both an independent makeup and has been comprised of an appropriate number of members for an organization of its size and resources. Only in the last year has the board been comprised of fewer than four persons, although a number of possible candidates have been reviewed and appointments are awaiting the resolution of this matter. A majority of the Board members are independent—they have no financial interest in any CAI transaction with any outside entity, including Greg Mortenson and/or MC Consulting. The Board minutes consistently discussed fluctuations in its size and makeup, as well as needs for additional board members. CAI agrees that best practices dictates closer attention to board size and independence and is pledged to maintain attention to those areas.

The Board met formally and in person, at a minimum, two to three times each year, and held telephonic meetings, as well, in between those regular meetings. The minutes reflect that the Board was consistently provided detailed financial information about CAI and its domestic and overseas operations, including its expenditures for such operations. CAI's Board meetings reflect discussions on addressing supporting documentation for credit card charges. The financial statements the Board was supplied at each meeting and the interim reports consistently made by staff persons stood as the primary support for most of the Board's decisions. Nothing exists to indicate that the Board could not and should not have relied upon—or made business decisions based upon—this information.

The Board faced a "Hobson's choice": How far could they press the resolution of these problems on behalf of CAI to achieve compliance on receipt documentation and procedural compliance? That is the crucial real world context within which the Board exercised its business judgment on these matters and it did so at a time when the mission of the charity was experiencing worldwide acclaim, robust donations, and stunning successes in Central Asia. Greg Mortenson maintained a near non-stop travel schedule, which clearly redounded to the benefit of the charity. As co-founder, he is the face of CAI's mission and he was the key person responsible for the overwhelming success of both the charity's domestic education and outreach mission and its mission to bring education to remote parts of Central Asia—a level of success that the Board knew far exceeded anyone's hopes or expectations. . . .

CAI's history reflects a small organization with limited staff that experienced unprecedented growth during a very short time. As its overseas school placement and global public outreach missions expanded exponentially, the staff and the Board were consistently working to improve the overall management and operations of the organization, including consistent additional oversight by an outside accountant and continued diligence in preparing staff/personnel and board policy manuals.

Over the past eighteen months, the Board has undertaken persistent, focused efforts to address the problems identified by the OAG. In doing so, CAI has demonstrated its commitment to operating transparently and within all practical best practices, as well as continuing to operate within the strictures of Montana law. This record of improvement is incontrovertible. Under the terms of the Settlement Agreement, experienced management will be in place to secure compliance in concert with an expanded board. CAI believes that the steps it has initiated, as well as the additional voluntary compliance undertakings it has agreed to with the Attorney General justify confidence in the charity by public officials and the public.

QUESTIONS

1. Should an author who writes a memoir about his experience with a nonprofit be entitled to the royalties, or do they belong to the nonprofit?
2. If Mortenson's arrangement with the board concerning royalties was reasonable and he and the board had actually followed that arrangement, would the agreement have been void or voidable under MNCA 3rd Ed.? Would it have been a violation of the duty of loyalty?
3. Did the board members who resigned in 2002 because they saw these problems, which did not come to public scrutiny for nine more years, fulfill their fiduciary duties sufficiently by quitting? What else could they have done?
4. Until recently, issues of board members' fiduciary duties have been state-law matters. Should they instead be federal issues? Should they be both federal and state issues? As mentioned above, the tax information form that most tax-exempt organizations file with the IRS, Form 990, asks several questions about the organization's governance practices.

V. ENFORCEMENT OF DIRECTORS' DUTIES

Although directors have definite legal duties, it is not always easy to enforce them. Several barriers exist. First, as we have seen above, the fiduciary standard is rather low. Second, even if the standard has been breached, courts can be reluctant to impose heavy sanctions. Third, state and federal statutes often limit directors' liability, especially if the directors are performing their services free of charge. Fourth, nonprofit corporations often offer to indemnify their directors, hold directors' and officers' liability insurance, or both. Finally, for the most part, other directors and state attorney generals are the only ones who can obtain standing to challenge whether directors have breached their fiduciary duties.[18]

That said, the possibility for personal liability is real, and the increased attention to nonprofit governance appears to be translating into actual judgments against defendants. In the *Sibley* case, above, the court declined to award damages or to remove the board members. In *Lemington,* which was decided 41 years later, the directors were responsible for more than $2 million in damages, even though they did not personally profit from the transaction.

---

[18] Many breaches of fiduciary duty also lead to violations of federal tax law, so the IRS may revoke an organization's tax exemption or impose excise taxes on board members for the same acts that constitute a breach of fiduciary duty. The laws and procedures that can give rise to those actions are covered primarily in Chapters 9 and 12. Despite the IRS's questions about good governance in Forms 1023 and 990, it remains up to the states to regulate breaches of fiduciary duties.

The policy tension is between the need to attract good people to serve on boards of directors, almost always without pay, and the need for an enforcement scheme ensuring that the directors carry out their fiduciary duties. Following are a sampling of statutes and cases that illustrate this tension.

STERN V. LUCY WEBB HAYES NATIONAL TRAINING SCHOOL FOR DEACONESSES

381 F. Supp. 1003 (1974)

[*Editor's Note:* The substantive part of this case appears in section III of this chapter.]

[The court] must now consider the appropriate relief in light of its finding that the defendant trustees have breached their fiduciary duties of care and loyalty to the Hospital. . . .

The function of equity is not to punish but merely to take such action as the Court in its discretion deems necessary to prevent the recurrence of improper conduct....

In attempting to balance the equities under the circumstances shown by the record, there are a number of factors which lead the Court to feel that intervention by injunction should be limited. First, the defendant trustees in this case constitute but a small minority of the full Sibley Board. Yet, in several respects, the responsibility for past failures adequately to supervise the handling of Hospital funds rests equally on all Board members. Second, it is clear that the practices criticized by plaintiffs have, to a considerable extent, been corrected and that the employees and trustees who were principally responsible for lax handling of funds have died or have been dismissed. Third, there is no indication that any of the named trustees were involved in fraudulent practices or profited personally by lapses in proper fiscal supervision, and, indeed, the overall operation of the Hospital in terms of low costs, efficient services and quality patient care has been superior. Finally, this case is in a sense one of first impression, since it brings into judicial focus for the first time in this jurisdiction the nature and scope of trustee obligations in a nonprofit, non-member charitable institution incorporated under D.C. Code §29-1001 et seq.

The Court is well aware that it must take proper steps to insure a clean break between the past and the future. Personnel changes and a recent greater awareness of past laxity are encouraging, as is the addition of Article XXVIII to the Hospital's by-laws, but good intentions expressed post-litem must be accompanied by concrete action. Accordingly, it is desirable to require by injunction that the appropriate committees and officers of the Hospital present to the full Board a written policy statement governing investments and the use of idle cash in the Hospital's bank accounts and other funds, and establish a procedure for the periodic reexamination of existing investments and other financial arrangements to insure compliance with Board policies. No existing financial relationships should be continued unless consistent with established policy and found by disinterested members of the Board to be in the Hospital's best interests. In addition, each trustee should fully disclose his affiliation with banks, savings and loan associations and investment firms now doing business with the Hospital.

Removal of the defendant trustees from the Sibley Board would be unduly harsh, and this will not be ordered. These trustees are now completing long years of service and they will soon become less active in the day-to-day affairs of the Hospital because of age or illness. It would unduly disrupt the affairs of the Hospital abruptly to terminate their relationship with that institution. Others must soon take over their roles in carrying forward the Hospital's affairs, and it is therefore unnecessary to interfere by order of removal or disqualification with a transition that is necessarily already taking place due to other immutable factors. . . .

The Hospital would be well advised to restrict membership on its Board to the representatives of financial institutions which have no substantial business relationship with the Hospital. The best way to avoid potential conflicts of interest and to be assured of objective advice is to avoid the possibility of such conflicts at the time new trustees are selected.

As an additional safeguard, the Court will require that each newly-elected trustee read this Opinion and the attached Order. Compliance with this requirement must appear in a document signed by the new trustee or in the minutes of the Sibley Board. In view of the circumstances disclosed by the record it will be desirable, in addition, to require public disclosure which will further insure that the Board's recently-avowed good intentions are faithfully carried out. To this end, the Court will direct that prior to each meeting of the full Board the members of the Board shall receive, at least one week in advance, a formal written statement prepared by the Hospital's Treasurer or Comptroller disclosing in detail the full extent of all business done by the Hospital since the last Board meeting with any bank, savings and loan association, investment service or other financial institution with which any trustee or officer of the Hospital is affiliated as a trustee, director, principal officer, partner, general manager or substantial shareholder. Moreover, all such dealings shall be summarized by the Hospital's auditors in their annual audit and a copy of the annual audit shall be made available on request for inspection by any patient of the Hospital at the Hospital's offices during business hours. Such arrangements should continue for a period of five years.

MODEL NONPROFIT CORPORATION ACT, 3D ED. (2008), §§8.33, 8.51, 8.52, AND 8.57

---

§8.33. Directors' Liability for Unlawful Distributions

(a) A director who votes for or assents to a distribution made in violation of this [act] is personally liable to the nonprofit corporation for the amount of the distribution that exceeds what could have been distributed without violating this [act] if the party asserting liability establishes that when taking the action the director did not comply with Section 8.30.

(b) A director held liable under subsection (a) for an unlawful distribution is entitled to:

(1) contribution from every other director who could be held liable under subsection (a) for the unlawful distribution; and

(2) recoupment from each person of the pro-rata portion of the amount of the unlawful distribution the person received, whether or not the person knew the distribution was made in violation of this [act].

(c) A proceeding to enforce:

(1) the liability of a director under subsection (a) is barred unless it is commenced within two years after the date on which the distribution was made; or

(2) contribution or recoupment under subsection (b) is barred unless it is commenced within one year after the liability of the claimant has been finally adjudicated under subsection (a).

§8.51. Permissible Indemnification

(a) Except as otherwise provided in this section, a nonprofit corporation may indemnify an individual who is a party to a proceeding because he is a director against liability incurred in the proceeding if:

(1) the individual:

(i) acted in good faith; and

(ii) reasonably believed:

(iii) in the case of any criminal proceeding, had no reasonable cause to believe his or her conduct was unlawful; or

(2) the individual engaged in conduct for which broader indemnification has been made permissible or obligatory under a provision of the articles of incorporation (as authorized by section 2.02(b)(8)).

(b) A director's conduct with respect to an employee benefit plan for a purpose the director reasonably believed to be in the interests of the participants in, and the beneficiaries of, the plan is conduct that satisfies the requirement of subsection (a)(1)(ii)(B).

(c) The termination of a proceeding by judgment, order, settlement, or conviction, or upon a plea of nolo contendere or its equivalent, is not, of itself, determinative that the director did not meet the relevant standard of conduct described in this section.

(d) Unless ordered by a court under section 8.54(a)(3), a nonprofit corporation may not indemnify a director:

(1) in connection with a proceeding by or in the right of the corporation, except for reasonable expenses incurred in connection with the proceeding if it is determined that the director has met the relevant standard of conduct under subsection (a); or

(2) in connection with any proceeding with respect to conduct for which the director was adjudged liable on the basis that the director received a financial benefit to which the director was not entitled, whether or not involving action in an official capacity.

§8.52. Mandatory Indemnification

A nonprofit corporation must indemnify a director to the extent the director was successful, on the merits or otherwise, in the defense of any proceeding to which the director was a party because the director was a director of the corporation against reasonable expenses incurred by the director in connection with the proceeding.

§8.57. Insurance

A nonprofit corporation may purchase and maintain insurance on behalf of an individual who is or was a director or officer of the corporation, or who, while a director or officer of the corporation, serves or served at the corporation's request as a director, officer, partner, trustee, employee, or agent of another domestic or foreign corporation, partnership, joint venture, trust, employee benefit plan, or other entity, against liability asserted against or incurred by the individual in that capacity or arising from the individual's status as a director or officer, whether or not the corporation would have power to indemnify or advance expenses to the individual against the same liability under this [subchapter].

CALIFORNIA CORPORATIONS CODE, §5142

(A) Notwithstanding Section 5141, any of the following may bring an action to enjoin, correct, obtain damages for, or to otherwise remedy a breach of a charitable trust:

1. The corporation, or a member in the name of the corporation pursuant to Section 5710.
2. An officer of the corporation.
3. A director of the corporation.
4. A person with a reversionary, contractual, or property interest in the assets subject to such charitable trust.
5. The Attorney General, or any person granted relator status by the Attorney General.

The Attorney General shall be given notice of any action brought by the persons specified in paragraphs (1) through (4), and may intervene.

IN RE MILTON HERSHEY SCHOOL

---

590 Pa. 35, 911 A.2d 1258 (Pa. 2006)

Opinion: Mr. Justice EAKIN

In 1909, Milton and Catherine Hershey established the Milton Hershey School, a charitable institution, funded by the Milton Hershey School Trust. The deed of trust is the original agreement between the Hersheys, the Hershey Trust Company as Trustee, and the Managers of the Trust. The deed, as amended in 1976, provides that the Trust Company and the Board of Managers (which consists of members of the Board of Directors of the Trust Company), are to administer the Trust and have responsibility for all aspects of running the School and for managing the Trust's assets. The deed also states, "[a]ll children shall leave the institution and cease to be the recipients of its benefits upon the completion of the full course of secondary education being offered at the School." *In re Milton Hershey School*, 867 A.2d 674, 678 (Pa. Cmwlth. 2005) (quoting Deed of Trust, November 15, 1909, at 12-13).

In 1930, at Milton Hershey's direction, school alumni and a former superintendent formed The Milton Hershey School Alumni Association. The Association is composed mostly of School graduates, though it includes honorary and associate members. The Association is not a division of the School or Trust Company; it was not named in the deed of trust and is not an intended beneficiary of the Trust.

Around 1990, the Association believed the Trust's resources were being diverted from the purpose of helping orphaned children. The Association contacted the Attorney General, which investigated and concluded the Trust Company was not acting consistent with the Trust's intent. In 2002, the Attorney General, the School, and the Trust Company entered an agreement governing certain aspects of the administration of the Trust and the School.

In 2003, this agreement was modified, essentially rescinding the 2002 agreement. Following the modification, the Association commenced an action in the orphans' court, seeking rescission of the 2003 agreement, reinstatement of the 2002 agreement, and appointment of a guardian ad litem and trustee ad litem. The School and the Trust Company filed preliminary objections alleging the Association lacked standing to challenge the rescission of the 2002 agreement; the trial court granted the preliminary objections.

The Commonwealth Court, en banc, reversed in a four-to-three decision, finding the Association had a "special interest" in the complained-of actions of the Trustee that supported its standing to seek enforcement of the Trust. The court observed the Association was created at the direction of the Trust's primary settlor, with the purpose of promoting school interests and establishing and maintaining supplemental education programs and activities for students.... It also summarized the Association's efforts to preserve School traditions and Trust assets, including prompting of the Attorney General to address perceived improprieties, and expending its own financial resources to aid that investigation....

The court acknowledged standing generally requires a "substantial, direct, and immediate interest" in the subject matter of the litigation. Id., at 684 (quoting *William Penn Parking Garage, Inc., v. City of Pittsburgh*, 464 Pa. 168, 346 A.2d 269 (Pa. 1975). It observed in charitable trusts, courts have fashioned a "special interest" doctrine, consistent with the Restatement (Second) of Trusts.... The court then implemented a five-part test to determine special interest standing in the charitable trust setting, which requires consideration of:

(1) the extraordinary nature of the acts complained of and the remedy sought;
(2) the presence of fraud or misconduct on the part of the charity or its directors;
(3) the attorney general's availability or effectiveness;
(4) the nature of the benefited class and its relationship to the charity; and
(5) subjective, case-specific circumstances.

... The court found this test struck the best balance, preventing unnecessary litigation involving charities while assuring the philanthropic purposes underlying trusts are maintained. Id.

Applying this test, the court found the circumstances here to be extraordinary, citing the need for reform administration of Trust assets, the decrease in the number of children the School served vis-a-vis over $5 billion in Trust assets, and the Association's instrumental role in addressing problems in the Trust's administration.... The court delineated the 70-year relationship between the Association and the Trust, including their common founder, the membership's successful participation in School affairs, its ongoing bonds with students, the location of the Association's offices on Trust lands, the Association's administration of student-related activities and graduate assistance programs, and the Association's intimate knowledge of the type of care provided at the School....

The court indicated the risk of vexatious or unreasonable litigation was "virtually non-existent," as the Association only sought reasons why the 2002 agreement was supplanted, when such agreement had resulted from an extensive investigation by the Attorney General (funded in part by the Association), which concluded the Trust's charitable purposes were being impeded.... The court also found the Association's efforts neither vexatious nor unreasonable.... Given the nature of the Trust and its status as the largest residential childcare charity in the world, the court concluded judicial scrutiny would advance the public interest in assuring the Trust is operating efficiently and effectively....

President Judge Colins, joined by Judges Cohn Jubelirer and Simpson, dissented, arguing the analysis should begin and end with the deed of trust, which endows the Board of Managers and the Trust Company with responsibility for School management and Trust administration, and which does not name the Association as an intended beneficiary.... The dissent pointed out that affording the Association standing interferes with the performance of the Attorney General's statutorily mandated duties.... The dissent also characterized the majority's holding as "a quantum leap" away from historical concepts of standing.

The facts are not in dispute. The Commonwealth Court found the trial court committed an error of law by granting the preliminary objections. We are left to decide whether the Commonwealth Court committed an error of law in its standing analysis.... As this is a purely legal question, our standard of review is de novo and scope of review is plenary....

The core concept of standing is that "a party who is not negatively affected by the matter he seeks to challenge is not aggrieved, and thus, has no right to obtain judicial resolution of his challenge." *City of Philadelphia v. Commonwealth*, 575 Pa. 542, 838 A.2d 566, 838 A.2d 566, 577 (Pa. 2003). A litigant is aggrieved when he can show a substantial, direct, and immediate interest in the outcome of the litigation. *William Penn Parking Garage, Inc.* at 280. A litigant possesses a substantial interest if there is a discernible adverse effect to an interest other than that of the general citizenry. It is direct if there is harm to that interest. Id. It is immediate if it is not a remote consequence of a judgment.

Private parties generally lack standing to enforce charitable trusts.... Since the public is the object of the settlor's beneficiaries in a charitable trust, private parties generally have insufficient interest in such trusts to enforce them. Those who may bring an action for the enforcement of a charitable trust include the Attorney General, a member of the charitable organization, or someone having a special interest in the trust.... A person whose only interest is that interest held in common with other members of the public cannot compel the performance of a duty the organization owes to the public. The question here is whether the Association had such a special interest in the enforcement of the Trust. . . .

[A] written trust exists here, specifically excluding School graduates from being recipients of the Trust's benefits. The Association is not mentioned in the Trust, and the bulk of the Association's members are specifically excluded from receiving the benefits of the Trust. To give the Association "special interest" standing where the settlors of the Trust specifically denied beneficiary status to its members, would surely contravene the settlors' intent expressed through their written trust. See *In re Milton Hershey School* at 691 (Colins, P.J., dissenting).

We find the Association did not have a special interest sufficient to vest it with standing. Nothing in this litigation would affect the Association itself; it loses nothing and gains nothing. The Association's intensity of concern is real and commendable, but it is not a substitute for an actual interest. Standing is not created through the Association's advocacy or its members' past close relationship with the School as former individual recipients of the Trust's benefits. The Trust did not contemplate the Association, or anyone else, to be a "shadow board" of graduates with standing to challenge actions the Board takes....

The Attorney General is granted the authority to enforce charitable trusts.... Current law allowed the Association, an outside group, to urge the Attorney General to enforce the Trust. However, the Association's disagreement with the

Attorney General's decision to modify the 2002 agreement does not vest the Association with standing to challenge that decision in court. Ultimately, the Association's dismay is more properly directed at the Attorney General's actions and decisions; it is insufficient to establish standing here.

We hold the Association did not have standing to bring this action. Order reversed. Jurisdiction relinquished.

NOTES AND QUESTIONS

1. Why did the *Stern* court impose such a weak remedy? Is there a temptation for courts to be lenient in a breach of fiduciary duty case in the nonprofit sector?

2. Would the *Stern* case be decided differently today? Is *Lemington* representative of increased governance scrutiny, or is it an outlier? It is generally assumed that breaches of the duty of care, without a corresponding breach of the duty of loyalty, will lead to removal from the board, but not monetary damages. In *People v. Manor*, 2013 IL App. (1st) 113132-U (2013), for example, the board member who used charitable assets for personal use was required to pay $2 million, while the board members who failed to supervise her or file the annual registration and annual financial report lost their positions on the board. The nonprofit was also forced to dissolve. *Lemington* appears to go further than this, however. The board member defendants were jointly and severally liable for damages, even though they did not engage in the violations of the duty of loyalty, as the officer defendants did. Could the *Lemington* award be particularly high because of the "deepening insolvency" tort or is it a sign of things to come?

   In 2015, the New York Attorney General Eric Schneiderman announced that he had settled with the directors of the Victor E. Perley Fund. That organization had drastically changed its purpose, allowed the director to profit personally from the organization, and overseen a decline in assets from $3.7 million to $1 million over five years. The settlement agreement acknowledged that even those who were not involved in the conflicted transactions were jointly and severally liable for the damages. Newspaper accounts of the settlement suggest that the trustees who violated the duty of care were the ones who eventually paid the damages because the others were judgment proof. Fortunately for them, their insurance made the payment. Erik Enquist, *After Looter of Charity Commits Suicide, Board Members Pay the Price*, CRAIN'S BUSINESS (April 30, 2015).

3. Did the second *Hershey* case come to the correct conclusion? What is the policy behind making it difficult to obtain standing to sue a board member? A 2015 case reaffirmed this standing rule. In *Harvard Climate Justice Coalition v. Harvard College* [2015 Mass. Super. LEXIS 30, 32 Mass. L. Rep. 529 (2015)], a suit brought by seven Harvard students claiming that the university mismanaged its charitable funds and intentionally invested in abnormally dangerous activities was dismissed because the students lacked standing. Is there a way to expand standing without violating those policies?

See Evelyn Brody, *From the Dead Hand to the Living Dead: The Conundrum of Charitable-Donor Standing*, 41 GA. L. REV. 1183 (2007).

4. UPMIFA does not permit donor standing, and a Missouri court enforced this provision under the Missouri version of the law by denying the donors standing even though they had reason to believe that nearly half the funds in their gift had not been spent in accordance with the terms of their gift. *Hardt v. Vitae Foundation*, 302 S.W.2d 133 (Mo. 2009).

5. If standing to sue is difficult to obtain and courts are reluctant to impose remedies when a breach has occurred, are nonprofit corporations truly protected from bad governance? Are other remedies available? How should courts and legislators resolve this tension? *See* American Law Institute, PRINCIPLES OF THE LAW OF NONPROFIT ORGANIZATIONS, TENTATIVE DRAFT NO. 1 (2008). For an example of a case that granted standing to the donor's widow, see *Smithers v. St. Luke's Roosevelt Hospital*, 723 N.Y.S.2d 426 (N.Y. App. Div. 2001).

6. Board members could also be liable for damages if the §501(c)(3) has failed to withhold federal income taxes and social security taxes from employees' wages. 26 U.S. Code §6672. The Internal Revenue Code makes an exception for honorary board members of tax-exempt organizations who are unpaid, do not handle the day-to-day operations of the organization, and are unaware of the tax liability, so long as someone within the organization remains liable for paying the tax.

PROBLEM

Use the following facts to discuss the breaches of fiduciary duties that existed at the school described below and the remedies that you think should be imposed. Assume that MNCA, 3d Ed., is in effect and that the cases in this chapter are from Model State, USA, even if they conflict with each other.

Mikala School is a private coeducational school in Model State, USA. It serves 3,000 children of Native American descent from kindergarten to twelfth grade. The school began in 1900 with a generous gift from Maria Kailua's estate. Her will provided the funds for a school that serves children of Native American descent who live in Model State, USA. Over the past century, through fortuitous investment, the corpus of the gift has grown so large that the school now has a $12 billion endowment. Each year, the endowment yields hundreds of millions of dollars in interest and dividends.

Mikala School is currently governed by a board that consists of 10 politically connected individuals. One is a former speaker of the state legislature, another is a former president of the state senate, and a third is a close confidant of the current governor. The state Supreme Court justices, who were selected by politicians, in turn appoint the board of the Mikala School.

The board oversees the school and its investments. The school owns thousands of acres of real estate, including beachfront hotels, shopping centers, and a golf course. It is also heavily invested in Wall Street hedge funds, Chinese banks, and offshore reinsurance companies. The school pays each board member $1 million a year for overseeing the school and its investments.

Recently, some law students have been looking into the affairs of the school. They discovered that each board member receives $1 million in compensation, even though most charity boards do not receive a dime for their services. They also found that the school serves only 6% of the eligible children in the state. One of the trustees, Julie Lokelei, named herself principal of the school last year, and by all accounts, she is woefully unqualified. The association that accredits private schools in the state recently characterized the atmosphere at the school under her direction as "oppressive and intimidating."

The law students also found a story of mismanagement and malfeasance of the financial affairs. For example, the school recently invested in an Internet dating service, but it insisted that the brother-in-law of one of the board members receive a six-figure consulting contract as part of the deal. When asked about this investment, the chair of the board responded that they thought this individual would best protect their investment. The board also hired a state senator as special projects officer, but the senator used the position for personal, rather than business, projects. Among the "business" expenses for which he received reimbursement were expenses incurred during several evenings spent at a strip club. When the students questioned these payments, the school asked for repayment and then promptly increased the senator's salary by the exact amount as the improper expenses plus taxes. An outside audit also showed that the school was getting a 2% return on its investment at a time that the average return was 10%.

The students contacted the local newspaper with their findings, but the newspaper ignored them. They then persuaded an alternative newspaper to publish their findings, and once the findings became public, the state attorney general began looking into the matter. The board of the school responded by looking into the possibility of moving to an Indian reservation, where the school could avoid the state scrutiny. It has not yet done so.

What, if any, breaches of fiduciary duty do you see? What remedies, if any, would help get this school back on track?

[*Editor's Note:* This problem is based on the governance problems of the Bishop Estate in Hawaii in the late 1990s. Princess Bernice Pauahi Bishop's will placed much of the land in Hawaii in a trust to be used for the benefit of the Kamehameha School for native Hawaiians. By the late 1990s, the trust was worth approximately $10 billion. Its trustees, powerful and well connected politically, were also benefiting personally instead of overseeing the school. The saga was the topic of a segment on *60 Minutes* on April 30, 2000, and much has been written about the scandal. *See* Samuel King and Randolph Roth, *Broken Trust: Greed, Mismanagement, and Political Manipulation at America's Largest Charitable Trust* (Univ. of Hawaii Press 2006); Gavan Daws & Na Leo o Kamehameha, *Wayfinding Through the Storm: Speaking Truth to Power at Kamehameha Schools, 1993-1999* (Watermark 2009).]

CHAPTER 4

TAX-EXEMPT PURPOSES OF §501(c)(3) ORGANIZATIONS

Purposes of this chapter:

- Examine and critique the theoretical bases for tax exemption
- Introduce §501(c)(3) and the organizational and operational tests
- Attempt to define "charitable" purposes in general and in the context of hospitals, disaster relief, and educational institutions
- Examine the special challenges of recognizing tax exemption for religious purposes

To think about as you read:

Art museums usually have no trouble obtaining §501(c)(3) recognition, but they do not fit easily within the commonsense definition of the words used in the statute. Assuming that no art museum has ever received §501(c) recognition, how would you convince the Internal Revenue Service (IRS) that your client, the local museum, deserves to be recognized? Which theory of tax exemption works best for your client? What language from the statute, the regulations, and the cases you are reading would be helpful? If you are creating your own virtual §501(c)(3) organization, think about the same questions with regard to your organization.

I. INTRODUCTION

We have introduced the concept of nonprofit organizations and the legal framework for starting nonprofits at the state level. We now turn to the topic of federal tax exemption. Section 501(c) of the Internal Revenue Code specifies 29 types of organizations that are exempt from federal income taxation. One of those types, the 501(c)(3) organization, makes up the largest number of tax-exempt organizations.[1] Section 501(c)(3) organizations are both tax-exempt and able to accept tax-deductible contributions. Non-501(c)(3) organizations—such as labor unions, chambers of commerce, country clubs, and fraternities—may be tax exempt, but donations to those organizations are not tax deductible.[2]

This book concentrates on §501(c)(3) organizations. For the next several chapters, you will parse the statute, look at its regulations, and read cases and IRS materials that help explain the statute. This initial chapter concerning §501(c)(3) organizations will examine the rationale for tax exemption and focus on acceptable purposes and activities for these organizations. The chapter also discusses the process of applying for recognition of §501(c)(3) status through Form 1023. Although an organization seeking §501(c)(3) recognition must show the IRS that it intends to follow all the statute's requirements, realistically, early-stage organizations will be able to be specific only about their purposes and planned activities.

This chapter begins with a discussion of the rationales for charitable tax exemption. It then provides an overall look at IRC §501(c)(3) and introduces the organizational and operational tests. Next, it examines the meaning of the term "charitable"—the way the term is used in the statute and the regulations, as well as public policy exceptions to the concept. The rest of the chapter examines the permissible purposes for charitable tax exemption in the context of specific types of nonprofit organizations, including health care, disaster relief, educational, religious, and legal organizations. The chapter ends with a sample Form 1023, the Application for Recognition of Exemption.

II. RATIONALES FOR CHARITABLE TAX EXEMPTION

Why does the Internal Revenue Code provide an exemption from the federal income tax for certain types of institutions? The first article below suggests that historical reasons explain which organizations qualify for tax-exemption and that a lack of a precise and explicit understanding of what constitutes charity underlies the entire sector. The next article discusses several prominent theories—the subsidy, income definition, capital formation, donative, and altruistic theories. A U.S. Supreme Court case, *Walz v. Tax Commission of City of New York*, 397 U.S. 664 (1970), which needed to grapple with the rationales for exemption in order to come to its conclusion, completes this section of the chapter.

---

[1] In April 2015, the IRS recognized over 1.5 million tax-exempt organizations. Approximately ¾ of these organizations (slightly over 1.15 million) are § 501(c)(3) organizations, the type of tax-exempt organization examined in this book. National Center for Charitable Statistics, *Quick Facts about Nonprofits*, citing NCCS Business Master File, 4/2015, http://nccs.urban.org/statistics /quickfacts.cfm, accessed May 9, 2016.

[2] Occasionally, a non-501(c)(3) organization, with a program that has 501(c)(3) purposes and activities, is permitted to accept tax-deductible donations for that program. An example would be a scholarship fund for orphans of firefighters that is part of a firefighters' organization.

STANLEY KATZ, SHOULD WE KILL THE GOOSE THAT LAID THE GOLDEN EGG? DO WE NEED A FUNCTIONAL DEFINITION OF CHARITY IN THE UNITED STATES?

NYU Conference on Elasticity of the Boundaries, Oct. 29, 2015

I want to make two points about the legal definition of charity from the perspective of a historian of philanthropy: the *first* is that in this country the institution of the philanthropic foundation came into existence without any explicit public policy determination of what it was or what it could and should do; the *second* is since there never has been any functional definition of the status of philanthropy as an institution, philanthropy has been and will continue to be strongly resistant to functional "reform." It is very hard to reform something you cannot even describe adequately. That is to say that philanthropy is a moving target for reformers, since it keeps subtly changing in form and public perception. As I hope will come clear later, the amorphous character of philanthropy as an institution has the advantage of permitting (or possibly encouraging) innovation. But the definitional flexibility of philanthropy simultaneously makes the institution exceedingly difficult to discuss critically or to shape through regulation. . . .

In the beginning [of the 20th century] came a new idea, philanthropy. . . . Philanthropy was the search for the underlying causes of the immediate problems that charity was trying to address. Philanthropy sought to eradicate illness, poverty, and social distress. Philanthropy sought to go to the root causes of these fundamental problems of society in order to enable us to completely eliminate them. Philanthropy sought national or international public policy change as its ultimate *modus operandi*. The philanthropist, so conceived, would invest his funds in a very different sort of way than the almsgiver.

The early philanthropists [such as John D. Rockefeller and Andrew Carnegie] needed an institutional vehicle in order to apply their funds efficiently to the rational analysis of a vast array of human problems, but no such organizational form existed at the time. Their consequent creation of what we now call the "private philanthropic foundation" was one of the great institutional innovations in American history. I think most of us assume that the foundation was somehow an old English charitable institution. Not so. There were of course charitable "foundations" of a variety of types in England and the United States, but the (endowed) grant-making foundation simply did not exist in 1880. Neither the organizational form nor its legal rationale existed until after the turn of the twentieth century. . . .

The extent to which the philanthropic foundation form proliferated in the United States is astounding. But what is most interesting is that Americans have avoided the English approach to defining and organizing charity, which was to insist upon a precise and explicit understanding of what constituted charity. The 1601 Elizabethan Statue of Charities is still the fundamental basis of the law of charities in the United Kingdom. This statute, which has of course been altered somewhat over the years, establishes a highly specific and prescriptive definition of charity. Its famous preamble was a rag-tag list of traditional charitable practices, from "the relief of the aged, impotent and poor people" to "aid or ease of any poor inhabitants concerning payments of fifteens." British judges over the years have accepted that there are "other purposes beneficial to the community, not falling under any of the [traditional categories]," but the concept of charity was understood to be bounded.[3] In the recent past, the British have also created an independent agency, now the Charity Commission, to supervise and regulate the charitable system. This is the way in which legal institutions affecting the public interest are established and maintained in most parts of the world, and we Americans could have gone that route. But we did not. In effect we permitted private legal action to create a public institution (the private philanthropic foundation), which we have only subsequently defined and regulated – and through the federal income tax system rather than a specialized independent agency. The result, as I will try to show, is that it has been very difficult in the United States to specify precisely what a philanthropist can or cannot do. It is hard to say whether the vagueness of the definition is deliberate or inadvertent, though it may be both. While this is thought by some to be the genius of our system, I want to argue that our approach has some significant functional problems.

After the Sixteenth Amendment was ratified in February 1913, we Americans consigned charitable giving the federal tax code and adopted many of the key legal conceptions of state charity law, including the notion of tax exemption. In consequence, charitable organizations are now categorized by federal law as "tax exempt"— we thus define charities by what they are not, rather than what they are. The result is that we do not have a formal substantive definition of charity/philanthropy. The law tells people what they cannot do (self-dealing, surplus distributing) rather than what they can do. Over time, the default has dominated; philanthropists are assumed to be doing the permissible, unless it is quite clear that their philanthropy is impermissible. It is not entirely unfair to say that our legal policy position is that it should be legal to make a charitable gift for any purpose that is not contrary to explicit legal rules. In practice, this means that the philanthropist can give for any purpose that is neither criminal nor clearly violates some section of the Internal Revenue Code. The default is that most genuinely non-self-aggrandizing gifts are charitable. Marion Fremont-Smith concludes her most recent book by saying the "rationale for the existing system" of American charity law is "to afford freedom to charitable fiduciaries to manage while assuring the public that charitable funds will not be diverted for private gain or used recklessly." No other country that I am aware of permits such wide philanthropic discretion.

The unarticulated assumption has been that the law of charities should support the benevolently public-serving purposes of private wealth. Philanthropy is

---

[3] [FN i] Marion R. Fremont-Smith, *Governing Nonprofit Organizations: Federal and State Law and Regulation*, HARVARD UNIVERSITY PRESS, 2004, pp.118-119.

"private power for the public good," as Ellen Lagemann has said.[4] The further (unspoken) assumption is that the state does well not to inquire too closely into how wealthy individuals choose to serve the public with their wealth. That's the unarticulated rationale for our system, or so many Americans, especially wealthy Americans, think. A further hidden assumption—perhaps the reason why we have done so little to tamper with this so-called system—is that we worry that philanthropy may be the goose that laid the golden egg, and that by closely inspecting the egg we may in fact kill the goose. If we question philanthropy, we may weaken it, and perhaps it will disappear altogether. Warren Buffett, upon being asked critically about his notions of philanthropy, has responded several times, "Well, what would you like me to do with my wealth, leave it to my children?" Buffett knows, and we know, that most Americans prefer that he dedicate his wealth (or, more honestly, power) to public purposes.

ROB ATKINSON, THEORIES OF THE FEDERAL INCOME TAX EXEMPTION FOR CHARITIES: THESIS, ANTITHESIS, AND SYNTHESES

27 Stetson L. Rev. 395, 402-404, 408-409, and 415-419 (1997)

The Thesis: Traditional Subsidy Theory/Public Benefit Theory

The traditional subsidy theory of the tax exemption for charities answers the first of our two questions—Why do charities warrant special treatment?—by pointing to their provision of two kinds of public benefits. The first of these I will call primary public benefits, since they are thought to inhere in the particular activities that the organization undertakes. Charities generate primary public benefits either by providing goods or services that are deemed to be inherently good for the public, or by delivering ordinary goods or services to those who are recognized as being especially needy. Healthcare and education are examples of products deemed to be inherently good; providing them to anyone, irrespective of need, is considered to produce public benefits. Providing food and shelter for the poor or otherwise disadvantaged is an example of benefitting an especially needy class; it makes no difference that the goods provided are themselves mundane. In summary, charities provide primary public benefits in two ways: especially good goods to ordinary people, and ordinary goods to the especially deserving.

Beyond these primary public benefits, charities are said to provide a second kind of public benefit, which I will call "meta-benefits." These benefits derive not from either *what* product is produced or to *whom* it is distributed, but rather from *how* it is produced or distributed. Traditional theory has identified two ways charities provide such "meta-benefits." In the first place, they are said to deliver goods and services more efficiently, more innovatively, or otherwise better than other suppliers. In the second place, charities' very existence is said to promote

---

[4] [FN iii] Ellen Condliffe Lagemann, *Private Power for the Public Good*, Wesleyan University Press, 1983.

pluralism and diversity, which are taken to be either inherently desirable or intimately related to our liberal democratic values. On this view, the charitable exemption is an indirect subsidy by which the government encourages organizations engaging in activities that promote the public good by providing the primary goods and meta-benefits I have outlined. This view, which is pretty much the foundation of present law, has several things to commend it. In the first place, it promises a single standard that unifies the field. Moreover, it is a standard that seems in accord with our intuitive notion of charity, in its broader, philanthropic meaning. The notion of "public benefit" corresponds nicely to love of humanity in general. Finally, the public benefit theory grafts the rationale of the tax exemption onto the more ancient root of the trust law definition of charity....

Antithesis: Bittker and Rahdert's Income Definition Theory

Problems with the traditional theory led Bittker and Rahdert to deny one of its central assumptions—the notion that the tax exemption is a subsidy—and to turn this negation into a positive theory of the exemption. If the tax exemption could be viewed not as a subsidy of some good—primary or otherwise—that the organization provides, but rather as a recognition that the revenue thus exempted is for some reason not appropriately included in the tax base, the problems of the traditional subsidy theory would be avoided. The search for a link between retained earnings and the purpose for favoring the tax-exempt organization would be less exigent, and criticisms of the general inefficiency of tax subsidies would be beside the point. Moreover, if charities' income is not measurable or not properly included in the tax base for reasons internal to the tax system, then the paradox of charities' being more favorably treated than their for-profit counterparts disappears, along with the need for a substantive standard of charitability.

After canvassing the early legislative history, Bittker and Rahdert conclude that charities and other nonprofits had been exempted primarily because the income tax could only logically be levied on activities undertaken for profit. Bittker and Rahdert accept this nascent rationale as essentially sound, and elaborate it into a full-blown exemption theory. They identify two fundamental problems with taxing the income of such organizations: first, their net income cannot be made to fit under any workable tax definition of income, and second, even if it could, no appropriate tax rate could be applied to them.

With respect to the definition of income, Bittker and Rahdert point to problems on both the revenue and the expenditure sides of the ledger. On the revenue side, the basic issue is whether to treat dues and contributions for tax purposes as the equivalent of business income or, alternatively, as gifts or capital contributions. If dues and contributions are treated as the latter, Bittker and Rahdert maintain, they are excluded from the computation of gross income under provisions of the tax code generally applicable to individuals and for-profit corporations.

On the disbursements side, one basic issue is whether expenditures for the conduct of the organization's program should be deductible as analogous to ordinary and necessary business expenses or nondeductible as not intended to make a profit; another is whether the current charitable deduction could be stretched or amended to cover such payments. If either of these basic issues is resolved in favor of deductibility, as Bittker and Rahdert suggest they should be, the taxable income of charitable organizations will essentially be reduced to zero, since all their assets are ultimately dedicated to their organizational programs. Thus, even if a workable definition of charitable organizations' income could be developed, the game would not be worth the candle.

Furthermore, Bittker and Rahdert argue that, even if a workable definition of their income could be developed, there would be insurmountable problems in finding the appropriate rate at which to tax it under either current theory of appropriate tax rates, the "benefit" or "ability to pay" theories. The primary reason for this difficulty is that the rate should ideally reflect the individual rates of the organizations' beneficiaries, many of whom are likely to be poor and thus "over-taxed" by any rate. Thus, if the game of taxing charities were to be played, the predictable losers would be their beneficiaries....

Hansmann's Capital Formation Theory

Hansmann's capital formation theory . . . rests on his descriptive account of the function of nonprofit firms in a capitalist economy in which for-profits are the norm. Hansmann argues that nonprofits tend to arise as the most efficient suppliers of goods and services when the normal for-profit provision fails for a particular set of reasons. Economic theory tells us that consumers usually know what goods and services they want to buy, that they are usually able to tell whether they got what they paid for, and that competition among for-profit suppliers usually ensures that they are paid the lowest possible price.

But sometimes these conditions are not met; sometimes the market fails. . . . Hansmann identifies three basic forms of contract failure. . . . [They include providing relief for the needy, as in a disaster relief situation, and complex personal services, such as education and healthcare. It is difficult to evaluate the effectiveness of the services in both of these cases. Contract failure also occurs with public goods, as in listener-sponsored radio, which create the opportunity for free riders to enjoy goods and services without paying for them. See Chapter 1, Part III.]

[I]n each of the three forms of contract failure he identifies, Hansmann maintains that the nonprofit form, with the nondistribution constraint as its essential characteristic, gives consumers the assurance that their difficulty in evaluating output will not be exploited to enhance distributable profits. From this descriptive analysis, it is tempting to draw the normative conclusion that nonprofits should be encouraged by the indirect subsidy of a tax exemption to develop in industries that exhibit contract failure. . .

Hansmann maintains that there is a less immediately apparent, but ultimately more satisfactory, reason for exempting the net revenues of such nonprofits from income taxation. This encouragement is needed because nonprofits, by definition forbidden to distribute net profits, are barred from a primary source of capital for expansion, equity investment. Moreover, they are likely to be unable to expand to an optimal size using either borrowed capital, donated capital, or retained earnings. The exemption of their income from taxation is an appropriate and effective form of encouragement, since it helps offset this disadvantage in access to capital by increasing nonprofits' ability to retain net earnings for expansion. If this is how nonprofits will use their enhanced net revenues, and if we accept the implicit normative premise that, other things being equal, efficient allocation of resources is to be encouraged, then this is an entirely appropriate conclusion....

Hall and Colombo's Donative Theory

To see how Hall and Colombo justify their donative theory in economic terms, we must return to Hansmann's argument that the greater efficiency of nonprofits in some industries is not itself a sufficient reason to warrant treating them more favorably under the tax laws than their for-profit counterparts. His reason for requiring something more is summed up in the rhetorical question "Why can consumers not be trusted to select nonprofit rather than proprietary producers on their own in those situations in which nonprofits are to be expected to offer more reliable service?" A critical assumption here is that, with the problems of contract failure redressed by nonprofits through the nondistribution constraint, their customers will purchase the amount of goods and services from them that maximizes their marginal utility, and hence a socially optimal level of production will occur. Patrons quite literally get what they pay for, and thus can be depended upon to buy as much as, and no more than, they want.

Hall and Columbo nicely isolate a flaw in this reasoning: while it may be true of commercial nonprofits, those financed by the sale of goods and services to those who consume them, it is probably not true of donative nonprofits, those through which patrons are buying goods or services to be consumed by strangers or by the public at large. Donative nonprofits may not produce an optimal level of output because wealth redistribution, an integral component of their output, is in some respects a public good. To the extent that donors' utility is tied to the receipt of benefits by others, rather than the act of giving itself, donors will be tempted to free-ride on the gifts of other donors. Accordingly, what the donors are really interested in buying—the provision of goods or services free or below cost to others—will probably be chronically undersupplied. Thus, in the case of donative nonprofits, Hall and Columbo conclude that subsidization is economically justified.

Hall and Colombo's analysis produces a justification for the tax exemption that is significantly narrower than Hansmann's with respect to both donative and commercial nonprofits. . . ., [I]n describing the implementation of their theory, Hall and Colombo insist that even donative organizations, in order to continue to qualify for the exemption, would have to receive an average of one third of their annual support from donations. This condition would bar the exemption of most private foundations, both operating and grant-making, and perhaps many heavily endowed and fee-supported public charities like museums and schools.

With respect to commercial nonprofits, the donativity theory calls for an even greater narrowing, compared both to Hansmann and to existing law. Hansmann would extend the exemption to a potentially large class of commercial nonprofits that supply complex goods and services that a substantial number of customers feel more comfortable buying from nonprofits on account of the difficulties of directly assessing quality themselves. Hall and Colombo, on the other hand, see no evidence of donations in the case of such commercial nonprofits, and thus find no room for them in an exemption designed to overcome the free-rider problems associated with donative financing.

Atkinson's Altruism Theory

My justification shares Hall and Colombo's focus on donations but differs in its scope and its ultimate rationale. To take the former first, I, unlike Hall and Colombo, find a donative element in commercial nonprofits, and in commercial nonprofits that supply garden variety goods, not just those goods that Hansmann identifies as complex and difficult for the consumer to evaluate. To find an element of donativity (or, as I prefer to call it, altruism) here, we must look on the supply side. How does capital get into such firms? If pooled by buyers, the resulting organization is a mutual benefit nonprofit or a cooperative, an organization in which the consumer-members are primarily interested in helping themselves.

But if the capital is provided by non-purchasers, that provision itself is altruistic. Whenever an organization with the potential to return profit to its founders is set up on a nonprofit basis, the founders have necessarily forgone that potential profit. The net revenues that otherwise would have been distributable to its founders are now committed to the purposes for which the organization was created. Moreover, as long as the organization continues to abide by the nondistribution constraint, its potential profits are available for subsidizing the purchases of its patrons. Thus, the founders' initial contribution of their potential earnings has an ongoing aspect; the organization embodies their altruism. As long as it remains nonprofit, this element of altruism remains, even if all other factors of production must be purchased at market prices. This makes for an exemption that is extremely, perhaps shockingly, broad; broader not only than Hansmann and Hall and Colombo, but also than present law.

WALZ v. TAX COMMISSION OF CITY OF NEW YORK

---

397 U.S. 664 (1970)

Mr. Chief Justice BURGER delivered the opinion of the Court.

Appellant, owner of real estate in Richmond County, New York, sought an injunction in the New York courts to prevent the New York City Tax Commission from granting property tax exemptions to religious organizations for religious properties used solely for religious worship. The exemption from state taxes is authorized by Art. 16, §1, of the New York Constitution, which provides in relevant part:

> Exemptions from taxation may be granted only by general laws. Exemptions may be altered or repealed except those exempting real or personal property used exclusively for religious, educational or charitable purposes as defined by law and owned by any corporation or association organized or conducted exclusively for one or more of such purposes and not operating for profit.

The essence of appellant's contention was that the New York City Tax Commission's grant of an exemption to church property indirectly requires the appellant to make a contribution to religious bodies and thereby violates provisions prohibiting establishment of religion under the First Amendment which under the Fourteenth Amendment is binding on the States.

Appellee's motion for summary judgment was granted and the Appellate Division of the New York Supreme Court, and the New York Court of Appeals affirmed. We noted probable jurisdiction…, and affirm.

II

The legislative purpose of a property tax exemption is neither the advancement nor the inhibition of religion; it is neither sponsorship nor hostility. New York, in common with the other States, has determined that certain entities that exist in a harmonious relationship to the community at large, and that foster its "moral or mental improvement," should not be inhibited in their activities by property taxation or the hazard of loss of those properties for nonpayment of taxes. It has not singled out one particular church or religious group or even churches as such; rather, it has granted exemption to all houses of religious worship within a broad class of property owned by nonprofit, quasi-public corporations which include hospitals, libraries, playgrounds, scientific, professional, historical, and patriotic groups. The State has an affirmative policy that considers these groups as beneficial and stabilizing influences in community life and finds this classification useful, desirable, and in the public interest. Qualification for tax exemption is not perpetual or immutable; some tax-exempt groups lose that status when their activities take them outside the classification and new entities can come into being and qualify for exemption.

Governments have not always been tolerant of religious activity, and hostility toward religion has taken many shapes and forms—economic, political, and sometimes harshly oppressive. Grants of exemption historically reflect the concern of authors of constitutions and statutes as to the latent dangers inherent in the imposition of property taxes; exemption constitutes a reasonable and balanced attempt to guard against those dangers. . . . We cannot read New York's statute as attempting to establish religion; it is simply sparing the exercise of religion from the burden of property taxation levied on private profit institutions.

We find it unnecessary to justify the tax exemption on the social welfare services or "good works" that some churches perform for parishioners and others—family counseling, aid to the elderly and the infirm, and to children. Churches vary substantially in the scope of such services; programs expand or contract according to resources and need. As public-sponsored programs enlarge, private aid from the church sector may diminish. The extent of social services may vary, depending on whether the church serves an urban or rural, a rich or poor constituency. To give emphasis to so variable an aspect of the work of religious bodies would introduce an element of governmental evaluation and standards as to the worth of particular social welfare programs, thus producing a kind of continuing day-to-day relationship which the policy of neutrality seeks to minimize. Hence, the use of a social welfare yardstick as a significant element to qualify for tax exemption could conceivably give rise to confrontations that could escalate to constitutional dimensions.

Determining that the legislative purpose of tax exemption is not aimed at establishing, sponsoring, or supporting religion does not end the inquiry, however. We must also be sure that the end result—the effect—is not an excessive government entanglement with religion. The test is inescapably one of degree. Either course, taxation of churches or exemption, occasions some degree of involvement with religion. Elimination of exemption would tend to expand the involvement of government by giving rise to tax valuation of church property, tax liens, tax foreclosures, and the direct confrontations and conflicts that follow in the train of those legal processes.

Granting tax exemptions to churches necessarily operates to afford an indirect economic benefit and also gives rise to some, but yet a lesser, involvement than taxing them. In analyzing either alternative, the questions are whether the involvement is excessive, and whether it is a continuing one calling for official and continuing surveillance leading to an impermissible degree of entanglement. Obviously a direct money subsidy would be a relationship pregnant with involvement and, as with most governmental grant programs, could encompass sustained and detailed administrative relationships for enforcement of statutory or administrative standards, but that is not this case. The hazards of churches supporting government are hardly less in their potential than the hazards of government supporting churches; each relationship carries some involvement rather than the desired insulation and separation. We cannot ignore the instances in history when church support of government led to the kind of involvement we seek to avoid.

The grant of a tax exemption is not sponsorship since the government does not transfer part of its revenue to churches but simply abstains from demanding that the church support the state. No one has ever suggested that tax exemption has converted libraries, art galleries, or hospitals into arms of the state or put employees "on the public payroll." There is no genuine nexus between tax exemption and establishment of religion.... The exemption creates only a minimal and remote involvement between church and state and far less than taxation of churches. It restricts the fiscal relationship between church and state, and tends to complement and reinforce the desired separation insulating each from the other.

Separation in this context cannot mean absence of all contact; the complexities of modern life inevitably produce some contact and the fire and police protection received by houses of religious worship are no more than incidental benefits accorded all persons or institutions within a State's boundaries, along with many other exempt organizations. The appellant has not established even an arguable quantitative correlation between the payment of an ad valorem property tax and the receipt of these municipal benefits.

All of the 50 States provide for tax exemption of places of worship, most of them doing so by constitutional guarantees. For so long as federal income taxes have had any potential impact on churches—over 75 years—religious organizations have been expressly exempt from the tax. Such treatment is an "aid" to churches no more and no less in principle than the real estate tax exemption granted by States. Few concepts are more deeply embedded in the fabric of our national life, beginning with pre-Revolutionary colonial times, than for the government to exercise at the very least this kind of benevolent neutrality toward churches and religious exercise generally so long as none was favored over others and none suffered interference.

It is significant that Congress, from its earliest days, has viewed the Religion Clauses of the Constitution as authorizing statutory real estate tax exemption to religious bodies.... It appears that at least up to 1885 this Court, reflecting more than a century of our history and uninterrupted practice, accepted without discussion the proposition that federal or state grants of tax exemption to churches were not a violation of the Religion Clauses of the First Amendment. As to the New York statute, we now confirm that view. Affirmed.

Mr. Justice BRENNAN, concurring.

[I]n my view, the history, purpose, and operation of real property tax exemptions for religious organizations must be examined to determine whether the Establishment Clause is breached by such exemptions....

History is particularly compelling in the present case because of the undeviating acceptance given religious tax exemptions from our earliest days as a Nation. Rarely, if ever has this Court considered the constitutionality of a practice for which the historical support is so overwhelming....

II

Government has two basic secular purposes for granting real property tax exemptions to religious organizations. First, these organizations are exempted because they, among a range of other private, nonprofit organizations contribute to the well-being of the community in a variety of nonreligious ways, and thereby bear burdens that would otherwise either have to be met by general taxation, or be left undone, to the detriment of the community....

Appellant seeks to avoid the force of this secular purpose of the exemptions by limiting his challenge to "exemptions from real property taxation to religious organizations on real property used exclusively for religious purposes." Appellant assumes, apparently, that church-owned property is used for exclusively religious purposes if it does not house a hospital, orphanage, weekday school, or the like. Any assumption that a church building itself is used for exclusively religious activities, however, rests on a simplistic view of ordinary church operations. As the appellee's brief cogently observes, "the public welfare activities and the sectarian activities of religious institutions are ... intertwined.... Often a particular church will use the same personnel, facilities and source of funds to carry out both its secular and religious activities."

Second, government grants exemptions to religious organizations because they uniquely contribute to the pluralism of American society by their religious activities. Government may properly include religious institutions among the variety of private, nonprofit groups that receive tax exemptions, for each group contributes to the diversity of association, viewpoint, and enterprise essential to a vigorous, pluralistic society.... To this end, New York extends its exemptions not only to religious and social service organizations but also to scientific, literary, bar, library, patriotic, and historical groups, and generally to institutions "organized exclusively for the moral or mental improvement of men and women." The very breadth of this scheme of exemptions negates any suggestion that the State intends to single out religious organizations for special preference. The scheme is not designed to inject any religious activity into a nonreligious context, as was the case with school prayers. No particular activity of a religious organization—for example, the propagation of its beliefs—is specially promoted by the exemptions. They merely facilitate the existence of a broad range of private, non-profit organizations, among them religious groups, by leaving each free to come into existence, then to flourish or wither, without being burdened by real property taxes.

III

Although governmental purposes for granting religious exemptions may be wholly secular, exemptions can nonetheless violate the Establishment Clause if they result in extensive state involvement with religion. Accordingly, those who urge the exemptions' unconstitutionality argue that exemptions are the equivalent of governmental subsidy of churches. General subsidies of religious activities would, of course, constitute impermissible state involvement with religion.

Tax exemptions and general subsidies, however, are qualitatively different. Though both provide economic assistance, they do so in fundamentally different ways. A subsidy involves the direct transfer of public monies to the subsidized enterprise and uses resources exacted from taxpayers as a whole.... Tax exemptions, accordingly, constitute mere passive state involvement with religion and not the affirmative involvement characteristic of outright governmental subsidy....

IV

Against the background of this survey of the history, purpose, and operation of religious tax exemptions, I must conclude that the exemptions do not "serve the essentially religious activities of religious institutions.".....

[*Editor's Note:* The concurring opinion of Mr. Justice HARLAN is omitted.]

Mr. Justice DOUGLAS, dissenting...

The financial support rendered here is to the church, the place of worship. A tax exemption is a subsidy. Is my Brother Brennan correct in saying that we would hold that state or federal grants to churches, say, to construct the edifice itself would be unconstitutional? What is the difference between that kind of subsidy and the present subsidy?...

Churches perform some functions that a State would constitutionally be empowered to perform. I refer to nonsectarian social welfare operations such as the care of orphaned children and the destitute and people who are sick. A tax exemption to agencies performing those functions would therefore be as constitutionally proper as the grant of direct subsidies to them. Under the First Amendment a State may not, however, provide worship if private groups fail to do so....

That is a major difference between churches on the one hand and the rest of the nonprofit organizations on the other. Government could provide or finance operas, hospitals, historical societies, and all the rest because they represent social welfare programs within the reach of the police power. In contrast, government may not provide or finance worship because of the Establishment Clause any more than it may single out "atheistic" or "agnostic" centers or groups and create or finance them.

The Brookings Institution, writing in 1933, before the application of the Establishment Clause of the First Amendment to the States, said about tax exemptions of religious groups:

Tax exemption, no matter what its form, is essentially a government grant or subsidy. Such grants would seem to be justified only if the purpose for which they are made is one for which the legislative body *would be equally willing to make* a direct appropriation from public funds equal to the amount of the exemption. This test would not be met except in the case where the exemption is granted to encourage certain activities of private interests, which, if not thus performed, would have to be assumed by the government at an expenditure at least as great as the value of the exemption. (Emphasis added.)

Since 1947, when the Establishment Clause was made applicable to the States, that report would have to state that the exemption would be justified only where "the legislative body could make" an appropriation for the cause. . . .

Direct financial aid to churches or tax exemptions to the church qua church is not, in my view, even arguably permitted.... If believers are entitled to public financial support, so are nonbelievers. A believer and nonbeliever under the present law are treated differently because of the articles of their faith. Believers are doubtless comforted that the cause of religion is being fostered by this legislation. Yet one of the mandates of the First Amendment is to promote a viable, pluralistic society and to keep government neutral, not only between sects, but also between believers and nonbelievers. The present involvement of government in religion may seem de minimis. But it is, I fear, a long step down the Establishment path. Perhaps I have been misinformed. But as I have read the Constitution and its philosophy, I gathered that independence was the price of liberty.

I conclude that this tax exemption is unconstitutional.

NOTES AND QUESTIONS

1. The *Walz* case concerned property tax exemption, not exemption from income tax, which §501(c)(3) addresses. For a discussion of whether charitable organizations should be exempt from property taxes, and if so, whether the standard should be the same as the standard for federal income tax exemption, see Part XI, Sec. C.

2. *Walz* also dealt with a religious organization. Are the reasons for granting tax exemptions for religious organizations the same as or different from the reasons for granting exemption to other charitable organizations?

3. Bruce Hopkins, an expert on tax exemption, believes that the decision to provide tax exemption to charitable organizations is a matter of political philosophy rather than tax policy. This decision reflects the pluralistic values of the United States because the tax-exempt sector provides an alternative to government. He has written, "the various provisions of the federal and state tax exemption system exist as a reflection of the affirmative policy of American government to refrain from inhibiting by taxation the beneficial activities of qualified tax-exempt organizations acting in community and other public interests." Bruce Hopkins, *Law of Tax-Exempt Organizations*, 11th ed. (Wiley Publishers, 2015), p. 12. *See also* Eric C. Chaffee, *Collaboration Theory: A Theory of the Charitable Tax Exempt Nonprofit Corporation*, 49 U.C. DAVIS LAW REVIEW __ (forthcoming, 2016), available at http://ssrn.com/abstract=2694366 ("charitable tax exempt nonprofit corporations are collaborations among the state governments, federal government, and individuals to promote the public good").

4. Do any of the theories described above adequately explain why charitable organizations are accorded tax exemption? Think of an art museum or, if you have created a fictional organization, consider that organization. Which, if any, of the theories explains why art museums are recognized as tax exempt? If you have created a nonprofit as part of this course, do any of the theories explain why your organization should be tax exempt?

5. Would it be possible to have different rationales for different types of charities? As you read the rest of the materials in this chapter, contemplate whether that is, in fact, the situation.

6. For further reading, see Philip T. Hackney, *What We Talk About When We Talk About Exemption*, 33 VA TAX REV 115 (2013); Miranda Fleisher, *Equality of Opportunity and the Charitable Tax Subsidies*, 91 B.U. L. REV. 603 (2011); Daniel Halperin, *Is Income Tax Exemption for Charities a Subsidy?* 64 TAX L. REV. 283 (2011); Evelyn Brody, *Of Sovereignty and Subsidy: Conceptualizing the Charity Tax Exemption*, 23 J. CORP. L. 585 (1998); Nina Crimm, *An Explanation of the Federal Income Tax Exemption for Charitable Organizations: A Theory of Risk Compensation*, 50 FLA. L. REV. 419 (1998);

III. INTRODUCTION TO SECTION 501(c)(3)

A large portion of the rest of this book will deal with IRC §501(c)(3), which is presented below. The emphasized portion details the purposes and activities of §501(c)(3) organizations. The introductory material also includes the Treasury Regulation that defines the word "charitable" and a discussion of the organizational and operational tests.

A. AN INTRODUCTION TO THE STATUTE AND ITS REGULATIONS

INTERNAL REVENUE CODE §501

(a) Exemption from taxation

An organization described in subsection (c) or (d) or section 401(a)[5] shall be exempt from taxation under this subtitle....

(c) List of exempt organizations

The following organizations are referred to in subsection (a):

(3) Corporations, and any community chest, fund, or foundation, *organized and operated* exclusively for *religious, charitable, scientific,*

---

[5] [Section 401(a) refers to employer-sponsored retirement plans for employees of state and local governments and certain tax-exempt entities.—*Ed.*]

testing for public safety, literary, or educational purposes, or to foster national or international amateur sports competition (but only if no part of its activities involve the provision of athletic facilities or equipment), or for the prevention of cruelty to children or animals, no part of the net earnings of which inures to the benefit of any private shareholder or individual, no substantial part of the activities of which is carrying on propaganda, or otherwise attempting, to influence legislation (except as otherwise provided in subsection (h)), and which does not participate in, or intervene in (including the publishing or distributing of statements), any political campaign on behalf of (or in opposition to) any candidate for public office (emphasis added).

TREASURY REGULATIONS §1.501(c)(3)-(2)

Charitable defined. The term charitable is used in section 501(c)(3) in its generally accepted legal sense and is, therefore, not to be construed as limited by the separate enumeration in section 501(c)(3) of other tax-exempt purposes which may fall within the broad outlines of charity as developed by judicial decisions. Such term includes: Relief of the poor and distressed or of the underprivileged; advancement of religion; advancement of education or science; erection or maintenance of public buildings, monuments, or works; lessening of the burdens of Government; and promotion of social welfare by organizations designed to accomplish any of the above purposes, or (i) to lessen neighborhood tensions; (ii) to eliminate prejudice and discrimination; (iii) to defend human and civil rights secured by law; or (iv) to combat community deterioration and juvenile delinquency. The fact that an organization which is organized and operated for the relief of indigent persons may receive voluntary contributions from the persons intended to be relieved will not necessarily prevent such organization from being exempt as an organization organized and operated exclusively for charitable purposes. The fact that an organization, in carrying out its primary purpose, advocates social or civic changes or presents opinion on controversial issues with the intention of molding public opinion or creating public sentiment to an acceptance of its views does not preclude such organization from qualifying under section 501(c)(3) so long as it is not an action organization of any one of the types described in paragraph (c)(3) of this section.

B. ORGANIZATIONAL AND OPERATIONAL TESTS

Section 501(c)(3) begins with language that requires the "nonprofit corporation, community chest, fund, or foundation" to be "organized and operated" for one or more of the statute's enumerated purposes. These words, "organized and operated," set forth the tests against which the other requirements of the statute are measured.

The first test, the organizational test, looks to the language of the governing documents (the articles of incorporation, articles of association, or trust instrument). It is not enough that the organization is run charitably; it must have specific language in its organizing documents. Section 501(c)(3)-1(b) of the Treasury Regulations requires the document to state the exempt purpose or purposes, agrees that the assets will continue to be used for exempt purposes upon dissolution, and refrains from stating anything that counters the requirements of the statute. Figure 4-1, from Form 1023, which is the form that an organization files in order to obtain §501(c)(3) recognition, illustrates these requirements for the organizational test.

Figure 4-1
Form 1023 Excerpt Illustrating the Organizational Test

Part III   **Required Provisions in Your Organizing Document**

The following questions are designed to ensure that when you file this application, your organizing document contains the required provisions to meet the organizational test under section 501(c)(3). Unless you can check the boxes in both lines 1 and 2, your organizing document does not meet the organizational test. DO NOT file this application until you have amended your organizing document. Submit your original and amended organizing documents (showing state filing certification if you are a corporation or an LLC) with your application.

1   Section 501(c)(3) requires that your organizing document state your exempt purpose(s), such as charitable, religious, educational, and/or scientific purposes. Check the box to confirm that your organizing document meets this requirement. Describe specifically where your organizing document meets this requirement, such as a reference to a particular article or section in your organizing document. Refer to the instructions for exempt purpose language. Location of Purpose Clause (Page, Article, and Paragraph): _____ □

2a   Section 501(c)(3) requires that upon dissolution of your organization, your remaining assets must be used exclusively for exempt purposes, such as charitable, religious, educational, and/or scientific purposes. Check the box on line 2a to confirm that your organizing document meets this requirement by express provision for the distribution of assets upon dissolution. If you rely on state law for your dissolution provision, do not check the box on line 2a and go to line 2c. □

2b   If you checked the box on line 2a, specify the location of your dissolution clause (Page, Article, and Paragraph). Do not complete line 2c if you checked box 2a. _____

2c   See the instructions for information about the operation of state law in your particular state. Check this box if you rely on operation of state law for your dissolution provision and indicate the state: _____ □

The second test, the operational test, looks at the way that the organization is run. In other words, appropriate language in the governing document is not sufficient to meet the requirements of §501(c)(3); the organization must also operate in a way that meets the statute's requirements. The Treasury Regulations require that the organization engage "primarily in activities which accomplish one or more of such exempt purposes specified in section 501(c)(3)." The organization must also meet the other requirements of the statute. Treas. Reg. §501(c)(3)-1(c). For most of the remainder of this chapter, we will examine permissible purposes and activities. At the beginning of an organization's life cycle, the organizational test is necessarily more important than the operational test. As the organization begins and maintains its operations, however, the operational test will come into play, and its requirements should be kept in mind as the organization plans its activities.

IV. "CHARITABLE" AND THE PUBLIC POLICY LIMITATION

The *Bob Jones* case, excerpted below, raises several questions about the purposes of tax exemption, the meaning of the term "charitable," the importance of public policy, and the respective roles of Congress, the courts, and the IRS. This case consolidated two similar cases, one concerning Bob Jones University's §501(c)(3) status, the other concerning the status of Goldsboro Christian Schools. Both were Christian educational institutions that made racially based decisions. Goldsboro excluded black students from its schools, while Bob Jones, which had originally also excluded blacks, admitted students of all races but banned interracial marriage or dating.

Until 1970, the IRS granted tax-exempt status to all private schools under §501(c)(3) without regard to their admissions policies, but in 1971, it announced it would no longer continue this policy. Revenue Ruling 71-447 provided:[6]

> Both the courts and the Internal Revenue Service have long recognized that the statutory requirement of being organized and operated exclusively for religious, charitable, ... or educational purposes was intended to express the basic common law concept [of charity].... All charitable trusts, educational or otherwise, are subject to the requirement that the purpose of the trust may not be illegal or contrary to public policy.... [T]he policy of the United States is to discourage discrimination in such schools.... Therefore, a school not having a racially nondiscriminatory policy as to students is not "charitable" within the common law concepts reflected in sections 170 and 501(c)(3) of the Code and in other relevant Federal statutes and accordingly does not qualify as an organization exempt from Federal income tax.

The IRS notified Bob Jones University of this new policy, and after some legal wrangling,[7] the IRS revoked Bob Jones University's exempt status in 1976, retroactive to 1970. The university paid federal unemployment taxes and then sued for a refund. The government counterclaimed for $489,675.59 plus interest, which it claimed equaled the unpaid federal taxes for the years 1971 through 1975.

The district court held for Bob Jones University. It found that the IRS did not have the power to revoke the university's exempt status, that it had violated its own rulings and procedures, and that it had infringed on the school's rights under the religion clauses of the First Amendment.

---

[6] ["A 'revenue ruling' is an interpretation by the Service that has been published in the Internal Revenue Bulletin. It is the conclusion of the Service on how the law is applied to a specific set of facts. Revenue rulings are published for the information and guidance of taxpayers, Service personnel, and other interested parties." Rev. Proc. 2010-4, 2010-1 I.R.B. 122. —*Ed.*]

[7] [Bob Jones had asked for administrative assurances that its exempt status would not be revoked and eventually sued to enjoin the IRS from revoking its tax-exempt status. The Supreme Court held that it could not review a tax case before the tax had been assessed or collected, and so Bob Jones University was left without reassurance. *Bob Jones University v. Simon*, 416 U.S. 725 (1974). —*Ed.*]

A divided Court of Appeals for the Fourth Circuit reversed, concluding that §501(c)(3) should be understood within the context of the common law of charitable trusts. An organization could not be considered "charitable" if it acted contrary to public policy. The court found that Bob Jones University's racial discrimination violated public policy and remanded the case for reinstatement of the government's counterclaim. *United States v. Bob Jones University*, 639 F.2d 147 (4th Cir. 1980).

Goldsboro Christian Schools, Inc. never received recognition of its §501(c)(3) status, and in 1972, the IRS found that it was not entitled to such status. The Goldsboro Christian Schools then paid unemployment taxes for one employee and sued for a refund. The district court held that the racially discriminatory practices, even if sincerely held, "violate clearly declared federal policy, and, therefore, must be denied the federal tax benefits flowing from qualification under Section 501(c)(3)," regardless of the reason for the discrimination. The Fourth Circuit affirmed, and the Supreme Court granted certiorari in both the *Bob Jones* and the *Greensboro Christian Schools* cases. Its opinion follows.

BOB JONES UNIVERSITY V. UNITED STATES

461 U.S. 574 (1983)

Chief Justice BURGER delivered the opinion of the Court.

We granted certiorari to decide whether petitioners, nonprofit private schools that prescribe and enforce racially discriminatory admissions standards on the basis of religious doctrine, qualify as tax-exempt organizations under §501(c)(3) of the Internal Revenue Code of 1954....

II

A

In Revenue Ruling 71-447, the IRS formalized the policy first announced in 1970, that §170 and §501(c)(3) embrace the common law "charity" concept. Under that view, to qualify for a tax exemption pursuant to §501(c)(3), an institution must show, first, that it falls within one of the eight categories expressly set forth in that section, and second, that its activity is not contrary to settled public policy.

Section 501(c)(3) provides that "[c]orporations ... organized and operated exclusively for religious, charitable ... or educational purposes" are entitled to tax exemption. Petitioners argue that the plain language of the statute guarantees them tax-exempt status. They emphasize the absence of any language in the statute expressly requiring all exempt organizations to be "charitable" in the common law sense, and they contend that the disjunctive "or" separating the categories in §501(c)(3) precludes such a reading. Instead, they argue that if an institution falls within one or more of the specified categories it is automatically entitled to exemption, without regard to whether it also qualifies as "charitable." The Court of Appeals rejected that contention and concluded that petitioners' interpretation of the statute "tears section 501(c)(3) from its roots." *United States v. Bob Jones University, supra*, 639 F.2d, at 151.

It is a well-established canon of statutory construction that a court should go beyond the literal language of a statute if reliance on that language would defeat the plain purpose of the statute....

Section 501(c)(3) therefore must be analyzed and construed within the framework of the Internal Revenue Code and against the background of the Congressional purposes. Such an examination reveals unmistakable evidence that, underlying all relevant parts of the Code, is the intent that entitlement to tax exemption depends on meeting certain common law standards of charity—namely, that an institution seeking tax-exempt status must serve a public purpose and not be contrary to established public policy.

This "charitable" concept appears explicitly in §170 of the Code.[8] That section contains a list of organizations virtually identical to that contained in §501(c)(3). It is apparent that Congress intended that list to have the same meaning in both sections. In §170, Congress used the list of organizations in defining the term "charitable contributions." On its face, therefore, §170 reveals that Congress' intention was to provide tax benefits to organizations serving charitable purposes. The form of §170 simply makes plain what common sense and history tell us: in enacting both §170 and §501(c)(3), Congress sought to provide tax benefits to charitable organizations, to encourage the development of private institutions that serve a useful public purpose or supplement or take the place of public institutions of the same kind.

Tax exemptions for certain institutions thought beneficial to the social order of the country as a whole, or to a particular community, are deeply rooted in our history, as in that of England. The origins of such exemptions lie in the special privileges that have long been extended to charitable trusts....

[*Editor's Note:* The Court quoted several cases between 1861 and 1878 that emphasized that charitable uses include those that serve the law and public policy.]

These statements clearly reveal the legal background against which Congress enacted the first charitable exemption statute in 1894: charities were to be given preferential treatment because they provide a benefit to society. . . .

A corollary to the public benefit principle is the requirement, long recognized in the law of trusts, that the purpose of a charitable trust may not be illegal or violate established public policy....

When the Government grants exemptions or allows deductions all taxpayers are affected; the very fact of the exemption or deduction for the donor means that other taxpayers can be said to be indirect and vicarious "donors." Charitable

---

[8] [Section 170 is the provision that permits tax-deductible donations to certain organizations. Its language tracks the language of §501(c)(3) in many respects. We will discuss §170 in Chapter 5 of this book.—*Ed.*]

exemptions are justified on the basis that the exempt entity confers a public benefit—a benefit which the society or the community may not itself choose or be able to provide, or which supplements and advances the work of public institutions already supported by tax revenues. History buttresses logic to make clear that, to warrant exemption under §501(c)(3), an institution must fall within a category specified in that section and must demonstrably serve and be in harmony with the public interest.[9] The institution's purpose must not be so at odds with the common community conscience as to undermine any public benefit that might otherwise be conferred.

B

We are bound to approach these questions with full awareness that determinations of public benefit and public policy are sensitive matters with serious implications for the institutions affected; a declaration that a given institution is not "charitable" should be made only where there can be no doubt that the activity involved is contrary to a fundamental public policy. But there can no longer be any doubt that racial discrimination in education violates deeply and widely accepted views of elementary justice.... Over the past quarter of a century, every pronouncement of this Court and myriad Acts of Congress and Executive Orders attest a firm national policy to prohibit racial segregation and discrimination in public education....

There can thus be no question that the interpretation of §170 and §501(c)(3) announced by the IRS in 1970 was correct.... Whatever may be the rationale for such private schools' policies, and however sincere the rationale may be, racial discrimination in education is contrary to public policy. Racially discriminatory educational institutions cannot be viewed as conferring a public benefit within the "charitable" concept discussed earlier, or within the Congressional intent underlying §170 and §501(c)(3).

C

Petitioners contend that, regardless of whether the IRS properly concluded that racially discriminatory private schools violate public policy, only Congress can alter the scope of §170 and §501(c)(3). Petitioners accordingly argue that the IRS overstepped its lawful bounds in issuing its 1970 and 1971 rulings.

Yet ever since the inception of the tax code, Congress has seen fit to vest in those administering the tax laws very broad authority to interpret those laws. In an area as complex as the tax system, the agency Congress vests with administrative responsibility must be able to exercise its authority to meet changing conditions and new problems. . . .

---

[9] [FN 19] The Court's reading of §501(c)(3) does not render meaningless Congress' action in specifying the eight categories of presumptively exempt organizations, as petitioners suggest. See Brief of Petitioner Goldsboro Christian Schools 18-24. To be entitled to tax-exempt status under §501(c)(3), an organization must first fall within one of the categories specified by Congress, and in addition must serve a valid charitable purpose.

Congress, the source of IRS authority, can modify IRS rulings it considers improper; and courts exercise review over IRS actions. In the first instance, however, the responsibility for construing the Code falls to the IRS. . . .

Guided, of course, by the Code, the IRS has the responsibility, in the first instance, to determine whether a particular entity is "charitable" for purposes of §170 and §501(c)(3). This in turn may necessitate later determinations of whether given activities so violate public policy that the entities involved cannot be deemed to provide a public benefit worthy of "charitable" status. We emphasize, however, that these sensitive determinations should be made only where there is no doubt that the organization's activities violate fundamental public policy.

On the record before us, there can be no doubt as to the national policy.... The correctness of the Commissioner's conclusion that a racially discriminatory private school "is not 'charitable' within the common law concepts reflected in ... the Code," Rev. Rul. 71-447, 1972-2 Cum. Bull., at 231, is wholly consistent with what Congress, the Executive and the courts had repeatedly declared before 1970. Indeed, it would be anomalous for the Executive, Legislative and Judicial Branches to reach conclusions that add up to a firm public policy on racial discrimination, and at the same time have the IRS blissfully ignore what all three branches of the Federal Government had declared.... Clearly an educational institution engaging in practices affirmatively at odds with this declared position of the whole government cannot be seen as exercising a "beneficial and stabilizing influenc[e] in community life," *Walz v. Tax Comm'n, supra*, 397 U.S., at 673, 90 S. Ct., at 1413, and is not "charitable," within the meaning of §170 and §501(c)(3). We therefore hold that the IRS did not exceed its authority when it announced its interpretation of §170 and §501(c)(3) in 1970 and 1971.

D

The actions of Congress since 1970 leave no doubt that the IRS reached the correct conclusion in exercising its authority. It is, of course, not unknown for independent agencies or the Executive Branch to misconstrue the intent of a statute; Congress can and often does correct such misconceptions, if the courts have not done so. Yet for a dozen years Congress has been made aware—acutely aware—of the IRS rulings of 1970 and 1971....

Ordinarily, and quite appropriately, courts are slow to attribute significance to the failure of Congress to act on particular legislation.... Here, however, we do not have an ordinary claim of legislative acquiescence. Only one month after the IRS announced its position in 1970, Congress held its first hearings on this precise issue. Equal Educational Opportunity: Hearings before the Senate Select Comm. on Equal Educational Opportunity, 91st Cong., 2d Sess. 1991 (1970). Exhaustive hearings have been held on the issue at various times since then....

Nonaction by Congress is not often a useful guide, but the nonaction here is significant. During the past 12 years, there have been no fewer than 13 bills introduced to overturn the IRS interpretation of §501(c)(3). Not one of these bills has emerged from any committee, although Congress has enacted numerous other amendments to §501 during this same period, including an amendment to

§501(c)(3) itself. Tax Reform Act of 1976, Pub. L. 94-455, §1313(a), 90 Stat. 1520, 1730 (1976). It is hardly conceivable that Congress—and in this setting, any Member of Congress—was not abundantly aware of what was going on. In view of its prolonged and acute awareness of so important an issue, Congress' failure to act on the bills proposed on this subject provides added support for concluding that Congress acquiesced in the IRS rulings of 1970 and 1971....

The evidence of Congressional approval of the policy embodied in Revenue Ruling 71-447 goes well beyond the failure of Congress to act on legislative proposals. Congress affirmatively manifested its acquiescence in the IRS policy when it enacted the present §501(i) of the Code, Act of October 20, 1976, Pub. L. 94-568, 90 Stat. 2697 (1976). That provision denies tax-exempt status to social clubs whose charters or policy statements provide for "discrimination against any person on the basis of race, color, or religion."[10] Both the House and Senate committee reports on that bill articulated the national policy against granting tax exemptions to racially discriminatory private clubs. S. Rep. No. 1318, 94th Cong., 2d Sess., 8 (1976); H.R. Rep. No. 1353, 94th Cong., 2d Sess., 8 (1976), U.S. Code Cong. & Admin. News 1976, p. 6051.

Even more significant is the fact that both reports focus on this Court's affirmance of *Green v. Connally, supra*, as having established that "discrimination on account of race is inconsistent with an *educational institution's* tax exempt status." S. Rep. No. 1318, *supra*, at 7-8 and n. 5; H.R. Rep. No. 1353, *supra*, at 8 and n. 5 (emphasis added), U.S. Code Cong. & Admin. News, p. 6058. These references in Congressional committee reports on an enactment denying tax exemptions to racially discriminatory private social clubs cannot be read other than as indicating approval of the standards applied to racially discriminatory private schools by the IRS subsequent to 1970, and specifically of Revenue Ruling 71-447.

III

Petitioners contend that, even if the Commissioner's policy is valid as to nonreligious private schools, that policy cannot constitutionally be applied to schools that engage in racial discrimination on the basis of sincerely held religious beliefs.[11] As to such schools, it is argued that the IRS construction of §170 and §501(c)(3) violates their free exercise rights under the Religion Clauses of the First Amendment. This contention presents claims not heretofore considered by this Court in precisely this context.

---

[10] [FN 26] Prior to the introduction of this legislation, a three-judge district court had held that segregated social clubs were entitled to tax exemptions. *McGlotten v. Connally*, 338 F. Supp. 448 (D.D.C. 1972). Section 501(i) was enacted primarily in response to that decision. See S. Rep. No. 1318, 94th Cong., 2d Sess., 7-8 (1976); H.R. Rep. No. 1353, 94th Cong., 2d Sess., 8 (1976), U.S. Code Cong. & Admin. News 1976, p. 6051.

[11] [FN 28] The District Court found, on the basis of a full evidentiary record, that the challenged practices of petitioner Bob Jones University were based on a genuine belief that the Bible forbids interracial dating and marriage. 468 F. Supp., at 894. We assume, as did the District Court, that the same is true with respect to petitioner Goldsboro Christian Schools. See 436 F. Supp., at 1317.

This Court has long held the Free Exercise Clause of the First Amendment an absolute prohibition against governmental regulation of religious beliefs. . . . As interpreted by this Court, moreover, the Free Exercise Clause provides substantial protection for lawful conduct grounded in religious belief.... However, "[n]ot all burdens on religion are unconstitutional.... The state may justify a limitation on religious liberty by showing that it is essential to accomplish an overriding governmental interest." *United States v. Lee*, 455 U.S. (1982) (citations omitted)....

On occasion this Court has found certain governmental interests so compelling as to allow even regulations prohibiting religiously based conduct. . . . Denial of tax benefits will inevitably have a substantial impact on the operation of private religious schools, but will not prevent those schools from observing their religious tenets.

The governmental interest at stake here is compelling. As discussed in Part II(B), *supra*, the Government has a fundamental, overriding interest in eradicating racial discrimination in education,[12] discrimination that prevailed, with official approval, for the first 165 years of this Nation's history. That governmental interest substantially outweighs whatever burden denial of tax benefits places on petitioners' exercise of their religious beliefs. The interests asserted by petitioners cannot be accommodated with that compelling governmental interest, ... and no "less restrictive means," ... are available to achieve the governmental interest.[13]

IV

The remaining issue is whether the IRS properly applied its policy to these petitioners. Petitioner Goldsboro Christian Schools admits that it "maintain[s] racially discriminatory policies," Brief of Petitioner, Goldsboro Christian Schools, No. 81-1, at 10, but seeks to justify those policies on grounds we have fully discussed. The IRS properly denied tax-exempt status to Goldsboro Christian Schools.

Petitioner Bob Jones University, however, contends that it is not racially discriminatory. It emphasizes that it now allows all races to enroll, subject only to its restrictions on the conduct of all students, including its prohibitions of association between men and women of different races, and of interracial

---

[12] [FN 29] We deal here only with religious schools—not with churches or other purely religious institutions; here, the governmental interest is in denying public support to racial discrimination in education. As noted earlier, racially discriminatory schools "exer[t] a pervasive influence on the entire educational process," outweighing any public benefit that they might otherwise provide.

[13] [FN 30] Bob Jones University also contends that denial of tax exemption violates the Establishment Clause by preferring religions whose tenets do not require racial discrimination over those which believe racial intermixing is forbidden. . . . The IRS policy at issue here is founded on a "neutral, secular basis," and does not violate the Establishment Clause. In addition, as the Court of Appeals noted, "the uniform application of the rule to all religiously operated schools *avoids* the necessity for a potentially entangling inquiry into whether a racially restrictive practice is the result of sincere religious belief."*United States v. Bob Jones Univ.*, 639 F.2d 147, 155 (CA4 1980) (emphasis in original).

marriage. Although a ban on intermarriage or interracial dating applies to all races, decisions of this Court firmly establish that discrimination on the basis of racial affiliation and association is a form of racial discrimination.... We therefore find that the IRS properly applied Revenue Ruling 71-447 to Bob Jones University.[14]

The judgments of the Court of Appeals are, accordingly, *Affirmed.*

Justice POWELL, concurring in part and concurring in the judgment.

I join the Court's judgment, along with part III of its opinion holding that the denial of tax exemptions to petitioners does not violate the First Amendment. I write separately because I am troubled by the broader implications of the Court's opinion with respect to the authority of the Internal Revenue Service (IRS) and its construction of §§170(c) and 501(c)(3) of the Internal Revenue Code.

I

. . . [T]here is force in Justice Rehnquist's argument that §§170(c) and 501(c)(3) should be construed as setting forth the only criteria Congress has established for qualification as a tax-exempt organization. Indeed, were we writing prior to the history detailed in the Court's opinion, this could well be the construction I would adopt. But there has been a decade of acceptance that is persuasive in the circumstances of this case, and I conclude that there are now sufficient reasons for accepting the IRS's construction of the Code as proscribing tax exemptions for schools that discriminate on the basis of race as a matter of policy. . . .

The statutory terms are not self-defining, and it is plausible that in some instances an organization seeking a tax exemption might act in a manner so clearly contrary to the purposes of our laws that it could not be deemed to serve the enumerated statutory purposes. And, as the Court notes, if any national policy is sufficiently fundamental to constitute such an overriding limitation on the availability of tax-exempt status under §501(c)(3), it is the policy against racial discrimination in education. Finally, and of critical importance for me, the subsequent actions of Congress present "an unusually strong case of legislative acquiescence in and ratification by implication of the [IRS's] 1970 and 1971 rulings" with respect to racially discriminatory schools. Ante, at 2033. In particular, Congress' enactment of §501(i) in 1976 is strong evidence of agreement with these particular IRS rulings.

II

I therefore concur in the Court's judgment that tax-exempt status under §§170(c) and 501(c)(3) is not available to private schools that concededly are

---

[14] [FN 32] Bob Jones University also argues that the IRS policy should not apply to it because it is entitled to exemption under §501(c)(3) as a "religious" organization, rather than as an "educational" institution. The record in this case leaves no doubt, however, that Bob Jones University is both an educational institution and a religious institution. As discussed previously, the IRS policy properly extends to all private schools, including religious schools. See n. 29, *supra.* The IRS policy thus was properly applied to Bob Jones University.

racially discriminatory. I do not agree, however, with the Court's more general explanation of the justifications for the tax exemptions provided to charitable organizations. The Court states:

> Charitable exemptions are justified on the basis that the exempt entity confers a public benefit—a benefit which the society or the community may not itself choose or be able to provide, or which supplements and advances the work of public institutions already supported by tax revenues.... The institution's purpose must not be so at odds with the common community conscience as to undermine any public benefit that might otherwise be conferred.

With all respect, I am unconvinced that the critical question in determining tax-exempt status is whether an individual organization provides a clear "public benefit" as defined by the Court. Over 106,000 organizations filed §501(c)(3) returns in 1981.... I find it impossible to believe that all or even most of those organizations could prove that they "demonstrably serve and [are] in harmony with the public interest" or that they are "beneficial and stabilizing influences in community life." Nor am I prepared to say that petitioners, because of their racially discriminatory policies, necessarily contribute nothing of benefit to the community. It is clear from the substantially secular character of the curricula and degrees offered that petitioners provide educational benefits.

Even more troubling to me is the element of conformity that appears to inform the Court's analysis. The Court asserts that an exempt organization must "demonstrably serve and be in harmony with the public interest," must have a purpose that comports with "the common community conscience," and must not act in a manner "affirmatively at odds with [the] declared position of the whole government." Taken together, these passages suggest that the primary function of a tax-exempt organization is to act on behalf of the Government in carrying out governmentally approved policies. In my opinion, such a view of §501(c)(3) ignores the important role played by tax exemptions in encouraging diverse, indeed often sharply conflicting, activities and viewpoints. As Justice Brennan has observed, private, nonprofit groups receive tax exemptions because "each group contributes to the diversity of association, viewpoint, and enterprise essential to a vigorous, pluralistic society." *Walz, supra*, at 689, 90 S. Ct., at 1421 (Brennan, J., concurring). Far from representing an effort to reinforce any perceived "common community conscience," the provision of tax exemptions to nonprofit groups is one indispensable means of limiting the influence of governmental orthodoxy on important areas of community life. . . .

I do not suggest that these considerations always are or should be dispositive. Congress, of course, may find that some organizations do not warrant tax-exempt status. In this case I agree with the Court that Congress has determined that the policy against racial discrimination in education should override the countervailing interest in permitting unorthodox private behavior.

I would emphasize, however, that the balancing of these substantial interests is for *Congress* to perform. I am unwilling to join any suggestion that the Internal Revenue Service is invested with authority to decide which public policies are sufficiently "fundamental" to require denial of tax exemptions. Its business is to administer laws designed to produce revenue for the Government, not to promote "public policy."... As Justice Blackmun has noted,

> where the philanthropic organization is concerned, there appears to be little to circumscribe the almost unfettered power of the Commissioner. This may be very well so long as one subscribes to the particular brand of social policy the Commissioner happens to be advocating at the time..., but application of our tax laws should not operate in so fickle a fashion. Surely, social policy in the first instance is a matter for legislative concern....

III

The Court's decision upholds IRS Revenue Ruling 71-447, and thus resolves the question whether tax-exempt status is available to private schools that openly maintain racially discriminatory admissions policies. There no longer is any justification for *Congress* to hesitate—as it apparently has—in articulating and codifying its desired policy as to tax exemptions for discriminatory organizations. Many questions remain, such as whether organizations that violate other policies should receive tax-exempt status under §501(c)(3). These should be legislative policy choices. It is not appropriate to leave the IRS "on the cutting edge of developing national policy."... The contours of public policy should be determined by Congress, not by judges or the IRS.

Justice REHNQUIST, dissenting.

The Court points out that there is a strong national policy in this country against racial discrimination. To the extent that the Court states that Congress in furtherance of this policy could deny tax-exempt status to educational institutions that promote racial discrimination, I readily agree. But, unlike the Court, I am convinced that Congress simply has failed to take this action and, as this Court has said over and over again, regardless of our view on the propriety of Congress' failure to legislate we are not constitutionally empowered to act for them.

In approaching this statutory construction question the Court quite adeptly avoids the statute it is construing. This I am sure is no accident, for there is nothing in the language of §501(c)(3) that supports the result obtained by the Court....

With undeniable clarity, Congress has explicitly defined the requirements for §501(c)(3) status. An entity must be (1) a corporation, or community chest, fund, or foundation, (2) organized for one of the eight enumerated purposes, (3) operated on a nonprofit basis, and (4) free from involvement in lobbying activities and political campaigns. Nowhere is there to be found some additional, undefined public policy requirement.

The Court first seeks refuge from the obvious reading of §501(c)(3) by turning to §170 of the Internal Revenue Code which provides a tax deduction for contributions made to §501(c)(3) organizations.... The Court seizes the words "charitable contribution" and with little discussion concludes that "[o]n its face, therefore, §170 reveals that Congress' intention was to provide tax benefits to organizations serving charitable purposes," intimating that this implies some unspecified common law charitable trust requirement.

The Court would have been well advised to look to subsection (c) where, as §170(a)(1) indicates, Congress has defined a "charitable contribution."...

Plainly, §170(c) simply tracks the requirements set forth in §501(c)(3). Since §170 is no more than a mirror of §501(c)(3) and, as the Court points out, §170 followed §501(c)(3) by more than two decades, *ante*, at 2026, n. 10, it is at best of little usefulness in finding the meaning of §501(c)(3).

Making a more fruitful inquiry, the Court next turns to the legislative history of §501(c)(3) and finds that Congress intended in that statute to offer a tax benefit to organizations that Congress believed were providing a public benefit. I certainly agree. But then the Court leaps to the conclusion that this history is proof Congress intended that an organization seeking §501(c)(3) status "must fall within a category specified in that section *and must demonstrably serve and be in harmony with the public interest.*" To the contrary, I think that the legislative history of §501(c)(3) unmistakably makes clear that *Congress has decided* what organizations are serving a public purpose and providing a public benefit within the meaning of §501(c)(3) and has clearly set forth in §501(c)(3) the characteristics of such organizations. In fact, there are few examples which better illustrate Congress' effort to define and redefine the requirements of a legislative act....

One way to read the opinion handed down by the Court today leads to the conclusion that this long and arduous refining process of §501(c)(3) was certainly a waste of time, for when enacting the original 1894 statute Congress intended to adopt a common law term of art, and intended that this term of art carry with it all of the common law baggage which defines it. Such a view, however, leads also to the unsupportable idea that Congress has spent almost a century adding illustrations simply to clarify an already defined common law term.

Another way to read the Court's opinion leads to the conclusion that even though Congress has set forth *some* of the requirements of a §501(c)(3) organization, it intended that the IRS additionally require that organizations meet a higher standard of public interest, not stated by Congress, but to be determined and defined by the IRS and the courts. This view I find equally unsupportable. Almost a century of statutory history proves that Congress itself intended to decide what §501(c)(3) requires.... The IRS certainly is empowered to adopt regulations for the enforcement of these specified requirements, and the courts have authority to resolve challenges to the IRS's exercise of this power, but Congress has left it to neither the IRS nor the courts to select or add to the requirements of §501(c)(3). . . .

But simply because I reject the Court's heavy-handed creation of the requirement that an organization seeking §501(c)(3) status must "serve and be in harmony with the public interest," does not mean that I would deny to the IRS the usual authority to adopt regulations further explaining what Congress meant by the term "educational." The IRS has fully exercised that authority in 26 CFR. §1.501(c)(3)-1(d)(3)....

I have little doubt that neither the "Fagin School for Pickpockets" nor a school training students for guerrilla warfare and terrorism in other countries would meet the definitions contained in the regulations.

Prior to 1970, when the charted course was abruptly changed, the IRS had continuously interpreted §501(c)(3) and its predecessors in accordance with the view I have expressed above....

In 1970 the IRS was sued by parents of black public school children seeking to enjoin the IRS from according tax-exempt status under §501(c)(3) to private schools in Mississippi that discriminated against blacks. The IRS answered, consistent with its long standing position, by maintaining a lack of authority to deny the tax-exemption if the schools met the specified requirements of §501(c)(3). Then ... in the face of a preliminary injunction, the IRS changed its position and adopted the view of the plaintiffs. . . .

Perhaps recognizing the lack of support in the statute itself, or in its history, for the 1970 IRS change in interpretation, the Court finds that "[t]he actions of Congress since 1970 leave no doubt that the IRS reached the correct conclusion in exercising its authority," concluding that there is "an unusually strong case of legislative acquiescence in and ratification by implication of the 1970 and 1971 rulings." The Court relies first on several bills introduced to overturn the IRS interpretation of §501(c)(3). But we have said before, and it is equally applicable here, that this type of congressional inaction is of virtually no weight in determining legislative intent. These bills and related hearings indicate little more than that a vigorous debate has existed in Congress concerning the new IRS position....

This Court continuously has been hesitant to find ratification through inaction. . . . . Few cases would call for more caution in finding ratification by acquiescence than the present one. The new IRS interpretation is not only far less than a long standing administrative policy, it is at odds with a position maintained by the IRS, and unquestioned by Congress, for several decades prior to 1970. The interpretation is unsupported by the statutory language, it is unsupported by legislative history, the interpretation has led to considerable controversy in and out of Congress, and the interpretation gives to the IRS a broad power which until now Congress had kept for itself. Where in addition to these circumstances Congress has shown time and time again that it is ready to enact positive legislation to change the tax code when it desires, this Court has no business finding that Congress has adopted the new IRS position by failing to enact legislation to reverse it. . . .

Petitioners are each organized for the "instruction or training of the individual for the purpose of improving or developing his capabilities," 26 CFR §1.501(c)(3)-1(d)(3), and thus are organized for "educational purposes" within the meaning of §501(c)(3). Petitioners' nonprofit status is uncontested. There is no indication that either petitioner has been involved in lobbying activities or political campaigns. Therefore, it is my view that unless and until Congress affirmatively amends §501(c)(3) to require more, the IRS is without authority to deny petitioners §501(c)(3) status. For this reason, I would reverse the Court of Appeals.

NOTES AND QUESTIONS

1. After the *Bob Jones* case, the IRS issued guidelines that require §501(c)(3) schools to demonstrate a racially nondiscriminatory policy in their governing documents and materials provided to the public. Schools must actively publicize their nondiscriminatory policies and keep records showing their compliance with these rules. *See* Rev. Proc. 75-50, 1975-2 C.B. 578. Few organizations have lost their tax exemption as a result of this limitation, however. Calhoun Academy in South Carolina lost its tax exemption because it failed to show that it carried out, in good faith, its nondiscriminatory policy toward black schoolchildren. *Calhoun Academy v. Commissioner*, 94 T.C. 284 (1990). At least two other private schools have had their exemption revoked for similar reasons. *See* PLR 200909064; PLR 201033039.[15] The IRS also determined that a privately administered trust cannot be recognized as exempt if its governing instrument restricts beneficiaries to "worthy and deserving white persons over the age of sixty who were residents of a certain city and did not have sufficient income from other sources for their comfort and support." PLR 8910001. How this public policy limitation extends to other situations remains uncertain, however. The following questions will help you define the parameters of this limitation.

2. The Kamehameha Schools in Hawaii give preference in admissions to applicants of Native Hawaiian ancestry. After *Bob Jones*, should they lose their §501(c)(3) tax-exempt status on public policy grounds? The Kamehameha Schools' admissions policy was at the center of a federal antidiscrimination suit, which was settled before it went to the Supreme Court. In 2006, the Ninth Circuit determined by a vote of 8-7 that the policy did not violate 42 U.S.C. §1981. *Doe v. Kamehameha Schools/Bernice Pauahi Bishop Estate*, 470 F.3d 827 (9th Cir. 2006), *cert. dismissed*, 550 U.S. 931 (2007). Is it possible that the organization (which receives no federal funds) does not deserve its tax exemption, even if the policy is valid under 42 U.S.C. §1981? If the case had been overturned on appeal, would it automatically follow that the Kamehameha Schools should lose its tax exemption on public policy grounds?

---

[15] PLR stands for "private letter ruling." The IRS explains its meaning as follows:

> A "letter ruling" is a written statement issued to a taxpayer by the Service's Employee Plans Technical office or Exempt Organizations Technical office that interprets and applies the tax laws or any nontax laws applicable to employee benefit plans and exempt organizations to the taxpayer's specific set of facts. Once issued, a letter ruling may be revoked or modified for any number of reasons, as explained in section 13 of this revenue procedure, unless it is accompanied by a "closing agreement."

Rev. Proc. 2010-4, 2010-2 I.R.B. 234.

3. Should *Bob Jones* be extended to organizations that engage in gender discrimination or sexual orientation discrimination? Does the Supreme Court's decision in *Obergefell v. Hodges,* 135 S. Ct. 2584, 83 U.S.L.W. 4592 (2015) shed light on this question? It held that the Due Process and Equal Protection clauses of the 14th Amendment protect the right for same-sex couples to marry. Does it make a difference if the nonprofit is a school or a religious organization? *See* Laurie Goodstain and Adam Liptak, *Schools Fear Gay Marriage Ruling Could End Tax Exemptions* NY TIMES (June 24, 2015); Kat Lucero, *Bob Jones Decision Difficult to Apply to Same-Sex Marriage Case,* 75 EXEMPT ORG. TAX REV. 674 (2015).

4. In a footnote that is not included in the *Bob Jones* excerpt above, the majority wrote: "[A] band of former military personnel might well set up a school for intensive training of subversives for guerrilla warfare and terrorism in other countries; in the abstract, that 'school' would qualify as an 'educational' institution. Surely Congress had no thought of affording such an unthinking, wooden meaning to §170 and § 501(c)(3) as to provide tax benefits to 'educational' organizations that do not serve a public, charitable purpose."[16] The dissent responded, "I have little doubt that neither the 'Fagin School for Pickpockets' nor a school training students for guerrilla warfare and terrorism in other countries would meet the definitions contained in the regulations." Do you agree with either the majority or the dissent? Why did you come to this conclusion? What if the organization was doing good work, but some of its funds got into the hands of terrorists? What if the goal is to teach individuals who have been associated with terrorism better ways of dealing with conflict, such as mediation?

5. For further reading on the public policy limitation, see Amy Moore, *Rife with Latent Power: Exploring the Reach of the IRS to Determine Tax-Exempt Status According to Public Policy Rationale in an Era of Judicial Deference,* 56 S. TEX. L. REV. 117, (2015); David A. Brennen, *The Power of the Treasury: Racial Discrimination, Public Policy, and "Charity" in Contemporary Society,* 33 U.C. DAVIS L. REV. 389 (2000); Miriam Galston, *Public Policy Constraints on Charitable Organizations,* 3 VA. TAX REV. 291 (1984); David A. Brennen, *Race-Conscious Affirmative Action by Tax-Exempt 501(c)(3) Corporations After* Grutter *and* Gratz, 77 ST. JOHN'S L. REV. 711 (2003); Johnny Rex Buckles, *Reforming the Public Policy Doctrine,* 53 KAN. L. REV. 397 (2005).

6. For further reading on the *Bob Jones* case, see Olatunde Johnson, *The Story of Bob Jones University v. United States,* in STATUTORY INTERPRETATION STORIES (William Eskridge & Elizabeth Grant eds., Foundation Press 2010);

---

[16] *Bob Jones v. U.S.,* 461 U.S. 574, 591, n.18 (1983).

Neal Devins, *Symposium: The Canon(s) of Constitutional Law: On Casebooks and Canons, or Why Bob Jones University Will Never Be Part of the Constitutional Law Canon,* 7 CONST. COMMENT. 285 (2000); Douglas Laycock, *Observation, Tax Exemptions for Racially Discriminatory Religious Schools,* 60 TEX. L. REV. 249 (1982).

V. SECTION 501(c)(3) PURPOSES: HEALTH CARE

Although health care is not one of the enumerated purposes for which §501(c)(3) status is conferred, many hospitals and medical clinics are organized as §501(c)(3)s. Traditionally, hospitals offered a fair amount of charity care, and therefore, they qualified as having a "charitable" purpose. *See* Rev. Rul. 56-185, 1956-1 C.B. 202. Once Medicare and Medicaid become prevalent, however, and it appeared that charity care might no longer be needed, the IRS articulated the "community benefit" standard, which remains important today. Rev. Rul. 69-545, 1969-2 C.B. 117. The *IHC Health Plans* case, which follows, describes this standard and builds upon it. In 2010, Congress refined that standard further by adding §501(r) to the tax code, a portion of which is reproduced in Part A below.

This community benefit standard has its critics. They claim that many, if not most, §501(c)(3) hospitals act very much like their for-profit counterparts and provide very little charitable care. A study of California hospitals between 2011 and 2014 estimated that nonprofit hospitals dedicated, on average, 1.9% of their revenues on charity care. This figure compared to 1.4% in for-profit hospitals.[17] An earlier study by the IRS found similar percentages when uncompensated care (uncollected bills and discounted services to privately or governmentally insured patients) was removed from the tally.[18] Compounding these statistics have been stories of callous treatment of patients who are unable to pay their bills and exorbitant salaries of doctors and hospital administrators.[19] Critics decry the lack of a definitive definition of "public benefit" and claim that society is not receiving sufficient public benefit to justify the estimated $24.6 billion[20] that tax-exempt hospitals save in state and local taxes each year.

---

[17] Erica Valdovinos, Sidney Le, and Renee Y. Hsia, *In California, Not-For-Profit Hospitals Spent More Operating Expenses on Charity Care Than For-Profit Hospitals Spent,* 34 HEALTH AFF. 1296 (2015).

[18] IRS Exempt Organization Hospital Study, Final Report, February 2009.

[19] *See, e.g.,* Jay Hancock, *Senate Critic of Nonprofit Hospitals Blasts CEO Bonuses,* ST. LOUIS POST DISPATCH (June 13, 2013); *See also,* "Sen. Chuck Grassley of Iowa is asking questions of a Missouri non-profit hospital that reportedly sues large numbers of low-income people over treatment bills instead of working with patients to offer reasonable payment plans for medical care," News Release, Jan. 15, 2015, http://www.grassley.senate.gov/news/news-releases/grassley-seeks-answers-non-profit-hospital-over-billing-lawsuits, accessed May 9, 2016.

[20] Sara Rosenbaum, David A. Kindig, Jie Bao, Maureen K. Byrnes, and Colin O'Laughlin, *The Value of the Nonprofit Hospital Tax Exemption Was $24.6 Billion in 2011,* 34 HEALTH AFFAIRS 1225 (2015).

Sec. 501(r) was enacted to curb some of these problems and to provide data that will allow for a stronger standard for "community benefit." Several states have gone even further than their federal counterparts and are denying state tax exemption for certain hospitals altogether. Part B discusses this development, and Part C then examines the public policy implications of the community benefit standard and tax exemption for hospitals in general.

A. HEALTH CARE AS A CHARITABLE PURPOSE

IHC HEALTH PLANS, INC. V. COMM'R OF INTERNAL REVENUE

325 F.3d 1188 (10th Cir. 2003)

TACHA, Chief Circuit Judge.

[*Editor's Note:* The issue in this case was whether three health maintenance organizations (HMOs) deserved recognition as §501(c)(3) charitable organizations. An HMO is a type of health insurance designed to reduce health costs by restricting the medical providers to a specific group and requiring the primary care doctor to make all referrals. The HMOs in question were IHC Health Plans ("Health Plans"), a state-licensed HMO[21], and its subsidiaries, IHC Care ("Care") and IHC Group ("Group"), both of which carried on functions that could not legally be performed by the other or by their parent corporation.

Health Plans was a dominant force in the Utah insurance market. In 1999, it enrolled approximately 20% of Utah's total population in its various plans. It also enrolled 50% of Utah's total Medicaid population in its Medicaid-managed care program. It determined premiums for small employer groups by adjusting its rates for risk factors such as age and gender, and it used a "past claims experience" method for larger employers.

Care and Group offered their plans to employers with more than 100 employees and determined their premiums. They also using an adjusted community rating methodology, as required for all federally qualified HMOs.

After the IRS revoked Health Plans's tax exemption under §501(c)(3) and issued a final adverse determination letter denying §501(c)(3) recognition for Care and Group, the three HMOs brought suit in the U.S. Tax Court, seeking a declaratory judgment reversing the commissioner's adverse determinations. The Tax Court affirmed the commissioner's conclusions, and this appeal followed.]

B. Overview of Applicable Law

"Our analysis must start from the proposition that exemptions from income tax are a matter of legislative grace." *Mutual Aid Ass'n of Church of the Brethren*

---

[21] Health Plans was also a preferred provider organization (PPO), another type of insurance company that encourages its customers to use doctors within its network.

v. United States, 759 F.2d 792, 794 (10th Cir. 1985) (citation omitted). Thus, we must narrowly construe exemptions from taxation.... In this case, petitioners seek exemption under 26 U.S.C. §501(c)(3).

Under section 501(c)(3), an organization must meet three requirements in order to qualify for tax exemption: "(1) the corporation must be organized and operated exclusively for exempt purposes; (2) no part of the corporation's net earnings may inure to the benefit of any shareholder or individual;[22] and (3) the corporation must not engage in political campaigns or, to a substantial extent, in lobbying activities."... In this case, the sole question we must consider is whether Health Plans, Care, and Group operated exclusively for exempt purposes within the meaning of section 501(c)(3).

C. Whether Health Plans, Care, and Group Operated for a Charitable Purpose

This inquiry requires us to address two basic questions. First, we must consider whether the purpose proffered by petitioners qualifies as a "charitable" purpose under section 501(c)(3). "The term 'charitable' is used in section 501(c)(3) in its generally accepted legal sense and is ... not to be construed as limited by the separate enumeration in section 501(c)(3)." 26 C.F.R. §1.501(c)(3)-1(d)(2). An organization will not be considered charitable, however, "unless it serves a *public rather than a private interest*." 26 C.F.R. §1.501(c)(3)-1(d)(1)(ii) (emphasis added).

Second, we must determine whether petitioners in fact operated *primarily* for this purpose....

In this case, the Tax Court concluded that "the promotion of health for the benefit of the community is a charitable purpose," but found that neither Health Plans, Care, nor Group operated primarily to benefit the community. For the reasons set forth below, we agree....

1. The Promotion of Health as a Charitable Purpose

In defining "charitable," our analysis must focus on whether petitioners' activities conferred a *public* benefit. 26 C.F.R. §1.501(c)(3)-1(d)(1)(ii) ("An organization is not organized or operated exclusively for [an exempt purpose] ... unless it serves a public rather than a private interest."). The public-benefit requirement highlights the *quid pro quo* nature of tax exemptions: the public is willing to relieve an organization from the burden of taxation in exchange for the public benefit it provides. ... As the Supreme Court has recognized, "[c]haritable exemptions are justified on the basis that the exempt entity confers a *public benefit*—a benefit which the society or the community may not itself choose or be able to provide, or which supplements and advances the work of public institutions already supported by tax revenues." *Bob Jones Univ. v. United States*, 461 U.S. 574, 591 (1983) (emphasis added).

---

[22] [FN 9] This element can be viewed as a corollary to the public-benefit requirement under section 501(c)(3)'s definition of "charitable," discussed *infra*.

a. Evolution of the "Community Benefit" Standard

The IRS has long recognized that nonprofit hospitals may be exempt as "charitable" entities under section 501(c)(3).... Early on, the touchstone for exemption was the provision of free or below-cost care. *Id.* at 217. In 1956, the IRS published Rev. Rul. 56-185, 1956 WL 11273, which provided that a hospital "must be operated to the extent of its financial ability for those not able to pay for the services rendered and not exclusively for those who are able and expected to pay."

By the last part of the twentieth century, however, with the advent of Medicare and Medicaid and the increased prevalence of private insurance, nonprofit hospitals moved away from this "relief of poverty" function. "The financing of their services evolved in parallel, from primary dependence on the generosity of religious orders and charitable donors, to almost exclusive reliance on payments for services rendered." M. Gregg Bloche, *Health Policy below the Waterline: Medical Care and the Charitable Exemption*, 80 MINN. L. REV. 299, 300 (1995).

In 1969, in response to the nonprofit hospital's changing function, the IRS modified its position regarding charity care. In Rev. Rul. 69-545, which modified 56-185, the IRS removed "the requirement [] relating to caring for patients without charge or at rates below cost." In its discussion, the IRS stated:

> The promotion of health, like the relief of poverty and the advancement of education and religion, is one of the purposes in the general law of charity that is deemed beneficial to the community as a whole even though the class of beneficiaries eligible to receive a direct benefit from its activities does not include all members of the community, such as indigent members of the community, provided that the class is not so small that its relief is not of benefit to the community. Rev. Rul. 69-545.

The hospital in question provided hospital care for all persons in the community able to pay either directly or through third-party insurers. The IRS also noted, however, that the hospital operated an emergency room open to all persons *regardless of ability to pay*. In addition, the hospital used surplus funds to improve patient care and finance medical training, education, and research. Based on these factors,[23] the IRS concluded that the hospital was "promoting the health of a class of persons ... broad enough to benefit the community."

---

[23] [FN 14] The specific facts of the nonprofit hospital in Revenue Ruling 69-545 are as follows:

Hospital A is a 250-bed community hospital. Its board of trustees is composed of prominent citizens in the community. Medical staff privileges in the hospital are available to all qualified physicians in the area, consistent with the size and nature of its facilities. The hospital has 150 doctors on its active staff and 200 doctors on its courtesy staff. It also owns a medical office building on its premises with space for 60 doctors. Any member of its active medical staff has the privilege of leasing available office space. Rents are set at rates comparable to those of other commercial buildings in the area.

Finally, in Revenue Ruling 83-157, the IRS amplified its prior ruling in 69-545. The hospital in 83-157 was identical to the hospital in 69-545, except that it did not operate an emergency room open to all regardless of ability to pay. In eschewing any rigid test under section 501(c)(3), the IRS made clear that although "[g]enerally, operation of a full time emergency room providing emergency medical services to all members of the public regardless of their ability to pay for such services is strong evidence that a hospital is operating to benefit the community ... other significant factors ... may be considered." Rev. Rul. 83-157. The IRS went on to conclude that the hospital did in fact operate for the benefit of the community, noting that the hospital treated patients participating in Medicare and Medicaid and applied any surplus funds to improve facilities, equipment, and patient care, and advance its medical training, education, and research.

Thus, under the IRS's interpretation of section 501(c)(3), in the context of health-care providers, we must determine whether the taxpayer operates *primarily for the benefit of the community*.[24] And while the concept of "community benefit" is somewhat amorphous, we agree with the IRS, the Tax Court, and the Third Circuit that it provides a workable standard for determining tax exemption under section 501(c)(3).

b. Defining "Community Benefit"

In giving form to the community-benefit standard, we stress that "not every activity that promotes health supports tax exemption under §501(c)(3). For example, selling prescription pharmaceuticals certainly promotes health, but pharmacies cannot qualify for ... exemption under §501(c)(3) on that basis alone." Rev. Rul. 98-15, 1998 WL 89783. In other words, engaging in an activity that promotes health, *standing alone*, offers an insufficient indicium of an organization's purpose. Numerous for-profit enterprises offer products or services that promote health.

Similarly, the IRS rulings in 69-545 and 83-157 demonstrate that an organization cannot satisfy the community-benefit requirement based solely on

---

The hospital operates a full-time emergency room and no one requiring emergency care is denied treatment. The hospital otherwise ordinarily limits admissions to those who can pay the cost of their hospitalization, either themselves, or through private health insurance, or with the aid of public programs such as Medicare. Patients who cannot meet the financial requirements for admission are ordinarily referred to another hospital in the community that does serve indigent patients.

The hospital usually ends each year with an excess of operating receipts over operating disbursements from its hospital operations. Excess funds are generally applied to expansion and replacement of existing facilities and equipment, amortization of indebtedness, improvement in patient care, and medical training, education, and research.

[24] [FN 16] In interpreting these three rulings, court decisions have highlighted several factors relevant under the "community benefit" analysis. These factors include: (1) size of the class eligible to benefit; (2) free or below-cost products or services; (3) treatment of persons participating in governmental programs such as Medicare or Medicaid; (4) use of surplus funds for research or educational programs; and (5) composition of the board of trustees....

the fact that it offers health-care services to all in the community[25] in exchange for a fee.[26] Although providing health-care products or services to all in the community is necessary under those rulings, it is insufficient, standing alone, to qualify for tax exemption under section 501(c)(3). Rather, the organization must provide some additional "plus."

This plus is perhaps best characterized as "a benefit which the society or the community may not itself choose or be able to provide, or which supplements and advances the work of public institutions already supported by tax revenues." *Bob Jones Univ.*, 461 U.S. at 591, 103 S. Ct. 2017. Concerning the former, the IRS rulings provide a number of examples: providing free or below-cost services, see Rev. Rul. 56-185; maintaining an emergency room open to all, regardless of ability to pay, see Rev. Rul. 69-545; and devoting surpluses to research, education, and medical training, see Rev. Rul. 83-157. These services fall under the general umbrella of "positive externalities" or "public goods."[27] Concerning the latter, the primary way in which health-care providers advance government-funded endeavors is the servicing of the Medicaid and Medicare populations....

c. Quantifying "Community Benefit"

Difficulties will inevitably arise in quantifying the required community benefit. The governing statutory language, however, provides some guidance. Under section 501(c)(3), an organization is not entitled to tax exemption unless it operates for a charitable *purpose*. Thus, the existence of some incidental community benefit is insufficient. Rather, the magnitude of the community benefit conferred must be sufficient to give rise to a strong inference that the organization operates *primarily for the purpose of benefitting the community.* *Geisinger I*, 985 F.2d at 1219.

Thus, our inquiry turns "not [on] the nature of the activity, but [on] the *purpose* accomplished thereby." Of course, because of the inherent difficulty in determining a corporate entity's subjective purpose, we necessarily rely on objective indicia in conducting our analysis.... In determining an organization's

---

[25] [FN 17] We recognize that certain health-care entities provide specialized services, which are not required by "all" in the community, and we do not mean to foreclose the possibility that such entities may qualify as "charitable" under section 501(c)(3). As the IRS recognized in Rev. Rul. 83-157: Certain specialized hospitals, such as eye hospitals and cancer hospitals, offer medical care limited to special conditions unlikely to necessitate emergency care and do not, as a practical matter, maintain emergency rooms. These organizations may also qualify under section 501(c)(3) if there are present similar, significant factors that demonstrate that the hospitals operate exclusively to benefit the community.

[26] [FN 18] At least where the fee is above cost. We express no opinion on whether an enterprise that sold health-promoting products or services entirely at or below cost would qualify for tax exemption under 501(c)(3).

[27] [FN 19] Under the Treasury Department's view, for-profit enterprises are unlikely to provide such services since " 'market prices ... do not reflect the benefit [these services] confer on the community as a whole.'... Thus, the provision of such 'public goods'—at least when conducted on a sufficiently large scale—arguably supports an inference that the enterprise is responding to some inducement that is not market-based."

purpose, we primarily consider the manner in which the entity carries on its activities.

d. The Resulting Test

In summary, under section 501(c)(3), a health-care provider must make its services available to all in the community *plus* provide additional community or public benefits. The benefit must either further the function of government-funded institutions or provide a service that would not likely be provided within the community but for the subsidy. Further, the additional public benefit conferred must be sufficient to give rise to a strong inference that the public benefit is the *primary purpose* for which the organization operates. In conducting this inquiry, we consider the totality of the circumstances. With these principles in mind, we proceed to review the Tax Court's decision in the present case.

2. The Tax Court Correctly Defined "Charitable" and Applied the Appropriate Legal Test under 501(c)(3)

Petitioners first contend that the Tax Court erred in its conclusion regarding the applicable law. Based upon our discussion *supra*, we disagree. The Tax Court correctly recognized the "promotion of health for the benefit of the community" as a charitable purpose. . . . Further, the Tax Court considered the community-benefit requirement based on the totality of the circumstances. . . . Thus, the Tax Court did not err in determining the applicable law.

3. The Tax Court Correctly Concluded That Petitioners Do Not Operate Primarily to Promote Health for the Benefit of the Community

Petitioners next argue that the Tax Court erred in concluding that petitioners did not operate primarily for the benefit of the community. We disagree.

a. Nature of the Product or Service and the Character of the Transaction

In this case, we deal with organizations that do not provide health-care services directly. Rather, petitioners furnish group insurance entitling enrollees to services of participating hospitals and physicians. Petitioners determine premiums using two methods: (1) an adjusted community rating for individuals and small employers; and (2) past-claims experience for large employers. Thus, . . . petitioners primarily perform a "risk-bearing function.". . . [T]he commercial nature of this activity inspire[s] doubt as to the entity's charitable purpose. . . .

b. Free or Below-Cost Products or Services

The fact that an activity is normally undertaken by commercial for-profit entities does not necessarily preclude tax exemption, particularly where the entity offers its services at or below-cost. But petitioners provide virtually no free or below-cost health-care services. All enrollees must pay a premium in order to receive benefits. As the Eighth Circuit has recognized, "[a]n organization which does not extend some of its benefits to individuals financially unable to make the required payments [generally] reflects a commercial activity rather than a charitable one." *Federation Pharmacy Servs., Inc. v. C.I.R.*, 625 F.2d 804, 807 (8th Cir. 1980).[28] Further, the fact that petitioners in no way subsidize dues for those who cannot afford subscribership distinguishes this case from the HMOs in *Sound Health Ass'n v. C.I.R.*, 71 T.C. 158 (1979), and *Geisinger I*, 985 F.2d at 1219.

We acknowledge, as did the Tax Court, that petitioners' "adjusted community rating system[] likely allowed its enrollees to obtain medical care at a lower cost than might otherwise have been available." Again, however, selling services at a discount tells us little about the petitioners' *purpose*. "Many profitmaking organizations sell at a discount." *Federation Pharmacy*, 72 T.C. at 692, *aff'd* 625 F.2d 804 (8th Cir. 1980). In considering price as it relates to an organization's purpose, there is a qualitative difference between selling at a discount and selling below cost.[29]

In sum, petitioners' sole activity is arranging for health-care services in exchange for a fee. To elevate the attendant health benefit over the character of the transaction would pervert Congress' intent in providing for charitable tax exemptions under section 501(c)(3). Contrary to petitioners' insinuation, the Tax Court did not accord dispositive weight to the absence of free care. Neither do we. Rather, it is yet another factor that belies petitioners' professions of a charitable purpose.

c. Research and Educational Programs

Nothing in the record indicates that petitioners conducted research or offered free educational programs to the public. This bolsters our conclusion that petitioners did not operate for the purpose of promoting health for the benefit of the community.

d. The Class Eligible to Benefit

(1) Health Plans

As the Tax Court noted, "[Health Plans] offered its [coverage] to a broad cross-section of the community including individuals, the employees of both large and small employers, and individuals eligible for Medicaid benefits." *Health Plans*, 82 T.C.M. at 604. In fact, in 1999 Health Plans' enrollees

---

[28] [This case held that a nonprofit pharmacy could not be recognized as a §501(c)(3) tax-exempt charity, even though its services improved health in the area and it provided special discount rates for handicapped and senior citizens, because it was primarily a commercial venture that operated in competition with other pharmacies.—*Ed.*]

[29] [FN 26] Further, as the Tax Court noted, "the benefit associated with these cost savings is more appropriately characterized as a benefit to petitioner[s]' enrollees as opposed to the community at large." *Care*, 82 T.C.M. at 625; *Group*, 82 T.C.M. at 615.

represented twenty percent of Utah's total population and fifty percent of Utah residents eligible for Medicaid benefits.[30]

Nevertheless, even though almost all Utahans were potentially eligible to enroll for Health Plans coverage, the self-imposed requirement of membership tells us something about Health Plans' operation. As the Third Circuit noted in *Geisinger I*:

> The community benefitted is, in fact, limited to those who belong to [the HMO] since the requirement of subscribership remains a condition precedent to any service. Absent any additional indicia of a charitable purpose, this self-imposed precondition suggests that [the HMO] is primarily benefitting itself (and, perhaps, secondarily benefitting the community) by promoting subscribership throughout the areas it serves.

985 F.2d at 1219. Further, while the absence of a large class of potential beneficiaries may preclude tax-exempt status, its presence standing alone provides little insight into the organization's purpose. Offering products and services to a broad segment of the population is as consistent with self promotion and profit maximization as it is with any "charitable" purpose.

(2) Care and Group

Neither Care nor Group offered their health plans to the general public. Rather, both Care and Group limited their enrollment to employees of large employers (employers with 100 or more employees). Thus, as the Tax Court found, "[Care and Group] operate[d] in a manner that substantially limit[ed] [the] universe of potential enrollees." Based on this finding, the Tax Court correctly concluded that neither Care nor Group promoted health for the benefit of the community.

e. Community Board of Trustees

Finally, we consider petitioners' board composition. Prior to 1996, Health Plans' bylaws provided that "[a] plurality of Board members shall represent the buyer-employer community and an approximately equal number of physicians and hospitals representatives shall be appointed." As the IRS noted, Health Plans' pre-1996 bylaws skewed control towards subscribers, rather than the community at large. In 1996, however, Health Plans amended its bylaws to require that a majority of board members be disinterested and broadly representative of the community.

It makes little difference whether we consider petitioners' board prior to 1996 or following the amendments. Even if we were to conclude petitioners' board broadly represents the community, the dearth of any actual community benefit in this case rebuts any inference we might otherwise draw.

---

[30] [FN 29] We acknowledge that Health Plans' service to Utah's Medicaid community provides some community benefit. The relevant inquiry, however, is not "whether [petitioner] benefitted the community at all ... [but] whether it primarily benefitted the community, as an entity must in order to qualify for tax-exempt status."*Geisinger I*, 985 F.2d at 1219.

4. Conclusion

For the above reasons, we agree with the Tax Court's conclusion that petitioners, standing alone, do not qualify for tax exemption under section 501(c)(3).

26 U.S. CODE § 501(r)

(r) Additional requirements for certain hospitals.

(1) In general. A hospital organization to which this subsection applies shall not be treated as described in subsection (c)(3) unless the organization—

(A) meets the community health needs assessment requirements described in paragraph (3),

(B) meets the financial assistance policy requirements described in paragraph (4),

(C) meets the requirements on charges described in paragraph (5), and

(D) meets the billing and collection requirement described in paragraph (6). . . .

(3) *Community health needs assessments.*

(A) In general. An organization meets the requirements of this paragraph with respect to any taxable year only if the organization—

(i) has conducted a community health needs assessment which meets the requirements of subparagraph (B) in such taxable year or in either of the 2 taxable years immediately preceding such taxable year, and

(ii) has adopted an implementation strategy to meet the community health needs identified through such assessment.

(B) Community health needs assessment. A community health needs assessment meets the requirements of this paragraph if such community health needs assessment—

(i) takes into account input from persons who represent the broad interests of the community served by the hospital facility, including those with special knowledge of or expertise in public health, and

(ii) is made widely available to the public.

(4) *Financial assistance policy.* An organization meets the requirements of this paragraph if the organization establishes the following policies:

(A) Financial assistance policy. A written financial assistance policy which includes—

(i) eligibility criteria for financial assistance, and whether such assistance includes free or discounted care,

(ii) the basis for calculating amounts charged to patients,

(iii) the method for applying for financial assistance,

(iv) in the case of an organization which does not have a separate billing and collections policy, the actions the organization may take in the event of non-payment, including collections action and reporting to credit agencies, and

(v) measures to widely publicize the policy within the community to be served by the organization.

(B) Policy relating to emergency medical care. A written policy requiring the organization to provide, without discrimination, care for emergency medical conditions (within the meaning of section 1867 of the Social Security Act (42 U.S.C. 1395dd)) to individuals regardless of their eligibility under the financial assistance policy described in subparagraph (A).

(5) *Limitation on charges.* An organization meets the requirements of this paragraph if the organization

(A) limits amounts charged for emergency or other medically necessary care provided to individuals eligible for assistance under the financial assistance policy described in paragraph (4)(A) to not more than the amounts generally billed to individuals who have insurance covering such care, and

(B) prohibits the use of gross charges.

(6) *Billing and collection requirements.* An organization meets the requirement of this paragraph only if the organization does not engage in extraordinary collection actions before the organization has made reasonable efforts to determine whether the individual is eligible for assistance under the financial assistance policy described in paragraph (4)(A). . . .

B. STATE PRESSURES ON TAX-EXEMPT HOSPITALS

The issue of which test, if any, should apply to determine tax exemption for hospitals is also alive at the state level, where large amounts of property tax are at issue. Both state legislatures and state courts have been active in the past few years.

For example, the Illinois Supreme Court denied a property tax exemption to Provena Covenant Medical Center in 2010. *Provena Covenant Medical Center v. Dept. of Rev.*, 925 N.E.3d 1131 (Ill. 2010).[31] The case had begun in 2003, when the local Board of Review denied Provena's request for continuation of its property tax exemption on the ground that the hospital did not provide enough charity care in 2002 to merit its $1.1 million in property tax exemptions.

In 2002, the hospital spent less than 7% of its revenue on charity care. Only 302 of 110,000 people admitted to the hospital received any reduction in their bills based on charitable considerations. Uninsured patients were charged the "established rates," which were far higher than the rates that insured patients paid, so that even when patients were granted "charitable" discounts, the hospital expected to generate a surplus. The hospital also used a tactic called "body

---

[31] This opinion has no precedential value because, even though the five justices who did not recuse themselves agreed that Provena should lose its property tax exemption, they did not agree on the rationale for this decision, and the plurality opinion did not constitute a majority. Nonetheless, the opinion sets out the parameters of the debate about the community benefit standard, and is worth considering from that perspective.

attachment" for bill collection: those who did not pay their hospital debt and missed a court date were arrested and taken to jail. Their bond money was then applied to the hospital debt. If the hospital could not collect the fees, it would then call the bad debt its "charity care."

The plurality opinion of the Illinois Supreme Court found that the hospital could not meet three of the five tests necessary for property tax exemption: (1) that it derives its funds mainly from private and public charity; (2) that it dispenses charity to all who need and apply for it; and (3) that it does not put obstacles in the way of those who needed its charitable benefits. Provena Hospital failed the first test because it relied on fees instead of donations. Nor could it show that it dispensed charity to all who need it because it offered so little charity care and made a profit on its discounted care. Further, its decision to accept Medicare and Medicaid patients made good business sense and was not charitable. Finally, the community services that Provena offered, such as ambulance service, medical education, emergency services training, and volunteer initiatives, did not count as "charitable." The court stated, "[W]hile all of these activities undoubtedly benefit the community, community benefit is not the test. Under Illinois law, the issue is whether the property at issue is used exclusively for a charitable purpose." The plurality also declared that Provena Hospitals was "required to demonstrate that its use of the property helped alleviate the financial burdens faced by the county or at least one of the other entities supported by the county's taxpayers."

Even though all the justices agreed to the denial of property tax exemption, two justices disagreed with the plurality's reasoning. These justices would deny the exemption because they did not see any evidence that Provena Hospital "engaged in outreach efforts to communicate the availability of charity care and encouraged patients to apply." They disagreed with the plurality's conclusion that the amount of charity care was *de minimis*, however, because nothing in the statute mentioned a quantitative definition of charity. They pointed out the dangers of usurping the legislature's role and the complexities surrounding a decision to quantify charity care.

The Illinois legislature took note and passed a law in 2011 that requires nonprofit hospitals that wish to keep their property tax exemption to provide charity care that is equal to or greater than the amount of property tax they would otherwise have paid. ILCS 200/15-86. The definition of charitable care is quite broad, and Provena Hospital has regained its tax-exempt status under this standard. Illinois was the fourth state to impose measurable charity care requirements in return for tax exemption, after Utah, Texas, and Pennsylvania.[32]

In 2015, a New Jersey tax court took a different approach in revoking the property tax exemption of the Morristown Memorial Hospital. *AHS Hosp. Corp. d/b/a Morristown Memorial Hospital v. Town of Morristown*, 28 N.J. Tax 456

---

[32] T.J. Sullivan and Eric Berman, *Illinois Legislature Clarifies Requirements for Non-Profit Hospital Property Tax Exemption, Increases Charity Care Requirements*, NATL. L REV. (June 18, 2012).

(2015). At issue was whether Morristown Memorial Hospital qualified for property tax exemption under N.J.S.A. 54:4-3.6. 1. The court applied a three-part test to determine if the requirements of this statute were met: "(1) [the owner of the property] must be organized exclusively for the [exempt purpose]; (2) its property must be actually and exclusively used for the tax-exempt purpose; and (3) its operation and use of its property must not be conducted for profit." p. 46. The court found that the first two tests were met, but that the third was not, because most of the hospital property was used for for-profit purposes.

In making its determination, the court looked at the way that the hospital conducted business and its complicated corporate structure. Its medical staff included physicians employed by the hospital with incentive compensation provisions in their contracts; physicians who were in for-profit practice for themselves; and physicians with exclusive contracts to provide services to the hospital's patients on a for-profit basis. The hospital also owned several for-profit physician practices and made loans to several of its for-profit subsidiaries. The court concluded, "The court finds that the operation and use of the subject property was conducted for a for-profit purpose, and advanced the activities of for-profit entities. By entangling and commingling its activities with for-profit entities, the Hospital allowed its property to be used for forbidden for profit activities." p. 514.

The court also presented a lengthy history of tax-exempt hospitals, noting their evolution from "charities for the diseased poor and the mentally ill" to "peculiar hybrids . . . [that] carried on their affairs much more like a business." This history caused the court to dismiss the hospital's claim that it should receive tax-exemption for historical reasons.

Finally, the court expressed its concern with excessive compensation, noting that the CEO had made $12.5 million over three years, and the chief administrative officer and general counsel each made more than $1.5 million per year.

The court concluded its 88-page opinion with, "If it is true that all non-profit hospitals operate like the Hospital in this case, as was the testimony here, then for purposes of the property tax exemption, modern non-profit hospitals are essentially legal fictions. . . . Accordingly, if the property tax exemption for modern non-profit hospitals is to exist at all in New Jersey going forward, then it is a function of the Legislature and not the courts to promulgate what the terms and conditions will be." pp. 536-537.

In late 2015, the parties settled the lawsuit, with the Morristown Medical Center agreeing to pay taxes on 24% of its property from 2016 to 2025, along with a $15 million payment for back taxes. Andrew Kitchemann, *Deal Strips Morristown Medical Center of Some of Its Tax-Exempt Status*, N.J. SPOTLIGHT (Nov. 21, 2015).

C. PUBLIC POLICY CONCERNS

STATEMENT OF JOHN COLOMBO, TESTIMONY BEFORE THE FULL COMMITTEE OF THE HOUSE COMMITTEE ON WAYS AND MEANS

May 26, 2005

Problems with Community Benefit

In retrospect, the community benefit standard for exemption has proven to be an unmitigated disaster both as tax law and as health care policy. As law, the main problem with the standard is that it lacks accountability; the standard simply does not require any measurable difference in behavior from a for-profit entity. Under the 1969 and 1983 rulings, a hospital is eligible for tax exemption if it has a community board, open medical staff, and treats Medicare/Medicaid patients. None of these criteria, however, focus on actual performance differences between exempt and for-profit hospitals—for example, even for-profit health care providers treat Medicaid patients. This lack of substantive criteria to differentiate an exempt nonprofit hospital from a for-profit one is undoubtedly what led the IRS to litigate the meaning of the standard in HMO cases—after all, if simply treating paying patients is a charitable purpose, then any for-profit health care provider is a "charity" under this standard. Yet the recent "health care plus" formulation of the 10th Circuit doesn't really add much to what we already knew. Perhaps it is now clear from the *IHC* case that simply treating paying patients isn't enough to get exemption, but even in 1983 the IRS opined that "the application of any surplus to improving facilities, equipment, patient care, and medical training, education, and research, indicate that the hospital is operating exclusively to benefit the community." In short, virtually anything a nonprofit hospital does with surplus funds might be a community benefit, and even supporters of the community benefit standard have admitted that definitions of community benefit remain "inconsistent, narrow, fragmented and only loosely related to the ways in which communities actually affect the health of their residents."

What we do know is that many of the behaviors touted by the nonprofit hospitals community as "community benefits" are really nothing more than what any good business would do to lure paying customers or stay in tune with their customer base. Hospitals, for example, claim that community needs assessments and community health education programs are "community benefits." But a community-needs assessment is analogous to market research regarding what services are in most demand; if a local automobile dealer did a "community needs assessment" for transportation services, we'd call this a marketing study. Similarly, many health education and screening programs, such as a pre-natal care program, are also good business—women who enroll in a particular hospital's pre-natal education program are very likely to choose that hospital for delivery services—which the hospital will make money on.

Finally, the community benefit standard ignores the fact that taxes paid by for-profit hospitals themselves constitute a major community benefit. In fact, one academic study noted that if we included the taxes paid by for-profit hospitals as a community benefit, for-profit hospitals actually provide *more* community benefits than their nonprofit counterparts.

So we are entitled to ask, I think, "What are we getting for the billions per year that we lose in tax revenues as a result of exemption?" The answer to this is that as a legal matter, we are getting nothing specific other than nonprofit form and a community board. Community benefit does not provide us with a benchmark against which we can hold nonprofits accountable for their performance; instead we simply trust nonprofits to do a better job by virtue of their form.

Now we might be happy with this "trust us" approach if we really believed that nonprofit form was inherently superior to for-profit form for the delivery of health services, so that no accountability was needed. . . . But . . . [e]mpirical studies on quality of care, costs of care, and free care for the poor show decidedly mixed results, with some studies finding in favor of nonprofits and others finding in favor of for-profits. . . .

As health policy, this lack of accountability also leads to the inevitable horror stories. In my own back yard, the Illinois Department of Revenue recently revoked state property tax exemption for Provena-Covenant Hospital in Urbana, Illinois. The reason was that for some period of time, Provena essentially hid its charity care program from patients. [Colombo recounted that Provena billed all its patients, counted its uncollected debt as its charity care, and aggressively collected its debt] The most distressing thing about Provena-Covenant for me as an expert on federal tax exemption is that throughout this entire ordeal, Provena kept touting in the press reports that even though the State of Illinois had revoked its property tax exemption, *it still met the standards for exemption under federal tax law—and Provena's statement on this point was absolutely correct.* From a federal tax perspective, I think we should be both embarrassed and horrified that an organization operating the way Provena did nevertheless could legitimately claim it had met federal exemption standards under the community benefit test.

Alternatives to Community Benefit

If community benefit isn't the answer, then the next question concerns what alternatives are available. I think there are three possibilities, each of which admittedly carry some drawbacks but uany of which are better than our current law.

A. A Strict Charity Care Standard

One alternative to the community benefit standard is to return to a charity care formula for hospital tax exemption. At least one state, Texas, has enacted specific charity care standards for exempt hospitals. A strict charity care approach certainly would provide an administrable standard of accountability for nonprofit hospitals. In crafting such a standard, however, a number of practical issues [regarding how to measure charity care and how much would be necessary] would have to be resolved. . . . . These issues are simply matters of policy choices and certainly can be resolved, but they in fact must be resolved in order for a charity care standard to work.

In addition, there are some more general policy questions with respect to a charity care approach. First, since free care has to be provided by reallocating revenues from other sources, some commentators argue that this essentially involves a "hidden tax" on paying patients and 3d-party and government insurers. Moreover, this "tax" is being assessed by private actors (hospitals) instead of through normal democratic processes.

Second, whether charity care is available and how much is available will be dictated by the local market and the success (or lack thereof) of hospitals in that market in reallocating revenues from other sources. Thus availability of care may vary enormously depending on geographic location.

Third, while a strict charity care standard is a viable solution to the accountability problem with tax exemption, it should not be viewed as a total solution to health care for the uninsured poor. . . . Certainly, having more charity care is better than having less, but it is not a complete solution to health care for the uninsured.

B. Replacing Community Benefit with a More Accountable Standard

A second possibility is to replace the community benefit standard with something more flexible than the strict charity care approach, but which has more specific behavioral guidelines that would provide more accountability than the community benefit standard. For example, the Catholic Hospital Association once promulgated guidelines for its members limiting "community benefits" to behavior that would not be duplicated by the for-profit sector. Another approach along these lines . . . could also involve providing usual health services to a medically-underserved population (e.g., an HMO formed to bring health services to a medically-underserved area) or providing services to the general population that were previously unavailable or under-provided. Thus a particular entity that formulated a plan to provide expanded AIDS treatment (a service identified in empirical work as unprofitable and hence under-provided) and met minimum financial commitments to such treatment might be rewarded with exemption. The downside of this approach is that it provides less clarity and therefore less stringent accountability than a strict charity care standard. In effect it introduces some "fuzziness" as compared to a strict charity care standard in order to achieve more flexibility.

C. Repeal the Community Benefit Standard

The final possibility would be to repeal the community benefit test. Under this alternative, a few hospitals that met other traditional standards of charity could remain exempt—for example, academic medical centers would remain exempt as educational institutions under Code Section 501(c)(3); and a few organizations such as the Mayo Clinic might be able to make the case that they are primarily engaged in medical (scientific) research and hence would be exempt for that purpose. Similarly, a clinic whose primary purpose was to serve the poor would be exempt as a poor relief charity. Most private nonprofit hospitals, however, would lose exemption under this approach, because their primary purpose would not be education, research or poor relief (rather, their primary purpose is to provide health services for a fee), but that is not necessarily a bad thing. . . . Of course, the downside of such entity-neutral incentives is that such incentives would be complicated to enact and administer, requiring agreement by Congress or a duly-delegated agency on the exact policy initiatives that this approach would subsidize. Because of the need for national political agreement, the direct incentives approach in the long run may be less desirable than an approach focused on more specific local community needs—for example, a particular community might need charity care more than it needs a burn unit.

One of the hardest things for human beings to do is to let go of the past. Prior to WWII, hospitals were essentially homeless shelters for the poor, often run by religious orders and staffed with volunteers. Today they are multi-million or in many cases multi-billion-dollar fee-for-service businesses. The reasons that justified exemption for hospitals in 1928 simply don't exist anymore, and I think that this Committee should carefully reconsider whether multi-billion-dollar fee-for-service businesses should be eligible for tax exemption at all. At the very least, shouldn't we replace community benefit with some specific behavioral standard that will provide accountability and enable us to answer with certainty the question posed earlier, "What are we getting for our money?"

JILL R. HORWITZ, TESTIMONY BEFORE THE COMMITTEE OF THE HOUSE COMMITTEE ON WAYS AND MEANS

May 26, 2005

Mr. Chairman, in its review of the tax-exempt sector, this Committee has heard many distinguished witnesses discuss the legal requirements governing nonprofit organizations, the advantages that come with nonprofit status, and whether nonprofit organizations provide sufficient public benefits to justify these advantages. These are particularly important questions for the hospital industry, where for-profit, nonprofit, and government hospitals operate side by side companies, and are subject to the same health care regulations. Superficially, they resemble each other so much that a patient admitted to a hospital is unlikely to be able to tell whether it is a for-profit or a nonprofit.

However, whether you find differences between nonprofit and for-profit hospitals depends on where you look. Most studies of hospital ownership have examined financial measures, and have found little difference among hospital types. For example, research has shown that nonprofit and for-profit hospitals are quite similar in their costs, sources of capital, exercise of market power, and adoption of certain types of technology. Although for-profit hospitals pay higher wages and offer incentives to top managers, nonprofits are increasingly using performance-based pay as well. Finally, during the early 1990s for-profit hospitals and nonprofits had similar margins, although for-profit margins were higher than those of nonprofits by the late 1990s. There is some evidence that in the most recent years the average nonprofit hospital had a negative income per admission, while the average for-profit had a positive income per admission.

Such financial measures, however, provide an incomplete picture of a hospital. Because they are first and foremost providers of care for the sick and injured, to evaluate whether nonprofit hospitals earn their keep we must also know how hospitals differ in the *medical care* they provide.

In my research on medical services, I have found large, systematic, and long-standing differences among hospital types. For-profit hospitals are more likely than their nonprofit counterparts to offer the most profitable services, and less likely than either nonprofits or government hospitals to offer services that are unprofitable yet valuable, even essential.

I will offer a few examples. Psychiatric emergency care is considered an extremely unprofitable service, both because of low reimbursements and because its patients tend to be poor and uninsured. Comparing hospitals that are similar in terms of size, teaching status, location, and market characteristics, for-profit hospitals were 7 percentage points less likely than nonprofits and 15 percentage points less likely than government hospitals to offer psychiatric emergency services.

Compare these results to open heart surgery, a service so profitable that it is often referred to as the hospital's "revenue center." For-profit hospitals are over 7 percentage points more likely than similar nonprofit hospitals and 13 percentage points more likely than government hospitals to provide open-heart surgery.

Perhaps what is most striking about for-profit hospitals is how strongly and quickly they respond to changes in financial incentives. The best illustration of this comes from a set of post-acute care services, such as home health-care and skilled nursing services, whose profitability changed sharply over time. These services became highly profitable in the early 1990s, then reversed and became less profitable with the 1997 Balanced Budget Act. All three types of hospitals increased their offerings of home health care when it became profitable, but for-profits did so to a striking degree. From 1988 to 1996, the probability of a for-profit hospital offering home health services more than tripled—from 17.5 percent to 60.9 percent. During the same period, nonprofit and government hospitals increased their investment at a much lower rate (nonprofits went from 40.9 to 51.7 percent, government hospitals went from 38.1 to 51.9 percent). When these services became unprofitable, for-profits were also quick to exit the market, roughly 5 times quicker than nonprofits. This finding provides evidence that for-profits move quickly and strongly in response to financial incentives. . . .

The most important aspect of these findings is that nonprofits are more willing than for-profits to offer services even though they happen to be unprofitable. These services include not just psychiatric emergency care, but also child and adolescent psychiatric care, AIDS treatment, alcohol and drug treatment, emergency rooms, trauma services, and obstetric care.

There are a few clear implications of these findings for the question of whether nonprofits provide valuable benefits to society. First, if the mix of medical services available in a community is strongly determined by the profitability of the services, this is potentially worrisome for all patients—rich and poor, insured and uninsured. Patients need what they need, depending on their medical condition not on the price of a service. Even rich and insured patients sometimes need services that are unprofitable for hospitals to offer.

As I noted above, nonprofits are more likely to offer a trauma center than for-profit hospitals with similar characteristics. One hopes never to be in a serious car crash. But survivors are more likely close to a trauma center if the accident takes place just outside a nonprofit hospital.

Second, extreme responsiveness to financial incentives can be quite costly to the government. Medicare spending per patient and increases in spending rates are higher in for-profit hospital markets than others. This can be explained by investments such as home health. For example, during that period of ramped up provision of home health care services, home health visits per Medicare beneficiary increased by nearly a factor of seven, and payments for those services ballooned. Government spending on post-acute care went from 3 percent of Medicare hospital payments to 26 percent. This increase was not patients getting better care, but hospitals double-dipping—receiving two reimbursements for the same treatment.

Perhaps more troubling is evidence that the relative responsiveness to financial incentives has led to fraudulent billing through a practice known as "up-coding." Up-coding occurs when a hospital shifts a patient's diagnosis to one that receives higher reimbursement from Medicare. For example, a hospital may label a case of pneumonia as a case of pneumonia with complications, at increased cost to the government of about $2,000 per discharge. Although all types of hospitals have done this, for-profit hospitals have done this more than nonprofit hospitals. Moreover, up-coding is contagious. Nonprofit hospitals are more likely to up-code when they have for-profit hospital neighbors than when they do not.

As a final point on differences in hospital behavior, let me say a word about charity care. Over the past fifty years, the legal requirements for nonprofit hospitals seeking tax exemption have increasingly shifted from narrow requirements that hospitals relieve poverty to broader demonstrations of charitable benefit. Yet, public attention to the provision of what is called "charitable care" has remained robust. Whether nonprofit and for-profit hospitals differ in their provision of charity care is difficult to say—in large part because what is typically measured is overall uncompensated care. Uncompensated care provided by hospitals represents items that most of us would not consider charitable. These include bills left unpaid by patients who have the ability to pay or discounts to insurance companies.

Given these measurement difficulties, credible evidence shows that hospital types do not differ much in the provision of uncompensated care. Even these results are hard to interpret because for-profit hospitals locate in relatively better-insured areas. My main point in discussing charity care is that although free care for those who are unable to afford it is important, other differences—in services, in quality, in medical innovation—are valuable to all members of society.

Hospital Competition

Do nonprofit hospitals have anti-competitive effects, or represent unfair competition to for-profits? The arguments about competition boil down to the idea that the nonprofit tax exemption is either unfair or distortionary. An older generation of research claimed, for example, that the tax exemption gives nonprofits an extra financial boost that makes it difficult for for-profits to compete. Newer research has dismissed this notion by demonstrating that income tax exemptions do not lower input prices. Furthermore, as an empirical matter, if there were anti-competitive effects we would not see mixed markets with both for-profit and nonprofit hospitals, but we do. . . .

The best evidence shows that nonprofit hospitals, rather than using their financial savings to offset inefficient management or lower prices to drive for-profit competitors out of business, provide unprofitable and essential services that are valuable to society. These come not only in the form of more valuable medical services like trauma care, but also in training physicians and nurses. It is the vigorous competition *among* nonprofit hospitals that has produced virtually all the medical innovations on which we rely. Imagine where we would be without the first small pox vaccination developed at the nonprofit Harvard Medical School or the first brain surgery at Johns Hopkins. We can thank nonprofits for robotic surgery, pacemakers, artificial skin, kidney transplants, and new technology to save premature infants. Finally, along with the competition among nonprofit hospitals, having for-profits in the mix provides another dimension of competition, competition between organizational types.

An important lesson of the research I have summarized today is that what you find depends on where you look. If you look at financial behavior, you will find few differences that justify tax exemption. If you look at medical treatment, you will find some striking differences of the sort that need to be included in any thorough discussion of nonprofit benefits.

Thank you for the opportunity to testify today.

NOTES AND QUESTIONS:

1. Was the *IHC* case decided correctly? If HMOs bring down the cost of health care and therefore make health care more accessible to all, are they not providing a "community benefit?" The court distinguishes HMOs from hospitals on the ground that HMOs do not provide direct care. Does that distinction make a difference on a policy level?

2. Professors Colombo and Horowitz testified about the charitable exemption for hospitals in 2005, several years before the Affordable Care Act (ACA) and §501(r) became effective. Do these changes make their testimony

irrelevant? The percentage of uninsured in the United States dropped from 18% in fall 2013 to 11.9% in spring 2015, and hospitals saved $7.4 billion in charity care in 2014 because more patients were insured. [33] Is the prediction that there will no longer be a need for charity care actually coming true? If that is the case, is charity care itself now irrelevant?

3. Does §501(r) solve, or at least take a step in the direction toward solving, the problems with the community benefit standard? If so, how does it do so? If not, what do you suggest? Is "charity care" a viable alternative to the "community benefit test"? Can you think of an alternative suggestion or is tax exemption for hospitals an anachronism?

4. For further reading, see Daniel B. Rubin, Simone R. Singh, and Gary J. Young, *Tax-Exempt Hospitals and Community Benefit: New Directions in Policy and Practice*, 36 ANNUAL REVIEW OF PUBLIC HEALTH 545 (2015); Mary Crossley, *Health and Taxes: Hospitals, Community Health, and the IRS*, YALE JOURNAL OF HEALTH POLICY, LAW, AND ETHICS (forthcoming; http://ssrn.com/abstract=2573821; Jill R. Horwitz, *Why We Need the Independent Sector: The Behavior, Law, and Ethics of Not-for-Profit Hospitals*, 50 UCLA L. REV. 1345 (2003); John D. Colombo, *Why We Need an Alternative to Community Benefit: Evidence from the IRS Hospital Compliance Project Final Report*, 63 EXEMPT ORG. TAX REV. 479 (2009).

VI. SECTION 501(c)(3) PURPOSES: DISASTER RELIEF

Organizations geared toward disaster relief obtain §501(c)(3) status because they have a "charitable" purpose. You will remember that the definition of "charitable," as spelled out in Treas. Reg. §1.501(c)(3)-(2), includes: "Relief of the poor and distressed or of the underprivileged." Since September 11, 2001, this area of the law has received a great deal of attention. Hurricanes, earthquakes, wildfires, tornadoes, droughts, and floods keep this topic in the news. Violence against humans is also sometimes handled through disaster relief agencies. The terrorist attacks on the World Trade Center and the Pentagon may be the most obvious situation in which disaster relief agencies became involved, but, unfortunately, it is not the only such instance.

Legal issues arising from these disasters include whether an individual with sufficient economic resources is nonetheless entitled to this form of assistance and whether an employer can provide relief to its employees. In response to these questions, the IRS has published several courses and materials,[34] including Publication 3833, an excerpt of which is reproduced below.

---

[33] Jenna Levy, *In U.S., Uninsured Rate Dips to 11.9% in First Quarter*, GALLUP WELL-BEING (April 13, 2015); Yasmeen Abutaleb, *U.S. Hospitals' Uncompensated Care Fell by $7.4 Billion in 2014: Government*, REUTERS (March 23, 2015).

[34] Links to those courses and materials can be found at "Disaster Relief Resources for Charities and Contributors," http://www.irs.gov/Charities-&-Non-Profits/Charitable-Organizations /Disaster-Relief-Resources-for-Charities-and-Contributors, accessed May 9, 2016.

INTERNAL REVENUE SERVICE, DISASTER RELIEF, PROVIDING ASSISTANCE THROUGH CHARITABLE ORGANIZATIONS

Publication 3833 (Rev 12-2014)

Charitable organizations can serve disaster victims and those facing emergency hardship situations in a variety of ways.

AID TO INDIVIDUALS—Organizations may provide assistance in the form of funds, services, or goods to ensure that victims have the basic necessities, such as food, clothing, housing (including repairs), transportation, and medical assistance (including psychological counseling). The type of aid that is appropriate depends on the individual's needs and resources. Disaster relief organizations are generally in the best position to determine the type of assistance that is appropriate.

For example, immediately following a devastating flood, a family may be in need of food, clothing, and shelter, regardless of their financial resources. However, they may not require long-term assistance if they have adequate financial resources. Individuals who are financially needy or otherwise distressed are appropriate recipients of charity. Financial need and/or distress may arise through a variety of circumstances. Examples include individuals who are:

- temporarily in need of food or shelter when stranded, injured, or lost because of a disaster
- temporarily unable to be self-sufficient as a result of a sudden and severe personal or family crisis, such as victims of violent crimes or physical abuse
- in need of long-term assistance with housing, childcare, or educational expenses because of a disaster
- in need of counseling because of trauma experienced as a result of a disaster or a violent crime

AID TO BUSINESSES—Disaster assistance may also be provided to businesses to achieve the following charitable purposes:

- to aid individual business owners who are financially needy or otherwise distressed
- to combat community deterioration
- to lessen the burdens of government

An exempt charity can accomplish a charitable purpose by providing disaster assistance to a business if:

- the assistance is a reasonable means of accomplishing a charitable purpose; and
- any benefit to a private interest is incidental to the accomplishment of a charitable purpose

Once a damaged business has been restored to viability or a newly attracted business is self-supporting, further assistance from a charity is no longer appropriate. Charities that aid businesses should have criteria and procedures in place to determine when aid should be discontinued.

EXAMPLE: As a result of a tornado, the central business district of a community is severely damaged. Because of the devastation, the area has become blighted. No single business wants to begin restoration efforts until it can be assured that the whole business district will be restored. A charity may provide funds to begin rebuilding the infrastructure of the district, such as for roads, sidewalks, parks, sewers, and power lines. This type of assistance would accomplish a charitable purpose by combating community deterioration. Any benefit to the business is incidental to the public purpose accomplished by the charity's program of assistance to the community.

CHARITABLE CLASS—The group of individuals that may properly receive assistance from a tax-exempt charitable organization is called a "charitable class." A charitable class must be large enough or sufficiently indefinite that the community as a whole, rather than a pre-selected group of people, benefits when a charity provides assistance. For example, a charitable class could consist of all the individuals in a city, county or state. This charitable class is large enough that the potential beneficiaries cannot be individually identified and providing benefits to this group would benefit the entire community.

If the group of eligible beneficiaries is limited to a smaller group, such as the employees of a particular employer, the group of persons eligible for assistance must be indefinite. To be considered to benefit an indefinite class, the proposed relief program must be open-ended and include employees affected by the current disaster and those who may be affected by a future disaster. Accordingly, if a charity follows a policy of assisting employees who are victims of all disasters, present or future, it would be providing assistance to an indefinite charitable class. If the facts and circumstances indicate that a newly established disaster relief program is intended to benefit only victims of a current disaster without any intention to provide for victims of future disasters, the organization would not be considered to be benefiting a charitable class.

Because of the requirement that exempt organizations must serve a charitable class, a tax-exempt disaster relief or emergency hardship organization cannot target and limit its assistance to specific individuals, such as a few persons injured in a particular fire. Similarly, donors cannot earmark contributions to a charitable organization for a particular individual or family.

EXAMPLE 1: Linda's baby, Todd, suffers severe burns in a fire requiring costly treatment that Linda cannot afford. Linda's friends and co-workers form the Todd Foundation to raise funds from fellow workers, family members, and the general public to meet Todd's expenses. Since the organization is formed to assist a particular individual, it would not qualify as a charitable organization.

Consider this alternative case: Linda's friends and co-workers form an organization to raise funds to meet the expenses of an open-ended group consisting of all children in the community injured by disasters where financial help is needed. Neither Linda nor members of Linda's family control the charitable organization. The organization controls the selection of aid recipients and determines whether any assistance should be provided to Todd. Potential donors are advised that, while funds may be used to assist Todd, their contributions might well be used for other children who have similar needs. The organization does not accept contributions specifically earmarked for Todd or any other individual. The organization, formed and operated to assist an indefinite number of current and future disaster victims, qualifies as a charitable organization....

EXAMPLE 2: A hurricane causes widespread damage to property and loss of life in several counties of a coastal state. Over 100,000 homes are damaged or destroyed by high winds and flooding. The group of people affected by the disaster is large enough so that providing aid to this group benefits the public as a whole. Therefore, a charitable organization can be formed to assist persons in this group since the eligible recipients comprise a charitable class.

EXAMPLE 3: A hurricane causes widespread damage to property and loss of life in several counties of a coastal state. In one of the affected counties, an existing charitable organization has an ongoing program that provides emergency assistance to residents of the county. A small number of residents of this county suffered significant injury or property damage as a result of the storm. The organization provided assistance to some of these individuals. The organization's assistance was provided to a charitable class because the group of potential recipients is indefinite in that it is open-ended to include other victims of future disasters in the county.

NEEDY OR DISTRESSED TEST—Generally, a disaster relief or emergency hardship organization must make a specific assessment that a recipient of aid is financially or otherwise in need. Individuals do not have to be totally destitute to be financially needy; they may merely lack the resources to obtain basic necessities. Under established rules, charitable funds cannot be distributed to individuals merely because they are victims of a disaster. Therefore, an organization's decision about how its funds will be distributed must be based on an objective evaluation of the victims' needs at the time the grant is made. The scope of the assessment required to support the need for assistance may vary depending upon the circumstances.

A charity may provide crisis counseling, rescue services, or emergency aid such as blankets or hot meals in the immediate aftermath of a disaster without a showing of financial need. Providing such services to the distressed in the immediate aftermath of a disaster serves a charitable purpose regardless of the financial condition of the recipients. However, as time goes on and people are able to call upon their individual resources, it may become increasingly appropriate for charities to conduct individual financial needs assessments. For example, if a charity intends to provide three to six months of financial assistance to families to pay for basic housing because of a disaster or emergency hardship, it would be required to make an assessment of financial need before disbursing aid. While those who may not have the resources to meet basic living needs may be entitled to such assistance, those who do not need continued assistance should not use charitable resources.

NO AUTOMATIC RIGHT TO CHARITY AID—An individual who is eligible for assistance because the individual is a victim of a disaster or emergency hardship has no automatic right to a charity's funds. For example, a charitable organization that provides disaster or emergency hardship relief does not have to make an individual whole, such as by rebuilding the individual's uninsured home destroyed by a flood, or replacing an individual's income after the person becomes unemployed as the result of a civil disturbance. This issue is especially relevant when the volume of contributions received in response to appeals exceeds the immediate needs. A charitable organization is responsible for taking into account the charitable purposes for which it was formed, the public benefit of its activities, and the specific needs and resources of each victim when using its discretion to distribute its funds.

SHORT-TERM AND LONG-TERM ASSISTANCE—Often charitable organizations (or programs of existing charities) are established as a result of a particular disaster where both short-term and long-term assistance might be required. The following types of assistance, if based on individual need, would be consistent with charitable purposes:

- assistance to allow a surviving spouse with young children to remain at home with the children to maintain the psychological well-being of the family
- assistance with elementary and secondary school tuition and higher education costs to permit a child to attend school
- assistance with rent, mortgage payments or car loans to prevent loss of a primary home or transportation that would cause additional trauma to families already suffering
- travel costs for family members to attend funerals and to provide comfort to survivors

EXAMPLE: A group of individuals are killed in a fire in a large office complex. A charitable organization was previously formed to assist needy individuals in the surrounding region. The charity determines that some victims' spouses and dependents lack adequate resources to meet immediate basic needs; others have resources to meet these needs, but will likely have a continuing need for counseling, medical, housing, childcare, and education expenses. In this circumstance, the organization can grant funds to assist in meeting current and continuing needs. The organization can also set aside funds for possible future needs. However, when payments are made out of the set-aside funds, they must be based on needs of victims' families that exist at the time the payments are made....

Employer-Sponsored Assistance Programs

Frequently, employers fund relief programs through charitable organizations aimed at helping their employees cope with the consequences of a disaster or personal hardship. As noted above, all charitable organizations, including those that provide disaster relief, must demonstrate that they serve a public rather than a private interest and serve a charitable class. In the past, employer-sponsored organizations were considered to enhance employee recruitment and retention, resulting in private benefit to sponsoring employers. In addition, there were concerns that employers could exercise undue influence over the selection of recipients. For these reasons, special rules apply to employer-sponsored charities. Employer-sponsored charities sometimes establish emergency hardship funds to help employees who have been the victims of crime or a personal loss such as a fire or a sudden death in the family.

Not all employer-sponsored charitable organizations are permitted to provide assistance to employees and their families in any type of emergency hardship situations. The types of benefits a charitable organization can provide through an employer-sponsored assistance program depend on whether the employer-sponsored organization is a public charity, a donor advised fund, or a private foundation. When an employer-sponsored organization provides assistance to employees, certain limitations apply that help to ensure that such aid does not result in impermissible private benefit to the employer.

NOTES AND QUESTIONS

1. Is the test for determining whether a disaster relief organization should be recognized as tax exempt under §501(c)(3) the same test as for health care organizations? What are the similarities and the differences?
2. Discussions of the legal issues surrounding disaster relief can be found in Danshera Cords, *Charity Begins at Home? An Exploration of the Systemic Distortions Resulting from Post-Disaster Giving Incentives*, 44 RUTGERS L.J. (2014); Catherine E. Livingston, *Disaster Relief Activities of Charitable Organizations*, 35 EXEMPT ORG. TAX REV. 153 (2002); Robert A. Katz, *A Pig in a Python: How the Charitable Response to September 11 Overwhelmed the Law of Disaster Relief*, 36 IND. L. REV. 251 (2003); and Elizabeth Boris and Eugene Steurle, AFTER KATRINA: PUBLIC EXPECTATION AND CHARITIES' RESPONSE (Urban Institute 2006), www.urban.org /publications/311331.html.

VII. SECTION 501(c)(3) PURPOSES: THE CONCEPT OF "CHARITABLE"

The term "charitable" is broad enough to encompass most types of §501(c)(3) organizations. The regulations enumerate several purposes that are "charitable," but they also specify that "the term 'charitable' is used ... in its generally accepted legal sense and is, therefore, not to be construed as limited by the separate enumeration in section 501(c)(3)." Treas. Reg. §1.501(c)(3)-1(d)(2). This chapter has only touched the surface of "charitable" organizations in its examination of health care and disaster relief organizations as such organizations. It has, however, given you a way to approach the question of whether an organization's primary purpose can be classified as "charitable" under §501(c)(3).

An organization that fits easily within one of the charitable functions enumerated in §501(c)(3) presents a relatively easy case. Soup kitchens and organizations providing vocational assistance to the unemployed, for example, have as their purpose the "[r]elief of the poor and distressed or of the underprivileged." A volunteer fire department is "lessening the burdens of Government." An organization devoted to historic preservation is encouraging the "promotion of social welfare" in its efforts to "combat community deterioration." And a civil rights group promotes social welfare in its efforts to "eliminate prejudice and discrimination." Even religious and educational organizations can be "charitable" because their purposes include the "advancement of religion" and the "advancement of education or science." These organizations also fit within the separate categories of "religion" and "education," of course.

PROBLEMS

Following are some problems that ask you to put on the hat of an IRS examiner. Should you issue a positive determination letter, recognizing each organization as a §501(c)(3) organization that has a "charitable" purpose? What is your reasoning behind this decision? If you do not have sufficient information to make a decision, what questions would you ask? If your response is to deny recognition as a §501(c)(3) organization, what facts would you need to make you change your mind? After each fact pattern are resources that you could use to help make your decision, but also consider the theoretical reasons for tax exemption and the principles used in determining whether health care and disaster relief organizations should be recognized as having a "charitable" purpose under IRC §501(c)(3).

1. *Environmental protection:* The Pevnick Land Trust is an organization that Jason Pevnick started last year in order to preserve the back 40 acres of his 100-acre farm in perpetuity. The land is not particularly ecologically sensitive, but Pevnick foresees the day on which suburban creep will arrive in his area. The nearest town, a suburb of Large Metropolis, is 20 miles away. The 40 acres are not farmed. *See* Rev. Rul. 76-204, 1976-1 C.B. 152; Rev. Rul. 78-384, 1978-2 C.B. 174; *Dumaine Farms v. Comm'r*, 73 T.C. 650 (1980).

2. *Legal aid:* Pass the Bar is a legal organization devoted to providing basic legal advice to middle-income people. In an attempt to make the customer feel comfortable, the setting is in a bar, not a traditional legal office. Customers pay $25 for each consultation, which comes with a free soft drink and pretzels. The fee does not begin to cover costs. Pass the Bar plans to make up the difference through charitable donations and by winning attorneys' fees from opposing parties. Pass the Bar's founder, Margherita Drinker, explained on Form 1023, "The poor have legal aid and the wealthy

have more lawyers than they need. The middle class has been neglected." Rev. Rul. 75-74, 1975-1 C.B. 152; Rev. Proc. 92-59, 1992-2 C.B. 411. *See also* Ruth McCambridge, *Bookstore & 2 Legal Services Law Firms Opt for the Nonprofit Form*, NONPROFIT QUARTERLY (April 14, 2016); Kathryn Sabett, *What's Money Got to Do With It? Public Interest Lawyering and Profit*, 91 DEN. U.L. REV. 441 (2014); Ann Southwork, *Conservative Lawyers and the Contest over the Meaning of "Public Interest Law*," 52 UCLA L. REV. 1223 (2005).

3. *Sperm donation clinic:* Friendly Fertility Clinic, a nonprofit corporation founded by Simon Says, provides Mr. Says's sperm free of charge to women seeking to become pregnant through artificial insemination or in vitro fertilization. The clinic seeks tax exemption as a §501(c)(3) charitable organization because it operates exclusively for the charitable purpose of promoting health. *See Free Fertility Foundation v. Comm'r*, 135 T.C. No. 2 (2010).

VIII. SECTION 501(c)(3) PURPOSES: EDUCATIONAL ORGANIZATIONS

"Educational" purposes are specifically listed as valid §501(c)(3) purposes, and the "advancement of education" is also part of the meaning of the word "charitable." "Education" includes far more than formal schooling. Correspondence courses, museums, lectures, and other organizations routinely fall within the definition of "educational" as spelled out in Treas. Reg. §1.501(c)(3)-1(d)(3), excerpted below. Nevertheless, definitional problems can arise, as is shown in the *American Campaign Academy* case, also excerpted below.

A more difficult issue with regard to education, however, is determining the boundary between "education" and "propaganda." The regulation defining "educational," which is reproduced below, attempts to define that boundary by stating, "An organization may be educational even though it advocates a particular position or viewpoint so long as it presents a sufficiently full and fair exposition of the pertinent facts as to permit an individual or the public to form an independent opinion or conclusion." In 1980, the D.C. Circuit Court of Appeals held the "full and fair exposition test" to be unconstitutionally vague [*Big Mama Rag, Inc. v. United States*, 631 F.2d 1030 (D.C. Cir. 1980)]. In response to *Big Mama Rag* and after a second case grappling with this issue, *National Alliance v. United States*, 710 F.2d 868 (D.C. Cir. 1983), the IRS issued Revenue Ruling 86-43, which set forth the "methodology" test for determining whether an advocacy organization is educational as defined in §1.501(c)(3). The *Nationalist Movement v. Comm'r* case below applied this methodology test and affirmed its constitutionality.

TREASURY REGULATIONS §1.501(c)(3)-1(d)(3)

---

(3) Educational defined—

(i) In general. The term educational, as used in section 501(c)(3), relates to:

(a) The instruction or training of the individual for the purpose of improving or developing his capabilities; or

(b) The instruction of the public on subjects useful to the individual and beneficial to the community. An organization may be educational even though it advocates a particular position or viewpoint so long as it presents a sufficiently full and fair exposition of the pertinent facts as to permit an individual or the public to form an independent opinion or conclusion. On the other hand, an organization is not educational if its principal function is the mere presentation of unsupported opinion.

(ii) Examples of educational organizations. The following are examples of organizations which, if they otherwise meet the requirements of this section, are educational:

- Example 1. An organization, such as a primary or secondary school, a college, or a professional or trade school, which has a regularly scheduled curriculum, a regular faculty, and a regularly enrolled body of students in attendance at a place where the educational activities are regularly carried on.
- Example 2. An organization whose activities consist of presenting public discussion groups, forums, panels, lectures, or other similar programs. Such programs may be on radio or television.
- Example 3. An organization which presents a course of instruction by means of correspondence or through the utilization of television or radio.
- Example 4. Museums, zoos, planetariums, symphony orchestras, and other similar organizations.

AMERICAN CAMPAIGN ACADEMY V. COMM'R

---

92 T.C. 1053 (1989)

NIMS, Chief Judge:

Petitioner, American Campaign Academy (also referred to hereinafter as petitioner or the Academy), is a Virginia corporation incorporated by Jan W. Baran, General Counsel of the National Republican Congressional Committee, on January 24, 1986, exclusively for charitable and educational purposes, . . .

As its primary activity, petitioner operates a school to train individuals for careers as political campaign professionals. Petitioner's school maintains a regularly scheduled curriculum, a regular faculty, and a full-time enrolled student body at the facilities it occupies. Petitioner claims that it is the only school to exclusively offer a highly concentrated and extensive campaign training curriculum. Similar campaign management courses are offered by [numerous colleges and universities.] Petitioner has no connection with any of these training programs.. . . .

The Academy stated on its Application for Recognition of Exemption (Form 1023) that it was an "outgrowth" of the course of instruction run by the NRCC [National Republican Congressional Committee.] NRCC contributed physical assets such as furniture and computer hardware to the Academy. Two of the Academy's six full-time faculty were previously involved in the NRCC's training program. One of the Academy's three initial directors, Joseph Gaylord, is the Executive Director of the NRCC. Another initial director, John C. McDonald, is a member of the Republican National Committee....

The Academy does not train candidates nor participate in, nor intervene in, any political campaign on behalf of any candidate. Neither does the Academy engage in any activities tending to influence legislation. Moreover, while the Academy actively refers resumes and provides recommendations of graduates to requesting campaigns, it assumes no formal placement responsibilities....

No training materials developed by the NRCC are used by the Academy. Rather, the Academy has generally hired its own faculty, developed its own courses and enhanced the training curriculum. . . .

The Academy has more applicants for admission than its physical facilities can accommodate. Thus, its admissions criteria are competitive. The Academy seeks to admit applicants who have a strong commitment to professional campaign involvement on the Congressional level....

Each applicant provides the Academy with the details of his or her qualifications. . .. And while applicants are not required to formally declare their political affiliation to attend the Academy, such affiliations may often be deduced from the campaign experiences and political references contained in the application. Applicants may freely volunteer their political party affiliation. The Academy maintains no records indicating the number of applicants who are Republicans, Democrats, associated with other parties, or independent.

Completed applications for admission to the Academy are evaluated by an admission panel. The Academy has no requirement that a member of the admission panel be affiliated with any particular political party. However, the Academy believes that a substantial number of the members of its admission panel are affiliated with the Republican party. The Academy does not discriminate on the basis of race, color, national, or ethnic origin in admitting students, in administering its educational policies and school-sponsored programs, or in granting financial assistance....

Mastery of coursework requires students to attend daily classes from 9:00 a.m. to 5:30 p.m., and to complete demanding case studies, role playing assignments, research projects and various homework exercises. Periodic evaluations are given to measure each student's performance. Students who fail to adequately perform may be dismissed from the program. To encourage students to concentrate their efforts on mastering the presented materials, students are prohibited from holding full or part-time jobs during their 10-week enrollment. Students admitted to the Academy are not charged tuition and receive a nominal weekly stipend during their course of study.

Following graduation, Academy students are expected to apply their newly acquired knowledge and skills in a political campaign. If a graduate fails to put forth a good faith effort to secure a position in a campaign, the Academy may withhold its recommendation. Approximately 80 percent of the Academy's graduates served on political campaigns during 1986....

Funding for the Academy's activities has been exclusively provided by the National Republican Congressional Trust (NRCT), an organization that collects political contributions and uses such funds for purposes approved by the Federal Election Commission. No funding has been received from any candidate's campaign committee. NRCT funding through August, 1987, reached $972,000. The Academy has estimated that 90 percent of its funding is expended to run its school. The remaining 10 percent of funding has been dedicated to research and the publishing of reports, pamphlets, books, or other materials to be made available to the general public....

Operational Test

The operational test of section 1.501(c)(3)-1(c)(1), Income Tax Regs., is designed to insure that the organization's resources and activities are devoted to furthering exempt purposes. The operational test examines the actual purpose for the organization's activities and not the nature of the activities or the organization's statement of purpose....

The Treasury Regulations specify three conditions which must be satisfied for an organization to meet the operational test.... First, the organization must be primarily engaged in activities which accomplish one or more of the exempt purposes specified in section 501(c)(3). Second, the organization's net earnings must not be distributed in whole or in part to the benefit of private shareholders or individuals. Third, the organization must not be an "action" organization, i.e., one which devotes a substantial part of its activities attempting to influence legislation, or participates or intervenes, directly or indirectly, in any political campaign. *Section.*

Respondent does not contend that petitioner's earnings inure to the benefit of private shareholders or individuals, or that petitioner is an action organization. Rather, respondent recognizes on brief that "Academy would ... be described in section 501(c)(3) so long as it serves a public interest as required by section 1.501(c)(3)-1(d)(1)(ii) [Income Tax Regs.]." Thus, the sole issue for declaration is whether respondent properly determined that petitioner failed to satisfy the first condition of the operational test by not primarily engaging in activities which accomplish exempt purposes.

Operating Primarily for Exempt Purposes

To establish that it operates primarily in activities which accomplish exempt purposes, petitioner must establish that no more than an insubstantial part of its activities does not further an exempt purpose.... The presence of a single substantial nonexempt purpose destroys the exemption regardless of the number or importance of the exempt purposes. *Better Business Bureau v. United States*, 326 U.S. 279, 283 (1945)....

Respondent contends that petitioner's activities substantially benefit the private interests of Republican party entities and candidates, thereby advancing a nonexempt private purpose. Petitioner counters that ... the private benefits, if any, conferred on various Republican entities and candidates were incidental to the exempt public educational purposes its activities further.[35]

Presence of Private Benefits

Having determined that nonincidental benefits conferred on disinterested persons may serve private interests, we now consider whether respondent erred in determining that petitioner conferred nonincidental private benefits upon Republican entities and candidates. Section 1.501(c)(3)-1(d)(1)(ii), Income Tax Regs. Petitioner contends that Rev. Rul. 76-456, 1976-2 C.B. 151, prescribes the proper characterization of all benefits conferred by organizations engaging in its type of activities. In this revenue ruling, an organization collected, collated and disseminated information concerning general campaign practices on a nonpartisan basis. The organization also furnished "teaching aids" to political science and civics teachers. Emphasizing the organization's nonpartisan nature, respondent determined that the organization exclusively served a public purpose by encouraging citizens to increase their knowledge and understanding of the election process and participate more effectively in their selection of government officials....

In contrast to the nonpartisan activities conducted by the organization in Rev. Rul. 76-456, *supra*, respondent determined and we find that petitioner conducted its educational activities with the partisan objective of benefiting Republican candidates and entities. Petitioner was incorporated by Jan W. Baran, General Counsel of the NRCC on January 24, 1986. In April, 1986, petitioner stated in its Application for Recognition of Exemption that its training program was an outgrowth of the program run by the NRCC.

Petitioner's activities have been exclusively funded by the National Republican Congressional Trust. Two of petitioner's three initial directors had significant ties to the Republican party: . . . . Petitioner's bylaws empowered this Republican majority of the Board to "have general charge of the affairs, property

---

[35] [Petitioner also maintained, unsuccessfully, that respondent erred in denying its exemption application by incorrectly applying the private benefit analysis of §1.501(c)(3)-1(d)(1)(ii), Income Tax Regs., to persons other than a "private shareholder or individual" within the meaning of §1.501(a)-1(c), Income Tax Regs. We will revisit this case again when we discuss the private benefit doctrine in Chapter 9.—*Ed.*]

and assets of the Corporation." Under their general charge the Academy instituted a curriculum that included studies of the "Growth of NRCC, etc." and "Why are people Republicans."

Following the reorganization of petitioner's curriculum after the 1986 election, additional partisan topics such as "Other Republican givers lists," "How some Republicans have won Black votes," and "NRCC/RNC/NRSC/State Party naughtiness" were added. The Academy's curriculum failed to counterbalance the Republican party focus of these courses with comparable studies of the Democratic or other political parties.

Petitioner does not require that its admission panel members be affiliated with a particular political party, but believes that a substantial number of the panel members are affiliated with the Republican party. Likewise, while no particular political affiliation is required of students, the two political references solicited by petitioner on its application for admission often permit the admission panel to deduce the applicant's political affiliation. In turn, knowledge of an applicant's political affiliation provides the admission panel with a means of limiting enrollment to applicants who are likely to subsequently work in Republican organizations and campaigns.

Petitioner was asked by respondent to identify the affiliation of the candidates served by its graduates. Petitioner responded that although graduates are not required to remain in contact with Academy following graduation, "some" graduates chose to report their whereabouts. To the "best" that petitioner could determine, these graduates served on campaigns of candidates who were predominantly affiliated with the Republican party.

The administrative record reveals that 119 of 120 graduates reported their whereabouts to petitioner.... The June-September, 1986, newsletters disclosed that 85 Academy graduates worked in approximately 98 Congressional and Senatorial candidate campaigns.... The political affiliations of the candidates served by petitioner's graduates were readily available to petitioner from the public records maintained by the Federal Election Commission....

A showing that petitioner's graduates served in Congressional and Senatorial campaigns of candidates from both major political parties in substantial numbers would have significantly aided petitioner's contention that its activities only benefited nonselect members of a charitable class. Nevertheless, petitioner did not see fit to include in the administrative record any specific example of a graduate working for a Democratic Senatorial or Congressional candidate..... Consequently, it is reasonable to infer from petitioner's omission that the affiliation information, had it been included, would have revealed the Republican affiliation of the candidates.

Based upon our review of the administrative record, we find that petitioner operated to advance Republican interests. We also find that the placement of 85 of petitioner's graduates in the campaigns of 98 Republican Senatorial and Congressional candidates conferred a benefit on those candidates. Petitioner's partisan purpose distinguishes the case at bar from Rev. Rul. 76-456. Likewise, petitioner's partisan purpose differs significantly from the nonpartisan educational purpose advanced by a university through means of a political science course which required each student to participate for a two-week period in the political campaign of a candidate of his or her choice....

Petitioner next contends that because all educational programs inherently benefit both the student by increasing his or her skills and future earnings and the eventual employer who profits from the services of trained individuals, the educational benefits it provides should not be construed as prohibited private benefits. (Hereinafter, we will refer to the benefits conferred on the students as primary private benefits and the benefits conferred on the employers as secondary benefits.) In support of this contention, petitioner cites several revenue rulings granting exempt status to training programs and educational facilities sponsored by various industry and professional organizations....

Petitioner argues that the above rulings establish that organizations which restrict benefits to identified classes demarked by industrial or geographic limitations may, nonetheless, qualify as exempt if the benefited class is broad enough to represent the community. Moreover, petitioner argues that since Republican entities and candidates arguably represent the interests of a class consisting of hundreds of organizations and millions of citizens, the benefits accruing to this class should be construed as public in nature.

Respondent does not quarrel with the notion that exempt educational organizations must inherently confer private benefits on participating individuals. Indeed, he recognizes that an educational organization exists to confer primary private benefits by instructing or training individuals for the purpose of improving or developing his or her capabilities. Section 1.501(c)(3)-1(d)(3)(i), Income Tax Regs. Moreover, respondent does not assert that the pool of potential students is so narrowly drawn that the Academy would confer a proscribed primary private benefit. See *Bob Jones University v. United States*, 461 U.S. at 597 and cases cited therein.

Instead, respondent objects to the secondary benefit accruing exclusively to the Republican entities and candidates who employ petitioner's skilled alumni. Respondent contends that where the training of individuals is focused on furthering a particular targeted private interest, the conferred secondary benefit ceases to be incidental to the providing organization's exempt purposes. By contrast, respondent contends that when secondary benefits are broadly distributed, they become incidental to the organization's exempt purposes.

Respondent asserts that the case at bar differs from the circumstances described in revenue rulings cited by petitioner. Significantly, respondent contends that the secondary benefit provided in each ruling was broadly spread among members of an industry (i.e., employers of union members within an industry, banks within an urban area, members and designees of a local bar association), as opposed to being earmarked for a particular organization or person. The secondary benefit in each of the cited rulings was therefore incidental to the providing organization's exempt purpose.

Based upon his determination that petitioner targeted Republican entities and candidates to receive the secondary benefit through employing its alumni, respondent concludes that the secondary benefit provided by petitioner was not incidental and that more than an insubstantial part of petitioner's activities were performed to further a nonexempt purpose. We agree with respondent....

Petitioner cites no authority in support of its contention that size alone transforms a benefited class into a charitable class. On the contrary, we believe a qualitative as opposed to a quantitative analysis is more appropriate in assessing the charitable characteristics of a benefited class....

Class size is only one factor to be considered in our qualitative analysis; it is not the sole determinant. Accordingly, petitioner must show that Republican entities and candidates possess charitable characteristics in order that the entities and candidates be deemed members of a charitable class. See section 1.501(c)(3)-1(d)(2), Income Tax Regs., for a noninclusive list of charitable characteristics: poor, distressed, underprivileged, religious, educational, scientific, etc. The large size of the Republican party, which petitioner submits is ultimately benefited by its graduates, does not diminish the need for such showing. Petitioner has not established that the specific Republican entities and candidates which benefited by its educational programs were members of a charitable class.

Moreover, even were we to find political entities and candidates to generally comprise a charitable class, petitioner would bear the burden of proving that its activities benefited the members of the class in a nonselect manner.... The administrative record and the partisan affiliation of the candidates served fail to establish that petitioner broadly distributed its secondary benefits among political entities and candidates in a nonselect manner.

Petitioner contends that the infusion of competent campaign workers into the overall political system will benefit the entire community by bolstering confidence in the American electorate. We do not disagree. It is clear, however, that not all organizations which incidentally enhance the public good will be classified as "public" organizations within the meaning of section 501(c)(3). One need only glance at the other types of organizations described in section 501(c) for examples of "nonpublic" organizations which often do much to enhance the public good: private clubs, fraternal societies, veterans' organizations, labor organizations, cemetery companies, etc.... Thus, while petitioner may incidentally benefit the public, we conclude that the administrative record and the partisan affiliation of the candidates served by petitioner's graduates in the 1986 election fully support respondent's determination that petitioner confers substantial private benefits on Republican entities and candidates.

Petitioner contends that should we determine that a private benefit is conferred on Republican entities and candidates, such benefit is incidental and collateral to its primary purpose of benefiting the general public. . . . Petitioner reasons that absent an ability to control [whether] its students [work for Republican organizations and candidates], it lacks the ability to control the conferral of secondary benefits attributable to such employment. Therefore, the secondary benefits conferred on Republicans are the result of happenstance and should in the opinion of petitioner be treated as merely incidental to its exempt purpose of educating campaign professionals.

Petitioner cites no compelling authority in support of its contention that nonincidental benefits must be controllable by the organization. Moreover, as discussed previously, we find the administrative record supports respondent's contention that petitioner was formed with a substantial purpose to train campaign professionals for service in Republican entities and campaigns, an activity previously conducted by NRCC. Petitioner has failed to persuade us that this is not the case. Secondary benefits which advance a substantial purpose cannot be construed as incidental to the organization's exempt educational purpose. Indeed, such a construction would cloud the focus of the operational test, which probes to ascertain the purpose towards which an organization's activities are directed and not the nature of the activities themselves.... Had the record established that the Academy's activities were nonpartisan in nature and that its graduates were not intended to primarily benefit Republicans, we would have a different case. We are not, however, deciding such a case.

Accordingly, we conclude that petitioner is operated for the benefit of private interests, a nonexempt purpose. Because more than an insubstantial part of petitioner's activities further this nonexempt purpose, petitioner has failed to establish that it operates exclusively for exempt purposes within the meaning of section 501(c)(3). Consequently, petitioner is not entitled to an exemption from taxation under section 501(a). Decision will be entered for the respondent.

THE NATIONALIST MOVEMENT V. COMM'R

102 T.C. 558 (1994), aff'd 37 F.3d 216 (5th Cir. 1994),
cert. denied, 513 U.S. 1192 (1994)

HAMBLEN, Chief Judge: Respondent determined that petitioner, The Nationalist Movement (sometimes abbreviated as TNM), does not qualify for exemption from Federal income taxation under section 501(c)(3). Petitioner has challenged respondent's determination by invoking the jurisdiction of this Court for a declaratory judgment pursuant to section 7428(a). The parties agree that petitioner has exhausted the administrative remedies available within the Internal Revenue Service (IRS) and has timely filed its petition in this Court. See sec. 7428(b).

... The statutory issues, which relate to whether petitioner operates exclusively for exempt purposes within the meaning of section 501(c)(3), are: (2) Whether, without regard to specific activities, petitioner more than incidentally serves a private interest rather than a public interest; and (3) whether, in view of petitioner's specific activities, including publication and distribution of a monthly newsletter, petitioner operates exclusively for charitable and/or educational purposes. The constitutional issues are: (4) Whether Rev. Proc. 86-43, 1986-2 C.B. 729, is unconstitutionally vague or overbroad on its face, or otherwise unconstitutional as applied, in contravention of the 1st, 5th, and 14th Amendments; and (5) whether respondent has violated due process and equal protection rights by treating petitioner differently than others similarly situated.

Background

... In applying for a State charter as a nonprofit corporation, which Mississippi approved on June 8, 1987, petitioner's incorporators stated the purposes of the organization as follows:

> To promote democracy and the rights of the American people; to uplift those who work, the poor, the sick, the aged and the distressed; to strengthen the Constitution, nationality, independence and freedom of the nation; to advance social justice; to charter and organize chapters and kindred organizations, all as a 501(c)(3) tax-exempt organization....

The charter showed the domicile of the organization as "c/o Richard Barrett," followed by a Mississippi address....

Through its spokespeople, supporters, and other means of disseminating information, petitioner advocates social, political, and economic change in the United States. More specifically, petitioner espouses a "pro-majority" philosophy, which generally favors those Americans who are white, Christian, English-speaking, and of northern European descent. In a pamphlet entitled "Why Join The Nationalist Movement?," the enclosed membership application states:

> I apply for membership in The Nationalist Movement vowing freedom as the highest virtue, America as the superlative nation, Christianity as the consummate religion, social justice as the noblest pursuit, English as the premier language, the White race as the supreme civilizer, work as the foremost standard and communism as the paramount foe.

Petitioner's pro-majority philosophy is intended to counteract minority "tyranny," which supposedly takes the form of special favors and privileges for minority groups, such as hiring quotas and affirmative action....

Petitioner's view of the appropriate Government in the United States is a majority rule, winner-take-all democracy. In this regard, petitioner favors voting in at least some elections and on certain policy matters, such as busing and immigration, by means of nationwide initiatives and referenda. To petitioner, foreigners and domestic minorities are generally considered "unassimilable" and "incompatible," and petitioner favors voluntary emigration or repatriation for these people.

Petitioner often encourages its supporters to collect food and clothing for, and otherwise assist, the poor, sick, and elderly. Petitioner includes Christian observances in its public activities and sometimes conducts ceremonies that center around the raising of an American flag or the laying of memorial wreaths.

[*Editor's Note:* The opinion outlines Richard Barrett's book, the organization's platform on issues relating to the topics above, a fundraising letter, the organization's newsletter, and its legal defense fund, all of which furthered the viewpoints described above.]

Petitioner formally applied for exemption under section 501(c)(3) by filing Form 1023, dated December 5, 1987, with the IRS. Barrett was petitioner's representative throughout the administrative process. After several exchanges of correspondence, at least two telephone conferences, and three proposed adverse ruling letters, the IRS issued a final adverse ruling dated March 27, 1991, stating as the reasons:

> Your activities demonstrate that you are not operated exclusively for exempt charitable or educational purposes as required by section 501(c)(3). Furthermore, you are operated in furtherance of a substantial nonexempt, private purpose.

Discussion

Section 501(a) generally exempts from Federal income taxation those organizations described in section 501(c), which includes corporations— "organized and operated exclusively for religious, charitable, scientific, testing for public safety, literary, or educational purposes, ... no part of the net earnings of which inures to the benefit of any private shareholder or individual, no substantial part of the activities of which is carrying on propaganda, or otherwise attempting, to influence legislation, ... and which does not participate in, or intervene in ... any political campaign on behalf of (or in opposition to) any candidate for public office." [Sec. 501(c)(3).] Contributions to organizations described in section 501(c)(3) are generally deductible to donors. Sec. 170(a)(1) and (c)(2).

Largely through constitutional arguments, petitioner here disputes respondent's determination that it does not qualify for exemption under section 501(c)(3). Petitioner also maintains that, consistent with section 501(c)(3), it operates exclusively for charitable and educational purposes....

[*Editor's Note:* After determining that the organization does not operate exclusively for charitable purposes, the court turned to the issue of whether it operates exclusively for educational purposes.]

B. Educational Purpose

1. Constitutional Issues

Petitioner, which devotes most of its briefs to constitutional arguments, maintains that the ... revenue rulings and revenue procedure relied upon by the IRS during the administrative process are unconstitutional, both facially and as applied....

Respecting petitioner's claims of vagueness and overbreadth, we will limit our consideration to Rev. Proc. 86-43, *supra*, which addresses whether advocacy by an organization is educational within the meaning of section 501(c)(3)....

a. Background of Rev. Proc. 86-43

The regulation at the focus of petitioner's constitutional arguments is section 1.501(c)(3)-1(d)(3)(i), Income Tax Regs., which provides:

> (3) Educational defined—(i) In general. The term "educational," as used in section 501(c)(3), relates to—

(a) The instruction or training of the individual for the purpose of improving or developing his capabilities; or (b) The instruction of the public on subjects useful to the individual and beneficial to the community. An organization may be educational even though it advocates a particular position or viewpoint so long as it presents a sufficiently full and fair exposition of the pertinent facts as to permit an individual or the public to form an independent opinion or conclusion. On the other hand, an organization is not educational if its principal function is the mere presentation of unsupported opinion.

Big Mama Rag, Inc. v. United States, 631 F.2d 1030 (D.C. Cir. 1980), which involved a feminist-oriented organization that published a monthly newspaper as its primary activity, addressed the constitutionality of the regulation. The court there concluded that the regulation is unconstitutionally vague in violation of the First Amendment, in part because the "full and fair exposition" standard is too imprecise to engender objective application.... In so holding, the court rejected proposals calling for "objective" line-drawing between unsupported opinion and fact and between emotional appeals and appeals to the mind....

The same court later considered the exempt status of an organization concerned with preserving the racial and cultural heritage of white Americans of European ancestry. In *National Alliance v. United States*, 710 F.2d 868 (D.C. Cir. 1983), the court focused on membership bulletins and monthly newsletters, concluding that the material did not fit within any reasonable interpretation of the statutory term "educational," regardless of the constitutionality of the regulation.

Later still, in section 3 of Rev. Proc. 86-43, *supra*, the IRS set forth the criteria to be used in determining whether advocacy is educational under section 501(c)(3):

.01 The Service recognizes that the advocacy of particular viewpoints or positions may serve an educational purpose even if the viewpoints or positions being advocated are unpopular or are not generally accepted.

.02 Although the Service renders no judgment as to the viewpoint or position of the organization, the Service will look to the method used by the organization to develop and present its views. The method used by the organization will not be considered educational if it fails to provide a factual foundation for the viewpoint or position being advocated, or if it fails to provide a development from the relevant facts that would materially aid a listener or reader in a learning process.

.03 The presence of any of the following factors in the presentations made by an organization is indicative that the method used by the organization to advocate its viewpoints or positions is not educational.

1. The presentation of viewpoints or positions unsupported by facts is a significant portion of the organization's communications.
2. The facts that purport to support the viewpoints or positions are distorted.

3. The organization's presentations make substantial use of inflammatory and disparaging terms and express conclusions more on the basis of strong emotional feelings than of objective evaluations.

4. The approach used in the organization's presentations is not aimed at developing an understanding on the part of the intended audience or readership because it does not consider their background or training in the subject matter.

.04 There may be exceptional circumstances, however, where an organization's advocacy may be educational even if one or more of the factors listed in section 3.03 are present. The Service will look to all the facts and circumstances to determine whether an organization may be considered educational despite the presence of one or more of such factors. [*Id.* at 729-730.]

The four factors in section 3.03 of the revenue procedure had earlier been the foundation of an IRS "methodology test," which was advanced during the course of the *National Alliance* litigation as an elaboration of the "full and fair exposition" standard previously deemed unconstitutionally vague in *Big Mama Rag, Inc., v. United States, supra. National Alliance v. United States, supra* at 870, 874. The court in National Alliance had found it unnecessary to resolve whether the methodology test would cure the vagueness of the regulation. *Id.* at 875-876.

b. Constitutionality of Rev. Proc. 86-43

Despite the apparent similarity between petitioner and the organization in National Alliance, we decline to decide this case based on an analysis of whether petitioner was educational within any reasonable interpretation of the statutory term, which was the approach utilized by the court in National Alliance. At the time the National Alliance case was decided, the methodology test was merely an argument raised by the IRS in the context of that litigation. Id. at 870. In contrast, the methodology test subsequently has been published as Revenue Procedure 86-43, supra. Although revenue procedures are not binding on this Court, they do constitute official statements of IRS procedure. Accordingly, we cannot avoid, as did the court in National Alliance, considering the constitutionality of the revenue procedure's methodology test as applied by respondent to petitioner.

The essence of petitioner's argument is that, by denying tax exemption, respondent is attempting to suppress ideas with which she does not agree. Petitioner further contends that its viewpoints are constitutionally protected as commentary on issues of public concern.

Denial of a tax exemption for engaging in speech consisting of "dangerous ideas" can be a discriminatory limitation on free speech.... A nondiscriminatory denial of a tax benefit, however, not aimed at suppressing speech content, does not infringe First Amendment rights.... Tax exemption is a privilege derived from legislative grace, not a constitutional right.... The Supreme Court has rejected "the notion that First Amendment rights are somehow not fully realized unless they are subsidized by the State."

The constitutional foundation of the void-for-vagueness doctrine is due process, which requires, first, fair notice of proscribed conduct and, second, explicit standards for Government officials who might otherwise engage in arbitrary and discriminatory enforcement.... The Supreme Court has expressed greater tolerance for laws with civil rather than criminal sanctions because of the relative severity of the consequences.... However, because of the potential chilling effect on constitutionally protected expression, the doctrine "demands a greater degree of specificity" in its First Amendment applications....

Under the overbreadth doctrine in the context of the First Amendment, a court may find a law void on its face for sweeping too broadly and thereby restricting or punishing speech that is constitutionally protected.... Because an overly broad law may inhibit free speech, even a party whose speech would be legitimately subject to regulation under a narrower law may have standing to assert the rights of others.... The overbreadth must be substantial relative to the legitimate sweep of a law, however, before invalidation is appropriate....

Under one branch of the overbreadth doctrine, a law may be void for granting overly broad discretion to a decisionmaker, such as a licensing authority or a police officer.... In this type of situation, "every application creates an impermissible risk of suppression of ideas."... A law granting excessive licensing discretion fosters a threat of official censorship that may intimidate people into censoring their own speech....

Petitioner makes clear that its main constitutional objection to Rev. Proc. 86-43, 1986-2 C.B. 729, is excessive administrative discretion, which is an analytical link between the doctrines of vagueness and overbreadth. Indeed, the two are "logically related and similar doctrines."... Our analysis, accordingly, does not follow two separate paths.

Our starting point is *Big Mama Rag, Inc. v. United States*, 631 F.2d 1030, 1034 (D.C. Cir. 1980), in which the court, prior to publication of the revenue procedure, held the "full and fair exposition" standard in section 1.501(c)(3)-1(d)(3)(i), Income Tax Regs., unconstitutionally vague. We note first that the same court later spoke approvingly, albeit in dictum, about the informal methodology test that served as the forerunner of the published revenue procedure:

> [S]tarting from the breadth of terms in the regulation, application by IRS of the Methodology Test would move in the direction of more specifically requiring, in advocacy material, an intellectually appealing development of the views advocated. The four criteria tend toward ensuring that the educational exemption be restricted to material which substantially helps a reader or listener in a learning process. The test reduces the vagueness found by the Big Mama decision. [National Alliance v. United States, 710 F.2d at 875.]

This positive view of the methodology test, and hence the revenue procedure, does not appear to be inconsistent with the reasoning in Big Mama Rag. The court in the latter case was concerned that the standard in section 1.501(c)(3)-

1(d)(3), Income Tax Regs., seemed to incorporate the individualistic and unascertainable reactions of members of the public. Big Mama Rag, Inc. v. United States, supra at 1037 (citing principally Coates v. City of Cincinnati, 402 U.S. 611 (1971)). The revenue procedure, however, is not phrased in terms of individual sensitivities similar to those in Coates, which involved an ordinance prohibiting sidewalk conduct "annoying to persons passing by." The court was also troubled by the uncertainty surrounding the disqualifying degree of "unsupported opinion"; namely, whether it had to be the "principal function" of the organization. The revenue procedure now clarifies that viewpoints unsupported by facts may preclude an educational purpose if such presentations constitute a "significant portion of the organization's communications," even if such presentations are not the organization's principal function. Rev. Proc. 86-43, supra at 730.

Petitioner apparently reads the revenue procedure to require organizations to present and rebut opposing views, and it is certainly true that such a presentation does not detract from educational status.... The revenue procedure, however, does not by its terms require this type of presentation, and we see this omission as tending to lessen administrative discretion. Because the IRS does not condition educational status under the revenue procedure on the presentation of opposing views, the IRS is not called upon to evaluate how accurately or completely an organization presents such views.

Petitioner also contends that the discretion for "exceptional circumstances" granted the IRS in section 3.04 of the revenue procedure is a factor that aggravates the unconstitutionality. Petitioner's interpretation of the provision is that the IRS may reject tax exemption "on its own whim" if an organization "does not curry its favor." Contrary to petitioner's reading, however, this provision is clearly written as a second chance for an organization that fails one or more of the specific standards. In other words, the exercise of IRS' discretion can only resurrect tax exemption, not displace it. If anything, then, the provision appears to favor respondent's constitutional defense of the revenue procedure....

Elsewhere, the Supreme Court has acknowledged that one consideration in a vagueness challenge is whether it would have been practical to draft more precisely.... Congress did not intend the word "educational" in section 501(c)(3) to embrace every ongoing dissemination of information, National Alliance v. United States, 710 F.2d at 873, and the term is not easily defined with precision. Id.; Big Mama Rag, Inc. v. United States, 631 F.2d at 1035, 1040.

In our view, Rev. Proc. 86-43, 1986-2 C.B. 729, is not unconstitutionally vague or overbroad on its face, nor is it unconstitutional as applied. Its provisions are sufficiently understandable, specific, and objective both to preclude chilling of expression protected under the First Amendment and to minimize arbitrary or discriminatory application by the IRS. The revenue procedure focuses on the method rather than the content of the presentation. In contrast, it was the potential for discriminatory denials of tax exemption based on speech content that caused the Court of Appeals for the District of Columbia Circuit to hold that the vagueness of the "full and fair exposition" standard violates the First

Amendment. Big Mama Rag., Inc. v. United States, supra at 1034 & n. 7, 1040 & n. 19; see National Alliance v. United States, supra. Petitioner has not persuaded us that either the purpose or the effect of the revenue procedure is to suppress disfavored ideas. See Regan v. Taxation with Representation of Wash., 461 U.S. at 548.

2. Newsletter as Educational

[*Editor's Note:* Although petitioner used language that paralleled Example 2 of Treasury Regulation § 1.501(c)(3)-1(d)(3)(ii) when it maintained both that its principal educational activities were "discussions, forums, and television interviews," and that the newsletter was an insubstantial activity, the court found that the newsletter was, in fact, a substantial activity. The next question was whether the organization should be categorized as an advocacy or an educational institution.]

The test contained in the revenue procedure focuses on "the method used by the organization to develop and present its views." Id. at 729. Under this test, "The method used by the organization will not be considered educational if it fails to provide a factual foundation for the viewpoint or position being advocated, or if it fails to provide a development from the relevant facts that would materially aid a listener or reader in a learning process." Id. at 729-730. In order to provide guidance under this test, the revenue procedure lists four factors relating to the presentations made by the organization, and states that the presence of any of these factors "is indicative that the method used by the organization to advocate its viewpoints or positions is not educational." Id. at 730.

The first listed indicator of a noneducational method is that "The presentation of viewpoints or positions unsupported by facts is a significant portion of the organization's communications." Id. at 730. Without question, the newsletter does present viewpoints unsupported by facts, as exemplified by the purportedly "common sense" standards advocated for Justices of the Supreme Court, including "No odd or foreign name" and "No beard." Moreover, in its listing of those groups of people who should be excluded from United States citizenship, the newsletter includes, with no further explanation, "Boat people, wetbacks, and aliens who are incompatible with American nationality and character, such as Nicaraguan refugees or Refusnik immigrants." An additional example is found in the newsletter"s "Q & A" section. In response to the question "WHAT IS 'BLACK HISTORY' MONTH ANYHOW?" the newsletter's complete response was as follows: "No such thing. Nary a wheel, building or useful tool ever emanated from non-white Africa. Africanization aims to set up a tyranny of minorities over Americans."

Although some viewpoints presented in the newsletters are based on purported facts, and the newsletters contain some apparently neutral communications, such as the listing of upcoming events, the above examples, as well as others, demonstrate that a significant portion of the newsletters consists of the presentation of viewpoints unsupported by facts. See also National

Alliance v. United States, 701 F.2d at 873 ("As the truth of the view asserted becomes less and less demonstrable, ... 'instruction' or 'education' must, we think, require more than mere assertion and repetition.").

The second factor mentioned as indicative of a noneducational method is that "The facts that purport to support the viewpoints or positions are distorted." Rev. Proc. 86-43, supra at 730. As an example of distorted facts, the newsletter in July 1990 stated that the Anti-Defamation League "recently called for Nationalists to be prosecuted and even killed for pamphleteering and exercising free speech." Further on, the article implied that the "killed" reference was an extrapolation by the writer or editor from the quoted phrases "must be stopped" and "pay the price." This type of distortion, however, is presumably less serious than one not apparent on its face. Although such latent distortions may exist in the newsletters, they are not readily apparent from the record. Respondent, for her part, neither emphasizes the distortion factor on brief nor points to specific distorted or erroneous facts. In the totality of these circumstances, we are unable to conclude whether or not the newsletter fails the distortion standard.

The third indicator of a noneducational method is as follows: "The organization's presentations make substantial use of inflammatory and disparaging terms and express conclusions more on the basis of strong emotional feelings than of objective evaluations." Id. This practice is prevalent in petitioner's newsletters. For example, petitioner refers to "queers" and "perverts" in the newsletter. In a vocabulary information sheet distributed by petitioner to supporters, these two words are described as good for "dramatic emphasis" and at least somewhat "caustic."

In addition, the words "invasion" and "invaders" often appear in the newsletter, usually to describe the January 1987 march in Forsyth County, Georgia, and its "black-power" participants. The November 1987 newsletter urged readers to prepare "to purify the ground defiled by the ... Invaders." Similarly, an audio cassette distributed by petitioner was entitled "We Cleanse This Ground of the Invaders' Stain." Barrett himself was quoted in the January 1988 newsletter as saying: " 'Just say no' to the never-ending demands of rioters, looters, burners and invaders." In the same issue and other issues of the newsletter, those resisting the "invaders" were characterized as "patriots" and "martyrs." A "patriot," as defined in petitioner's vocabulary information sheet, is "A lover of his country; a Nationalist."

Based upon these and similar examples, we conclude that petitioner's newsletter comes within the terms of the third of the factors in the revenue procedure that are indicative of a noneducational method.

The fourth and final disqualifying factor is as follows: "The approach used in the organization's presentations is not aimed at developing an understanding on the part of the intended audience or readership because it does not consider their background or training in the subject matter." Rev. Proc. 86-43, 1986-2 C.B. at 730.

The administrative record leaves no doubt that young people are at least a substantial portion of petitioner's intended readership for the newsletter. The average age of petitioner's members, who have an automatic subscription to the newsletter, is in the low twenties. In addition, petitioner's literature refers to young people in glowing terms such as "mainstay" and "seedbed." Direct appeals in the newsletter to young readers include the solicitation of volunteers to work at headquarters or to become Strikers and an occasional short "Inspiration to Youth" segment. In addition to the many references to "youth and workers" and "youth and working people" in the newsletter, other indirect indications that young people are intended readers include articles about activities of students, skinheads, and Strikers, articles about recruitment efforts directed toward skinheads and other "youth," and articles about the youth-oriented priorities of headquarters personnel.

Petitioner derives much of its ideological impetus from the civil unrest of the 1960s. The newsletter, not surprisingly, often refers to news and events from that period, including legislation such as the Civil Rights Act and the Voting Rights Act. King, whose activities are the subject of so many negative references in the newsletter, was assassinated in 1968. Young readers, by virtue of age alone, might have a somewhat limited "background or training in the subject matter." We conclude that petitioner's newsletter does not educate its readership in the manner required by section 501(c)(3).

Accordingly, petitioner's newsletter is not in furtherance of an educational purpose within the meaning of section 501(c)(3) and section 1.501(c)(3)-1(d)(3), Income Tax Regs. Further, as earlier described, the publication and distribution of the newsletter comprise a substantial part of petitioner's overall activities. We therefore conclude that petitioner fails the operational test of section 1.501(c)(3)-1(c)(1), Income Tax Regs.

NOTES AND QUESTIONS

1. Neither the statute nor the regulations defines the word "educational." Do you think that a definition is necessary, or can the meaning of the term be decided on a case-by-case basis? Can you come up with a definition?

2. Do you agree with the court's conclusion and its reasoning in the *Nationalist Movement* case? Does the methodology test solve the problems that the "full fair and exposition" test presented? If not, can you suggest an alternative?

3. In *Fund for the Study of Econ. Growth and Tax Reform v. IRS*, 161 F. 3d 755 (D.C. Cir. 1998), the D.C. Circuit upheld an IRS ruling denying tax exemption to an organization that was set up to study the flat tax because it was an action organization rather than an educational organization. "Based on the record before us, the court could reasonably conclude that the Commission had not set out to study tax reform generally and only later concluded that a flat tax was preferable to the present system of taxation. Rather, the indications are that the Commission assumed a conclusion—the preferability of a flat tax—and then tried to sell this conclusion both to Congress and the President, and to the public more broadly." *Id.* at 761. See also PLR 201408030, in which the IRS refused to recognize an organization formed to conduct research on issues affecting low- and moderate-income

communities as exempt under IRC § 501(c)(3) because it was engaged "in substantial non-exempt advocacy and legislative activities similar to those of action organizations."

4. The following is a mission statement from an environmental organization: "X is an independent, campaigning organization that uses non-violent, creative confrontation to expose global environmental problems, and force solutions for a green and peaceful future. Its goal is to ensure the ability of the Earth to nurture life in all its diversity." Does this organization have an "educational" purpose under §501(c)(3) and its regulations? Does it, instead, have a "charitable" purpose? Or is the purpose one that should not be tax exempt at all?

5. Would the following mission statement qualify an organization as educational? "We, as families of soldiers who have died as a result of war, are organizing to be a positive force in our world to bring our country's sons and daughters home from Iraq, to minimize the human cost of this war, and to prevent other families from the pain we are feeling as the result of our losses."

6. In recent years, Congress, the IRS, and state legislators have begun to question the activities of wealthy institutions of higher education, whose tuition is beyond the means of most students. In 2014, 56 colleges and universities had endowments worth more than $1 billion. Harvard's endowment alone was $37.4 billion. Several of these schools actually pay their investment advisors more than they pay out in tuition assistance. Victor Fleischer, *Stop Universities from Hoarding Money*, N.Y. TIMES (Aug. 19, 2015). And if one considers this tax exemption a subsidy, the government subsidizes some of these private colleges far more than it supports state public institutions of higher education. Princeton University, for example, receives $105,000 in government appropriations and tax subsidies per student, whereas Rutgers University, New Jersey's flagship public university, receives $12,300 per student. Jorge Klor de Alva and Mark Schneider, *Rich Schools, Poor Students: Tapping Large University Endowments to Improve Student Outcomes*, Nexus Research (2015). Not all endowments are large, however. A 2008 IRS compliance check found that 89% of colleges and universities have endowment funds, with the average market value of $187 million. IRS, COLLEGE AND UNIVERSITIES COMPLIANCE PROJECT: FINAL REPORT (2013).

When this book went to press, such endowments remained tax-exempt, but the pressure to find some tax revenues within those endowments was increasing. In 2016, the chairs of both the Senate Finance Committee and the House Ways and Means Committee sent joint letters to those institutions of higher learning with endowments of $1 billion or more, asking a series of questions about their activities. Matt Rocheleau, *Federal Lawmakers Query Colleges on Endowments*, BOSTON GLOBE (Feb. 11, 2016). A Connecticut legislator went so far as to introduce a bill to tax that portion of a university's endowment that is not being used for mission-related purposes, if the school's endowment is greater than $10 billion. Connecticut has one university with such a large endowment—Yale University. Janet Lorin, *Legislation Would Impose State Tax on Yale's Endowment Returns*, BLOOMBERG BUSINESS, (March 23, 2015). And the *New York Times* published an op-ed recommending that universities with endowments greater than $100 million be required to spend at least 8% of that endowment on educational purposes each year. Victor Fleisher, *supra.*

7. The concern about these large private universities has spread beyond concern about the endowment. In 2011, four townspeople sued Princeton University for revocation of property tax exemption, in *Fields v. Trustees of Princeton University*, claiming that the university was engaged in commercial activities, ranging from patent royalties, catering, computer sales, and travel agency services. Princeton already pays $2.5 million in voluntary payments in lieu of property taxes. David Voreacos and Susan Decker, *Princeton Patent Royalties Spark Suit over Tax Exemption*, BLOOMBERG NEWS (Sept. 3, 2013).[36] In the pretrial stage, the university lost several procedural appeals, including whether it had the burden of proving it deserved the property tax exemption. *Fields v. Trustees of Princeton Univeristy*, 28 N.J. Tax 574 (2015). As this book went to press, the parties were preparing for trial, which was scheduled for October 2016. *See Center Files Second Amicus Brief in Princeton Property Tax Exemption Case*, NJNonprofits.org (Jan. 12, 2016); Stephanie Cumings, *2 Universities Prevail in Challenges to Their Property Tax Exemptions*, 77 EXEMPT ORG. TAX REV. 227 (2016).

8. Circulation in most newspapers has dropped dramatically over the past decade. Some have suggested that the way to save newspapers would be to convert them into §501(c)(3) organizations. Assuming that this would be a wise economic decision, would the ordinary daily newspaper have a "charitable" purpose within the meaning of §501(c)(3)? *See* Richard Picard, Valerie Belair-Gagnon, Sofia Ranchordas, Adam Aptowitzer, Roderick Flynn, Franco Papandrea, and Judith Townend, *The Impact of Charity and Tax Law and Regulation on Not-for-Profit News Organizations*, Reuters Institute for the Study of Journalism (March 2016) available at http://ssrn.com/abstract=2754832; Marion Fremont-Smith, *Can Nonprofits Save Journalism? Legal Constraints and Opportunities*, 65 EXEMPT ORG. TAX REV. 468 (2009). A second question is whether large donations would jeopardize the impartiality of the news. Larry Kaplan, *The Latest News Organization to Go Nonprofit Raises Further Impartiality Issues*, NONPROFIT QUARTERLY (Jan. 17, 2016).

9. For further reading on educational §501(c)(3)s, see Erika Lunder, *501(c)(3) Organizations: What Qualifies as "Educational"?* CGL. RES. SERV. (Aug. 21, 2012); Lynn Lu, *Flunking the Methodology Test: A Flawed Tax-Exemption Standard for Educational Organizations That "Advocate a Particular Position or Viewpoint,"* 29 N.Y.U. REV. L. & SOC. CHANGE 377 (2004);

---

[36] See Part XI below for a discussion of Payments in Lieu of Taxes, often called PILOTs.

Daniel Shaviro, *From Big Mama Rag to National Geographic: The Controversy Regarding Exemptions for Educational Publications*, 41 TAX L. REV. 693 (1986).

IX. SECTION 501(c)(3) PURPOSES: RELIGIOUS ORGANIZATIONS

"Religious" purposes are among those enumerated in §501(c)(3). Additionally, the regulations that define "charitable" include the "advancement of religion" as part of the definition of that term. Treas. Reg. §1.501 (c)(3)-1(d)(2). Nevertheless, neither the statute nor the regulations define the term "religious." Undoubtedly, constitutional concerns explain this absence—to delve too deeply into someone's religious beliefs would violate the First Amendment. On the other hand, without some definition of religion, anyone could claim to have organized a religion and obtain the tax benefits of a §501 (c)(3) organization. The following cases show how some courts have wrestled with this problem.[37] As you read them, consider whether these courts succeeded in creating tests that avoid value judgments about whether a set of beliefs constitutes a religion. Is it possible to do so? Is there another way to decide that a religious organization should not have §501(c)(3) status without addressing the definitional issue?

A "church" is a type of "religious" organization that receives additional favorable tax treatment. Like other religious organizations, churches are exempt from income tax and can accept tax-deductible organizations. Additionally, however, churches need not apply for exempt status, nor do they need to file the annual reporting document (Form 990) that other §501(c)(3) organizations with at least $25,000 in gross receipts must file. Churches are also automatically categorized as public charities instead of private foundations, and they receive far more protection in an IRS audit than other §501(c)(3) religious organizations. These differences will be discussed in later chapters, but the definition of a "church" is discussed in *Foundation of Human Understanding v. United States*, 614 F.3d 1383 (2010), which is excerpted following two cases that discuss the requirements for finding that an organization has a religious purpose under §501(c)(3).

---

[37] The *Holy Spirit Association* case involves New York property tax exemption instead of §501(c)(3), but the state tax exemption statute is similar enough to §501(c)(3) that the analysis for one statute could be used for the other.

HOLY SPIRIT ASSOCIATION V. TAX COMMISSION

55 N.Y.2d 512; 435 N.E.2d 662; 450 N.Y.S.2d 292 (N.Y. 1982)

In determining whether a particular ecclesiastical body has been organized and is conducted exclusively for religious purposes, the courts may not inquire into or classify the content of the doctrine, dogmas, and teachings held by that body to be integral to its religion but must accept that body's characterization of its own beliefs and activities and those of its adherents, so long as that characterization is made in good faith and is not sham. On this principle, it must be concluded that the Unification Church has religion as its "primary" purpose inasmuch as much of its doctrine, dogmas, and teachings and a significant part of its activities are recognized as religious, and in good faith, it classifies as religious the beliefs and activities which the Tax Commission (Commission) and the court below have described as political and economic.

The Holy Spirit Association for the Unification of World Christianity (the Church) is one of more than 120 national Unification Churches throughout the world propagating a common religious message under the spiritual guidance of the Reverend Sun Myung Moon, the Unification movement's founder and prophet. The Church was organized as a California nonprofit corporation in 1961, and since 1975 has maintained its headquarters in New York City.

In March, 1976 the Church applied to the Tax Commission of the City of New York under section 421 (subd 1, par [a]) of the New York Real Property Tax Law[38] for exemption from real property taxes for the tax year beginning July 1, 1976 of three properties title to which it had acquired in 1975.... Following hearings, the Tax Commission on September 21, 1977, by a vote of 4 to 3 denied the application. The majority concluded that, "although the applicant association does in certain respects bespeak of a religious association, it is in our opinion so threaded with political motives that it requires us to deny its application." Having concluded that the Church was not organized or conducted exclusively for religious purposes, the majority of the Commission had no occasion to consider whether the three properties were used exclusively for religious purposes. The dissenting members of the Tax Commission, explicitly declining to judge the validity or content of the religious beliefs of the Church or its adherents or to submit the Church's theology to analysis, concluded that the Church was organized exclusively for religious purposes and that the three properties in question were used exclusively for statutory purposes. The dissenters would therefore have granted the application.

---

[38] [FN 1] New York Real Property Tax Law (§421): "1. (a) Real property owned by a corporation or association organized or conducted exclusively for religious, charitable, hospital, educational, moral, or mental improvement of men, women, or children or cemetery purposes, or for two or more such purposes, and used exclusively for carrying out thereupon one or more of such purposes, either by the owning corporation or association or by another such corporation or association as hereinafter provided, shall be exempt from taxation as provided in this section."

[*Editor's Note:* The church sought relief from the New York Supreme Court, which transferred the proceeding to the Appellate Division. The Appellate Division remanded the matter for a hearing by a Special Referee, who concluded that the church's primary purpose is religious, but the commission did not act arbitrarily or capriciously in its determination. The Appellate Division then affirmed the report of the Special Referee.] Because that court, in reviewing the determination of the Commission invoked erroneous legal principles (as did the majority of the Commission in ruling on the Church's application for tax exemption), we now reverse.

It is appropriate at the threshold to delineate our holding in this case—to make explicit what we are not as well as what we are called on to decide. We are not called on to determine whether the Church has any real religious purpose or whether any of its doctrine, dogmas, and teachings constitute a religion. In this case it is recognized that at least many of the beliefs and a significant part of the activities of the Church are religious and that the Unification movement at least in part is a religion. The determination of the Tax Commission, the report of the Special Referee, the opinion at the Appellate Division, and now the arguments of the Tax Commission in our court all, at least implicitly, accept this proposition.

The issue that we confront is a narrower one—is the Church, many of whose beliefs and activities are religious, organized and conducted primarily[39] for religious purposes within the contemplation of section 421 (subd 1, par [a])? This, as understood by the Tax Commission and the Appellate Division, turns on whether the Church is engaged in so many or such significant nonreligious activities as to warrant the conclusion that its purpose is not primarily religious. More specifically, the issue is whether the activities which have been found to be "political" and "economic" are for the purposes of that statute to be classified as secular rather than religious.

When, as here, particular purposes and activities of a religious organization are claimed to be other than religious, the civil authorities may engage in but two inquiries: Does the religious organization assert that the challenged purposes and activities are religious, and is that assertion bona fide? Neither the courts nor the administrative agencies of the State or its subdivisions may go behind the declared content of religious beliefs any more than they may examine into their validity. This principle was firmly established in *Watson v. Jones*, 13 Wall. [80 U.S.] 679, 728, 20 L. Ed. 666, when the Supreme Court declared that "[t]he law knows no heresy, and it committed to the support of no dogma, the establishment of no sect."...

We turn then to the first avenue of inquiry allowed us, namely, whether the Church asserts that its religious doctrine and teachings embrace the challenged activities. We quote the statement with respect to the history and doctrine, dogmas and teachings of the Church from the brief of the Church in our court (without its footnote references to sources in the record).

---

[39] [FN 2] The statute uses the adverb "exclusively," but we have held that it connotes "principally" or "primarily" (*Matter of Association of Bar of City of N.Y. v. Lewisohn*, 34 N.Y.2d 143, 153).

The Unification movement has its origins in Korea as one of the host of revivalist Christian religions that flourished there in the aftermath of the forty-year Japanese occupation (1905-1945), during which Korean religions were suppressed. Common to many of these new, patriotic religions was the theme of Korea as the modern Holy Land, birthplace of the new Messiah. This theme likewise animates the religion founded by the Reverend Moon.

Unification theology is based on the teachings of the Old and New Testaments as clarified by revelations held to have been received by the Reverend Moon directly from Jesus Christ beginning in 1936, and subsequently recorded by his followers in the book *Divine Principle*. Central to *Divine Principle* is the millenialist conviction that the time has come for the forces of God to reclaim the earth from the forces of Satan, and to restore "the Kingdom of God on earth."

According to Unification theology, the "great promise of Christianity" is "the return of Christ"—"not as a visiting God but as a sinless man"—to complete the work Jesus began 2,000 years ago. Unification faith holds that "when Jesus came he was the Messiah," the perfect image of God. Through the Resurrection, the Church believes, Jesus brought "spiritual salvation," but the physical institutions of this world—beginning with the family—remained unredeemed; in the Church's view, it is for the new Messiah to restore a Bride and establish the True Family serving as the foundation for ending "the existence of evil in the world," and to accomplish "not only spiritual but also physical" salvation for mankind. Adherents of the Unification faith look to the Reverend Moon to accomplish this task.

In Unification doctrine, every temporal sphere—political, cultural, and economic—is a battleground for the forces of God and the forces of Satan. God-denying Communism is deemed a singularly potent evil, threatening to overwhelm the forces of God just as Cain overwhelmed Abel; the division between North and South Korea is seen as a central providential instance of the struggle between the sons of Adam. Other temporal controversies also assume crucial spiritual significance in Unification theology.

Committed to the view that men and women need no "mediator between themselves and God," Unification faith makes no provision for a "priestly class." All members of the Church, for example, are qualified to conduct prayer services and other religious activities. Church members fall into two categories—some 7,000 members, serving the Church full-time, are engaged in some combination of evangelical, educational, pastoral, and fund-raising activities, and rely upon the Church or local Church units to meet their material needs; the remaining 30,000 members accept the tenets of the Church as their faith but devote less than full-time efforts to the Church. Representing a movement that proclaims an urgent millenialist gospel, the Church appeals primarily, but not exclusively, to the young.

There can be no doubt on the record before us that the Church has amply demonstrated that it does indeed assert that those beliefs and activities which the Tax Commission and the Appellate Division have found to be political and economic are of the essence of its religious doctrine and program. This has been the finding at every stage of this matter. The Special Referee reported that "the petitioner's theological doctrines bind petitioner to a course of political activism," that "petitioner believes that the physical world consisting of science and economics as well as the spiritual world consisting of religion have developed in accordance with 'God's providence' and that 'religion and economy relate to social life through politics,'" that "it is petitioner's religious tenet that the republican form of government with separate or coequal powers held by the legislative, judicial and executive branches of government is a Satanic principle and that these three governmental branches under the present political system must be brought under a single controlling force as a condition for the second coming of the Messiah"; that "according to the Divine Principle, the forces of Satan must be subdued and Korea unified under the type of political environment where religions and science are unified in order to make the world ready for the second coming of the Messiah"; and that "it also appears that petitioner is opposed to the constitutionally mandated separation of church and State." Following a recital of illustrative examples of "political" activities, the report continues, "The petitioner's involvement in these political activities is not an escalated mobilization in behalf of a political cause. Each activity is consistent with the expression of political motives set forth in the Divine Principle and is part of an over-all plan and it is petitioner's deployment of its cadre and administrators for these activities that mark its involvement in political causes." "One of the principal tenets advanced in the Divine Principle is that there be complete integration of all economic, social and religious activities."

The Appellate Division described the referee as reporting, "that petitioner's primary purpose is religious, but that petitioner's theology, as expressed in Reverend Moon's writings binds it to a course of political activity." That court itself concluded that "religious and nonreligious themes are inextricably intertwined in the doctrine," and that, "[therefore], despite the religious content of the doctrine, and the leitmotif of religion with which the eclectic teachings are tinged, the doctrine, to the extent that it analyzes and instructs on politics and economics has substantial secular elements."

We conclude that it has been sufficiently demonstrated that what have been characterized below as political and economic beliefs and activities are in the view of the Church integral aspects of its religious doctrine and program.

We turn then to the second avenue of our restricted inquiry. No serious question can be raised on the record before us that the Church has demonstrated the sincerity and the *bona fides* of its assertions that in its view the political beliefs and activities of the Church and its members and the efforts which they devote to fund raising and recruitment are at the core of its religious beliefs. The Tax Commission found that the Church "does in certain aspects bespeak of a religious association"; the Special Referee reported that the Church's "primary purpose is religious" and that "it is religious in nature and nothing contained in this report should be considered as constituting a comment on the sincerity or lack of sincerity with which any members of [the Church] practices his faith." The Appellate Division concluded "that one of [the Church's] purposes is religious." We do not confront in this case an organization every aspect of whose claim to being religious is challenged, and whose *bona fides* might accordingly be said to be suspect.

The error of the majority of the Tax Commission, of the Special Referee and of the majority at the Appellate Division is that each asserted the right of civil authorities to examine the creed and theology of the Church and to factor out what in its or his considered judgment are the peripheral political and economic aspects, in contradistinction to what was acknowledged to be the essentially religious component. Each then took the view that beliefs and activities which could be objectively accurately described by knowledgeable outsiders as "political" and "economic" were by that fact precluded from being classified as "religious."

As stated, it is not the province of civil authorities to indulge in such distillation as to what is to be denominated religious and what political or economic. It is for religious bodies themselves, rather than the courts or administrative agencies, to define, by their teachings and activities, what their religion is. The courts are obliged to accept such characterization of the activities of such bodies, including that of the Church in the case before us, unless it is found to be insincere or sham.

Applying this principle, we conclude that on the record before us, as a matter of law, the primary purpose of the Church (much of whose doctrine, dogmas, and teachings and a significant part of whose activities are recognized as religious) is religious and that the determination of the Tax Commission to the contrary is both arbitrary and capricious and affected by error of law.

Determinations with respect to the use to which each of the three individual properties is put, however, cannot be made as a matter of law. Accordingly, inasmuch as such determinations should be made in the first instance by the Tax Commission rather than by the courts, the case must be remitted to the Supreme Court with directions to it to remand to the Tax Commission to make determination as to the use of each of the three properties in conformity with the views expressed in this opinion.

For the reasons stated, the judgment of the Appellate Division should be reversed, without costs, and the case remitted to Supreme Court for further remand in accordance with this opinion.

CHURCH OF THE CHOSEN PEOPLE V. UNITED STATES

548 F. Supp. 1247 (D. Minn. 1982)

...

Facts

Plaintiff Demigod Socko Pantheon (DSP) was incorporated in Minnesota on August 31, 1976. DSP filed federal income tax returns for tax years 1976, 1977, and 1978, and paid taxes in the amounts of $45.60, $1.40, and $425.00 for the respective years....

Although the IRS never ruled on the plaintiff's refund requests, the IRS denied the plaintiff's three applications for tax exempt status as a religious organization....

The plaintiff's articles of incorporation contain a list of several of the organization's purposes. According to Richard John Baker (Baker), an attorney for and Archon of the DSP,[40] the plaintiff's primary purpose and activity is the preaching of a doctrine called The Gay Imperative. The plaintiff defines The Gay Imperative as "the philosophic fundamental whereby the Gods direct that ever increasing numbers of persons expand their affectional preferences to encompass loving Gay relationships to hasten their full development for the control of overbreeding, and to ensure the survival of the human species and the multitude of terrestrial ecologies."...

At trial, Baker testified that The Gay Imperative includes the belief that there are three equally valid human pair-bonds: male-male, female-female, and male-female.... Adherents to The Gay Imperative believe that only 10 percent of the population has to reproduce in order to be self-fulfilled; another 10 percent of the population needs a female-female bond for self-fulfillment; and another 10 percent of the population needs a male-male bond for self-fulfillment. According to this doctrine, the remaining 70 percent of the population can be persuaded to join religions advocating any of the three pair-bonds....

The plaintiff's organization or structure is pyramidal. Archons occupy the highest governing positions in the DSP. Only Archons can be elected to serve in the corporate positions of president and secretary, but only members who are not Archons can be elected to serve as vice president and treasurer. According to Baker, Archons are divinely appointed and are not required to complete any formal training. During the period from 1976 to 1978, four individuals were Archons. Baker and J. Michael McConnell (McConnell) are the only Archons presently active in the DSP. Both testified at trial.[41] The plaintiff's organizational structure includes other functionaries known as proselytes, demigods, and heroes. Baker testified that during the period at issue he was not sure whether anyone served as a functionary. Baker stated that one person may have served as a proselyte and another person may have served as a demigod. Functionaries, like the members and officials, are only required to take one vow, which is to preach The Gay imperative to the "Chosen" and "breeders" alike.[42]

In addition to officers and functionaries, the plaintiff has members. The plaintiff presented conflicting evidence concerning the number of its members. In

---

[40] [FN 4] An Archon is "the ethical governor of a Pantheon," which is a sanctuary or sacred place.... According to the plaintiff's articles of incorporation, the DSP is governed by a board, called the Board of the People, which is composed of three to five Archons, who are divinely appointed, and up to five members, who are appointed by the Archons. The Archons elect one of their number to serve as the Prime Archon and the chairperson of the board.

[41] [FN 7] Baker testified that he and J. Michael McConnell are married to one another.

[42] [fn 8] The plaintiff defines "Chosen" as a person "befavored by the Gods, especially members of the Church of the Chosen People (usually not applied to breeders)...." Baker testified that the "Chosen" are the adherents of The Gay Imperative, and "breeders" are people who feel unfulfilled unless they produce a child or "carbon-copy," the term used by Baker, of themselves.

a letter to the IRS dated October 27, 1975, the plaintiff claimed to have 10 members. However, Baker testified that the plaintiff had no list of the members of the congregation. Baker also stated that the secretary of the DSP had not enrolled any members during the period at issue.

In addition to members, the plaintiff has, according to Baker, adherents who "identify" with the DSP and The Gay Imperative. The plaintiff maintains no record of the names or numbers of these adherents. Adherents are not required to attend any ceremonies, to participate in any instruction, or to read any publications. According to Baker, adherents are automatically trained by associating with members of the DSP.

The plaintiff possesses no outward characteristics that are analogous to those of other religions. The plaintiff has no published literature explaining its traditions. The plaintiff's doctrines are not formalized in any written equivalent of the Bible, Talmud, Koran, or Bhagavadgita. Nor does the plaintiff claim to have any oral literature reflecting its beliefs or history. During the years in question, the plaintiff conducted only two ceremonies. One of the ceremonies was a memorial to a gay victim; the other was the dedication of an archacy or subunit of the geographic area known as a Panarchate. The plaintiff held no regular religious services although it declared certain parts of an annual Gay Pride Week a "Festival of the Chosen." The plaintiff claims to have performed one marriage between two members of the same sex. The Minnesota Supreme Court has declared that such same sex "marriages" are not authorized and are in fact prohibited under Minnesota statutes. *Baker v. Nelson*, 291 Minn. 310, 191 N.W.2d 185, 186 (1971).

The plaintiff itself emphasizes the secular nature of its ideology. The plaintiff's sacerdotal functions are "all bodily functions normal to the adult human...." The plaintiff's secular nature is also revealed in its advertising....

Baker testified that the main activity of the plaintiff's adherents is preaching The Gay Imperative which can be done anywhere on the planet and encompasses all of daily life. This "preaching," according to Baker, involves attaining a state of consciousness that can be exhibited anywhere including walking down the street or at poker games. No words are required to "preach" the doctrine.

No clear distinction existed between the plaintiff's business affairs and those of Baker and McConnell. The plaintiff's income from donations and the sale of religious artifacts was used to pay the rent at 2929 South 40th Street, Minneapolis, Minnesota, in 1977. Baker and McConnell used the residence as their personal residence and only one room was occasionally used for church administrative matters. On a few occasions the residence was used for social gatherings by the plaintiff's adherents. The rent was not prorated to reflect a division between personal and church use. The plaintiff's revenues also were used to pay the utilities and telephone bills for the residence. In addition, the plaintiff paid for subscriptions to *Time* magazine, local newspapers, and other periodicals in Baker's and McConnell's names. The plaintiff's bank account was in Baker's name, not its own name.

Discussion

... In determining whether the plaintiff is entitled to an exemption, the Court must avoid any judgments concerning the truth or validity of the plaintiff's religious beliefs....

Even if the Court determines that the plaintiff organization and its adherents are sincere in their beliefs, they must still establish that their beliefs are religious in nature. The definitions of the words "religion" and "religious" are by no means free of ambiguity.... The United States Supreme Court has not established a clear standard for determining which beliefs are religious. The Supreme Court has, however, distinguished between personal secular philosophy and religious beliefs. *See, e.g., Wisconsin v. Yoder*, 406 U.S. 205, 216, 32 L. Ed. 2d 15, 92 S. Ct. 1526 (1972) (distinguishing between the religious belief of the Amish and personal philosophy of Thoreau).

In *Africa v. Commonwealth of Pennsylvania*, 662 F.2d 1025 (3d Cir.), cert. denied, 456 U.S. 908, 102 S. Ct. 1756, 72 L. Ed. 2d 165 (1982), the court set forth a three-part test for determining whether a plaintiff's goals are religious. The test addresses the questions of: (1) whether the beliefs address fundamental and ultimate questions concerning the human condition, (2) whether the beliefs are comprehensive in nature and constitute an entire system of belief instead of merely an isolated teaching, and (3) whether the beliefs are manifested in external forms.... Many courts use a definition by analogy approach, inquiring whether the beliefs espoused hold "the same important position for members of one of the new religions as the traditional faith holds for more orthodox believers...."

The Court concludes based on its findings of fact and the standard set forth in *Africa* that the plaintiff was not exclusively or substantially organized for religious purposes. During the period in question, The Gay Imperative, the plaintiff's only major doctrine, was a single-faceted doctrine of sexual preference and secular lifestyle. The plaintiff's ideology did not address the fundamental and ultimate questions concerning the human condition, such as the nature of good and evil, right and wrong, life and death.

The plaintiff's doctrine was not comprehensive in nature nor did it constitute an entire system of belief. Instead, the plaintiff narrowly focused on only one aspect of human existence—sexual preference. Despite the construction of an elaborate framework based on numerous borrowings from ancient Greek philosophy, the plaintiff's entire structure rested on the slim foundation of one teaching.

In addition, the plaintiff lacked external manifestations analogous to other religions during the period in question. It possessed no established history or literature, required no formal or informal education of its leaders, conducted no regular ceremonies, and possessed no identifiable membership beyond its small core of leaders. The plaintiff is prohibited by Minnesota law from conducting same-sex "marriages," one of the few activities the plaintiff performed that is analogous to those of mainstream religions.

The Court also concludes that the plaintiff was operated to benefit private individuals and thus, was not qualified for exemption on this basis. The entire rent for Baker and McConnell's residence was paid by the plaintiff even though the residence was not used substantially for religious purposes. The plaintiff's revenues provided other substantial personal benefits to Baker and McConnell that were unrelated to religious purposes.

The Court concludes that because the plaintiff was not organized and operated exclusively for religious purposes, the plaintiff was not entitled to tax exempt status under section 501(c)(3)....

FOUNDATION OF HUMAN UNDERSTANDING V. UNITED STATES

---

614 F.3d 1383 (Fed. Cir. 2010)

BRYSON, *Circuit Judge*.

The Foundation of Human Understanding ("the Foundation"), which describes itself as "based upon Judeo-Christian beliefs and the doctrine and teachings of its founder, Roy Masters," challenges a decision of the United States Court of Federal Claims that the Foundation did not qualify as a "church" under section 170(b)(1)(A)(i) of the Internal Revenue Code ("I.R.C."), 26 U.S.C. §170(b)(1)(A)(i), for the period from January 1, 1998, through December 31, 2000. We affirm.

I

[*Editor's Note:* The IRS recognized the Foundation as a 501(c)(3) religious organization in 1965. A few years later, the Foundation requested a ruling from the IRS that it was also a church, entitled to the additional benefits that a church receives. The IRS denied the request, but ultimately the U.S. Tax Court held that it qualified as a church because it conducted services three or four times a week in a building that it owned in Los Angeles; it also conducted services at a building and a ranch that it owned in Oregon; it operated a denominational school; and it conducted regular religious services for congregations ranging from 50 to 350 people that were served by an organized ministry. The Tax Court recognized that the foundation devoted substantial resources to nonchurch activities, such as disseminating its message through radio broadcasts and printed materials, but the court held that those activities did not overshadow the church activities.]

In the years following the Tax Court's decision, the Foundation underwent several changes. First, in 1991, Brighton Academy was separately incorporated and began to operate as a "private non-denominational Christian school" rather than a school based on the Foundation's doctrines. Next, during the mid-1990s, the Foundation sold its buildings in Los Angeles and Grants Pass, and, in the late 1990s, meetings at the Tall Timber Ranch became less frequent. The Foundation, however, continued to disseminate its messages through broadcast and print media, and it began to use the Internet for the same purpose.

[*Editor's Note:* In 2001, the IRS began a church-tax inquiry for the tax years 1998–2000. It determined that the Foundation was no longer a church, although it remained entitled to tax-exempt status under §501(c)(3) as a religious organization. The Foundation challenged that decision in the U.S. Court of Federal Claims. Both parties moved for summary judgment, and the court ruled in favor of the government. *Foundation of Human Understanding v. United States (Foundation II)*, 88 Fed. Cl. 203 (2009).]

... The court ... identified the two main analytical approaches that have been used to determine whether an institution is a "church" under section 170: a set of 14 criteria devised by the IRS,[43] and the so-called "associational test" adopted by several courts. The court expressed concern about the "14 criteria" approach on the ground that it "appears to favor some forms of religious expression over others in a manner in which, if not inconsistent with the letter of the Constitution, the court finds troubling when considered in light of the constitutional protections of the Establishment and Free Exercise Clauses." Nonetheless, the court looked to the 14 criteria for guidance and found that the Foundation satisfied some, but not all, of those criteria. For example, the court found that the Foundation had not established that it had a regular congregation or that it held regular services during the years at issue.

Even though the trial court referred to the 14 criteria in the course of its factual findings, it ultimately decided the case by applying the associational test, which defines a church as an organization that includes a body of believers who assemble regularly for communal worship. Specifically, the court found that the Foundation did not provide regular religious services to an established congregation and concluded that "[t]he extent to which [the] Foundation brings people together to worship is incidental to its main function" of spreading its message through publication and broadcasting. Relying on case law that treats publishing activities as insufficient to confer church status and denies church status to entities whose associational activities are merely incidental to their publishing and broadcasting activities, the trial court held that the Foundation did not qualify as a church under section 170. The Foundation appeals that decision.

---

[43] [FN 2] The 14 criteria have their origin in a 1979 speech by the IRS Commissioner, and the IRS has subsequently applied those factors in its section 170 determinations. *See Foundation I*, 88 T.C. at 1357. The 14 criteria are: (1) a distinct legal existence; (2) a recognized creed and form of worship; (3) a definite and distinct ecclesiastical government; (4) a formal code of doctrine and discipline; (5) a distinct religious history; (6) a membership not associated with any other church or denomination; (7) an organization of ordained ministers; (8) ordained ministers selected after completing prescribed studies; (9) a literature of its own; (10) established places of worship; (11) regular congregations; (12) regular religious services; (13) Sunday schools for religious instruction of the young; and (14) schools for the preparation of its ministers. The IRS also considers "any other facts and circumstances which may bear upon the organization's claim for church status."*Id.* at 1357-58.

II

Neither Congress nor the IRS has provided much guidance as to the meaning of the term "church" in I.R.C. §170 or what is required for an institution to qualify for that designation....

Nevertheless, some degree of consensus has emerged from court decisions. First, those courts that have addressed the issue largely agree that "Congress intended a more restricted definition for a 'church' than for a 'religious organization.' " Second, as several courts have noted, "[t]he means by which an avowedly religious purpose is accomplished [is what] separates a 'church' from other forms of religious enterprise." Third, the courts have relied mainly on the IRS's 14 criteria and on the associational test when addressing the distinction between a religious organization and a church under section 170.

With respect to the 14 criteria, we share the concerns expressed by the trial court and note that courts have generally declined to accept the 14 criteria as a definitive test for whether an institution qualifies as a church.... Courts have been more receptive to the associational test as a means of determining church status under section 170.

We agree that the associational test is an appropriate test for determining church status under section 170, although we recognize that the associational test and the "14 criteria test" substantially overlap.... [A]mong the most important of the 14 criteria are the requirements of "regular congregations" and "regular religious services." Thus, whether applying the associational test or the 14 criteria test, courts have held that in order to be considered a church under section 170, a religious organization must create, as part of its religious activities, the opportunity for members to develop a fellowship by worshipping together.

The Foundation asserts that a religious organization should be treated as a church under section 170 as long as "there is a body of followers beyond the scope of a 'family church' ... [who] seek the teachings of the organization and express or acknowledge an affiliation with its religious tenets." However, every religious organization has members who express an affiliation with the organization's tenets. For that reason, the Foundation's approach is at odds with the generally accepted principle that Congress intended a more restricted definition for a "church" than for a religious organization, especially in light of case law interpreting section 170 to require more than mere affiliation by a number of people with an organization espousing a particular belief system.

Therefore, in order to qualify as a church under section 170, the Foundation was required to establish that it met the associational test during the years at issue.[44] The trial court held that the Foundation failed to carry that burden. For the reasons given below, we agree with the court's conclusion.

---

[44] [FN 3] Because the IRS ruled that the Foundation qualified as a "religious organization" for purposes of I.R.C. §501(c)(3), the Foundation did not need to establish the sincerity or legitimacy of its religious beliefs.

III

A

... With respect to the Foundation's in-person services, the record shows that during the three-year audit period at issue the Foundation did not hold regular services at any location, including its facility at the Tall Timber Ranch in Selma, Oregon. During that period, the Foundation held 21 seminars in various locations throughout the United States, five of which took place at the Tall Timber Ranch. We agree with the government that the evidence regarding the seminars does not establish that the Foundation conducted regular meetings or had a regular congregation and therefore does not satisfy the associational test. First, the attendance of groups of people at occasional seminars in cities scattered across the country does not constitute a regular assembly of a cohesive group of people for worship. Second, as for the seminars at the Tall Timber Ranch, the Foundation has not shown that those five meetings in a three-year period enabled congregants to establish a community of worship. While the associational test does not demand that religious gatherings be held with a particular frequency or on a particular schedule, it does require gatherings that, by virtue of their nature and frequency, provide the opportunity for members to form a religious fellowship through communal worship. The Foundation has failed to show that the sporadic meetings conducted in various locations were sufficiently regular to satisfy that requirement. Moreover, the Foundation has presented no evidence regarding attendance or any other indication that a regular congregation gathered even for those occasional meetings during the three-year period at issue.

The Foundation points to a number of letters from individuals stating that they had received the Foundation's teachings and considered the Foundation to be their church. However, that evidence does not identify those who attended in-person meetings as opposed to those who received the Foundation's teachings through its electronic ministry. The evidence of attendance at Foundation meetings or services is thus insufficient to satisfy the associational test because it does not establish the frequency or nature of the meetings, the consistency of the congregation, or the extent to which those meetings enabled members to associate with each other in worship.

In sum, the record supports the trial court's finding that the in-person services conducted during the years in question were merely incidental to the Foundation's primary purposes, and were therefore insufficient to demonstrate that the Foundation was a "church" for tax purposes. Accordingly, we uphold the trial court's decision on that issue.

B

With respect to its "electronic ministry," the Foundation asserts that its members regularly assembled to worship as a "virtual congregation" by listening to sermons broadcast over the radio and the Internet at set times, referred to as "appointments to listen." However, disseminating religious information, whether through print or broadcast media, does not fulfill the associational role required to qualify as a "church" under section 170. The fact that all the listeners simultaneously received the Foundation's message over the radio or the Internet does not mean that those members associated with each other and worshiped communally. As the trial court observed, "[t]here is no evidence ... that [the Foundation's] adherents regard their experience while listening to [the Foundation's] broadcasts as a shared experience with other ... followers, or as a communal experience in any way." *Foundation II*, 88 Fed. Cl. at 232.

The Foundation argues that it satisfied the associational test because its electronic ministry included a "call-in" show that enabled individuals to call and interact with the Foundation's clergy over the telephone. Those conversations, according to the Foundation, were broadcast to listening congregants and subsequently transcribed for distribution. However, a call-in show, like other forms of broadcast ministry, does not provide individual congregants with the opportunity to interact and associate with each other in worship, and it therefore does not provide a basis for concluding that the Foundation's religious activities satisfied the associational test.

The Foundation relies on *Purnell v. Commissioner*, T.C. Memo 1992-289, 63 T.C.M. (CCH) 3037 (1992), for the proposition that its broadcasting activities qualified it as a "church without walls." In *Purnell*, however, the court found that the organization in question had regular congregations and regular services. The fact that the organization also served an irregular congregation by operating in part as a "street church" did not diminish its standing as a church under section 170. Under *Purnell*, an organization holds regular services with a regular congregation, it satisfies the associational test even if it also undertakes other activities, such as broadcasting, that would not qualify under the associational test if considered alone. In this case, by contrast, the Foundation has not established that it held regular services with a regular congregation. *Purnell* therefore provides no support for the Foundation's argument.

Because the Foundation failed to establish that, during the three-year period at issue, it qualified as a "church" within the meaning of I.R.C. §170, we uphold the trial court's decision sustaining the IRS's ruling....

AFFIRMED

NOTES AND QUESTIONS

1. In 2015, comedian John Oliver briefly set up his own church, Our Lady of Perpetual Exemption. He claimed that it met the 14-point test described in the *Foundation of Human Understanding* case because his studio was a house of worship, his audience the congregants, and they had a creed concerning the nature of fraudulent churches. He filed as a church in the state of Texas, but shut the church down within a few weeks and donated the funds to Doctors Without Borders. http://www.ourladyofperpetualexemption .com. Given the tests that you have studied for determining whether a religious organization should be exempt and whether that organization should be classified as a church, how would you anticipate the IRS would

have reacted if the organization had remained in existence and had been audited?

2. Can an online church qualify as a church under either the 14-point test or the associational test? Should it?

3. The First Church of Cannabis was formed in Indiana in 2015 after the state's Religious Freedom Restoration Act, which provides extra protections for religious practices, became law. A major sacrament of this religion involves smoking marijuana, which is illegal in Indiana. The church is founded on principles of love, respect, equality, and compassion. It does not have a deity at the top of the church, but it is guided by 12 tenets of faith, the New Deity Dozen. Although the church did not need to apply for recognition as a tax-exempt church, it decided to do so. Given what you have read above, do you think it meets the criteria to be both a religious organization and a church?

4. The Kansas Court of Appeals denied personal property tax exemption to the Westboro Baptist Church in 2008 for the truck that it used to protest homosexuality at church services, military funerals, government offices, political conventions, and other locations. *In re Westboro Baptist Church*, 40 Kan. App. 2d 27, 189 P.3d 535 (2008), *cert. denied* 287 Kan. 765 (2009). The court in that case held that the protesting activity was not exclusively religious because it was political. Do you agree that this is political activity? Even if you disagree with their opinions and actions, if their opinions are sincerely held, should we consider them religious? Further information about Westboro Baptist Church can be found at its website, http://www.godhatesfags.com.

5. A 2011 Illinois appellate court decision agreed with the Illinois Department of Revenue that the Armenian Church of Lake Bluff, Illinois, was not a church, and therefore must pay property taxes of $80,000 a year. The owners of a mansion in Lake Bluff, Illinois, had converted their home to a church when the wife became too disabled to leave home to attend services. The husband obtained a pastor's degree from an online religious site and began holding weekly services at the home, complete with church bulletins. The court found that it was insufficient to hold services from time to time for private contemplation. *Armenian Church of Lake Bluff v. Dep't of Revenue of Ill.*, 956 N.E.2d 479 (Il. App. 2011).

6. For further reading, see Lloyd Hitoshi Mayer, *Limits on State Regulation of Religious Organizations: Where We Are and Where We Are Going,* Notre Dame Legal Studies Paper No. 1521 (2015), available at http://ssrn.com/abstract=2627850; Joel Newman, *What Is a Church? A Look at Tax Exemptions for the Original Kleptonian Neo-American Church and the First Church of Cannabis,* LEXIS FEDERAL TAX J.Q. (Dec. 2015); James E. Vaughn, *Reaping Where They Have Not Sowed: Have American Churches Failed to Satisfy the Requirements for the Religious Tax Exemption?* 43 CATH. LAW. 29 (2004). *See also* Mark Oppenheimer, *Now's the Time to End Tax Exemptions for Religious Institutions,* TIME (June 28, 2015). The IRS

publishes guidance for churches and religious organizations at irs.gov/charities/churches/index.html.

X. OTHER SECTION 501(c)(3) PURPOSES

The three most common §501(c)(3) purposes are charitable, religious, and educational. The statute also allows organizations to be exempt from federal income tax under §501(c)(3) for scientific, literary, prevention of cruelty to animals, amateur sports, and public safety testing purposes. Literary organizations are the easiest to discuss, as no law exists on the topic. Evidently, all organizations that have a literary purpose can also be subsumed under charitable and educational purposes. *See* Walter N. Trenerry, *A Literary Pilgrim's Progress Along Section 501(c)(3)*, 51 A.B.A. J. 252 (1965).

There are almost as few public safety testing organizations as there are literary ones. Congress added public safety testing as a tax-exempt purpose after a federal appeals court denied income tax exemption to an organization that conducts tests and experiments and investigates the causes of insurance loss. A handful of §501(c)(3) organizations fit into this category. These are the only type of §501(c)(3) organizations for which donations are not tax deductible under IRC §170.

Determining whether a purpose is the prevention of cruelty to animals is relatively straightforward. Animal rescue organizations, organizations that help pay for spaying and neutering pets, and organizations seeking humane treatment of laboratory animals would all fall under this category.

Finally, the amateur sports category was added in 1976 to allow organizations that foster national or international sports competition, such as the Olympics, to be tax exempt under §501(c)(3). Organizations such as Little League teams were already recognized as charitable, but these other types of amateur organizations had been classified as §501(c)(4) social welfare organizations or §501(c)(6) business leagues.

XI. STATE AND LOCAL CHARITABLE TAX EXEMPTIONS

This chapter has focused on the purposes and activities that make an organization eligible for federal income tax exemption under I.R.C. §501(c)(3). Several of the cases have actually been state property tax cases, however: *Walz v. Tax Commission of City of New York*, 397 U.S. 664 (1970); *Holy Spirit Ass'n v. Tax Commission*, 55 N.Y.2d 512; 435 N.E.2d 662; 450 N.Y.S.2d 292 (N.Y. 1982); *Provena Covenant Medical Center v. Dept. of Rev.*, 925 N.E.3d 1131 (Ill. 2010), and *AHS Hosp. Corp. d/b/a Morristown Memorial Hospital v. Town of Morristown*, 2015 N.J. Tax LEXIS 12. Those cases were placed in the discussion about §501(c)(3) earlier in this chapter on the assumption that the state tax language and policies were similar enough to §501(c)(3) to shed light on the language and policies of the federal statute. This section of the chapter delves further into the similarities and differences between state and federal tax exemption.

This book covers §501(c)(3) so extensively that it is almost easy to forget that federal income taxes are but one of the many taxes that an organization might be required to pay. An organization with employees is responsible for payroll taxes,[45] and one that has engaged in profitable unrelated income activities must pay unrelated business income taxes. *See* Chapter 8 *infra*. In some cases, §501(c)(3) organizations will also be responsible for state or local taxes. A general description of the ways in which states approach income, sales and use, and property tax exemptions rules follows. The rules concerning those taxes vary widely by jurisdiction, however, and each §501(c)(3) organization must determine for itself which taxes it should pay.

These exemptions are not without cost to states and municipalities. It has been estimated that states forego $17–32 billion a year in property taxes, $7–9 billion in state income taxes, and $3.3 billion in sales taxes.[46] Financially strapped governments are considering eliminating or reducing some of these exemptions as one way to help balance the budget.

A. STATE INCOME TAX

States generally grant charitable exemptions from state income taxes to §501(c)(3) organizations.[47] Some states, such as Delaware, make the determination automatic. Del. Code Ann. Tit. 30, 1133. Others, such as California, incorporate federal tax exemption language into the statute, but they require a separate application for exemption. Cal. Rev. & Tax. §23701. Most states also have state provisions similar to the federal unrelated business income tax.

B. SALES AND USE TAXES

Sales and use taxes vary considerably from state to state. They are not as universal as income and property tax exemptions.[48] Some jurisdictions treat charitable organizations as ordinary taxpayers; some list organizations that are eligible for exemption from sales and use taxes; and others grant broad exemptions to charitable organizations. For a discussion of the policies behind

---

[45] Payroll taxes, if overlooked or deliberately left unpaid, can lead to a personal judgment against board members. 26 U.S. Code §6672. *See* Robert W. Wood, *Officers of Nonprofits Face Personal Liability for Taxes*, Forbes (Oct. 14, 2011).

[46] Maria Di Miceli, *Drive Your Own PILOT: Federal and State Constitutional Challenges to the Imposition of Payments in Lieu of Taxes on Tax-Exempt Entities*, 66 TAX LAW. 835 (2013).

[47] *Id*. Only 45 states have a corporate income tax. They all exempt charitable organizations from this tax.

[48] *Id*. A total of 24 states exempt purchases made by nonprofits from the sales tax, and another 16 exempt specific categories of nonprofits. In contrast, only 15 states exempt sales made by nonprofits.

exemptions for sales and use taxes for nonprofit organizations and a list of the rules in each jurisdiction, see Mark J. Cowan, *Nonprofits and the Sales and Use Tax*, 9 FLA. TAX REV. 1077 (2010); Melissa A. Walker & Linsey F. Sipult, *Nonprofit Sales Tax Exemption: Where Do States Draw the Line?* 40 NONPROFIT & VOLUNTARY SECTOR Q. 1005 (2011).

One cannot assume that an organization exempt from income tax under §501(c)(3) will also be exempt from sales and use taxes. In Wisconsin, for example, professional symphonies are subject to the sales tax because their concerts are considered entertainment events, not educational ones, even though they are characterized as educational organizations under §501(c)(3). *Milwaukee Symphony Orchestra Inc. v. Dep't of Revenue*, 781 N.W.2d 674 (Wis. 2010). Similarly, the Cascade Christian Center, a nonprofit church that operates a center for children in Washington state, did not notice a new law regarding sales tax exemptions and failed to comply. According to Avalara Consultants, the penalties, fines, and fees that the organization paid after being audited almost bankrupted the organization. *Nonprofits and Sales Tax*, An Avalara Q&A*, http://www.avalara.com/learn/whitepapers/nonprofits-and-sales-tax/, accessed May 10, 2016.

C. PROPERTY TAXES AND PILOTS

Although all states grant charitable tax exemptions for property taxes,[49] these exemptions have become increasingly controversial, and much of the change in tax-exempt charity law in recent years has been with regard to property taxes. We saw some of this change earlier in the chapter in the discussion of health care, educational, and religious purposes, but changes in property tax exemption generally affect all nonprofits in a locality. This section discusses the rationale behind property taxes, some recent legislative and case law developments, and Payments in Lieu of Taxes (PILOTS).

1. Rationales for Property Tax Exemptions

Why would local property tax exemptions be more troublesome than state or federal income tax exemptions? Is there a difference behind the rationales for these types of exemptions? One rationale for a property tax exemption is the subsidy theory—the work that the charity does is so worthwhile that it deserves an extra incentive to complete the work. That explanation may be true, but it does not explain why the charities that own the most real estate are the beneficiaries of this largesse. It is of no help at all to a charity that rents space.

---

[49] Evelyn Brody points out that 18 state constitutions mandate property tax exemption for charities; 25 state constitutions authorize the legislature to grant exemptions, and 7 state constitutions are silent on property tax exemptions for charities. The U.S. Constitution, which governs Washington, D.C., is silent as to whether charities should be exempt from property taxes in the District of Columbia. Evelyn Brody, *All Charities Are Property-Tax Exempt, but Some Are More Exempt than Others*, 44 NEW ENG. L. REV. 621, Appendix (2010).

One difference between property tax and income tax exemptions is that the test for property tax exemption has a dual focus. Like the income tax exemption test, it looks to the charitable purpose of the institution, but it also determines whether the charity uses the property for exempt purposes. This difference does not explain why the definition of "charity" might change from one context to another, however.

Another possible difference between the approach to state property exemption and federal income tax protection is that state and local governments face social problems, such as homelessness and poverty, more directly than the federal government. This puts additional pressure on the taxing authorities, legislatures, and courts to include a "charity care" requirement into the test for property tax exemption.

The most frequent way of looking at the differences between property and income tax exemptions is to examine the uses to which the government puts the property tax payments. Property taxes pay for water services, fire protection, garbage collection, and the like. Is it fair for an obviously wealthy tax-exempt organization with a great deal of land, such as a university or law school, to remove that land from the tax base? The university still avails itself of the municipal services, but does not pay for them. On the other hand, the income tax pays for governmental services, such as military protection, that tax-exempt organizations also use to their advantage. It may be that the connection between the tax payments and services granted is simply less immediately evident in the income tax context.

Perhaps the difference in attitude is based more on practical than theoretical concerns. Some localities have so much exempt property that there is barely any revenue available for the schools. Almost 80% of the property in Dayton, Ohio, for example, is exempt from property taxes.[50] State and local governments often have constitutional mandates to balance budgets, and the sluggish economy has sent all governmental entities in search of new revenue. A 2007 study that calculated the tax benefits of 27 hospital systems in the Chicago area sheds some light on these practical considerations. It found that these hospitals received $489 million in tax benefits—$44 million in federal income tax, $10 million in state income tax, $156 million in sales tax, and $279 million in property tax. It also found that the systems provided $175 million in charity care.[51] In other words, the community lost almost twice as much revenue as it received in return for

---

[50] Ken McLatchey, *Downtown Dayton: 80 Percent of Property Is Exempt from Taxes*, TRIBUNE BUSINESS NEWS (Aug. 29, 2015).

[51] CTBA, AN UPDATE: AN ANALYSIS OF THE TAX EXEMPTIONS GRANTED TO NON-PROFIT HOSPITALS IN CHICAGO AND THE METRO AREA AND THE CHARITY CARE PROVIDED IN RETURN (2009). National estimates for the annual value of secular tax-exempt property range from $9 billion to $15 billion. Churches' property tax exemption is probably worth another $3 billion to $5 billion. Joseph J. Cordes, Marie Gantz, and Thomas Pollak, *What Is the Property-Tax Exemption Worth?* PROPERTY TAX EXEMPTION FOR CHARITIES: MAPPING THE BATTLEFIELD 81 (Evelyn Brody ed., 2002); Woods Bowman & Marion R. Fremont-Smith, *Nonprofits and State and Local Governments*, in NONPROFITS AND GOVERNMENT: COLLABORATION AND CONFLICT 181, 202 (Elizabeth T. Boris & C. Eugene Steuerle eds., 2d ed. 2006).

community benefit. To add insult to injury, those who receive the benefit from nationally renowned hospitals, private schools, museums, and summer camps, are not even members of the local community. With these considerations in mind, the trend for local governments to try to narrow the property tax exemption is unsurprising. As Professor Evelyn Brody has pointed out, "State exemption requirements generally reflect more of a quid-pro-quo rationale [for granting exemption] than does federal exemption." Evelyn Brody, *All Charities Are Property-Tax Exempt, but Some Charities Are More Exempt Than Others*, 44 NEW ENG. L. REV. 621, 622 (2010).

This quid pro quo rationale raises several questions. Is it the correct test for property tax exemption? Is the exemption merely an acknowledgment of the economic return that the organization already brings the community? Should the only charities that receive property tax exemptions be those that "lessen the burdens of government"? Or should properties be accorded tax exemption because of intangible social benefits that they bring to the community?

2. Legislative and Case Law Development

As mentioned above, the property tax exemption statutes generally look both to the charitable purpose of the organization and to the use of the property in question. If the property is not used for charitable purposes, even if the organization is exempt, it is likely to pay property taxes. Thus, a tax-exempt school that charges faculty and students for parking may be able to avoid federal income taxes due to an exception to the unrelated business income tax rules,[52] but it will likely pay property taxes for the parking lot because the property is not being used for exempt purposes.

Recent case law has used this part of the statutory analysis to expand the property tax rolls. Although the property tax statutes under consideration were different, this analysis was, in essence, the basis of both the *Provena Hospital* and *AHS Hospital* decisions, described in Part V, Sec. C. above. Provena failed to provide enough charity care or help lessen the burdens of government, and the Morristown Memorial Hospital intertwined commercial activity with its tax-exempt activity to such an extent that the court found it could not differentiate the two purposes. In other words, despite their charitable purposes, these hospitals were not using the property for charitable purposes.

In addition to case law, states and localities are hoping that legislative changes can help bring in additional funds. In many ways, it is easier politically to remove a tax exemption than to raise taxes, and between 2011 and 2014, most states established task forces to examine their tax exemptions and credits.[53] As mentioned above, Illinois amended its statute to require hospitals to document that they provide a community benefit that is equal to or greater than the property tax they would otherwise pay. Other states proposed legislation that did not pass,

---

[52] Chapter 8 covers the unrelated business income tax rules.

[53] Jennifer DePaul, *Short on Revenue, State and Local Governments Turn to Nonprofits*, 71 STATE TAX NOTES 205 (2014).

but that are likely to be reintroduced. For example, New Hampshire considered legislation that would require nonprofits with more than $1.5 million in gross operating expenditures to pay the business enterprise tax. North Dakota considered legislation that would allow municipalities to levy special assessments on tax-exempt nonprofits for safety and emergency services, and the District of Columbia's Tax Revision Commission recommended that nonprofits pay a local services fee of $25 per quarter for each person they employ. None of these measures has passed into law, however.

In 2015, the governor of Maine, Paul LePage, used his proposed 2016–2017 budget to suggest a major change in state property tax exemption rules. His proposal would tax nonprofits with property valued at $500,000 or more at 50% of the tax that they would pay as for-profits. Houses of worship and smaller nonprofits would retain the traditional 100% property tax exemption. The governor predicted that this provision would generate at least $60 million in yearly revenue for the state's local municipalities. The budget was eventually passed without this provision.[54]

Pennsylvania is an interesting state to watch in this respect. In 2012, the Pennsylvania Supreme Court reaffirmed an earlier decision that set forth a five-part test for determining whether an entity is an 'institution of purely public charity' under the Pennsylvania Constitution. In *Mesivtah Eitz Chaim of Bobov, Inc. v. Pike County Board of Assessment Appeals*, 44 A.3d 3 (Pa. 2012), the issue was whether the plaintiff, a Jewish summer camp, would be tax-exempt under a broader test that the Pennsylvania legislature had adopted with the Purely Public Charity Act, 10 P.S. §§ 371-385 (Act 55). The Pennsylvania Court found that it was the final arbiter of constitutional interpretation in the state and rejected the legislature's test.

Instead, the court applied its earlier test that requires an organization requesting property tax exemption to (1) advance a charitable purpose; (2) donate or render gratuitously a substantial portion of its services; (3) benefit a substantial and indefinite class of persons who are legitimate subjects of charity; (4) relieve the government of some of its burden; and (5) be entirely free from a private profit motive. The court let stand the lower-case decision that denied the exemption on the ground that the summer camp did not relieve the government of some of its burden. *Mesivtah Eitz Chaim of Bobov, Inc. v. Pike County Bd. of Assessment Appeals*, 2009 Pa. Commw. Unpub. LEXIS 369.

The opinion has opened the door for cases that one would not have expected in earlier years. For example, in *Fayette Res., Inc. v. Fayette County Bd. of Assessment Appeals*, 107 A.3d 839 (Pa Commw. Ct. 2014), a §501(c)(3) that supports people with disabilities (in part by providing homes for them) was denied property tax exemption because its acceptance of Medicaid fees prevents it from showing that it donates a substantial portion of its services.

---

[54] Alanna Durkin, *Lepage Plan to Tax Nonprofits Getting National Attention*, PORTLAND PRESS HERALD, (March 8. 2015); Steve Mistler, *After Long, Fierce Fight, Maine Gets a Budget and Avoids a Shutdown*, PORTLAND PRESS HERALD (June 30, 2015).

The opinion has also unleashed a contest between the legislative and judicial branches of the government. A constitutional amendment has been proposed that will overrule the *Mesivtah Eitz Chaim* case and ensure that the legislature, not the courts, has the power to determine which organizations qualify for charitable tax exemption. Once the House passes the amendment, it will go to the voters for a decision. In general, large nonprofits favor the amendment because they assume that the legislature will reinstate the more liberal Act 55. Many municipalities favor the status quo because they expect to collect more property tax. It is unclear, however, if these assumptions are correct. No action occurred on this constitutional proposal in 2015. Evelyn Brody, *The 21st-Century Fight over Who Sets the Terms of the Charity Property Tax Exemption*, 77 EXEMPT ORG. TAX. REV. 259 (2016); Kevin Kearns, *The Property Tax Exemption in Pennsylvania: The Saga Continues*, 6 NONPROFIT POLICY FORUM 111 (2015).

In the meantime, cities and counties in Pennsylvania are busy adding more nonprofit organizations to their tax rolls. Allegheny County, the home of Pittsburgh, has been particularly aggressive. In 2013, it sent letters to 2,800 local nonprofits asking them to show that they used their property solely for charitable purposes. Almost 200 of them have been added to the tax rolls, either because they responded that they were taxable or because they did not respond at all. The county is reviewing the property of those that responded that they were pure public charities. *Pa. County's Review Puts Scores of Charities on Tax Rolls*, CHRON. PHIL. (Feb. 17, 2015).[55]

3. PILOTs (and SILOTs)

Whatever the purpose behind the property tax exemption, the pressures on the public purse are unlikely to abate soon. Some nonprofits and their communities have entered into Payments in Lieu of Taxes (PILOTs) or Services in Lieu of Taxes (SILOTs) agreements. A 2012 study found that at least 420 nonprofits in 218 localities in 28 states paid PILOTs. The northeastern United States accounted for 80% of these payments. Most payments are quite small, but 10 organizations account for the majority of the $92 million that is brought in annually—Harvard University, Yale University, Stanford University, Brown University, Boston University, Massachusetts General Hospital, Dartmouth College, Brigham and Women's Center, Massachusetts Institute of Technology, and Princeton University (in order of payments, beginning with the highest). Adam Langley, Daphne Kenyon, and Patricia C. Bailin, *Payments in Lieu of Taxes by Nonprofits*, Lincoln Institute of Land Policy (2012).

The property tax debate is of obvious importance to any nonprofit organization that owns its own property, as well as to local governments. It may

---

[55] In 2013, the city of Pittsburgh, itself in Alleghany County, sued the University of Pittsburgh Medical Center, claiming that it should pay payroll and property taxes. The suit was dismissed in 2014 on procedural grounds, and the city of Pittsburgh said it would negotiate PILOTS instead. Robert Zullo, *UPMC, City Drop Legal Fight over Taxes*, PITTSBURGH POST-GAZETTE (July 29, 2014). As of August 2015, they had not come to an agreement. Chelsea Wagner, *The City Should Challenge UPMC on Property Tax Exemptions*, PITTSBURG POST-GAZETTE (Aug. 7, 2015).

also be important for policymakers at the federal level, however. Despite the differences between federal income tax exemption and state property tax exemption, pressure exists at both levels of government to find more tax revenue and to resolve tensions that arise when nonprofit organizations engage in commercial activity without aiding the poor or lessening the burdens of government. The IRS and Congress will undoubtedly be watching developments at the state level, just as state policymakers will watch the IRS and Congress. Whether the standards for tax exemption at the state and federal levels will ultimately be uniform remains an open question.

For further reading on property tax exemptions for nonprofit organizations and PILOTS, see Evelyn Brody, *The 21st-Century Fight Over Who Sets the Terms of the Charity Property Tax Exemption*, 77 EXEMPT ORG. TAX. REV. 259 (2016); Eric Lustig, *A Continuing Look at Boston's Payment in Lieu of Taxes Program: Updated Version 2.0*, 50 NEW ENGL. L. REV. ON REMAND 1 (2015); Maria Di Miceli, *Drive Your Own PILOT: Federal and State Constitutional Challenges to the Imposition of Payments in Lieu of Taxes on Tax-Exempt Entities*, 66 TAX LAW. 835 (2013); Daphne A. Kenyon & Adam H. Langley, PAYMENTS IN LIEU OF TAXES: BALANCING MUNICIPAL AND NONPROFIT INTERESTS (Ann LeRoyer ed., 2010); Fan Fei, James Hines, and Jill Horwitz, *Are Pilots Property Taxes For Nonprofits?* Working Paper 21088, http://www.nber.org/papers/w21088, NATIONAL BUREAU OF ECONOMIC RESEARCH (2015).

XII. APPLICATION FOR RECOGNITION OF SECTION 501(c)(3) STATUS

With a few exceptions, organizations secure IRS recognition as §501(c)(3) organizations by filing a completed Form 1023 or 1023-EZ with the IRS. Churches[56] and public charities that normally have less than $5,000 in annual gross receipts are exempted from this requirement, but the vast majority of organizations need to file a version of Form 1023 within 27 months of their date of incorporation, so that their exemption will be retroactive to the date of incorporation.[57] Those who file after 27 months can obtain exemption from the date that the IRS determines the requirements of the statute are met. See IRC §508 and accompanying regulations.

Most organizations with annual gross receipts of less than $50,000 and total assets of less than $250,000 are eligible to complete Form 1023-EZ, a three page document that is much simpler to complete than Form 1023. *See* Rev. Proc.

---

[56] The statute exempts "churches, their integrated auxiliaries, and conventions or associations of churches" from the requirement of applying for recognition of §501(c)(3) status.

[57] If an organization has a legitimate reason for missing the 27-month deadline and has, in fact, been organized and operated as a §501(c)(3) organization during that time, the IRS may waive the deadline and make the exemption retroactive. If the IRS does not waive the 27-month filing requirement, however, the exemption will not begin until the date the IRS receives the filing.

2014-40. IR 2014-77. The form must be filed online at https://pay.gov /public/registration. The form is considerably simpler than the traditional Form 1023. It is also less expensive than the traditional form (the fee is $400 as opposed to $850). Yet not all lawyers recommend that eligible organizations file this form instead of the traditional Form 1023, and many believe this new form is a bad idea.

Why would someone who would otherwise qualify to submit Form 1023-EZ not decide to go this route? First, some of the questions ask about activities that are permissible, such as lobbying, but which encourage a "no" answer. Small organizations that might do an insignificant amount of lobbying, engage in financial transactions with the board, or conduct activities outside the United States, will want to complete Form 1023-EZ. Second, the organization might succeed beyond its dreams and receive more than $50,000 in revenue in its first few years. Although there is no penalty if the estimate was made in good faith and was reasonable, some fear that this type of success would trigger an audit, and it would be better to fill the complete form and avoid the audit. Finally, donors may steer away from organizations that filled out Form 1023-EZ, recognizing that there was less rigor in their application process. Ben Takis, *Who Should (And Should Not) File the 1023-EZ?* TAX-EXEMPT SOLUTIONS (July 14, 2014).

Is it a good idea to permit filing a simpler Form 1023? One of the purposes of the longer form is to educate budding organizations about the rules and requirements of §501(c)(3) status, and the three-page document is unable to perform that function thoroughly. The concern is that organizations that would otherwise not qualify will receive determination letters, and the process of revoking their exemption is difficult and expensive. Although the IRS has procedures in place to avoid such mistakes, concern remains. In 2015, the Taxpayer Advocate Service studied Form 1023-EZs filed in 20 states and found that 37% of the organizations receiving favorable determination letters from the IRS were not actually eligible for exempt status under the law. As a result, it recommended that the IRS revise Form 1023-EZ to require the addition of organizing documents, a description of actual or planned activities, and past or projected financial information. It also recommended that the IRS review this information before deciding whether to approve exemption applications. NATIONAL TAXPAYER ADVOCATE ANNUAL REPORT TO CONGRESS 2015.

Assuming that the IRS determines that the requirements of §501(c)(3) are met, it issues a letter of determination that recognizes the organization's tax exemption and its ability to accept tax-deductible contributions. It also addresses the issue of whether the organization is a public charity or a private foundation. In some instances, the IRS is able to make a final determination as to this categorization, but in other cases, the IRS issues an advance ruling that the organization is likely to be a public charity in five years, and it will revisit the issue at that time. This topic, one of the more complex in this book, will be discussed in Chapter 7.

An organization's letter of determination is a public document that must be made available to any individual or organization that asks to see it. It is also the document that organizations use to prove they are §501(c)(3) organizations to funders and others who need proof of their tax-exempt status. The public can rely on this letter of determination unless the IRS notifies the public that the organization is no longer a §501(c)(3) organization. Once the letter of determination has been issued, the IRS will include the organization in Publication 78, Cumulative List of Exempt Organizations. A searchable list of §501(c)(3) organizations is online at www.guidestar.org and www.irs.gov /charities/article/0,,id=96136,00.html.

PROBLEM: COMPLETING FORM 1023

Prepare a Form 1023 for your organization. This exercise has three purposes: (1) to introduce you to an important IRS form; (2) to help you learn how to convince the IRS that an organization has a tax-exempt purpose and that its activities will further that purpose; and (3) if you are in a course in which the students create virtual organizations, to create some more "facts" to be used in hypothetical questions throughout the course.

The form is available online at www.irs.gov/pub/irs-pdf/f1023.pdf. Before completing the form online, however, be sure that your Portable Document Format (PDF) program allows you to save changes to the form. If not, you will want to print out the form and complete it manually.

When you are engaged in the practice of law, you will need to consult the IRS's instructions for Form 1023 as you answer each question. This exercise does not ask you to do that, but please read the instructions carefully if you ever actually complete Form 1023. A helpful website for someone who is completing Form 1023 is http://501c3book.org. The publisher of that website has also written an e-book on the topic, Sandy Deja, *Prepare Your Own 501(c)(3) Application* (2016).

The following "instructions" should help you fill in the form for purposes of this exercise. After you have read a few more chapters, you will understand why the IRS asks each of these questions. For now, you should understand the questions about the purpose and activities of your organization and know how to answer them. Regarding issues that we have not yet covered, this exercise will either tell you how to answer the questions, tell you to skip them, or expect you to use common sense.

Please do not include any attachments, except the narrative description of activities in Part IV and the list of people (or classes of people) who receive benefits in Part VI. Despite the language of the form, do not attach your organizational documents, send a fee, send the 1023 checklist, or send any other requested attachments.

Part I: Identification of Applicant: Most of these questions are self-explanatory, and you can answer them however you want. Question 10 should be revised, as all §501(c)(3) organizations must now file a Form 990, so your answer should be "yes."

Part IV: Narrative Description of Your Activities: This is the most important question in this assignment, because this chapter focuses on proving that your organization's purposes and activities fit within the requirements of §501(c)(3). It is also the most important question if you are actually submitting the document to the IRS, because it gets to the heart of your organization. Use what you have learned from the readings and class discussions to explain your organization's activities in a way that will increase its chances for obtaining IRS approval.

Part V: Compensation and Other Financial Arrangements with Officers, Directors, Trustees, Employees, and Independent Contractors:

1. When you list officers, directors, and trustees, be consistent with your organizational documents.

2. Make up answers to the questions about highly paid employees and contractors. You can have them if you want (and if you make your budget large enough in Part IX), but you certainly do not have to do so.

3. Do not answer questions 4–9, although you may want to read them as a preview of the concerns that the IRS will have about financial arrangements, which we will cover later in this book.

Part VI: Your Members or Other Individuals and Organizations That Receive Benefits from You: If you answer "yes" to any of these questions, please answer the question in one sentence (or list). Remember that this response could have an effect on the IRS's perception of whether your organization's purpose is one that can be deemed tax exempt under §501(c)(3).

Part VIII: Your Specific Activities: Your organization does not support political candidates; it can attempt to influence legislation if you want, but if it does, indicate that it has elected to have the lobbying activities measured by filing Form 5766. Answer the rest of Part VIII. Your answer will be "no" to most questions, but some of you will answer "yes" to one or two of the questions. Do not worry about the explanations or attachments.

Part IX: Financial Data:

A. You should make up information for this part. This is an opportunity to learn a little about budgets. Do not worry if you do not know what to say. Your budget is irrelevant for the purposes of this course, unless we can use it to create hypothetical situations later. Completing this part now should encourage you to learn something about financial statements before you start your own nonprofit—or any organization, for that matter.

B. You have not yet completed a tax year, so you do not need to fill out the part about tax years.

Part X: Public Charity Status: These questions allude to topics covered in Chapter 7. For now, your organization is not a private foundation (question 1a) and you should check g, h, or i in question 5 (unless the organization is a church, school, or hospital, in which case you should check the correct box). In question 6, request an advance ruling. The answer to question 7 is "no"— the organization has not been in existence long enough.

RAISING MONEY

CHAPTER 5

CHARITABLE CONTRIBUTIONS

Purposes of this chapter:

- Introduce §170
- Explore rationales for the charitable contribution deduction
- Define the term "quid pro quo" and consider what constitutes a gift for tax purposes
- Introduce other charitable contribution issues
- Consider contractual issues that can arise in the charitable gifts context

To think about as you read:

You are the outside attorney to an art museum. Some wealthy donors would like to donate $100 million worth of paintings to the museum. They would like to take a tax deduction for the full amount today but hang the paintings in their homes for the next five years. At that point, they expect the paintings to be placed together in a wing of the museum named after the donors and to stay there forever. Can the art museum accommodate them? What should you do to protect the museum from future lawsuits?

I. INTRODUCTION

Up to this point, we have concentrated on the issues surrounding the creation of a nonprofit organization. We have examined whether an organization should be incorporated, focused on the issues surrounding incorporation, developed articles of incorporation and bylaws, examined the legal issues that can arise from these documents, and explored governance issues at the state-law level. We have also begun to explore issues surrounding tax exemption for charitable organizations, specifically the purposes and activities that fulfill the requirements of 26 USC §501(c)(3).

Funding the organization is the next major challenge—no matter how strong its mission, a nonprofit cannot stay in business for long without money. Section 501(c)(3) organizations raise money from individuals (Chapters 5 and 6), from foundations and alternatives to foundations (Chapter 7), and through commercial activity (Chapters 8 and 10). Each of these situations raises interesting and complex legal issues.

This chapter and the next cover the topic of raising funds from individuals from two different perspectives—which gifts are tax deductible (Chapter 5) and what rules an organization must follow when it solicits funds (Chapter 6).[1] The topic of tax-deductible contributions is often covered in income tax courses, where the focus is on the individual taking the deduction. Here, the focus is on the nonprofit corporation. Which of these organizations are eligible to receive tax-deductible contributions? When has an organization that is able to accept a tax-deductible contribution actually received a completed gift? What must the organization do to substantiate the gift?

By necessity, the topic of charitable contributions is covered cursorily. The law covering charitable contributions is extremely complex and cannot be covered completely in an introductory book to nonprofit corporation law. Therefore, this chapter covers relatively simple donor transactions. It does not tackle difficult issues of valuation, charitable bequests, or deferred giving.

II. RATIONALE FOR THE CHARITABLE CONTRIBUTION DEDUCTION

In 2014, Americans donated $358.38 billion to charity. Almost ¾ of that amount (72%) came from living individuals.[2] The rest came from testamentary gifts, foundations, and corporations. Only about 1/3 of individual taxpayers who donated these funds actually took advantage of the charitable tax deductions discussed in this chapter,[3] but their gifts accounted for approximately 4/5 of the total giving by individuals.[4] Thus, the money exempted from the tax system is considerable, and scholars and legislators debate its merits on a regular basis.

---

[1] Some of the charitable contribution rules are also applicable to gifts from corporations or other entities, but this chapter concentrates on individuals. In addition, the charitable solicitation laws discussed in Chapter 6 apply to solicitations from any person, corporation, or foundation, but because the laws are designed to protect individuals, the discussion of these rules is located in the section of this book that covers raising funds from individuals.

[2] Giving USA, 2015, GIVING USA FOUNDATION.

[3] A total of 68% of returns filed in 2014 claimed the standard deduction. Tax Policy Center, http://taxpolicycenter.org/taxfacts/displayafact.cfm?DocID=173&Topic2id=30&Topic3id=34, accessed May 11, 2016.

[4] Harvey P. Dale & Roger Colinvaux, *The Charitable Contributions Deduction: Federal Tax Rules,* 68 TAX LAW. 331, 359 (2015), citing the Giving USA statistics from 2013 reported in Giving USA 2014. Interestingly, 1/5 of that total came from those with adjusted gross income of more than $1 million a year, a group that represents 0.074% of the population.

The rationales set forth for the charitable contribution deduction tend to parallel the rationales for tax exemption that were set forth in Chapter 4. There is a public benefit theory (organizations that provide a public benefit deserve an additional subsidy beyond that of income tax exemption), an income tax theory (income that is not used for personal consumption should not be taxed), and a political philosophy theory (contributions to private philanthropy encourage pluralism, democracy, and innovation beyond that which can be provided by the government or for-profit sectors).

The charitable deduction was introduced in 1917, when Congress was increasing taxes to help pay for World War I. Congressional leaders were concerned that this tax increase would cause individuals to reduce or stop their contributions to charitable organizations unless the deduction was introduced. As Senator Henry Hollis from New Hampshire explained,

> Usually people contribute to charities and educational objects out of their surplus. After they have done everything else they want to do, after they have educated their children and traveled and spent their money on everything they really want or think they want, then, if they have something left over, they will contribute it to a college or to the Red Cross or for some scientific purposes. Now, when war comes and we impose these very heavy taxes on incomes, that will be the first place where the wealthy men will be tempted to economize, namely, in donations to charity. They will say, "Charity begins at home."[5]

This belief that tax deductions can spur charitable giving continues to influence legislators. In December 2015, for example, President Barack Obama signed the Protecting Americans from Tax Hikes (PATH) Act, which allows taxpayers who are at least 70½ years old to make tax-free distributions from their individual retirement accounts (IRAs) to charity. It also provides an enhanced deduction for contributions of food inventory and for conservation easements. These provisions, which had been in effect on a temporary basis, were made permanent because Congress believed that they had proven their effectiveness at encouraging giving.

Not all lawmakers believe that donors respond to charitable tax incentives. In 2015, for example, Governor Paul LePage of Maine recommended eliminating that state's charitable deduction provision. Part of his reasoning was that deductions are unimportant to taxpayers who donate to charitable organizations.[6]

Whether or not taxpayers are motivated by the charitable deduction, other policy issues arise. Is the charitable deduction fair? Does it actually give a bigger benefit to the wealthy? Do donors give for other reasons apart from the tax deduction? Is there a way to encourage giving, either without the deduction or with a changed system? Is it possible that it is structured in such a way that it has become "essential to the maintenance and perpetuation of the upper class in the United States," who use nonprofit activities as "the nexus of a modern power

---

[5] Remarks of Senator Hollis, 55 Cong. Rec. 6728 (1917).
[6] Steve Mistler, *LePage's 'Flood' of Charitable Giving from Income Tax Cut Is Disputed*, PORTLAND PRESS HERALD (Feb. 17, 2015).

elite"?[7] Following are excerpts from articles and some notes that address these issues.

JOHN COLOMBO, THE MARKETING OF PHILANTHROPY AND THE CHARITABLE CONTRIBUTIONS DEDUCTION: INTEGRATING THEORIES FOR THE DEDUCTION AND TAX EXEMPTION

36 WAKE FOREST L. REV. 657, 667-669, 678, and 682-685 (2001)

One rationale that could justify the "contribution or gift" limitation on deductibility is that the deduction is a reward for certain individual altruism that is particularly valued by our society.... [A] deduction serves as a reward for selfless behavior. Another, slightly different, variation of this theme is that a person who makes a charitable donation is less well-off or less able to pay taxes than one who does not; hence, a deduction is warranted on the grounds of horizontal equity....

The major problem with this theory, however, is identifying what behavior we should be inducing.... Presumably, we want to subsidize only "good" behavior by the contributor, which in turn creates two major difficulties. First, many academics within the social sciences argue that there is no such thing as altruism, and that behavior which is seemingly altruistic actually is motivated by self-interest. Second, even if people do act altruistically from time to time, because human motivations are terribly complex, developing an administrable legal test that could accurately isolate donations which are selflessly motivated in order to encourage them through the deduction would be practically impossible....

Finally, there are simple tax and legal policy problems with the "subsidizing altruism" rationale for the section 170 deduction. First, the deduction for charitable donations applies not only to individuals, but also to corporations. While one can imagine pure altruism as a motive for individual donors, ascribing purely altruistic motives to corporate philanthropy is difficult at best....

Second, as tax-expenditure analysts have previously noted, the deduction provides a financial reward for philanthropic behavior that varies with the donor's marginal tax bracket. This effect of the deduction means that the cost of giving is cheapest for those in the highest tax brackets; or put conversely, the size of the government subsidy increases as one's tax bracket goes up. If the deduction is meant to serve as a financial reward for philanthropic behavior, it is hard to see why rich folks ought to receive a proportionately greater benefit from such behavior than poor folks.

Third, ... the desire to subsidize altruistic behavior cannot be squared with the fact that a contribution deduction is available only in the case of transactions with exempt charities. Surely a person who anonymously gives to a relief fund to

---

[7] Tersa Odendahl, CHARITY BEGINS AT HOME: GENEROSITY AND SELF INTEREST AMONG THE PHILANTHROPIC ELITE (Basic Books, 1990).

aid a particular individual comes closer to the altruistic ideal than the multi-million-dollar capital gift to a major university, replete with commemorative plaques, signs, and the high-profile news conference. Yet under current law, the former is not deductible while the latter almost certainly is....

Despite suggestions that the section 170 deduction can be explained as an incentive for individual altruism and despite [the] suggestion that the deduction is consistent with the normative definition of the income tax base, the most widely accepted rationale for the section 170 deduction remains that the deduction helps subsidize the activities of charitable organizations. Legislative history indicates that the original deduction was primarily intended to insure that the "new" income tax did not seriously impair the flow of private funds to exempt charities; the particular motivation of the giver was not a subject of discussion. Similarly, later amendments to the charitable deduction provision to permit deductions for contributions by corporations came at a time (during the Great Depression) that "the federal government sought voluntary transfers from the private sector (i.e., nontax revenue) to fund needed social programs."

In fact, much of the academic work on the deduction over the past several decades has focused on whether the deduction is an efficient support mechanism for charitable activity. Because a contribution is deductible, the contributor saves the taxes that otherwise would have been due on the contribution, making its true economic cost to the contributor lower. By foregoing taxes that otherwise would have been due on the contribution, the government makes contributions cheaper and supplies an implicit subsidy to the recipient organization equal to the donor's marginal tax bracket....

An explanation for deductibility focused on its relationship to funding the underlying charitable entity also gives a plausible basis for the "upside-down" effect of the deduction. If, in fact, we are concerned only about insuring the flow of funds from private individuals to exempt organizations, making this behavior cheapest to those with the most money, and therefore the most capacity to transfer economic wealth to exempt entities, makes some sense.

One can argue, of course, that this government subsidization skews the influence of big donors and that the private funds subsidized in this manner disproportionately flow to certain kinds of organizations, particularly arts organizations. Empirical studies confirm that some organizations, particularly churches, are largely funded by relatively small donations from middle and lower-income groups, whereas arts and education organizations rely more heavily on large gifts from wealthy contributors.

Finally, focusing on subsidizing the exempt entity provides an explanation for why donations to private disaster relief are not deductible.... [M]ajor explanations for why charities are tax exempt focus to a great degree on the "spread" of societal benefits provided by these institutions. In effect, government policy regarding the contributions deduction reflects underlying policy decisions to provide governmental support only to organizations that provide broad societal benefits rather than benefits to a single individual. We give special status to contributions to the Red Cross not because of administrative efficiency but because we have some assurance that the governmental subsidy provided to the Red Cross will be spread across a broad cross-section of society and not go just to a single person.

ARIANNA HUFFINGTON, NOT ALL CHARITY IS CREATED EQUAL

Excerpt from FANATICS AND FOOLS: THE GAME PLAN FOR WINNING BACK AMERICA (Hyperion 2004), p. 293

I . . . once believed that the private sector—especially Republican multimillionaires who talk incessantly about less government—would rise to the occasion and provide the funding needed to replicate and sustain on a large scale the many private social programs that have proven successful. But I found out firsthand that it's much easier to raise money for fashionable cultural causes and prestigious educational institutions than for homeless shelters and mentoring programs for at-risk children. The annual $3,500-a-plate, black-tie ball for the Costume Institute of the Metropolitan Museum of Art raises enough money to buy plenty of warm winter coats for children in New York City. But instead the funds go to preserving and displaying the evening gowns of the social elite.

. . . If the private sector is to play a serious part in addressing social crises in America, we need to stop defining charitable giving as any tax-deductible contribution to any old 501(c)(3)—a classification that lumps together a struggling soup kitchen and a university with an endowment larger than the GDP of the poorest one hundred countries. There's a compelling reason for the government to not reward these donations equally. Just take a look at the Slate 60, the online magazine's answer to the Forbes 400. It's an annual list of America's top charitable givers. Year in and year out, the list is dominated by those giving to already flush universities and museums—often to fund buildings bearing the giver's name.

After I wrote about my objections to the buck-is-a-buck-is-a-buck standard of the Slate rankings, its then-editor, Michael Kinsley, suggested I come up with a formula for adjusting the list—correcting for true philanthropic spirit as one might correct for inflation. So in 2000 I devised a compassion index, or as Slate dubbed it, "the Slate 60 Huffington Virtue Remix." The Slate 60 is based on the principal of praise, but those on the uncorrected list got plenty of that. I thought it was time for a little humiliation.

The virtue remix awarded minus points for self-aggrandizing gifts that only serve to make the world of the superrich just a little nicer, and plus points for gifts that help overcome poverty, alleviate suffering, and turn lives around. For example: minus 10 percent for investing in buildings instead of people (with another 15 percent deduction if the gift goes to a building named after the donor); 20 percent off for "self-referential giving" directly connected to the donor's business interests; and a sliding scale of demerits based on the age of the donor at the time of giving—a.k.a the "What took you so long?" factor. A 10 percent bonus, on the other hand, was awarded for giving to K–12 education, where the crisis is, rather than to Ivy League colleges, where the prestige and the big bucks are. And there was a 15 percent bonus if giving time went along with the gift of money.

The effect of the index on that year's list was telling. Forty-three donors had more points taken away than added, while only four gained points A few donors dropped more than twenty places, and one moved up thirteen. The biggest hit was taken by William Porter, founder of the Internet brokerage E*Trade, and his wife, Joan. Their $25 million gift to MIT had placed them in a tie for the twenty-seventh spot on the original Slate 60, but they dropped thirty spots for donating a) to a building at b) an already well-endowed institution that c) is related to Mr. Porter's business and d) was named after himself.

Also feeling the sting of the index was Robert G. Mondavi, chairman of the Robert Mondavi Winery, who was docked 30 percent for his self-referential gift of $20 million to the American Center for Wine, Food, and the Arts in his hometown of Napa, California. After sniffing and sipping (and yes, spitting), I found the donation cheeky and vainglorious, with strong notes of venality, and a hint of disingenuousness. Then there was Elmer E. Rasmuson, the former chairman of the National Bank of Alaska, who was penalized 20 percent for waiting until his ninetieth birthday party to announce a $50 million gift to the Anchorage Museum of History and Art. Did Elmer hit eighty and think, I'd better wait, there might be a $50 million emergency just around the bend? On the brighter side of the remix, cell phone mogul Craig McCaw and his wife, Susan, moved up thirteen places for their $15 million to the Foundation for Community Development and the Nelson Mandela Foundation, striving to bring health care, economic development, and peace to Africa.

The original catalyst for the Slate 60 was Ted Turner's warning that the "superrich won't loosen up their wads because they're afraid they'll reduce their net worth and go down on the Forbes list." His corrective was "to honor the generous and shame the stingy." The next step is for us all to acknowledge the obvious: Not all generosity is created equal, and so we need to honor those among the generous whose sights extend beyond their own enclaves. Compassion and philanthropy can't fix America's problems on their own. But they fill an even smaller portion of the gap between rich and poor when they are directed where they are not urgently needed.

ARTHUR C. BROOKS, CHARITABLE EXPLANATION

Wall St. J. (Nov. 27, 2006), p. A-12

'Tis the season to give. Our mailboxes are filling with appeals from fine organizations and worthy causes, competing for our holiday spirit and tax-deductible dollars. Millions of Americans will answer the call, donating in December as much as a third of the quarter-trillion dollars we give away each year. Per capita, Americans give more in this single month than most nations give all year long.[8]

Before congratulating ourselves too heartily, however, note that charity is not a virtue shared by all. While 85 million American households give away money each year to nonprofit organizations, another 30 million do not. And this distinction goes beyond "formal" giving. Recent survey data reveal that people who fail to donate money to charities are only a third as likely as donors to give money to friends and strangers. Non-donors are half as likely as donors to give blood. They even are less honest: Non-donors are much less likely than donors to return change mistakenly given to them by a cashier. When it comes to charity, we are two nations.

Why does Giving America behave so differently from Non-Giving America? The answer, contrary to what you might be thinking, is not income; America's working poor give away at least as large a percentage of their incomes as the rich, and a lot more than the middle class. The charity gap is driven not by economics but by values.

Nowhere is the divide in values more on display than in religion, the frontline in our so-called "culture war." And the relationship between religion and charity is nothing short of extraordinary. The Social Capital Community Benchmark Survey indicates that Americans who weekly attend a house of worship are 25 percentage points more likely to give than people who go to church rarely or never. These religious folks also give nearly four times more dollars per year than secularists, on average, and volunteer more than twice as frequently.

It is not the case that these enormous differences are due simply to religious people giving to their churches. Religious people are more charitable with all sorts of nonreligious causes as well. They are 10 percentage points likelier than secularists to give money to explicitly nonreligious charities like the United Way, and 25 points more likely to volunteer for secular groups such as the PTA. Churchgoers were far likelier in 2001 to give to 9/11-related causes. On average, people of faith give more than 50% more money each year to non-church social welfare organizations than secularists do.

A second core value affecting charity shows up in the belief citizens have about the government's role in their lives. Some Americans (about a third) believe the government should do more to reduce income differences between the rich and poor—largely through higher taxation and social spending. Others (about 40%) do not favor greater forced income redistribution. This is a major difference in worldview—not just about taxation, but also about the perceived duty of individuals to take personal responsibility for themselves and others. This difference affects people's likelihood of voluntarily giving to charity. The

---

[8] [This statistic has held constant since this article was originally published. A total of 30% of the donations made online via the Network for Good site in 2014 were made in December, with 10% of the annual total donated in the last three days of the year. That statistic has held for three years in a row. http://www.networkforgood.com/nonprofitblog/2014-year-end-giving-results-in-big-win-online-for-nonprofits/, accessed May 11, 2016. —Ed.]

General Social Survey shows that people who oppose government income redistribution donate four times as much money each year as do redistribution supporters.

Note that the charity gap is not due to anything the government is actually doing; rather, to what people think the government should be doing—in other words, nothing more than a political opinion. This fact throws a wrench into the traditional stereotype that conservatives in America are hardhearted while liberals are the compassionate ones. In the words of one common 2004 campaign yard sign in my town, "Bush Must Go! Human need, not corporate greed." However, the General Social Survey indicates that people who opine that government is "spending too little money on welfare"—not a viewpoint typically associated with George W. Bush's supposedly venal supporters—are less likely to give food or money to a homeless person than people who oppose greater welfare spending. Regardless of which view on welfare is superior, ask yourself this: Who will personally do more for a poor person today?

A third key value affecting charity is reflected in family life. Couples, even when they earn the same amount as single people, are more likely to give to charity, and the simple act of raising children appears to stimulate giving as well—children help us fill the collection plate even as they drain our wallets. Further, family life is the ideal transmission mechanism for charitable values: Data show that people who see their parents behave charitably are far likelier to be charitable themselves as adults.

As you probably noticed, the values predicting private charity in America tend to smile on the political right. Conservatives are twice as likely as liberals to attend a house of worship regularly; conservatives are one third as likely as liberals to say the government should "do more" to reduce income inequality; conservatives also have about 40% more children than liberals. Furthermore, there is a fringe on today's political left that goes beyond simple neglect of charity, and openly condemns it, claiming it lets governments off the hook from having to pay for services. So while there may be nothing inherently charitable about political conservatism, today's conservatives do outperform liberals on most measures of private giving.

What does this mean in the wake of the Democratic takeover of Congress this month? Will the new Democratic majority look for ways to protect and expand private giving? Or will they allow cultural forces to manifest themselves in policies uncongenial to private giving—such as punitive regulation on private foundations, expanded public subsidies to nonprofits that squeeze out charity, and various schemes that lower disposable income among major givers?

But an even greater moral test is personal, not political. Left or right, secular or religious, single or married, the cultural forces of giving and non-giving are not destiny for any of us. Private charity is a choice: a choice to express our values in a private and singularly humane way. This is worth remembering as we hold requests for charitable support in our hands this month—and make the right choice.

NOTES AND QUESTIONS

1. Recent research has confirmed the finding in the Arthur Brooks piece above that those with fewer resources tend to be more generous in their charitable contributions than the wealthy. Rebecca Koenig, *Mismatch Between Need and Affluence*, CHRONICLE OF PHILANTHROPY (July 8, 2015); Paul Solman, *Why Tghose Who Feel They Have Less Give More* (PBS NEWS HOUR, June 21, 2013). (The Solman report also noted that studies show those who volunteer and spend time on charity live longer than their less charitable counterparts.) Do these findings suggest that we should change or eliminate the charitable tax deduction?

2. Taxpayers who do not itemize their deductions take a "standard deduction," which is a set amount that covers all deductions that the taxpayers could take, whether or not they actually qualify for these deductions. In other words, they have no tax incentive to make charitable contributions, and yet this group of taxpayers donates approximately 20% of the contributions each year. What is the public policy behind the decision to allow a standard deduction? Does it imply that people are not responsive to tax incentives? Should Congress try to find a way to allow nonitemizers to take charitable tax deductions, as well as the standard deduction or would that be "double-dipping"?

3. Proposals for limiting, removing, or altering the charitable tax deduction have grown stronger in the last few years. For example, every budget proposal that President Obama sent to Congress recommended a 28% cap on all personal income tax deductions for those who itemize their taxes. Alliance for Charitable Reform, M*ore of the Same for Charities in President's Final Budget*, PHILANTHROPY ROUNDTABLE, Feb. 9, 2016. If this proposal had become law, taxpayers would have combined all their itemized deductions and tax benefits, such as the charitable deduction and the mortgage deduction, and could then take advantage of those deductions, so long as they remained at or below 28% of their income. Others have proposed a tax credit instead of a deduction. A tax credit provides a credit for the donation against the taxpayer's total income. In this case, a $100 gift would eliminate $100 from a person's taxable income whether she is a millionaire or an individual of modest means. (A deduction, on the other hand, depends on the taxpayer's tax bracket.) Which public policy or public policies do these proposals represent? Why do you think they have not been passed into law?

4. The most vocal opponents of these proposals are in the nonprofit sector. They fear that this could be the beginning of the end for the entire charitable deduction. *See* Rick Cohen, *Editorial Essayists Weigh in on Donation Cap*, NONPROFIT QUARTERLY (April 27, 2013). For an interesting discussion between Daniel Mitchell of the Cato Institute and Diana Aviv of Independent Sector on the charitable deduction, see *Should We End the Tax Deduction for Charity?* WALL ST. J. (Dec. 14, 2012). The Hudson Institute also held an informative program on the *Charitable Deduction in American*

Political Thought in April 2013, audio available at http://www.hudson .org/events/1007-the-charitable-deduction-in-american-political-thought42013, accessed May 11, 2016.

5. Several articles on the topic have been published in the last few years. Khrista Johnson, *The Charitable Deduction Games: Catching Change*, 31 GA. STATE U. LAW REV. 291 (2015); Roger Colvinaux, *Rationale and Changing the Charitable Deduction*, TAX NOTES 1453 (2013); Joseph Rosenberg, *Composition of Tax-Deductible Charitable Contributions*, 132 TAX NOTES 1427 (2011); Alex Reid, *Renegotiating the Charitable Deduction*, 71 TAX ANALYSTS 21 (2013); C. Eugene Steuerle, *The Charitable Deduction: Policy and Analysis*, 24 N.Y.U. Nat'l Center on Philanthropy & L. Conf. sec. A (2012); Paul Valentine, *A Lay Word for a Legal Term: How the Popular Definition of Charity Has Muddled the Perception of the Charitable Deduction*, 89 NEB. L. REV. 997 (2011).

6. Empirical research can also inform the debate. *See* Brian D. Galle, *How Do Nonprofit Firms Respond to Tax Policy?* PUBLIC FINANCE REVIEW (forthcoming, 2016) (finding that the charitable deduction is less effective in helping firms raise funds than previously assumed) available at http://ssrn.com/abstract=2443621; Joseph Rosenberg et al., Urban Inst., *What's Been Happening to Charitable Giving Recently? A Look at the Data* (2011); David Joulfaian, *Is Charitable Giving by the Rich Really Responsive to the Income Tax?* (2011), *available at* http://ssrn.com/abstract =1952889; Michael Schuyler, PhD, & Stephen J. Entin, *Case Study #11: Deduction for Charitable Contributions, Tax Foundation* (Aug. 12, 2013) (Eliminating the charitable deduction would have a positive effect on the economy if tax rates were also cut.)

III. WHO OR WHAT IS A PROPER RECIPIENT OF A CHARITABLE GIFT?

Section 170 of the Internal Revenue Code sets forth the rules for the charitable tax deduction. The portion of §170 excerpted below clarifies which organizations are eligible to receive tax deductible gifts.

INTERNAL REVENUE CODE §170. CHARITABLE, ETC., CONTRIBUTIONS AND GIFTS

(a) Allowance of deduction

(1) General rule: There shall be allowed as a deduction any charitable contribution (as defined in subsection (c)) payment of which is made within the taxable year. A charitable contribution shall be allowable as a deduction only if verified under regulations prescribed by the Secretary....

(c) Charitable contribution defined: For purposes of this section, the term "charitable contribution" means a contribution or gift to or for the use of—

(1) A State, a possession of the United States, or any political subdivision of any of the foregoing, or the United States or the District of Columbia, but only if the contribution or gift is made for exclusively public purposes.

(2) A corporation, trust, or community chest, fund, or foundation—

(A) created or organized in the United States or in any possession thereof, or under the law of the United States, any State, the District of Columbia, or any possession of the United States;

(B) organized and operated exclusively for religious, charitable, scientific, literary, or educational purposes, or to foster national or international amateur sports competition (but only if no part of its activities involve the provision of athletic facilities or equipment), or for the prevention of cruelty to children or animals;

(C) no part of the net earnings of which inures to the benefit of any private shareholder or individual; and

(D) which is not disqualified for tax exemption under section 501(c)(3) by reason of attempting to influence legislation, and which does not participate in, or intervene in (including the publishing or distributing of statements), any political campaign on behalf of (or in opposition to) any candidate for public office.

A contribution or gift by a corporation to a trust, chest, fund, or foundation shall be deductible by reason of this paragraph only if it is to be used within the United States or any of its possessions exclusively for purposes specified in subparagraph (B).

NOTES AND QUESTIONS

1. William Tucker donated $100 to the local elementary school and then deducted that amount on his income tax return. Was that legal?

2. Sarah Costanza is interested in donating money to an organization that provides relief to Afghan people who are recovering from decades of war, and she wants to take a deduction for that donation. She has three choices: (1) Afghan Relief, an organization that is based in Afghanistan; (2) Afghan Support, a U.S.-based organization that sends funds to Afghanistan; and (3) Friends of Afghan Relief, a U.S.-based organization that is affiliated with Afghan Relief. Which option or options can provide her with the ability to take a charitable tax deduction?

3. The excerpt from §170 that is reproduced above describes the organizations that receive the vast majority of tax-deductible donations. It does not include three potential recipients of tax-deductible donations—organizations of war veterans, fraternal societies operating under a lodge system if the funds are used for charitable purposes, and cemetery or burial companies in certain situations. Nor does it include the special definitions of a qualified conservation easement. §170(h).

IV. WHAT IS A CHARITABLE GIFT?

Occasionally the question arises as to whether a donation is a gift or a payment for goods and services. Following are two Supreme Court cases that deal with this issue, along with several notes that expound on the concepts discussed in these cases.

UNITED STATES V. AMERICAN BAR ENDOWMENT

477 U.S. 105 (1986)

Justice MARSHALL delivered the opinion of the Court.

... The ... issue is whether the organization's members may claim a charitable deduction for the portion of their premium payments that exceeds the actual cost to the organization of providing insurance.

I

Respondent American Bar Endowment (ABE) is a corporation exempt from taxation under §501(c)(3) of the Code, which, with certain exceptions not relevant here, exempts organizations "organized and operated exclusively for ... charitable ... or educational purposes." ABE's primary purposes are to advance legal research and to promote the administration of justice, and it furthers these goals primarily through the distribution of grants to other charitable and educational groups. All members of the American Bar Association (ABA) are automatically members of ABE. The ABA is exempt from taxation as a "business league" under §501(c)(6).

ABE raises money for its charitable work by providing group insurance policies, underwritten by major insurance companies, to its members. Approximately 20% of ABE's members participate in the group insurance program, which offers life, health, accident, and disability policies. ABE negotiates premium rates with insurers and chooses which insurers shall provide the policies. It also compiles a list of its own members and solicits them, collects the premiums paid by its members, transmits those premiums to the insurer, maintains files on each policyholder, answers members' questions concerning insurance policies, and screens claims for benefits.

There are two important benefits of purchasing insurance as a group rather than individually. The first is that ABE's size gives it bargaining power that individuals lack. The second is that the group policy is experience rated. This means that the cost of insurance to the group is based on that group's claims experience, rather than general actuarial tables. Because ABA members have favorable mortality and morbidity rates, experience rating results in a substantially lower insurance cost. When ABE purchases a group policy for its members, it pays a negotiated premium to the insurance company. If, as is uniformly true, the insurance company's actual cost of providing insurance to the group is lower than the premium paid in a given year, the insurance company pays a refund of the excess, called a "dividend," to ABE. Critical to ABE's fundraising efforts is the fact that ABE requires its members to agree, as a condition of participating in the group insurance program, that they will permit ABE to keep all of the dividends rather than distributing them pro rata to the insured members.

It would be possible for ABE to negotiate lower premium rates for its members than the rates it has charged throughout the relevant period, and thus receive a lower dividend. However, ABE prices its policies competitively with other insurance policies offered to the public and to ABE members. In this way ABE is able to generate large dividends to be used for its charitable purposes. In recent years the total amount of dividends has exceeded 40% of the members' premium payments. ABE advises its insured members that each member's share of the dividends, less ABE's administrative costs, constitutes a tax-deductible contribution from the member to ABE. Thus the after-tax cost of ABE's insurance to its members is less than the cost of a commercial policy with identical coverage and premium rates....

III

Section 170 of the Code provides that a taxpayer may deduct from taxable income any "charitable contribution," defined as "a contribution or gift to or for the use of" qualifying entities, §170(c). The individual respondents contend that the excess of their premium payments over the cost to ABE of providing insurance constitutes a contribution or gift to ABE.

Many of the considerations supporting our holding that ABE's earnings from the insurance program are taxable also bear on the question whether ABE's members may deduct part of their premium payments. The evidence demonstrates, and the Claims Court found, that ABE's insurance is no more costly to its members than other policies—group or individual—available to them. Thus, as we have recognized, ABE's members are never faced with the hard choice of supporting a worthwhile charitable endeavor or reducing their own insurance costs.

A payment of money generally cannot constitute a charitable contribution if the contributor expects a substantial benefit in return.... However, as the Claims Court recognized, a taxpayer may sometimes receive only a nominal benefit in return for his contribution. Where the size of the payment is clearly out of proportion to the benefit received, it would not serve the purposes of §170 to deny a deduction altogether. A taxpayer may therefore claim a deduction for the difference between a payment to a charitable organization and the market value of the benefit received in return, on the theory that the payment has the "dual character" of a purchase and a contribution....

In Rev. Rul. 67-246, *supra*, the IRS set up a two-part test for determining when part of a "dual payment" is deductible. First, the payment is deductible only if and to the extent it exceeds the market value of the benefit received.

Second, the excess payment must be "made with the intention of making a gift." 1967-2 Cum. Bull., at 105. The Tax Court has adopted this test....

The Claims Court applied that test in this case, and held that respondents Broadfoot, Boynton, and Turner had not established that they could have purchased comparable insurance for less money. Therefore, the court held, they had failed to establish that the value of ABE's insurance to them was less than the premiums paid. Respondent Sherwood demonstrated that there did exist a group insurance program for which he was eligible and which offered lower premiums than ABE's insurance. However, Sherwood failed to establish that he was aware of that competing program during the years at issue. Sherwood therefore had failed to demonstrate that he met the second part of the above test—that he had intentionally paid more than the market value for ABE's insurance because he wished to make a gift.

The Court of Appeals, in reversing, held that the Claims Court had focused excessively on the taxpayers' motivation. In the Court of Appeals' view, the necessary inquiry was whether "the transaction was ... of a business and not a charitable nature," considering all of the circumstances. The Court of Appeals therefore remanded for redetermination under that standard.

We hold that the Claims Court applied the proper standard. The *sine qua non* of a charitable contribution is a transfer of money or property without adequate consideration. The taxpayer, therefore, must at a minimum demonstrate that he purposely contributed money or property in excess of the value of any benefit he received in return. The most logical test of the value of the insurance respondents received is the cost of similar policies. Three of the four individual respondents failed to demonstrate that they could have purchased similar policies for a lower cost, and we must therefore assume that the value of ABE's insurance to those taxpayers at least equals their premium payments. Had respondent Sherwood known that he could purchase comparable insurance for less money, ABE's insurance would necessarily have declined in value to him. Because Sherwood did not have that knowledge, however, we again must assume that he valued ABE's insurance equivalently to those competing policies of which he was aware. Because those policies cost as much as or more than ABE's, Sherwood has failed to demonstrate that he intentionally gave away more than he received.

IV

We ... hold that the individual taxpayers have not established that any portion of their premium payments to ABE constitutes a charitable contribution. Accordingly, we reverse the judgment of the Court of Appeals and remand to that court with instructions to ... affirm the judgment of the Claims Court with respect to the individual taxpayers. *It is so ordered.*

HERNANDEZ V. COMMISSIONER OF INTERNAL REVENUE

490 U.S. 680 (1989)

Justice MARSHALL delivered the opinion of the Court.

Section 170 of the Internal Revenue Code of 1954 (Code), 26 U.S.C. §170, permits a taxpayer to deduct from gross income the amount of a "charitable contribution." The Code defines that term as a "contribution or gift" to certain eligible donees, including entities organized and operated exclusively for religious purposes. We granted certiorari to determine whether taxpayers may deduct as charitable contributions payments made to branch churches of the Church of Scientology (Church) in order to receive services known as "auditing" and "training." We hold that such payments are not deductible.

I

Scientology was founded in the 1950's by L. Ron Hubbard. It is propagated today by a "mother church" in California and by numerous branch churches around the world. The mother Church instructs laity, trains and ordains ministers, and creates new congregations. Branch churches, known as "franchises" or "missions," provide Scientology services at the local level, under the supervision of the mother Church. Scientologists believe that an immortal spiritual being exists in every person. A person becomes aware of this spiritual dimension through a process known as "auditing." Auditing involves a one-to-one encounter between a participant (known as a "preclear") and a Church official (known as an "auditor"). An electronic device, the E-meter, helps the auditor identify the preclear's areas of spiritual difficulty by measuring skin responses during a question and answer session. Although auditing sessions are conducted one on one, the content of each session is not individually tailored. The preclear gains spiritual awareness by progressing through sequential levels of auditing, provided in short blocks of time known as "intensives."

The Church also offers members doctrinal courses known as "training." Participants in these sessions study the tenets of Scientology and seek to attain the qualifications necessary to serve as auditors. Training courses, like auditing sessions, are provided in sequential levels. Scientologists are taught that spiritual gains result from participation in such courses.

The Church charges a "fixed donation," also known as a "price" or a "fixed contribution," for participants to gain access to auditing and training sessions. These charges are set forth in schedules, and prices vary with a session's length and level of sophistication. In 1972, for example, the general rates for auditing ranged from $625 for a 12½-hour auditing intensive, the shortest available, to $4,250 for a 100-hour intensive, the longest available.... This system of mandatory fixed charges is based on a central tenet of Scientology known as the "doctrine of exchange," according to which any time a person receives something he must pay something back. In so doing, a Scientologist maintains "inflow" and "outflow" and avoids spiritual decline. The proceeds generated from auditing and training sessions are the Church's primary source of income. The Church promotes these sessions not only through newspaper, magazine, and radio advertisements, but also through free lectures, free personality tests, and leaflets. The Church also encourages, and indeed rewards with a 5% discount, advance payment for these sessions. The Church often refunds unused portions of prepaid auditing or training fees, less an administrative charge.

Petitioners in these consolidated cases each made payments to a branch church for auditing or training sessions. They sought to deduct these payments on their federal income tax returns as charitable contributions under §170. Respondent Commissioner, the head of the Internal Revenue Service (IRS), disallowed these deductions, finding that the payments were not charitable contributions within the meaning of §170.

Petitioners sought review of these determinations in the Tax Court.... The court found "no indication that Congress intended to distinguish the religious benefits sought by Hernandez from the medical, educational, scientific, literary, or other benefits that could likewise provide the quid for the quo of a nondeductible payment to a charitable organization." The court also rejected Hernandez's argument that it was impracticable to put a value on the services he had purchased, noting that the Church itself had "established and advertised monetary prices" for auditing and training sessions, and that Hernandez had not claimed that these prices misstated the cost of providing these sessions.... Hernandez's constitutional claims also failed.

The Ninth Circuit also found that the taxpayers had received a "measurable, specific return ... as a quid pro quo for the donation" they had made to the branch churches.... The Ninth Circuit also rejected the taxpayers' constitutional arguments....

II

Section 170, . . . requires a taxpayer claiming the deduction to satisfy a number of conditions. The Commissioner's stipulation in this case, however, has narrowed the statutory inquiry to one such condition: whether petitioners' payments for auditing and training sessions are "contribution[s] or gift[s]" within the meaning of §170.

The legislative history of the "contribution or gift" limitation, though sparse, reveals that Congress intended to differentiate between unrequited payments to qualified recipients and payments made to such recipients in return for goods or services. Only the former were deemed deductible. The House and Senate Reports on the 1954 tax bill, for example, both define "gifts" as payments "made with no expectation of a financial return commensurate with the amount of the gift." S. Rep. No. 1622, 83d Cong., 2d Sess., 196 (1954); H.R. Rep. No. 1337, 83d Cong., 2d Sess., A44 (1954), U.S. Code Cong. & Admin. News 1954, pp. 4017, 4180, 4831....

In ascertaining whether a given payment was made with "the expectation of any quid pro quo," ... the IRS has customarily examined the external features of the transaction in question. This practice has the advantage of obviating the need for the IRS to conduct imprecise inquiries into the motivations of individual taxpayers. The lower courts have generally embraced this structural analysis.... We likewise focused on external features in *United States v. American Bar Endowment*, to resolve the taxpayers' claims that they were entitled to partial deductions for premiums paid to a charitable organization for insurance coverage; the taxpayers contended that they had paid unusually high premiums in an effort to make a contribution along with their purchase of insurance. We upheld the Commissioner's disallowance of the partial deductions because the taxpayers had failed to demonstrate, at a minimum, the existence of comparable insurance policies with prices lower than those of the policy they had each purchased. In so doing, we stressed that "[t]he *sine qua non* of a charitable contribution is a transfer of money or property *without adequate consideration*....

In light of this understanding of §170, it is readily apparent that petitioners' payments to the Church do not qualify as "contribution[s] or gift[s]." As the Tax Court found, these payments were part of a quintessential *quid pro quo* exchange: in return for their money, petitioners received an identifiable benefit, namely, auditing and training sessions. The Church established fixed price schedules for auditing and training sessions in each branch church; it calibrated particular prices to auditing or training sessions of particular lengths and levels of sophistication; it returned a refund if auditing and training services went unperformed; it distributed "account cards" on which persons who had paid money to the Church could monitor what prepaid services they had not yet claimed; and it categorically barred provision of auditing or training sessions for free.... Each of these practices reveals the inherently reciprocal nature of the exchange.

Petitioners do not argue that such a structural analysis is inappropriate under §170, or that the external features of the auditing and training transactions do not strongly suggest a *quid pro quo* exchange.... Petitioners argue instead that they are entitled to deductions because a *quid pro quo* analysis is inappropriate under §170 when the benefit a taxpayer receives is purely religious in nature. Along the same lines, petitioners claim that payments made for the right to participate in a religious service should be automatically deductible under §170.

We cannot accept this statutory argument for several reasons. First, it finds no support in the language of §170. Whether or not Congress could, consistent with the Establishment Clause, provide for the automatic deductibility of a payment made to a church that either generates religious benefits or guarantees access to a religious service, that is a choice Congress has thus far declined to make. Instead, Congress has specified that a payment to an organization operated exclusively for religious (or other eleemosynary) purposes is deductible *only* if such a payment is a "contribution or gift." 26 U.S.C. §170(c). The Code makes no special preference for payments made in the expectation of gaining religious benefits or access to a religious service.... The House and Senate Reports on §170, and the other legislative history of that provision, offer no indication that Congress' failure to enact such a preference was an oversight.

Second, petitioners' deductibility proposal would expand the charitable contribution deduction far beyond what Congress has provided. Numerous forms of payments to eligible donees plausibly could be categorized as providing a religious benefit or as securing access to a religious service. For example, some taxpayers might regard their tuition payments to parochial schools as generating a religious benefit or as securing access to a religious service; such payments, however, have long been held not to be charitable contributions under §170.... Taxpayers might make similar claims about payments for church-sponsored counseling sessions or for medical care at church-affiliated hospitals that otherwise might not be deductible. Given that, under the First Amendment, the IRS can reject otherwise valid claims of religious benefit only on the ground that a taxpayers' alleged beliefs are not sincerely held, but not on the ground that such beliefs are inherently irreligious, ... the resulting tax deductions would likely expand the charitable contribution provision far beyond its present size. We are loath to effect this result in the absence of supportive congressional intent....

Finally, the deduction petitioners seek might raise problems of entanglement between church and state. If framed as a deduction for those payments generating benefits of a religious nature for the payor, petitioners' proposal would inexorably force the IRS and reviewing courts to differentiate "religious" benefits from "secular" ones. If framed as a deduction for those payments made in connection with a religious service, petitioners' proposal would force the IRS and the judiciary into differentiating "religious" services from "secular" ones. We need pass no judgment now on the constitutionality of such hypothetical inquiries, but we do note that "pervasive monitoring" for "the subtle or overt presence of religious matter" is a central danger against which we have held the Establishment Clause guards....

Accordingly, we conclude that petitioners' payments to the Church for auditing and training sessions are not "contribution[s] or gift[s]" within the meaning of that statutory expression.

IV

[After rejecting petitioners' claims based on the Establishment Clause and the Free Exercise Clause of the First Amendment], [w]e turn, finally, to petitioners' assertion that disallowing their claimed deduction is at odds with the IRS' longstanding practice of permitting taxpayers to deduct payments made to other religious institutions in connection with certain religious practices....

[P]etitioners ... make two closely related claims. First, the IRS has accorded payments for auditing and training disparately harsh treatment compared to payments to other churches and synagogues for their religious services: Recognition of a comparable deduction for auditing and training payments is necessary to cure this administrative inconsistency. Second, Congress, in modifying §170 over the years, has impliedly acquiesced in the deductibility of payments to these other faiths; because payments for auditing and training are indistinguishable from these other payments, they fall within the principle acquiesced in by Congress that payments for religious services are deductible under §170.

Although the Commission demurred at oral argument as to whether the IRS, in fact, permits taxpayers to deduct payments made to purchase services from other churches and synagogues, ... the Commissioner's periodic revenue rulings have stated the IRS' position rather clearly. A 1971 ruling, still in effect, states: "Pew rents, building fund assessments, and periodic dues paid to a church ... are all methods of making contributions to the church, and such payments "are deductible as charitable contributions within the limitations set out in section 170 of the Code." Rev. Rul. 70-47, 1970-1 Cum. Bull. 49 (superseding A.R.M. 2, Cum. Bull. 150 (1919)). We also assume for purposes of argument that the IRS also allows taxpayers to deduct "specified payments for attendance at High Holy Day services, for tithes, for torah readings and for memorial plaques." *Foley v. Commissioner*, 844 F.2d, at 94, 96.

The development of the present litigation, however, makes it impossible for us to resolve petitioners' claim that they have received unjustifiably harsh treatment compared to adherents of other religions. The relevant inquiry in determining whether a payment is a "contribution or gift" under §170 is, as we have noted, not whether the payment secures religious benefits or access to religious services, but whether the transaction in which the payment is involved is structured as a *quid pro quo* exchange. To make such a determination in this case, the Tax Court heard testimony and received documentary proof as to the terms and structure of the auditing and training transactions; from this evidence it made factual findings upon which it based its conclusion of nondeductibility, a conclusion we have held consonant with §170 and with the First Amendment.

Perhaps because the theory of administrative inconsistency emerged only on appeal, petitioners did not endeavor at trial to adduce from the IRS or other sources any specific evidence about other religious faiths' transactions. The IRS' revenue rulings, which merely state the agency's conclusions as to deductibility and which have apparently never been reviewed by the Tax Court or any other judicial body, also provide no specific facts about the nature of these other faiths' transactions. In the absence of such facts, we simply have no way (other than the wholly illegitimate one of relying on our personal experiences and observations) to appraise accurately whether the IRS' revenue rulings have correctly applied a *quid pro quo* analysis with respect to any or all of the religious practices in question. We do not know, for example, whether payments for other faiths' services are truly obligatory or whether any or all of these services are generally provided whether or not the encouraged "mandatory" payment is made.

The IRS' application of the "contribution or gift" standard may be right or wrong with respect to these other faiths, or it may be right with respect to some religious practices and wrong with respect to others. It may also be that some of these payments are appropriately classified as partially deductible "dual payments." With respect to those religions where the structure of transactions involving religious services is established not centrally but by individual congregations, the proper point of reference for a *quid pro quo* analysis might be the individual congregation, not the religion as a whole. Only upon a proper factual record could we make these determinations. Absent such a record, we must reject petitioners' administrative consistency argument.

Petitioners' congressional acquiescence claim fails for similar reasons. Even if one assumes that Congress has acquiesced in the IRS' ruling with respect to "[p]ew rents, building fund assessments, and periodic dues," Rev. Rul. 70-47, 1970-1 Cum. Bull. 49, the fact is that the IRS' 1971 ruling articulates no broad principle of deductibility, but instead merely identifies as deductible three discrete types of payments. Having before us no information about the nature or structure of these three payments, we have no way of discerning any possible unifying principle, let alone whether such a principle would embrace payments for auditing and training sessions. For the reasons stated herein, the judgments of the Courts of Appeals are hereby *Affirmed*.

Justice BRENNAN and Justice KENNEDY took no part in the consideration or decision of these cases.

Justice O'CONNOR, with whom Justice SCALIA joins, dissenting.

The Court today acquiesces in the decision of the Internal Revenue Service (IRS) to manufacture a singular exception to its 70-year practice of allowing fixed payments indistinguishable from those made by petitioners to be deducted as charitable contributions. Because the IRS cannot constitutionally be allowed to select which religions will receive the benefit of its past rulings, I respectfully dissent.

The cases before the Court have an air of artificiality about them that is due to the IRS' dual litigation strategy against the Church of Scientology (Church). As the Court notes, ... the IRS has successfully argued that the mother Church of Scientology was not a tax-exempt organization from 1970 to 1972 because it had diverted profits to the founder of Scientology and others, conspired to impede collection of its taxes, and conducted almost all of its activities for a commercial purpose. See *Church of Scientology of California v. Commissioner*, 83 T.C. 381 (1984), aff'd, 823 F.2d 1310 (CA9 1987), cert. denied, 486 U.S. 1015, 108 S. Ct. 1752, 100 L. Ed. 2d 214 (1988). In the cases before the Court today, however, the IRS decided to contest the payments made to Scientology under 26 U.S.C. §170 rather than challenge the tax-exempt status of the various branches of the Church to which the payments were made. According to the Deputy Solicitor General, the IRS challenged the payments themselves in order to expedite matters.... As part of its litigation strategy in these cases, the IRS agreed to several stipulations which, in my view, necessarily determine the proper approach to the questions presented by petitioners.

The stipulations, relegated to a single sentence by the Court, ... established that Scientology was at all relevant times a religion; that each Scientology branch to which payments were made was at all relevant times a "church" within the

274 | 5. Charitable Contributions

meaning of §170(b)(1)(A)(i); and that Scientology was at all times a "corporation" within the meaning of §170(c)(2) and exempt from general income taxation under 26 U.S.C. §501(a).... As the Solicitor General recognizes, it follows from these stipulations that Scientology operates for " 'charitable purposes' " and puts the "public interest above the private interest."... Moreover, the stipulations establish that the payments made by petitioners are fixed donations made by individuals to a tax-exempt religious organization in order to participate in religious services, and are not based on "market prices set to reap the profits of a commercial moneymaking venture."... The Tax Court, however, appears to have ignored the stipulations. It concluded, perhaps relying on its previous opinion in *Church of Scientology,* that "Scientology operates in a commercial manner in providing [auditing and training]. In fact, one of its articulated goals is to make money." 83 T.C., at 578. The Solicitor General has duplicated the error here, referring on numerous occasions to the commercial nature of Scientology in an attempt to negate the effect of the stipulations.

It must be emphasized that the IRS' position here is *not* based upon the contention that a portion of the knowledge received from auditing or training is of secular, commercial, nonreligious value. Thus, the denial of a deduction in these cases bears no resemblance to the denial of a deduction for religious-school tuition up to the market value of the secularly useful education received.... Here the IRS denies deductibility solely on the basis that the exchange is a *quid pro quo,* even though the *quid* is exclusively of spiritual or religious worth. Respondent cites no instances in which this has been done before, and there are good reasons why.

When a taxpayer claims as a charitable deduction part of a fixed amount given to a charitable organization in exchange for benefits that have a commercial value, the allowable portion of that claim is computed by subtracting from the total amount paid the value of the physical benefit received.... It becomes impossible, however, to compute the "contribution" portion of a payment to a charity where what is received in return is not merely an intangible, but an intangible (or, for that matter a tangible) that is not bought and sold except in donative contexts so that the only "market" price against which it can be evaluated is a market price that always includes donations. Suppose, for example, that the charitable organization that traditionally solicits donations on Veterans Day, in exchange for which it gives the donor an imitation poppy bearing its name, were to establish a flat rule that no one gets a poppy without a donation of at least $10. One would have to say that the "market" rate for such poppies was $10, but it would assuredly not be true that everyone who "bought" a poppy for $10 made no contribution. Similarly, if one buys a $100 seat at a prayer breakfast receiving as the *quid pro quo* food for both body and soul[,] it would make no sense to say that no charitable contribution whatever has occurred simply because the "going rate" for all prayer breakfasts (with equivalent bodily food) is $100. The latter may well be true, but that "going rate" *includes* a contribution.

Confronted with this difficulty, and with the constitutional necessity of not making irrational distinctions among taxpayers, and with the even higher standard of equality of treatment among *religions* that the First Amendment imposes, the Government has only two practicable options with regard to distinctively religious *quids pro quo:* to disregard them all, or to tax them all. Over the years it has chosen the former course. [*Editor's Note:* The dissent then listed several rulings in which pew rents, building fund assessments, and periodic dues were considered charitable contributions.]

These rulings, which are "official interpretation[s] of [the tax laws] by the [IRS]," Rev. Proc. 78-24, 1978-2 Cum. Bull. 503, 504, flatly contradict the Solicitor General's claim that there "is no administrative practice recognizing that payments made in exchange for religious benefits are tax deductible."...

There can be no doubt that at least some of the fixed payments which the IRS has treated as charitable deductions, or which the Court assumes the IRS would allow taxpayers to deduct, are as "inherently reciprocal," as the payments for auditing at issue here. In exchange for their payment of pew rents, Christians receive particular seats during worship services.... Similarly, in some synagogues attendance at the worship services for Jewish High Holy Days is often predicated upon the purchase of a general admission ticket or a reserved seat ticket.... Religious honors such as publicly reading from Scripture are purchased or auctioned periodically in some synagogues of Jews from Morocco and Syria.... Mormons must tithe their income as a necessary but not sufficient condition to obtaining a "temple recommend," *i.e.*, the right to be admitted into the temple.... A Mass stipend—a fixed payment given to a Catholic priest, in consideration of which he is obliged to apply the fruits of the Mass for the intention of the donor—has similar overtones of exchange. According to some Catholic theologians, the nature of the pact between a priest and a donor who pays a Mass stipend is "a bilateral contract known as *do ut facias*. One person agrees to give while the other party agrees to do something in return." 13 New Catholic Encyclopedia, Mass Stipend, p. 715 (1967). A finer example of a *quid pro quo* exchange would be hard to formulate. . . .

[R]espondent . . . attempts to reconcile his previous rulings with his decision in these cases by relying on a distinction between direct and incidental benefits in exchange for payments made to a charitable organization. This distinction, adumbrated as early as the IRS' 1919 ruling, recognizes that even a deductible charitable contribution may generate certain benefits for the donor. As long as the benefits remain "incidental" and do not indicate that the payment was actually made for the "personal accommodation" of the donor, the payment will be deductible. It is respondent's view that the payments made by petitioners should not be deductible under §170 because the "unusual facts in these cases ... demonstrate that the payments were made primarily for 'personal accommodation.' "... Specifically, the Solicitor General asserts that "the rigid connection between the provision of auditing and training services and payment of the fixed price" indicates a *quid pro quo* relationship and "reflect[s] the value that petitioners expected to receive for their money." *Id.*, at 16.

There is no discernible reason why there is a more rigid connection between payment and services in the religious practices of Scientology than in the religious practices of the faiths described above. Neither has respondent explained why the benefit received by a Christian who obtains the pew of his or her choice by paying a rental fee, a Jew who gains entrance to High Holy Day services by purchasing a ticket, a Mormon who makes the fixed payment necessary for a temple recommend, or a Catholic who pays a Mass stipend, is incidental to the real benefit conferred on the "general public and members of the faith," BNA Daily Report, at J-3, while the benefit received by a Scientologist from auditing is a personal accommodation. If the perceived difference lies in the fact that Christians and Jews worship in congregations, whereas Scientologists, in a manner reminiscent of Eastern religions, gain awareness of the "immortal spiritual being" within them in one-to-one sessions with auditors, *ante,* at 2140-2141, such a distinction would raise serious Establishment Clause problems....

Given the IRS' stance in these cases, it is an understatement to say that with respect to fixed payments for religious services "the line between the taxable and the immune has been drawn by an unsteady hand."... This is not a situation in which a governmental regulation "happens to coincide or harmonize with the tenets of some or all religions," ... but does not violate the Establishment Clause because it is founded on a neutral, secular basis.... Rather, it involves the differential application of a standard based on constitutionally impermissible differences drawn by the Government among religions. As such, it is best characterized as a case of the Government "put[ting] an imprimatur on [all but] one religion."... That the Government may not do. . . .

On a more fundamental level, the Court cannot abjure its responsibility to address serious constitutional problems by converting a violation of the Establishment Clause into an "administrative consistency argument" ... with an inadequate record. It has chosen to ignore both longstanding, clearly articulated IRS practice, and the failure of the respondent to offer any cogent, neutral explanation for the IRS' refusal to apply this practice to the Church of Scientology. Instead, the Court has pretended that whatever errors in application the IRS has committed are hidden from its gaze and will, in any event, be rectified in due time.

In my view, the IRS has misapplied its longstanding practice of allowing charitable contributions under §170 in a way that violates the Establishment Clause. It has unconstitutionally refused to allow payments for the religious service of auditing to be deducted as charitable contributions in the same way it has allowed fixed payments to other religions to be deducted.... [T]he IRS' application of the *quid pro quo* standard here—and only here—discriminates against the Church of Scientology. I would reverse the decisions below.

NOTES AND QUESTIONS

1. The quid pro quo doctrine is not absolute. The value of certain small items, such as a mug or a T-shirt given in return for a gift, may be ignored. In 2016, donors could receive gifts with a wholesale value of $10.60 and still deduct the entire amount of their donation, so long as their gift was at least $53. Larger donors could receive larger gifts, without having to prorate the

deduction, but the gifts could never exceed $106 or 2% of the gift, whichever is lower. Exceptions to the quid pro quo doctrine are also made for intangible religious benefits (benefits from an organization operated exclusively for religious purposes that are not usually sold in commercial transactions) and for donor recognition, including naming rights. IRS Pub. No. 1771, CHARITABLE CONTRIBUTIONS—SUBSTANTIATION AND DISCLOSURE REQUIREMENTS 7-8 (Rev. 3-2016).

2.   Shortly after winning this case at the Supreme Court level and after winning several other cases related to whether the church itself should retain its tax exemption, the Internal Revenue Service (IRS) entered into a closing agreement with the Church of Scientology that reinstated its tax-exempt status and allowed it to accept charitable donations. Commentators at the time claimed that the agreement eviscerated the *Hernandez* decision. *See e.g.,* Jerome Kurtz, *Former IRS Commissioner Says IRS Should Fully Explain Its Settlement with Church of Scientology*, 10 EXEMPT ORG. TAX REV. 235 (1994). A copy of that closing agreement can be found in *Closing Agreement Between IRS and Church of Scientology*, 19 EXEMPT ORG. TAX REV. 227 (1998).

3.   After the IRS reinstated the tax-exempt status of the Scientology Church, Michael and Maria Sklar tried to deduct 55% of the tuition they paid to their children's religious school on the basis that this amount represented the proportion of the school day allocated to religious education. When the IRS disallowed the deduction, the Sklars claimed that §501(c)(3) allowed an exception to the quid pro quo rule for purely religious benefits. They also claimed that the IRS was treating them inconsistently if they disallowed this deduction but allowed a deduction for Scientologist practice, thus creating both administrative and constitutional inconsistency. If you were the court, how would you rule? *See Sklar v. Comm'r,* 282 F. 3d 610 (9th Cir. 2002) and *Sklar v. Commissioner,* 549 F.3d 1252 (9th Cir. 2008), *cert. denied* 558 U.S. 829 (2009).

4.   For further reading on the *Hernandez* case, the IRS settlement with Church of Scientology, and deductions for gifts from donors who receive religious benefits, see Paul Horwitz, *Scientology in Court: A Comparative Analysis and Some Thoughts on Selected Issues in Law and Religion*, 47 DEPAUL L. REV. 85 (2004); Gregg D. Polsky, *Can Treasury Overrule the Supreme Court?* 84 B.U. L. REV. 185 (2004). This book covers a second case dealing with the Church of Scientology in Chapter 9, *Church of Scientology of California v. Comm'r,* 823 F.2d 1310 (9th Cir. 1987), *cert. denied* 486 US 1015 (1988). For more information on the Church of Scientology, see Janet Reitman, INSIDE SCIENTOLOGY: THE STORY OF AMERICA'S MOST SECRETIVE RELIGION (Mariner Books, Houghton Mifflin Harcourt Publishers, 2013); GOING CLEAR: SCIENTOLOGY AND THE PRISON OF BELIEF, AN HBO SPECIAL (2015).

5.   The IRS and courts have found examples of quid pro quo arrangements in gifts of conservation easements. *See Seventeen Seventy Sherman St., LLC v.*

Comm'r, T.C. Memo 2014-124 (taxpayer received a city development agreement in return for the easement) and *Pollard v. Comm'r*, T.C. Memo 2013-38 (easement was in return for the county's granting a subdivision exemption). For an introduction to the law regarding charitable easements, see F. Cheever & Nandy McLaughlin, *An Introduction to Conservation Easements in the United States: A Simple Concept and a Complicated Mosaic of Law*, J. Law, Prop. & Society (2015).

6. The IRS publishes Publication 526, which provides information on how to claim a charitable deduction, which organizations are eligible to accept such deductions, and which contributions qualify for this deduction. https://www.irs.gov/pub/irs-pdf/p526.pdf.

V. A BRIEF OVERVIEW OF OTHER CHARITABLE CONTRIBUTION ISSUES

The cases and statute above have concentrated on eligible donees and what constitutes a completed gift. Numerous other legal issues can arise with regard to charitable contributions. Some of them are discussed below.

Amount of deduction. As is clear from the cases above, donations to charitable organizations are only tax deductible to the extent that the gift exceeds the fair market value of any goods or services received in return. Rev. Rul. 67-246, 1967-2 C.B. 104. Charities must provide a written disclosure to a donor who receives goods or services in excess of $75 in return for a single contribution. Such disclosure is not required if the goods or services are a token amount, can be classified as membership benefits, or are intangible religious benefits. The regulations spell out the definitions of these terms, but they basically allow organizations to provide items such as inexpensive mugs or calendars to donors, free admission to members, and entrance to paid religious events without providing a written disclosure.

Services. Individuals who give their time, rather than their money or property, cannot deduct the value of those services. They can deduct the expenses they incurred while donating time to a qualified organization, however. Treas. Reg. §1.170A-1(g).

Timing of the deduction. A cash charitable contribution is deductible in the year that it is paid regardless of the taxpayer's accounting method. Treas. Reg. §1.170A-1(a). Note that a check is delivered when it is given or mailed to the charitable organization, even if it cleared at a later date, because the donor relinquishes control when the check is mailed. A pledge to a charitable organization is deductible when the pledge is paid, not when it is pledged. Treas. Reg. §1.170A-1(b).

Unconditional gift. A charitable gift is deductible only if it is given unconditionally to a charity. The donor cannot retain control of the funds, and the gift cannot be subject to any conditions, unless that condition is so remote that it is unlikely to happen. Treas. Reg. §1.170A-1(e).

Percentage limitations and carryovers. In order to avoid the possibility that a taxpayer could completely avoid federal income tax by making charitable contributions, Congress has limited the charitable contribution deduction to a percentage of the taxpayer's net income. Donors who provide gifts of cash and ordinary income to "publicly supported" charities—such as schools, hospitals, churches, and other organizations that receive most of their support from the public—must limit their charitable contribution deductions to 50% of their net income. Gifts to private foundations, on the other hand, must be limited to 30% of the taxpayer's net income.[9] These percentage limitations can become quite complicated when a taxpayer provides gifts to both types of organizations or provides gifts that are subject to capital gains treatment. In addition, the excess of the contribution over the allowable deduction can be carried forward for five years. These rules are beyond the scope of this course, but an attorney for the organization receiving large contributions should be aware that these limitations may be relevant to the donor. *See* 26 IRC §§170(b)(1)(A), (b)(1)(B), (d)(1).

Substantiation requirements. Section 170(f)(8) requires taxpayers to receive a contemporaneous written acknowledgment from the organization receiving the charitable contribution before taking the charitable deduction. Although the donor is responsible for obtaining this acknowledgment, good donor relations mandate that the recipient organization provide such acknowledgments as a matter of course. The acknowledgment must include (1) the name of the organization, (2) the amount of cash contributed, (3) a description (but not the value) of any noncash property that was contributed, (4) whether the organization provided any return benefits, (5) a description and good faith estimate of the value of any goods or services provided to the donor in exchange for making the gift, and (6) a statement that the goods or services provided in exchange for the gift are intangible religious benefits, if that is the case. IRS Pub. 1771 explains these provisions.

The IRS and courts are quite strict about these requirements. One couple produced an acknowledgment letter for a $22,000 gift, but the IRS challenged the deduction because the letter did not state whether goods or services were provided by the charity in return. Even though the couple corrected that omission, the tax court disallowed the deduction and assessed additional taxes and penalties for not following proper procedures in a timely manner. *Durden v. IRS,* T.C. Memo. 2012-140. Another couple's $18.5 million donation was disallowed because the gift of real estate did not include a contemporaneous appraisal. Even though they later commissioned an appraisal letter, which confirmed that the

---

[9] This book will discuss the differences between these types of charities in Chapter 7.

land was worth more than $20 million, and the land was sold within a year in an arms-length transaction for $23 million, the deduction was disallowed. *Mohamed v. IRS*, T.C. Memo. 2012-152. *See also French v. Comm'r*, T.C. Memo. 2016-53. For a discussion of the policies behind this rule, current cases, and suggestions for reform, see Ellen P. Aprill, *Reforming the Charitable Contribution Substantiation Rules*, 14 FLORIDA TAX REVIEW 275 (2013).

Noncash contributions. Determining the amount of the charitable contribution becomes more complicated when the donation is property rather than cash. The rules regarding the treatment of long-term capital gain property and ordinary income-producing property are also beyond the scope of this text. The basic rule about the deduction being limited to the fair market value of the item remains, however. Treas. Reg. §1.170A-1(c). Unfortunately, a 2012 Treasury Inspector General for Tax Administration report found that the majority of claims for noncash charitable contributions are reported incorrectly, and the IRS rarely challenges these valuations. It made several recommendations for improvement. Treasury Inspector General for Tax Administration, *Many Taxpayers Are Still Not Complying with Noncash Charitable Contribution Reporting Requirements*, Ref. No. 2013-40-009 (Dec. 20, 2012).

The IRS has not been reluctant to challenge valuations of façade and conservation easements, however. In 2014, both the Second and Fifth Circuits upheld U.S. Tax Court rulings against donors. The Second Circuit denied the entire façade easement donation in *Scheidelman v. Comm'r*, 755 F.3d 148 (2d Cir. 2014), and the Fifth Circuit dramatically reduced the value of the donation in *Whitehouse Hotel Limited Partnership v. Comm'r*, 755 F.3d 236 (5th Cir. 2014). The penalties for undervaluation can be quite expensive—20% for a negligent or substantial understatement of income tax and 40% for a gross valuation misstatement. IRC §6662. In *Legg v. Commissioner*, 145 T.C. No. 13 (Dec. 7, 2015), that 40% penalty was applied to a conservation easement case. For a discussion of these valuation difficulties, see Nancy McLaughlin, *Conservation Easements and the Valuation Conundrum*. 19 FLA. TAX REV. (forthcoming, 2016).

PROBLEM

John Joseph is a staunch supporter of his local museum. He volunteers often, helping to appraise paintings, which saves the museum thousands of dollars on appraisers. Recently, he paid $150 to attend a benefit for the museum. The event included drinks, dinner, and dancing, and it was a huge success. Not only did 250 people attend, but all the people involved with the benefit donated their goods and services, so the museum could pocket 100% of the proceeds. If these goods and services had not been donated, the museum would have had to spend $75 per person. Part of the evening's entertainment was a raffle. John spent $5 on his raffle and won a Jaguar. The next day, he donated his old minivan to the art museum. He figured that was the least he could do to thank them for his new car, and he figured he would get a tax break for the donation. After all, the *Kelley Blue Book* estimated the value of his minivan at $5,000. John knows that he will have to pay taxes on the Jaguar, but he is counting on charitable deductions to offset these taxes. Can he deduct his ticket to the charity event? If so, can he deduct the entire amount? Can he deduct the $5 raffle ticket? The *Blue Book* value of the car? The value of his volunteer services to the museum? What if he decides to donate $100,000 to the museum, with the condition that a wing of the museum be named after him? Can he deduct the $100,000?

VI. ISSUES OF DONOR INTENT

Disagreements with donors over the meaning of a gift can lead to expensive, embarrassing, and damaging legal disputes. In the past few years, several lawsuits have alleged that nonprofit organizations have ignored donors' wishes. The *Milton Hershey School* case excerpted in Chapter 3, *In re Milton Hershey Sch.*, 807 A.2d 324 (Pa. Commw. 2002), was one such instance. Such disputes can also arise if the donor does not live up to his or her end of the bargain. If a donor reneges on a pledge, the charitable organization must decide whether to sue to recover the amount that has been pledged. Organizations have difficult decisions if a donation comes from "tainted" funds as well. Should organizations refuse or return funds from questionable sources so they can honestly say all their funds are consistent with the integrity of their mission? Or do they have an obligation to accept and retain the donation in order to keep the organization financially healthy?

Following is a case concerning a decision to change the name of a dormitory, as well as some notes and hypothetical questions that should draw out the legal, ethical, and public relations problems that these situations can pose.

TENNESSEE DIVISION OF THE UNITED DAUGHTERS OF THE CONFEDERACY V. VANDERBILT UNIVERSITY

---

174 S.W.3d 98 (Tenn. App. 2005)

Opinion by: WILLIAM C. KOCH, JR. This appeal involves a dispute stemming from a private university's decision to change the name of one of its dormitories. An organization that donated part of the funds used to construct the dormitory filed suit in the Chancery Court for Davidson County, asserting that the university's decision to rename the dormitory breached its seventy-year-old agreement with the university and requesting declaratory and injunctive relief and damages. Both the university and the donor filed motions for summary judgment. The trial court, granting the university's motion, determined that the university should be permitted to modify the parties' agreement regarding the dormitory's name because it would be "impractical and unduly burdensome" to require the university to continue to honor the agreement. The donor organization appealed. We have determined that the summary judgment must be reversed because the university has failed to demonstrate that it is entitled to a judgment as a matter of law. Furthermore, based on the essentially undisputed facts, we have determined that the donor is entitled to a partial summary judgment because the university has breached the conditions placed on the donor's gift and, therefore, that the university should be required to return the present value of the gift to the donor if it insists on renaming the dormitory.

[*Editor's Note:* The court then provided some background for the case. It explained that the Tennessee General Assembly had incorporated the George Peabody College for Teachers (Peabody College) in 1909. When Peabody College decided to construct a new campus near Vanderbilt University, the Tennessee Division of the United Daughters of the Confederacy (U.D.C.) offered to help build a dormitory. Over the next few years, Peabody College and U.D.C. entered into three contracts that were germane to this lawsuit. In 1914, U.D.C. offered to raise $50,000 for the new dorm, so long as "the trustees agreed to allow women descendants of Confederate soldiers nominated by the Tennessee U.D.C. to live in the dormitory rent-free and to pay other dormitory expenses on an estimated cost basis." In 1927, the parties agreed that the building would be called "Confederate Memorial Hall," that the parties would agree on the plans and specifications for the building, and that U.D.C. would turn over funds as it raised them if the college invested the sums, paid interest on them, and returned the sums deposited, with interest, if U.D.C. recalled them. Finally, in 1933, the parties entered into their last agreement. By this time, the entire $50,000 had been raised, but the parties decided jointly that the $50,000 should be added to other funds to create a larger dormitory. Their third contract reflected these changes and expressly ratified and affirmed the earlier ones. The parties reiterated that the first two floors of the dormitory would be used for women descendants of Confederate soldiers and agreed that the building would include an inscription naming it the "Confederate Memorial Hall."]

[O]n June 1, 1935, Peabody College held a dedication ceremony for the new dormitory.... From 1935 until the late 1970's, women descendants of Confederate soldiers nominated by the Tennessee U.D.C. and accepted by Peabody College lived in Confederate Memorial Hall rent-free.... By the time [Peabody College merged with Vanderbilt University in 1979], only four students nominated by the Tennessee U.D.C. were still living in Confederate Memorial Hall. Vanderbilt allowed these four students to continue living there at a reduced rental rate, but after they graduated, no other students nominated by the Tennessee U.D.C. were allowed to live in Confederate Memorial Hall rent-free or at a reduced rate....

E. Gordon Gee became the new chancellor of Vanderbilt in July 2000. In conversations with Vanderbilt students, faculty, and alumni over the next two years, the name of Confederate Memorial Hall was repeatedly identified as a major impediment to the progress of the university. In June 2002, ... Chancellor

Gee, without consulting the Tennessee U.D.C., ... decided to change the name of "Confederate Memorial Hall" to "Memorial Hall," and his decision was made public in the fall of 2002.... [*Editor's Note:* Chancellor Gee had the support of the students, faculty, alumni, and trustees.]

On October 17, 2002, the Tennessee U.D.C. filed suit against Vanderbilt for breach of contract in the Chancery Court for Davidson County. The Tennessee U.D.C. alleged that it had fully performed its obligations under the 1913, 1927, and 1933 contracts and that Vanderbilt's renaming of Confederate Memorial Hall constituted a breach of those contracts. The Tennessee U.D.C. sought an injunction to prevent Vanderbilt from removing the inscription on the pediment on the front of the building, a declaratory judgment specifying Vanderbilt's rights and obligations to the Tennessee U.D.C., and compensatory damages in an amount to be shown at trial....

The trial court heard the parties' summary judgment motions on September 22, 2003, and filed a memorandum opinion on September 30, 2003. The memorandum opinion, as well as the final order filed on October 9, 2003, granted Vanderbilt's motion for summary judgment and denied the Tennessee U.D.C.'s motion for partial summary judgment. The trial court framed the issue as "whether Vanderbilt has shown a sufficient basis for modification of the parties' contracts to allow Vanderbilt to remove the name, 'Confederate' from the building on Vanderbilt's Peabody campus." The trial court [first] ... found from the parties' course of dealing that the Tennessee U.D.C. and Peabody College intended the building to be named "Confederate Memorial Hall."

The trial court then addressed whether changes in society would excuse Vanderbilt from continuing to comply with the contractual naming obligation. The court noted that in the years between the signing of the contracts and the present, racial segregation had been declared unconstitutional, racial discrimination had been outlawed, Vanderbilt had integrated its student body, and a stigma had become attached to the name "Confederate" because of the Confederacy's association with the institution of slavery. The trial court concluded that it would be "impractical and unduly burdensome for Vanderbilt to continue to perform that part of the contract pertaining to the maintenance of the name 'Confederate' on the building, and at the same time pursue its academic purpose of obtaining a racially diverse faculty and student body." The court found that Vanderbilt had "carried its burden of proof for modification of the contracts," declared that Vanderbilt sufficiently complied with its obligations under the 1913 and 1927 contracts by installation and maintenance of the plaque by the entrance to Confederate Memorial Hall, and held that, aside from the plaque, Vanderbilt could remove the name "Confederate" from the building without any further obligation to the Tennessee U.D.C. The Tennessee U.D.C. appealed....

Donors often seek to impose conditions on gifts to charitable organizations.... A conditional gift is enforceable according to the terms of the document or documents that created the gift.... If the recipient fails or ceases to comply with the conditions, the donor's remedy is limited to recovery of the gift.... Because noncompliance results in a forfeiture of the gift, the conditions must be created by express terms or by clear implication and are construed strictly....

Taking all three contracts together, the gift from the Tennessee U.D.C. to Peabody College was subject to three specific conditions. First, Peabody College was required to use the gift to construct a dormitory on its campus conforming to plans and specifications approved by the Tennessee U.D.C. Second, Peabody College was required to allow women descendants of Confederate soldiers nominated by the Tennessee U.D.C. and accepted by Peabody College to live on the first and second floors of the dormitory without paying rent and paying all other dormitory expenses on an estimated cost basis. Third, Peabody College was required to place on the dormitory an inscription naming it "Confederate Memorial." The contracts do not specify the duration of these conditions. In such circumstances, the court must determine whether a duration can be inferred from the nature and circumstances of the transaction.... Given the nature of the project and the content of the conditions, we conclude that these conditions were not meant to bind Peabody College forever but instead were to be limited to the life of the building itself. Thus, as long as the building stands, these three conditions apply to the gift....

Vanderbilt's claim that the placement of a plaque by the entrance to the building describing the contributions of the Tennessee U.D.C. to the original construction constitutes substantial performance with the inscription condition cannot be taken seriously. The determination of whether a party has substantially performed depends on what it was the parties bargained for in their agreement.... Here, the 1933 contract expressly and unambiguously required Peabody College to place an inscription on the building naming it "Confederate Memorial," and we have already concluded that the parties intended the inscription to remain until the building was torn down. Peabody College complied with the condition by placing a large inscription in stone on the pediment of the building reading "Confederate Memorial Hall." Peabody College did so in conformity with Peabody College's own 1934 construction drawings which show these words in large incised lettering on the pediment of the building.

Vanderbilt continued to comply fully with this condition from its 1979 merger with Peabody College until 2002 when it announced its plans to remove the word "Confederate" from the building's pediment. It is doubtful that a party such as Vanderbilt that has willfully changed course after over twenty years of compliance with the literal terms of an agreement could ever rely on the doctrine of substantial performance.... Even if it could, no reasonable fact-finder could conclude that replacing a name written in stone in large letters on the pediment of a building with a plaque by the entrance constitutes substantial performance of a requirement to do the former.

Vanderbilt's argument that it should be excused from complying with the inscription condition contained in the 1933 contract because the Tennessee U.D.C. has already received enough value for its original contribution to the construction of the building is likewise without merit. The courts must interpret contracts as they are written, ... and will not make a new contract for parties who have spoken for themselves.... The courts do not concern themselves with the wisdom or folly of a contract, ... and are not at liberty to relieve parties from contractual obligations simply because these obligations later prove to be burdensome or unwise....

By entering into the 1913, 1927, and 1933 contracts, Peabody College necessarily agreed that the value of the gift it was receiving was worth the value of full performance of the conditions of the gift.... In short, Vanderbilt's unilateral assessment that Peabody College gave away too much in the 1913, 1927, and 1933 agreements does not constitute a legal defense that would excuse Vanderbilt from complying with the conditions of the original gift.

Vanderbilt's assertion that principles of academic freedom allow it to keep the gift from the Tennessee U.D.C. while ignoring the conditions attached to that gift is equally unavailing. As Vanderbilt correctly notes in its brief on appeal, the United States Supreme Court has long been solicitous of the independence of private colleges from government control.... However, the source of the obligation at issue in this case is not the government but Vanderbilt itself....

Moreover, we fail to see how the adoption of a rule allowing universities to avoid their contractual and other voluntarily assumed legal obligations whenever, in the university's opinion, those obligations have begun to impede their academic mission would advance principles of academic freedom. To the contrary, allowing Vanderbilt and other academic institutions to jettison their contractual and other legal obligations so casually would seriously impair their ability to raise money in the future by entering into gift agreements such as the ones at issue here.

... [W]here a donee fails or ceases to comply with the conditions of a gift, the donor's remedy is limited to recovery of the gift. However, it would be inequitable to allow Vanderbilt to "return" the gift at issue here simply by paying the Tennessee U.D.C. the same sum of money the Tennessee U.D.C. donated in 1933 because the value of a dollar today is very different from the value of a dollar in 1933. To reflect the change in the buying power of the dollar, the amount Vanderbilt must pay to the Tennessee U.D.C. in order to return the gift should be based on the consumer price index published by the Bureau of Labor Statistics of the United States Department of Labor.... Thus, on remand, if Vanderbilt continues to elect not to comply with the terms of the gift, it must pay the Tennessee U.D.C. in today's dollars the value of the original gift in 1933.

In settling on this method of accounting for the changed value of the Tennessee U.D.C.'s original contribution, we have considered and rejected an approach that would require Vanderbilt to pay simple or compound interest on the original contribution....

This court is well aware of the strong passions this case has generated on both sides. The depth of feeling is understandable given that the case touches on issues of heritage, identity, and racial justice.... What this court has done is to resolve the existing legal dispute between the parties according to neutral principles of law. Our decision should not be viewed as an endorsement of either

Vanderbilt's decision to change the name or the Tennessee U.D.C.'s desire to perpetuate it.

NOTES AND QUESTIONS

1. In *Adler v. SAVE*, 432 N.J. Super.101 74 A.3d 41 (2013), the New Jersey Appellate Court ordered a no-kill animal shelter to return $50,000 that Bernard and Jeanne Adler had donated between 2002 and 2006 with the express provision that the shelter would use the money for an expansion, named after the Adlers, that had space for large dogs and older cats. In 2006, the shelter announced it was merging with another charity and would no longer build the expansion, and it refused to return the funds to the Adlers. The court found that the shelter had rededicated the gift to "a purpose materially unrelated to plaintiffs' original purpose, without even attempting to ascertain from plaintiffs what, in their view, would be 'a charitable purpose as nearly possible' to their particular original purpose." *See also Register v. Nature Conservancy*, 2014 U.S. Dist. LEXIS 170852 (court found that donor's $1 million gift to preserve a specific property was a restricted gift as a matter of law, but that issues of fact still remained as to whether the Nature Conservancy had violated those restrictions.)

2. Art museums that face financial difficulties can always improve their cash flow by selling one or more pieces of art. Whether such an action is legally feasible often rests on the donor's intent. In recent years, Brandeis College, the Detroit Museum of Art, the Corcoran Gallery, and Fisk University have faced these issues. S*ee* Emily Lanza, *Comment, Breaking Up Is Hard to Do: The Sale of a Charitable Art Donation*, 66 TAX LAW. 483 (2013); Robert Cooper, Deaccessioning and Donor Intent—Lessons Learned *from* Fisk's Stieglitz Collection, Columbia Law School Charities Regulation and Oversight Project Policy Conference on "The Future of State Charities Regulation" (2013). Chapter 13 also discusses the Corcoran and Detroit cases.

3. In 2015, Joan Weill offered to donate $20 million to Paul Smith's College in upstate New York on the condition that its name be changed to Joan Weill–Paul Smith College. In a case of donor intent interfering with donor intent, it turns out the college is named after an earlier benefactor whose will specified that the school should bear his name forever. Paul Smith's board, the State Board of Regents, and the Charitable Donations Bureau of the New York State Attorney General's Office supported the name change, and an alumni group that opposed the change was denied standing in the suit. Nonetheless, the New York State Supreme Court refused to approve this change, and Joan Weill decided not to make the gift. Kristen Hussey, *After Ruling, Paul Smith's College Won't Get Weils' $20 Million Gift*, NY TIMES, Oct. 22, 2015. Another case of donor intent interfering with donor intent occurred in 2014 when David Geffen offered Lincoln Center $100 million if it would rename Avery Fisher Hall after him. Lincoln Center paid Avery Fisher's

heirs $15 million to settle their lawsuit over this change. The hall is being renovated for $500 million and will reopen in 2021. Felix Salmon, *Naming Wrongs*, SLATE (March 6, 2015), http://www.slate.com/articles/business /moneybox/2015/03/david_geffen_gives_100_million_to_lincoln_center_wh y_the_sale_of_naming.html, accessed May 31, 2016.

4. In 2008, Princeton University settled a "donor intent" lawsuit with the Robertson family, the heirs of one of its donors. The initial gift of $35 million in 1961 had grown to almost $800 million by 2007. The gift was designed "to strengthen the Government of the United States ... by improving the facilities for the training and education of men and women for government service...." In 2002, some members of the donor's family brought suit, claiming that Princeton diverted more than $200 million to activities unrelated to the mission and that it had placed very few graduates in government foreign-policy positions. Although Princeton never agreed to the plaintiffs' version of the facts, it did agree to pay the Robertsons $40 million to cover their legal fees and to pay an additional $50 million so that the Robertsons could begin a separate institution to prepare students for government service called the Robertson Foundation for Government. The parties agreed to dissolve the Robertson Foundation and to grant Princeton control over the remaining funds in an endowment to support the Woodrow Wilson School. For comments on and descriptions of the case, see Iris J. Goodwin, *Ask Not What Your Charity Can Do for You: Robertson v. Princeton Provides Liberal-Democratic Insights into the Dilemma of Cy Pres Reform*, 51 ARIZ. L. REV. 75 (2009); Neil Freeman, THE ROBERTSON V. PRINCETON CASE: TOO IMPORTANT TO BE LEFT TO THE LAWYERS (Hudson Institute 2009); Victoria Bjorklund, *Robertson v. Princeton—Perspective and Context*, EO TAX J. (Mar./Apr. 2009).

5. *"Tainted" funds.* Should a Native American philanthropy accept donations from the Original Americans Foundation, a foundation started by the owner of the Washington Redskins? In 2014, one nonprofit group raising money for a skate park rejected such an offer,[10] while a second accepted a gift to build a playground.[11] A third nonprofit, the cash-strapped Indian Finals National Rodeo, accepted a $200,000 donation from the Original Americans Foundation in 2014 and then requested a gift of $527,000 the next year. Four days after sending that request, they changed their mind and wrote to the foundation:

> After much soul searching, we have decided that we cannot in good conscience accept resources from you on the terms you have offered, no matter how desperately we need it. That is because, as you know, the resources you are offering are not truly philanthropic—they come with the

---

[10] Felicia Fonseca, *Tribe Rejects Offer From Redskins, Calls It "Blood Money"* (NBC4, July 21, 2014).
[11] Erik Brady, *Montana Indian Tribe Happy To Take Redskins' Money*, USA TODAY (July 31, 2014).

expectation that we will support the racial slur that continues to promote your associated professional football team's name...

There is some suggestion, denied by the Indian Finals National Rodeo, that the wealthy Oneida Indian tribe either offered to make up the difference or to introduce other donors if the rodeo would refuse the gift and denounce the foundation.[12]

These types of issues arise regularly, and the decisions associated with them are not easy. The Girl Scouts of Western Washington faced a dilemma in 2015 when offered a $100,000 gift on the condition that the gift not be used to support transgender girls. The troop refused the gift and then publicized its reasons for the refusal as it launched a fundraising campaign that raised more than $300,000 in four days. Natalie Schachar, *Girl Scouts Reject Anti-Transgender Gift, Then Triple the Money*, L.A. TIMES (July 3, 2015).

When allegations that Bill Cosby had raped several women surfaced in 2015, schools that had accepted support from him faced decisions about whether to sever their relationship and return any funds that he and his wife had donated. *See* Ruth McCambridge, *More Schools Cut Ties with Cosby*, NONPROFIT QUARTERLY (Sept. 14, 2015). And in 2012, two military charities refused donations from a donor who had written a firsthand account of the raid that killed Osama Bin Laden because the donor did not submit his work to the Pentagon for review before publication, as he had been required to do. John Hudson, *Second Charity Refuses Donations from Navy SEAL Author*, ATLANTIC WIRE (Sept. 10, 2012). The donor had publicized that he would donate all proceeds to three military charities. If you were on the board of the third charity and now had the opportunity to receive all the proceeds, would you accept the gift?

6. *Enforceability of pledges.* When someone makes a pledge of a multiyear donation, the nonprofit organization must account for the gift as if it had been received in its entirety. If the donor later reneges on this promise, the organization's finances will suffer, as well as any programs that had been earmarked for benefits from the donor's largesse. Should the nonprofit sue the donor for the funds? Does the board have a fiduciary duty to see that the organization does all that is legally possible to obtain the funds? Gary Clark and Brandon Meyer, *Pledges to a Charity: Can They Be Enforced and When Should They Be?* 82 OK. BAR ASSN. J. 147 (2011); Budig, Butler, & Murphy, *Pledges to Nonprofit Organizations: Are They Enforceable and Must They Be Enforced?* 27 U.S.F. L. REV. 47 (1992).

7. *Standing.* Chapter 3 covered the issue of standing in the context of bringing a lawsuit to enforce the board's fiduciary duties. Standing issues also arise in "donor intent" cases. On the one hand, it is unlikely that anyone has a

---

[12] John Cox & Michael Rosenwald, *Why Did Indian Rodeo Reject "Redskins" Name and Dan Snyder's Money?* WASH. POST (Sept. 17, 2015); Rick Cohen, *Rejecting a Tainted Grant: Dan Snyder Just Can't Save Face*, NONPROFIT QUARTERLY (Sept. 22, 2015).

stronger interest in ensuring that a gift is used according to the donor's instructions than the donor. On the other hand, the donor has made a complete gift and no longer has control over that gift. Allowing a donor to bring suit could undermine the concept of a completed gift and allow meddling in the internal affairs of the organization receiving the gift. If, however, the attorney general, who is authorized to bring suit, cannot or will not do so, allowing donor standing could be an important accountability tool.

Most states do not allow donors to bring suit. *See Hardt v. Vitae Foundation*, 302 S.W.3d 133 (Mo. App. 2010) (Nov. 10, 2009) [gift allegedly not being spent in accordance with conditions, but the Uniform Prudent Management of Institutional Funds Act (UPMIFA) does not grant standing to donors]. There are exceptions, however. *See, e.g., Smithers v. St. Luke's—Roosevelt Hospital Center*, 281 A.D.2d 127, 723 N.Y.S.2d 425 (Sup. Ct. App. Div. 2001) (widow of donor granted standing to challenge decision of alcoholism treatment center built with donor's funds to sell the building and move funds to a general account). Note that the Robertson family members in the *Robertson* case, *supra*, had standing because they were on the board of the Robertson Foundation, a separate supporting organization that provided funds for the Woodrow Wilson School at Princeton University. Their relationship to the donor was irrelevant. For more thoughts on donor standing, *see* Reid Kress Weisbord and Peter DeScioli, *The Effects of Donor Standing on Philanthropy: Insights from the Psychology of Gift-Giving*, 45 GONZ. L. REV. 225 (2010).

8. *Donor-advised funds.* Chapter 7 covers donor-advised funds, which are charitable funds that donors set up at a public charity (the sponsoring organization). The donor is entitled to an immediate federal income tax deduction for the entire gift because the donation is to a public charity. The sponsoring organization then educates the donors about community needs and charities and accepts nonbinding grant recommendations from the original donor before it makes grants to other organizations from the donor-advised fund. The sponsoring organization also invests the funds and takes care of all tax, legal, and accounting matters. Since 2006, donor-advised funds have been quite carefully regulated due to concerns that these funds could circumvent the completed-gift requirement for charitable donations.

9. *Cy pres.* Chapter 13 discusses the issue of cy pres, the doctrine requiring that funds for which it is impossible to fulfill the initial purpose be used for a purpose that is as close to the original one as possible. That issue arises when an organization dissolves, merges, or transforms into a for-profit organization, which is why that discussion is in the final chapter. The discussion is also applicable to this chapter. Times change, and the donor's intent cannot be followed exactly, even when the original recipient organization remains active. For example, a provision that requires funds to be used for white women (which you will read about in the following problem) is a restriction that has become impossible given current laws. In *Tennessee Division of the United Daughters of the Confederacy v. Vanderbilt*

University, 174 S.W.3d 98 (Tenn. App. 2005), excerpted above, the Vanderbilt plaintiffs had hoped that changed circumstances would give them a cy pres justification to change the name of the dormitory, but they did not prevail.

A PROBLEM BASED ON *HOWARD V. ADMINISTRATORS OF THE TULANE EDUCATIONAL FUND*

In 1886, Josephine Newcomb donated funds to Tulane University to establish the H. Sophie Newcomb Memorial College in memory of her daughter. She also left the majority of her estate to the school when she died in 1901. In 2006, Tulane decided to merge Sophie Newcomb Memorial College with Tulane to gain administrative efficiencies and help the school recover from the devastation of Hurricane Katrina. The Newcomb endowment, then worth $40 million, would be used to support the H. Sophie Newcomb Memorial College Institute, an academic center designed to enhance women's education at Tulane. Relatives of Josephine Newcomb brought suit to challenge this action, maintaining that the closure of the H. Sophie Newcomb Memorial College violated the conditions of Ms. Newcomb's gift.[13] Assume that you are the judge who must determine whether the conditions have been violated. Following are excerpts from Ms. Newcomb's original inter vivos gift and her will. Do you rule that Tulane has violated the terms of the gift? Why or why not?

A letter dated October 11, 1886, from Ms. Newcomb to Tulane stated:

> In pursuance of a long cherished design to establish an appropriate memorial of my beloved daughter H. Sophie Newcomb, deceased, I have determined ... to entrust to your Board the execution of my design. Feeling a deep personal sympathy with the people of New Orleans, and a strong desire to advance the cause of female education in Louisiana, and believing also that I shall find in the Board selected by the benevolent Paul Tulane, the wisest and safest custodian of the fund I propose to give, I hereby donate to your Board the sum of One hundred thousand dollars, to be used in establishing the H. Sophie Newcomb Memorial College, in the Tulane University of Louisiana for the higher education of white girls and young women. I request that you will see that the tendency of the institution shall be in harmony with the fundamental principles of the Christian religion, and to that end that you will have a chapel or assembly room in which Christian worship may be observed daily for the benefit of the students. But I desire that the worship and instruction shall not be of a sectarian or denominational character. I further request that the education given shall look to the practical side of life, as well as to literary excellence. But I do not mean in this my act of donation to impose upon you restrictions which will allow the intervention of any person or persons to control, regulate or interfere with your

---

[13] The Louisiana Supreme Court issued an opinion in 2008, holding that "would-be heirs" could have standing to bring suit and remanding the case so the heirs could prove their status. The excerpts from the inter vivos gift and will are from that opinion, *Howard v. Administrators of the Tulane Educational Fund,* 86 So. 2d 47 (La. 2008). In 2010, a divided Louisiana appellate court held that Tulane was not legally obligated to keep the college open. *Montgomery v. Administrators of the Tulane Educational Fund* 2009-1670 (La. App. 4 Cir. 10/13/10), 2010 La. App. LEXIS 1384.

disposition of this fund, which is committed fully and solely to your care and discretion with entire confidence in your fidelity and wisdom.

Her will stated, in part:

Aware as I am, of the uncertainty of life, I, Josephine Louise Newcomb, widow of Warren Newcomb, do make this my last will and testament.

First. I have resided of late years in different places, but have made the City of New Orleans my permanent home, because I here witness and enjoy the growth of the H. Sophie Newcomb Memorial College, a department of the Tulane University of Louisiana which I have founded, and has been named in honor of the memory of my beloved daughter.

I have implicit confidence that the "Administrators of the Tulane Educational Fund" will continue to use and apply the benefactions and property I have bestowed and may give for the present and future development of this department of the University known as the H. Sophie Newcomb Memorial College which engrosses my thoughts and purposes, and is endeared to me by such hallowed associations.

Second. I have no forced heirs, I owe no debts; and I hereby revoke all wills of a date anterior to this. I hereby make the following special legacies and bequests: [*Editor's Note:* Ms. Newcomb then provides funds to a cemetery and two individuals.]...

Third. With the exception of the special legacies and bequests herein above stated and made, I hereby give and bequeath to the "Administrators of the Tulane Educational Fund" of New Orleans, the whole of the property, real, personal, and mixed, of which I am now possessed or which I may leave at the time of my death, and to that end and purpose, I do hereby name and constitute the said "Administrators of the Tulane Educational Fund" to be my universal legatee....

CHAPTER 6

CHARITABLE SOLICITATIONS

Purposes of this chapter:

- Examine ways that the state regulates charitable solicitation activities
- Determine the effectiveness of and limitations on state regulatory schemes
- Examine complexities that the Internet brings to these regulatory schemes
- Explore alternative ways to regulate charitable solicitation

To think about as you read:

In recent months, the headlines of the newspapers in your state have exposed what they are calling a charitable scam. Heat for the Hungry, a §501(c)(3) charitable organization, has been using Freddie Fundraiser to solicit funds that will help poor families heat their homes this winter. Freddie has used the telephone and the Internet to make his pitch. He has raised $1 million, only $20,000 of which has gone to Heat for the Hungry. Yesterday's headline, "There Oughtta Be a Law," has caught your attention because you are a state legislator. Should you sponsor the Model Act Concerning the Solicitation of Funds for Charitable Purposes, which is reproduced in this chapter, in your state? What other legislation, if any, would you propose to help ensure that funds raised for Heat the Hungry reach the poor families? How does your legislation avoid the First Amendment concerns described in Section IV in this chapter?

I. INTRODUCTION

In 2014, Americans donated more than $358 billion to charities.[1] Unfortunately, stories about unscrupulous individuals or organizations that are using the illusion of charity to raise money from unsuspecting individuals are all too frequent. In

---

[1] According to Giving USA, AAFRC Trust for Philanthropy, *Giving USA 2015,* Americans gave $358.38 to charity in 2014, a 7.1% growth over 2013.

2015, for example, all 50 states, the District of Columbia, and the Federal Trade Commission (FTC) filed suit against four cancer organizations and some of their officers, claiming that they had bilked consumers out of $187 million by falsely claiming that the money would be used to help cancer patients.[2]

The *Tampa Bay Times* did an exposé on the nation's 50 worst charities in 2013, finding in part: "Over a decade, one diabetes charity raised nearly $14 million and gave about $10,000 to patients. Six spent nothing at all on direct cash aid. . . . Florida-based Project Cure has raised more than $65 million since 1998, but every year has wound up owing its fundraiser more than what was raised. According to its latest financial filing, the nonprofit is $3 million in debt."[3] Also in 2013, Bobby Thompson (evidently an alias of John Donald Cody) was sentenced to 28 years and fined $6.3 million for scamming donors out of more than $100 million by raising funds for a nonexistent charity, U.S. Navy War Vets.[4]

This chapter covers charitable solicitation laws—their purpose, their effectiveness, and the constitutional issues that they raise. It begins with a consideration of state law requirements, including a model act and an article that describes one state's efforts to eliminate charitable fraud. It then considers whether current law is sufficient to regulate charitable giving in the digital age. Finally, it covers the constitutional issues surrounding the regulation of charitable solicitations.

II. STATE LAW REQUIREMENTS

A. The Model Act and Enforcement Difficulties

Most states have charitable solicitation laws that are designed to prevent and penalize abuses. The laws vary from state to state, but in general, they follow similar patterns. They typically apply to three types of charitable fundraisers: (1)

---

[2] FTC press release, *FTC, All 50 States and D.C. Charge Four Cancer Charities with Bilking over $187 Million from Consumers* (May 19, 2015). The FTC settled that suit a year later, with a $75.8 million judgment against two of the charities and the founder, James Reynolds. The charities were to be dissolved and their assets liquidated. James Reynolds agreed to a lifetime ban from paid nonprofit work and charitable fundraising, as well as a ban from managing charitable assets amd serving on a charity's board of directors. An earlier agreement shut down the other two organizations. FTC Press Release, FTC, *States Settle Claims Against Two Entities Claiming to Be Cancer Charities* (March 30, 2016).

[3] Chris Hundley and Kendall Taggart, *America's 50 Worst Charities*, Tampa Bay Tribune (June 6, 2013).

[4] Brian Albrecht, *Bobby Thompson Sentenced to 28 Years in Prison for Veterans Charity Scam*, Cleveland Plain Dealer (Dec. 16, 2013). That sentence was later reduced to 27 years. Ida Lieskovsky, *Bobby Thompson's Sentence Reduced by One Year in Veterans Charity Scam*, Cleveland Plain Dealer (2015). *See* http://www.raffa.com/Fraud/Blogs/Pages/default.aspx, accessed Sept. 27, 2015, for additional reports of charitable wrongdoing.

charities that raise funds, (2) fundraising consultants who advise charities about fundraising, and (3) paid fundraising solicitors who do actual fundraising for charities. (The terms and definitions vary from state to state, but these three functions are similar in most states.) These statutes cover any request for charitable gifts. They require fundraising charities, consultants, and solicitors to register with the state charitable officials and file annual reports, including financial reports. Most states require anyone conducting fundraising on behalf of another to have a written contract specifying the purpose of the agreement, the services that will be provided, and the basis for the fee. Some states also require fundraising consultants or solicitors to post a bond. Small charities, churches, educational institutions, lawyers, accountants, investment advisors, employees, and volunteers are often exempt from these charitable solicitation laws.

Following are excerpts from "A Model Act Concerning the Solicitation of Funds for Charitable Purposes," which the National Association of Attorneys General and the National Association of State Charity Officials adopted in 1986. Currently, 39 states and the District of Columbia require individuals and organizations engaged in charitable solicitations to register with the state. And 37 of those jurisdictions allow the fundraisers to use a uniform form to complete the registration, although 13 of those states have additional requirements. [5]

Although each state's rules are different, many are similar to the Model Act, which follows.

A MODEL ACT CONCERNING THE SOLICITATION OF FUNDS FOR CHARITABLE PURPOSES (1986)

[*Editor's Note:* Blank lines are to be filled in with the name of the administering agency unless the context otherwise applies.]

Section 1. Definitions

(a) "Charitable organization" means:

(1) Any person determined by the Internal Revenue Service to be a tax-exempt organization pursuant to section 501(c)(3) of the Internal Revenue Code; or

(2) Any person who is or holds himself out to be established for any benevolent, educational, philanthropic, humane, scientific, patriotic, social welfare or advocacy, public health, environmental conservation, civic or other eleemosynary purpose or for the benefit of law enforcement personnel, firefighters, or other persons who protect the public safety, or any person

[5] *See* The Unified Registration Statement, Multi-State Filer Project, www.multistatefiling.org/n_appendix.htm, and Affinity Fundraising, Registration, *Charitable Registration State Map*, http://www.fundraisingregistration.com/index. php?option=com_content &view=article&id=19&Itemid=28, accessed May 11, 2016.

who in any manner employs a charitable appeal as the basis of any solicitation or an appeal which has a tendency to suggest there is a charitable purpose to any such solicitation.

(b) "Person" means an individual, corporation, association, partnership, trust, foundation, or any other entity, however styled.

(c) "Solicit" and "solicitation" mean the request directly or indirectly for money, credit, property, financial assistance, or other thing of any kind or value on the plea or representation that such money, credit, property, financial assistance, or other thing of any kind or value, or any portion thereof, will be used for a charitable purpose or benefit a charitable organization.... A solicitation shall be deemed to have taken place whether or not the person making the same receives any contribution.

(d) "Charitable purpose" means:

(1) Any purpose described in Internal Revenue Code section 501(c)(3); or

(2) Any benevolent, educational, philanthropic, humane, scientific, patriotic, social welfare or advocacy, public health, environmental conservation, civic or other eleemosynary objective, or an objective that benefits law enforcement personnel, firefighters, or other persons who protect the public safety.

(e) "Contribution" means the grant, promise or pledge of money, credit, property, financial assistance or other thing of any kind or value in response to a solicitation. It does not include bona fide fees, dues or assessments paid by members, provided that membership is not conferred solely as consideration for making a contribution in response to a solicitation.

(f) "Fund raising counsel" means a person who for compensation plans, manages, advises, consults, or prepares material for, or with respect to, the solicitation in this state of contributions for a charitable organization, but who does not solicit contributions and who does not employ, procure, or engage any compensated person to solicit contributions. No lawyer, investment counselor, or banker who advises a person to make a contribution shall be deemed, as a result of such advice, to be a fund raising counsel. A bona fide salaried officer, employee, or volunteer of a charitable organization shall not be deemed to be a fund raising counsel.

(g) "Paid solicitor" means a person who for compensation performs for a charitable organization any service in connection with which contributions are, or will be, solicited in this state by such compensated person or by any compensated person he employs, procures, or engages, directly or indirectly, to solicit. No lawyer, investment counselor, or banker who advises a person to make a charitable contribution shall be deemed, as the result of such advice, to be a paid solicitor. A bona fide salaried officer employee or volunteer of a charitable organization shall not be deemed to be a paid solicitor.

(h) "Commercial Co-venturer" means a person who for profit is regularly and primarily engaged in trade or commerce other than in connection with soliciting for charitable organizations or purposes and who conducts a charitable sales promotion.

(i) "Charitable Sales Promotion" means an advertising or sales campaign, conducted by a commercial co-venturer, which represents that the purchase or use of goods or services offered by the commercial co-venturer will benefit, in whole or in part, a charitable organization or purpose.

Section 2. Annual Registration Requirement for Charitable Organizations

(a) Every charitable organization, except those granted exemption in section 4 of this act, which intends to solicit in this state or have contributions solicited in this state on its behalf by other charitable organizations, commercial co-venturers, or paid solicitors shall, prior to any solicitation, file a registration statement with the _____ upon a form prescribed by the _____. Said registration statement shall be refiled on or before the fifteenth day of the fifth calendar month after the close of each fiscal year in which such charitable organization solicited in this state. The _____ shall examine each registration to determine whether the applicable requirements of this section relating to the same are satisfied. The _____ shall notify the charitable organization within ten days of its receipt of any deficiencies therein, otherwise it shall be deemed approved as filed. No charitable organization required to be registered under this section shall solicit prior to registration.

(b) A registration statement shall be signed and sworn to under penalties of perjury by two authorized officers including the chief fiscal officer of the charitable organization....

(e) Every charitable organization required to register shall pay a fee of _____ dollars with each registration.

Section 3. Annual Financial Report; Audit Requirement

(a) Every charitable organization required to register with the _____ shall file an annual financial report. The annual financial report shall include: a balance sheet; a statement of support, revenue, expenses and changes in fund balance; a statement of functional expenses at least broken into program, management and general, and fund raising; and such other information as the _____ may require....

(b) The annual financial report of every charitable organization which received more than _____ thousand dollars in gross revenue during its most recently completed fiscal year shall be accompanied by an audited financial statement prepared in accordance with generally accepted accounting principles which has been examined by an independent certified public accountant for the purpose of expressing an opinion thereon. Said _____ thousand dollar audit requirement may hereafter by adjusted by regulation.

Section 4. Exemptions

The following shall not be required to file a registration statement:

(a) Persons that are exempt from filing a federal annual information return pursuant to Internal Revenue Code section 6033(a)(2)(A)(i) and (iii) and Internal Revenue Code section 6033(a)(2)(C)(i).

(b) Political parties, candidates for federal or state office and political action committees required to file financial information with federal or state elections commissions.

(c) Charitable organizations which do not intend to or do not actually raise or receive gross revenue, excluding government grants, in excess of _____ thousand dollars during a fiscal year or do not receive contributions from more than ten persons during a fiscal year, if all of their functions, including solicitation, are carried on by persons who are unpaid for their services and if no part of their assets or income inures to the benefit of, or is paid to, any officer or member; provided, if the gross revenue, excluding government grants, whether accrued or received during any fiscal year, exceeds _____ thousand dollars, or if the charitable organization shall receive contributions from more than ten persons during any fiscal year, it shall, within thirty days after the date thereof, register with and report to the _____ as required by sections 2 and 3.

Section 5. Requirements for Fund Raising Counsel

(a) There shall be a contract between a charitable organization and a fund raising counsel which shall be in writing and shall be filed by the fund raising counsel with the _____ prior to the performance by the fund raising counsel of any material services pursuant to it. The contract shall contain such information as will enable the _____ to identify the services the fund raising counsel is to provide, including whether the fund raising counsel will at any time have custody of contributions....

Section 6. Registration, Contract, and Disclosure Requirements for Paid Solicitors

(a) A paid solicitor shall register with the _____ prior to engaging in any solicitation. Applications for registration or re-registration shall be in writing, under oath, in the form prescribed by the _____ and shall be accompanied by a fee in the amount of _____ dollars. The application shall contain such information as the _____ shall require. Each registration is valid for one year and may be renewed for additional one year periods upon application and payment of the fee.

(b) A paid solicitor shall, at the time of making application for registration and renewal of registration, file with and have approved by the _____ a bond, in which the paid solicitor shall be the principal obligor in the sum of

_____ thousand dollars, with one or more responsible sureties whose liability in the aggregate as such sureties will at least equal that sum....

(c) Prior to the commencement of each solicitation campaign the paid solicitor shall file with the _____a completed "Solicitation Notice" on forms prescribed by the _____. . .

(d) (1) There shall be a contract between a paid solicitor and a charitable organization which shall be in writing, shall clearly state the respective obligations of the paid solicitor and the charitable organization and shall state the amount of the gross revenue from the solicitation campaign that the charitable organization will receive. Said amount shall be expressed as a fixed percentage of the gross revenue or as a reasonable estimate of the gross revenue....

(f) Within 90 days after a solicitation campaign has been completed, and on the anniversary of the commencement of a solicitation campaign lasting more than one year, the paid solicitor and the charitable organization shall file with the _____ a joint financial report for the campaign, including gross revenue and an itemization of all expenses incurred. The report shall be completed on a form prescribed by the _____. The report shall be signed by an authorized official of the paid solicitor and an authorized official from the charitable organization and they shall certify, under oath, that it is true to the best of their knowledge....

(h) Each contribution in the custody of the paid solicitor shall, in its entirety and within five days of its receipt, be deposited in an account at a bank or other federally insured financial institution. The account shall be in the name of the charitable organization with whom the paid solicitor has contracted and the charitable organization shall have sole control of all withdrawals from the account....

Section 7. Charitable Sales Promotions

(a) Every charitable organization which agrees to permit a charitable sales promotion to be conducted by a commercial co-venturer on its behalf shall file with _____ a notice of such promotion prior to its commencement within this state. Such notice shall state the names of the charitable organization and commercial co-venturer, that they will conduct a charitable sales promotion, and the date such promotion is expected to commence.

(b) Every charitable organization which agrees to permit a charitable sales promotion to be conducted in its behalf shall, prior to the commencement of the charitable sales promotion within this state, obtain a written agreement from the commercial co-venturer which shall be available to the _____ upon request. The agreement shall be signed by an authorized representative of the charitable organization and the commercial co-venturer....

(c) The final accounting for the charitable sales promotion is to be kept by the commercial co-venturer for three years after the final accounting date and shall be available to the _____ upon request.

(d) The commercial co-venturer shall disclose in each advertisement for the charitable sales promotion the dollar amount or percent per unit of goods or services purchased or used that will benefit the charitable organization or purpose.

ROBERT E. COOPER, JR., WHY TAKING LEGAL ACTION AGAINST CHARITY FRAUD IS SO HARD

Chronicle of Philanthropy (JULY 23, 2015)

When all 50 states and the Federal Trade Commission joined together in May to sue Cancer Fund of America and three related charities for fraud after a four-year investigation, some commentators asked, "What took so long?"

As a former state attorney general, I thought, "What an accomplishment!" In my experience, state nonprofit regulation presents formidable structural, financial, and legal challenges that make this first broad-based enforcement action a significant milestone.

When I was appointed Tennessee attorney general in 2006, one of my biggest surprises was the scope and complexity of the office's nonprofit work. I knew the office had a broad portfolio, but I did not expect to litigate over a multimillion-dollar university art collection, foundation mismanagement, or misuse of nonprofit corporations. I should not have been surprised, since the nonprofit sector is estimated to account for 5percent of the nation's gross domestic product and 10 percent of its private-sector work force.

State attorneys general frequently collaborate on enforcing consumer protection, false claims, and antitrust laws. For example, 49 states and the federal government negotiated a highly publicized $25-billion consumer-protection settlement in 2012 with the five largest U.S. banks over allegations of fraud in servicing home mortgages. But in the nonprofit area, while many states have strong individual traditions of enforcement, broad collective action has been absent, at least until now.

So why did the states need four years to pull together the case against Cancer Fund of America and three related entities, which the complaint alleges were engaged in "massive, nationwide fraud" in their fundraising for cancer victims? After all, the defendants raised over $187 million from 2008 to 2012, and less than 3 percent went to cancer patients, according to the complaint.

First, there are structural challenges to nonprofit enforcement. In many states, nonprofit regulation is spread among multiple offices. For example, Tennessee's attorney general enforces the state's nonprofit statute, while the secretary of state enforces the charitable-solicitation statute and handles nonprofit registration and reporting.

The cancer-charity fraud case reflects this complexity. The complaint identifies 50 state attorneys general, the attorney general of the District of Columbia, eight secretaries of state, the Rhode Island Department of Business

Regulation, and the Utah Division of Consumer Protection as participants in the lawsuit. As the number of responsible parties multiplies, cases inevitably move more slowly, and matters are more likely to fall through the cracks.

Second, nonprofit cases have financial challenges that other civil enforcement does not. Consumer cases, for example, are frequently brought against well-capitalized for-profit entities and often result in recoveries that state enforcement agencies can use to fund future cases. In the 2012 mortgage-servicing settlement, my office received $1.8 million for its work.

In contrast, during my eight years as attorney general, none of our charitable-litigation recoveries went to fund the office's enforcement efforts.

Nonprofit enforcement, particularly involving fraudulent solicitation, often involves entities whose assets have been dissipated before a suit is ever filed. And recoveries, whether large or small, are more likely to be directed to bona fide charities than applied to the costs of investigation and litigation. This result respects the defrauded donors' charitable intent, which is good legal policy and the right thing to do, but it does not help pay for future enforcement.

The cancer-charities case appears to be following the same path. According to the pleadings, the government will collect only a fraction of the settlement judgments against individual defendants because of their inability to pay. What little is recovered from the settling entities will likely be distributed to legitimate charities.

The lack of a reliable funding stream for nonprofit enforcement work is a problem in an era of shrinking state budgets. Because nonprofit fraud does not generally attract the same public interest as criminal protection or consumer enforcement, there is less political pressure to invest scarce resources there.

Even without financial incentives, all 50 states recognized the need to stop the alleged fraud at the four related cancer charities, so donors would no longer be cheated and funds would not be diverted from legitimate charities. The settlement shut down two entities and placed permanent solicitation bans on three individuals. That leads to the third challenge facing the states: Fraudulent solicitation cases like these are difficult to prove.

The U.S. Supreme Court has set a high First Amendment bar for governments seeking to limit speech related to charitable solicitation. As a result, the line between constitutionally protected speech and fraudulent solicitation can be hard to define. Exorbitant fundraising costs and paltry charitable spending are not enough. The government must prove fraud to make a case, which takes considerable time and resources.

Even before the 50-state lawsuit was filed, several states had obtained judgments against Cancer Fund of America over the years. But when one state succeeded, the business simply moved its focus to another. That is why collective enforcement action was necessary. And the key to such action is enhancing the states' ability to coordinate and share nonprofit information more efficiently.

Some of that work is already under way:

The National Association of State Charity Officials [NASCO] and the Charities Project of the Columbia Law School National State Attorneys General program provide important venues where state nonprofit-enforcement officials compare notes and collaborate.

The National Association of Attorneys General, the membership organization of state attorneys general, works with NASCO and is financially supporting the Cancer Fund of America litigation.

The Columbia Charities Project and the Urban Institute's Center on Nonprofits and Philanthropy are close to finishing the first national survey of state charities regulators, which will provide the most detailed information to date on the nature and mission of these offices and the challenges they confront.

The most important advancement in collective enforcement, however, may be NASCO's Single Portal project. The portal will offer a nationwide, web-based registration and filing system for nonprofits and their professional fundraisers and provide a central repository of regulatory data for officials, academics, policy makers, and the public. The project is working on a funding plan to launch the website. When the website goes live, a nonprofit will no longer be able to move from state to state to escape its past.[6]

Federal agencies obviously play critical roles in multistate nonprofit enforcement. The FTC provided key support in pursuing the Cancer Fund of America case. NASCO is talking with the IRS and Treasury Department about making nonprofit tax data more accessible to state officials.

But state regulators are on the front line in regulating nonprofits in our federal system. It is a challenging job that demands greater efficiency, enhanced transparency, and stronger enforcement — all of which require money. While some of those resources must come from the states, the nonprofit community also needs to play a greater part. Let's honor the generosity of America's donors by finding the means to investigate and file the next multistate lawsuit or, better yet, to stop the fraud before a lawsuit is needed.

B. Cause-Related Marketing

Cause-related marketing, or embedded marketing, occurs when a business promises to give a portion of its proceeds to charity. The term "cause-related marketing" was coined in 1983 when American Express agreed to support the Statue of Liberty Restoration project by donating a penny for every card transaction and $1 for every new card issued. The company donated almost $2

---

[6] [The filing portal's website is http://mrfpinc.org. It is discussed further in the "Notes and Questions" at the end of this section.—*Ed.*]

million in four months. During that time, consumer card usage grew by 27%, and new applications increased 45%.[7]

Such arrangements are increasingly popular. You are probably familiar with the products that support Susan G. Komen for the Cure, the breast cancer awareness organization. These products are accompanied by the pink ribbon that signifies Susan G. Komen for the Cure. Similarly, Red.org has teamed up with several retailers to raise funds to fight AIDS in Africa. These types of efforts are likely to continue to grow because a large majority of Americans express an interest in seeing more products, services, and retailers support charitable causes.[8] As the chief executive officer (CEO) of Benevity, a company that has created an embeddable microdonation platform, has said, "Our vision is that soon, giving back to the community or the cause of your choice will be as easy and prevalent as leaving a tip at a restaurant."[9]

Despite the popularity of embedded giving, some scholars, commentators, and reporters are concerned about the lack of transparency surrounding these arrangements. It is often unclear what percentage of the proceeds goes to charity and which charities benefit. The Model Act, *supra*, addresses cause-related marketing in Section 7, Charitable Sales Promotions. (Its term is "commercial co-venture.") Do you think this is sufficient regulation? In 2010, approximately 20 states had commercial co-venture statutes similar to this one. They all required written contracts with the charity, and 11 of them also required the marketing to disclose how much of the goods or services purchased would go to charity, either as a dollar amount or as a percentage of the value. A few states also required the commercial co-venturer to post a bond, and several of them require the charity to file a copy of the contract with the state, as well.[10] Since 2010, Maine repealed its commercial co-venture statute and South Carolina added one. New York also published "Five Best Practices for Transparent Cause Marketing" in 2012 in an effort to use education as a tool to encourage transparency.[11]

Whether or not commercial co-ventures are covered by a special state statute, they must make truthful statements in their marketing. In 1999, Yoplait yogurt announced it would donate 50 cents to the Breast Cancer Research Foundation for every lid that customers sent to the company. The contract between Yoplait

---

[7] Edward Chansky, *For Goodness Sake: Legal Regulation and Best Practices in the Field of Cause Marketing*, 28 NYSB INSIDE 13 (2010).

[8] 2010 Cone Cause Evolution Study, www.coneinc.com/news/request.php?id=3350.

[9] Benevity, Benevity to Power Innovation in Corporate Giving (Sept. 29, 2010), http://www.benevity.com/press-releases/benevity-to-power-innovation-in-corporate-giving, accessed June 1, 2016.

[10] Edward Chansky, *supra* n. 7 at 13. According to Jason Kohout, *Legal Issues in Cause-Related Marketing*, NATIONAL LAW REVIEW (April 14, 2015), more than half the states had commercial co-venture statutes in 2015.

[11] M. Lackritz-Peltier, *New Year, New Ventures: Keeping up with Charitable Sales Promotions*, NONPROFIT LAW MATTERS (Jan. 19, 2016), http://www.nonprofitlawmatters.com.

and the Breast Cancer Research Foundation capped the contribution at $100,000, and that is what Yoplait paid the charity. Customers had sent in more than 8 million lids, however, and the Georgia attorney general intervened to ensure that the charity received what the company claimed it would receive.[12]

Finally, the nonprofit itself must also be careful when it enters into these agreements. It could face issues concerning unrelated business income or excess benefit transactions, concepts that will be discussed in Chapters 8 and 9, respectively.

For a discussion of issues surrounding cause-related (or embedded) marketing, see Sarah Dadush, *Profiting in (Red): The Need for Enhanced Transparency in Cause-Related Marketing*, 42 N.Y.U. J. INT'L L. & POL. 1269 (Summer 2010); Lucy Bernholz, *Embedded Giving, Bad for You, Bad for Change*, PHILANTHROPY 2173, http://philanthropy.blogspot.com/2010/10/embedded-giving-bad-for-you-bad-for.html. *See also* Dayna Harpster, *Some Pink Products Do Little for Cancer Research*, USA TODAY, Oct. 31, 2010.

NOTES AND QUESTIONS

1. What state interests do charitable solicitation statutes protect? How well do they accomplish this purpose? How likely are fraudulent organizations to register and tell the truth on these forms? Have the states devised a bureaucratic solution that catches only the good guys?

2. The charitable solicitation statutes are designed, in part, to protect the charities themselves, but the charities often complain that complying with charitable solicitation statutes is expensive and time consuming, especially if they need to register in more than one state. A total of 36 states and the District of Columbia have adopted the Unified Registration Statement (URS), which allows charities to consolidate their reporting requirements. Only three other states—Florida, Colorado, and Oklahoma—regulate charitable solicitation but do not accept the URS. However, 14 jurisdictions require supplemental forms in addition to the URS, and each state has its own filing fee. The form and instructions can be found at http://www.multistatefiling.org. As this book went to press, 12 states were working with National Association of State Charity Officials (NASCO) and the National Association of Attorneys General to create and pilot a single charitable registration portal. This initiative was mentioned in the Cooper article above, and interested parties can follow its progress at http://www.nasconet.org/category/single-portal/ and http://mrfpinc.org/.

3. As the Cooper article points out, enforcement is hampered, in part, by a lack of funds. Although state charity officials could always use more funding, the advent of the Internet has created a relatively inexpensive way for states to inform the public about charities. Several states allow consumers to search for information about individual charities online, publicize their enforcement

---

[12] Chansky, *supra* n. 1 at 13.

efforts online, or both. *See, e.g.*, California Office of Attorney General, Registry of Charities, http://rct.doj.ca.gov/MyLicenseVerification /Search.aspx?facility=Y; NYS Attorney General's Charities' Bureau, www.charitiesnys.com; and Hawaii Professional Fundraising System, http://ag.hawaii.gov/tax/.

4. Another difficulty in enforcement has been the privacy restrictions that prevented authorities from sharing information. The Pension Protection Act of 2006 included a provision that allows the IRS to share information about charitable organizations with state charity officials, upon written request from the appropriate state official. Pension Protection Act of 2006, Pub. L. No. 109-280, §1224, 120 Stat. 780 (2006). Unfortunately, the states have not found this provision to be adequate, and 43 state attorneys general asked in 2012 that it be amended to allow further sharing of information. That letter is available at http://www.nasconet.org/fedstate-information-sharing-letter/ naag-info-share-letter/.

5. For further reading, see Richard Steinberg, *Economic Perspectives on Regulation of Charitable Solicitation*, 39 CASE W. RES. L. REV. 775 (1989); Jamie Usry, CHARITABLE SOLICITATION WITH THE NONPROFIT SECTOR: PAVING THE REGULATORY LANDSCAPE FOR FUTURE SUCCESS (Center for Public Policy and Administration, University of Utah 2008); www.givingforum.org/policy/regulators.html. A good infographic on the state of charitable solicitation laws is https://www.harborcompliance.com /information/fundraising-compliance-infographic.

6. Some commentators claim that social enterprises, discussed in Chapters 2 and 10, should be regulated by charitable solicitation acts or are already covered by such acts. Do you agree? For a discussion of these issues, see Robert T. Esposito, *Charitable Solicitation Acts: Maslow's Hammer for Regulating Social Enterprise*, 11 N.Y.U. J. L. & BUS. 463 (2015); Dana Brakman Reiser, *Regulating Social Enterprise*, 14 UC DAVIS BUS. L. J. 231 (2014); and John E. Tyler, *State Attorney General Regulation of Charitable Hybrid Forms: To Be or Not to Be Charitable* (2013). *See also* 2013 Columbia Law School Charities Regulation and Oversight Project Policy Conference on "The Future of State Charities Regulation," http://ssrn.com/abstract=2414192 or http://dx.doi.org/10.2139/ssrn.2414192.

III. CHARITABLE SOLICITATION IN THE DIGITAL AGE

An organization raising funds over the Internet is arguably raising funds in every jurisdiction in the world. Unfortunately, the charitable solicitation statutes were drafted before the advent of the Internet, and, most state statutes have not been modified. With the advent of social media, cell phone solicitations, and crowdfunding, this situation has gotten even more complex. How does the Model Act reproduced above apply to an organization that asks for gifts over the Internet or over a cell phone? Is it flexible enough to adapt to changing technologies? What are the practical effects on the state charity officials and on the charities themselves of including newer types of solicitation in state charitable solicitation statutes?

These questions are not idle ones. According to Blackbaud's 2015 Charitable Giving Report, online donations now make up 7.1% of all donations, and they are growing at the rate of 9.2% a year (compared to traditional fundraising, which is growing at the rate of 1.6% a year). Nearly 14% of gifts came from mobile devices in 2015.[13] Online growth is also coming from traditional web pages, from web portals such as Network for Good, from employee giving pages, and from peer-to-peer pages, which are driven by social connections.[14] The ALS Ice Bucket Challenge of 2014, which raised over $100 million for the ALS Association, is an example of this latter type of gift. [15]

In 2001, NASCO promulgated the Charleston Principles to provide guidance for states grappling with questions concerning online fundraising. Excerpts of these principles are reproduced below. Nearly 15 years later, only two states had adopted the guidelines into their charitable solicitation regulations, and critics were claiming that the principles had not kept up with changing technologies. Richard H. Levey, *Technology Evolves Fundraising, But Charleston Principles Remain Unchanged*, NONPROFIT QUARTERLY (Oct. 15, 2014). Does this mean the principles are a failure? Why do you think so few states have adopted them? Assuming that the Charleston Principles were satisfactory when the only new technology was the Internet, do they cover newer technologies, such as Twitter, Facebook, and phone apps that can be used for charitable solicitation?

THE CHARLESTON PRINCIPLES: GUIDELINES ON CHARITABLE SOLICITATIONS USING THE INTERNET

National Association of State Charity Officials (2001)

I. General Principles

A. These Principles are offered as a guide to states as to when charities, and their fundraisers, fundraising counsel and commercial co-venturers may be required to register, or may be subject to enforcement action, and in what jurisdictions, with regard to charitable solicitations via the Internet. States are encouraged to use these Principles to develop common policies to implement

---

[13] Steve McLaughlin, BLACKBAUD CHARITABLE GIVING REPORT: HOW NONPROFIT FUNDRAISING PERFORMED IN 2015, https://www.blackbaudhq.com/corpmar/cgr/how-nonprofit-fundraising-performed-in-2015.pdf, accessed May 11, 2016.

[14] NetworkforGood, *The Network for Good Digital Giving Index*, 2014 Year in Review, http://www.networkforgood.com/digitalgivingindex/, accessed May 11, 2016.

[15] ALS Press Release, ALS Association Expresses Sincere Gratitude to Over Three Million Donors (Aug. 29, 2014), http://www.alsa.org/news/media/press-releases/ice-bucket-challenge-082914.html, accessed May 11, 2016.

their specific state laws, but these Principles are not necessarily the views of any particular individual, office, or state, nor do they state an official policy position of NASCO. These Principles recognize that the laws of individual states vary, and that implementation of these Principles may also vary....

D. The basic premise of these Principles is this: Although existing state laws govern charitable solicitations on the Internet, in many instances the use of the Internet raises new questions that state charity officials must answer in order to effectively carry out their statutory missions. Therefore, state charity officials should require registration of those over whom their state courts could constitutionally assert personal jurisdiction to enforce a registration requirement. State charity officials and those who solicit contributions using the Internet should note that in actions to enforce state laws against deceptive charitable solicitations, including fraud and misuse of charitable funds, jurisdiction typically exists over some organizations not required to register in the state....

III. Application of Registration Requirements to Internet Solicitation

A. Entities That Are Domiciled Within the State

1. An entity that is domiciled within a state and uses the Internet to conduct charitable solicitations in that state must register in that state. This is true without regard to whether the Internet solicitation methods it uses are passive or interactive, maintained by itself or another entity with which it contracts, or whether it conducts solicitations in any other manner.

2. An entity is domiciled within a particular state if its principal place of business is in that state.

B. Entities That Are Domiciled Outside the State

1. An entity that is not domiciled within a state must register in accordance with the law of that state if:

3. An entity that solicits via e-mail into a particular state shall be treated the same as that solicits via telephone or direct mail, if the soliciting party knew or reasonably should have known that the recipient was a resident of or was physically located in that state.

4. Questions may arise as to whether individual charities are required to register in a particular state when the operator of a Web site through which contributions for that charity are solicited or received is required to register, but the charity itself would not independently satisfy the criteria of Principle III(B)(1)(b). As to such charities:

C. General Exclusions from Registration

1. Maintaining or operating a Web site that does not contain a solicitation of contributions but merely provides program services via the Internet—such as through a public information Web site—does not, by itself, invoke a registration requirement. This is true even if unsolicited donations are received.

2. Entities that provide solely administrative, supportive, or technical services to charities without providing substantive content, or advice

concerning substantive content, are not required to register. Such service providers

NOTES AND QUESTIONS

1. In 2014, Detroit began shutting off water to homes that had failed to pay their water bills. A Twitter campaign that sought volunteers to pay these bills began in July 2014. Within three weeks, 3,000 donors had pledged support and 300 Detroit residences had reached out for help. Adam Ganucheau, *Twitter Campaign Tries to Keep Detroit Water Flowing*, USA TODAY (July 25, 2014). Given the charitable solicitation law in the casebook or the one in your state, is this activity covered? If so, who should register and pay the fee to the state? Another innovation to appear during Detroit's financial crisis is a crowdfunding platform for public-private partnerships called Patroncity.org. Does this raise any charitable solicitation concerns? *See* Rich Tafel, *The Empire Strikes Back! CrowdGranting Is Giving Power Back to the People*, HUFFINGTON POST (Jan. 5, 2016), http://www.huffingtonpost.com /rich-tafel/the-empire-strikes-back-c_b_8914024.html.

2. Jeremiah Souza used Facebook to raise $20,000 for the Missleton Cancer Society in memory of his friend Frieda, who died of cancer last year. He told his Facebook friends what he was doing, collected the money, and turned it over to the cancer society. Assuming that the Model Act was enacted in his state, did he have a legal obligation to contract with Missleton before he began raising funds and to register as a fundraising solicitor? *See* Nicole Wallace, *Fund Raising via Personal Web Sites Grows—But So Do Risks of Misuse*, CHRON. PHILANTHROPY (June 14, 2007). According to the *Chronicle of Philanthropy*, 58% of charities use Facebook to raise funds, 42% use Twitter, 36% raise funds through YouTube, 18% try blogging, and 15% use text messaging. Noelle Barton, *How the Chronicle's Annual Survey of Online Fund Raising Was Compiled*, CHRON. PHILANTHROPY (Aug. 18, 2010). Does the Model Act that is reproduced above cover any of these social networking methodologies?

IV. CONSTITUTIONAL ISSUES

States' efforts to regulate charitable solicitation are restricted by First Amendment concerns. The U.S. Supreme Court has decided four cases dealing with charitable solicitation laws, each of which has confirmed that charitable solicitation activities have full First Amendment constitutional protection. The first, *Village of Schaumburg v. Citizens for a Better Environment*, 444 U.S. 620 (1980), concerned a village ordinance that prohibited charitable organizations from soliciting for funds unless they used at least 75% of their receipts for "charitable purposes." The Court noted that charitable solicitation is not the same as purely commercial speech because the request for funds is generally intertwined with informative and persuasive speech that seeks support for particular causes or views. Thus, charitable solicitation is accorded First Amendment protection, and governments seeking to regulate such solicitation must show that the regulation is narrowly tailored to advance a significant governmental interest. In *Schaumburg*, the governmental interests in protecting the public from fraud, criminal conduct, and invasions of privacy were considered substantial, but they were "only peripherally promoted by the 75-percent requirement and could be sufficiently served by measures less destructive of First Amendment interests." *Id.* at 636. With respect to fraudulent activity, the Court noted that legitimate organizations that are primarily involved in research, education, or advocacy would likely spend more than 25% of their receipts on fundraising, salary, and overhead, especially if they use paid staff to conduct the research and the fundraising. The government cannot include these legitimate organizations with fraudulent ones, without a more precise measure of the difference. Moreover, the government could use other measures to achieve its interest in preventing fraud. Criminal statutes that forbid fraud could be applied, and the requirement of full disclosure would allow the donors to make their own decisions.

Similarly, the 75% requirement was not narrowly tailored to the interest in protecting public safety and privacy because there was no evidence that organizations that spent more on overhead were more likely to intrude on privacy or public safety than those who met the 75% requirement. These privacy concerns could be addressed by less restrictive measures, such as trespass statutes or "no solicitation" signs that homeowners could post on their property. Thus, the village ordinance was unconstitutionally overbroad.

Four years later, the Supreme Court decided *Secretary of State of Maryland v. Joseph H. Munson Co., Inc.*, 467 U.S. 947 (1984), which concerned Maryland's statute that prohibited charitable organizations from engaging in any fundraising activities if they paid or agreed to pay as expenses more than 25% of the amount raised, but which provided a waiver if that limitation effectively prevented the organization from raising contributions. The Court found that "the waiver provision does not save the statute." *Id.* at 962. The waiver provision did not give relief to charitable organizations whose costs were high because they were discussing public issues or whose cause was unpopular. Moreover, the statute assumed that high solicitation costs were equivalent to fraud—an assumption with no basis in fact. Finally, the court reiterated its position in *Schaumburg* that "concerns about unscrupulous professional fundraisers, like concerns about fraudulent charities, can and are accommodated directly, through disclosure and registration requirements and penalties for fraudulent conduct." *Id.*, at fn. 16.

The third case, *Riley v. National Federation of the Blind of North Carolina, Inc.*, 487 U.S. 781 (1988), concerned a North Carolina statute that allowed professional fundraisers to charge a "reasonable fee" according to a three-tiered schedule: any fee up to 20% of the gross receipts of the charitable solicitation was reasonable; any fee falling in the range of 20% to 35% was excessive and unreasonable if the campaign did not involve dissemination of information, discussion, or advocacy; and any fee in excess of 35% was excessive and unreasonable unless the professional fundraiser could demonstrate that the purpose of the solicitation was to support the dissemination of information, discussion, or advocacy *and* that its ability to engage in those activities would be significantly diminished in the absence of the fee charged. The statute also required professional fundraisers to disclose to potential donors the identity of the charitable organization for whom it worked and the portion of the charitable solicitation revenues that the professional fundraiser would retain. Finally, it required professional fundraisers to obtain a license before making charitable solicitations in North Carolina. The Supreme Court determined that all these requirements were contrary to the First Amendment, except for the requirement that fundraisers disclose their identity and that of the organization for which they work.

The Court reiterated its position that charitable solicitation is protected speech and that using percentages to determine the legality of the professional fundraiser's fee was not narrowly tailored to the state's interest in preventing fraud. As there is no connection between the funds retained by the fundraiser and fundraising fraud, the statute cannot be narrowly drawn, even with a three-tiered approach. And once again, an antifraud law and requirements to disclose financial information are more narrowly tailored to achieve the interest in preventing fraud. The statute's provision that the fundraiser could rebut the presumption that the fees were excessive did not make the statute constitutional. Requiring fundraisers to litigate before engaging in advocacy or dissemination of information "necessarily" chills speech, either by driving them out of North Carolina or discouraging them from advocacy and the dissemination of information.

Requiring fundraisers to disclose the percentage of contributions actually given to the charities also violates the First Amendment because it alters the content of the fundraiser's speech and that speech is fully protected, even if it only relates to the fundraiser's profit from the contribution. The Court reasoned that the commercial aspects of the fundraiser's speech are "inextricably intertwined with otherwise fully protected speech." Thus, the interests advanced by this restriction must be compelling and the means selected to promote or achieve those interests must be narrowly tailored.

North Carolina claimed the interest advanced by the Solicitations Act was to dispel donor misconceptions that the money they contributed will ultimately go to the charity for which the funds were solicited. The Court found that this interest was not as weighty as the state asserted, however, because the charity receives benefit from the solicitation, even if it does not receive the funds, when the solicitation is combined with advocacy and the dissemination of information. Moreover, the person being solicited should be aware that some of the money would go to the fundraiser because the fundraiser must explain his or her professional status to potential donors, and the donor could always ask whether the solicitor would receive some of the funds. The Court noted that this restriction was discriminatory against organizations that need to hire outside fundraisers because organizations with in-house fundraisers would be able to carry out the identical solicitation, even if its costs and expenses were high. Requiring professional fundraisers to make these unfavorable disclosures will result in unsuccessful solicitations, and "the predictable result" is that professional fundraisers will be encouraged to leave the state or refrain from engaging in solicitations. Once again, financial disclosure and antifraud laws would be more narrowly tailored ways of achieving the state's interest.

Finally, the Court found that licensure requirement for professional fundraisers also violated the First Amendment because, although the state may impose time, place, or manner restrictions on speech, it may not license speech without providing a time limit within which the license must be granted.

This was the state of the law when *Madigan v. Telemarketing Associates, Inc.*, which is reproduced below, came before the Supreme Court. The Illinois attorney general brought suit against fundraisers who retained 85% of the proceeds of their fundraising endeavors. *Madigan* did not solve all issues relating to charitable fundraising, however, as the *Fraternal Order of Police*, which is also reproduced below, attests.

MADIGAN V. TELEMARKETING ASSOCIATES, INC.

538 U.S. 600 (2003)

OPINION: Justice GINSBURG delivered the opinion of the Court.

I

Defendants below, respondents here, Telemarketing Associates, Inc., and Armet, Inc., are Illinois for-profit fundraising corporations wholly owned and controlled by defendant-respondent Richard Troia. Telemarketing Associates and Armet were retained by VietNow National Headquarters, a charitable nonprofit corporation, to solicit donations to aid Vietnam veterans. In this opinion, we generally refer to respondents, collectively, as "Telemarketers."

The contracts between the charity, VietNow, and the fundraisers, Telemarketers, provided that Telemarketers would retain 85 percent of the gross receipts from donors within Illinois, leaving 15 percent for VietNow. Under the agreements, donor lists developed by Telemarketers would remain in their "sole and exclusive" control. Telemarketers also brokered contracts on behalf of VietNow with out-of-state fundraisers; under those contracts, out-of-state fundraisers retained between 70 percent and 80 percent of donated funds, Telemarketers received between 10 percent and 20 percent as a finder's fee, and VietNow received 10 percent. Between July 1987 and the end of 1995, Telemarketers collected approximately $7.1 million, keeping slightly more than

$6 million for themselves, and leaving approximately $1.1 million for the charity.[16]

In 1991, the Illinois Attorney General filed a complaint against Telemarketers in state court. The complaint asserted common-law and statutory claims for fraud and breach of fiduciary duty. It alleged, *inter alia*, that the 85 percent fee for which Telemarketers contracted was "excessive" and "not justified by expenses [they] paid." Dominantly, however, the complaint concerned misrepresentation.

In the course of their telephone solicitations, the complaint states, Telemarketers misleadingly represented that "funds donated would go to further VietNow's charitable purposes." Affidavits attached to the complaint aver that Telemarketers told prospective donors their contributions would be used for specifically identified charitable endeavors; typical examples of those endeavors include "food baskets given to vets [and] their families for Thanksgiving," paying "bills and rent to help physically and mentally disabled Vietnam vets and their families," "job training," and "rehabilitation [and] other services for Vietnam vets." One affiant asked what percentage of her contribution would be used for fundraising expenses; she "was told 90% or more goes to the vets." Another affiant stated she was told her donation would not be used for "labor expenses" because "all members are volunteers." Written materials Telemarketers sent to each donor represented that contributions would "be used to help and assist VietNow's charitable purposes."

The 15 cents or less of each solicited dollar actually made available to VietNow, the Attorney General charged, "was merely incidental to the fund raising effort"; consequently, she asserted, "representations made to donors [that a significant amount of each dollar donated would be paid over to VietNow for its purposes] were knowingly deceptive and materially false, constituted a fraud, and were made for the private pecuniary benefit of [Telemarketers]."

Telemarketers moved to dismiss the fraud claims, urging that they were barred by the First Amendment. The trial court granted the motion, and the dismissal order was affirmed, in turn, by the Illinois Appellate Court and the Illinois Supreme Court. The Illinois courts placed heavy weight on three decisions of this Court: *Schaumburg v. Citizens for a Better Environment*, 444 U.S. 620, 63 L. Ed. 2d 73, 100 S. Ct. 826 (1980); *Secretary of State of Md. v. Joseph H. Munson Co.*, 467 U.S. 947, 81 L. Ed. 2d 786, 104 S. Ct. 2839 (1984); and *Riley v. National Federation of Blind of N. C., Inc.*, 487 U.S. 781, 101 L. Ed. 2d 669, 108 S. Ct. 2667 (1988). Each of the three decisions invalidated state or local laws that categorically restrained solicitation by charities or professional fundraisers if a high percentage of the funds raised would be used to cover administrative or fundraising costs.

The Illinois Supreme Court acknowledged that this case, unlike *Schaumburg*, *Munson*, and *Riley*, involves no prophylactic provision proscribing any charitable

---

[16] [FN 1]The petition for certiorari further alleges that, of the money raised by Telemarketers, VietNow in the end spent only about 3 percent to provide charitable services to veterans.

solicitation if fundraising costs exceeded a prescribed limit. Instead, the Attorney General sought to enforce the State's generally applicable antifraud laws against Telemarketers for "specific instances of deliberate deception." "However," the court said, "the statements made by [Telemarketers] during solicitation are alleged to be 'false' only because [Telemarketers] retained 85% of the gross receipts and failed to disclose this information to donors." The Attorney General's complaint, in the Illinois Supreme Court's view, was "in essence, an attempt to regulate [Telemarketers'] ability to engage in a protected activity based upon a percentage-rate limitation"—"the same regulatory principle that was rejected in *Schaumburg*[,] *Munson*, and *Riley*."

"High solicitation costs," the Illinois Supreme Court stressed, "can be attributable to a number of factors." In this case, the court noted, Telemarketers contracted to provide a "wide range" of services in addition to telephone solicitation. For example, they agreed to publish a newsletter and to maintain a toll-free information hotline. Moreover, the court added, VietNow received "nonmonetary benefits by having [its] message disbursed by the solicitation process," and Telemarketers were directed to solicit "in a manner that would 'promote goodwill' on behalf of VietNow." Taking these factors into account, the court concluded that it would be "incorrect to presume ... [any] nexus between high solicitation costs and fraud."

The Illinois Supreme Court further determined that, under *Riley*, "fraud cannot be defined in such a way that it places on solicitors the affirmative duty to disclose to potential donors, at the point of solicitation, the net proceeds to be returned to the charity." Finally, the court expressed the fear that if the complaint were allowed to proceed, all fundraisers in Illinois would be saddled with "the burden of defending the reasonableness of their fees, on a case-by-case basis, whenever in the Attorney General's judgment the public was being deceived about the charitable nature of a fund-raising campaign because the fund-raiser's fee was too high." The threatened exposure to litigation costs and penalties, the court said, "could produce a substantial chilling effect on protected speech." We granted certiorari.

II

The First Amendment protects the right to engage in charitable solicitation.... The Court has not previously addressed the First Amendment's application to individual fraud actions of the kind at issue here. It has, however, three times considered prophylactic statutes designed to combat fraud by imposing prior restraints on solicitation when fundraising fees exceeded a specified reasonable level. Each time the Court held the prophylactic measures unconstitutional. [*Editor's Note:* The Court then summarized the three previous cases discussed above in the Introduction to this section.]

III

A

The Court's opinions in *Schaumburg, Munson,* and *Riley* took care to leave a corridor open for fraud actions to guard the public against false or misleading charitable solicitations. As those decisions recognized, and as we further explain below, there are differences critical to First Amendment concerns between fraud actions trained on representations made in individual cases and statutes that categorically ban solicitations when fundraising costs run high. See Part III-B, *infra.* Simply labeling an action one for "fraud," of course, will not carry the day. For example, had the complaint against Telemarketers charged fraud based solely on the percentage of donations the fundraisers would retain, or their failure to alert potential donors to their fee arrangements at the start of each telephone call, *Riley* would support swift dismissal. A State's Attorney General surely cannot gain case-by-case ground this Court has declared off limits to legislators.

Portions of the complaint in fact filed by the Attorney General are of this genre. As we earlier noted, however, the complaint and annexed affidavits, in large part, alleged not simply what Telemarketers failed to convey; they also described what Telemarketers misleadingly represented.... [*Editor's Note:* The court then listed several misrepresentations alleged in the complaint.]

Fraud actions so tailored, targeting misleading affirmative representations about how donations will be used, are plainly distinguishable, as we next discuss, from the measures invalidated in *Schaumburg, Munson,* and *Riley.* So long as the emphasis is on what the fundraisers misleadingly convey, and not on percentage limitations on solicitors' fees *per se,* such actions need not impermissibly chill protected speech.

B

In *Schaumburg, Munson,* and *Riley,* the Court invalidated laws that prohibited charitable organizations or fundraisers from engaging in charitable solicitation if they spent high percentages of donated funds on fundraising—whether or not any fraudulent representations were made to potential donors. Truthfulness even of all representations was not a defense. In contrast to the prior restraints inspected in those cases, a properly tailored fraud action targeting fraudulent representations themselves employs no "broad prophylactic rule," *Schaumburg,* 444 U.S., at 637 (internal quotation marks and citation omitted), lacking any "nexus ... [to] the likelihood that the solicitation is fraudulent," *Riley,* 487 U.S., at 793. Such an action thus falls on the constitutional side of the line the Court's cases draw "between regulation aimed at fraud and regulation aimed at something else in the hope that it would sweep fraud in during the process." *Munson,* 467 U.S., at 969-970. The Illinois Attorney General's complaint, in this light, has a solid core in allegations that home in on affirmative statements Telemarketers made intentionally misleading donors regarding the use of their contributions.

Of prime importance, and in contrast to a prior restraint on solicitation, or a regulation that imposes on fundraisers an uphill burden to prove their conduct lawful, in a properly tailored fraud action the State bears the full burden of proof. False statement alone does not subject a fundraiser to fraud liability. As restated in Illinois case law, to prove a defendant liable for fraud, the complainant must show that the defendant made a false representation of a material fact knowing that the representation was false; further, the complainant must demonstrate that the defendant made the representation with the intent to mislead the listener, and succeeded in doing so. Heightening the complainant's burden, these showings must be made by clear and convincing evidence.

Exacting proof requirements of this order, in other contexts, have been held to provide sufficient breathing room for protected speech. As an additional safeguard responsive to First Amendment concerns, an appellate court could independently review the trial court's findings. What the First Amendment and our case law emphatically do not require, however, is a blanket exemption from fraud liability for a fundraiser who intentionally misleads in calls for donations.

The Illinois Supreme Court in the instant case correctly observed that "the percentage of [fundraising] proceeds turned over to a charity is not an accurate measure of the amount of funds used 'for' a charitable purpose." But the gravamen of the fraud action in this case is not high costs or fees, it is particular representations made with intent to mislead. If, for example, a charity conducted an advertising or awareness campaign that advanced charitable purposes in conjunction with its fundraising activity, its representation that donated funds were going to "charitable purposes" would not be misleading, much less intentionally so. Similarly, charitable organizations that engage primarily in advocacy or information dissemination could get and spend money for their activities without risking a fraud charge.

The Illinois Attorney General here has not suggested that a charity must desist from using donations for information dissemination, advocacy, the promotion of public awareness, the production of advertising material, the development or enlargement of the charity's contributor base, and the like. Rather, she has alleged that Telemarketers attracted donations by misleading potential donors into believing that a substantial portion of their contributions would fund specific programs or services, knowing full well that was not the case. Such representations remain false or misleading, however legitimate the other purposes for which the funds are in fact used.

We do not agree with Telemarketers that the Illinois Attorney General's fraud action is simply an end run around *Riley*'s holding that fundraisers may not be required, in every telephone solicitation, to state the percentage of receipts the fundraiser would retain. It is one thing to compel every fundraiser to disclose its fee arrangements at the start of a telephone conversation, quite another to take fee arrangements into account in assessing whether particular affirmative representations designedly deceive the public.

C

Our decisions have repeatedly recognized the legitimacy of government efforts to enable donors to make informed choices about their charitable contributions. In *Schaumburg*, the Court thought it proper to require "disclosure of the finances of charitable organizations," thereby to prevent fraud "by informing the public of the ways in which their contributions will be employed." In *Munson*, the Court reiterated that "disclosure of the finances of a charitable organization" could be required "so that a member of the public could make an informed decision about whether to contribute." And in *Riley*, the Court said the State may require professional fundraisers to file "detailed financial disclosure forms" and may communicate that information to the public.

In accord with our precedent, as Telemarketers and their *amici* acknowledge, in "almost all of [the] states and many localities," charities and professional fundraisers must "register and file regular reports on activities[,] particularly fundraising costs." These reports are generally available to the public; indeed, "many states have placed the reports they receive from charities and professional fundraisers on the Internet." Telemarketers do not object on First Amendment grounds to these disclosure requirements.

Just as government may seek to inform the public and prevent fraud through such disclosure requirements, so it may "vigorously enforce... antifraud laws to prohibit professional fundraisers from obtaining money on false pretenses or by making false statements." High fundraising costs, without more, do not establish fraud. And mere failure to volunteer the fundraiser's fee when contacting a potential donee, without more, is insufficient to state a claim for fraud. But these limitations do not disarm States from assuring that their residents are positioned to make informed choices about their charitable giving. Consistent with our precedent and the First Amendment, States may maintain fraud actions when fundraisers make false or misleading representations designed to deceive donors about how their donations will be used.

For the reasons stated, the judgment of the Illinois Supreme Court is reversed, and the case is remanded for further proceedings not inconsistent with this opinion....

Justice SCALIA, with whom Justice THOMAS joins, concurring.

The question presented by the petition for certiorari in this case read as follows: "Whether the First Amendment categorically prohibits a State from pursuing a fraud action against a professional fundraiser who represents that donations will be used for charitable purposes but in fact keeps the vast majority (in this case 85 percent) of all funds donated." I join the Court's opinion because I think it clear from the opinion that if the *only* representation made by the fundraiser were the one set forth in the question presented ("that donations will be used for charitable purposes"), and if the *only* evidence of alleged failure to comply with that representation were the evidence set forth in the question presented (that the fundraiser "keeps the vast majority (in this case 85 percent) of all funds donated"), the answer to the question would be yes.

It is the teaching of *Riley v. National Federation of Blind of N. C., Inc.*, 487 U.S. 781 (1988), and *Secretary of State of Md. v. Joseph H. Munson Co.*, 467 U.S. 947, 966 (1984), that since there is such wide disparity in the legitimate expenses borne by charities, it is not possible to establish a maximum percentage that is reasonable. It also follows from that premise that there can in general be no reasonable expectation on the part of donors as to what fraction of the gross proceeds goes to expenses. When that proposition is combined with the unquestionable fact that one who is promised, without further specification, that his charitable contribution will go to a particular cause must reasonably understand that it will go there *after* the deduction of legitimate expenses, the conclusion must be that the promise is not broken (and hence fraud is not committed) by the mere fact that expenses are very high. Today's judgment, however, rests upon a "solid core" of misrepresentations that go well beyond mere commitment of the collected funds to the charitable purpose.

FRATERNAL ORDER OF POLICE, N.D. STATE LODGE V. STENEHJEM

---

431 F.3d 591 (8th Cir. 2005), *cert. denied*, 547 U.S. 1129 (2006)

WOLLMAN, Circuit Judge.

I

This case involves a facial challenge to North Dakota Century Code Chapter 51-28 (the "Act"), which prohibits certain telephone solicitations of North Dakota residents who register with the state's "do-not-call" list. Plaintiffs are nonprofit organizations who rely on professional charitable solicitors for their fundraising.

The Act exempts telephone solicitations made by charitable organizations if "the telephone call is made by a volunteer or employee of the charitable organization" and the caller makes specified disclosures. N.D. Cent. Code §51-28-01(7) (2003). [17]…

II

We review *de novo* the district court's grant of judgment on the pleadings as to the unconstitutionality of the Act…. Because professional charitable solicitation is fully protected speech, *see Riley v. Nat'l Fed'n of the Blind of*

---

[17] [FN 2]The Act also exempts calls made with a resident's prior written consent; by or on behalf of any person with whom the resident has an established personal or business relationship; by or on behalf of pollsters unless the call is made through an automatic dialing-announcing service; by individuals soliciting without the intent to complete the solicitation on the phone but who will follow up with a face-to-face meeting; and by or on behalf of a political party, candidate, or other group with a political purpose.

North Carolina, Inc., 487 U.S. 781, 796 (1988), we begin our analysis by determining whether the North Dakota regulation is content neutral or content based....

[I]t is evident that the Act is content neutral. First, North Dakota has not distinguished between professional and in-house charitable solicitors because of any disagreement with the message that would be conveyed, for the message would be identical regardless of who conveyed it. Second, the regulation can be justified without reference to the content of the regulated speech, for North Dakota's interest is in protecting residential privacy.

Although the Act appears to make a subject matter distinction between advocacy and solicitation, . . . the interest in residential privacy "is not limited to the ringing of the phone; rather, how invasive a phone call may be is also influenced by the manner and substance of the call." *F.T.C. v. Mainstream Mktg. Servs., Inc.*, 345 F.3d 850, 855 (10th Cir. 2003) (per curiam). Because solicitation may reasonably be viewed as more invasive than advocacy, we conclude that the Act is a content-neutral regulation....

III

The test appropriate for regulation of professional charitable solicitation is derived from *Village of Schaumburg v. Citizens for a Better Environment*, 444 U.S. 620, 636 (1980). Although the Supreme Court has not specified whether the *Schaumburg* test is an intermediate scrutiny review of a content-neutral regulation, we have interpreted it as such....

We observed in *Pryor* that the *Schaumburg* test is "obviously very similar" to the time, place, and manner test enunciated in *Ward*.[18] We then considered: (a) whether the State had a sufficient or "legitimate" interest; (b) whether the interest identified was "significantly furthered" by a narrowly tailored regulation; and (c) whether the regulation substantially limited charitable solicitations.

A

The first question under *Pryor* is whether the State has a sufficient or legitimate interest. We have held that residential privacy is a "significant" government interest, particularly when telemarketing calls "are flourishing, and becoming a recurring nuisance by virtue of their quantity." *Van Bergen v. Minnesota*, 59 F.3d 1541, 1555 (8th Cir. 1995). The rationale underlying the North Dakota regulation falls within this significant interest.

B

We next consider whether North Dakota's regulation is narrowly tailored. "The requirement of narrow tailoring is satisfied so long as the regulation

---

[18] [The Court is referring to *Nat'l Fed'n of the Blind of Arkansas, Inc. v. Pryor*, 258 F.3d 851(8th Cir. 2001), and *Ward v. Rock Against Racism*, 491 U.S. 781 (1989).—*Ed.*]

promotes a substantial interest that would be achieved less effectively absent the regulation and the means chosen does not burden substantially more speech than is necessary to further the [state's] content-neutral interest." *Krantz v. City of Fort Smith*, 160 F.3d 1214, 1219 (8th Cir. 1998) (citations omitted). When a content-neutral regulation does not entirely foreclose any means of communication, it may satisfy the tailoring requirement even though it is not the least restrictive or least intrusive means of serving the statutory goal.

North Dakota's goal of ensuring residential privacy would be achieved less effectively if the legislature exempted professional charitable solicitors from the Act. Seeking to balance the interest of callers against the privacy rights of subscribers, the legislature distinguished between in-house and professional charitable solicitors. North Dakota contends that the distinction is based upon the sheer volume of calls because "[a] charity using paid professional telemarketers is typically able to dial substantially more residential telephone numbers than if the charity used its own volunteers and employees." In this facial challenge, we are reluctant to second-guess the North Dakota Legislature's judgment that professional charitable solicitors intrude more regularly on residents' privacy than volunteers or employees and that the Act is a necessary means of enabling its citizens to halt these intrusions.

The Fourth Circuit recently upheld the Federal Trade Commission's (FTC's) charity-specific do-not-call provision. *Nat'l Fed'n of the Blind v. F.T.C.*, 420 F.3d 331, 341 (4th Cir. 2005). Like the statute at issue here, the FTC regulation applied to professional charitable solicitors and exempted in-house or volunteer solicitors. The court held that the regulations struck an appropriate balance between "[t]he rights of charities and telefunders to communicate with potential donors" and "the right of those donors to enjoy residential peace." *Id.* at 349-50. Accordingly, the court held that the provision was "a permissible governmental response to a legitimate and substantial public concern." *Id.* at 350. We find the Fourth Circuit's analysis persuasive, and we join in it in upholding the distinction between professional charitable solicitors and in-house charitable solicitors.

The appellees argue that this distinction renders the Act underinclusive because a ringing phone disrupts residential privacy whether the caller is a volunteer or a professional. They claim that the exemption of in-house charitable fundraisers demonstrates that the Act is not related to residential privacy. Although exceptions from an otherwise legitimate regulation of speech may undermine the government's reasons for the regulation, *City of Ladue v. Gilleo*, 512 U.S. 43, 52, 114 S. Ct. 2038, 129 L. Ed. 2d 36 (1994), we do not perceive that to be the case here. North Dakota's do-not-call statute does not give one side of a debate an advantage over the other, but rather it reduces the total number of unwelcome telephone calls to private residences. "[T]he validity of the regulation depends on the relation it bears to the overall problem the government seeks to correct, not on the extent to which it furthers the government's interest in an individual case." *Ward*, 491 U.S. at 801, 109 S. Ct. 2746. In the case before us, the overall problem is the intrusion on residential privacy caused by unwanted telephone solicitation. We are satisfied that the Act furthers the state's interest in preserving residential privacy.

Additionally, the Act does not burden more speech than is necessary to further the State's interest in residential privacy. The place to which a regulation applies must be taken into account in determining whether a statute is narrowly tailored.... Accordingly, we find it relevant that the Act applies only to personal residences. Further, a content-neutral and viewpoint-neutral opt-in provision like the one here limits the degree of government interference with First Amendment interests.... Although the opt-in nature of the Act is not dispositive, we find it important that the Act's restriction is triggered only when a resident joins the do-not-call registry. Absent this affirmative private action, there is no restriction on a charity's use of professional charitable solicitors. Because the Act prohibits only calls to unwilling residents in their homes, we hold that the Act is narrowly tailored to serve the government's substantial interest in protecting residential privacy.

Finally, the Act need not be the least restrictive means to satisfy the tailoring requirement.... Although exempting all charitable solicitations from the Act or requiring a charity-specific do-not-call list would be less restrictive than North Dakota's regulation, we are not convinced that the existence of these options renders the Act unconstitutional. Because this narrowly drawn, content-neutral statute does not entirely foreclose any means of communication, we are satisfied that the Act is sufficiently tailored to pass constitutional muster.

C

We turn, then, to the final consideration under *Pryor*, whether North Dakota's regulation substantially limits charitable solicitations. We conclude that it does not. The Act prohibits calls to the homes of residents who have chosen not to receive calls from professional charitable solicitors. The Act does not foreclose all means of charitable solicitation directed at these residents. Employees or volunteers may solicit funds from all North Dakota residents, and professionals may solicit funds from residents who have not registered with the state's do-not-call list. Further, the charities may launch fundraising campaigns through the mail or in person. Although the Act restricts charitable solicitation, it leaves open several alternative channels of communication. Accordingly, we conclude that the Act does not substantially limit charitable solicitation.

IV

Appellees argue that the Act is overbroad because it "makes no legitimate effort to distinguish telemarketing calls affecting residential privacy and innocuous speech" and it prevents unknown charities from soliciting North Dakota residents who have registered with the state's do-not-call list.... "For a statute to fail on overbreadth grounds, 'there must be a realistic danger that the statute itself will significantly compromise recognized First Amendment protection of parties not before the Court.'" *Pryor*, 258 F.3d at 856 (quoting *City*

Council v. Taxpayers for Vincent, 466 U.S. 789, 801, 104 S. Ct. 2118, 80 L. Ed. 2d 772 (1984)). The North Dakota statute does not present that danger. When North Dakota citizens register on the do-not-call list, they choose to exclude telephone solicitation from their homes. The registrants have decided that the Act's banned phone calls intrude on their residential privacy. Further, unknown charities will be treated the same as the appellees. Appellees simply cannot support their claim that the Act impermissibly curtails the First Amendment rights of parties not before this court.

Conclusion

... North Dakota's narrowly tailored do-not-call statute significantly furthers the state's interest in residential privacy. The Act does not substantially limit charitable solicitations and is not unconstitutionally overbroad....

NOTES AND QUESTIONS

1. Look again at the Model Act reproduced above. Does it have any constitutional difficulties? Do any parts of this statute seem to be responding to the Supreme Court's decisions concerning charitable solicitation statutes?

2. Oregon, Florida, Arizona, and Maine changed their solicitation laws in 2013 and 2014. Maine and Arizona became less restrictive, while Oregon and Florida became more so. Arizona repealed its requirement that charities register with the state but retained the requirement that veterans' organizations register and made clear that contracted fundraisers that engaged in unlawful solicitation activities would be committing a felony. HB 2457, enacted Sept. 13, 2013. In Maine, organizations that solicit funds below a stated threshold no longer need to register with the state, and nonprofits do not need to include their IRS determination letters when they register. Wilmette Elder and Bernstein Shur, *Charitable Solicitation Requirements Are Changing in Maine*, Martindale.com (Aug. 5, 2014).

   In Oregon, the attorney general has the authority to disqualify charities from receiving tax-deductible contributions for Oregon income tax purposes if they spend more than 70% of their donations on management and fundraising over three years. ORS §128.760 (2013). *See Oregon Charity Law Punishes Nonprofits That Spend Too Much Money On Overhead*, HUFFINGTON POST (July 1, 2013). Florida's new law is similar. It requires all nonprofits soliciting funds in the state, no matter how small, to register. If a nonprofit with revenues above $1 million spends less than 25% on program costs, it faces additional reporting requirements and must explain why the ratio is so low. Florida Department of Agriculture and Consumer Services, Charitable Giving In Florida (2014).

   Why are some states lessening the regulation on charities and some getting stricter? Is either the Florida or the Oregon statute constitutional? Why or why not?

3. As part of the USA Patriot Act, which was passed in response to the September 11, 2001, attacks, Congress amended the Telemarketing and Consumer Fraud and Abuse Prevention Act, 15 U.S.C. §6101 et seq. to include charitable solicitations, which had been exempted from the original sales call rules. The rules require charitable solicitors to state the purpose of their call and the name and address of the charity at the beginning of the call. Is this requirement constitutionally sound? Why do you think that charities were exempted when the Telemarketing and Consumer Fraud and Abuse Prevention Act was first passed? Is that distinction constitutionally required?

4. Some states require professional fundraisers to post a bond before beginning solicitation on behalf of a charity, a requirement that is not applicable to volunteer fundraisers. Such a provision was upheld in *Heritage Publishing v. Fishman*, 634 F. Supp. 1489 (D. Minn. 1986), but found unconstitutional in *American Target Advertising v. Giani*, 199 F. 3d 1241 (9th Cir. 2000), *cert. denied*, 531 U.S. 811 (2000). Given the cases described above, how would you decide such a case, and on what basis?

5. *Nat'l Fed'n of the Blind v. FTC*, 420 F.3d 331 (4th Cir. 2005), *cert. denied*, 126 S. Ct. 2058 (2006), which is quoted in *Fraternal Order of Police*, dealt with the do-not-call registry rules, which imposed limitations on professional telemarketers who solicit donations on behalf of nonprofit organizations, but not on volunteers or in-house callers. The Fourth Circuit held that these rules are constitutionally permissible, and the Supreme Court denied certiorari. Are these two cases consistent with the other First Amendment charitable solicitation cases that you have read?

6. For further reading, see James Fishman, *Who Can Regulate Fraudulent Charitable Solicitation?* 13 PITT. TAX REV. 1 (2015); John D. Inazu, *Making Sense of Schaumburg: Seeking Coherence in First Amendment Charitable Solicitation Law*, 92 MARQ. L. REV. 551 (2009); Michael Hoefges, *Telemarketing Regulation and the Commercial Speech Doctrine*, 32 J. LEGIS. 50 (2005); Edward J. Schoen and Joseph S. Falchek, *The Do-Not-Call Registry Trumps Commercial Speech*, 2005 MICH. ST. L. REV. 483 (2005); Errol Copilevitz, *The Historical Role of the First Amendment in Charitable Appeals*, 27 STETSON L. REV. 457 (1997); Frederick Zufelt, *Recent Development: National Federation of the Blind v. Federal Trade Commission: The Fourth Circuit's Uncertain Scrutiny of the Telemarketing Sales Rule*, 85 N.C. L. REV. 1241 (2007); Marcus Wilbers, *Note: Residential Privacy and Free Speech: Competing Interests in Charitable Solicitation Regulation*, 71 MO. L. REV. 1177 (2006).

CHAPTER 7

PRIVATE FOUNDATIONS AND THEIR ALTERNATIVES

Purposes of this chapter:

- Introduce the distinction between public charities and private foundations
- Provide an overview of the special tax rules for private foundations
- Introduce donor-advised funds and supporting organizations
- Consider policies behind the distinction between a public charity and a private foundation

To think about as you read:

You are advising a very wealthy family about their options with regard to the $50 million that they would like to use for charitable purposes. If they would like to start a private foundation, what rules will they have to follow? If they prefer to start a public charity, what efforts will they have to undertake to ensure that they do not become a private foundation? What are the advantages and disadvantages of each? Under what circumstances would you recommend they start a donor-advised fund or a supporting organization instead of a private foundation?

I. INTRODUCTION

Section 501(c)(3) organizations are classified for tax purposes as either public charities or private foundations. This chapter discusses the tax implications of that distinction, but before beginning that discussion, it is helpful to know that private foundations are usually funded by a single person or a small group of funders and serve as grant-making organizations. Sometimes private foundations exist because organizations that would prefer to be public charities do not obtain funding from a sufficiently large group of investors. In tax terms, they do not have sufficient "public support." These two types of organizations are functionally quite different, but they must follow the same tax rules.

We study the laws surrounding foundations for several reasons. First, although this book concentrates on public charities, private foundations are important nonprofit corporations, and a course on nonprofit corporations should expose you to their rules. Second, public charities should be aware of the rules that they will need to follow if they do not qualify for public charity status. Third, the private foundation rules are the basis for several relatively new provisions that are applicable to public charities, such as the excess benefit transaction rules, the excise tax on political activity, and the rules for donor-advised funds and supporting organizations.[1] Finally, private foundations and their alternatives (donor-advised funds, supporting organizations, and community foundations) are important sources of funds for public charities.

The Internal Revenue Code defines a "private foundation" as a §501(c)(3) organization that is not a public charity. IRC §509(a) sets forth complicated definitions for the four types of public charities. Before tackling those definitions, this chapter discusses the history behind the enactment of the statute that distinguished private foundations from public charities, and sets forth the rules that private foundations must follow. The chapter then explores the two most common types of public charities—§509(a)(1) traditional public charities and §509(a)(2) "gross receipts" public charities. The chapter ends with a discussion of organizations that function in many ways as alternatives to private foundations, but which remain public charities—community foundations, donor-advised funds, and §509(a)(3) supporting organizations.[2] This material can be quite difficult, but if you read the historical excerpt carefully enough to understand the perceived abuses that Congress was trying to curtail when it adopted these rules, and work through each of the examples, you should be able to understand it and be well positioned to learn the rules that you will encounter later in the book that are based on the private foundation rules.

II. HISTORY BEHIND THE CREATION OF THE PRIVATE FOUNDATION RULES

TANYA D. MARSH, A DUBIOUS DISTINCTION: RETHINKING TAX TREATMENT OF PRIVATE FOUNDATIONS AND PUBLIC CHARITIES

22 Va. Tax Rev. 137, 138-139, 142-144, and 148-152 (2002)

The American nonprofit sector has its origins in the 1601 Statute of Charitable Uses, in which Queen Elizabeth I authorized the establishment of private perpetual funds to support specific religious and charitable institutions.

---

[1] Excess benefit transactions are discussed in Chapter 9, excise taxes for political activity in Chapter 11, and donor-advised funds and supporting organizations in section V of this chapter.

[2] John Colombo's testimony in Chapter 1 introduced the distinction between private foundations and public charities and described the policy reasons behind this distinction.

These perpetual foundations were and are somewhat remarkable in a legal tradition that places restrictions on a dead man's ability to control his wealth from beyond the grave. The public benefit and the religious roots of philanthropy justify such exceptions to the rationale underlying the Rule Against Perpetuities. Perhaps due to the great cultural respect for altruism and "good works," the American legal system largely has neglected or refused to govern nonprofit organizations outside of the purview of the Internal Revenue Code (Code).

Since Queen Elizabeth I's day, the definition of a foundation has been most simply a perpetual gift to benefit a particular charity or group of deserving persons. Such an expansive definition could encompass the entire nonprofit sector. However, when Congress authored the current regulations concerning the nonprofit sector in 1969, it divided the traditional foundation category into two parts. Congress perceived a sharp division between private foundations, such as the high-profile Ford Foundation, Carnegie Corporation, and Kellogg Foundation; and public charities, organizations that the public more broadly supports through donations, such as the Salvation Army, Red Cross, and California Community Foundation. Congress intended the private/public distinction to serve as a proxy for the amount of control a donor retained over her gift after dedicating it to philanthropy and taking the corresponding tax deduction....

Wealthy Americans always have contributed generously to their communities, especially funding the establishment and perpetuation of churches, hospitals, and schools; however, organized and national philanthropy in the United States did not begin in earnest until the Industrial Revolution enabled individuals to amass great fortunes. Some of these self-made millionaires, most famously the steel tycoon Andrew Carnegie, believed that the accumulation of wealth carried the moral imperative to improve the conditions of society. A number of wealthy robber barons used their fortunes to establish foundations they hoped would promote their "personal visions of ... society" in perpetuity.

While American philanthropists established only five general foundations in the nineteenth century, Carnegie and John D. Rockefeller not only inspired a generation of tycoon-philanthropists, but they invented the organized philanthropy of the twentieth century. Both Carnegie and Rockefeller believed that philanthropy, as opposed to personal charity, required knowledge, skills, and a professional staff. These pioneers also believed that by funding scientific research and endowing institutions they could eliminate social ills.

The first four decades of the twentieth century gave birth to large numbers of foundations, including the W. K. Kellogg Foundation in 1930, and the Lilly Endowment in 1937. The prosperity of the decade following World War II encouraged the endowment of a number of large foundations, like the Ford Foundation. In the 1950s, the foundation movement exploded and the number of foundations with assets of more than $ 1 million doubled. The tax structure in place in the middle of the twentieth century made foundations an attractive shelter for great wealth, and too many pseudo-philanthropists received tax benefits without actually engaging in philanthropy. These very public manipulations drew the attention of Congress, which passed the Tax Reform Act of 1969 (1969 Act) in order to rein in private foundations....

In the decades after World War II, economic expansion, high income tax rates, and significant estate taxes fueled an explosion in the number of private foundations. While most of the new foundations were legitimate charitable enterprises, many were little more than abusive tax shelters. In 1950, President Harry S. Truman captured public anger at those manipulating the system when he complained to Congress that private foundations were "a cloak for speculative business ventures."

Public sentiment encouraged Congress to pass the first real effort to regulate nonprofit organizations through the Code. In order to discourage people from using foundations for private gain, Congress moved to revoke section 501(c)(3) status from "charities that engaged in 'prohibited transactions' (specified acts benefiting substantial contributors), or whose undistributed income was unreasonable in amount or duration, used to a substantial degree for nonexempt purposes, or invested in a manner jeopardizing their exempt purposes." Congress exempted several types of traditional charities (e.g., schools, churches, hospitals) but did not attempt to justify why these organizations should not be covered by the new restrictions. "By asserting that the new self-dealing rules were applicable to 'organizations which are manipulated to the private advantage of [their] substantial donors,' the 1950 committee reports implied that charitable organizations subjected to these rules were more prone to this type of abuse than those exempted." This language suggests that as early as 1950, Congress recognized distinctions between different types of nonprofit organizations and their varying levels of vulnerability to abuse by donors. The beginning of the private/public distinction as a proxy for the pivotal variable, level of donor control, originated in this 1950 legislation.

Congress further amended the Code in 1954 and 1964 in efforts to distinguish between categories of charitable organizations to a greater degree and to prevent various subversions of charitable intent. . . . [These changes] rely on a perceived distinction between private and public charities, which were rooted in a number of assumptions that favored the public grouping over the private. Charities that receive their support from a number of donations rather than from a single source, for example, could be considered to have a public mandate for their activities. The rationales for the 1954 and 1964 legislation foreshadowed the sweeping changes that came in 1969.

The 1969 Act, which is imbedded in the Code and administered by the Internal Revenue Service (Service), is primarily regulatory legislation aimed at private foundations despite the trappings of tax legislation. Its enactment represented a major departure from the laissez-faire attitude that had long characterized the American government's relationship with the nonprofit sector and instituted a number of rules aimed at curbing the abuses noticed by President Truman and Congress as early as 1950.

To populists, private foundations represented the arrogance and greed of a wealthy, mainly East Coast, elite. In 1961, Representative Wright Patman, a

Democrat from Texas, began a series of high-profile investigations into the activities of private foundations. Patman and his supporters concluded that large foundations without countervailing accountability possessed too much financial and political power and that wealthy Americans were using foundations to abuse tax laws. At Representative Patman's insistence, the Treasury Department investigated private foundations but concluded in a 1965 report that most private foundations did not abuse the tax system and did fulfill an important social function. However, the Treasury Department did identify several problems in the private foundation world that justified congressional attention, including dangerous concentrations of economic and social power in private foundations, instances of donors and their families using foundations for private gain, inappropriate business holdings by foundations, and an "undue lag between the charitable gift generating the tax benefit (the transfer of wealth to the foundation) and the use of the funds for charitable purposes." Although the 1965 Treasury report identified only modest problems, it encouraged Representative Patman's committee to issue new reports in 1966, 1967, and 1968, which "presented a stream of new allegations and cases of flagrant foundation misconduct."

On February 18, 1969, Representative Patman's personal crusade took on new significance when the House Ways and Means Committee opened hearings on the question of tax-exempt foundations. Representative Patman was the first witness before the Committee, and he set the tone for the discussion:

> Today, I shall introduce a bill to end a gross inequity which this country and its citizens can no longer afford: the tax-exempt status of the so-called privately controlled charitable foundations, and their propensity for domination of business and accumulation of wealth. Put most bluntly, philanthropy—one of mankind's more noble instincts—has been perverted into a vehicle for institutionalized, deliberate evasion of fiscal and moral responsibility to the nation. This has been accomplished by tax immunities granted by the U.S. Congress. The use of the tax-free status ... reveals the continuing devotion of some of our millionaires to greed, rather than conversion to graciousness....

On the second day of the hearings, Representative John J. Rooney, a Democrat from New York City, testified that private foundations could be used to undermine democracy. In a previous campaign, explained Representative Rooney, a wealthy opponent used his own private foundation to make tax-free donations to politically influential groups to encourage them to get out the vote. Thus, his opponent's campaign was "subsidized by all United States taxpayers and in defiance, if not in violation, of laws governing campaign moneys." Representative Rooney warned the committee that the same thing "can—and probably will—happen in your districts. In fact, the appeal of this political gimmick is a threat to every officeholder, in Congress or elsewhere, who does not have access to a fat bankroll or to a business or to a tax-exempt foundation."

On the third day, Ford Foundation president McGeorge Bundy was scheduled to testify. Bundy was one of the most controversial figures in the philanthropic world in 1969. Under his leadership, the Ford Foundation gave money to organizations to support efforts to increase African-American voter registration and assisted an allegedly militant Mexican-American organization to enter local politics. Only a week before the hearings began, The New York Times reported that the Ford Foundation made grants totaling $ 131,000 to eight prominent members of the late Senator Robert F. Kennedy's staff. According to a Ford Foundation press release, they intended these grants, personally approved by Bundy, " 'to ease the transition from public to private life [by providing] up to a year of leisure and freedom from immediate financial concern.' "

The committee members began by firing questions at Bundy regarding the Kennedy staff grants. He attempted to defend the grants as purely "educational" rather than personal or political—an argument undermined both by common sense and the Ford Foundation's own press release. Throughout his testimony, Bundy "conveyed a strong impression of arrogance and condescension." One congressman remarked, " 'I went into that hearing this morning basically friendly to the foundations; I came out feeling that if Bundy represents the prevailing attitude among them, they are going to have to be brought down a peg. For all their Ph.D.'s, they are not above the law.' "

Although the turbulent first days of the hearings gave way to more sober testimony and reflection by committee members, the tone had been set and the perceived privileges and excesses of private foundations were under attack. Eventually, Congress drafted legislation with the intent of curbing the power, influence, and flexibility of private foundations. The House and Senate passed different versions of the tax bill, and a conference committee hammered out a compromise act. After much deliberation, Congress finalized the 1969 Act on December 23, 1969.

III. OVERVIEW OF FEDERAL TAX TREATMENT OF PRIVATE FOUNDATIONS

In layman's terms, a "foundation" is a charitable organization funded by an individual or a small group of individuals, typically a wealthy family or a successful corporation. The initial gift is usually stock from the company that the family founded, or from the corporation that is creating the foundation. Although the organization could raise money once it is founded, most foundations do not seek funding from outsiders. Instead, they use investment income to pay expenses and provide grants to public charities. Providing grants to public charities and other "qualifying organizations" is such a large and important part of a foundation's activities that one tongue-in-cheek definition of a foundation is that it is "a large body of money completely surrounded by people who want more."[3] This chapter will concentrate on the most typical form of private foundation—the endowment foundation, which relies on investment income. In

---

[3] Dwight Macdonald, THE FORD FOUNDATION: THE MEN AND THE MILLIONS (Reynal 1956), p. 3.

May 2016, the 10 largest foundations in the United States were all endowment foundations.[4]

Many §501(c)(3) organizations choose to be set up as private foundations, even though they enjoy less favored tax treatment than public charities. Private foundations are a good vehicle for individuals and families who want to spread charitable giving over time (possibly forever). In the 20 years between 1993 and 2012, despite two recessions, the number of foundations more than doubled, to 86,192, and their assets grew almost fivefold, to $715 billion.[5] In 2014, $41.6 billion was donated to private foundations, and the foundations in turn granted almost $60 billion to other charities.[6]

Following is a summary of the tax rules that private foundations must follow. These rules are extremely complex and could be the basis of an entire course. They are introduced here, however, because students need to understand the different rules that the two different types of §501(c)(3) organizations must follow, and because some of the concepts relating to private foundations have been introduced into public charity law. As you read these rules and the article that follows, consider whether they resolve the problems that concerned Congress when it passed the legislation. Also consider what additional plans and financial records that your organization will need to track if it is classified as a foundation instead of as a public charity.

A. SPECIAL RULES FOR PRIVATE NONOPERATING FOUNDATIONS[7], AND SOME PROBLEMS

The 1969 legislation described in the article above created a series of excise taxes covering self-dealing, mandatory payouts, business holdings, investment practices, and various expenditures. It also created an excise tax on investment income as a way to pay for the additional scrutiny that these rules would require. Except for the excise tax on investment income, the other taxes are avoidable. If

---

[4] Foundation Center, http://foundationcenter.org/findfunders/topfunders/top100assets.html, accessed June 1, 2016. The top 10 include the Bill and Melinda Gates Foundation, the Ford Foundation, the J. Paul Getty Trust, the Robert Wood Johnson Foundation, William and Flora Hewlett Foundation, W. K. Kellogg Foundation, Lilly Endowment, Inc., David and Lucile Packard Foundation, Gordon and Betty Moore Foundation, and Bloomberg Philanthropies. They range from $6.55 billion to $44.3 billion in assets. Six years earlier, the top 10 foundations, nine of which remain on the list in 2016, held assets ranging from $4.5 billion to $29.9 billion in assets.

[5] The 2012 statistics are from Foundation Stats, Foundation Center, http://data.foundationcenter.org/about.html#about, last accessed May 12, 2016. The 1993 statistics (41, foundations with $155.6 billion in assets) are from the SOI Tax Stats—Domestic Private Foundation and Charitable Trust Statistics, http://www.irs.gov/uac/SOI-Tax-Stats-Domestic-Private-Foundation-and-Charitable-Trust-Statistics, accessed May 12, 2016.

[6] The Giving Institute, *Giving USA 2015 Press Release,* June 15, 2015.

[7] Private foundations can themselves be classified into two groups—operating and nonoperating. Most private foundations are nonoperating foundations. Although the rules for both types of foundations are more stringent than the rules for public charities, the rules for operating foundations are not quite as stringent as the rules for nonoperating foundations. Section III.C, *infra,* discusses operating foundations.

the foundation stays within the self-dealing, mandatory payouts, business holdings, investment practices, and expenditure rules, it pays no other excise taxes. After an initial violation, it must pay a moderate tax. If that matter is not corrected and the initial tax is not paid in a timely manner, a more onerous tax is assessed. Finally, if the actions continue to be willful, flagrant, or repeated, a termination tax, which will effectively terminate the foundation's existence, is imposed. Following is a description of those rules, along with hypothetical questions to help you understand them. Some of the hypothetical facts are deliberately vague so that you can discuss what would happen with different interpretations of the facts.

1. Excise Tax on Investment Income (§4940)

When the 1969 legislation was introduced, Congress passed a tax on investment income that would provide the Internal Revenue Service (IRS) with sufficient funds to enforce these provisions. The tax is currently set at 2% of the organization's net investment income, although an organization can reduce its tax to 1% by paying out more "qualifying distributions"[8] than its historical average. As mentioned above, these taxes are not avoidable. Rather, they act somewhat like income taxes on a foundation's investment income.

Hypothetical Example 1. A few years ago, John Ambrose donated his fortune to Haven, a nonoperating grant-making foundation devoted to providing grants to organizations working to eradicate AIDS. Haven's accountants have determined that its net investment income is $1 million. Assuming that Haven has not made any extra qualifying distributions, what will it have to pay in investment income excise taxes?

2. Self-Dealing (§4941)

Subject to certain exceptions, a private foundation cannot engage in any prohibited transactions with "disqualified persons." Disqualified persons[9] are:

- The person who creates the foundation
- Directors, officers, trustees of the foundation, and the manager or executive director of the foundation
- Substantial contributors (those who have given more than $5,000 in the applicable tax year, provided that the $5,000 exceeds 2% of the total contributions from the inception of the foundation through the close of the tax year in which the gift or bequest is made)

---

[8] Qualifying distributions are defined in the paragraph about minimum distribution requirements, §4942 below.

[9] Section 4946 defines the term "disqualified persons." This definition is relevant for the self-dealing rules described here, for supporting organizations, and for the public support test of §509(a)(2). The same term is used in the context of an excess benefit transaction, but the definition is slightly different. That concept will be discussed in Chapter 9.

- A person who owns more than 20% of a business that is a substantial contributor
- Family members of a disqualified person (parents, spouses, children, children's spouses, grandchildren, and grandchildren's spouses)
- Corporations or business entities controlled by a disqualified person or a group of disqualified persons

Generally, foundation assets cannot be used to enter into a financial transaction between the foundation and a disqualified person. Such transactions include, but are not limited to, selling or leasing of property, loaning money, furnishing goods or services, and using the foundation's facilities. These transactions are forbidden, even if they do not result in any gain to the disqualified person. The regulations provide a few exceptions, such as a transaction in which no money exchanges hands or one that was carried out for a charitable purpose. In addition, a disqualified person may receive compensation or reimbursement of expenses if the disqualified person's activities are reasonable and necessary in carrying out the charitable purposes of the foundation. Unless the transaction falls within one of the exceptions, however, there is an absolute prohibition against self-dealing.

Note that the term "disqualified persons" is defined quite broadly. It includes people who could have a direct conflict of interest if they transacted business with the organization, as well as people and organizations that have a close enough relationship to another disqualified person that a business relationship between those people or entities and the foundation could be a form of indirect self-dealing. Section 4941 is designed to prevent transactions from taking place indirectly that would otherwise be prohibited.

Also, substantial contributors retain their status as substantial contributors, even if they cease all involvement with the foundation. The only way to stop being treated as such is to allow at least 10 years to pass, during which neither the substantial contributor nor any related person contributes to the foundation or acts as the foundation manager. In addition, the aggregate amount contributed to the foundation by a disqualified person (and related persons and entities) must be insignificant compared to the aggregate amount of contributions made to the private foundation by one other person.

For example, Jeremiah Jeffreys contributed $10,000 to the Shore Foundation on September 14, 2005. At that time, the aggregate amount the foundation had collected was $100,000. Jeffreys was a substantial contributor at that point—his gift was larger than $5,000 and more than 2% of the total that the organization had raised at that point. He would remain a substantial contributor to that foundation for the rest of his life unless, for at least 10 years, neither he nor any related person nor entity contributed to or ran the organization, and someone else had donated so much to the Jeffreys Foundation that Jeremiah Jeffreys' contribution was insignificant compared to that person's contribution. If Jeffreys and his relatives stopped supporting the foundation through contributions, management, and governance in 2005, and Warren Buffett, who had no blood ties or personal relationship to Jeffreys, donated $10 million to the Jeffreys Foundation, Jeffreys would probably cease being a substantial contributor in 2015. Such a situation is unlikely to happen.

If self-dealing occurs, the initial tax on the self-dealer is 10% of the amount involved. In addition, if the foundation manager (executive director, trustee, or other person in control of the foundation) knowingly participated in the self-dealing, he or she must pay 5% of the self-dealing amount. The initial foundation manager tax cannot exceed $20,000, however. If the self-dealing is not corrected in a timely fashion and the tax paid, a second, additional tax of 200% can be imposed on the self-dealer and a 10% tax (up to $40,000) on the foundation manager. If the organization continues with willful, repeated violations, a tax that will result in involuntary termination of the foundation will be imposed.

This provision may be the most important excise tax. It prevents the people who control a private foundation from taking unfair advantage of the organization or its assets. It has also become the basis of the intermediate sanctions provisions for public charities, which will be discussed in Chapter 9.

Hypothetical Example 2. In 2000, Sherman Woyzek contributed $1 million to the Jamal Foundation, a §501(c)(3) private foundation started by Jason Jamal with a $3 million gift a few months earlier. Woyzek and Jamal were acquaintances but had no business or familial ties. No one else ever contributed another dime to the foundation. Jamal remained on the board and managed the foundation, but Woyzek never contributed another dime, served on the board, or managed the foundation. No one else, including Jamal, ever made another contribution to the foundation. In 2015, Woyzek, an insurance salesman, wants to sell insurance to the foundation. Can he do so without exposing himself or the foundation manager to excise taxes?

Hypothetical Example 3. The Hayes Performing Arts Center was endowed with funds from Natalie Fassie as a §501(c)(3) private foundation. Her gift was so generous that the center never charged for its plays. After one of the plays, Ms. Fassie purchased the sets and costumes used in the production from the foundation for $5,000. The sale was not open to the public, and the fair market value of the set and costumes was $6,000. Is this transaction allowed under the Internal Revenue Code? If not, what is the penalty? If the center had sold the set and costumes to the administrative assistant instead of to Ms. Fassie, would the same result occur? What if Fassie's husband took the company car on vacation? Would the result be different if her boyfriend took the car on vacation?

Hypothetical Example 4. Last January, Angelina Jolie and Bono entered into a contest to see which one of them would give a larger donation to Global Odyssey, an international educational organization. In the end, Global Odyssey found itself a $15 million private foundation. (They each contributed $7.5 million. No one else made any contributions.) They both now work as executives at the organization, and they pull in salaries of $50,000 and $75,000, respectively. Do you see any legal problems with this arrangement?

3. Minimum Distribution Requirements (§4942)

Private foundations must make a minimum distribution of their assets each year, so that they cannot avoid using their assets for charitable purposes by hiding their wealth in these vehicles. Within 12 months after the end of each fiscal year, each private foundation must make "qualifying distributions" in an amount equal to or greater than 5% of the fair market value of the foundation's assets that are not used directly to carry out the foundation's exempt purposes. This rule is also stated as the requirement that the foundation pay out at least 5% of its net investment assets.

Qualifying distributions include grants, direct charitable activities, reasonable expenses needed to administer a grant program, program-related investments, and special projects approved by the IRS. Grants to other nonoperating endowment foundations are not usually considered qualifying distributions.

If a private foundation does not make its minimum distribution requirement within the specified time, it could be required to pay an excise tax of 30% of the undistributed amount. And if that tax remains unpaid at the end of the correction period, it must pay a tax of 100% of the undistributed amount. These excise taxes are in addition to distributing the undistributed amount.

Hypothetical Example 5. Think Pink is a §501(c)(3) private foundation that averaged $10 million in net investment assets in fiscal year 2014. Within 12 months after the end of that year, it provided grants worth $100,000 to breast cancer charities. It also spent $400,000 on rent, salary, travel expenses, and office supplies for administering the grant program. Has it met its minimum distribution requirement? If not, what should happen?

4. Excess Business Holdings (§4943)

Private foundations are often capitalized with stock from a corporation. If the foundation owns all, or even a significant part, of the corporation, it could have an incentive to run the business instead of working to achieve its charitable purpose. This concern has led to the requirement that a private foundation may only own a certain percentage of the stock and securities of a business—generally 20%. That 20% combines the ownership of the private foundation with that of the disqualified persons. If the private foundation and the disqualified persons own too large a share of a business enterprise, that excess is called an "excess business holding." A private foundation with excess business holdings has 90 days to fix the situation unless a gift or bequest causes this situation, in which case it has five years to divest itself. It can, in some situations, obtain an additional five years to diversify if it can show a "good-faith" effort to do so earlier. Like the self-dealing tax, the initial tax is 10% of the value of the excess holding, and the secondary tax is 200% if the problem is not corrected in a timely manner.

Hypothetical Example 6. Six years ago, the Outterson Family Foundation was created with stock from Tech-Savvy, Inc., which had been owned by Sara Outterson, her siblings, and her parents. The Outterson Foundation has never sold any of the Tech-Savvy stock. At the end of the current tax year, the Outterson Family Foundation owns 10% of the voting shares of Tech-Savvy stock. Sarah owns 5%, as do each of her two siblings and each of her parents. Does the foundation have any excess business holdings issues?

5. Jeopardizing Investments (§4944)

A private foundation must exercise prudence and good business judgment in investing a foundation's assets so that it does not invest its funds in ways that could jeopardize the foundation's ability to carry out its charitable purposes. Such a use of funds would be called a "jeopardizing investment." A determination of whether an investment is jeopardizing is made on an investment-by-investment basis, taking into account the private foundation's portfolio as a whole. If the rule is violated, both the organization and the funder could be liable for a 10% excise tax.

Section 4944 specifies that program-related investments do not count as jeopardizing investments.. A program-related investment (PRI) is an investment made for the purpose of furthering a foundation's tax-exempt purpose. It can take the form of a loan, an equity position, a loan guarantee, or any other transaction in which the foundation has an economic interest, so long as (1) its primary purpose is the accomplishment of a charitable purpose; (2) it does not have any purpose that would be prohibited under the private foundation rules, such as lobbying or intervention in a political campaign; and (3) the investment does not have the production of income or the appreciation of property as a significant purpose. PRIs have become an increasingly important way to finance social enterprises, which are discussed in Chapters 2 and 10.

Hypothetical Example 7. The Rochester Foundation owns 5% of the stock in Photo-Age, a large photography company, which comprises its entire investment portfolio. (In other words, the Rochester Foundation has no other investments.) As of the beginning of the year, the Photo-Age stock was worth $100 million. Unfortunately, Photo Age has not been as quick to adapt to the digital age as its competitors, and its stock declined 20% last year. Is the Rochester Foundation's investment in Photo Age a jeopardizing investment? Would it also be a jeopardizing investment if the stock had risen?

6. Taxable Expenditures (§4945)

A "taxable expenditure" is an expenditure made for a noncharitable purpose. Taxable expenditures include payments for political campaigns and lobbying, certain grants to individuals, and grants to non–501(c)(3) public charities unless the foundation exercises "expenditure responsibility" with respect to the grant.[10] Such procedures include obtaining advance approval from the IRS under certain circumstances, making inquiries about the grantee, requiring reports from the grantee, and entering into a contract with the grantee that ensures that the grantee will use the grant funds for charitable purposes. The excise tax rules also help ensure that private foundations follow these rules by imposing a 10% initial tax on the organization and any foundation manager who knowingly made the taxable expenditure.

Hypothetical Example 8. E-Squared is a §501(c)(3) private foundation devoted to improving the environment. Last year, it funded a research project to determine how carbon dioxide emissions affect the environment. The report included information on legislation pending before the California legislature that would severely limit carbon emissions from cars and air conditioners. The report commented favorably on this legislation without analyzing its advantages, disadvantages, or economic costs. Was the report a taxable expenditure?

7. Charitable Contribution Deduction Rules (§170)

Chapter 5 noted that gifts of cash and ordinary income property to public charities are subject to an annual limitation of 50% of the adjusted gross income, with a five-year carryover of any excess. Gifts to private foundations, on the other hand, are limited to 30% adjusted gross income. Limits on the deductibility of charitable contributions for gifts of long-term capital gain property to private foundations and for gifts of appreciated assets are also more stringent for private foundations than for public charities. This rule does not make a difference for most donors, but it could for some.

Hypothetical Example 9. Frank Farmer owns a farm worth $1 million, which is exactly what he paid for it. His adjusted gross income over a five-year period will be $100,000 a year. Will he be able to deduct the entire $1 million if he donates the farm to a private foundation? Will it make a difference if he donates the farm to a public charity?

8. Required Restrictions in a Foundation's Founding Documents (§508)

Private foundations must include provisions in their governing documents that recognize the special private foundation excise taxes, in addition to the provisions about charitable purposes and nondistribution that all §501(c)(3)

---

[10] §4945(h) defines "Expenditure responsibility" as requiring the private foundation "to exert all reasonable efforts and to establish adequate procedures—(1) to see that the grant is spent solely for the purpose for which made, (2) to obtain full and complete reports from the grantee on how the funds are spent, and (3) to make full and detailed reports with respect to such expenditures to the Secretary [of the Treasury]."

organizations must contain. 26 U.S.C.A. § 508(e). IRS Publication 557 provides sample language for these provisions.

9. Terminating a Private Foundation (§507)

If a foundation is terminated involuntarily, it faces a termination tax equal to the lower of (1) the aggregate historical tax benefits of exemption to the foundation and its substantial contributors (dating back to its origin) plus interest, or (2) the value of the net assets of the foundation. Such a termination would occur only for "willful repeated acts" or a "willful and flagrant act or failure to act." §507(a)(2)(A). The IRS has the authority to abate the termination tax if the private foundation distributes all its net assets to one or more public charities.

A private foundation may also terminate voluntarily by distributing all its assets to one or more public charities or by operating as a public charity itself. It must give notice to the IRS and follow special regulations to make this change.

Hypothetical Example 10. Although the Brecon Foundation, a low-income housing organization, received an advance determination as a §501(c)(3) public charity when it began seven years ago, it never met either of the public support tests described below. A few years ago, it was reclassified as a §501(c)(3) private foundation. Its founder, Brian Ivy, has engaged in numerous incidents of self-dealing and has willfully disregarded all orders to pay excise taxes. Had the Brecon Foundation been a for-profit corporation, it would have paid $100,000 in corporate income tax for each of the 10 years of its existence. Its net assets are now worth $50,000. How much, if anything, does the Brecon Foundation owe the IRS?

10. Abuses

RICK COHEN, TIME TO STOP EXCUSING THE INEXCUSABLE: FOUNDATION TRUSTEES WHO PLAY BY THEIR OWN RULES

Nonprofit Quarterly (Dec. 21, 2003)

Illustrating the latest example of eyebrow-raising foundation behavior, the *Boston Globe* recently reported that the H. N. and Frances C. Berger Foundation invested $100 million of Foundation resources in distressed Texas real estate. The payoff? $4.2 million in "profit sharing bonuses" for the foundation's seven trustees. Stories like this—and there are many of them—are hardly the publicity philanthropy needs.

Without a doubt, foundation scandals involve only a small fraction of grantmakers. But good foundations don't deserve to be dragged down by the unscrupulous actors in their midst. It's time to notice the red flags and wake up foundation trustees to the highest possible standards of foundation probity.

Foundation boards have to do what's right, not just what's within the boundaries of the law. After all, that's what they expect of the nonprofits they fund.

Trustee Fees

Numerous foundations pay trustees quite hefty sums for doing as little as showing up at a couple of board meetings each year. . . . The worst examples publicized in the press recently include: The Paul and Virginia Cabot Charitable Trust in Massachusetts paid trustee Paul C. Cabot $1.4 million in 2001 (including an extra $200,000 he needed for his daughter's wedding in Boca Grande, Florida); . . . the Statler Foundation paid each of its trustees $20,429 in 2001 for selecting 32 grant applicants, and . . . the George W. McManus Foundation in Maryland, . . . paid its board president and trustees more than it granted to charities. . . .

In defense of the practice, former Kellogg Foundation executive Joel Orosz suggests, "Foundations that pay trustee fees generally get what they pay for." In other words, if the foundation doesn't pay for quality on the board, it won't get it. That's a troubling, backhanded slap at all the foundation trustees who donate their board service because they truly believe that foundation boards should be voluntary.

In some foundations, trustees are compensated to carry out functions that would otherwise have to be done by staff. Setting aside for a moment the rather generous valuation of the time of some foundation trustees, the action is fundamentally a conflict of interest. If a foundation trustee is working as the equivalent of staff, who is going to tell the trustee-staff person that he or she is doing the job poorly, needs to be retrained, or ought to be terminated?

Fees might be justifiable if they were intended to diversify the racial, ethnic and social class composition of foundation boards. But most recipients of trustee fees are hardly working stiffs and rarely people of color. . . . [T]here is no evidence that trustee fees have been used primarily to create a discernible impact on the democratization of foundation governance.

Trustee Self-Dealing

In America's heartland of Peoria, Illinois, the local press ran a series of articles on the scandalous finances and investments of the Bielfeldt family and their foundation. Local nonprofits were appreciative of the $25 million the Bielfeldt Foundation had given away over its 17 years to charities such as the Peoria Ballet, the Peoria Area World Affairs Council, the George Washington Carver Center and CHOICES Youth Outreach. But they were unaware that the foundation paid family members, primarily Gary Bielfeldt, and businesses owned by or run by the Bielfeldt family $21 million for investment services.

In 2002 alone, the foundation paid Gary Bielfeldt, his son, and their firms more than $3 million for investment advice, while paying out only $1.2 million in grants. Between 2001 and 2002, the foundation's assets plunged 46 percent, while it continued to pay fees and commissions of almost $2 million to Bielfeldt family members. In the same time period, according to the Peoria Star Journal., the average drop in assets of other Illinois foundations was only 6 percent. Don't ask the Bielfeldts to manage your 401(k). The Star Journal cited experts who suggested that the self-dealing practices of the Bielfeldts might be entirely legal. This is the big loophole in [the foundation excise tax] rules. The[y] are basically a tax on foundation insiders (officers, directors, trustees and their families) for the use of a charity's tax-exempt status resources for inappropriate private personal gain.

While most of the philanthropic attention on [these rules] has focused on the salaries of foundation executive directors, [they] also cover trustee fees. When foundation trustees provide actual services—legal, accounting, investment—to their institutions for a fee, they will be penalized only if they receive an "excess benefit" from the transaction. . . . The fact that the Bielfeldts seem to have squandered the foundation's assets with alacrity in a one-year period does not seem to affect the "reasonableness" of their charges to the foundation. As long as they can say that the foundation's payments to the Bielfeldts for their investment services were generally similar to those paid for services by other organizations in "similar circumstances," they meet the market test. . . .

Trustee Self-Granting

The swirl of controversy around the Ewing Marion Kauffman Foundation in Kansas City, Missouri, includes allegations that the foundation made a grant to the organization of one of its board members. He abstained but did not recuse himself from the board meeting approving the grant. He subsequently voted to save the job of the foundation's controversial executive director in a 4-3 vote. Did the $50,000 grant sway his vote? Hard to say. Did it look lousy to the readers of the *Kansas City Star?* Probably.

Grants to board members' organizations are hardly unknown, but the practice is becoming increasingly visible to nonprofits. . . [T]he Yawkey Foundation, established by Red Sox owners Tom and Jean Yawkey from the sales proceeds of the team for $420 million . . . approved a $15 million grant to Boston College, where the Yawkey chairman is a trustee, the college chancellor is on the Yawkey Foundation board, and another person is on both the Yawkey and BC boards. A *New York Times* article described the recent behavior of the John Stauffer Charitable Trust, which paid each of its trustees $130,000, not including legal fees paid to the law firm of one of the trustees, and made nine grants, five to universities where two Stauffer trustees were also board members and another serves as a vice president emeritus.

Nonprofit grant applicants are obviously at a distinct disadvantage when competing with foundation board members for grants, regardless of whether the trustees recuse themselves from deliberations, simply abstain from the vote or momentarily step out of the meeting room during the final headnodding. Tilting the grantmaking rules to favor foundation insiders doesn't do much toward fairness, especially when the insider games are basically hidden from sight.

Trustees' Discretionary Grants

Foundation trustees sometimes forget that they're working with other people's money, "other people" meaning the public. It's not Monopoly money, but tax-exempt money that the public has entrusted to the governing boards of foundations to use to benefit communities and the nation.

In some foundations, trustees are given their own pots of money to allocate as they see fit, with little or no connection to the mission of the foundation and frequently little or no due diligence other than checking that the grant recipients have 501(c)(3) status.

The practice might end up with grants made to trustees' alma maters or their favorite houses of worship (with c3 fiscal agents) or who knows where. . . .Some well-respected institutional as well as family foundations allocate as much as 40 percent or more of their grant funds to trustee discretionary grant pools.

Of course, the entire board might be tempted to treat foundation assets as discretionary play money. The foundation associated with Florida Atlantic University gave the president of FAU a parting gift of a $42,000 red Corvette, running the gift through a hidden payment to the president's wife. In Oklahoma City, the Kerr Foundation favors a $44,000 Jaguar, the Arthur S. DeMoss Foundation of West Palm Beach has a $36 million Bombardier jet used to ferry board chairperson Nancy DeMoss and her daughter and the Samuel Roberts Noble Foundation favors a less expensive Cessna Bravo jet. These expenditures make a mockery of the charitable purposes of the foundations.

Finding Solutions

Imagine the nonprofit [grantee] submitting a proposal to a foundation with a budget line that includes payments to board members. Try including a line that calls for paying the board members for professional services rendered. Does the word "rejected" come to mind? . . .

. . .It is impossible to think of foundations tolerating anything like these practices among [grantees].

Have some foundations lost their charitable compass? . . . What might be done to clean up philanthropy . . ., short of a Sarbanes-Oxley law for foundations?

- *End the practice of paying compensation to foundation trustees.*

Trustee fees are not the same as reimbursing board members for expenses incurred in attending foundation meetings—or replacing the lost wages of working people who might be invited to join foundation boards. Pablo Eisenberg has proposed alternatives such as paying trustees a nominal sum or severely penalizing foundations that exceed a reasonable trustee compensation limit.. . . That might be politically more feasible than simply ending the practice. But most foundation trustees are hardly in need of the extra cash. . . .

- *Link the foundation excise tax to federal and state oversight and enforcement.*

. . . The excise tax was originally a mechanism to pay for the IRS role in this sector, but the revenues, now in the hundreds of millions of dollars per year, simply go into the general treasury. More IRS activity alone cannot answer the accountability problems of the sector. But the IRS has to be part of the solution, as do the charity officers in the offices of state attorneys general, who may well be much closer than the IRS to spotting foundation problems. . . .

- *Toughen up [foundation excise rules].*

Of course, enforcement begs the question of "enforcing what?" There is far too much leeway in the [excise tax] provisions. Beefing them up would give trustees, foundations and their trade associations tougher standards to meet, which, like most law-abiders, they will do without the prod of an IRS audit finding. . . .

- *Add backbone to trade association standards.*

The philanthropic trade associations face a challenging balancing act. On one hand, they want to keep their members—and their dues—in the organization, and that means not criticizing them. On the other, they have to establish ethical benchmarks for the association, its members and the profession. The alternative is to sanction errant members whose behavior tarnishes everyone. The time is now for the philanthropic trade associations to get into gear and develop something more than milquetoast ethical standards that address self-dealing and self-enrichment schemes that circumvent the Intermediate Sanctions rules in the foundation world.

- *Remember the true responsibility of foundation board stewardship.*

. . . It's time for all foundation trustees around the nation to be embarrassed by this stuff, to see that their reputations are sullied by the behavior of their miscreant peers. They won't be able to look the other way in the future, because all of us—the mainstream press, state attorneys general, maybe the Internal Revenue Service, nonprofit grant recipients, and nonprofit watchdogs—will be looking and prepared to speak out. It is time to stop excusing the inexcusable. . . .

B. PRIVATE OPERATING FOUNDATIONS AND A PROBLEM

A "private operating foundation (POF)" is a separate type of private foundation that is somewhat of a hybrid between a public charity and a nonoperating or grant-making private foundation. Like a public charity, a POF engages in charitable or educational activities rather than in distributing grants. Like a private foundation, the POF is generally funded by an individual or a small group of funders, and it has too much investment income to qualify as a public charity. The tests for determining whether an organization qualifies as a POF are as complex as the other tests that we have discussed in this chapter so far. The organization must use at least 85% of its income to perform its own charitable activities and also meet one of three other tests:

1. The assets test, which requires at least 65% of the foundation's assets to be devoted to exempt function activities, functionally related businesses, or both
2. The endowment test, which requires the foundation to show that it normally spends at least two-thirds of its minimum investment return on its exempt activities (two-thirds of 5% is 3.3% of its investment assets)
3. The support test, which requires the foundation to show that it receives support from the general public and from five or more exempt organizations that are not related to each other

If an organization qualifies as a POF, it receives more favorable tax treatment than private, nonoperating foundations in many respects. For example:

1. Gifts made to POFs qualify for the same level of deductions as do gifts to public charities—up to 50% of the donor's income base for gifts of cash or ordinary income property. They are not limited to 30% of the donor's income base for such gifts, as other foundations are.
2. POFs are not required to make the annual minimum distribution (5% of investment assets) that nonoperating foundations must make.
3. Private, nonoperating foundations that provide grants to POFs can count these grants as "qualifying distributions" in terms of satisfying the annual payout requirement.
4. Private, nonoperating foundations that provide grants to POFs do not need to exercise the same expenditure responsibility as is required when they provide grants to other private nonoperating foundations.
5. Some POFs are exempt from the 2% excise tax on investment income. (Determining which POFs qualify as "exempt operating foundations" is beyond the scope of this book.)

In other respects, however, a POF is still a type of private foundation, subject to the restrictions that apply to private foundations. The following problem, drawn from the pages of a newspaper in 2006, will give you an opportunity to apply some of the principles that you have been reading about in this chapter.

PROBLEM

In 2006, the California attorney general investigated the Getty Trust, a POF that runs a research institute, a library, an art conservation program, a grant-making office, and the J. Paul Getty Museum in Los Angeles. Presumably, the

IRS investigated as well.[11] Among the allegations that local and national newspapers publicized were the following:

- The president of the Getty Trust, Barry Munitz, received compensation that exceeded $1 million a year. He traveled extensively and luxuriously at Getty's expense. For example, he used Getty money to buy a $72,000 Porsche Cayenne, repeatedly flew first class, stayed in $1,000-a-night hotels, and asked his assistants to express-mail umbrellas when he traveled.
- Munitz authorized grants and uses of the trust's money without obtaining proper approval. Some of these payments were spent on Munitz's pet projects, which seemed unrelated to Getty's mission. For example, he set up the Getty Chess Project Office and flew a chess-playing trust security guard to Israel to observe the Kasparov Chess Academy.
- The Getty Trust sold property to a billionaire friend of Munitz's for $700,000, below its appraised value.
- In 1999 and 2000, Munitz presented more than $20,000 in gifts of art to four departing trustees, even after the trust's attorney advised against these gifts. (Other board members later repaid part of this expense.)
- The Getty's former antiquities curator faced trial in Italy on charges of trafficking in looted antiquities. She also took out a personal loan from an art dealer with whom she had done millions of dollars in museum business.
- The *Los Angeles Times* stated, "Subsequent disclosures of Munitz's lavish compensation, travel, and other perks—many of them unheard of in the philanthropic field—were equally shocking. Getty money seemed to have changed uses during his tenure, since the annual average spent buying art— the lifeblood of the institution—had simultaneously declined by one-third when adjusted for inflation."[12]

Assuming that the allegations were true, answer the following questions:

1. Why is the Getty Trust a POF instead of a private foundation or a public charity? (Don't do the math. Use your common sense.)
2. Which of the private foundation rules discussed above continue to apply to this POF, and which ones are irrelevant because the Getty Trust meets the POF tests?
3. Which of the rules that a POF must follow have been violated?
4. What remedy should apply?
5. From the information provided, does the Getty Trust appear to be in any danger of losing its status as a POF? If so, what difference would that make? Are any of the issues discussed earlier in the book relevant in this situation?

---

[11] Because the IRS does not publicize its investigations, we do not know whether it did in this case, but for purposes of thinking about this problem, assume that it did consider these issues.

[12] The quote is from Christopher Knight, *At Getty Trust, the Trust Part Is Lacking*, LA TIMES (Nov. 15, 2005). The rest of the information in this problem is from that article and from Jason Felch, Robin Fields, and Louise Roug, *The Munitz Collection*, LA TIMES (June 10, 2005), p. A-2.

NOTES AND QUESTIONS

1. To prevent abuses like those described in the *Nonprofit Quarterly* article above, would it be better to adopt more stringent legislation, do a better job of enforcing existing law, or improve educational efforts directed at foundations? What type of legislation would you enact?

2. Is it a good idea to require a minimum distribution requirement? Why do you think 5% was chosen as the minimum distribution?

3. As was mentioned in Chapter 2, Mark Zuckerberg, the founder of Facebook, and his wife, Priscilla Chan, have decided to forego (at least for the time being) a private foundation when they engage in philanthropic activities. Instead, they will work through a limited liability company (LLC), the Chan Zuckerberg Initiative. What business and tax reasons would they have for making this decision? Why are some members of the traditional philanthropic community critical of, or at least skeptical of, this decision? Do you agree, as at least one prominent nonprofit scholar has said, that this is "the end of philanthropy as we know it"? *See* Leslie Lenkowsky, *Ending Philanthropy as We Know It*, WALL ST. JOURNAL (Dec. 2, 2015); Felix Salmon, *Mark Zuckerberg Wants to Change the World Again: You Got a Problem with That?* FUSION, (Dec. 3, 2015); Daniel Harris, Matthew Brady, *The Chan Zuckerberg Initiative: The Pros and Cons of LLCs in Charitable Giving*, WELLS FARGO (Dec. 23, 2015). The Chan Zuckerberg Initiative's Facebook page is https://www.facebook.com/chanzuckerberginitiative.

4. Are private foundations the only §501(c)(3) organizations that should be required to make minimum distributions? Harvard University, for example, announced in 2015 that its endowment was $37.6 billion, up by $10 billion from 2010.[13] Should it be required to spend some of that endowment on "qualifying distributions"? Does your answer change if you learn that it lost $11 billion between 2008 and 2009? Why might one come up with a different answer about minimum distributions for Harvard than for the Ford Foundation? For further discussion of university endowments, see the notes following Part VIII of Chapter 4.

IV. PUBLIC POLICY CONSIDERATIONS WITH REGARD TO PRIVATE FOUNDATIONS

The private foundation rules discussed in Part III were designed to prevent the types of abuses that Congress felt could arise when an organization is funded and controlled by a single person or a small group of people. (Remember that a

---

[13] The 2015 statistic is from FINANCIAL REPORT, FY 2015 (Harvard University, Oct. 29, 2015) http://finance.harvard.edu/files/fad/files/_fy15harvard_finreport_.pdf?m=1446159221. These numbers compare to a $27.6 million endowment in 2010, as it emerged from the Great Recession. Harvard Management Company Management Report, 2010, Updated Message from the CEO, at http://piketty.pse.ens.fr/files/capital21c/xls/RawDataFiles/WealthReportsEtc/USUniversities/Harvard/Harvard2010EndowmentReport.pdf, accessed May 12, 2016.

corporation can be a person in this context.) What has happened since then is that most foundations follow a very similar pattern. They are set up to last in perpetuity[14] by giving away a maximum of 5% of their net investment income each year. These gifts are generally either made to well-established nonprofits such as Harvard University (which received both a $350 million and a $400 million gift between September 2014 and June 2015)[15] or to programs that seem innovative to the grant-makers. The grants for programs rarely cover overhead expenses, and long-term grant relationships are unusual, so that the funded programs will need to find another source of income when the grant commitment is over. Meanwhile, the foundations invest the other 95% of their assets (the part they are not required to distribute) the same way as other investment managers, which means that the vast majority of their assets are not devoted to charitable purposes. Critics have begun to question some of the assumptions surrounding private foundations, and some foundations are beginning to make changes. Following is a discussion of these issues.

Should foundations last forever? Traditionally, the answer has been "yes." The idea is to save for a rainy day and to make sure that the resources are available in times of need. In addition, the money earned on investments should increase the amount that is paid out over time. Although the vast majority of foundations are set up to last forever, some scholars, commentators, and even funders of foundations are beginning to question this response. The Bill and Melinda Gates Foundation, for example, is set to wind up within 20 years of its founders' deaths.[16] Those who question perpetuity for foundations ask why we should wait until tomorrow to solve a problem that can be solved today. Some problems, like climate change, may not be solvable if we wait 50 years before addressing them. And it seems cruel to wait to eradicate a disease that could be stopped within a few years. Even if new technology to eradicate that disease will be available later, these critics maintain that we should have faith that a new generation of philanthropists will step forward at that time. The critics have also noted that foundations did not do a particularly good job of meeting charitable needs during the rainy days of the 2008–2009 recession, when the need for charitable resources increased considerably.[17] Although some foundations indeed increased their giving, others retrenched. Their own investments were hard hit, and if they were to stay in business forever, they believed that they needed to reduce their charitable distributions.

---

[14] According to a 2009 survey by the Foundation Center, only 11.2% of foundations are intended to have a limited lifespan. Loren Renz and David Wocheck, *Perpetuity or Limited Lifespan?* The Foundation Center (2009).

[15] Mariel Klein, *A $400 Million Gift, and Accompanying Scrutiny,* HARVARD CRIMSON (July 7, 2015).

[16] Gates Foundation, *Who We Are, Foundation Trust,* http://www.gatesfoundation.org/Who-We-Are/General-Information/Financials/Foundation-Trust, last accessed May 12, 2016.

[17] Charitable grants by foundations fell by 8.9% between 2008 and 2009. Giving USA Foundation, Giving USA, Executive Summary 2010, http://www.pursuantmedia.com/givingusa/0510/export/GivingUSA_2010_ExecSummary_Print.pdf, accessed June 1, 2016.

The critics make another point that appeals to some founders of foundations. Once the founder has died, no one else can ensure that his or her wishes are followed. Even if the children work to follow their parent's wishes, times change, and it can be impossible to know what Mom or Dad would have wanted in today's world. The more time that elapses after the founder's death, the more difficult it is to follow the founder's wishes.[18]

Whether foundations should be perpetual or not, is 5% the correct payout amount? Congress created the 5% limitation because over time, a foundation will earn at least 5% on its investment, which will allow the foundation to stay in business forever. Some critics question this policy. First, it is unclear whether the 5% payout calculation is correct. Professor Brian Galle's empirical study shows that foundations are earning much more money and growing much more quickly than earlier studies suggested—a finding that implies that the law could require a much higher annual payout without sacrificing the perpetuity concept.[19] Second, the 5% payout requirement includes the operating expenses of the foundations, which the critics believe should not be included in the payout requirement because the overhead expenditures are not charitable. Third, the 5% can include program-related investments, which can earn a profit for the foundation. Critics fear that foundations will steer their funds toward their investments and could ultimately take funds away from charities that need gifts. Finally, the rule has had the unintended effect of making 5% a maximum payout instead of a minimum. The median foundation payout rate in 2010 was 5.1%.[20]

Should foundations have a different investment strategy than for-profit investors? Proponents of the status quo point out that if the purpose of the foundation is to stay in business forever, and the investment managers have a fiduciary duty to engage in prudent investments, then they need to follow the best investment strategy possible. And if they make more money in investments, that will make more money available to the charity. Critics question this assumption. They maintain that private foundations have an obligation, at the least, to do no harm, and some foundations have begun to divest themselves of investments that they see as harmful. Among the more interesting incidents of this trend is the Rockefeller Foundation's decision to divest itself from fossil fuels, even though it

---

[18] Critics include Brian Galle, *Pay It Forward? Law and the Problem of Restricted Spending Philanthropy*, forthcoming 93 WASH. UNIV. L. REV. (2016); Ray Madoff, IMMORTALITY AND THE LAW: THE RISING POWER OF THE AMERICAN DEAD (Yale Univ. Press 2011); Arthur Schmidt, *Escaping the Perpetuity Mindset*, NONPROFIT Q. (Dec. 9. 2009). Defenders of the status quo include Ronna Brown and Leslie Lin, *The Legitimacy of Foundations in Perpetuity, Philanthropy* New York (Oct. 14, 2014); Paul Brest and Hal Harvey, MONEY WELL SPENT: A STRATEGIC PLAN FOR SMART PHILANTHROPY 259-266 (2008); Joel L. Fleishman, THE FOUNDATION: A GREAT AMERICAN SECRET 236-248 (2007)

[19] B. Galle, *supra*, n. 18, at 35-40.

[20] Internal Revenue Service, *Statistics of Income, Domestic Private Foundations, 2010*, http://www.irs.gov/pub/irs-soi/2010PrivateFoundationsOneSheet.pdf. Foundation Source reported in its 2015 annual report that the foundations in its study averaged an 11.8% payout. Foundation Source, *2015 Annual Report on Private Foundations*. http://www.foundationsource.com/resources /library/2015-annual-report/.

began with stock from Standard Oil.[21] Others claim that foundations should make positive investments that reflect their mission, either in the form of program-related investments or mission-related investments.[22]

What relationship should foundations have with grantees? The relationship between foundations and grantees is, by definition, an imbalanced one because the organization that holds the purse strings can dictate the terms of the agreement. Some of those terms can actually hamper the effectiveness of the recipient organizations. For example, foundations generally provide funds for innovative programs, but not for tried and true programs or for overhead; i.e., staff salaries, computers, buildings, and electricity. They also often require reporting on the program's effectiveness without sufficiently covering the cost of these reports.[23] Although many foundations are working on improving this aspect of the foundation-grantee relationship, there remains the question of whether the foundation or the grantee is the actual change agent. Some foundations are more hands-on than others. The Bill and Melinda Gates Foundation, for example, prioritizes the issues that it plans to address, identifies the strategies, and, in essence, commissions work to implement these strategies. Other foundations see their role more as a supporting one. They believe that they are providing resources to enable the real experts—the charities themselves. For further information, see Ruth McCambridge, *The Strategic Philanthropy Crowd: Qualified Apologies-R-Us*, NONPROFIT QUARTERLY (April 6, 2016); E. Schmidt, *Don't Bite the Hand that Feeds You*, CHARITY CHANNEL'S GRANTS AND FOUNDATIONS REVIEW (July 20, 2005).

V. DISTINCTION BETWEEN PUBLIC CHARITY AND PRIVATE FOUNDATION

Section 501(c)(3) organizations are presumed to be private foundations unless they can show that they are public charities, as described in §509(a) (1)-(4). Congress determined that these four types of public charities are both supported by and accountable to the general public, and thus are less susceptible to abuse than private foundations, which depend on a single person or a small group of persons for their support. Unless an organization can show that it fits within one of these provisions, it will be subject to the private foundation rules discussed above: tighter restrictions on the deductibility of charitable contributions, excise taxes on investment income, prohibitions on self-dealing, minimum distribution

---

[21] John Schwartz, *Rockefellers, Heirs to an Oil Fortune, Will Divest Charity of Fossil Fuels*, NY TIMES (Sept. 21, 2014).

[22] James P. Joseph and Andras Kosaras, *New Strategies for Leveraging Foundation Assets*, 20 Tax'n of Exempts 22 (2008); Bruce DeBoskey, *Should Foundations be "All-In" on Their Charitable Missions?*, DENVER POST (May 12, 2013); Ron Cordes, *How Philanthropies Invest Money Is Just as Important as How They Make Grants*, CHRONICLE OF PHILANTHROPY (Sept.24, 2014).

[23] Nonprofit Finance Fund, 2015 State of the Nonprofit Sector Survey, http://nonprofitfinancefund.org/state-of-the-sector-surveys, last accessed May 12, 2016.

requirements, restrictions on excess business holdings, and prohibitions on speculative investments.

The rules for determining which organizations are §509 public charities are, as the Tax Court has said, "frighteningly complex."[24] Yet they are crucial because they determine which tax rules an organization must follow throughout its lifetime. In broad terms, §509(a)(1) "public support" organizations obtain most of their support from donations, while §509(a)(2) "gross receipts" charities collect receipts from the public in the form of admissions, sales of merchandise, and/or performances of services, in addition to charitable contributions. Section 509(a)(3)–supporting organizations are organized and controlled for the benefit of another public charity. Even though they are usually endowed by an individual or family, and, in many respects act as alternatives to private foundations, they are considered public charities themselves because of their close relationship with a public charity. Supporting organizations are discussed in the last section of this chapter, "Alternatives to Foundations." Section 509(a)(4) testing for public safety organizations will not be discussed, as they are too specialized and numerically insignificant to be covered.

The materials that follow in this section of the chapter discuss the first two types of public charities, §509(a)(1) traditional public charities and §509(a)(2) gross receipts public charities, in some detail. The vast majority of public charities fall within one of these two categories. Following are the relevant statutes, along with a discussion of their application and some examples. If you try to work through the examples yourselves before you look at the answers, you will end up with a better understanding of the concepts. The notes and questions at the end of this section of the chapter will also help you solidify your understanding of the concepts. As you consider these provisions, consider whether the public support that these organizations receive shelters them from the abuses that the private foundation rules are designed to prevent.

A. STATUTES CONCERNING PRIVATE FOUNDATION/ PUBLIC CHARITY DISTINCTION

INTERNAL REVENUE CODE §509(A) PRIVATE FOUNDATION DEFINED

(a) General rule. For purposes of this title, the term "private foundation" means a domestic or foreign organization described in section 501(c)(3) other than—

(1) an organization described in section 170(b)(1)(A) (other than in clauses (vii) and (viii);

(2) an organization which—

---

[24] *Friends of the Society of Servants of God v. Comm'r*, 75 T.C. 209 (1980).

(A) normally receives more than one-third of its support in each taxable year from any combination of—

(i) gifts, grants, contributions, or membership fees, and

(ii) gross receipts from admissions, sales of merchandise, performance of services, or furnishing of facilities, in an activity which is not an unrelated trade or business . . . not including such receipts from any person, or from any bureau or similar agency of a governmental unit (as described in section 170(c)(1)), in any taxable year to the extent such receipts exceed the greater of $5,000 or 1 percent of the organization's support in such taxable year, from persons other than disqualified persons (as defined in section 4946) with respect to the organization, from governmental units described in section 170(c)(1), or from organizations described in section 170(b)(1)(A) (other than in clauses (vii) and (viii)), and

(B) normally receives not more than one-third of its support in each taxable year from the sum of—

(i) gross investment income (as defined in subsection (e)) and

(ii) the excess (if any) of the amount of the unrelated business taxable income . . . over the amount of the tax imposed by section 511.

(3) an organization which—

(A) is organized, and at all times thereafter is operated, exclusively for the benefit of, to perform the functions of, or to carry out the purposes of one or more specified organizations described in paragraph (1) or (2),

(B) is—

(i) operated, supervised, or controlled by or in connection with one or more organizations described in paragraph (1) or (2).

(ii) supervised or controlled in connection with one or more such organizations, or (iii) operated in connection with one or more such organizations, and

(C) is not controlled directly or indirectly by one or more disqualified persons (as defined in section 4946) other than foundation managers and other than one or more organizations described in paragraph (1) or (2); and

(4) an organization which is organized and operated exclusively for testing for public safety.

INTERNAL REVENUE CODE §170(B)(1)-A

(A) General rule. Any charitable contribution to—

(i) a church or a convention or association of churches,

(ii) an educational organization which normally maintains a regular faculty and curriculum and normally has a regularly enrolled body of pupils or students in attendance at the place where its educational activities are regularly carried on,

(iii) an organization the principal purpose or functions of which are the providing of medical or hospital care or medical education or medical research, if the organization is a hospital, or if the organization is a medical research organization directly engaged in the continuous active conduct of medical research in conjunction with a hospital, and during the calendar year in which the contribution is made such organization is committed to spend such contributions for such research before January 1 of the fifth calendar year which begins after the date such contribution is made,

(iv) an organization which normally receives a substantial part of its support (exclusive of income received in the exercise or performance by such organization of its charitable, educational, or other purpose or function constituting the basis for its exemption under section 501(a)) from the United States or any State or political subdivision thereof or from direct or indirect contributions from the general public, and which is organized and operated exclusively to receive, hold, invest, and administer property and to make expenditures to or for the benefit of a college or university which is an organization referred to in clause (ii) of this subparagraph and which is an agency or instrumentality of a State or political subdivision thereof, or which is owned or operated by a State or political subdivision thereof or by an agency or instrumentality of one or more States or political subdivisions,

(v) a governmental unit referred to in subsection (c)(1),

(vi) an organization referred to in subsection (c)(2) which normally receives a substantial part of its support (exclusive of income received in the exercise or performance by such organization of its charitable, educational, or other purpose or function constituting the basis for its exemption under section 501(a)) from a governmental unit referred to in subsection (c)(1) or from direct or indirect contributions from the general public.

B. DISCUSSION AND EXAMPLES OF §509(a)(1) TRADITIONAL PUBLIC CHARITIES

Of the four types of public charities, more organizations fall into the §509(a)(1) category than into any of the others. Section 509(a)(1) includes six types of charities. Five of them are easily recognizable: churches, educational organizations, medical organizations (providing medical or hospital care or providing medical research), development foundations for public universities, and governmental units. The sixth category, "an organization receiving a substantial part of its support from governmental units or from contributions from the general public," is more complex. The regulations for §509(a)(1) set out two subtests that allow the IRS to determine whether an organization receives substantial support from governmental or public contributions: (1) the mechanical test and (2) the facts and circumstances test. An organization needs to meet only one of these tests to be classified as a §509(a)(1) traditional charity.

1. Inherently Public Organizations

Churches, educational institutions, hospitals, medical research organizations, development foundations for public universities, and governmental units automatically receive §509(a)(1) status.[25] These organizations do not need to prove that they are financially supported by the general public because, by their nature, they are accountable to the general public. The assumption is that these institutions need to convince the general public that they are fulfilling their mission in order to stay in business, and therefore, they are not susceptible to the abuses that led to the enactment of the private foundation rules.

Example: The Phoenix Center is a school for at-risk boys, with a regular faculty and student body. The boys attend regularly scheduled classes and follow a regular curriculum. Since its inception five years ago, the center has raised $1 million. Steve Svajian donated $500,000; Darren Abernathy donated the other $500,000. The school has not had any other income. Is the Phoenix Center a public charity or private foundation?

Answer: The Phoenix Center is a public charity because schools are automatically public charities.[26]

2. Testing Period

Organizations that want to be classified as public charities need not meet the public charity tests described below when they first apply for recognition as §501(c)(3) organizations. Few, if any, organizations begin with a broad base of public support, so the regulations allow five years before organizations must meet this test. From then on, organizations that obtained the initial classification of a public charity must show on their tax information forms (Form 990) that they have received sufficient public support to retain the public charity classification.[27]

---

[25] Governmental units are not §501(c)(3) organizations, but they are treated as public charities instead of private foundations in this situation.

[26] The same result would occur if the Phoenix Center had been a hospital, a church, a development foundation for a public university, or a governmental unit because the Code assumes these organizations are publicly supported without examining the actual sources of support. An organization with this financial history that does not fit into one of the five categories enumerated as automatic public charities, however, would not be able to meet either the mechanical test or the facts and circumstances test described below. In the §509(a)(1) traditional charities test, only 2% of the total support could be attributed to either donor in the numerator of the equation, so the ratio would be 4%—far less than the one-third ratio that is needed in the mechanical test or the 10% in the facts and circumstances test. In the §509(a)(2) test, neither donor's gift could be attributed in the numerator at all because they would be "substantial contributors." Under these facts, there is also no income from tuition to change the ratio. Therefore, the §509(a)(2) test is not met, either.

[27] The rules surrounding the testing period were more complex for organizations that obtained their tax exemptions prior to 2008.

These organizations need not meet the test every year, however. An organization must show that its support for the current fiscal year and the previous four years meets either the mechanical test or the facts and circumstances test described below. Also, if an organization meets a public support test for one year, it will be treated as a publicly supported organization for both the current year and the next year.

Example: Elder Aide Legal Services was recognized as a §501(c)(3) tax-exempt organization many years ago, and it obtained an advance ruling that it would be treated as a public charity for the first five years of its existence. Since that time, it has always maintained its status as a public charity due to its ability to meet the public support test under §170(b)(1)(a)(2). Elder Aide is now preparing to file its Form 990 for the 2016 tax year. Which years will it use to calculate its status as a public charity on its Form 990? Assume that the calculations for the public support test on this year's Form 990 demonstrate that Elder Aide remains a public charity. If it has a particularly poor fundraising campaign the next year and cannot meet the public support test when it completes its tax information form, will it be classified as a private foundation for that year?

Answer: Elder Aide must show its public support for 2012, 2013, 2014, 2015, and 2016 on its Form 990. Assuming that it meets the public support test for 2016, it will continue to be treated as a public charity in 2017, even if its fund-raising shortfalls cause it to flunk the public support test in 2017. If it has a second year in which it fails to meet either public support test, however, it will lose its status as a public charity and be treated as a private foundation instead.

3. Mechanical Test

An organization satisfies the mechanical test if at least one-third of its total support over the course of five years comes from the government, from indirect or direct contributions from the general public, or from a combination of these sources. In other words, the ratio of the public support (defined as support from the government plus support from the public) to total support needs to be at least one-third. It can be written as an equation:

$$\frac{\text{Public support (from the government and from the public)}}{\text{Total support}} > \frac{1}{3}$$

Unfortunately, the rules for determining what constitutes public support and total support are rather complex. First, receipts from admissions, tuitions, sales, services, or rental of facilities that are collected in furtherance of the organization's exempt purpose cannot be included in either part of the equation, because this test measures support from contributions, not receipts. Capital gains are also kept from both parts of the equation, as are unusual grants, which will be discussed later in this chapter.

The first calculation is to determine *total support* (total income). Total support includes:

1. Gifts, grants, and contributions (including bequests) from individuals, public charities, private foundations, and other nonprofit organizations
2. Government grants made to enable the organization to benefit the public
3. Membership fees paid for general support of the organization
4. Net income from unrelated business activities
5. Gross investment income (so long as it does not include capital gains income)
6. Tax revenues levied on behalf of the organization and either paid to it or expended on its behalf
7. The value of governmental services or facilities furnished to an organization (e.g., free rent)

The next calculation is the determination of *public support*, which includes:

1. Gifts, grants, and contributions
2. Government grants
3. Membership fees
4. Tax revenues levied for the benefit of the organization
5. The value of services or goods furnished for the benefit of the organization

Note that investment income and unrelated business income are *not* included as public support, as they are considered nonpublic, nongovernmental support. In addition, donations from private sources (e.g., individuals, corporations, trusts, or private foundations) are included in public support only to the extent that they do not exceed 2% of the total support received by the organization over the testing period. Contributions from government entities and other public charities are not subject to this 2% limitation, so their entire contributions are included as public support, even if they are quite large.

The public support then becomes the numerator of the fraction and the total support is the denominator. If that fraction is greater than one-third (33 1/3%), the mechanical test is met. Although this calculation is complex, remember that it is a "mechanical test." In other words, it is simply a matter of plugging the correct numbers into the equation. The following example can help make this point clear.

Example: Since its inception five years ago, Hampton Resettlement Organization has received the following support:

- $250,000 from Bereket Tesfu
- $250,000 in other contributions (1,000 gifts of $250 each)
- $250,000 in government grants
- $50,000 in gross investment income (no capital gains income)
- $150,000 net unrelated business income
- $100,000 in exempt income

Does it qualify as a §509(a)(1) public charity under the mechanical test?

Answer:

1. Determine what is not included in total support (denominator) or public support (numerator).
   a. Exempt income: $100,000
   b. Capital gains: $0
   c. Unusual grants: $0
2. Determine the total support:
   a. Gifts, grants, and contributions: $250,000 + $250,000
   b. Government grants: $250,000
   c. Membership fees: $0
   d. Net income from unrelated business activities: $150,000
   e. Gross investment income (but not capital gains income): $50,000
   f. Tax revenues levied on behalf of the organization and either paid to it or expended on its behalf: $0
   g. Value of governmental services or facilities furnished to an organization, (i.e., free rent): $0
   Total support calculation: 250,000 + 250,000 + 250,000 + 150,000 + 50,000 = $1,000,000.
3. Calculate 2% of total support: .02 × $1,000,000 = $20,000
4. Determine what is *not* included in public support (the numerator):
   a. The excess of any gift or grant from individuals, corporations or foundations that exceeds 2% of the total support. Thus, $230,000 of Bereket Tesfu's gift will be excluded and only $20,000 included. The other gifts from individuals are smaller than $20,000, so they will be included in full, as will the government grant.
   b. Unrelated business income: $150,000
   c. Gross investment income: $ 100,000
   d. Contributions of services for which no deduction is allowed: $0
   Public support calculation: 20,000 + 250,000 + 250,000 + = *$520,000*

5. Ratio : $\dfrac{\text{Allowable part of contributions + government support}}{\text{All sources of income except exempt purposes income}}$

$$= \frac{520,000}{1,000,000} > \frac{1}{3}$$

Thus, Hampton Resettlement meets the mechanical test and qualifies as a §509(a)(1) organization.

If Hampton Resettlement had not met the mechanical test, the facts and circumstances test described below is also a possibility. But before one gives up on the mechanical test, another possibility should be considered. The regulations allow an organization to exclude an unusual grant from both parts of the public support fraction if including the grant would cause the organization to fail the public support test. The Treasury Regulations define an "unusual grant" as a contribution or bequest that is (1) attracted by the public-supported nature of the organization, (2) is unusual or unexpected in amount, (3) and which, because of its size, would adversely affect the foundation's publicly supported status.

Example: Assume that the facts above, except that the $250,000 in other contributions came from an unexpected grant from a foundation that had learned about Hampton Roads Resettlement on the Internet.

Answer: The first two requirements are met, so the question is whether that grant would make Hampton Roads Resettlement fail the mechanical test. The total support will remain the same, at $1 million, but the public support will be different because only $20,000 of that large, unexpected gift would normally be included as public support. The fraction of public support to total support would then be $290,000/$1,000,000. That does not equal one-third, so the mechanical test would not be met. All is not lost if the mechanical test is not met, however. In this case, the unexpected grant could be an unusual grant, or the organization could try to meet the facts and circumstances test.

4. Facts and Circumstances Test

The facts and circumstances test requires that an organization:

1. Normally receive at least 10% of its support from direct and indirect contributions from the general public, governmental units, or a combination of the public and the government
2. Be organized and operated in a manner that will attract new public or governmental support on a continuous basis
3. Be able to show additional facts and circumstances that demonstrate broad public support

The first two of these requirements are straightforward. The 10% test is met in the same manner as the mechanical test—by finding the ratio between public support and total support. The organization can demonstrate that it is organized and operated to attract new public or governmental support on a continuous basis through an active fundraising program and/or a membership program. The third requirement, that the organization show additional facts and circumstances that demonstrate broad public support, leaves more to a fact finder's discretion. The regulations list five factors that can show such additional facts and circumstances, and they state that the weight accorded to any one of them may differ depending on the nature and purpose of the organization and the length of time it has been in existence. Those factors are (1) the percentage of financial support (the closer it is to 33 1/3%, the more likely the organization will meet this test); (2) sources of support (it is better to have a variety of financial supporters); (3) representative governing body (a board that represents the community is preferable to a narrow group); (4) availability of public facilities or services and public participation (services that benefit the general public on a continuing basis are better than those that address a small group); and (5) additional factors pertinent to membership organizations (membership organizations that attract a broad cross section of the public are more likely to meet the test than narrowly focused organizations).

Example: Over the past five years, the Calvin Coolidge Institute (CCI) has promoted the historical legacy and political philosophy of Calvin Coolidge. It has provided its educational information to anyone who is interested in Coolidge and has provided funds for research and publications, without regard to age, race, gender, or national origin. It has solicited funds from the general public via letters, e-mails, phone calls, and the Internet. It also seeks funds from foundations. CCI's board consists of Richard Norton Smithson, Leeann Edwards, George Wilson, Roberto Novaki, Jamie Douglas, Mary Romney, and Vito Fosselli. It is not a membership organization. It has received the following support:

- $550,000 from George Wilson
- $250,000 in government grants
- $50,000 in investment income
- $150,000 net unrelated business income
- $100,000 in exempt income

Answer:

1. Determine the ratio:
   a. Total support is $1 million (550,000 + 250,000 + 50,000 + 150,000).
   b. 2% of the total support is $20,000.
   c. Public support includes 2% of a larger personal grant and 100% of a government grant (20,000 + 250,000)
   d. $$\frac{20,000 + 250,000}{1,000,000} = \frac{270,000}{1,000,000} = 27\% <33^{1}/_{3}\%> \; 10\%$$

2. Is CCI organized and operated so as to attract public or governmental support? Yes.
3. Are there additional facts and circumstances to suggest the organization is oriented to the public?
   a. The percentage of support is close to one-third.
   b. The sources of support are not particularly broad.
   c. The board of directors is diverse.
   d. The organization provides services to the general public.

The organization probably meets the facts and circumstances test, as it meets most of the factors listed in the regulations. In general, the more an organization's funds come from smaller donors, the government, or other public charities as opposed to large individual donors or foundations, the more likely it is that the organization is going to obtain public charity status under the traditional charities §509(a)(1) test. It is not a difficult test for most organizations to meet, and therefore, most public charities qualify under this classification.

C. DISCUSSION AND EXAMPLES OF §509(a)(2) GROSS RECEIPTS CHARITIES

An organization that receives a substantial part of its support from exempt function activities, such as ticket sales, sales of merchandise, or performances of services can qualify as a §509(a)(2) gross receipts charity. To qualify as this type of public charity, an organization must meet the requirements of two tests: (1) the positive support test and (2) the negative investment income test. The testing period is the same as the testing period for §509(a)(1) organizations. The legislative history indicates that this provision was intended to cover "symphony societies, garden clubs, alumni associations, Boy Scouts, Parent-Teacher Associations, and many other membership organizations." Report No. 91-413, page 41, of House Ways and Means Committee. Such organizations, as you can see in footnote 29, might not meet the §509(a)(1) test because they do not rely exclusively on donations, but they still attract "public support" in the form of gross receipts.

1. Positive Support Test

An organization meets the positive support test if it "normally" receives more than one-third of its total support from a combination of gifts, grants, contributions, membership fees, admission charges, and fees from the performance of exempt function activity. The fraction can be written as:

$$\frac{\text{Positive support}}{\text{Total support}} = \frac{\text{Gifts} + \text{grants} + \text{contributions} + \text{exempt function income}}{\text{Total support}} > 1/3$$

The definition of "total support" here is broader than it is under §509(a)(1) because it includes exempt function income. Total support for §509(a)(2) includes:

1. Gifts, grants, contributions, and membership fees
2. Gross receipts from admissions, sales of merchandise, performance of services, or furnishing of facilities in an activity that is related to the organization's exempt purpose
3. Net income from unrelated business activities
4. Gross investment income, excluding capital gains
5. Tax revenues levied for the organization's benefit and either paid to or expended on behalf of the organization
6. The value of services or facilities furnished by the government specifically to the organization without charge

Positive support includes gifts, grants, contributions, and membership fees received from governmental sources, public charities, or any other person who is not a disqualified person with respect to the organization. It also includes the gross receipts from the conduct of exempt functions, with some exceptions, as described below.

Two rules complicate the determination of positive support. First, contributions from disqualified persons are not included at all. (The term "disqualified persons" was defined in section III.B above.) Generally, anyone who contributes 2% or more of the total support is a disqualified person.[28] Thus, a §501(c)(3) theater with $50,000 in contributions over its lifetime would not be able to include any part of a gift of $10,000 from a single contributor as part of its public support in the tax year that it received the gift. The second rule is that gross receipts are not included in this definition of positive support to the extent that they exceed the greater of $5,000 or 1% of the organization's total support for that year. Therefore, if one person had bought all 600 tickets at $100 apiece for the only theatrical performance at a §501(c)(3) theater, and the theater received no other support that year, only $60 of those gross receipts would be included in the theater's public support. These requirements are intended to ensure that the organization creates and maintains a broad-based program of generating income instead of relying on a single patron or a very small group of customers.

2. Negative Investment Income Test

An organization attempting to meet the requirements of the §509(a)(2) "gross receipts" organization test must meet the positive support test *and* the negative investment income test. This negative test provides that no more than one-third of an organization's total support may consist of gross investment income and net unrelated business taxable income minus the amount paid for unrelated business income tax. Congress was concerned that an organization that was mostly supported by investment income would be susceptible to the abuses that it was trying to curb in the private foundation area, so it created this limitation.

The following example will illustrate these §509(a)(2) tests.

Example: Since the inception of Professional Police Management Resources five years ago, it has received the following support:

- $250,000 contribution from Amy Ginger
- $50,000 government grant
- $50,000 in investment income
- $150,000 in net unrelated business income (from sales of *Rockford* and *Columbo* paraphernalia)
- $500,000 in exempt income from tuition for police training, $100,000 of which is from Adrian Monk.

---

[28] Section 4946, described in section III.B *supra*, defines "disqualified person." It covers substantial contributors (those who have provided 2% of the contributions), as well as directors, officers, trustees, and the manager or executive director of the organization. It also includes family members of disqualified persons, a person who owns more than 20% of a business that is a substantial contributor, and corporations or business entities controlled by a disqualified person.

Answer: §509(a)(2) gross receipts test:[29] Public support > 1/3 and gross investment income < 1/3.

3. Calculating the Positive Support Test

1. Determine total support, which includes gifts and grants from the public, gross receipts from admissions, sales of merchandise, performance of services, or the furnishing of facilities. Thus, the total support = $250,000 from the single contribution + $50,000 government grant + $50,000 investment income + $150,000 net unrelated business income + $500,000 in exempt income = $1,000,000.

2. Determine whether there are any substantial contributors (that is, those who have contributed more than 2% of the total support ever received by the organization). Amy Ginger's contribution is 25% of the total support. Thus, it is more than 2% of the total support and cannot be included in the numerator.

3. Determine whether there are any excess exempt function revenues. Exempt function revenues received from one source are not counted toward public support if they exceed $5,000 or 1% of the organization's support, whichever is higher. Note that 1% of $1 million is $10,000. Adrian Monk's payments exceed both $5,000 and 1% of the organization's support. Therefore, only $10,000 of his gross receipts can be counted in the numerator. (This assumes that all the income came in one year, and that in the other years, there was none, because this calculation is done on a yearly basis.)

4. Determine what is not included as "public support."

    a. Unrelated business income
    b. Investment income
    c. Any contribution from a "substantial contributor"
    d. Excess exempt function revenues (any payment over $5,000 and 1% of an organization's support in a single year)

5. Calculate the public support:

---

[29] If you are interested in how this problem would work with the §509(a)(1) test, the calculations follow.

Mechanical test:

- Total support (denominator) = 250,000 + 50,000 + 50,000 + 150,000 = 500,000
- 2% of 500,000 = 10,000
- Numerator: 10,000 + 50,000
- Ratio: $\dfrac{10,000 + 50,000}{500,000} = \dfrac{60,000}{500,000}$ < 1/3

Facts and Circumstances Test:

The ratio (12%) is more than 10%, but not by much. Professional Police's Form 1023 shows that it serves police officers and charges tuition to the general public. It has a small board (Amy Ginger, James Rockford, and L. T. Columbo). It also seeks funding from foundations and the government. Given the low ratio and its small, nonrepresentative board, Professional Police is smart to use the §509(a)(2) test to qualify as a public charity, as it will probably not qualify as a §509(a)(1) public charity.

$$\frac{50,000 + 400,000 + 10,000}{250,000 + 50,000 + 150,000 + 500,000} = \frac{460,000}{1,000,000} > \frac{1}{3}$$

6. Therefore, Professional Police meets the public support test. It must also meet the investment income test, however, if it is to qualify as a 509(a)(2) public charity.

4. Calculating the Negative Investment Income Test

1. Determine the total support, which is identical to total support under the positive support test: $1,000,000.
2. Determine the investment income: investment funds plus net unrelated business income, $150,000 + $50,000 = $200,000.
3. Determine the fraction:

$$\frac{150,000 + 500,000}{1,000,000} = \frac{200,000}{1,000,000} < \frac{1}{3}$$

Professional Police meets the negative investment income test, as well as the positive support test. Therefore, it qualifies as a public charity under §509(a)(2).

D. SUMMARY OF §509(a)(1) AND §509(a)(2) TESTS

The two most prevalent types of public charities are the §509(a)(1) traditional charities and the §509 (a)(2) gross receipts charities.

1. §509(a)(1) Traditional Charities

Traditional charities have three ways of meeting the §509(a)(1) requirements. First, five types of organizations automatically qualify as §509(a)(1) traditional charities: churches, educational organizations, hospitals and medical research organizations, development foundations for public charities, and governmental units. An organization that qualifies as one of these types of organizations never has to prove that it is publicly supported. Other organizations can meet the §509(a)(1) requirements of public support through the second and third ways of proving public support under §509(a)(1)—that is, either the mechanical test or the facts and circumstances test.

The mechanical test requires that the organization prove that at least one-third of its funds over a five-year period come from governmental or public contributions. Contributions from non-public sources that are greater than 2% of the organization's total support (the denominator) are only included as public support (the numerator) to the extent that they are equal to or less than 2% of the total support that the organization has received in the testing period. Exempt income is never included in the calculation.

An organization that does not meet the mechanical test can still qualify under the facts and circumstances test. The organization must have total support of more than 10% (the closer to 33 1/3%, the better); it must be set up to attract new support on a continuous basis; and other factors should point to the public nature of the organization—for example, the board is widely representative of the public, the facilities are open to the public, and the sources of support are varied.

2. §509(a)(2) Gross Receipts Charities

If an organization receives a large portion of its funds in exempt income, it should look to the gross receipts test, which requires an organization to meet both the public support test and the investment income test. The public support test for gross receipts organizations is calculated somewhat differently from the public support test for traditional charities. The ratio is still one-third, but there are three major differences: (1) all income, including exempt income, is included in the calculations; (2) substantial contributions, which are calculated differently than they are in §509(a)(1), are eliminated entirely from the numerator; and (3) gross receipts from any person or governmental unit that exceed the greater of $5,000 or 1% of total support for that year can only be counted to the greater of $5,000 or 1% of the total support. The one-third public support test is an absolute minimum, as there is no facts and circumstances test to fall back on. In addition, the organization must meet the negative investment income test—that is, the investments funds and the unrelated business income cannot exceed one-third of the total support of the organization.

NOTES AND QUESTIONS

1. Would it be easier for the organization that you created as part of this class to be classified as a §509(a)(1) traditional public charity or as a §509(a)(2) "gross receipts" charity? Why? If you did not create an organization for this class, which type of public charity best fits the typical art museum? Why?

2. Play for the Future, an organization devoted to youth sports, has had the following revenues over the past five years: $100,000 in tickets to sporting events (1,000 customers paid $100 each); $100,000 in fees for tennis lessons ($20,000 customers paid $5 each); and $200,000 in gross investment income. Assume that the tickets and lessons are both exempt purpose income. Does Play for the Future have any problems remaining a public charity?

3. Clean Start receives all its income from the sale of baby clothes. It is arguing with the IRS over whether those receipts come from exempt income or unrelated business income. That distinction makes sense for tax purposes, as we will see in Chapter 8. Is this factor also important for Clean Start's status as a public charity or a private foundation? Why or why not?

4. Elder Care has had the following receipts over the last five years: $50,000 in small contributions (1,000 contributions of $50 each) and $950,000 in a one-time contribution. Is it a public charity or a private foundation?

5. Over the past five years, Undergraduate Financial Assistance has received total contributions equal to $100,000. Of that $100,000, $25,000 is from small contributions from the general public (1,000 gifts of $25), and $75,000 is from the United Way, a local §501(c)(3) public charity. Is Undergraduate Financial Advisors a public charity or a private foundation?

6. Over the past five years, Women's Financial Independence Project has received total contributions equal to $100,000. Of that $100,000, $25,000 is from small contributions from the general public (1,000 gifts of $25), and $75,000 is from the Ford Foundation, a §501(c)(3) private foundation. Is Women's Financial Independence Project a public charity or a private foundation?

VI. ALTERNATIVES TO FOUNDATIONS

The Internal Revenue Code classifies foundations and charities on the basis of their support instead of on their functions. As we saw in the first part of this chapter, the §501(c)(3) organizations with the least public support (namely, private foundations) face the most stringent regulations. Despite these regulations, private foundations remain a useful vehicle for donors and foundation managers who wish to retain control over the investment of the foundation's assets and its grant-making decisions.

Not everyone who wishes to keep some control over assets and grant-making decisions must follow all the private foundation rules, however, because some vehicles that allow donors to give away charitable funds over time can meet one or more of the public charity tests. Supporting organizations, for example, are automatically classified as public charities under §509(a)(3). They are stand-alone charities, but they must always be closely affiliated with another charity. Donor-advised funds, another alternative, cannot be stand-alone entities. They are usually component funds of a community foundation or funds within a larger gift fund established by an investment company.[30] In the years leading up to 2006, Congress became concerned about abuses of these vehicles, and it passed the Pension Protection Act of 2006 (PPA) to resolve perceived loopholes. The following materials introduce the rules surrounding supporting organizations (SOs) and donor-advised funds, describe community foundations and institutional charitable gift funds, and examine the factors that a philanthropist may consider when deciding whether to place his or her gift in a private foundation, supporting organization, donor-advised fund, or public charity.

---

[30] Examples include the Fidelity Charitable Gift Fund, the Schwab Charitable Fund, and the Vanguard Charitable Endowment Program.

A. INTRODUCTION TO SUPPORTING ORGANIZATIONS

Supporting organizations (SOs) are defined in §509(a)(3). Remember that §509 identifies the four types of public charities,[31] and that §501(c)(3) organizations that do not fit within these categories are classified as private foundations. We studied §509(a)(1) and 509(a)(2) organizations earlier in this chapter, when we explored the two public support tests. Instead of the public support test, §509(a)(3) organizations gain their public charity status by being closely connected to another public charity. The SO must provide financial and/or programmatic support to this other public charity. It must also cede some of its structural and operational control to that organization. The organization that receives the support and has the control is called the "supported" organization.

The IRS explains on its website:

> A supporting organization is a charity that carries out its exempt purposes by supporting other exempt organizations, usually other public charities. This classification is important because it is one means by which a charity can avoid classification as a private foundation, a status that is subject to a more restrictive regulatory regime. Of course, supporting another public charity is not enough by itself to warrant status as a public charity – many private foundations support public charities as well. A supporting organization generally warrants public charity status because it has a relationship with its supported organization sufficient to ensure that the supported organization is effectively supervising or paying particular attention to the operations of the supporting organization.

http://www.irs.gov/Charities-&-Non-Profits/Section-509(a)(3)-Supporting-Organizations

People create SOs for a variety of reasons. A common reason is to create a "friends of" organization for an arts organization, hospital, or school. The board of the supported organization is busy running the main organization, and therefore the SO can raise money, provide snacks at intermission, and perform other ancillary functions for the supported organization. An SO can also manage a large endowment or even conduct a capital campaign for the supported organization. Such a structure allows major donors to determine fund-raising strategies and investment policies as board members of the SO, while allowing the supported organization's board to run the original organization. Sometimes a donor or the supported organization wants to protect the assets in a major gift from liability. If the supported organization engages in activities that makes it susceptible to tort liability, for example, a properly structured SO's assets cannot be accessed through litigation. A donor who is skeptical about whether the supported organization will honor the donor's intent for a restricted gift may also want to create an SO, as might a donor who wants to place the family company in the charitable stream without having to sell all the assets. In these latter two cases, the SO is a viable alternative to the private foundation. It is a grant-making

---

[31] Section 509(a)(4) provides public charity status to "an organization which is organized and operated exclusively for testing for public safety" as a public charity. This category is too small to be discussed in this book.

institution without significant public support of its own, but because of its close affiliation to a public charity, it is classified as a public charity.

In 2006, according to the IRS, there were 21,095 SOs, holding $371.5 billion in assets, and providing $28 billion in support to the SOs.[32] Not all the support provided by SOs is in the form of grants. SOs also pool and manage investments for supported organizations, provide real estate management services, and offer facilities at no or reduced rent.

The rules surrounding SOs, first promulgated in 1969, became stricter and more complex in 2006, after passage of the PPA. This law attempted to close loopholes that congressional testimony and newspapers suggested were being exploited by SOs. The allegations were similar to those Congress heard in 1969, shortly before it created strict rules for private foundations—that donors used SOs as vehicles for charitable deductions for assets that would never enter the charitable stream, and that SOs were making large loans to members of the board of directors.[33] The new law specified stricter rules for SOs, bringing them closer in line to those that private foundations must follow. Following is a short summary of the tests an organization must meet to be classified as a SO and the rules that it must follow.

1. Tests All SOs Must Meet

All SOs must meet four tests to be classified as a §509(a)(3) SO: (1) an organizational test, (2) an operational test, (3) a relationship test, and (4) a disqualified person control test. An SO meets the organizational test by stating in its organizational documents that its purpose is limited to operating exclusively for the benefit of, to perform the functions of, or to carry out the purposes of one or more IRC §509(a)(1) or §509(a)(2) organizations. It meets the operational test by engaging solely in activities that support one or more publicly supported organizations. All §501(c)(3) organizations must meet organizational and operational tests, but SOs must also meet two other tests. The disqualified person control test requires that the SO not be controlled directly or indirectly by disqualified persons (generally a substantial contributor, his or her family members, or an entity owned at least 35% by a disqualified person). In other words, an organization with five board members—three of whom are a substantial contributor, her husband, and her daughter—would fail this test because disqualified persons control a majority of the votes on the board. Finally, the relationship test requires that the SO have one of three types of relationships with at least one supported organization. Depending on the test that it meets, the

---

[32] Dept. of the Treasury, Report to Congress on Supporting Organizations and Donor Advised Funds (Dec. 2011), http://www.treasury.gov/resource-center/tax-policy/documents/supporting-organizations-and-donor-advised-funds-12-5-11.pdf.

[33] *See, e.g.,* Jane G. Gravelle, Proposals for Reform of Donor-Advised Funds, Testimony Before Senate Finance Committee on Charities and Charitable Giving (April 5, 2005); Stephanie Strom, *Big Tax Break Often Bypasses Idea of Charity*, N.Y. TIMES, April 25, 2005, p. A-1; Harvy Lipman and Grant Williams, *Donors Set up Grant-Making Groups, Then Borrow Back Their Gifts*, CHRON. PHILANTHROPY (Feb. 5, 1994).

SO will then be classified as a Type I, Type II, or Type III SO. Type III SOs are further classified as functionally integrated and nonfunctionally integrated. The distinction can be important because different types of SOs follow different rules.

One rule that all SOs must follow is a prohibition against the SO's providing any grant, loan, compensation, or other similar payment to a substantial contributor, a close relative of the substantial contributor, or a 35% controlled entity. Thus, SOs are prohibited from paying substantial contributors a salary that reflects the fair market value of the work that they are performing for the SO—a rule that is stricter than the rule for private foundations. Such payments are considered automatic excess benefit transactions under IRC §4958, a provision that we will study in Chapter 9. In effect, this is a self-dealing provision for SOs.

2. Type I SOs

Type I SOs (see Figure 7-1) are "operated, supervised, or controlled by" one or more supported public charities. §509(a)(3)(b)(i). The IRS regulations compare this relationship to a parent-subsidiary relationship, because the supported organization appoints a majority of the board of the SO. Treas. Reg. §1.509(a)-4(f)(2). The Robertson Foundation, which was discussed in Chapter 5 in the context of a dispute concerning donor intent, was a Type I SO. Princeton University was its supported organization. According to the articles of incorporation of the SO (Roberts Foundation), Princeton appointed four members of the board of directors and the Robertsons appointed three. Because the supported organization appointed a majority of the board of the SO, it was classified as a Type I organization.[34]

SOs that meet this relationship test as well as the other three tests described above, will be labeled Type I SOs and will be public charities that need not follow the private foundation rules described earlier in this chapter. A Type I SO will lose its public charity status, however, if it accepts gifts from a person that directly or indirectly controls (alone, or together with family members and 35% controlled organizations) the governing body of a supported organization. For example, John Johnson, his wife, and his daughter are three of the five board members of Johnson Child Abuse Prevention, a §509(a)(1) public charity. Johnson Child Abuse Prevention is the supported organization of Child Savers, a Type I SO that owns several safe houses, which Johnson Child Abuse Prevention uses rent-free for its programs. Child Savers' organizational documents allow Johnson Child Abuse Prevention to name the entire board of directors, and no one in the Johnson family is on the Child Savers' board. Thus, assuming that Child Savers continues to operate as specified in its organizational documents, Child Savers has met all four tests to be a Type I SO. The Johnsons cannot make a donation to Child Savers, however. They control the supported organization,

---

[34] For a discussion of its status as an SO and excerpts from the Robertson Foundation's request for classification as a §509(a)(3) public charity by reason of being an SO controlled by the university within the meaning of §509(a)(3) of the Internal Revenue Code, see http://www.princeton.edu /robertson/about/tax_status.

Figure 7-1
Type I Supporting Organizations[35]

SUPPORTED ORGANIZATION

Board of Supported Organization (beneficiary organization)

1. Appoints the majority of board of supporting organization, which leads to
2. Substantial degree of directions over SO policies, programs, and activities

SUPPORTING ORGANIZATION

Board of Supporting Organization (receives public charity status because of relationship with supported organization)

1. Provides financial and operational support to supported organization

and so any gift from them to the Johnson Family SO will create a private foundation instead of a SO. Why do you think Congress instituted this rule?

3. Type II SOs

Type II (see Figure 7-2) organizations are "supervised or controlled in connection with" one or more of their supported organizations. §509(a)(3)(B)(ii). They are considered brother/sister organizations because they have overlapping boards, such that the control or management of the SO is vested in the same people that control or manage the supported organization. For example, the founder of the Feira Vacuum Coater Company donated 1,000 shares in his stock to the Feira Foundation, a Type II SO that supports Main Street Community Hospital. The Feira Foundation's bylaws specify that members of its board of

---

[35] This chart has been adapted from GAO, Tax Exempt Organizations: Collecting More Data on Donor-Advised Funds and Supporting Organizations Could Help Address Compliance Challenges (GAO-06-799) (2006). The smiley faces represent board members, and the shaded faces represent overlapping board members.

directors shall at all times consist of the chief executive officer (CEO) of Main Street Community Hospital, the chair of the board, and three other individuals who are also members of the hospital's board of directors at the time they serve on the Feira Foundation board.

Figure 7-2
Type II Supporting Organizations

SUPPORTED ORGANIZATION

Board of Supported Organization (beneficiary organization)

1. Overlapping boards. A majority of SO board are also members of supported organization's board, which leads to
2. A substantial degree of directions over SO policies, programs, and activities

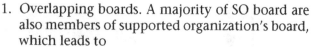

SUPPORTING ORGANIZATION

Board of Supporting Organization (receives public charity status because of relationship with supported organization)

1. Provides financial and operational support to supported organization

In Chapter 3, you read about the Milton Hershey School Trust, an endowment left by Milton Hershey to oversee and promote the Hershey School, in the context of the fiduciary responsibilities of the board of directors. It is also relevant in the context of SOs. In 1969, when Congress passed the Tax Reform Act of 1969, this trust could not pass the public support test. Although schools are automatically public charities, the Hershey Trust was not a school. It was instead an endowment that oversaw and supported a school, a classic SO. Had Congress not included the SO as a type of public charity, the Hershey School Trust would have been a private foundation, subject to the excess business holding rules, and it would have had to diversify its holdings in the Hershey Company. Evidently, Congress had the Hershey Trust in mind when it created

SOs, because it did not see the need for this endowment to follow the strict rules for private foundations.[36]

In 1969, the Hershey Trust was a Type II SO, and it was probably the basis for the first example in the Treasury Regulations describing Type II SOs:

> A, a philanthropist, founded X school for orphan boys (a publicly supported organization). At the same time A founded X school, he also established Y trust into which he transferred all of the operating assets of the school, together with a substantial endowment for it. Under the provisions of the trust instrument, the same persons who control and manage the school also control and manage the trust. The sole function of Y trust is to hold legal title to X school's operating and endowment assets, to invest the endowment assets and to apply the income from the endowment to the benefit of the school in accordance with direction from the school's governing body. Under these circumstances, Y trust is organized and operated for the benefit of X school and is supervised or controlled in connection with such organization within the meaning of §509(a)(3). The fact that the same persons control both X and Y insures Y's responsiveness to X's needs.

Treas. Reg. 1-509(a)(4)(h) Example 1.

In both Type I and Type II SOs, the overlapping boards suggest that the SO is close enough to (and controlled sufficiently by) the supported organization to allow the SO to achieve the same public charity status that the supported organization holds. Do you think that this relationship ensures that the abuses that Congress fears will occur if an individual or family controls a §501(c)(3) organization will be averted? Why or why not?

4. Type III SOs

Type III (see Figure 7-3) SOs are "operated in connection with" the supported charity. §509(a)(3)(B)(iii). To meet this test, an SO must prove that it is responsive to the needs of the publicly supported organization and has an integral or significant involvement in the affairs of the publicly supported organization. The board of a Type III SO need not overlap with or be appointed by the board of the supported organization, as is the case in a Type I or Type II SO. This disconnect between the boards led some to conclude that Type III organizations needed more regulation to prevent abuse. As a result, all Type III SOs must follow stricter rules than their Type I and Type II cousins. Furthermore, the PPA created two subcategories of Type III SOs—those that are functionally integrated with their supported organizations, and those that are nonfunctionally integrated. The "functionally integrated" Type III SOs are exempt from some of the restrictive rules imposed on the nonfunctionally integrated SOs.

---

[36] Evelyn Brody, *Whose Public? Parochialism and Paternalism in State Charity Law Enforcement*, 79 IND. L.J. 937 (2004).

Figure 7-3
Type III Supporting Organizations

SUPPORTED ORGANIZATION	*Board of Supported Organization*

1. Responsiveness test
   Is the relationship between the organizations such that the supporting organization has a significant voice in investment policies and operations of the supporting organization, including the timing and manner of selecting grant recipients? AND
2. Integral Part test
   a. The supporting organization performs activities that carry out the purposes or functions of the supported organization that the supported organization would carry out itself **"but for"** this support (functionally integrated) OR
   b. SO provides sufficient funds to the supported organization to assure the supported organization's **attentiveness** to the SO non-functionally integrated.

SUPPORTING ORGANIZATION	*Board of Supporting Organization*

1. Provides financial and operational support

SOs must meet two tests to qualify as Type III SOs: (1) the "responsiveness" and (2) the "integral part" tests.[37] The responsiveness test is meant to guarantee that the supported organization will have the ability to influence the SO's

---

[37] Nora Jones and Amanda Blaising would include the notification requirement described as a special requirement for Type III SOs below as a third requirement. Nora Jones and Amanda Blaising, IRS Final and Temporary Regulations for Type III Supporting Organizations: The Integral Part Test for Functionally Integrated Type III Supporting Organizations, TAX EXEMPT ORGANIZATIONS LAW Update (May 2013).

activities. It requires one of three relationships: (1) the SO appoints at least one board member of the SO; (2) the two organizations share a board member; or (3) the people running the two organizations maintain a close and continuous working relationship. By virtue of this relationship, a supported public charity plays a significant role in the SO's investment policies; the timing and terms of grants, the selection of recipients, and other decisions concerning income or assets would have the ability to influence the SO's activities.

The integral part test demonstrates that the SO is an integral part of the organization it supports. This test can be met in one of two ways, the first of which qualifies the SO as a functionally related SO, and the second of which makes it a nonfunctionally related SO in two ways: (1) by carrying out a function or purpose of the supported organization that the supported organization would otherwise carry out directly (the "but for" test), or (2) by providing sufficient funding or other benefits to the supported organization, such that the supported organization will pay significant attention to the operations of the supported organization.

For example, Promoting Infant Well-Being would be a Type III functionally integrated SO if it met the other tests for a Type III SO and ran the infant daycare program at the three daycares that it supports. The daycares would otherwise run their own infant programs. These facts allow Promoting Infant Well-Being to show it meets the "but for" test. If, instead of running the daycares, Promoting Infant Well-Being grants a substantial amount of money each year to these daycares, it would be a nonfunctionally related Type III SO. Promoting Infant Well-Being is a Type III SO in either circumstance because only one of the integral part tests must be met.

Once a Type III SO has been identified, it must pay attention to the special rules for Type III SOs. All Type III SOs must notify their publicly supported organizations about their activities annually, and they are forbidden from supporting foreign charities.[38] They will also lose their SO status (and become private foundations) if they accept gifts from persons who control the supported organization, a requirement that Type I SOs also face.

Nonfunctionally integrated Type III SOs, those that meet the integral part test through monetary gifts, face additional rules that bring them closer to private foundations in terms of regulation. They are subject to the same excess business holding rules that private foundations follow. Thus, nonfunctionally integrated Type III SOs cannot own more than 20% of the stock in one corporation. As a result, donors who want to place all the assets of a closely held corporation in a charitable entity without selling the stock can no longer use this type of entity to bypass the private foundations rules on excess business holdings. In addition, nonfunctionally integrated Type III SOs must meet annual payout requirements similar to those made by private foundations.

---

[38] The supported organizations of Type I and Type II can be foreign organizations only if the foreign organizations are already recognized as §501(c)(3) organizations or if they are described in §501(c)(3), but Type III organizations cannot support any foreign organizations.

Further, private foundations cannot include grants made to Type III SOs that are not functionally integrated as qualifying distributions under IRC 4942 unless they exercise expenditure responsibility. In other words, they cannot count these grants as part of their 5% payout requirement. This rule prevents foundations from using SOs to avoid their payout requirement by making their grants to public charities that also have no payout requirement. These payout rules do not apply to functionally integrated Type III SOs, however. Functionally integrated Type III SOs have no annual payout requirements or excess business holding rules, and private foundations may treat grants to them as qualifying distributions.[39] Why do you think Congress made this distinction? Given the complexities of being a Type III non–functionally related SO, can you think of any reason to become or remain organized in this way? Would it be better to become or convert to a private foundation?

PROBLEM

To test your understanding of SOs, label the following as a Type I SO, Type II SO, non–functionally integrated Type III SO, functionally integrated Type III SO, or a private foundation.

1. The founder of the Juarez Foundation, James Juarez, wants the Juarez Foundation to be an SO of Esme University. The foundation's organizational documents state that it will support Esme University and that Esme University's board can appoint the Juarez Foundation's board. The university names Juarez, his wife, his daughter, and four people from the community who are not related to the Juarez family as the board of the Juarez Foundation. The Juarez Foundation works closely with the university and provides funds to the university every year.

2. Assume that the facts are the same as in question 1, but the board composition is slightly different. The university names James Juarez, his wife, and his daughter along with two others from the community who have no affiliation with the Juarez family.

3. Assume that the facts are the same as in question 1, but Esme University names only one person to the board. James Juarez meets with university officials every other year to discuss the Juarez Foundation's contributions, which amount to at least 5% of the foundation's assets annually. The university uses the funds for a theater program. These funds are not the theater program's main support, but it could not continue the program without the foundation's support.

4. Assume that the facts are the same as in question 3, but James Juarez meets with a group of board members of the university monthly to discuss the

---

[39] Nonoperating private foundations cannot count grants given to any SO as part of their payout requirement if one or more disqualified persons of the private foundation directly or indirectly controls such supporting organization or one of its supported organizations. In addition, all foundations must exercise expenditure responsibility with regard to any SO.

foundation's investment policies and recommendations as to the allocations of the foundation's gifts to the university and its students. The Juarez Foundation has taken on the role of maintaining the buildings in the university, a role that the university would have to undertake if the Juarez Foundation had not done so.

5. Assume that the facts are the same as in question 4, but instead of maintaining buildings, the Juarez Foundation's funds underwrite the installation and display of a painting by James Juarez in the university's art museum. The university has a significant art collection and would not otherwise have this painting, but the gifts from the foundation make the display possible. The Juarez Foundation distributes at least 5% of its assets annually to Esme University, but that amount is very small compared to the university's entire budget.

B. DONOR-ADVISED FUNDS AND SPONSORING ORGANIZATIONS

1. Donor-Advised Funds

A *donor-advised fund* is a charitable fund that a donor sets up at another public charity (the sponsoring organization). The donor is entitled to an immediate federal income tax deduction for the entire gift because the donation is to that other public charity. The sponsoring organization then educates the donors about community needs and charities and accepts nonbinding grant recommendations from the original donor before it makes grants to other organizations from the donor-advised fund. The sponsoring organization invests the funds and takes care of all tax, legal, and accounting matters.

These funds have grown substantially in the last 20 years, in part because they offer some of the advantages of private foundations. The donor may make nonbinding grant recommendations without the administrative and investment burdens of a private foundation. The donor has given up control because his grant recommendations are nonbinding, but the sponsoring organization almost always follows the donor-advisor's recommendation.

According to the National Philanthropic Trust, 238,293 donor-advised funds held more than $70 billion in assets in fiscal year 2014. The number of donor-advised funds increased 8.8% between 2013 and 2014. Grants from these funds totaled $12.49 billion, which represented a 21.9% payout rate.[40]

The PPA provided the first codified definition of a donor-advised fund, which is reproduced below.

---

[40] National Philanthropic Trust, *Growth in Recent Years*, 2015 DONOR-ADVISED FUND REPORT (2015). Experts do not agree on the method for determining payout rate, but every method finds that the overall payout rate for donor-advised funds is higher than that of private foundations. Alex Daniels, *Donor-Advised Funds Continue Rapid Growth*, CHRONICLE OF PHILANTHROPY, Nov. 9, 2015.

Section 4966(d)(2) (A) IN GENERAL.—Except as provided in subparagraph (B) or (C), the term "donor advised fund" means a fund or account—

(i) which is separately identified by reference to contributions of a donor or donors,

(ii) which is owned and controlled by a sponsoring organization, and

(iii) with respect to which a donor (or any person appointed or designated by such donor) has, or reasonably expects to have, advisory privileges with respect to the distribution or investment of amounts held in such fund or account by reason of the donor's status as a donor.

(B) EXCEPTIONS. The term "donor advised fund" shall not include any fund or account

(i) which makes distributions only to a single identified organization or governmental entity, or

(ii) with respect to which a person described in subparagraph (A)(iii) advises as to which individuals receive grants for travel, study, or other similar purposes, if—

(I) such person's advisory privileges are performed exclusively by such person in the person's capacity as a member of a committee all of the members of which are appointed by the sponsoring organization,

(II) no combination of persons described in subparagraph (A)(iii) (or persons related to such persons) control, directly or indirectly, such committee, and

(III) all grants from such fund or account are awarded on an objective and nondiscriminatory basis pursuant to a procedure approved in advance by the board of directors of the sponsoring organization, and such procedure is designed to ensure that all such grants meet the requirements of paragraphs (1), (2), or (3) of section 4945(g).

Basically, a donor-advised fund is a separately identified fund that is owned and controlled by a sponsoring organization and that permits a donor to have advisory privileges as to the distribution or investment of fund assets. The fund's sponsoring organization is a tax-exempt organization that is not a private foundation and that maintains one or more donor-advised funds. As we shall see, community foundations and the large charitable gift funds are two major categories of sponsoring organizations.

Donor-advised funds came under increasing scrutiny in the years preceding 2006. As with SOs, critics claimed that these funds were simply clever mechanisms for avoiding stringent private foundation rules. Without minimum distribution requirements, for example, donors could receive a charitable contribution deduction for a gift that lived forever within a charitable gift fund and was never used for a charitable purpose. Reports of individuals using the donor-advised funds for personal purposes also surfaced, as did reports of "round-tripping," in which a donor-advised fund contributed to a foundation, which then made a contribution to the donor-advised fund to satisfy the foundation's minimum distribution requirement.[41]

The PPA addressed some of the issues described above by placing restrictions on donor advised funds that are similar to those that private foundations face. The issues that it addressed are discussed below, and the issues that remain are discussed later in the chapter.

Self-dealing Provisions Donors, donor advisors, and close relatives of donors and donor advisors are forbidden from advising on a distribution that results in their receiving a "more than incidental benefit." §4967. Anyone who provides such advice and then benefits from it is subject to an excise tax of 125% of the benefit. A separate excise tax may be imposed on the fund manager who agreed to make a distribution knowing there would be a return benefit.

Example: Judy Smith recommends that her donor-advised fund should make a grant to the Animal Rescue Organization (ARO). If the fund makes this grant, the ARO agrees to reward Judy with two kittens, free veterinary care for the lifetime of the kittens, and a year's supply of cat food. Although regulations defining an "incidental benefit" have not yet been drafted, the kittens, veterinary care, and food would likely be considered to be more than an incidental benefit, and both Judy and the organization manager at the donor-advised fund's SO could be subject to the excise tax.

The PPA also prohibits donor-advised funds from making a grant or loan, paying compensation, reimbursing expenses, or making a similar payment to a donor, a donor advisor or their close relatives. Such transactions are called "automatic excess benefit transactions." This rule builds on, but is more stringent than, the excess benefit rules that apply to public charities.[42] They are also more stringent than the self-dealing provisions for private foundations because there are no exceptions. If, for example, the community foundation that is the sponsoring organization for Judy Smith's donor-advised fund allows her donor-advised fund to loan Judy $500, that $500 would be an automatic excess benefit transaction, even if all the terms were fair and made through arms-length negotiations. Judy would have to return the entire amount and pay an excise tax. Those at the community foundation who authorized the loan could also be subject to an excise tax.

Taxable Distribution The PPA also added penalties for taxable expenditures, a concept borrowed from the private foundation rule that covers expenditures made for noncharitable purposes. Donor-advised funds cannot provide grants to individuals,[43] nor can grants have noncharitable purposes. Donor-advised funds are also forbidden from giving a grant to a non–functionally integrated Type III

---

[41] Gravelle, *supra* n. 33 at 357.

[42] Chapter 9 discusses excess benefit transactions and intermediate sanctions. SOs must also follow this rule, as we saw in the discussion of SOs, *infra.*

[43] Donor-advised funds can provide scholarship funds and employer-sponsored disaster relief funds, provided that certain measures are taken to ensure no self-dealing occurs.

SO or to any SO or private foundation in which the donor or donor advisor directly or indirectly controls a supported organization of the SO. This rule addresses the self-dealing and "round-tripping" concerns described above. The managers of the sponsoring organization must exercise expenditure responsibility to ensure that the gifts are charitable and these rules are followed. If these rules are violated, the sponsoring organization must pay an excise tax for each taxable distribution that it makes from a donor-advised fund, and any fund manager of the sponsoring organization who made the distribution, knowing that it was taxable, is liable as well.

Example: Several years ago, Jorge Estavan donated $100,000 to the Fidelity Charitable Gift Fund to set up a donor-advised fund in his name. This year, he makes two recommendations. He would like his gift fund to "donate" $10,000 to his alma mater to pay his son's tuition. He also recommends that it donate $25,000 to the Jorge Estavan Private Foundation, which needs more cash to meet the 5% payout rule for private foundations. It turns out that most of the assets in the Jorge Estavan Private Foundation are illiquid, and the foundation does not have sufficient funds to meet the payout requirement without an infusion of additional cash. If the Fidelity Charitable Gift Fund agrees to either donation, both Jorge and the fund manager would be liable for excise taxes.

Excess Business Holdings Another concept borrowed from the foundations rules is the excess business holdings rule. A donor-advised fund and the disqualified persons with respect to that donor-advised fund cannot own more than 20% of the stock and securities of a corporation. Any excess of that limitation is considered an "excess business holding" and is subject to an excise tax. The definition of a disqualified person includes the donor and any person appointed or designated by a donor who has or reasonably expects to have advisory privileges with respect to the distribution of grants or investment of assets.

Example: Irene Li donated 30% of the stock of the company that she founded, Li Holdings, to set up a donor-advised fund in her local community foundation. The community foundation will need to sell enough of that stock to bring the holdings below a 20% ownership of the company in order to avoid an excise tax.

Restrictions on Charitable Contribution Deductions The IRS will not allow a charitable income tax deduction for a contribution to a donor-advised fund if the sponsoring organization is a non–functionally integrated Type III SO.[44] In other words, someone who is setting up a donor-advised fund and expects an income tax deduction for contributions to that fund should use a community foundation, a charitable gift fund, or another established charity as its sponsoring

---

[44] Income tax deductions will also be denied if the sponsoring organization is a war veterans' organization, a fraternal organization, or a cemetery company.

organization instead of a non–functionally integrated Type III SO. Which potential abuse was Congress addressing with this provision?

Annual Returns Sponsoring organizations for donor-advised funds must include information on their annual tax information returns[45] that describes the number of donor-advised funds they own, the aggregate value of the assets those funds hold and the aggregate contributions to and grants from such organizations. What concern about donor-advised funds is this provision designed to address?

2. Sponsoring Organizations

Any §501(c)(3) charitable organization, except a non–functionally integrated Type III SO, can be a sponsoring organization. Some churches and institutions of higher learning administer donor-advised funds, but the regulations are too complex and the possibility of making a mistake that will either engender excise taxes or lead to a revocation of tax exemption is too great for most charities to become sponsoring organizations. The most common vehicles for managing donor-advised funds are community foundations and charitable gift funds.

Community Foundations

Community foundations typically work within a specific community to make grants to other charitable organizations and engage in programmatic grant making. In these respects, they are like private foundations. Unlike private foundations, however, they receive funds from a sufficiently large group of people to have public charity status and avoid the private foundation rules. Community foundations offer a number of types of funds for donors,[46] but donor-advised funds are among the most popular. When community foundations receive donor-advised funds, they become sponsoring organizations of these funds.

Community foundations can also become supported organizations for §509(a)(3) SOs. So long as the SOs carry out the purpose of and are controlled by the community foundation, the SO can maintain its §501(c)(3) public charity status. If the community foundation selects the majority of board members, it will maintain the requisite control for a Type I SO. The community foundation also typically provides administrative support, including financial reports, audits, and tax preparation services.

Community foundations are growing rapidly, in large part because of donor advised funds. Between 2008 and 2014, the total assets held by community foundations almost doubled, from $38 billion to $71 billion. In 2014, community foundations received $8.3 billion in donations and contributed $5.5 billion to other charities. Approximately half the community foundation assets were held in

---

[45] The tax information form, Form 990, is discussed in Chapter 12.

[46] These funds include the unrestricted general fund, field-of-interest funds, and scholarship funds.

donor-advised funds, and one-third of the contributions that they made came from these funds.[47]

Charitable Gift Funds

In 1992, Fidelity Investments began its Fidelity Gift Fund, which provided a new way to utilize the donor-advised model that community foundations had invented in the 1930s. These charitable gift funds are basically holding organizations for the donor-advised funds that the clients of the financial service company have created. Since 1992, all major financial services companies have created similar charitable entities. These charitable gift funds are separate §501(c)(3) organizations that can pool the funds in such a way that the organization will maintain its public charity status.

By 2015, Fidelity Gift Fund was essentially tied for first place with the United Way as the largest charity in the United States.[48] That year, four charitable gift funds—the Fidelity Charitable Gift Fund, Schwab Charitable Fund, Vanguard Charitable Endowment Program, and National Christian Fund— were among the top 10 charities in terms of funds raised from private sources in the United States. The Silicon Valley Community Foundation, which holds many large donor-advised funds, was also in the top 10, and a fifth charitable gift fund, Goldman Sachs Fund, held the 11th place. [49]

Some donors find it easier to create a donor-advised fund within such a charitable gift fund than to go to a community foundation. First, the convenience of combining other financial services with charitable giving is appealing to some (even though the for-profit investment firms are kept strictly separate from the nonprofit charitable funds). Second, these funds are national in scope and have a wider geographic area than most community foundations. Third, it is widely perceived that these funds are less likely to educate donors or scrutinize a grant recommendation than a community foundation.[50]

Other donors prefer the local community foundation, however, precisely because it has a charitable presence within the community. Community foundations generally host a wide variety of funds, along with donor-advised funds, and they use their own endowments to make grants within the community.

---

[47] CF Insights, S*ustained Growth in an Expanding Field, 2014 Columbus Survey Findings,* FOUNDATION CENTER (2015).

[48] The United Way brought in $3.87 billion in donations, and Fidelity $3.85 billion. CHRONICLE OF PHILANTHROPY, *The 2015Philanthropy 400* (Oct. 29, 2015), https://philanthropy.com/specialreport/The-2015-Philanthropy-400/73, accessed April 11, 2016.

[49] *Id.*

[50] Despite the perception that charitable gift funds scrutinize recommendations less carefully than community foundations, the large gift funds make clear that they will not provide grants for preexisting pledges, school tuition, political contributions, and other types of grants that are not permitted under the Internal Revenue Code.

3. Donor-Advised Funds in Action

ALAN CANTOR, STRINGS ON DONOR-ADVISED FUNDS ARE MAKING CHARITY SUPPORTERS ANGRY

Chronicle of Philanthropy, Aug.12, 2015

Donor-advised funds are often promoted as "giving, simplified" or charitable checkbooks. That is true in many ways. Donor-advised funds allow donors to contribute stock shares in one fell swoop, for instance. The donors can then oversee the charitable distribution at their leisure, while sponsoring organizations like Fidelity Charitable or a community foundation keep the books. Yes, in some ways donor-advised funds are indeed simple.

But as the number of donor-advised funds has increased, so too have the challenges for nonprofits and the donors themselves. That's because there are some very real legal restrictions on how grants from donor-advised funds can be distributed. These restrictions are increasingly causing headaches and inefficiencies for nonprofits, while giving rise to misunderstanding and resentment between those organizations and their donors.

What's behind the confusion? Well, donor-advised funds are, technically, just that—funds whose use is advised, not directed, by donors. The final decision-making about grants is legally up to the sponsoring organization, whether a community foundation, a religious federation, or a commercial gift fund.

In practice, the donor-advisers pretty much have carte blanche to recommend grants to any charitable organization they want—fund sponsors make that very clear in their marketing materials—but there are two lines that cannot be crossed even by the most pliant of sponsors. First, grants from donor-advised funds cannot be used if the donor gets any sort of personal benefit. Second, a donor cannot use a donor-advised fund to redeem a personal pledge.

Those seem like modest restrictions, but as they play out, significant issues arise. Here are some examples, not ripped from the headlines (nonprofit leaders are far too discreet—or timid—to complain publicly), but taken from actual examples people have brought to my attention over the last few months.

Missing premium syndrome. A national conservation group has traditionally offered premiums to people who make big gifts. Recently the organization tempted donors by letting them know that donors who gave at least $2,500 would receive a particularly attractive thank-you gift. The donors responded generously, but many of them did so through their donor-advised funds—the source they have come to rely on for charitable gifts of that size.

Many of these donors then grew livid with the organization when staff members explained that because the donors had given through their donor-advised funds, they were ineligible to receive the gift. If the organization had sent the premium to the members, they explained, it would have violated the rule against providing personal benefits for a donor-advised fund gift. . . .

Not-such-a-gala-event tension. Nonprofits make the big money at gala dinners not from people paying $100 or even $250 a head to attend, but from sponsorship gifts of $5,000, $10,000, $50,000, or (in gala meccas like New York City or San Francisco) even more. Sponsorships provide the donors with perks, of course, the most common being a table or two of guests in exchange for, say, a $5,000 gift.

A few free meals in return for a $5,000 gift would seem like an incidental benefit, but the rules governing donor-advised funds make it clear that those plates of coq au vin constitute an inappropriate benefit for the donor-adviser. A staff member at a major cultural organization told me there are a growing number of donors who want to make sponsorship gifts through their donor-advised funds, but who are reluctant to give up any of the perks.

That's creating a challenging dynamic. "People no longer want to write a big check," the development director explained to me. "They like the simple, painless aspect of giving through their donor-advised funds. And when they find out the rules prohibit the donor-advised funds from underwriting sponsorships with benefits, they're either a) mad at me, b) unwilling to be a sponsor any longer, or c) both of the above."

The pledge-that-isn't accounting. In the good old days (I'm talking about all of 20 years ago), donors to a capital campaign would sign a three-year pledge at $100,000 a year. Today, if that same donor is ready to commit to a three-year, $300,000 gift but wants to use her donor-advised fund—well, she can't, because of the prohibition against using such funds to fulfill a personal pledge. A lot of organizations have the donor sign an "intent-to-donate" form that's sort of a pledge form-lite—a moral obligation, but not a legally binding one, and it is not recorded as a pledge in the institution's financial statements.

Along with the annoyance of essentially having to keep two sets of books (one for tracking the campaign progress, which would list this as a $300,000 gift or pledge and one for the official financial statements, which would only list the $100,000 portion of the gift that arrived in year one), the intent-to-donate-sort-of-pledge can create real financial challenges for the nonprofit.

Most notably, if the gift is for a building campaign and the organization needs to borrow funds to keep the project running on time and under budget, it can't use the commitments from donor-advised funds as collateral because the intention to donate is not a legally binding pledge. And as more and more of the major gifts take this form, the project can get delayed and the costs can escalate.

NOTES AND QUESTIONS

Test your understanding of donor-advised funds and their sponsoring organizations by answering the following questions:

1. You are on the board of your local community foundation. The donor to a donor-advised fund has recommended that a gift of $43,900 be given to

Nonantum Law School, where his youngest son is a first-year law student. Do you have an obligation as a board member to ensure that this is truly a gift and not a tuition payment? What if you are the executive director and not a board member? What liability might you or your organization face?

2. Many gifts to colleges are actually gifts to fundraising SOs of those colleges. If a donor of a donor-advised fund recommends that a gift be given to her alma mater, what kind of due diligence must the administrators of the fund do to determine whether the money will, in fact, go to an SO, and if so, what type of SO is involved?

3. If a donor to a donor-advised fund wants to give a big enough gift to his alma mater that he gets to join an elite giving society, can he do so through his donor-advised fund? What if he writes a personal check for any special privileges that he might get from that society, so that charitable funds are not being used for special privileges?

4. You are an attorney for the Mandvi Art Museum. Last week, John Jones pledged that he would donate $100,000 to the museum, to be paid over five years. The first check for $20,000 arrived today from the John Jones Donor-Advised Fund of Local Community Foundation. Why might you advise your client not to cash the check and to require Mr. Jones to pay the pledge personally? Why might your client want to resist your advice?

C. POLICY ISSUES REMAINING WITH SUPPORTING ORGANIZATIONS AND DONOR-ADVISED FUNDS

The PPA did not tackle some of the more difficult issues surrounding donor-advised funds and SOs. Instead, it asked the Secretary of the Treasury to report on four questions:

1. Are existing charitable deductions for donor-advised funds appropriate considering the use of contributions or the use for the benefit of the donor?

2. Should donor-advised funds be subject to a payout ratio?

3. Is an advisory role in the investment or distribution of donated funds consistent with a completed gift?

4. Do these issues apply to other charitable gifts?

The report that was issued in 2011 used information from 2006 and was generally favorable to donor-advised funds. It found that donors give up sufficient control when making the gift to allow a charitable deduction. It also found that the advisory role is consistent with a completed gift. As for the payout rate, it found that the average payout rate for sponsoring organizations of donor-advised funds was 9.3% of assets, which is a higher payout rate than that for private foundations. The report determined that "it would be premature to make a recommendation regarding distribution requirements for [donor-advised funds] on the basis of this first year of reported data." Finally, the report concluded that these issues apply to other charitable gifts because "issues relating to type, extent, and timing of the use of charitable contributions, and the appropriateness of the existing charitable contribution rules, are the same for all public charities. Similarly, issues relating to when a charitable gift is considered complete are common to all charitable organizations." Dept. of the Treasury, REPORT TO CONGRESS ON SUPPORTING ORGANIZATIONS AND DONOR-ADVISED FUNDS (Dec. 2011),

A 2012 Congressional Research Service Report using 2008 information drew some different conclusions. It pointed out that donors to donor-advised funds effectively have control over the distributions and sometimes over investments, which makes them similar to private foundations and brings into question whether these are completed gifts. It found an average payout rate of 13.1%, but noted that "a [donor-advised fund] sponsor can have a high average payout rate although many accounts have little or no payout." It provided several possibilities as remedies: (1) requiring sponsoring organizations to make charitable contributions if an account did not meet minimum distribution requirements by year's end; (2) requiring a minimum distribution over a period of time; (3) applying private foundation rules to donor-advised funds; and (4) restricting the duration of donor advisory rights or of the donor-advised funds themselves. The report also discussed the need for better reporting, so that researchers could determine whether individual accounts are being abused. Even if Congress does not want to require reporting at the level of the individual donor-advised fund, it can ask the sponsoring organizations to report which percentage of accounts made no distributions (or at best, very small ones) and what part of the distributions was spent on investment fees and administrative costs. Molly Sherlock and Jane Gravelle, AN ANALYSIS OF CHARITABLE GIVING AND DONOR-ADVISED FUNDS (Cong. Res. Serv. 2012). http://www.fas.org/sgp/crs/misc /R42595.pdf.

Congress has not acted on these issues, but the policy questions remain. In 2014, David Camp, the Chair of the House Ways and Means Committee, released a tax reform discussion draft that would have introduced to eliminated Type II and Type III SOs and required a 5% payout for donor-advised funds.[51] Although that legislation did not pass, reform of donor-advised funds and SOs is likely to become part of any tax reform package. Meanwhile, commentator discussion, especially about donor-advised funds, has continued.[52]

Given the complexity of these rules, some commentators have suggested that SOs and donor-advised funds should simply follow the same rules that private

---

[51] http://waysandmeans.house.gov/UploadedFiles/Statutory_Text_Tax_Reform_Act_of_2014_ Discussion_Draft__022614.pdf.

[52] See, e.g., Hudson Institute, "Donor-Advised Funds: Warehouses of Wealth?" (May 22, 2013), http://www.hudson.org/index.cfm?fuseaction=publication_details&id=9634; Lewis B. Cullman, Stop the Misuse of Philanthropy, NEW YORK REVIEW OF BOOKS (Sept. 25, 2014); Leon Neyfakh, Donor-Advised Funds: Where Charity Goes to Wait, BOSTON GLOBE (Dec. 1, 2013); Howard Husock, Why Donor-Advised Funds Can Increase Charitable Giving, INSIDE PHILANTHROPY (April 23, 2015).

foundations follow.[53] Others have noted that this complexity, combined with the increasing use of excise taxes for public charities, has rendered the distinction between public charities and private foundations inadequate, and that all public charities should follow the same rules as private foundations.[54]

D. COMPARING THE OPTIONS

As we have seen, donor-advised funds and SOs can be alternatives for private foundations, but the rules for each are somewhat different and are not easy to tackle. Why would one choose one grant-making entity over another when setting up a mechanism that allows one to donate funds in the present but distribute them over time? As an advisor to a philanthropist, or a philanthropist yourself, you will have several factors to consider. Table 7-1 is intended to help with that decision.

Table 7-1

	PRIVATE FOUNDATION	DONOR-ADVISED FUND	TYPE I AND II SO	TYPE III SO	PUBLIC CHARITY (DIRECT GIFT)
Donor control over distributions	Most donor control	Donor recommendation	Might be a board member, but donor does not have control	Might be a board member, but donor does not have control	None, though charity must follow donor intent
Cost to set up and administer	Expensive	Less expensive because it is a fund within a larger charity, so there are economies of scale	Expensive	Expensive, especially non-functionally integrated Type III SOs	Donor has no cost

---

[53] Johnny Rex Buckles, *Should the Private Foundation Excise Tax on Failure to Distribute Income Generally Apply to "Private Foundation Substitutes"?* 44 NEW ENG. L. REV. 493 (2010); Buzz Schmidt, *Time for a New Foundation for Philanthropy,* ALLIANCE MAG. (June 1, 2015).

[54] See, *e.g.,* Marion R. Fremont-Smith, *Is It Time to Treat Private Foundations and Public Charities Alike?* 52 EXEMPT ORG. TAX REV. 236 (2006).

Table 7-1 (*Cont'd*)

	PRIVATE FOUNDATION	DONOR-ADVISED FUND	TYPE I AND II SO	TYPE III SO	PUBLIC CHARITY (DIRECT GIFT)
Flexibility in changing charities to which funds can be distributed	Yes	Yes	No Supported organization has control over board Donor cannot control supported organiza-tion in Type I SO	Possibly Less control by supported organization, but must still be responsive and integral part Donor cannot control supported organization	None Gift goes to chosen charity
Deductibility of gift	Less than public charity	Maximum deductibility	Maximum deductibility	Maximum deductibility	Maximum deductibility
Can substantial contributor be reimbursed for expenses, receive salary at fair market value?	Yes. This is an exception to self-dealing provision.	No	No	No	Yes, so long as it is fair market value
Payout requirement	Yes	No, but being studied	No	Yes, for non–functionally integrated	No
Excess business holding rule	Yes	No, but being studied	No, unless the Type II SO accepts gifts from person who controls supported organization	Yes	
Annual excise tax	Yes	No	No	No	No
Gifts to foreign entities	Yes, if exercise expenditure responsibility	Yes, if exercise expenditure responsibility	Yes	No	Yes

PROBLEM

Assume that your client, Buarno Michelangelo, has a burning passion for Renaissance art and wants to ensure that his $20 million is used to support Renaissance art for at least another 1,000 years. He can donate the money directly to Renaissance Art Museum, with instructions that the fund be used in perpetuity, or he can set up a private foundation, a donor-advised fund, or an SO. If he sets up an SO, he will also need to determine which type best fits his interests. Depending on his priorities, he will undoubtedly make different choices. If he wants to support Medieval Art Museum perpetually, for example, his decision will be different than if he wants flexibility to support other museums at a later point. He will also consider how much control he wants over future distributions. If the desire for control is high, he may want to start a private foundation, but he must balance that interest against the possibility of receiving a smaller tax deduction, the additional rules of a private foundation, and the extra costs of running the organization and following the rules. Consider the following situations that might apply to Michelangelo and determine how each of them would affect his decision.

1. Michelangelo wants to spend full time on this endeavor. He is independently wealthy and does not need to be paid for his work, but it would be nice to get paid.
2. Michelangelo realizes that the best Renaissance art is abroad, and he may want to see some of his money at work abroad.
3. Michelangelo knows that he is a terrible investment manager. He does not want to worry about managing the funds himself, and he does not want to supervise directly the investment manager.
4. Michelangelo plans to contribute his share (50%) of a closely held corporation.
5. Michelangelo plans to contribute $20 million worth of Renaissance art and no cash. He does not want to see the art sold.

NOTES AND QUESTIONS

1. As mentioned above, the Robertson Foundation was a Type I SO for which Princeton University appointed a majority of the board of directors. One of the plaintiffs' allegations in the lawsuit concerning whether Princeton had followed the donor's intent was that the board members appointed by Princeton had an inherent conflict of interest and were not devoted to the Robertson Foundation. In essence, they were identifying a structural conflict of interest in Type I SOs. Do you agree that that conflict exists? If so, how can it be resolved? Another issue in that lawsuit was that the Robertsons paid their litigation expenses from a §501(c)(3) private nonoperating foundation. One of the purposes of that foundation was to support the Robertson Foundation. Is paying litigation expenses a method of pursuing this charitable purpose, or does it amount to self-dealing, as some have suggested? *See* Ben Gose, *Family Uses Nonprofit Funds to Pay Legal*

Expenses in Princeton U Case, CHRONICLE OF PHILANTHROPY (October 24, 2007).

2. For further reading on this general topic, see Stephanie B. Casteel, *Philanthropy and Choice of Grant-Making Entity in a Changing World*, 23 PROB. & PROP. 52 (2009); Terry W. Knoepfle, *The Pension Protection Act of 2006: A Misguided Attack on Donor-Advised Funds and Supporting Organizations*, 9 FLA. TAX REV. 221 (2009). Articles on SOs include Richard S. Gallagher et al., *New Regulations on Type III Supporting Organizations Flesh Out Complex Requirements*, 118 J. Tax'n 255 (2013); David M. Flynn and Noel A. Fleming, *Private Foundation or Public Charity? Type III Supporting Organizations After the PPA*, 108 J. TAX'N 365 (2008). An article on the law of community foundations is Mark Sidel, *Recent Developments in Community Foundation Law: The Quest for Endowment Building*, 85 CHI.-KENT L. REV. 657 (2010).

3. Donor-advised funds also continue to pique scholarly and practitioner interest. Papers from a 2015 conference held by Boston College School of Law's Forum on Philanthropy, *The Rise of Donor-Advised Funds: Should Congress Respond?* are hosted online at https://www.bc.edu/schools/law /newsevents/events/philanthropy-forum/events/donor-advised-funds-program-.html. *See also* John R. Brooks, *The Missing Tax Benefit of Donor-Advised Funds*, 150 TAX NOTES 1013 (2016) (finding that donor-advised funds generate, at best, a small tax benefit and may often generate a tax cost to donors); Jorge Lopes and Courtney Nash, *Proposed Guidance for Donor-Advised Funds*, 2014 CA. TAX LAWYER 14 (2014); Michael J. Hussey, *Avoiding Misuse of Donor-Advised Funds*, 58 CLEV. ST. L. REV. 59 (2010).

4. Charitable remainder trusts, charitable lead trusts, and pooled income funds are other ways to combine charity and a tax break. They are beyond the scope of this book, however. A short description of some the tax implications of these split income trusts can be found at https://www.irs.gov/uac/SOI-Tax-Stats-Split-Interest-Trust-Statistics.

CHAPTER 8

RAISING FUNDS FROM COMMERCIAL ACTIVITIES

Purposes of this chapter:

- Consider the role of commercial activity in §501(c)(3) organizations
- Explore the amount of acceptable commercial activity in a §501(c)(3) organization
- Learn to identify unrelated business income as well as its exceptions and modifications
- Understand the complexities of the unrelated business income tax (UBIT) scheme

To think about as you read:

If you have created a virtual §501(c)(3) organization, consider what commercial activities your organization might want to undertake and how you will structure these activities to avoid losing your tax exemption and minimize (or avoid altogether) paying unrelated business income taxes. If you have not created a virtual organization, imagine that you represent a young art museum that needs to bring in more revenue than you can get through donations and grants alone. What recommendations would you make to the board, and what cautionary tales would you tell?

I. INTRODUCTION

Section 501(c)(3) requires that an organization be organized and operated *exclusively* for a charitable purpose. Increasingly, however, nonprofit organizations receive at least part of their funding from commercial activity. In 2012, almost 3/4 of the $1.65 trillion in revenues that §501(c)(3) public charities reported on their Form 990 [the tax information form that §501(c)(3) organizations must file annually] came from fees for goods and services.[1] Hospital and tuition fees accounted for 2/3 of these fees, but other nonprofit organizations are quite creative and bold in their pursuit of commercial funds. The Museum of Modern Art reported more than $26 million in sales in FY 2012, over $4 million of which was unrelated to its exempt purpose.[2] Some megachurches have restaurants, Starbucks, and even gyms.[3] Even smaller organizations have bake sales, bingo games, and other commercial ventures.

This chapter begins with articles documenting this increase and questioning its impact on the nonprofit sector. It then discusses the two major legal issues that arise from commercial activity:

- Whether the activity is of such a nature that the organization should lose its tax exemption
- Whether the proceeds should be taxed as unrelated business income.[4]

While the term "exclusively" need not be interpreted literally, commercial activity can be substantial enough that the organization is not being operated for charitable purposes. In such instances, the organization will lose its §501(c)(3) tax-exempt status. Unfortunately, the Treasury Regulations, Revenue Rulings, and case law are not as clear as one would like in either drawing the line between permissible and impermissible activities or creating a test for determining where the line should be drawn. The materials that follow show several possible approaches—asking whether a substantial amount of revenue is unrelated to the exempt purpose, determining whether a "commercial hue" exists, and asking whether the organization's charitable program is "commensurate in scope" with the organization's financial resources. As you will see, none of these approaches provides much certainty for organizations that are trying to determine how much commercial activity is too much.

Assuming that the commercial activities are not enough to cause an organization to lose its tax-exempt status, the proceeds from those activities could still be taxed. The unrelated business income tax rules require tax-exempt organizations to pay a tax on the proceeds from trades or businesses that are both regularly carried on and not related to the organization's tax-exempt purpose. There are a number of exceptions and exemptions from this tax. For example, businesses conducted by volunteers, sales of donated items, businesses created for the convenience of the organization's constituents, and passive income all escape the unrelated business income tax. Once an organization has determined what should be classified as unrelated business income, it can deduct its expenses

---

[1] Brice S.McKeever and Sarah L. Pettijohn, THE NONPROFIT SECTOR IN BRIEF 2014: PUBLIC CHARITIES, GIVING, AND VOLUNTEERING (Urban Institute, 2014).

[2] Museum of Modern Art's 2012 Form 990, accessed at http://www.guidestar.org, May 14, 2016.

[3] Elizabeth Bernstein, *Holy Frappucino!* WALL ST. J., Aug. 31, 2001, at W1.

[4] Additional questions are raised when §501(c)(3) organizations enter into complex commercial transactions, such as joint ventures and for-profit subsidiaries. These issues will be discussed in Chapter 10, after we have covered inurement and intermediate sanctions.

from its income. Given the exceptions and the deductibility of expenses, many tax-exempt organizations with significant nonexempt commercial activity pay no taxes.

II. NONPROFIT COMMERCIAL ACTIVITY: POLICY CONSIDERATIONS

BURTON WEISBROD, THE PITFALLS OF PROFITS

Stan. Soc. Innovation Rev. (Winter 2004), pp. 40-47

For more than 150 years, the Young Men's Christian Association has helped Americans stay in shape. The association's Boston affiliate opened the first gym in the country in 1851. Forty years later, a YMCA physical fitness instructor in Springfield, Mass., James Naismith, invented basketball so his young charges would have a game to play indoors during the winter. In 1895, another Y instructor, who considered basketball too strenuous for older members, came up with the game of volleyball.

Since the 19th century, the YMCA has morphed into a health-and-fitness goliath. In 2001, this tax-exempt organization had revenues of $4.1 billion, making it the largest nonprofit, in terms of earned income, in the United States. Today, many of the more than 2,400 local Y's in the country boast basketball courts, swimming pools, jogging tracks, and well-equipped weight rooms.

These familiar neighborhood institutions are under heavy fire, however, for an increasing presence in upscale areas. Private health clubs, like Bally's, have sued Y's for unfair competition, claiming that as a tax-exempt charity, the YMCA is able to undercut private operators' prices enough to siphon away a significant amount of profitable business. "The feeling is that it's an uneven playing ground," said Brooke MacInnes, spokeswoman for the International Health, Racquet, and Sportsclub Association, a trade group. "We're talking about multimillion dollar facilities with the best of equipment, the best of programs."

Critics say that Y's are abandoning their traditional mission of serving low-income neighborhoods. The Y counters that its mission is to serve people of all income levels, not just the poor, and that its upscale affiliates often subsidize memberships for low-income families.

The Y's expansion into affluent neighborhoods raises the question of whether it has become overly commercialized and whether it deserves its tax-exempt status. The rationale behind tax breaks for nonprofits is that nonprofits render goods and services that are valuable for society, ones that no for-profit company would provide because they would be unprofitable. Because for-profit gyms could not make money by providing high-quality exercise facilities in inner cities and because providing such a service is socially valuable, in theory society subsidizes nonprofit Y's to open gyms in those areas.

The Y's expansion into new markets is just one example of how nonprofits are becoming increasingly commercialized. By commercialized, I mean the degree to which nonprofits rely on revenues other than donations or grants. (A "pure" nonprofit is one that depends entirely on contributions, gifts, or grants from private individuals, foundations, or governments.) The commercial activities of nonprofits span the gamut from charging user fees to forging marketing relationships with for-profits to generating revenues from businesses unrelated to the nonprofit's mission. While these commercial activities do not necessarily produce conflicts with a nonprofit's mission, the danger is omnipresent.

The Y's expansion into affluent neighborhoods, for instance, may be generating revenue in the long run while simultaneously directing its money and commitment away from upgrading existing facilities in inner cities in the short run. Although the right balance between generating appropriate revenues and becoming commercialized may be a matter for debate, taxpayers and public policymakers should be concerned. In general, because of the various legal and reputational risks involved, nonprofits should avoid commercial activities—whether they be joint ventures with for-profit companies, unrelated businesses that subsidize the nonprofit's core activities, or other revenue-maximizing behaviors—that distract them from providing public goods at unprofitable rates. To make up the revenue shortfall, I believe that the tax code should be modified to encourage more individual donations to charitable groups—while at the same time restricting forays into commercialism. . . .

A World of Minefields

At a minimum, nonprofits risk their good name when they forge partnerships with for-profits. Ethicists argued that the AMA's deal with Sunbeam was inappropriate because it was unethical for a physician's group dedicated to the public good to be paid to endorse commercial wares. The incident turned into a major debacle for the AMA. More than 2,700 members quit, costing the association more than $1 million in dues. "It was a PR nightmare in that the media and the members, and ultimately the AMA, realized that we were doing something that we shouldn't have been doing," said an AMA spokesman. The association's chief executive and several other ranking officials lost their jobs. Sunbeam later sued for breach of contract, and the AMA wound up paying more than $10 million to settle the case.

Similarly, while supporters of [University of California] Berkeley's contract with Novartis said it would bring the plant biology department much needed cash, give professors access to sophisticated equipment, and help the university win other research funding, critics said it could compromise the faculty's independence and skew research priorities. In 2000, the *Atlantic Monthly* spotlighted the deal in an unflattering article headlined "The Kept University."...

Some nonprofits have lost tax-exemption status as a consequence of their commercial forays, like St. David's Health Care System did in 2000. The controversy began when St. David's formed its partnership with Columbia/HCA

Healthcare. After a two-year audit, the IRS ruled that by linking itself with a profit-making company without retaining clear control, St. David's had forfeited its nonprofit status and had to start paying taxes. St. David's paid more than $1.1 million in back taxes, interest, and penalties for 1996 alone. Although a jury eventually ruled to restore St. David's nonprofit status, the lengthy legal struggle drained funds that the medical center had earmarked for Austin-area charities, such as clinics for the poor.[5]

Lately, the suspicion that certain nonprofits are not upholding their end of the bargain by providing enough socially valuable goods has raised a stir in Washington. Allegations of nonprofit hospitals charging underinsured patients more than they charge patients enrolled in HMOs led U.S. Rep. Bill Thomas (R. Calif.), chairman of the House Ways and Means Committee, to hold hearings in June to determine whether medical centers are violating their duty to provide charitable care.

In short, the drive for profit exposes nonprofits to the charge of losing sight of their social goals. Devoting significant resources and staff time to beefing up a bank account may compromise the nonprofit's ability to carry out its mission. Looking into the future, it is likely that "missions of nonprofits engaged in commercial activities will grow more ambiguous through time. New demands on senior management to pay attention not only to nonprofit but to for-profit goals, the adoption of new structures such as joint ventures that create mixed missions and messages for participating entities, and the tendency of senior management to look at activities from the perspective of their contribution to revenues may create an environment in which nonprofits must work especially hard to keep their charitable mission in daily focus. Increased responsibility will likely fall on boards of directors of commercial nonprofits to ensure that a dilution of charitable mission does not occur...."

Mechanisms to encourage donations, by altering tax law, are readily available. Mechanisms to discourage commercial activity, however, are more challenging. Outright prohibition of any activity that generates "sales" would have vast and uncertain consequences, but the use of tax instruments to discourage all commercial activity—not merely unrelated business activity, which is already subject to taxation—deserves exploration. We should also explore how a shift in public policy that encourages donations rather than commercialism would affect the various industries in which nonprofits operate. For universities, user fees in the form of tuition are a major source of revenue, while user fees are of little import for soup kitchens. But as these issues are examined, we should not forget that nonprofits require some kind of funding for their social missions; it would be counterproductive to constrain commercial revenue-producing activity without also relaxing constraints on donations. Reshaping the pattern of nonprofits' revenue should not be a pretext for constricting this valuable economic sector.

---

[5] [The *St. David's* case is reproduced in Chapter 10, *infra.—Ed.*]

III. SECTION 501(c)(3) CONSIDERATIONS ABOUT COMMERCIAL ACTIVITY

The statutes and regulations reprinted below provide language to help institutions and their attorneys determine when an organization's commercial activities are so paramount that the organization should lose (or be denied) §501(c)(3) tax-exempt status. As you read the cases below, try to determine whether the courts correctly applied this language. Do you have a better suggestion for making this determination? The cases exemplify the reasoning that courts use to determine whether an organization is too commercial to become or remain a §501(c)(3) organization. Part C introduces a 1964 Revenue Ruling that provides a third test.

A. STATUTES AND REGULATIONS

INTERNAL REVENUE CODE §501(C)(3)

Corporations ... organized and operated *exclusively* for religious, charitable, scientific, testing for public safety, literary, or educational purposes, or to foster national or international amateur sports competition (but only if no part of its activities involve the provision of athletic facilities or equipment), or for the prevention of cruelty to children or animals.... [Emphasis added.]

TREASURY REGULATIONS §1.501(C)(3)-1(C)(1)

An organization will be regarded as operated exclusively for one or more exempt purposes only if it engages primarily in activities which accomplish one or more of such exempt purposes specified in section 501(c)(3). An organization will not be so regarded if more than an insubstantial part of its activities is not in furtherance of an exempt purpose.

TREASURY REGULATIONS §1.501(C)(3)-1(E)

An organization may meet the requirements of section 501(c)(3) although it operates a trade or business as a substantial part of its activities, if the operation of such trade or business is in furtherance of the organization's exempt purpose or purposes and if the organization is not organized or operated for the primary purpose of carrying on an unrelated trade or business, as defined in section 513. In determining the existence or nonexistence of such primary purpose, all the circumstances must be considered, including the size and extent of the trade or business and the size and extent of the activities which are in furtherance of one or more exempt purposes.

B. IS THE ACTIVITY SO COMMERCIAL THERE IS NO EXEMPT PURPOSE?

ZAGFLY, INC. v. COMMISSIONER OF INTERNAL REVENUE

T.C. Memo 2013-29 (2013), affirmed 603 Fed. Appx. 638 (9th Cir. 2015)

GUY, Special Trial Judge:

Petitioner was organized as a California nonprofit corporation in March 2010. Petitioner's articles of incorporation state in part: "The specific purpose of this corporation is to establish Internet platforms that will enable the general public to direct the proceeds of their activities to charitable causes." . . .

Initially, petitioner intends to create a Web site and sell flowers as part of an established network of florists. As a flower broker, petitioner anticipates that it will earn a sales commission of approximately 10% to 20% of the purchase price of the flowers it sells, . . . and it expects to sell flowers at market rates. . . .

Petitioner indicated that it would "suggest that our users allocate a small percentage (10% to 20%) of the profits (i.e., 1% to 2% of the purchase price) from their flower purchase to supporting our nonprofit. . . . Petitioner's "goal is to cover all operating costs with philanthropic donations so that all user generated revenue * * * can be directed to the charitable causes our users wish to support."
. . .

Respondent contends that petitioner does not qualify as an exempt organization under section 501(a) on the . . . grounds that . . .petitioner will not operate exclusively for an exempt purpose as required by section 501(c)(3). Petitioner asserts that although it "will fulfill its purpose by engaging in activities that others engage in for commercial gain," its primary motivation is charitable. Petitioner maintains that its "'business' will not generate a financial profit since it will be supplying the good of charitable contribution to its users commensurate in scope with its operational revenue." In short, petitioner contends that its primary purpose is not to operate a trade or business but rather is a charitable one--to facilitate the donation of its profits to other charitable organizations.

. . . The record reflects that petitioner's primary activity will be to operate a Web site through which its customers may purchase flowers at market prices from a network of florists. Petitioner intends to engage in this sales-based business, in direct competition with commercial flower brokers, on a regular and continuous basis with the ultimate aim of maximizing profits in the form of commissions paid on each transaction that it completes. See *Commissioner v. Groetzinger*, 480 U.S. 23, 35 (1987) (a trade or business is an activity that is continuous and regular and is undertaken with the primary purpose of deriving income or profit). Thus, contrary to petitioner's position, its primary activity is not a charitable one, but rather it is a commercial activity that amounts to an unrelated trade or business within the meaning of section 513.

Selling flowers at market prices on the Internet is not substantially related to an exempt purpose under section 501(c)(3), except insofar as it provides petitioner with income that it intends to distribute to charitable organizations. . . . Because petitioner will not be operated exclusively for an exempt purpose, it does not qualify as an organization that is exempt from Federal income taxation under section 501(a).

C. COMMERCIALITY DOCTRINE

BETTER BUSINESS BUREAU OF WASHINGTON, D.C., INC. V. UNITED STATES

326 U.S. 279 (1945)

Mr. Justice MURPHY delivered the opinion of the Court.

Here our consideration is directed to the question of whether the petitioner, the Better Business Bureau of Washington, D.C., Inc., is exempt from social security taxes as a corporation organized and operated exclusively for scientific or educational purposes within the meaning of Section 811(b)(8) of the Social Security Act.[6]

From the stipulated statement of facts it appears that petitioner was organized in 1920 as a non-profit corporation under the laws of the District of Columbia. It has no shares of stock and no part of its earnings inures to the benefit of any private shareholder or individual. Its officers are elected annually from its membership; they have merely nominal duties and are paid no salary. Only the managing director and a small number of employees are paid. Membership is open to "any person, firm, corporation or association interested in better business ethics" as may be elected by the board of trustees and pay "voluntary subscriptions" or dues.

The charter of petitioner states that "the object for which it is formed is for the mutual welfare, protection and improvement of business methods among merchants and other persons engaged in any and all business or professions and occupations of every description whatsoever that deal directly or indirectly with the public at large, and for the educational and scientific advancements of business methods among persons, corporations or associations engaged in business in the District of Columbia so that the public can obtain a proper, clean, honest and fair treatment in its dealings or transactions with such merchants, tradesmen, corporations, associations or persons following a profession and at the same time protecting the interest of the latter classes of businesses to enable such as are engaged in the same to successfully and profitably conduct their business and for the further purpose of endeavoring to obtain the proper, just, fair and effective enforcement of the Act of Congress approved May 29th, 1916,

---

[6] [This statute mirrored §101(6) of the Internal Revenue Code, the predecessor to the current §501(c)(3).—*Ed.*]

otherwise known as 'An Act to prevent fraudulent advertising in the District of Columbia.' "

In carrying out its charter provisions, petitioner divides its work roughly into five subdivisions:

(1) Prevention of fraud by informing and warning members and the general public of the plans and schemes of various types of swindlers.
(2) Fighting fraud by bringing general and abstract fraudulent practices to the attention of the public.
(3) Elevation of business standards by showing and convincing merchants that the application of "the doctrine of caveat emptor is not good business" and by showing and convincing them that misleading advertising, extravagant claims and price comparisons are not good business.
(4) Education of consumers to be intelligent buyers.
(5) Cooperation with various governmental agencies interested in law enforcement.

Information which the petitioner compiles is available to anyone without charge and is communicated to the members and the public by means of the radio, newspapers, bulletins, meetings and interviews. This information is also exchanged with the approximately eighty-five other Better Business Bureaus in the United States.

After paying the social security taxes for the calendar years 1937 to 1941, inclusive, petitioner filed claims for refunds, which were disallowed. This suit to recover the taxes paid was then filed by petitioner in the District Court, which granted a motion for summary judgment for the United States. The court below affirmed the judgment ... and we granted certiorari, the Tenth Circuit Court of Appeals having reached a contrary result in *Jones v. Better Business Bureau of Oklahoma City*, 123 F.2d 767.

Petitioner claims that it qualifies as a corporation "organized and operated exclusively for ... scientific ... or educational purposes ... no part of the net earnings of which inures to the benefit of any private shareholder or individual" within the meaning of §811(b)(8) of the Social Security Act and hence is exempt from payment of social security taxes. No serious assertion is made, however, that petitioner is devoted exclusively to scientific purposes. The basic contention is that all of its purposes and activities are directed toward the education of business men and the general public. Merchants are taught to conduct their businesses honestly, while consumers are taught to avoid being victimized and to purchase goods intelligently. We join with the courts below in rejecting this contention....

In this instance, in order to fall within the claimed exemption, an organization must be devoted to educational purposes exclusively. This plainly means that the presence of a single noneducational purpose, if substantial in nature, will destroy the exemption regardless of the number or importance of truly educational purposes. It thus becomes unnecessary to determine the correctness of the educational characterization of petitioner's operations, it being apparent beyond dispute that an important, if not the primary, pursuit of petitioner's organization is to promote not only an ethical but also a profitable business community. The exemption is therefore unavailable to petitioner.

The commercial hue permeating petitioner's organization is reflected in its corporate title and in the charter provisions dedicating petitioner to the promotion of the "mutual welfare, protection and improvement of business methods among merchants" and others and to the securing of the "educational and scientific advancements of business methods" so that merchants might "successfully and profitably conduct their business." Petitioner's activities are largely animated by this commercial purpose. Unethical business practices and fraudulent merchandising schemes are investigated, exposed and destroyed. Such efforts to cleanse the business system of dishonest practices are highly commendable and may even serve incidentally to educate certain persons. But they are directed fundamentally to ends other than that of education. Any claim that education is the sole aim of petitioner's organization is thereby destroyed.

The legislative history of §811(b)(8) of the Social Security Act confirms the conclusion that petitioner is not exempt under that section. This provision was drawn almost verbatim from §101(6) of the Internal Revenue Code, dealing with exemptions from income taxation. And Congress has made it clear from its committee reports that it meant to include within §811(b)(8) only those organizations exempt from the income tax under §101(6). Significantly, however, Congress did not write into the Social Security Act certain other exemptions embodied in the income tax provisions, especially the exemption in §101(7) of "business leagues, chambers of commerce, real-estate boards, or boards of trade." Petitioner closely resembles such organizations and has, indeed, secured an exemption from the income tax under §101(7) as a "business league." Thus Congress has made, for income tax exemption purposes, an unmistakable demarcation between corporations organized and operated exclusively for educational purposes and those organizations in the nature of business leagues and the like. Its manifest desire to include only the former within the meaning of §811(b)(8) of the Social Security Act prevents us from construing the language of that section to include an organization like petitioner.

Moreover, in amending the Social Security Act in 1939, Congress created certain new exemptions by providing, inter alia, that an organization exempt from income taxes under any of the subdivisions of §101 of the Internal Revenue Code was also exempt from social security taxes as to those employees receiving no more than $45 in a calendar quarter. The Congressional committee reports referred specifically to "business leagues, chambers of commerce, real estate boards, [and] boards of trade" as being included among those organizations exempt from income taxes and affected by this new partial exemption from social security taxes. The inescapable inference from this is that such organizations, of which petitioner is an example, remain subject to social security taxes as to higher paid employees. No contention has been made that any of petitioner's employees are within the low-paid category.

Finally, a Treasury regulation defining an educational organization as "one designed primarily for the improvement or development of the capabilities of the individual" for purposes of §101(6) of the Internal Revenue Code was in effect at the time when Congress used that section in framing §811(b)(8) of the Social Security Act. An identical definition has been promulgated under §811(b)(8) and petitioner admittedly does not meet its terms. Under the circumstances the administrative definition is "highly relevant and material evidence of the probable general understanding of the times and of the opinions of men who probably were active in the drafting of the statute." *White v. Winchester Club*, 315 U.S. 32, 41 (1942). It lends persuasive weight to the conclusion we have reached.

For the foregoing reasons, the judgment of the court below is affirmed.

PRESBYTERIAN AND REFORMED PUBLISHING CO. V. COMMISSIONER OF REVENUE

743 F.2d 148 (3d Cir. 1984)

ADAMS, Circuit Judge.

This is an appeal from a decision of the United States Tax Court affirming the Internal Revenue Service's (IRS) revocation of tax-exempt status for a religiously-oriented publishing house. The Tax Court's decision affirming the termination of the publisher's 52-year-old tax-exemption under 26 U.S.C. §501(c)(3) (1982) was based on its conclusion that the publisher had become a profitable venture with only an attenuated relationship to the church with which it claims an affiliation. For the reasons set forth below, the decision of the Tax Court will be reversed.

I

In 1931, the Presbyterian and Reformed Publishing Company (P & R) was incorporated to "state, defend and disseminate (through every proper means connected with or incidental to the printing and publishing business) the system of belief and practice taught in the Bible, as that system is now set forth in the Confession of Faith and Catechisms of the Presbyterian Church in the United States of America." P & R's charter requires that any income otherwise available as a dividend be used to improve its publications, extend their influence, or assist institutions "engaged in the teaching or inculcating" of the "system of belief and practice" of the Orthodox Presbyterian Church (OPC).

The IRS granted P & R tax-exempt status in 1939, stating, "Your actual activities consist of publishing a religious paper known as 'Christianity Today,' a Presbyterian journal devoted to stating, defending, and furthering the gospel. Your income is derived from subscriptions, contributions and gifts and is used to defray maintenance and general operating expenses."

From the beginning, P & R has been closely linked—although not formally affiliated—with the OPC, a Presbyterian group dedicated to its view of reformed Presbyterian theology and, in particular, to the doctrine of Biblical Christianity set forth in the Westminster Confession of Faith. P & R's central editorial criterion is whether a book chosen for publication would make a "worthy contribution ... to the reformed [Presbyterian] community." One independent publisher characterized P & R's books as lacking in "common ground" with the "nonreformed mind" and "offensive" to all but the "truly reformed."

One of P & R's three incorporators and original directors founded the OPC in 1932, one year after P & R's incorporation. Seven of P & R's nine directors are either officials at Westminster Theological Seminary of Philadelphia or pastors of OPC or OPC-affiliated denominations. On January 1, 1976, P & R changed its charter to specify OPC's seminary, the Westminster Theological Seminary of Philadelphia, as the recipient of all P & R assets in case of dissolution, citing Westminster's common dedication to Biblical Christianity and the Westminster Confession.

The organizational structure of P & R further underscores its close ties to the OPC. Since 1931, the publishing house has been run by three successive generations of the Craig family. Samuel, Charles, and Bryce Craig each worked without compensation at what amounted to a family concern whose business was conducted at the Craigs' kitchen table; all three Craigs were ministers. The record is devoid of evidence indicating any lessening of ties between P & R and the OPC.

From its inception until 1969, the company could claim no income over and above expenses. Indeed, the Craigs themselves often contributed personal funds in order to keep the corporation afloat (Samuel donated $500 in 1939 and $3,000 in 1954; Charles donated a total of $19,600 from 1955 to 1963). Until 1973, P & R relied exclusively on volunteers to help the Craigs with editing, packing, shipping, and clerical work.

Beginning in 1969, however, P & R experienced a considerable increase in economic activity as a result of the sudden and unexpected popularity of books written by Jay Adams, a Westminster Theological faculty member. P & R reported gross profits of over $20,000 for 1969, almost twice as much in 1970, and subsequent escalations culminating in over $300,000 in gross profits in 1979.... By 1979, P & R had seven paid employees assisting Bryce Craig, one with a salary of $12,500, and five with salaries under $6,250 (all five full-time employees were OPC officials or members). Bryce Craig himself began receiving a salary of $12,000 in 1976, which increased, to $15,350 by 1979.

As early as March 2, 1974, P & R notified the Internal Revenue Service that it was accumulating surplus cash as a "building fund." In 1976, P & R used this fund to purchase 5½ acres of land in Harmony, New Jersey, close to both an OPC community and Harmony Press, the printer for both P & R and OPC. In 1978, construction of a combined warehouse and office building in Harmony was completed at a cost of $263,000; an additional $27,000 was spent in 1979 for equipment.

After an audit, the IRS issued a revocation of P & R's tax-exempt status in 1980 on the grounds that P & R was not "operating exclusively for purposes set forth in 501(c)(3)" and was "engaged in a business activity which is carried on similar to a commercial enterprise." The IRS made this revocation retroactive, to apply from January 1, 1969 onward.

The Tax Court affirmed the revocation... but held that the IRS abused its discretion in making the revocation retroactive to 1969. Instead, it set the effective revocation date at 1975, based upon its declaration that as of that year P & R "had acquired a truly commercial hue" and the company "was aware... that IRS agents had been raising serious questions [about its exemption]."... To support its determination that P & R came to be "animated" by a substantial commercial [and thus nonexempt] purpose" in 1975, ... the Tax Court relied primarily on three lines of evidence: first, P & R's "soar[ing] net and gross profits" between 1969 and 1979; second, the fact that P & R set prices which generated "consistent and comfortable net profit margins," rather than lowering prices to encourage a broader readership; and, third, P & R's purchase and sale of books to and from Baker Book Stores (a commercial publishing house), which "must have ... overlapp[ed] in subject matter" with commercial publishers.... The Tax Court deemed this sufficient to support the proposition that P & R was in "competition with commercial publishers."[7]

On P & R's motion for reconsideration, the Tax Court issued a second opinion on April 8, 1983, leaving its prior judgment intact and rejecting P & R's argument that its "profit" figures should have been adjusted to reflect accumulations for the building fund. The Tax Court suggested that the new building furthered commercial purposes as much as religious purposes, and noted that "gross profit margins" did not fall after the building was completed.... Finally, the Tax Court emphasized that P & R's accumulations exceeded its expenditures for the new building. P & R's motion to reconsider also sought to distinguish its OPC-affiliated activity from that of generic Christian publishers. The Tax Court rejected this point, stating that "the denominational or

---

[7] [FN 2] Other activities as well indicate that petitioner was animated by a substantial commercial purpose. It consciously attempted to transform itself into a more mainline commercial enterprise: It searched out more readers; it employed paid workers; it dropped money-losing plans; it paid substantial royalties; it made formal contracts with some authors; and, of course, it expanded into a new facility from which it could continue to reap profits. Further, petitioner was not affiliated or controlled by any particular church organization and this nondenominational character "contributes to the resemblance between its publishing activities and those of commercial, non-exempt publishers of Christian literature with whom ... [it] competes." *Inc. Trustees of Gospel Wkr. Soc. v. United States*, [510 F. Supp. 374,] 379, n. 16 [D.D.C. (1981)].

Petitioner argues that it accumulated profits to expand so that it could publish more books and thus reach more readers. We recognize that petitioner used a large amount of its accumulated profits for the new Harmony facility; this new facility probably aided petitioner in increasing its productivity and distribution. Such increase, however, may also be indicative of a commercial enterprise. We are not convinced that one of the significant reasons for expansion was not the commercial one of wishing to expand production for profit....

nondenominational character of an organization has never been a controlling criterion."...

II

The principal issue we must address is at what point the successful operation of a tax-exempt organization should be deemed to have transformed that organization into a commercial enterprise and thereby to have forfeited its tax exemption. The Tax Court answered this question by looking at the composite effects of the broad-scale increase in commercial activity, the accumulation of capital, the company's "profitability," and the development of a professional staff. Although these indicia of non-exempt business activity are all relevant, we are troubled by the inflexibility of the Tax Court's approach. It is doubtful that any small-scale exempt operation could ever increase its economic activity without forfeiting tax-exempt status under such a definition of non-exempt commercial character. Thus, we believe that the statutory inclusion or exclusion of P & R should be considered under a two-prong test: first, what is the purpose of an organization claiming tax-exempt status; and, second, to whose benefit does its activity inure?

This two-prong inquiry is drawn directly from the wording of §501(c)(3) and the legislative history of its enactment. The statute explicitly cites as qualifying for tax exemption those entities "organized exclusively for religious, charitable ... or educational purposes." Indeed, the statute's original sponsor cited the religious publishing house as the archetypal example of the contemplated tax-exempt organization. In the words of the sponsor, Senator Bacon:

> [T]he corporation which I had particularly in mind as an illustration at the time I drew this amendment is the Methodist Book Concern, which has its headquarters in Nashville, which is a very large printing establishment, and in which there must necessarily be profit made, and there is a profit made exclusively for religious, benevolent, charitable, and educational purposes, in which no man receives a scintilla of individual profit.....

This passage directly supports the two-part test set forth today. The legislative history refers to a "very large printing establishment ... in which there must necessarily be profit made" as within the scope of the exemption. Significantly, Senator Bacon's remarks point to the purpose of the publishing house and the absence of personal profit, rather than the volume of business, as the hallmarks of non-taxable activity. Assuming that large religious or educational publishers may qualify for an exemption, and assuming that not all such publishers are created as large entities, the question becomes one of defining the standards by which the growth in volume of a publisher will not in itself jeopardize the tax exemption.

In the case at hand, the "purpose" prong of the two-part test is the more difficult to administer. Therefore, we will turn first to the question of inurement, and then return to the question of purpose.

A

In order to qualify for a §501(c)(3) exemption, "no part of an organization's net earnings may inure to the benefit of any private shareholder or individual."... There is no basis in the record for concluding that P & R's increased commercial activity inured to the personal benefit of any individual.... Therefore, if P & R is to be denied tax-exempt status, it must be as a result of the first prong of the test set forward today: the purpose of P & R would have to be incompatible with §501(c)(3).

B

In order to come within the terms of §501(c)(3), an organization seeking tax-exempt status must establish that it is organized "exclusively" for an exempt purpose. In the leading case elucidating the purposes considered exempt under §501(c)(3), the Supreme Court in *Better Business Bureau v. U.S.*, 326 U.S. 279, 283, 66 S. Ct. 112, 114, 90 L. Ed. 67 (1945), stated, "[t]he presence of a single [non-exempt] purpose, ... substantial in nature, will destroy the exemption." The Court found that the Better Business Bureau of the District of Columbia was not exempt because a substantial purpose was "the mutual welfare, protection and improvement of business methods among merchants." *Id.* at 281. Nevertheless, *Better Business Bureau* is a relatively straightforward case because of the presence of an explicit non-exempt commercial purpose by the organization claiming the exemption. P & R, to the contrary, claims that it is animated by no commercial motive and therefore falls squarely within the statutory exemption. Thus, the Tax Court's decision in the present case rests on the evaluation of what it deemed to be the true but unspoken motive of P & R.

Any exploration of unarticulated or illicit purpose necessarily involves courts in difficult and murky problems. When the legality of an action depends not upon its surface manifestation but upon the undisclosed motivation of the actor, similar acts can lead to diametrically opposite legal consequences. In the field of equal protection law, for instance, similar state actions having disproportionate impacts upon minorities may be upheld or struck down depending upon the weighing of various indicia of "discriminatory intent."...

The difficulties inherent in any legal standard predicated upon the subjective intent of an actor are further compounded when that actor is a corporate entity. In such circumstances, courts forced to pass upon a potentially illicit purpose have looked for objective indicia from which the intent of the actor may be discerned....

The Tax Court properly framed the inquiry as to whether P & R's purpose was within §501(c)(3) as follows: "Where a nonexempt purpose is not an expressed goal, courts have focused on the manner in which activities themselves are carried on, implicitly reasoning that an end can be inferred from the chosen means. If, for example, an organization's management decisions replicate those of commercial enterprises, it is a fair inference that at least one purpose is commercial, and hence nonexempt. And if this nonexempt goal is substantial, tax exempt status must be denied. Clearly, petitioner's conduct of a growing and very profitable publishing business must enbue [sic] it with some commercial hue. How deep a tint these activities impart can best be evaluated by looking at certain factors deemed significant in cases involving religious publishing companies, as well as in other pertinent cases....

There are two aspects of the Tax Court's opinion regarding P & R's purpose that require careful examination. First is the Tax Court's conclusion that "petitioner was not affiliated or controlled by any particular church and [that] this nondenominational character 'contributes to the resemblance between its publishing activities and those of commercial, non-exempt publishers of Christian literature with whom ... [it] competes.'" ... Given the close connection between P & R and the OPC, the absence of formal control of P & R by any particular church is not dispositive of the question of the fundamental ties between its goals as a publishing house and the dogma espoused by the OPC. In *Inc. Trustees*, the court's decision that a gospel-oriented press failed to qualify for §501(c)(3) status did not turn on the extent of the press' formal affiliation with a church. Rather, the court focused on the virtually complete cessation of religious activity by the church, the church's unexplained accumulation of millions of dollars, and the fact that some officers of the affiliated publishing concern were drawing salaries ranging from $42,000 to over $100,000. The Tax Court itself seems to have recognized the non-dispositive nature of formal affiliation in its decision on the motion for reconsideration, where it stated, "the denominational or nondenominational character of an organization has never been a controlling criterion."

The second point, P & R's accumulation of "profits," causes greater difficulty. Although the profits of P & R constituted only one of the factors enumerated and discussed by the Tax Court in its opinion, the memorandum filed upon P & R's motion for reconsideration makes clear that the Tax Court's principal concern was the "presence of substantial profits."... The Tax Court computed P & R's profits by subtracting the cost of goods sold from the gross sales of books to arrive at the gross profits. The sum of other expenses was in turn subtracted from the gross profits to derive the net profit schedule used by the Tax Court in determining P & R's profitability.... These net profits peaked at $106,180 in 1975, the year the Tax Court decided that P & R had acquired a truly commercial character. On reconsideration, the Tax Court added that the gross profits margin of P & R did not fall even after the new building was constructed....

We do not read §501(c)(3) or its legislative history to define the purpose of an organization claiming tax-exempt status as a direct derivative of the volume of business of that organization. Rather, the inquiry must remain that of determining the purpose to which the increased business activity is directed. As the Tax Court itself observed, "the presence of profitmaking activities is not per se a bar to qualification of an organization as exempt if the activities further or accomplish an exempt purpose." *Aid to Artisans, Inc. v. Commissioner*, 71 T.C. 202, 211

(1978).[8] Despite the long history of §501(c)(3) and the numerous organizations that have claimed its coverage, no regulation or body of case law has defined the concept of "purpose" under this provision of the Tax Code with sufficient clarity to protect against arbitrary, ad hoc decision-making.

The Tax Court's analysis of P & R's accumulation of profits in the present context could, absent a clearer articulation of the legal standard for tax-exempt status, lead to such arbitrary or ad hoc treatment. We are particularly concerned that although the Tax Court acknowledged that P & R informed the IRS as early as March 2, 1974 of its accumulation of funds to purchase or build an office and warehouse, the opinion tabulates the company's cash-on-hand, and cites this as an important factor in concluding that P & R was motivated by a non-exempt purpose.

There is no doubt that unexplained accumulations of cash may properly be considered as evidence of commercial purpose.... In light of the clear notice to the IRS of P & R's need to expand its physical capacity, the claim that the accumulated profits would be used for this purpose, and the recognition by the IRS of such expansion as a legitimate reason for cash accumulation, we are unable to affirm the Tax Court's determination that P & R's cash-on-hand situation was a strong indicator of a non-exempt purpose....

Although we recognize that the Tax Court is entitled to deference in determining the existence of a substantial, non-exempt purpose, that court must focus on facts which indicate a purpose falling outside the ambit of section 501(c)(3). In this case, the Tax Court focused primarily on two factors—the lack of affiliation with a particular church and the accumulation of profits. As we have shown, neither factor indicates the presence of a non-exempt purpose here. Therefore, we must consider the balance of the record to determine whether all the evidence taken together supports a finding of non-exemption. Such an examination reveals no additional evidence of improper motives.

III

Two competing policy considerations are present in situations where tax-exempt organizations begin to expand the scope of their profit-generating activities. On the one hand, the simple act of accumulating revenues may properly call into question the ultimate purpose of an organization ostensibly dedicated to one of the enumerated pursuits under §501(c)(3). On the other hand, success in terms of audience reached and influence exerted, in and of itself, should not jeopardize the tax-exempt status of organizations which remain true to their stated goals.

---

[8] [FN 5] *Fides Publishers Ass'n v. U.S.*, 263 F. Supp. 924 (N.D. Ind. 1967), relied upon by the Tax Court below, would seem to suggest otherwise. The court in *Fides* upheld the revocation of a religious publisher's exempt status on the ground that the publisher made a profit. 263 F. Supp. at 935. Insofar as *Fides* is read to suggest a *per se* profits rule, we decline to accept its reasoning as contrary to the history and language of §501(c)(3). However, *Fides* may be distinguishable on the facts. In that case, the publisher offered no reason for its accumulation of earnings. In the immediate case, P & R clearly explained its need to expand to the IRS and the Tax Court.

Our concern is that organizations seeking §501(c)(3) status may be forced to choose between expanding their audience and influence on the one hand, and maintaining their tax-exempt status on the other. If this were a stagnant society in which various ideas and creeds preserve a hold on a fixed proportion of the population, this concern would evaporate. A large religious institution with a broad base of support, such as one of the more established churches, could be the springboard for large-scale publishing houses dedicated to advancing its doctrines and be assured of qualifying for §501(c)(3) coverage. A small denomination, such as the OPC, could then have within its penumbra only a small-scale operation run off a kitchen table. In such circumstances, any attempt by a publisher adhering to the views of the small denomination to expand its scope of activities would properly raise questions relating to its continued eligibility for tax-exempt status.

This view does not reflect either the dynamic quality of our society or the goals that generated the grant of tax-exempt status to religious publishers. The sudden popularity of an erstwhile obscure writer, such as Jay Adams, cannot, by itself, be the basis for stating that P & R has departed from its professed purpose any more than an increase in congregations would call into question the OPC's continued designation as a church. Such a standard would lead to an inequitable disparity in treatment for publishers affiliated with mainstream churches as opposed to small offshoots.

Accordingly, the decision of the Tax Court will be reversed.

AIRLEE FOUNDATION V. IRS

283 F. Supp. 2d 58 (D.D.C. 2003)

SULLIVAN, District Judge.

Introduction

Plaintiff in this case, Airlie Foundation ("Airlie") seeks a declaratory judgment against defendant, the Internal Revenue Service ("IRS") under section 7428 of the Internal Revenue Code of 1986 (26 U.S.C. §7428) as amended (the "Code" or "IRC"), that it (i) is an organization described in sections 170(c) and 501(c)(3) of the Code; (ii) is not a private foundation pursuant to section 509(a)(2) of the Code; and (iii) is exempt from federal income tax beginning January 1, 1995.

Plaintiff argues that the IRS applied "an unprecedented and poorly reasoned *per se* test" in determining that it did not qualify for tax-exempt status because it did not provide conference services for governmental and charitable patrons as fees "substantially below its costs." Plaintiff contends that, had the IRS applied the correct legal standard and considered "all of the relevant facts and circumstances," it "would have been compelled to recognize Airlie as exempt."

Defendant maintains that it rightly denied plaintiff's application for recognition as a tax-exempt organization. It argues that, while plaintiff may conduct a limited number of charitable and educational activities, "those...are incidental to [its] primary activity, which is the operation of a conference center in a manner consistent with that of a commercial business."... Pending before the Court are plaintiff's and defendant's cross-motions for Summary Judgment.

Facts

Plaintiff is a Virginia non-stock corporation created in 1960...and recognized by the IRS as a tax exempt organization in 1963. It was organized to accomplish the following purposes:

(a) To study, promote, encourage and foster knowledge, understanding and appreciation of (i) the interrelationships which exist in the physical and social sciences, and (ii) the significance of unifying and integrating the knowledge gained about the physical and social sciences, in attaining for the people in the United States richer, happier and fuller lives; and to disseminate knowledge and basic factual material relating to the foregoing so that adults in the United States may healthily exercise their mental faculties, better understand the society in which they live, and live harmoniously in a changing environment [and]

(b) In the field of adult education, to associate together and promote cooperation among administrators, scholars, scientific and professional groups, and others to engage in research, gather basic factual information, and publish and otherwise disseminate in any and all forms the results thereof; to conduct an educational conference center for groups and organizations that have an educational purpose and to hold, initiate, sponsor, aid in managing and directing, and to assist cooperative groups or organizations in holding, [sic] meetings, assemblies, seminars and conferences of a local, state, or national character; and by these and other means to arrive at and disseminate impartial and authoritative findings on questions of national and international importance, and thus to stimulate the growth of informed opinion with a view to preserving and strengthening the democratic processes and principles of freedom.

Plaintiff carries out its mission principally by organizing, hosting, conducting, and sponsoring educational conferences on its facilities.... It has played a role in the development of programs in areas as diverse as civil and human rights, international relations, public policy, the environment, medical education, mental health and disability.... Plaintiff sponsors events such as lectures, concerts, and art shows free of charge and provides meeting space for non-profit organizations, overnight accommodations for participants of its cultural programs, and public use of its grounds for large-scale charitable events.... Besides operating the conference center, plaintiff provides in-kind and administrative support for environmental studies conducted on its facilities by the

International Academy for Preventative Medicine, Inc. Plaintiff receives a monthly fee of $12,500 for its services.

... On average, plaintiff hosts about 600 groups per year. It derives approximately 85 percent of its operating revenue from fees paid by these clients and approximately eight percent from its endowment.... An average of 20 percent of Airlie's conference events are for government clients, 50 percent from nonprofit and/or educational clients, and 30-40 percent for "other" users. At most, ten percent of plaintiff's clients use its facility for private events and another ten percent at most represent private commercial clients pursuing their private interests....

Plaintiff maintains that "[t]he decision to serve principally the governmental and nonprofit sector rather than the commercial for-profit sector reflects a deliberate choice by the Foundation's Board at its creation as the most effective way to accomplish its educational and charitable purposes."... According to industry data from 1999, plaintiff's average daily rate was almost twenty percent lower than the average rates for nearby conference centers.... The expected operating pre-tax profit margin for a commercial conference center should be approximately twenty percent of gross revenues. Plaintiff's actual operations during the years 1995-1998 reflected a pre-tax profit margin of barely four percent after excluding grants, investment income and unusual items. "In other words, the Foundation uses the investment income from its endowment to subsidize its conference and its other public benefit activities."...

In response to an inquiry by IRS, plaintiff provided a daily list of all patrons that used its facilities during 1999. The data revealed that, of the 651 events in 1999, plaintiff fully subsidized 4.75 percent and partially subsidized another 12.5 percent.... Subsidies varied depending on the patrons, but included discounts of ten percent, nearly 50 percent and 80 percent....

Plaintiff has traditionally operated on a break-even basis. While it did earn net income and pay more than $1.3 million in federal and state income taxes, its investment income during those years exceeded its four-year net excess of revenues over expenses....

In the late 1970s, the IRS commenced an investigation of Airlie. The agency's main concern surrounded the nature and extent of financial benefits flowing from plaintiff to its founder, the late Murdoch Head. The IRS also looked into plaintiff's conference activities. On November 3, 1988, the IRS revoked its recognition of plaintiff's tax-exempt status under section 501(c)(3), retroactive to January 1, 1976. The agency's stated grounds for removal were (i) that plaintiff's earnings inured to the benefit of its founder, Murdoch Head, and to his family; and (ii) that plaintiff operated its conference center activity for a non-exempt, commercial purpose. In 1993, this Court denied plaintiff's challenge to that determination. *See Airlie Found. v. United States*, 826 F. Supp. 537 (D.D.C. 1993). In its opinion, the district court explicitly stated that "it is not necessary to address the IRS' determination that [Airlie] was operating its conference center as a commercial enterprise." *Id.* at 539 n. 2. The D.C. Circuit affirmed in a *per curiam* decision. *Airlie Found. v. United States*, 55 F.3d 684 (D.C. Cir. 1995)....

On February 3, 1998, having decided to make an effort to regain its exempt status, plaintiff participated in a "pre-filing" conference with IRS representatives. At that conference, the agency identified three potential issues that could be raised by a new Airlie exemption application: (i) whether there were improper financial benefits to Airlie insiders or other private interests; (ii) whether Airlie's relationship with the Head family was appropriate; and (iii) whether Airlie's conference-related activities were undertaken for commercial purposes.... On August 6, 1999, plaintiff applied to the IRS for recognition as a Section 501(c)(3) tax-exempt entity. The IRS denied plaintiff's application on January 24, 2002, finding that plaintiff operated its conference center for a commercial purpose....

Discussion

... As defendant concedes that plaintiff was organized for an exempt purpose, only the operational test is at issue in this case.... The operational test requires both that an organization engage "primarily" in activities that accomplish its exempt purpose and that not more than an "insubstantial part of its activities" further a non-exempt purpose.... Though an incidental non-exempt purpose will not automatically disqualify an organization, the "presence of a single [nonexempt] purpose, if substantial in nature, will destroy the exemption, regardless of the number or importance of truly [exempt] purposes." *Better Business Bureau of Washington, D.C. v. United States*, 326 U.S. 279, 283, 66 S. Ct. 112, 90 L. Ed. 67 (1945); *Airlie*, 826 F. Supp. at 549. In cases where an organization's activities could be carried out for either exempt or nonexempt purposes, courts must examine the *manner* in which those activities are carried out in order to determine their true purpose....

In applying the operational test, courts have relied on what has come to be termed the "commerciality" doctrine.... In many instances, courts have found that, due to the "commercial" manner in which an organization conducts its activities, that organization is operated for nonexempt commercial purposes rather than for exempt purposes. Among the major factors courts have considered in assessing commerciality are competition with for profit commercial entities; ... extent and degree of below cost services provided; pricing policies; and reasonableness of financial reserves.... Additional factors include, *inter alia*, whether the organization uses commercial promotional methods (e.g., advertising) and the extent to which the organization receives charitable donations.

Plaintiff contends that, considering the various "commercialism" factors that courts have identified in conjunction with an "overall facts and circumstances" test, its "present conference activities are undertaken principally to advance the educational and charitable purposes for which Airlie was organized...." Plaintiff submits that its conference activities differ substantially from those of commercial, taxable conference centers in the following respects:

- Airlie's conference fees are comparable to, and in some respects lower than, those of other nonprofit conference centers and substantially lower than those of commercial conference centers.
- Airlie engages in very little advertising. Its limited promotional activities via the web are less commercial even than those of other nonprofit conference centers that are tax-exempt.
- Airlie has not accumulated its reserves unreasonably. "To the contrary, Airlie's management has acted prudently to maximize Airlie's educational and charitable activities in light of the serious financial limitations presented by its largely break-even operations since revocation of exemption, its inability to solicit tax-deductible contributions, its reliance on its investment income to subsidize conference activities, its plans to acquire substantial additional property for its environmental preserve, and the depletion of its endowment to fund its 1998 real estate purchase."...

According to defendant, the administrative record clearly demonstrates that the "commercial hue" of plaintiff's conference center activities disqualifies it as a tax exempt organization pursuant to Section 501(c)(3). The IRS asserts that "there is little dispute that the lectures, concerts, art shows and other activities sponsored by plaintiff are merely incidental in comparison to that activity."... Defendant relies heavily on a 1997 appraisal of plaintiff's facilities, which found that:

> The Airlie Center primarily competes with conference centers located in the Washington, D.C. area. In addition, the subject competes to some extent with upscale specialty inns such as the Inn at Perry Cabin. The Airlie Center also derives substantial income from weddings and special events. The competitive conference centers typically derive a much smaller percentage of their income from these services. The subject primarily competes with local motels and fellowship halls in Fauquier County.

As it is clear from the facts that plaintiff engages in conduct of both a commercial and exempt nature, the question whether it is entitled to tax-exempt status turns largely on whether its activities are conducted *primarily* for a commercial or for an exempt purpose. Parties are correct in asserting that *BSW Group, Inc. v. Comm'r*, 70 T.C. 352, 358 (1978), provides the most relevant case authority.

BSW Group involved the operation of a business purportedly formed for the purpose of providing consulting services primarily in the fields of rural-related policy and program development. Petitioner's consulting clients were to be tax-exempt organizations and not-for-profit organizations who were to become aware of petitioner's services through word of mouth rather than traditional advertisement. *BSW Group*, 70 T.C. at 354-55. Petitioner's general policy was to provide its consulting services at or close to cost, but fees were to be sufficiently high as to enable petitioner to retain at least a nominal administrative fee over and above the amount payable to individual consultants. *Id.* at 355. In concluding, "with reluctance," *id.* at 360, that BSW Group was not an exempt organization, the Tax Court focused on the fact that the organization's "overall fee policy [was] ... to recoup its costs and ... realize some profit," that the organization competed with commercial firms, that it had not received or solicited voluntary contributions, and that it had failed to limit its clientele to organizations which were themselves exempt under Section 501(c)(3). Notably, while petitioner's fee structure in that case reflected ability to pay, it did not appear that the organization planned ever to charge a fee less than cost. *Id.* at 358-60.

In the present case, plaintiff admits that its primary activity is the operation of a conference center. Like petitioner in *BSW Group*, plaintiff acts as an intermediary and does not directly benefit the public. As was the case in *BSW Group*, plaintiff's conference patrons are not limited to tax-exempt entities. According to the booking report for 1999, the year in which plaintiff applied to the IRS for tax exempt status, in fact, approximately 30-40 percent of plaintiff's patrons were of a private or corporate nature. While plaintiff in the instant case has made profits ranging from an average of four percent up to ten percent, unlike petitioner in *BSW Group*, it provided more than 17 percent of its 1999 conferences for fees covering less than total costs. As the Tax Court correctly stated in the case of *IHC Health Plan Inc. v. Comm'r*, 325 F.3d 1188 (10th Cir. 2003), cited by defendant, "there is a qualitative difference between selling at a discount and selling below cost." *IHC*, 325 F.3d at 1200. The fact that plaintiff's conference center derives substantial income from weddings and special events and competes with a number of commercial, as well as non-commercial, entities constitutes strong evidence, pursuant to *BSW Group*, of a commercial nature and purpose. Furthermore, though plaintiff contends that most of its bookings are the result of word-of-mouth referrals, it maintains a commercial website and has paid significant advertising and promotional expenses....

While plaintiff was organized for an exempt purpose, the Court cannot find, under the totality of the circumstances, that it is operated similarly. Having considered the facts before it, the Court is not persuaded that plaintiff has met its burden of demonstrating that an incorrect determination was made by the Internal Revenue Service. While certain factors—including plaintiff's fee structure and subsidization practice—are indicative of non-commercial characteristics, others—such as the nature of its clients and competition, its advertising expenditures and the substantial revenues derived from weddings and special events on the premises—strongly suggest that the agency was correct in revoking the foundation's tax exempt status. The final determination letter underscores the IRS' proper understanding and application of the "operations test":

> You have failed to establish that you are operated exclusively for charitable or educational purposes within the meaning of section 501(c)(3) of the Code. You are not exempt because you are operated in a manner not significantly distinguishable from a commercial endeavor. By operating in the manner described, you are furthering a substantial nonexempt purpose.

The IRS' conclusion is fully supported by the totality of circumstances as set forth in the administrative record. While plaintiff's organizational purpose is exempt and the foundation operates, in important respects, in an exempt fashion, there is a distinctive "commercial hue" to the way Airlie carries out its business.

For the reasons outlined herein, the Court finds that defendant IRS is entitled to summary judgment against plaintiff Airlie.

D. COMMENSURATE IN SCOPE DOCTRINE

REV. RUL. 64-182, 19640-2, C.B. 186-187

A corporation organized exclusively for charitable purposes derives its income principally from the rental of space in a large commercial office building which it owns, maintains and operates. The charitable purposes of the corporation are carried out by aiding other charitable organizations, selected in the discretion of its governing body, through contributions and grants to such organizations for charitable purposes. Held, the corporation is deemed to meet the primary purpose test of section 1.501(c)(3)-1(e)(1) of the Income Tax Regulations, and to be entitled to exemption from Federal income tax as a corporation organized and operated exclusively for charitable purposes within the meaning of section 501(c)(3) of the Internal Revenue Code of 1954, where it is shown to be carrying on through such contributions and grants a charitable program commensurate in scope with its financial resources.

IRS GEN. COUNS. MEM. 34682 (NOV. 17, 1971)[9]

It is evident, as reflected in the questions which you have asked, that your concern with the position in the ... ruling centers principally around two fundamental issues respecting charitable qualification under section 501(c)(3) of organizations engaged in unrelated trade or business. The first is how much unrelated trade or business an organization may engage in under the limitations of the "primary purpose" provision of Regulations 1.501(c)(3)-1(e) without defeating qualification for charitable status under section 501(c)(3). The second is how much charity an organization must do in relation to a given amount of resources in order to fulfill the operational requirements of charitable status under the ... concept of the "primary purpose" limitation. [*Editor's Note:* The

---

[9] [General Counsel Memoranda are documents prepared by the Office of the Chief Counsel that "contain the reasons behind the adoption of revenue rulings, private letter rulings, and technical advice memoranda" and have "important precedential value in determining future tax questions."*Taxation with Representation Fund v. IRS*, 485 F. Supp. 263 at 266 (D.D.C. 1980). The IRS zealously guards the anonymity of the taxpayers, which explains the use of the word "you" instead of a name in this memorandum.—*Ed.*]

memorandum stated that the answer to both questions is that there is no categorical rule.] ...

We believe, fundamentally, ... that charity property must be administered exclusively in the beneficial interest of the charitable purposes to which it is dedicated. The duties and limitations growing out of that principle, and the remedies for their violation, are essentially equitable in nature, and cannot be reduced to mechanical rules of application....

Consequently, if there is substantial evidence of real, charitable purpose—that is, a purpose to accomplish a charitable objective of substance and one that is not a sham or inconsequential in the light of the organization's resources—in the manner of administration of an organization's resources, including the endeavors respecting the devotion of property to the production of income, and no compelling proof to the contrary, there is no tenable legal basis for saying that an organization's "primary purpose" in respect to the administration of its properties—i.e., its operations—is other than charitable.

On the other hand, if there is a lack of evidence that the full beneficial use of property is being applied to the accomplishment of any such charitable end—either currently or in the reasonably determinable future, then doubt is raised as to whether the properties are being administered exclusively in the beneficial interest of any charitable object or to "effectuate" the charitable purposes to which it is dedicated. This, of course, is the same as the question of whether the organization is being "operated" exclusively for charitable purpose within the terms of the charity provisions of the Code....

[T]he ultimate determination in application of the "primary purpose" requirement of the regulations is one of the presence or the absence of evidence of purpose to accomplish a charitable end or object in the administration of an organization's property—not a comparison of the "amount" of one kind of purpose or activity with another kind of purpose or activity. In that respect, the idea of an organization carrying on a charitable program "reasonably commensurate with its resources" was not expressed in the ... case with any idea that it would serve as a precise indicator of charitable purpose or precise gauge as to when an organization's "primary purpose" is charitable and when an organization's "primary purpose" is to carry on unrelated trade or business. It was simply meant to convey the point that we have attempted to clarify here: Namely, that if an organization is carrying on a real and substantial charitable program reasonably commensurate with its resources, that is just about the most conclusive evidence one could have as to charitable purpose of an organization in the administration of its properties.

The idea of a charitable program "reasonably commensurate" with an organization's financial resources is admittedly not a precise concept. Nevertheless, there are situations in which men of reasonable judgment would agree that a particular program either does broadly meet such standard or does not even remotely meet such standard. Those were the types of cases at which the ... rule was principally directed.

NOTES AND QUESTIONS

1. Another "commercial hue" case is *Family Trust of Massachusetts v. United States*, 722 F.3d 355 (DC Cir. 2013) (trustee of pooled trusts denied exemption because its activities were too commercial). For further reading on this commerciality issue, see Lloyd Hitoshi Mayer, *The "Independent" Sector: Fee-for-Service Charity and the Limits of Autonomy*, 65 VAND. L. REV. 51 (2012); John D. Colombo, *Making and Spending Money in Nonprofits: Reforming Internal Revenue Code Provisions on Commercial Activity by Charities*, 76 FORDHAM L. REV. 67 (2007); R. Charles Miller, *Comment: Rendering unto Caesar: Religious Publishers and the Public Benefit Rule*, 134 U. PA. L. REV. 433 (1986).

2. Professor Weisbrod's article questioned the wisdom of commercialization of the nonprofit sector and suggested enterprise and tax incentives to discourage commercial activity. In 2012, an empirical study that examined the tax forms of 700 New York City social service organizations confirmed his hypothesis. The study found that organizations that engaged in unrelated business activities spent less on their exempt-purpose activities. Rebecca Tekula, SOCIAL ENTERPRISE: INNOVATION OR MISSION DISTRACTION? (2012). *See* David Zax, *The Thin Mint Paradox*, FAST COMPANY (Nov. 10, 2010).

3. Weisbrod is not the only one questioning whether YMCAs have become too commercial. In 2014, YMCAs in Idaho, Kansas, and Colorado successfully fought off attempts to require them to pay property taxes after competitors complained about their unfair advantage. The Colorado opinion was affirmed by the Colorado Court of Appeals in 2016. It granted the YMCA of the Rockies a religious exemption from local property taxes. *Grand Cnty. Bd. of Comm'rs v. Colo. Prop. Tax Adm'r*, 2016 COA 2, 2016 Colo. App. LEXIS 20 (Colo. Ct. App. 2016).

   Do the localities complaining about commercialization have a point? Nationally, the YMCA has revenues of $6.6 billion, $4.7 billion of which comes directly from fees for goods and services.[10] Has the YMCA become so commercial that it should lose its tax exemption? Why or why not? Do the religious origins of this organization affect your decision? What additional information would help you make this determination?

4. Later in this chapter, you will read a case concerning whether the National Collegiate Athletic Association (NCAA) should have paid unrelated business income tax on the advertising revenue from the program for the Final Four basketball tournament. You will also read about corporate sponsorships of college athletic events. The NCAA is big business. The NCAA"s 2014 Form 990 revealed almost $900 million in program service revenues, $12 million

---

[10] The statistic is from *The 2015 NPT Top 100* (Nonprofit Times, 2015). For information on the tax controversies, see Rick Cohen, *Kansas Rejects Tax-Exempt Status for For-Profit Fitness Clubs*, NONPROFIT QUARTERLY (May 5, 2014); Rick Cohen, *New YMCA Property Tax Controversy: The Y as a Religious Institution*, NONPROFIT QUARTERLY (Aug. 21, 2014); and Harrison Berry, *YMCA Tax Exemption Reinstated, Ada County Commissioners Reverse Earlier Action*, BOISE WEEKLY (July 3, 2014).

in investments, and \$3 million in contributions. The form also indicated that "the primary purpose of the NCAA is to maintain intercollegiate athletics as an integral part of the educational program and the athlete as an integral part of the student body." In your opinion, is the NCAA in danger of losing its §501(c)(3) status for being too commercial under any of the tests described above?

5. The Internal Revenue Service (IRS) used the "commensurate in scope" test in the 1964 Revenue Ruling reproduced above, but it has never adopted regulations that could make the test useful to charities, the IRS, and the courts. In 2014, the Advisory Committee on Tax Exempt and Government Entities recommended "that the IRS open a regulation project to: (1) formalize the commensurate test articulated in Rev. Rul. 64-182; and (2) to reject application of the commerciality test." Advisory Committee on Tax Exempt and Government Entities, 2014 REPORT OF RECOMMENDATIONS (June 17, 2014). For further discussion of this test, see Testimony of John D. Colombo, House Committee on Ways and Means, Subcommittee on Oversight (July 25, 2012); Tavis Blais & Cristopher T. Bird, *Should the Commensurate Test Force Greater Spending by Public Charities?*, 63 EXEMPT ORG. TAX REV. 31 (April 2009)' John D. Colombo, *Commercial Activity and Charitable Tax Exemption*, 44 WM. & MARY L. REV. 487 (2002).

6. Questions about the effect of commercial activity on tax exemption can, and are, also raised at the state and local levels. As discussed in Chapter 4, the Morristown Medical Center and Princeton University have both faced challenges to their property tax exemptions, on the grounds that their activities were too commercial. In late 2015, Morristown Medical Center settled its suit, agreeing to pay \$15.5 million in back taxes and penalties, plus annual property taxes on 24% of the hospital's property from 2016 to 2025. As this book went to press, the Princeton case was preparing for trial, which was scheduled for October 2016.

IV. UNRELATED BUSINESS INCOME

In the 1930s and 1940s, nonprofit organizations were free to engage in business activities, so long as the profits were used for charitable or other exempt purposes. The Supreme Court promulgated this "destination of income" test in *Trinidad v. Sagrada Orden*, 263 U.S. 578 (1924). Sagrada Orden was a Philippine religious order that received the bulk of its income from large real estate and securities holdings, but it had smaller revenues from the sale of wine, chocolates, and other articles for use within its religious missions. The Insular Collector of the Philippine Islands (then under U.S. jurisdiction) maintained that although the organization was organized and operated for exempt purposes, it was not exclusively operated for those purposes. The court held that the predecessor to §501(c)(3) in effect at the time permitted exempt organizations to have income and "said nothing about the source of the income, but makes the destination the ultimate test of exemption." In other words, so long as the destination of the income was to a charitable organization, the income would not be taxed.

After this case, several organizations entered into commercial activities, often through separate entities called "feeders," which distributed the profits to their tax-exempt owners. The best known of the cases questioning these arrangements was *C. F. Mueller Co. v. Comm'r*, 190 F.2d 120 (3d Cir. 1951). C. F. Mueller was the nation's largest manufacturer of noodles and macaroni. It distributed all its profits to New York University's law school, a practice the third circuit found fully consistent with its tax-exempt status because all its profits were being used for tax-exempt purposes.

In 1950, Congress responded by establishing the unrelated business income tax (UBIT). It also made feeder organizations that engage in a trade or business for profit ineligible for exemption if the only reason for exemption is that their profits are destined for charitable purposes. The legislative history suggests that Congress was concerned with unfair competition,[11] although the language of the statute does not mention competition. The need for revenue to finance the Korean War was probably also a consideration. The law has evolved over the years, so that churches, social clubs, and fraternal beneficiary societies that were initially exempt from the tax are now included, and several specialized exemptions have been added.

Many of the unrelated business income statutory provisions are reproduced below. The definition of unrelated business income has three key elements: (1) income from a trade or business (2) that is regularly carried on by the organization and (3) is not substantially related to the performance of the organization's tax-exempt functions.

The three cases that follow the statutes stress each of these parts of the definition in turn. Determining whether the income is derived from profit-seeking activities not related to an organization's exempt purposes is the most difficult of the three issues to apply. Not only are the regulations rather abstract, but the determinations are very fact specific. In many museum stores, for example, the determination of whether something is related to the tax-exempt purpose is made on an item-by-item basis.

Three activities are specifically excluded from the definitions of an unrelated trade or business: any trade or business (1) in which substantially all the labor is performed by unpaid volunteers; (2) that is carried on primarily for the convenience of members, students, officers, or employees of a §501(c)(3) organization, a state college, or a university; and (3) which consists of selling donated merchandise, such as a thrift shop. Several other specialized exceptions are also provided in the statute. They include bingo, certain sponsorship

---

[11] Representative John Dingell had warned that unless Congress took action, "the macaroni monopoly will be in the hands of the university ... and eventually all the noodles produced in this country will be produced by corporations held or created by universities." Hearings Before the House Comm. on Ways and Means, 81st Cong., 2d Sess. 579-580 (1950).

payments that are not advertising, distribution of low-cost items as part of fund-raising solicitations, and other, more specialized exceptions (such as the rental of telephone poles). The corporate sponsorship regulations are included in this chapter.

Finally, the Code contains numerous "modifications," which, in effect, exempt all passive income from UBIT, provided that the income is not derived from debt-financed property or from controlled organizations. Thus, passive investment income, rents, royalties, research income, and payments from a controlled organization are generally exempt from unrelated business taxable income (UBTI). The *Sierra Club* case in section IV.F discusses the meaning of the royalty modification.

Despite (or perhaps because of) these complicated rules and regulations, only 2.7% of the nonprofit organizations that filed Forms 990 in 2008 reported any unrelated business income that year. The total reported unrelated business income in 2008 was $10.3 billion. After deducting business expenses, only half the organizations reporting UBTI paid any tax, and in total, they paid $336 million.[12]

A. UBIT Statutes

INTERNAL REVENUE CODE §511 IMPOSITION OF TAX ON UNRELATED BUSINESS INCOME OF CHARITABLE, ETC., ORGANIZATIONS

(a) Charitable, etc., organizations taxable at corporation rates.

(1) Imposition of tax. There is hereby imposed for each taxable year on the unrelated business taxable income (as defined in section 512) of every organization described in paragraph (2) a tax computed as provided in section 11. In making such computation for purposes of this section, the term "taxable income" as used in section 11 shall be read as "unrelated business taxable income."

(2) Organizations subject to tax.

(A) Organizations described in sections 401(a) and 501(c). The tax imposed by paragraph (1) shall apply in the case of any organization (other than a trust described in subsection (b) or an organization described in section 501(c)(1)) which is exempt, except as provided in this part or part II (relating to private foundations), from taxation under this subtitle by reason of section 501(a).

(B) State colleges and universities. The tax imposed by paragraph (1) shall apply in the case of any college or university which is an agency or instrumentality of any government or any political subdivision thereof, or

---

[12] Katherine Toran, *The Unrelated Business Income Tax*, Urban Institute Center on Nonprofits and Philanthropy (2013).

which is owned or operated by a government or any political subdivision thereof, or by any agency or instrumentality of one or more governments or political subdivisions. Such tax shall also apply in the case of any corporation wholly owned by one or more such colleges or universities....

INTERNAL REVENUE CODE §512

(a) Definitions. For purposes of this title—

(1) General rule: Except as otherwise provided in this subsection, the term "unrelated business taxable income" means the gross income derived by any organization from any unrelated trade or business (as defined in section 513) regularly carried on by it, less the deductions allowed by this chapter which are directly connected with the carrying on of such trade or business, both computed with the modifications provided in subsection (b)....

(b) Modifications: The modifications referred to in subsection (a) are the following:

(1) There shall be excluded all dividends, interest, payments with respect to securities loans..., amounts received or accrued as consideration for entering into agreements to make loans, and annuities, and all deductions directly connected with such income.

(2) There shall be excluded all royalties....

(3) In the case of rents—

(A) Except as provided in subparagraph (B), there shall be excluded—

(i) all rents from real property . . .

(ii) all rents from personal property . . . leased with such real property, if the rents attributable to such personal property are an incidental amount of the total rents received or accrued under the lease, determined at the time the personal property is placed in service

(B) Subparagraph (A) shall not apply—

(i) if more than 50 percent of the total rent received or accrued under the lease is attributable to the personal property described in subparagraph A(ii), or

(ii) if the determination of the amount of such rent

depends in whole or in part on the income or profits derived by any person from the property leased (other than an amount based on a fixed percentage or percentages of receipts or sales).

(C) There shall be excluded all deductions directly connected with rents excluded under subparagraph (A).

(4) Notwithstanding paragraph (1), (2), (3), or (5), in the case of debt-financed property ... there shall be included, as an item of gross income derived from an unrelated trade or business, the amount ascertained under section 514(a)(1), and there shall be allowed, as a deduction, the amount ascertained under section 514(a)(2).

(5) There shall be excluded all gains or losses from the sale, exchange, or other disposition of property other than—

(A) stock in trade or other property of a kind which would properly be includible in inventory if on hand at the close of the taxable year or

(B) property held primarily for sale to customers in the ordinary course of the trade or business....

(7) There shall be excluded all income derived from research for (A) the United States, or any of its agencies or instrumentalities, or (B) any State or political subdivision thereof; and there shall be excluded all deductions directly connected with such income.

(8) In the case of a college, university, or hospital, there shall be excluded all income derived from research performed for any person, and all deductions directly connected with such income.

(9) In the case of an organization operated primarily for purposes of carrying on fundamental research the results of which are freely available to the general public, there shall be excluded all income derived from research performed for any person, and all deductions directly connected with such income....

INTERNAL REVENUE CODE §513. UNRELATED TRADE OR BUSINESS

(a) General rule.

The term "unrelated trade or business" means, in the case of any organization subject to the tax imposed by section 511, any trade or business the conduct of which is not substantially related (aside from the need of such organization for income or funds or the use it makes of the profits derived) to the exercise or performance by such organization of its charitable, educational, or other purpose or function constituting the basis for its exemption under section 501 (or, in the case of an organization described in section 511(a)(2)(B), to the exercise or performance of any purpose or function described in section 501(c)(3)), except that such term does not include any trade or business—

(1) in which substantially all the work in carrying on such trade or business is performed for the organization without compensation; or

(2) which is carried on, in the case of an organization described in section 501(c)(3) or in the case of a college or university described in section 511(a)(2)(B), by the organization primarily for the convenience of its members, students, patients, officers, or employees, or, in the case

of a local association of employees described in section 501(c)(4) organized before May 27, 1969, which is the selling by the organization of items of work-related clothes and equipment and items normally sold through vending machines, through food dispensing facilities, or by snack bars, for the convenience of its members at their usual places of employment; or

(3) which is the selling of merchandise, substantially all of which has been received by the organization as gifts or contributions....

(c) Advertising, etc., activities.

For purposes of this section, the term "trade or business" includes any activity which is carried on for the production of income from the sale of goods or the performance of services. For purposes of the preceding sentence, an activity does not lose identity as a trade or business merely because it is carried on within a larger aggregate of similar activities or within a larger complex of other endeavors which may, or may not, be related to the exempt purposes of the organization. Where an activity carried on for profit constitutes an unrelated trade or business, no part of such trade or business shall be excluded from such classification merely because it does not result in profit....

(h) Certain distributions of low cost articles without obligation to purchase and exchanges and rentals of member lists.

(1) In general.

In the case of an organization which is described in section 501 and contributions to which are deductible under paragraph (2) or (3) of section 170(c), the term "unrelated trade or business" does not include—

(A) activities relating to the distribution of low cost articles if the distribution of such articles is incidental to the solicitation of charitable contributions, or

(B) any trade or business which consists of—

(i) exchanging with another such organization names and addresses of donors to (or members of) such organization, or

(ii) renting such names and addresses to another such organization. . . .

(3) Distribution which is incidental to the solicitation of charitable contributions described.

For purposes of this subsection, any distribution of low cost articles by an organization shall be treated as a distribution incidental to the solicitation of charitable contributions only if—

(A) such distribution is not made at the request of the distributee,

(B) such distribution is made without the express consent of the distributee, and

(C) the articles so distributed are accompanied by—

(i) a request for a charitable contribution (as defined in section 170(c)) by the distributee to such organization, and

(ii) a statement that the distributee may retain the low cost article regardless of whether such distributee makes a charitable contribution to such organization.

B. TRADE OR BUSINESS

UNITED STATES V. AMERICAN BAR ENDOWMENT

477 U.S. 105 (1986)

Justice MARSHALL delivered the opinion of the Court.

The first issue in this case is whether income that a tax-exempt charitable organization derives from offering group insurance to its members constitutes "unrelated business income" subject to tax under §§511 through 513 of the Internal Revenue Code (Code), 26 U.S.C. §§511-513. The second issue is whether the organization's members may claim a charitable deduction for the portion of their premium payments that exceeds the actual cost to the organization of providing insurance.

[*Editor's Note:* The part of this case that discusses the charitable deduction issue is reproduced in Chapter 5. Recall that members of the American Bar Association purchased insurance from the American Bar Endowment. The proceeds were distributed to charitable organizations.]

II

We recently discussed the history and structure of the unrelated business income provisions of the Code in *United States v. American College of Physicians*, 475 U.S. 834 (1986). The Code imposes a tax, at ordinary corporate rates, on the income that a tax-exempt organization obtains from an "unrelated trade or business ... regularly carried on by it." §§512(a)(1), 511(a)(1). An "unrelated trade or business" is "any trade or business the conduct of which is not substantially related ... to the exercise or performance by such organization of its charitable, educational, or other purpose," §513(a). The Code thus sets up a three-part test. ABE's insurance program is taxable if it (1) constitutes a trade or business; (2) is regularly carried on; and (3) is not substantially related to ABE's tax-exempt purposes. Treas. Reg. §1.513-1(a), 26 CFR §1.513-1(a) (1985); *American College of Physicians, supra*, at 838-839. ABE concedes that the latter two portions of this test are satisfied. Its defense is based solely on the proposition that its insurance program does not constitute a trade or business.

A

In the Tax Reform Act of 1969, Pub. L. 91-172, 83 Stat. 487, Congress defined a "trade or business" as "any activity which is carried on for the production of income from the sale of goods or the performance of services," §513(c). The Secretary of the Treasury has provided further clarification of that definition in Treas. Reg. §1.513-1(b) (1985), which provides: "in general, any activity of [an exempt] organization which is carried on for the production of income and which otherwise possesses the characteristics required to constitute 'trade or business' within the meaning of section 162" is a trade or business for purposes of 26 U.S.C. §§511-513.

ABE's insurance program falls within the literal language of these definitions. ABE's activity is both "the sale of goods" and "the performance of services," and possesses the general characteristics of a trade or business. Certainly the assembling of a group of better-than-average insurance risks, negotiating on their behalf with insurance companies, and administering a group policy are activities that can be—and are—provided by private commercial entities in order to make a profit. ABE itself earns considerable income from its program. Nevertheless, the Claims Court and Court of Appeals concluded that ABE does not carry out its insurance program in order to make a profit.... Because ABE does not operate its insurance program in a competitive, commercial manner, the Claims Court decided, that program is not a trade or business. The Court of Appeals adopted this reasoning.

The Claims Court rested its conclusion on four factors. First, it found that "the program was devised as a means for fundraising and has been so presented and perceived from its inception." Second, the court found that the program's phenomenal success in generating dividends for ABE was evidence of noncommercial behavior. The court noted that ABE's insurance program has provided $81.9 million in dividends in its 28 years of operation, and concluded that such large profits could not be the result of commercial success, but must proceed from the generosity of ABE's members. Third, and most important, in the court's view, was the fact that ABE's members collectively had the power to change ABE's conduct of the insurance program so as to drastically reduce premiums. That the members had not done so was strong evidence that they sought to further ABE's charitable purposes by paying higher insurance rates than necessary. Fourth, because ABE did not underwrite insurance or act as a broker, it was not competing with other commercial entities.

It appears, then, that the Claims Court viewed ABE as engaging in two separate activities—the provision of insurance and the acceptance of contributions in the form of dividends. If so, the unspoken premise of the Claims Court's decision is that ABE's income is not a result of the first activity, but of the second. There is some sense to this reasoning; should ABE sell a product to its members for more than that product's fair market value, it could argue to the IRS that the members intended to pay excessive prices as a form of contribution, and that some formula should be adopted to separate the income received into taxable profits and nontaxable contributions. Even if we viewed it as appropriate for the federal courts to engage in such a quasi-legislative activity, however, there is no factual basis for the Claims Court's attempt to do so in this case.

B

We cannot agree with the Claims Court that the enormous dividends generated by ABE's insurance program demonstrate that those dividends cannot constitute "profits." Were ABE's insurance markedly more expensive than other insurance products available to its members, but ABE nevertheless kept the patronage of those members, we might plausibly conclude that generosity was the reason for the program's success. The Claims Court did not find, however, that this was the case. ABE prices its insurance to remain competitive with the rest of the market.... Thus ABE's members never squarely face the decision whether to support ABE or to reduce their own insurance costs.

The Claims Court concluded that "such profit margins [as ABE's] cannot be maintained year after year in a competitive market."... The court apparently reasoned that ABE's staggering success would inevitably induce other firms to offer similar programs to ABA members unless that success is the result of charitable intentions rather than price-sensitive purchasing decisions. It is possible, of course, that ABE's members genuinely intend to support ABE by paying higher premiums than necessary, and would pay those high premiums even if a competing group insurance plan offered very low premiums. But that is by no means the only possible explanation for the market's failure to provide competition for ABE. Lacking a factual basis for concluding that generosity is at the core of ABE's success, we can easily view this case as a standard example of monopoly pricing. ABE has a unique asset—its access to the ABA's members and their highly favorable mortality and morbidity rates—and it has chosen to appropriate for itself all of the profit possible from that asset, rather than sharing any with its members.

The argument that ABE's members could change the insurance program and receive the bulk of the dividends themselves if they so desired is unconvincing. Were ABE to give each member a choice between retaining his pro rata share of dividends or assigning them to ABE, the organization would have a strong argument that those dividends constituted a voluntary donation. That, however, is not the case here. ABE requires its members to assign it all dividends as a condition for participating in the insurance program. It is simply incorrect to characterize the assignment of dividends by each member as "voluntary" simply because the members theoretically could band together and attempt to change the policy....

The Claims Court also erred in concluding that ABE's insurance program did not present the potential for unfair competition. The undisputed purpose of the unrelated business income tax was to prevent tax-exempt organizations from competing unfairly with businesses whose earnings were taxed.... This case presents an example of precisely the sort of unfair competition that Congress intended to prevent. If ABE's members may deduct part of their premium payments as a charitable contribution, the effective cost of ABE's insurance will be lower than the cost of competing policies that do not offer tax benefits. Similarly, if ABE may escape taxes on its earnings, it need not be as profitable as its commercial counterparts in order to receive the same return on its investment. Should a commercial company attempt to displace ABE as the group policyholder, therefore, it would be at a decided disadvantage.

The Claims Court failed to find any taxable entities that compete with ABE, and therefore found no danger of unfair competition. It is likely, however, that many of ABE's members belong to other organizations that offer group insurance policies. Employers, trade associations, and financial services companies frequently offer group insurance policies. Presumably those entities are taxed on their profits, and their policyholders may not deduct any part of the premiums paid. Such entities may therefore find it difficult to compete for the business of any ABE members who are otherwise eligible to participate in these group insurance programs.

The only valid argument in ABE's favor, therefore, is that the insurance program is billed as a fundraising effort. That fact, standing alone, cannot be determinative, or any exempt organization could engage in a tax-free business by "giving away" its product in return for a "contribution" equal to the market value of the product. ABE further contends that it must prevail because the Claims Court found that ABE's profits represent contributions rather than business income.... The undisputed facts, however, simply will not support the inference that the dividends ABE receives are charitable contributions from its members rather than profits from its insurance program. Moreover, the Claims Court failed to articulate a legal rule that would permit it to split ABE's activities into the gratuitous provision of a service and the acceptance of voluntary contributions, and we find no such rule in the Code or regulations. Even if we assumed, however, that the court's failure to attach the label "trade or business" to ABE's insurance program constitutes a finding of fact, we would be constrained to hold that finding clearly erroneous....

Justice STEVENS, dissenting.

... "The problem at which the tax on unrelated business income is directed ... is primarily that of unfair competition." In considering the ABE insurance fundraising, then, it is appropriate to assume that, if the ABE were funded by operating a normal macaroni company and receiving an unfair competitive advantage from its tax exemption, it would be a "trade or business" within the Act and taxable. On the other hand, it is equally clear that, if the ABE simply provided insurance for ABA members at very low cost, and sent the insurance dividends with an urgent request that the dividends be assigned to the Endowment, the arrangement would not be a "trade or business," and would not be taxable. The central issue in this case is thus whether the ABE's insurance program should be viewed as akin to the macaroni company, and thus a "trade or business," or as akin to the dividend assignment request, and thus not a "trade or business."

I believe that the ABE's activities are far closer to the latter than the former for two reasons. First, there is no danger of unfair competition, the problem that the unrelated business tax addresses. Second, the program has functioned as a charitable fundraising effort, rather than as a business.

I

An understanding of the purpose of the unrelated business income tax exposes a basic error in the Court's analysis. As noted, that purpose is to protect commercial enterprises from the unfair competition that may be generated by the operation of competing businesses by tax-free organizations. There is no evidence in the record, despite more than three weeks of trial and numerous witnesses, to support the notion that the Endowment's provision of insurance to its members has had any competitive impact whatsoever. The Court relies on a parade of hypotheticals to justify its conclusion that there is some effect on competition....

The legislative history further underscores the fact that the ABE insurance operation poses none of the possible effects on competition that the unrelated business tax was intended to address. Congress has twice made clear that insurance programs by other nonprofit organizations are not subject to the unrelated business tax. When Congress substantially revised the unrelated business tax in 1969, the accompanying legislative history emphasized that the group insurance policies provided by fraternal organizations were not intended to be subject to the unrelated business tax. Similarly, when a question arose concerning the taxability of income from insurance programs administered by veterans' organizations, Congress enacted legislation to ensure that the insurance income would not be taxed. Indeed, Congress found the taxation of the veterans' insurance operations so contrary to its intent that it took the unusual step of making the 1972 amendment fully retroactive to 1969....

In short, a proper consideration of the purpose of the unrelated business tax leads to a conclusion that the ABE's insurance program is not a "trade or business."...

C. REGULARLY CARRIED ON

NATIONAL COLLEGIATE ATHLETIC ASS'N V. COMM'R OF INTERNAL REVENUE

914 F.2d 1417 (10th Cir. 1990)

I

The NCAA is an unincorporated association of more than 880 colleges, universities, athletic conferences and associations, and other educational organizations and groups related to intercollegiate athletics, for which it has been the major governing organization since 1906. The NCAA is also an "exempt organization" under section 501(c)(3) of the Code, and hence is exempt from federal income taxes. One of the purposes of the NCAA, as described in the organization's constitution, is "to supervise the conduct of ... regional and national athletic events under the auspices of this Association." Pursuant to this purpose, the NCAA sponsors some seventy-six collegiate championship events in twenty-one different sports for women and men on an annual basis. The most prominent of these tournaments, and the NCAA's biggest revenue generator, is the Men's Division I Basketball Championship. The tournament is held at different sites each year. In 1982, regional rounds took place at a variety of sites, and the Louisiana Superdome in New Orleans was the host for the "Final Four," the tournament's semifinal and final rounds. In that year, the Championship consisted of forty-eight teams playing forty-seven games on eight days over a period of almost three weeks. The teams played in a single-game elimination format, with each of the four regional winners moving into the Final Four.

The NCAA contracted with Lexington Productions, a division of Jim Host and Associates, Inc. ("Host" or "Publisher"), in 1981 to print and publish the program for the 1982 Final Four games. The purpose of such programs, according to the NCAA's then-director of public relations, is "to enhance the experience primarily for the fans attending the game.... [It also] gives the NCAA an opportunity to develop information about some of its other purposes that revolve around promoting sports [as a] part of higher education and demonstrating that athletes can be good students as well as good participants." . .

The "Official Souvenir Program" for the 1982 Final Four round of the tournament was some 129 pages long, and it featured pictures of NCAA athletes such as Michael Jordan and articles on the NCAA itself, on New Orleans, on individual athletes, on championships from prior years, and on the Final Four teams: Georgetown, Houston, Louisville, and North Carolina. Advertisements made up a substantial portion of the program, some of which were placed by national companies. Among the products and services so displayed were Buick automobiles, Miller beer, Texaco motor oil, Fuji film, Maxwell House coffee, Nike sneakers, McDonald's fast food, Coca-Cola soda, Xerox photocopiers, ESPN cable network, and Popeye's Famous Fried Chicken. Other advertisers were local New Orleans merchants. A number of the New Orleans advertisements, including those for restaurants, hotels, and rental cars, apparently were directed at out-of-town tournament attendees. But these advertisements were exceeded in number by those placed by New Orleans/Louisiana companies not specifically related to the tourist industry. Among the local advertisers were the Canal Barge Company, the National Bank of Commerce in Jefferson Parish, Breit Marine Surveying, Inc., Pontchartrain Materials Corp., McDermott Marine Construction, and Tri-Parish Construction & Materials, Inc.

The NCAA's total revenue from the 1982 Men's Division I Basketball Championship was $18,671,874. The NCAA reported none of this amount as unrelated business taxable income on its federal income tax return for the fiscal year ending August 31, 1982. The Commissioner mailed the NCAA a notice of deficiency in which he determined that the NCAA was liable for $10,395.14 in taxes on $55,926.71 of unrelated business taxable income from the program advertising revenue. The NCAA petitioned the tax court for a redetermination of the deficiency set forth by the Commissioner. The tax court determined that this revenue was unrelated business taxable income, and that it was not excludable from the tax as a royalty....

III

Section 511 of the Code imposes a tax on the unrelated business taxable income of exempt organizations. Section 512(a)(1) of the Code defines the term "unrelated business taxable income" as "the gross income derived by any organization from any unrelated trade or business ... regularly carried on by it...."

The NCAA's advertising revenue therefore must be considered unrelated business taxable income if: "(1) It is income from trade or business; (2) such trade or business is regularly carried on by the organization; and (3) the conduct of such trade or business is not substantially related (other than through the production of funds) to the organization's performance of its exempt functions." Treas. Reg. §1.513-1(a). If a taxpayer shows that it does not meet any one of these three requirements, the taxpayer is not liable for the unrelated business income tax.

The NCAA concedes that its program advertising was a "trade or business" not "substantially related" to its exempt purpose. The only question remaining, therefore, is whether the trade or business was "regularly carried on" by the organization. The meaning of the term "regularly carried on" is not defined by the language of the statute. Accordingly, we turn to the Treasury Regulations for assistance.

Section 1.513-1(c) of the Treasury Regulations provides a discussion of the phrase "regularly carried on." The general principles set out there direct us to consider "the frequency and continuity with which the activities productive of the income are conducted *and* the manner in which they are pursued." Treas. Reg. §1.513-1(c)(1) (emphasis added). As a cautionary note, the regulations emphasize that whether a trade or business is regularly carried on must be assessed "in light of the purpose of the unrelated business income tax to place exempt organization business activities upon the same tax basis as the nonexempt business endeavors with which they compete."

The regulations then move beyond the general principles and set out a process for applying the principles to specific cases. The first step is to consider the normal time span of the particular activity, and then determine whether the length of time alone suggests that the activity is regularly carried on, or only intermittently carried on. *See id.* §1.513-1(c)(2)(i). If the activity is "of a kind normally conducted by nonexempt commercial organizations on a *year-round* basis, the conduct of such [activity] by an exempt organization over a period of only a few weeks does not constitute the regular carrying on of trade or business." *Id.* (Emphasis added.) As an example of a business not regularly carried on, the regulations describe a hospital auxiliary's operation of a sandwich stand for only two weeks at a state fair. In contrast, the regulations deem the operation of a commercial parking lot every Saturday as a regularly-carried-on activity. *Id.*

If the activity is "of a kind normally undertaken by nonexempt commercial organizations only on a *seasonal* basis, the conduct of such activities by an exempt organization during a *significant portion* of the season ordinarily constitutes the regular conduct of trade or business." *Id.* (Emphasis added.) The operation of a horse racing track several weeks a year is an example of a regularly-conducted seasonal business, because such tracks generally are open only during a particular season. *Id.*

A primary point of contention in this case is whether the NCAA's advertising business is normally a seasonal or year-round one, and whether it is intermittent or not. The tax court noted that the Commissioner looked at the short time span of the *tournament*, concluded that it was as much a "seasonal" event as the operation of a horse racing track, and then argued that the time involved in the tournament program advertising made it a regularly carried on business. The court observed that the NCAA, which did not agree with the Commissioner's "season" conclusion, also focused on the tournament itself in contending that the event's short time span made the activity in question intermittent. The tax court rejected these arguments as "placing undue emphasis on the tournament itself as the measure for determining whether petitioner regularly carried on the business at issue. Although sponsorship of a college basketball tournament and attendant circulation of tournament programs are seasonal events, the 'trade or business' of selling advertisements is not."

We agree that to determine the normal time span of the activity in this case, we should consider the business of *selling advertising space*, since that is the business the Commissioner contends is generating unrelated business taxable income. There is no dispute that the tournament itself is substantially related to the NCAA's exempt purpose and so, unlike the horse racing track, it should not be the business activity in question. *See American College of Physicians*, 475 U.S. at 839 ("Congress has declared unambiguously that the *publication of paid advertising* is a trade or business activity *distinct* from the publication of accompanying ... articles") (emphasis added). Since the publication of advertising is generally conducted on a year-round basis, we conclude that if the NCAA's sale of program advertising was conducted for only a few weeks, that time period could not, standing alone, convert the NCAA's business into one regularly carried on.

In regard to the question of how long the NCAA conducted its advertising business, ... [t]he tax court held, and the Commissioner argues, that the amount of preliminary time spent to solicit advertisements and prepare them for publication is relevant to the regularly-carried-on determination, and that the length of the tournament is not relevant. This position is contrary to the regulations and to existing case law. The language of the regulations alone suggests that preparatory time should not be considered. The sandwich stand example in the regulations, for instance, included a reference only to the two weeks it was operated at the state fair. *See* Treas. Reg. §1.513-1(c)(a)(i). The regulations do not mention time spent in planning the activity, building the stand, or purchasing the alfalfa sprouts for the sandwiches.

The case closest to the one here also does not evaluate preparatory time. In that case, *Suffolk County Patrolmen's Benevolent Ass'n v. Commissioner*, 77 T.C. 1314 (1981), an exempt organization staged a professional vaudeville show every year as a fundraising event, using a company with which it had contracted. The organization derived the vast majority of its receipts from the sale of advertising in a program guide distributed to show patrons and to anyone who requested it. The shows generally consisted of three or four performances stretching over two weekends. The tax court found that preparation for the shows and the program, including the solicitation of advertisements, lasted eight to sixteen weeks, but it then emphasized that "nowhere in the regulations or the legislative history of the tax on unrelated business income is there any mention of time apart from the duration of the event itself.... The fact that an organization seeks to insure the success of its fundraising venture by beginning to plan and prepare for it earlier should not adversely affect the tax treatment of the income derived from the venture."

As in *Suffolk County*, the advertising here was solicited for publication in a program for an event lasting a few weeks. The NCAA did put on evidence as to the duration of that event. While the length of the tournament is irrelevant for purposes of assessing the normal time span of the business of selling advertising space, we hold that, contrary to the tax court's conclusion, the tournament must be considered the actual time span of the business activity sought to be taxed here. The length of the tournament is the relevant time period because what the NCAA was selling, and the activity from which it derived the relevant income, was the publication of advertisements in programs distributed over a period of less than three weeks, and largely to spectators. Obviously, the tournament is the relevant time frame for those who chose to pay for advertisements in the program. This case is unlike *American College of Physicians*, 475 U.S. at 836, where advertisements were sold for each issue of a monthly medical journal. Accordingly, we conclude that the NCAA's involvement in the sale of advertising space was not sufficiently long-lasting to make it a regularly-carried-on business solely by reason of its duration.

The next step of the regulation's analysis is to determine whether activities which are intermittently conducted are nevertheless regularly carried on by virtue of the manner in which they are pursued. In general, according to the regulations, "exempt organization business activities which are engaged in only discontinuously or periodically will not be considered regularly carried on if they are conducted without the competitive and promotional efforts typical of commercial endeavors." Treas. Reg. §1.513-1(c)(2)(ii). As an example of an activity not characteristic of commercial endeavors, the regulations refer to "the publication of *advertising in programs for sports events* or music or drama performances." *Id.* (Emphasis added.) The NCAA places considerable emphasis on this latter sentence....

[W]e fail to see what evidence in addition to the advertisements themselves the tax court could require. The regulations discuss the business of advertising but refer only to advertisements published in programs, and not to any efforts to secure the advertisements. In *Suffolk County*, the tax court disregarded all but the advertisements themselves and stated that it is "entirely reasonable for an exempt organization to hire professionals in an effort to insure the success of a fundraiser, and there are no indications [in the applicable statutes and regulations] ... that the use of such professionals would cause an otherwise infrequent intermittent activity to be considered regularly carried on." 77 T.C. at 1323.

The Commissioner's assertion that the advertisements themselves are of a commercial nature deserves more discussion. It is true that a number of the advertisements are virtually indistinguishable from those that might appear in magazines like *Sports Illustrated*. A substantial number of other advertisements, however, particularly those placed by Louisiana companies not engaged in the tourist industry, seem to us to resemble more closely the "complimentary contributions" of Suffolk County.

The difficult question of whether the NCAA's advertising is of the type envisioned as commercial in nature, or instead as consistent with that connected to the "sports events" referred to in the regulations, is not one which we must answer now, however. For the final step in the process spelled out by the regulations requires us to consider whether, promotional efforts notwithstanding, an intermittent activity occurs "so infrequently that neither [its] recurrence nor the manner of [its] conduct will cause [it] to be regarded as trade or business regularly carried on." Treas. Reg. §1.513-1(c)(2)(iii). We conclude that the advertising here is such an infrequent activity. The programs containing the advertisements were distributed over less than a three-week span at an event that occurs only once a year. We consider this to be sufficiently infrequent to preclude a determination that the NCAA's advertising business was regularly carried on.

Our conclusion is buttressed by the regulation's admonition that we apply the regularly-carried-on test in light of the purpose of the tax to place exempt organizations doing business on the same tax basis as the comparable nonexempt business endeavors with which they compete. *See* Treas. Reg. §1.513-1(c)(1). The legislative history of the unrelated business income tax also convinces us that we must consider the impact an exempt organization's trade or business might have on its competition. The tax was a response to the situation prevailing before 1950, when an exempt organization could engage in any commercial business venture, secure in the knowledge that the profits generated would not be taxed as long as the *destination* of the funds was the exempt organization. The *source* of those funds did not affect their tax status....

[A]nalyzing the business in question in terms of its possible effect on prospective competitors helps to explain why an activity can occur "so infrequently" as to preclude a designation as a business regularly carried on. While the operation of a parking lot on a weekly basis occurs sufficiently frequently to threaten rival parking lot owners, the hospital auxiliary's annual sandwich stand is too infrequent a business to constitute a threat to sandwich shop owners. The competition in this case is between the NCAA's program and all publications that solicit the same advertisers. The competition thus includes weekly magazines such as *Sports Illustrated* and other publications which solicit automobile, beverage, photocopier, and fried chicken advertisements, to name a few. Viewed in this context, we conclude that the NCAA program, which is published only once a year, should not be considered an unfair competitor for the publishers of advertising. Application of the unrelated business tax here therefore would not further the statutory purpose. We hold that the NCAA's advertising business was not regularly carried on within the meaning of the Code.

The decision of the tax court is REVERSED.

D. SUBSTANTIALLY RELATED TO CHARITABLE PURPOSE

UNITED STATES V. AMERICAN COLLEGE OF PHYSICIANS

475 U.S. 834 (1986)

Justice MARSHALL delivered the opinion of the Court.

A tax-exempt organization must pay tax on income that it earns by carrying on a business not "substantially related" to the purposes for which the organization has received its exemption from federal taxation. The question before this Court is whether respondent, a tax-exempt organization, must pay tax on the profits it earns by selling commercial advertising space in its professional journal, The Annals of Internal Medicine.

I

Respondent, the American College of Physicians, is an organization exempt from taxation under §501(c)(3) of the Internal Revenue Code. The purposes of the College, as stated in its articles of incorporation, are to maintain high standards in medical education and medical practice; to encourage research, especially in clinical medicine; and to foster measures for the prevention of disease and for the improvement of public health. The principal facts were stipulated at trial. In furtherance of its exempt purposes, respondent publishes The Annals of Internal Medicine (Annals), a highly regarded monthly medical journal containing scholarly articles relevant to the practice of internal medicine. Each issue of Annals contains advertisements for pharmaceuticals, medical supplies, and equipment useful in the practice of internal medicine, as well as notices of positions available in that field. Respondent has a longstanding policy of accepting only advertisements containing information about the use of medical products, and screens proffered advertisements for accuracy and relevance to internal medicine. The advertisements are clustered in two groups, one at the front and one at the back of each issue.

[At issue was $55,965 in taxes paid on the net income earned from advertising in 1975. Annals sued in the United States Claims Court for refund of the taxes.]

The Claims Court . . . concluded that the advertisements in Annals were not substantially related to respondent's tax-exempt purposes. . . . Accordingly, the court determined that the advertising proceeds were taxable.

The Court of Appeals for the Federal Circuit reversed. . . . The Court of Appeals believed that the trial court had focused too much on the commercial character of the advertising business and not enough on the actual contribution of the advertisements to the education of the journal's readers. It held that respondent had established the requisite substantial relation and its entitlement to exemption from taxation.... We granted the Government's petition for certiorari and now reverse.

II

The taxation of business income not "substantially related" to the objectives of exempt organizations dates from the Revenue Act of 1950. The statute was enacted in response to perceived abuses of the tax laws by tax-exempt organizations that engaged in profit-making activities. Prior law had required only that the profits garnered by exempt organizations be used in furtherance of tax-exempt purposes, without regard to the source of those profits. As a result, tax-exempt organizations were able to carry on full-fledged commercial enterprises in competition with corporations whose profits were fully taxable....

Nevertheless, Congress did not force exempt organizations to abandon all commercial ventures, nor did it levy a tax only upon businesses that bore no relation at all to the tax-exempt purposes of an organization, as some of the 1950 Act's proponents had suggested. Rather, in the 1950 Act it struck a balance between its two objectives of encouraging benevolent enterprise and restraining unfair competition by imposing a tax on the "unrelated business taxable income" of tax-exempt organizations.

"Unrelated business taxable income" was defined as "the gross income derived by any organization from any unrelated trade or business ... regularly carried on by it...." §512(a)(1). Congress defined an "unrelated trade or business" as "any trade or business the conduct of which is not substantially related ... to the exercise or performance by such organization of its charitable, educational, or other purpose or function constituting the basis for its exemption...." §513(a). Whether respondent's advertising income is taxable, therefore, depends upon (1) whether the publication of paid advertising is a "trade or business," (2) whether it is regularly carried on, and (3) whether it is substantially related to respondent's tax-exempt purposes.

III

A

Satisfaction of the first condition is conceded in this case, as it must be, because Congress has declared unambiguously that the publication of paid advertising is a trade or business activity distinct from the publication of accompanying educational articles and editorial comment.

In 1967, the Treasury promulgated a regulation interpreting the unrelated business income provision of the 1950 Act. The regulation defined "trade or business" to include not only a complete business enterprise, but also any component activity of a business. Treas. Reg. §1.513-1(b).... The new regulation segregated the "trade or business" of selling advertising space from the "trade or business" of publishing a journal, an approach commonly referred to as "fragmenting" the enterprise of publishing into its component parts, , , ,

[T]he Tax Reform Act of 1969, Pub. L. 91-172, 83 Stat. 487 (1969 Act) . . . specifically endorsed the Treasury's concept of "fragmenting" the publishing enterprise into its component activities, and adopted, in a new §513(c), much of the language of the regulation that defined advertising as a separate trade or business: "Advertising, etc., activities ... an activity does not lose identity as a trade or business merely because it is carried on ... within a larger complex of other endeavors which may, or may not, be related to the exempt purposes of the organization." 26 U.S.C. §513(c). The statute clearly established advertising as a trade or business, the first prong of the inquiry into the taxation of unrelated business income.

The presence of the second condition, that the business be regularly carried on, is also undisputed here. The satisfaction of the third condition, however, that of "substantial relation," is vigorously contested, and that issue forms the crux of the controversy before us.

B

According to the Government, Congress and the Treasury established a blanket rule that advertising published by tax-exempt professional journals can never be substantially related to the purposes of those journals and is, therefore, always a taxable business. Respondent, however, contends that each case must be determined on the basis of the characteristics of the advertisements and journal in question. Each party finds support for its position in the governing statute and regulations issued by the Department of the Treasury.

In its 1967 regulations, the Treasury not only addressed the "fragmentation" issue discussed above, but also attempted to clarify the statutory "substantially related" standard found in §513(a). It provided that the conduct of a tax-exempt business must have a causal relation to the organization's exempt purpose (other than through the generation of income), and that "the production or distribution of the goods or the performance of the services from which the gross income is derived must *contribute importantly* to the accomplishment of [the exempt] purposes." Treas. Reg. §1.513-1(d)(2), 26 CFR §1.513-1(d)(2) (1985) (emphasis added). In illustration of its new test for substantial relation, the Treasury provided an example [of an exempt organization that published a journal that included articles and other editorial information that that contributed importantly to its tax exempt purpose. The advertisements in that journal did not, however, contribute importantly to the exempt purpose.]

The Government contends both that Example 7 creates a *per se* rule of taxation for journal advertising income and that Congress intended to adopt that rule, together with the remainder of the 1967 regulations, into law in the 1969 Act. We find both of these contentions unpersuasive.

Read as a whole, the regulations do not appear to create the type of blanket rule of taxability that the Government urges upon us. On the contrary, the regulations specifically condition tax exemption of business income upon the importance of the business activity's contribution to the particular exempt purpose at issue, and direct that "[w]hether activities productive of gross income contribute importantly to the accomplishment of any purpose for which an organization is granted an exemption depends *in each case* upon the facts and circumstances involved," §1.513-1(d)(2) (emphasis added). Example 7 need not be interpreted as being inconsistent with that general rule. Attributing to the term "example" its ordinary meaning, we believe that Example 7 is best construed as an illustration of one possible application, under given circumstances, of the regulatory standard for determining substantial relation. . . .

[The court then explained why it could not hold that Treasury set out a *per se* statement of law or that Congress interpreted those regulations as creating a blanket rule when it intended to adopt that rule into law in the 1969 Act.]

. We agree, therefore, with both the Claims Court and the Court of Appeals in their tacit rejection of the Government's argument that the Treasury and Congress intended to establish a *per se* rule requiring the taxation of income from all commercial advertisements of all tax-exempt journals without a specific analysis of the circumstances.

IV

It remains to be determined whether, in this case, the business of selling advertising space is "substantially related"—or, in the words of the regulation, "contributes importantly"—to the purposes for which respondent enjoys an exemption from federal taxation. Respondent has maintained throughout this litigation that the advertising in Annals performs an educational function supplemental to that of the journal's editorial content.... Testimony of respondent's witnesses at trial tended to show that drug advertising performs a valuable function for doctors by disseminating information on recent developments in drug manufacture and use.... In addition, respondent has contended that the role played by the Food and Drug Administration, in regulating much of the form and content of prescription-drug advertisements, enhances the contribution that such advertisements make to the readers' education. All of these factors, respondent argues, distinguish the advertising in Annals from standard commercial advertising. Respondent approaches the question of substantial relation from the perspective of the journal's subscribers; it points to the benefit that they may glean from reading the advertisements and concludes that that benefit is substantial enough to satisfy the statutory test for tax exemption. The Court of Appeals took the same approach. It concluded that the advertisements performed various "essential" functions for physicians, 743 F.2d, at 1576, and found a substantial relation based entirely upon the medically related content of the advertisements as a group.

The Government, on the other hand, looks to the conduct of the tax-exempt organization itself, inquiring whether the publishers of Annals have performed the advertising services in a manner that evinces an intention to use the advertisements for the purpose of contributing to the educational value of the journal. Also approaching the question from the vantage point of the College, the Claims Court emphasized the lack of a comprehensive presentation of the material contained in the advertisements. It commented upon the "hit-or-miss nature of the advertising," ... and observed that the "differences between ads plainly reflected the advertiser's marketing strategy rather than their probable importance to the reader." "[A]ny educational function [the advertising] may have served was incidental to its purpose of raising revenue."

We believe that the Claims Court was correct to concentrate its scrutiny upon the conduct of the College rather than upon the educational quality of the advertisements. For all advertisements contain some information, and if a modicum of informative content were enough to supply the important contribution necessary to achieve tax exemption for commercial advertising, it would be the rare advertisement indeed that would fail to meet the test. Yet the statutory and regulatory scheme, even if not creating a *per se* rule *against* tax exemption, is clearly antagonistic to the concept of a *per se* rule *for* exemption for advertising revenue. Moreover, the statute provides that a tax will be imposed on "any trade or business the *conduct* of which is not substantially related," 26 U.S.C. §513(a) (emphasis added), directing our focus to the manner in which the tax-exempt organization operates its business. The implication of the statute is confirmed by the regulations, which emphasize the "manner" of designing and selecting the advertisements. See Treas. Reg. §1.513-1(d)(4)(iv), Example 7, 26 CFR §1.513-1(d)(4)(iv), Example 7 (1985). Thus, the Claims Court properly directed its attention to the College's conduct of its advertising business, and it found the following pertinent facts:

> The evidence is clear that plaintiff did not use the advertising to provide its readers a comprehensive or systematic presentation of any aspect of the goods or services publicized. Those companies willing to pay for advertising space got it; others did not. Moreover, some of the advertising was for established drugs or devices and was repeated from one month to another, undermining the suggestion that the advertising was principally designed to alert readers of recent developments [citing, as examples, ads for Valium, Insulin and Maalox]. Some ads even concerned matters that had no conceivable relationship to the College's tax-exempt purposes.

These facts find adequate support in the record. Considering them in light of the applicable legal standard, we are bound to conclude that the advertising in Annals does not contribute importantly to the journal's educational purposes. This is not to say that the College could not control its publication of advertisements in such a way as to reflect an intention to contribute importantly to its educational functions. By coordinating the content of the advertisements with the editorial content of the issue, or by publishing only advertisements reflecting new developments in the pharmaceutical market, for example, perhaps the College could satisfy the stringent standards erected by Congress and the Treasury. In this case, however, we have concluded that the Court of Appeals erroneously focused exclusively upon the information that is invariably conveyed by commercial advertising, and consequently failed to give effect to the governing statute and regulations. Its judgment, accordingly, is Reversed.

REVENUE RULING 73-105, 1973-1 C.B. 264

The sale of scientific books and city souvenirs by a museum of folk art exempt from tax under section 501(c)(3) of the Code constitutes unrelated trade or business even though other items sold in the museum shop are related to its exempt function.

Advice has been requested whether, under the circumstances described below, the sales activities of an art museum exempt from Federal income tax as an educational organization under section 501(c)(3) of the Internal Revenue Code of 1954 constitute unrelated trade or business within the meaning of section 513 of the Code.

The organization maintains and operates an art museum devoted to the exhibition of American folk art. It operates a shop in the museum that offers for sale of the general public: (1) reproductions of works in the museum's own collection and reproductions of artistic works from the collections of other art museums (these reproductions take the form of prints suitable for framing, postcards, greeting cards, and slides); (2) metal, wood, and ceramic copies of American folk art objects from its own collection and similar copies of art objects from other collections of art works; and (3) instructional literature concerning the history and development of art and, in particular, of American folk art. The shop also rents originals or reproductions of paintings contained in its collection. All of its reproductions are imprinted with the name of the artist, the title or subject matter of the work from which it is reproduced, and the museum's name.

Also sold in the shop are scientific books and various souvenir items relating to the city in which the museum is located.

Section 511(a) of the Code imposes a tax upon the unrelated business taxable income (as defined in section 512) of organizations exempt from Federal income tax under section 501(c)(3). Section 512(a) of the Code defines "unrelated business taxable income" as the gross income from any "unrelated trade or business" regularly carried on by the organization as computed in the manner provided in section 512.

The term "unrelated trade or business" is defined in section 513 of the Code as any trade or business the conduct of which is not substantially related (aside from the need of such organization for income or funds or the use it makes of the profits derived) to the exercise or performance by such organization of its exempt functions.

Section 1.513-1(d)(2) of the Income Tax Regulations provides that trade or business is "substantially related" to purposes for which exemption is granted only if the production or distribution of the goods from which the gross income is derived "contributes importantly" to the accomplishment of those purposes.

Section 513(c) of the Code and section 1.513-(b) of the regulations provide that trade or business includes any activity which is carried on for the production of income from the sale of goods. An activity does not lose its identity as trade or business merely because it is carried on within a larger aggregate of similar activities or within a larger complex of other endeavors which may not be related to the exempt purposes of the organization.

Thus, sales of a particular line of merchandise may be considered separately to determine their relatedness to the exempt purpose. Section 1.513-1(d)(2) of the regulations emphasizes that it is the particular facts and circumstances involved in each case which determines whether the activities in question contribute importantly to the accomplishment of any purpose for which the organization is exempt.

An art museum is exempt as an educational organization on the basis of its ownership, maintenance, and exhibition for public viewing of an art collection. The sale and rental of reproductions of works from the museum's own collection and reproductions of artistic works not owned by the museum contribute importantly to the achievement of the museum's exempt educational purpose by making works of art familiar to a broader segment of the public, thereby enhancing the public's understanding and appreciation of art. The same is true with respect to literature relating to art.

Accordingly, it is held that these sales activities do not constitute unrelated trade or business under section 513 of the Code.

On the other hand, scientific books and souvenir items relating to the city where the museum is located have no causal relationship to art or to artistic endeavor and, therefore, the sale of these items does not contribute importantly to the accomplishments of the subject organization's exempt educational purpose which, as an art museum, is to enhance the public's understanding and appreciation of art. The fact that some of these items could, in a different context, be held related to the exempt educational purpose of some other exempt educational organization does not change the conclusion that in this context they do not contribute to the accomplishment of this organization's exempt educational purpose.

Additionally, under the provisions of section 513(c) of the Code, the activity with respect to sales of such items does not lose identity as trade or business merely because the museum also sells articles which do contribute importantly to the accomplishment of its exempt function.

Accordingly, it is held that the sale of those articles having no relationship to American folk art or to art generally, constitutes unrelated trade or business under section 513 of the Code.

E. EXCEPTIONS AND MODIFICATIONS

As mentioned above, Congress included several exceptions to the definition of unrelated business. The first three of these exceptions are businesses conducted by volunteers, sales of donated items, and businesses created for the convenience of the organization's members, students, patients, officers, or employees. Thus, thrift stores, hospital cafeterias, and museum gift shops that are run by volunteers are all exempt from UBIT, even if they would otherwise fit the definition of unrelated business activities.

Other exceptions include games of chance run by a nonprofit organization (bingo), entertainment at fairs and expositions, certain trade show activities, low-cost articles provided to donors as part of a fundraising activity, mailing lists, certain associate member dues for a tax-exempt agricultural or horticultural organization, and corporate sponsorship payments. The regulations covering sponsorship payments are described below. Drawing the line between advertising, which is generally included in UBTI, and corporate sponsorship can be tricky.

In addition to the listed exceptions are several "modifications," which, although technically included in the definition of UBTI, have the effect of creating additional exceptions. Congress passed the UBIT provisions to address competition between for-profit and nonprofit organizations. It assumed that such business endeavors must be active for competition to exist. Thus, income acquired in a passive manner is not taxed as UBTI, and income derived from dividends, interest, annuities, and royalties is not taxed. Rental income can be excluded, so long as the tax-exempt lessor is not actively providing services along with the rent, such as cleaning services; the rent is not for personal property; and the rent is not a way to disguise income or profits. The rules concerning rental income are complex and beyond the scope of this course, but in general, they follow the premise that passive income is not taxed, but active pursuit of unrelated business income is taxed to the extent that UBTI is created. To complicate matters, none of these modifications prevents UBTI if the passive income is traceable to borrowed funds. The following case explores the boundaries between active and passive income.

1. Rental and Royalty Payments

SIERRA CLUB, INC. V. COMMISSIONER

86 F.3d 1526 (9th Cir. 1996)

WIGGINS, Circuit Judge

I

[Editor's Note: At issue in this case was whether income that the Sierra Club received in 1985, 1986, and 1987 from renting its mailing list and entering into an affinity credit card program constituted passive income or unrelated business taxable income. The Sierra Club had developed a mailing list over the years, which it decided to rent to others. It retained ownership over the list but hired others to maintain and administer it and to oversee the external uses of the list. For the tax years in question, it received almost $1 million for the rental of its mailing lists.

The affinity credit card program involved an agreement between the Sierra Club and American Bankcard Services, Inc. (ABS). ABS offered Sierra Club members a bank card with the name "Sierra Club" on the front of the card and the Sierra Club logo on the back. ABS agreed to pay a royalty fee of 0.5% of total sales for the use of the Sierra Club's name and logo. Subject to the Sierra Club's approval, ABS would develop and bear the costs of promotional materials for this program. The Sierra Club had the right to pay for the production and mailing costs associated with the solicitations to its members. If it chose that route, ABS would need to pay a higher percentage as the royalty fee.

The Commissioner issued a notice of deficiency for the 1986, 1986, and 1987 tax years. The Sierra Club paid the tax and challenged the determination in Tax Court. The Tax Court held that the income from both the mailing list and the affinity card constituted royalties. The Commissioner appealed.]

II

B.

The crux of the parties' dispute is how to define "royalties" for the purpose of I.R.C. §512(b)(2). A tax-exempt organization under I.R.C. §501(c) must pay taxes at normal corporate rates on "unrelated business taxable income." I.R.C. §511(a). UBTI is defined as "the gross income derived by any organization from any unrelated trade or business ... regularly carried on by it, less the deductions allowed ... both computed with the modifications provided in subsection (b)." I.R.C. §512(a)(1). Section 512(b)(2) provides that "there shall be excluded all royalties (including overriding royalties) whether measured by production or by gross or taxable income from the property, and all deductions directly connected with such income."

"Royalties" as used in §512(b)(2) is not further defined by statute or by regulation. Thus, we look to the "ordinary, everyday senses" of the word.... "[R]oyalty" commonly refers to a payment made to the owner of property for permitting another to use the property. The payment is typically a percentage of profits or a specified sum per item sold; the property is typically either an intangible property right—such as a patent, trademark, or copyright—or a right relating to the development of natural resources.[12]...

Revenue Ruling 81-178, relied upon by the parties, supports defining royalty as a payment which relates to the use of a property right. It states that "payments for the use of trademarks, trade names, service marks, or copyrights, whether or not payment is based on the use made of such property, are ordinarily classified as royalties for federal tax purposes."

The parties agree that the above definition of royalty is correct—up to this point. The Commissioner argues that "royalty" must be further defined, claiming that a payment for the use of intangible property is not necessarily a royalty *unless* the subject of the payment is "passive in nature." Sierra Club, on the other hand, contends that any payment for the use of an intangible property right constitutes a royalty. For the following reasons, we hold that under §512(b)(2) "royalties" are payments for the right to use intangible property. We further hold that a royalty is by definition "passive" and thus cannot include compensation for services rendered by the owner of the property.

First, the circuits that have considered whether or not income received by a tax-exempt organization constitutes royalties under §512(b)(2) have consistently excluded income received as compensation for services—income that is not "passive"—from royalty income. . . . [*Editor's Note:* The Court then discussed three appellate court cases that held that revenues were not royalty income because the organizations in question were too actively involved in the business, *Disabled American Veterans v. United States*, 227 Ct. Cl. 474, 650 F.2d 1178 (Ct. Cl. 1981); *Fraternal Order of Police, Ill. State Troopers, Lodge No. 41 v. Commissioner*, 883 F.2d 717 (7th Cir. 1987), and *Texas Farm Bureau v. United States*, 53 F.3d 120 (5th Cir. 1995).]

This distinction between payments for services and payments for the right to use an intangible property right is supported by Rev. Rul. 81-178. The ruling discusses and applies the exclusion of royalty income from UBTI in two factual scenarios. In the first, a tax-exempt organization of professional athletes solicits and negotiates licensing agreements which authorize the use of the organization's trademarks, trade names, service marks, as well as its members' names, photographs, likenesses and facsimile signatures; under the terms of the agreements, the organization has the right to approve the quality and style of the use of the licensed product. In the second, the same organization solicits and negotiates agreements to endorse the products and services offered by the other

---

[12] [FN 12] Thus, "royalty" is differentiated from "rent" by the nature of the property the owner is permitting another to use. *See id.* at 1297 (defining "rent" as "compensation or fee paid, usually periodically, for the use of any property, land, buildings, equipment, etc.").

party to the agreement; the agreements require personal appearances by the members of the organization. The ruling states that the income generated by the agreements in the first situation is royalty income within the meaning of §512(b). However, the income received in the second situation is not royalty income because the agreements "require the personal services of the organization's members in connection with the endorsed products and services." Rev. Rul. 81-178, 1981-2 C.B. 135.

Lastly, differentiating between passive royalty income and income which is compensation for services comports with the purpose of I.R.C. §§511-513. As discussed by the Commissioner, the imposition of the tax on unrelated business income was in response to a concern that tax-exempt organizations were competing unfairly with taxable businesses. . . . Certain categories of income, however, were excluded from UBTI because "[the] committee believed that they are 'passive' in character and are not likely to result in serious competition for taxable businesses having similar income." S. Rep. No. 2375, 81st Cong., 2d Sess., 28, 30-31 (1950).... The purpose of the tax on UBTI to prevent unfair competition coupled with the exclusion of income believed to be "passive" in character from that tax provides additional support for excluding payment for services from royalty income.

Sierra Club's argument against "narrowly" interpreting the definition of royalties in §512(b)(2) is threefold. First, Sierra Club argues that the IRS has previously rejected a "passivity test" in its own rulings. IRS internal memoranda, however, are not binding on the IRS or on this court ("Such informal, unpublished opinions of attorneys within the IRS are of no precedential value."). Second, Sierra Club [argues and] [w]e agree with Sierra Club that the legislative history, as well as the language of the statute, indicates that Congress intended to exclude "all royalties." Acknowledging this, however, does not aid in determining whether by definition "all royalties" *means* payments (for the use of a property right) that are passive in nature.

Third, Sierra Club claims that in order for the exception to UBTI to apply, the royalty income must be derived from an unrelated business activity, or it would not be taxable as UBTI in the first place. Thus, if the exclusion of royalties from UBTI were only meant to encompass passively derived royalties, §512(b)(2) would never apply. In other words, because a trade or business is defined to *exclude* passive activities, *see American Bar Endowment*, 477 U.S. at 110, 106 S. Ct. at 2429 ("Congress defined 'trade or business' as 'any activity which is carried on for the production of income from the sale of goods or the performance of services.'") (quoting I.R.C. §513(c)), a tax-exempt organization must be engaged in an active trade or business before a royalty could possibly be taxed under §511.

This last argument highlights why royalties should be defined as "passive" only to the extent that a royalty cannot be compensation for services. Sierra Club could be engaged in a trade or business such as manufacturing t-shirts. The income from selling the t-shirts would be taxable as UBTI. However, if Sierra Club copyrighted the designs on its t-shirts and then licensed the designs to a t-shirt manufacturer in exchange for a one percent royalty fee on gross sales, the royalty fees would be excluded from UBTI under §512(b)(2).

Thus, to the extent the Commissioner claims that a tax-exempt organization can do *nothing* to acquire such fees (*e.g.*, providing a rate sheet listing the fee charged for use of each copyrighted design or retaining the right to approve how the design is used and marketed), the Commissioner is incorrect. However, to the extent that Sierra Club appears to argue that a "royalty" is any payment for the use of a property right—such as a copyright—regardless of any additional services that are performed in addition to the owner simply permitting another to use the right at issue, we disagree.

In sum, we hold that "royalties" in §512(b) are defined as payments received for the right to use intangible property rights and that such definition does not include payments for services.

III.

Given the above definition of royalties, we must now decide whether the district court erred in granting summary judgment on the issue of whether the payments received by Sierra Club for one-time rentals of its lists constitute "royalties" or payments for services performed by Sierra Club.

The facts upon which the Tax Court based its decision are as follows. Sierra Club maintained its mailing lists in furtherance of its tax exempt function; it hired [others] to perform the task of maintaining the lists on a computerized data base . . . and to administer the rental of the lists. Sierra Club set the rates for the list rentals and retained the right to approve the content and date of the mailings of a list user. [The other parties marketed the lists, fulfilled the orders, and sorted and provided labels. They either received commissions or charged their services to the list user].

On these facts, the Tax Court held that it was undisputed that the income Sierra Club received for the rental of the lists was compensation for the use of its unique property—the mailing lists. The government argues that it does not matter that Sierra Club paid others to perform services such as sorting by zip code and providing the names on labels—Sierra Club was still in the business of selling and marketing its mailing lists. Sierra Club, on the other hand, correctly points out that it did not participate in any of the business activities that could be considered providing services. It did not market its lists, sort the lists, provide the lists on labels, or provide any other service to the list users. Nor did it pay [the company maintaining the lists] to perform these services. That company billed [the subcontractors] for these services, who in turn billed the list renter.

Moreover, Sierra Club did not pay [the marketer] to market the lists; rather, [the marketer] received a commission from each rental. Nonetheless, the Commissioner argues that this commission was deducted from the list rental fee, and therefore was the equivalent of Sierra Club paying [directly for] marketing services. Accordingly, the Commissioner would have us hold that any active effort to market intangible property—such as the right to use the names on the mailing lists—converts what was a royalty into a non-royalty, because the payment is obtained by active rather than passive conduct.

We find Sierra Club's position more persuasive. Sierra Club did not itself perform the services relating to the rental of mailing lists. Nor did it market the mailing lists. It did nothing more than collect a fee for the rental of its mailing lists. Thus, Sierra Club's activities with regard to the mailing list rentals were far less substantial than the activities other courts have found to prevent a claim that income was royalty income.... To hold otherwise would require us to hold that any activity on the part of the owner of intangible property to obtain a royalty, renders the payment for the use of that right UBTI and not a royalty.

We therefore affirm the Tax Court's grant of partial summary judgment on this issue because the income received by Sierra Club from the list rentals was royalty income and not payment for services....

2. IRC §513(i): Corporate Sponsorship Payments

In 1991, Mobil Oil paid $1.5 million to the Cotton Bowl Athletic Association (CBAA), a §501(c)(3) educational organization that sponsored one of football's more prominent bowl games, the Cotton Bowl. By the time that play started, the game had been renamed the Mobil Oil Cotton Bowl. Television announcers reported on the sponsorship, and the Mobil Oil logo appeared almost everywhere—on the field, on the players' jerseys, and around the stadium.

The CBAA considered the $1.5 million a sponsorship payment—a donation from a corporation that did not expect anything in return for the payment except recognition for its gift, much as a large individual donor might have naming rights to a building. The IRS, on the other hand, considered the $1.5 million to be a quid pro quo payment. In return for $1.5 million, Mobil Oil advertised its products in a nationally televised football game. Because advertisements are not related to CBAA's educational purpose, the IRS maintained that the income should be taxed as unrelated business income.[13]

The IRS pronouncement concerned nonprofits that depended on sponsorship payments, such as public radio and television, art museums, theaters, and even Little League teams. The opponents of this pronouncement were politically effective, and in 1997, Congress enacted §513(i), which excluded "qualified sponsorship payments" from unrelated business taxable income. Final regulations interpreting §513(i) were promulgated in 2002. Treas. Reg. §513-4.[14]

A qualified sponsorship payment (QSP) is "any payment by any person engaged in a trade or business with respect to which there is no arrangement or expectation that the person will receive any substantial return benefit." Treas.

---

[13] Technical Advice Memorandum (TAM) 9147007. The IRS did not reveal the names of the parties in the TAM, but Tax Notes revealed the name, and the TAM is now widely called the "Cotton Bowl ruling."

[14] The statute and final regulations were actually based on proposed regulations that the IRS drafted in 1993, ostensibly as a defensive measure against threatened congressional action. *See* Nathan Wirtshafter, *Note, Fourth Quarter Choke: How the IRS Blew the Corporate Sponsorship Game*, 27 LOY. L.A. L. REV. 1465 (1994).

Reg. §513-4(c). It does not matter whether the sponsored activity is related or unrelated to the organization's exempt purpose, or if the activity is temporary or permanent.

One goal of the regulations is to differentiate the acknowledgments of QSPs from advertisements. By their very nature, advertisements are payments in expectation of a return, and they are therefore automatically considered substantial return benefits. Distinguishing between an acknowledgment of a QSP and an advertisement can be difficult, however. The regulations state that no substantial return benefit occurs if the §501(c)(3) organization acknowledges the payment with the payor's name, logo, or product line. Treas. Reg. §1.513-(c)(2)(iv). Thus, a statement that "General Motors is a proud sponsor of this public television program" is an acknowledgment of the gift, not an advertisement.

The exempt organization can even display or distribute the payor's product. For example, a charity that serves drinks, refreshments, and prizes provided by its sponsor at a marathon can consider the drinks, refreshments, and prizes a QSP because they are a way of acknowledging the sponsorship within the meaning of the regulations. Funds spent providing the sponsor's address, phone number, or Internet address are also acceptable as QSPs. *Id.*

The payment will not be a QSP, however, if the acknowledgment includes qualitative or comparative language; price information or other indications of savings or value; an endorsement; or an inducement to purchase, sell, or use the products or services. Treas. Reg. §1.513-4(2)(v). In such a case, the payment would be classified as a substantial return benefit instead of a QSP. A 501(c)(3) trying to avoid paying UBIT would thus do well to avoid adding "Be sure to test-drive one of GM's superior new models" to the statement about its proud sponsorship.

The regulations spell out other factors that can help organizations structure the relationship so that the payment will be a QSP instead of a substantial return benefit. For example, the payment cannot be contingent on a certain degree of public exposure, such as broadcast ratings or the number of people attending an event. Treas. Reg. §1.513-4(e)(2). Nor can the payor include the "acknowledgment" in a regularly scheduled periodical or newspaper because that would be an advertisement. Treas. Reg. §1.513-4 (b). Although an acknowledgment can be included in printed material produced for the sponsored event, its publication in a regularly scheduled periodical constitutes an advertisement.

Advertising is not the only way that a payor could receive a substantial return benefit, however. If the payor gains the right to use an intangible asset of the exempt organization or if it receives something with a monetary return that is worth more than 2% of the sponsorship payments, it will receive a substantial return benefit. Treas. Reg. §1.513-4(iii)(D); Treas. Reg. §513-4(c)(2)(ii). Thus, for example, the exempt organization can provide the sponsor's executives with a free meal if the cost of those meals is less than 2% of the total amount the sponsor spends.

One of the more difficult situations addressed by the regulations concerned exclusivity agreements. The regulations state that an "exclusive sponsor" payment, in which the payor receives the right to be the only sponsor of the exempt organization's activity (or the only sponsor in a trade or industry), is a QSP so long as the only benefit that the payor receives is an announcement that it is the exclusive sponsor of an event. Treas. Reg. §1.513-4(c)(2)(vi)(A). An "exclusive provider" arrangement, however, in which the exempt organization agrees not to sell or use any competing products, services, or facilities in connection with the organization's activity, is a substantial return benefit. Do you see what that benefit is? What is the distinction between an "exclusive sponsor" and an "exclusive provider"?

The regulations also tackle the issue of whether an exempt organization's placing a link on its website to the sponsor's website is an acknowledgment of a QSP or a substantial return benefit. If an exempt organization acknowledges a sponsor on its website in the form of a link to the sponsor's website, without promoting the sponsor or advertising its merchandise, the link will be considered an acknowledgment. If, however, the charity approves of a statement on the sponsor's website that the charity endorses the sponsor's product, there is a substantial return benefit.

NOTES AND QUESTIONS

1. For a discussion of the public policy behind the unrelated business income tax, see John D. Colombo, *The IRS University Compliance Project Report on UBIT Issues: Roadmap for Enforcement...Reform...or Repeal?* National Center on Philanthropy and the Law, 2013. John Colombo and Evelyn Brody, *Of Sovereignty and Subsidy: Conceptualizing the Charity Tax Exemption*, 22 EXEMPT ORG. TAX REV. 421 (1998); Ethan G. Stone, *Adhering to the Old Line: Uncovering the History and Political Function of the Unrelated Business Income Tax*, 54 EMORY L.J. 1475 (2005); Henry Hansmann, *Unfair Competition and the Unrelated Business Income Tax*, 75 VA. L. REV. 605 (1989). For a video that explains UBIT concepts, see Benjamin Takis, *UBIT Basics*, NONPROFIT ACCOUNTING (March 3, 2015), available at http://www.nonprofitaccountingbasics.org/video/ubit-basics.

2. In 2013, the IRS released the Colleges and Universities Project Final Report (www.irs.gov/pub/irs-tege/CUCP_FinalRpt_042513.pdf), which discussed, among other things, the prevalence and underreporting of UBTI at colleges and universities. In 2008, the IRS sent surveys to 400 colleges and universities across the country, asking questions about unrelated business income, endowments, and compensation practices. After examining those results, it audited the returns of 34 of the responding colleges and universities. The IRS found that 60% of the colleges responding to the questionnaire had filed a Form 990-T (the tax form that exempt organizations with unrelated business must file) at some point. Among the organizations that were audited, fully 90% had underreported their UBTI. Most of the errors were in defining allowable expenses or miscalculating expenses, but

40% of the audited colleges and universities had misclassified activities by labeling them as related when they were actually unrelated. More than half of those institutions had sought advice from accountants, but the IRS disagreed with the accountants' conclusions. Following the release of this report, the Advisory Committee on Tax-Exempt and Government Entities suggested that the Treasury Department redesign the Form 990-T and provide additional guidance for public charities and tax examiners. ADVISORY COMMITTEE ON TAX EXEMPT AND GOVERNMENT ENTITIES (ACT) 2014 REPORT OF RECOMMENDATIONS.

3. Do the rules and tests described in this chapter provide enough distinction between the sectors? Would it be better to merge the sectors and have them follow the same set of rules? What should the tax consequences be in such a situation? *See* James E. Austin, Ezequiel Reficco, Enriqe Ogliastri, and Roberto Gutiérrez, *Notes on Convergence*, STAN. SOC. INNOVATION REV. (Feb. 2007); Anup Alani and Eric A. Posner, *The Case for For-Profit Charities*, 93 VA. L. REV. 2017, 2037-38 (2007). Along similar lines, are both the commerciality doctrine and the unrelated business income provisions actually necessary? If the UBTI is substantial, will it not be taxed at a corporate rate, as it would be if the §501(c)(3) organization lost its tax exemption?

4. Section IV of this chapter introduces unrelated business income by defining the concept and explaining exclusions and modifications. It does not discuss how one calculates the tax, however. An organization facing UBIT will subtract from gross unrelated business income all allocable deductions for business expenses, losses, deprecation, and other items "directly connected" with the unrelated business. Organizations can often use the expense allocation rules to avoid the tax altogether, As the statistics in the introduction to this section suggested, less than two percent of all §501(c)(3) organizations paid any unrelated business tax in 2008. All totaled, they paid slightly less than 1/3 of the amount they reported. ($336 million paid; $10.3 billion reported.)[15]

    Determining how to allocate expenses between related and unrelated activities can be particularly complicated. For example, in *Rensselaer Polytechnic Institute v. Comm'r*, 732 F.3d 1058 (2d Cir. 1984), the question was how to allocate the expenses of the field house, which the school used for both related (i.e., sports events) and unrelated (i.e., rock concerts) purposes. The court found that Rensselaer had allocated the expenses "on a reasonable basis," as required in Treas. Reg. §1.512 (a)-1(c). Needless to say, Rensselaer's allocation method produced far less tax than did the IRS's method.

5. For further reading on corporate sponsorships, see Ethan G. Stone, *Halos, Billboards, and the Taxation of Charitable Sponsorships*, 82 IND. L.J. 213 (2007); LaVerne Woods, *Tax Treatment of Corporate Sponsorship Payments*

---

[15] K. Toran, *supra* n. 12.

to Exempt Organizations: Final Regulations, 38 EXEMPT ORG. TAX REV. 205-210 (2002).

6. In recent years, college athletes have pushed to obtain compensation and to unionize. They have not yet been successful. *See O'Bannon v. NCAA*, 802 F. 3d 1049 (9th Cir. 2015) (holding that rules barring compensation to student athletes are subject to antitrust laws, but that in this situation, allowing the students to be paid cash compensation would violate their status as amateurs) and *Northwestern University and College Players Association*, 2015 NLRB LEXIS 613 (2015) (the NLRB refused to accept jurisdiction to determine whether the athletes could unionize as employees, which effectively ended their efforts to unionize). If college athletes eventually become employees as a legal matter, questions could arise as to whether the income from college sports should still be treated as related income. Erik Jensen, *Taking the Student out of Student-Athlete: College Sports and the Unrelated Business Income Tax*, 31 JOURNAL TAXATION OF INVESTMENTS 29 (2014); David van den Berg, *Push to Unionize Student Athletes Raises UBIT Questions For Schools*, 2014 TAX NOTES TODAY 32-4 (2014). For further discussion on college sports and the tax system, see Richard Schmalback, *Ending the Sweetheart Deal Between Big-Time College Sports and the Tax System* (March 17, 2014), available at http://scholarship.law.duke.edu/faculty _scholarship/3422/; John D. Colombo, *The NCAA, Tax Exemption, and College Athletics*, 2010 U. ILL. L. REV. 109 (2010).

PROBLEM

You are an IRS auditor concentrating on the activities of a tax-exempt university. Which of the following would you consider unrelated business income?

a. Tuition payments
b. Revenue from football ticket sales
c. Revenue from T-shirts with the team's logo, sold in the school's store
d. Revenue from royalties gained from the T-shirt company that used the school's logo on the T-shirts that it sells throughout the United States
e. Revenue from television broadcast rights for the football game
f. Revenue from parking fees charged to students and faculty
g. Revenue from a sponsorship agreement that requires a banner on the basketball court that proclaims, "Joe's Coffee—Have a Taste."

ISSUES WHILE RUNNING THE ORGANIZATION

CHAPTER 9

INUREMENT, PRIVATE BENEFIT, AND EXCESS BENEFIT TRANSACTIONS

Purposes of this chapter:

- Examine the restrictions within §501(c)(3) against profiting from a nonprofit
- Understand the limitations of using §501(c)(3) to police the sector
- Explore the intermediate sanctions provisions—how they work and whether they solve the limitations of using the private inurement provision to police the sector.
- Examine the relationship between §501(c)(3) and §4958
- Look at nonprofit compensation issues

To think about as you read:

As you have seen from the first page of this book, the main principle of this body of law is that one should not profit from a nonprofit. Assume that your organization, whether it is a virtual organization that you created or an art museum, is riddled with people who are trying to find a way to cheat the system. The board members, the executive director, the receptionist, the volunteers, and the outside vendors are all trying to make money off the nonprofit. Can they make any money without jeopardizing the organization's tax exemption? If so, how much is too much? Are the laws that you read about in this chapter sufficient to prevent them from receiving too much money from the nonprofit organization?

I. INTRODUCTION

This chapter introduces a unit on issues that are likely to arise once the nonprofit organization is actively carrying out its programs, as opposed to beginning operations or raising funds. This first chapter of the unit covers the topics of inurement, private benefit, and intermediate sanctions—the federal requirements that an organization's assets must continue to be used for charitable purposes.

The general concept that individuals and other organizations should not profit from a nonprofit organization has been part of this book since Chapter 1 introduced the nondistribution constraint. Each chapter since then has addressed the concept, at least indirectly. This chapter stresses the federal tax consequences of violating that constraint.

The operational test of §501(c)(3) requires that the nondistribution constraint remain in force throughout the lifetime of a 501(c)(3) organization. Two doctrines have emerged from §501(c)(3) to protect this principle—private inurement and private benefit. The private inurement doctrine comes directly from the language of the statute, while the private benefit doctrine is derived from the statute's regulations. These doctrines are related, and inurement is generally considered a type of private benefit. In both cases, the penalty for violating the doctrine is revocation of tax exemption.

In 1996, Congress passed "intermediate sanctions" legislation, which provides for economic sanctions against those who obtain "excess benefits" from the tax-exempt organization (IRC §4958). This legislation applies to §501(c)(3) and §501(c)(4) organizations. Modeled upon the excise tax provisions that private foundations face for self-dealing, the intermediate sanctions legislation imposes a tax on "disqualified persons" and "organizational managers" who receive "excess benefits" from the organization.

After the passage of the intermediate sanctions legislation, one of the issues that continued to trouble practitioners was the relationship between that law, which imposes the penalty of a tax instead of revocation of the tax exemption, and the private inurement and private benefit doctrines, which mandate revocation. In 2008, the Internal Revenue Service (IRS) issued final regulations that address this issue. Those regulations are reproduced at the end of this chapter. As a result, a typical approach when analyzing activity in which an insider seemingly benefits from the tax-exempt organization is to ask whether intermediate sanctions should apply and then ask whether enough of the factors in these regulations exist to warrant a revocation of exemption.

II. INUREMENT

The private inurement doctrine arises from the language in §501(c)(3) that states: "[N]o part of the net earnings of which inures to the benefit of any private shareholder or individual." Courts have been left to determine the meanings of each of those words, which are not immediately obvious. Should "no part" be construed literally? What if an insider steals a dollar bill from the organization? What are the "net earnings"? What is a "benefit"? Can private inurement occur even if no cash changes hands? Who is a "private shareholder or individual"? Finding a "shareholder" in a §501(c)(3) organization is almost literally impossible.[1] Perhaps because the penalty for private inurement is so harsh, it is rarely invoked, and thus neither the doctrine nor the theory behind it is particularly well defined. The following statutory and regulatory language, as well as the following cases, can shed some light on this doctrine.

INTERNAL REVENUE CODE §501(C)(3)

Corporations ... organized and operated exclusively for religious, charitable, scientific, testing for public safety, literary, or educational purposes, ... *no part of the net earnings of which inures to the benefit of any private shareholder or individual*, no substantial part of the activities of which is ... attempting, to influence legislation ... and which does not participate in, or intervene in ... any political campaign on behalf of (or in opposition to) any candidate for public office. (Emphasis added.)

TREASURY REGULATIONS §§1.501(a)-1(C) AND 1.501(C)(3)-1(C)(2)

1.501(c)(3)-1(c)(2)

Distribution of earnings. An organization is not operated exclusively for one or more exempt purposes if its net earnings inure in whole or in part to the benefit of private shareholders or individuals. For the definition of the words *private shareholder* or *individual*, see paragraph (c) of §1.501(a)-1.

1.501(a)-1(c)

Private shareholder or individual defined. The words *private shareholder* or *individual* in section 501 refer to persons having a personal and private interest in the activities of the organization.

UNITED CANCER COUNCIL, INC. V. COMM'R

---

165 F.3d 1173 (7th Cir. 1999)

POSNER, Chief Judge. The United Cancer Council is a charity that seeks, through affiliated local cancer societies, to encourage preventive and ameliorative approaches to cancer, as distinct from searching for a cure, which has been the emphasis of the older and better-known American Cancer Society, of which UCC is a splinter. The Internal Revenue Service revoked UCC's

---

[1] In rare cases, §501(c)(3) organizations can have "shareholders," but they cannot accept dividends or be owners in the normal sense of the word "shareholder."

charitable exemption and the Tax Court upheld the revocation, precipitating this appeal.

So far as relates to this case, a charity, in order to be entitled to the charitable exemption from federal income tax, and to be eligible to receive tax-exempt donations, must be "organized and operated exclusively for ... [charitable] purposes" and "no part of the net earnings of [the charity may] inure to the benefit of any private shareholder or individual."... The IRS claims that UCC (which is defunct) was not operated exclusively for charitable purposes, but rather was operated for, or also for, the private benefit of the fundraising company that UCC had hired, Watson & Hughey Company (W & H). The Service also claims that part of the charity's net earnings had inured to the benefit of a private shareholder or individual—W & H again. The Tax Court upheld the Service's second ground for revoking UCC's exemption—inurement—and did not reach the first ground, private benefit. The only issue before us is whether the court clearly erred ... in finding that a part of UCC's net earnings inured to the benefit of a private shareholder or individual.

It is important to understand what the IRS does not contend. It does not contend that any part of UCC's earnings found its way into the pockets of any members of the charity's board; the board members, who were medical professionals, lawyers, judges, and bankers, served without compensation. It does not contend that any members of the board were owners, managers, or employees of W & H, or relatives or even friends of any of W & H's owners, managers, or employees. It does not contend that the fundraiser was involved either directly or indirectly in the creation of UCC, or selected UCC's charitable goals. It concedes that the contract between charity and fundraiser was negotiated on an arm's length basis. But it contends that the contract was so advantageous to W & H and so disadvantageous to UCC that the charity must be deemed to have surrendered the control of its operations and earnings to the noncharitable enterprise that it had hired to raise money for it.

The facts are undisputed. In 1984, UCC was a tiny organization. It had an annual operating budget of only $35,000, and it was on the brink of bankruptcy because several of its larger member societies had defected to its rival, the American Cancer Society. A committee of the board picked W & H, a specialist in raising funds for charities, as the best prospect for raising the funds essential for UCC's survival. Another committee of the board was created to negotiate the contract. Because of UCC's perilous financial condition, the committee wanted W & H to "front" all the expenses of the fundraising campaign, though it would be reimbursed by UCC as soon as the campaign generated sufficient donations to cover those expenses. W & H agreed. But it demanded in return that it be made UCC's exclusive fundraiser during the five-year term of the contract, that it be given co-ownership of the list of prospective donors generated by its fundraising efforts, and that UCC be forbidden, both during the term of the contract and after it expired, to sell or lease the list, although it would be free to use it to solicit repeat donations. There was no restriction on W & H's use of the list. UCC agreed to these terms and the contract went into effect.

Over the five-year term of the contract, W & H mailed 80 million letters soliciting contributions to UCC. Each letter contained advice about preventing cancer, as well as a pitch for donations; 70 percent of the letters also offered the recipient a chance to win a sweepstake. The text of all the letters was reviewed and approved by UCC. As a result of these mailings, UCC raised an enormous amount of money (by its standards)—$28.8 million. But its expenses—that is, the costs borne by W & H for postage, printing, and mailing the letters soliciting donations, costs reimbursed by UCC according to the terms of the contract— were also enormous—$26.5 million. The balance, $2.3 million, the net proceeds of the direct-mail campaign, was spent by UCC for services to cancer patients and on research for the prevention and treatment of cancer. The charity was permitted by the relevant accounting conventions to classify $12.2 million of its fundraising expenses as educational expenditures because of the cancer information contained in the fundraising letters.

Although UCC considered its experience with W & H successful, it did not renew the contract when it expired by its terms in 1989. Instead, it hired another fundraising organization—with disastrous results. The following year, UCC declared bankruptcy, and within months the IRS revoked its tax exemption retroactively to the date on which UCC had signed the contract with W & H. The effect was to make the IRS a major creditor of UCC in the bankruptcy proceeding. The retroactive revocation did not, however, affect the charitable deduction that donors to UCC since 1984 had taken on their income tax returns.

The term "any private shareholder or individual" in the inurement clause of section 501(c)(3) of the Internal Revenue Code has been interpreted to mean an insider of the charity.... A charity is not to siphon its earnings to its founder, or the members of its board, or their families, or anyone else fairly to be described as an insider; that is, as the equivalent of an owner or manager. The test is functional. It looks to the reality of control rather than to the insider's place in a formal table of organization. The insider could be a "mere" employee—or even a nominal outsider, such as a physician with hospital privileges in a charitable hospital, ... or for that matter a fundraiser, *National Foundation, Inc. v. United States*, 13 Cl. Ct.486, 494-95 (1987)—though the court in that case rejected the argument that the fundraiser controlled the charity.

The Tax Court's classification of W & H as an insider of UCC was based on the fundraising contract. Such contracts are common. Fundraising has become a specialized professional activity and many charities hire specialists in it. If the charity's contract with the fundraiser makes the latter an insider, triggering the inurement clause of section 501(c)(3) and so destroying the charity's tax exemption, the charity sector of the economy is in trouble. The IRS does not take the position that every such contract has this effect. . . . What troubles it are the particular terms and circumstances of UCC's contract. It argues that since at the inception of the contract the charity had no money to speak of, and since, therefore, at least at the beginning, all the expenses of the fundraising campaign were borne by W & H, the latter was like a founder, or rather refounder (UCC was created in 1963), of the charity. The IRS points out that 90 percent of the contributions received by UCC during the term of the contract were paid to W & H to defray the cost of the fundraising campaign that brought in those contributions, and so argues that W & H was the real recipient of the contributions. It argues that because W & H was UCC's only fundraiser, the charity was totally at W & H's mercy during the five-year term of the contract— giving W & H effective control over the charity. UCC even surrendered the right to rent out the list of names of donors that the fundraising campaign generated. The terms of the contract were more favorable to the fundraiser than the terms of the average fundraising contract are.

Singly and together, these points bear no relation that we can see to the inurement provision. The provision is designed to prevent the siphoning of charitable receipts to insiders of the charity, not to empower the IRS to monitor the terms of arm's length contracts made by charitable organizations with the firms that supply them with essential inputs, whether premises, paper, computers, legal advice, or fundraising services.

Take the Service's first point, that W & H defrayed such a large fraction of the charity's total expenses in the early stages of the contract that it was the equivalent of a founder. Pushed to its logical extreme, this argument would deny the charitable tax exemption to any new or small charity that wanted to grow by soliciting donations, since it would have to get the cash to pay for the solicitations from an outside source, logically a fundraising organization. We can't see what this has to do with inurement. The argument is connected to another of the Service's points, that W & H was UCC's only fundraiser during the period of the contract. If UCC had hired ten fundraisers, the Service couldn't argue that any of them was so large a recipient of the charity's expenditures that it must be deemed to have controlled the charity. Yet in terms of the purposes of the inurement clause, it makes no difference how many fundraisers a charity employs. W & H obtained an exclusive contract, and thus was the sole fundraiser, not because it sought to control UCC and suck it dry, but because it was taking a risk; the exclusive contract lent assurance that if the venture succeeded, UCC wouldn't hire other fundraisers to reap where W & H had sown.

And it was only at the beginning of the contract period that W & H was funding UCC. As donations poured into the charity's coffers as a result of the success of the fundraising campaign, the charity began paying for the subsequent stages of the campaign out of its own revenues. True, to guarantee recoupment, the contract with W & H required UCC to place these funds in an escrow account, from which they could be withdrawn for UCC's charitable purposes only after W & H recovered the expenses of the fundraising campaign. But this is a detail; the important point is that UCC did not receive repeated infusions of capital from W & H. All the advances that W & H had made to UCC to fund the fundraising campaign were repaid. Indeed, it is an essential part of the government's case that W & H profited from the contract.

The other point that the Service makes about the exclusivity provision in the contract—that it put the charity at the mercy of the fundraiser, since if W & H stopped its fundraising efforts UCC would be barred from hiring another fundraiser until the contract with W & H expired—merely demonstrates the Service's ignorance of contract law. When a firm is granted an exclusive contract, the law reads into it an obligation that the firm use its best efforts to promote the contract's objectives.... If W & H folded its tent and walked away, it would be in breach of this implied term of the contract and UCC would be free to terminate the contract without liability.

The Service also misses the significance of the contract's asymmetrical treatment of the parties' rights in the donor list. The charitable-fundraising community distinguishes between "prospect files" and "house files." A prospect file is a list of people who have not given to the charity in question but are thought sufficiently likely to do so to be placed on the list of addressees of a direct-mail fundraising campaign. If the prospect responds with a donation, his or her name is transferred to the house file, that is, the list of people who have made a donation to the charity. A house file is very valuable, because people who have already donated to a particular charity are more likely to donate to it again than mere prospects are likely to donate to it for the first time. The house file's value to the charity is thus as a list of people who are good prospects to respond favorably to future solicitations. Its value to the fundraiser is quite different. The fundraiser is not a charity. The value to it of a house file that it has created is the possibility of marketing it (as a prospect file—but as a prospect file in which all the prospects are charitable donors rather than a mere cross-section of potential donors) to another charity that hires it. So it made perfect sense for the contract to give the fundraiser the exclusive right to use the UCC house file that it created in raising money for other charities, while reserving to UCC the right to use the house file to solicit repeat donations to itself.

The Service's point that has the most intuitive appeal is the high ratio of fundraising expenses, all of which went to W & H because it was UCC's only fundraiser during the term of the contract, to net charitable proceeds. Of the $28-odd million that came in, $26-plus million went right back out, to W & H. These figures are deceptive, because UCC got a charitable "bang" from the mailings themselves, which contained educational materials (somewhat meager, to be sure) in direct support of the charity's central charitable goal. A charity whose entire goal was to publish educational materials would spend all or most of its revenues on publishing, but this would be in support rather than in derogation of its charitable purposes.

Even if this point is ignored, the ratio of expenses to net charitable *receipts* is unrelated to the issue of inurement. For one thing, it is a ratio of apples to oranges: the gross expenses of the fundraiser to the *net* receipts of the charity. For all that appears, while UCC derived a net benefit from the contract equal to the difference between donations and expenses plus the educational value of the mailings, W & H derived only a modest profit; for we know what UCC paid it, but not what its expenses were. The record does contain a table showing that W & H incurred postage and printing expenses of $12.5 million, but there is nothing on its total expenses.

To the extent that the ratio of net charitable proceeds to the cost to the charity of generating those proceeds has any relevance, it is to a different issue, one not presented by this appeal, which is whether charities should be denied a tax exemption if their operating expenses are a very high percentage of the total charitable donations that they receive. To see that it's a different issue, just imagine that UCC had spent $26 million to raise $28 million, but that the $26 million had been scattered among a host of suppliers rather than concentrated on one. There would be no issue of inurement, because the Service would have no basis for singling out one of these suppliers as being in "control" of UCC (or the suppliers as a group, unless they were acting in concert). But there might still be a concern either that the charity was mismanaged or that charitable enterprises that generate so little net contribution to their charitable goals do not deserve the encouragement that a tax exemption provides. Recall that most of UCC's fundraising appeals offered the recipient of the appeal a chance to win a sweepstake, a form of charitable appeal that, we are told, is frowned upon. There may even be a question of how reputable W & H is (or was).... But these points go to UCC's sound judgment, not to whether W & H succeeded in wresting control over UCC from the charity's board.

UCC's low net yield is no doubt related to the terms of the fundraising contract, which were more favorable to the fundraiser than the average such contract. But so far as appears, they were favorable to W & H not because UCC's board was disloyal and mysteriously wanted to shower charity on a fundraiser with which it had no affiliation or overlapping membership or common ownership or control, but because UCC was desperate. The charity drove (so far as the record shows) the best bargain that it could, but it was not a good bargain. Maybe desperate charities should be encouraged to fold rather than to embark on expensive campaigns to raise funds. But that too is a separate issue from inurement. W & H did not, by reason of being able to drive a hard bargain, become an insider of UCC. If W & H was calling the shots, why did UCC refuse to renew the contract when it expired, and instead switch to another fundraiser?

We can find nothing in the facts to support the IRS's theory and the Tax Court's finding that W & H seized control of UCC and by doing so became an insider, triggering the inurement provision and destroying the exemption. There is nothing that corporate or agency law would recognize as control. A creditor of UCC could not seek the satisfaction of his claim from W & H on the ground that the charity was merely a cat's paw or alter ego of W & H ... The Service and the Tax Court are using "control" in a special sense not used elsewhere, so far as we can determine, in the law, including federal tax law. It is a sense which, as the amicus curiae briefs filed in support of UCC point out, threatens to unsettle the charitable sector by empowering the IRS to yank a charity's tax exemption simply because the Service thinks its contract with its major fundraiser too one-sided in favor of the fundraiser, even though the charity has not been found to have violated any duty of faithful and careful management that the law of nonprofit corporations may have laid upon it. The resulting uncertainty about the charity's ability to retain its tax exemption—and receive tax-exempt donations—

would be a particular deterrent to anyone contemplating a donation, loan, or other financial contribution to a new or small charity. That is the type most likely to be found by the IRS to have surrendered control over its destiny to a fundraiser or other supplier, because it is the type of charity that is most likely to have to pay a high price for fundraising services.... It is hard enough for new, small, weak, or marginal charities to survive, because they are likely to have a high expense ratio, and many potential donors will be put off by that. The Tax Court's decision if sustained would make the survival of such charities even more dubious, by enveloping them in doubt about their tax exemption.

We were not reassured when the government's lawyer, in response to a question from the bench as to what standard he was advocating to guide decision in this area, said that it was the "facts and circumstances" of each case. That is no standard at all, and makes the tax status of charitable organizations and their donors a matter of the whim of the IRS.

There was no diversion of charitable revenues to an insider here, nothing that smacks of self-dealing, disloyalty, breach of fiduciary obligation or other misconduct of the type aimed at by a provision of law that forbids a charity to divert its earnings to members of the board or other insiders. But what there may have been was imprudence on the part of UCC's board of directors in hiring W & H and negotiating the contract that it did. Maybe the only prudent course in the circumstances that confronted UCC in 1984 was to dissolve. Charitable organizations are plagued by incentive problems. Nobody owns the right to the profits, and therefore no one has the spur to efficient performance that the lure of profits creates. Donors are like corporate shareholders in the sense of being the principal source of the charity's funds, but they do not have a profit incentive to monitor the care with which the charity's funds are used. Maybe the lack of a profit motive made UCC's board too lax. Maybe the board did not negotiate as favorable a contract with W & H as the board of a profitmaking firm would have done. And maybe tax law has a role to play in assuring the prudent management of charities. Remember the IRS's alternative basis for yanking UCC's exemption? It is that as a result of the contract's terms, UCC was not really operated exclusively for charitable purposes, but rather for the private benefit of W & H as well. Suppose that UCC was so irresponsibly managed that it paid W & H twice as much for fundraising services as W & H would have been happy to accept for those services, so that of UCC's $26 million in fundraising expense $13 million was the equivalent of a gift to the fundraiser. Then it could be argued that UCC was in fact being operated to a significant degree for the private benefit of W & H, though not because it was the latter's creature. That then would be a route for using tax law to deal with the problem of improvident or extravagant expenditures by a charitable organization that do not, however, inure to the benefit of insiders.

That in fact is the IRS's alternative ground for revoking the exemption, the one the Tax Court gave a bye to. It would have been better had the court resolved that ground as well as the inurement ground, so that the case could be definitively resolved in one appeal. But it did not, and so the case must be remanded to enable the court to consider it. We shall not prejudge the proceedings on remand. The usual "private benefit" case is one in which the charity has dual public and private goals, see, e.g., *Better Business Bureau v. United States*, 326 U.S. 279,283 (1945); *Living Faith, Inc. v. Commissioner*, 950 F.2d 365 (7th Cir. 1991); *American Campaign Academy v. Commissioner*, supra, 92 T.C. at 1064-65, and that is not involved here. However, the board of a charity has a duty of care, just like the board of an ordinary business corporation, ... and a violation of that duty which involved the dissipation of the charity's assets might (we need not decide whether it would—we leave that issue to the Tax Court in the first instance) support a finding that the charity was conferring a private benefit, even if the contracting party did not control, or exercise undue influence over, the charity. This, for all we know, may be such a case.

Reversed and Remanded.

CHURCH OF SCIENTOLOGY OF CALIFORNIA V. COMM'R

823 F.2d 1310 (9th Cir. 1987), *cert. denied* 486 US 1015 (1988)

TANG, Circuit Judge:

The Church of Scientology (Church) appeals a judgment of the Tax Court which affirmed the Commissioner's assessment of tax deficiencies and late filing penalties against the Church for the years 1970, 1971 and 1972. At issue is whether the Commissioner properly revoked the Church's tax exempt status.

The Church was incorporated as a nonprofit corporation in the State of California in 1954. In 1957, the Commissioner recognized it as a tax exempt organization under §501(c)(3) of the Internal Revenue Code of 1954. The Commissioner revoked the Church's tax exempt status in 1967. The letter of revocation stated that the Church was "engaged in a business for profit," and was "operated in a manner whereby a portion of [its] earnings inure[d] to the benefit of a private individual," and was "serving a private, rather than a public interest."

On March 28, 1978, the Church filed suit in United States Tax Court challenging the Commissioner's determination of tax deficiency. In an extensive opinion, the Tax Court substantially upheld the determination of the Commissioner 83 T.C. 381 (1984). It held that the Church did not qualify for exemption from taxation under §§501(a) & 501(c)(3) because: (1) the Church was operated for a substantial commercial purpose; (2) its earnings inured to the benefit of L. Ron Hubbard, his family, and OTC, a private non-charitable corporation controlled by key Scientology officials; and (3) it violated well defined standards of public policy by conspiring to prevent the IRS from assessing and collecting taxes owed by the Church. The Court also upheld the validity of the Notice of Deficiency. Finally, the Court upheld the penalties for failure to file tax returns.

II

During the years in question, the Church of Scientology of California was the "Mother Church" of the many Scientology churches around the country. The Church propagated the Scientology faith, a religion founded by L. Ron Hubbard, through such means as the indoctrination of laity, training and ordination of ministers, creation of congregations, and provision of support to affiliated organizations.

Scientology teaches that the individual is a spiritual being having a mind and body. Part of the mind, called the "reactive mind" is unconscious and filled with mental images that are frequently the source of irrational behavior. Through the administration of a process known as "auditing" a parishioner, called a "pre-clear," is helped to erase his or her reactive mind and gain spiritual awareness. Auditing is administered individually by a trained "auditor." The auditor poses questions to the pre-clear and measures the latter's response with an electronic device call an "E-Meter" that is attached to the skin. The E-Meter assists in the identification of spiritual difficulty. Scientology teaches that spiritual awareness is achieved in stages. A disciple achieves different levels of awareness through additional auditing. The religion also offers courses to train auditors.

Scientology teaches that people should pay for whatever of value they receive. This is called the "Doctrine of Exchange." Toward the realization of this doctrine, branch churches exacted a "fixed donation" for training and auditing. Fixed donations were not based on ability to pay and with few exceptions, services were not given for free.

Scientology is an international religion with numerous churches around the world. In the 1970's, these churches were organized along hierarchical lines according to the level of services they were authorized to provide. Churches that delivered services at the lowest levels were called "franchises" and later "missions." "Class IV orgs" delivered auditing through "grade IV" and training through "level IV." "St. Hill organizations" and "advanced organizations" offered intermediate and higher level services. The branch known as "Flag" offered the highest level of training and auditing....

In addition to auditing and training, the Church provided assistance to prisoners, ex-offenders, the elderly, the mentally ill and drug addicts. On occasion, the Church assisted the poor and the sick. The Church performed christenings, funerals and wedding ceremonies free of charge, and conducted regular Sunday services. The Church's chaplain provided marriage and family counseling free of charge. The Church also provided free, a specialized form of auditing geared to help people in crisis.

Flag was the highest division of the California Church. It provided spiritual leadership. It also acted as the Church's administrative center. The Flag division was headquartered aboard the ship *Apollo,* which cruised the Mediterranean Sea and docked in various countries along its shores. L. Ron Hubbard, his wife, Mary Sue, and their family lived aboard the *Apollo* with other members of the ship's crew and staff. Besides performing the highest levels of auditing and training,

Flag staff members performed a variety of management functions [including issuing] policy letters, directives, and other kinds of administrative advice geared to improving local church operations, develop[ing] programs for improving the administration of local churches, [and sending] teams of specialists to help other units or churches experiencing management difficulties.

The Church derived income from four sources: (1) auditing and training; (2) sales of Scientology literature, recordings and E-meters; (3) franchise operations; and (4) management services. Franchise operators were required to remit ten percent of gross income to the Church. The Church offered its managerial services to branch organizations around the world for a fixed fee.

One of the policy directives of the Church was to "MAKE MONEY." The Church frequently engaged in aggressive promotion of its products and services. This promotion included market surveys and advertisements. In addition, the Church trained staff members in salesmanship techniques.

L. Ron Hubbard officially resigned his position as executive head of the California and other Scientology churches in 1966. Despite his official resignation, the Tax Court found that he continued to exert significant control over the Church by making policy statements, directives, and orders. In addition, his approval was required for all financial planning. He was the sole trustee of a major Scientology trust fund into which the Church made substantial payments. He or Mary Sue Hubbard were signatories on many Church bank accounts. During the tax years at issue, L. Ron Hubbard and Mary Sue Hubbard received salaries from the California Church and its affiliate, the United Kingdom Church [ranging from $20,249 in 1970 to $115,680 in 1972].

During these years, L. Ron Hubbard, Mary Sue Hubbard, and their four children resided for the most part aboard the *Apollo*. While aboard ship, the Church provided the Hubbards with free lodging, food, laundry, medical services, and vitamins.

The Church made royalty payments to L. Ron Hubbard for sales of his books, tapes, and E-Meters. The royalties amounted to ten percent of the retail price. The Church, for example, made $104,618.27 in royalty payments to Hubbard in 1972. Additionally, Church policy required that all work pertaining to Scientology and Dianetics be copyrighted to L. Ron Hubbard. As the result of this policy, a number of publications copyrighted by L. Ron Hubbard were actually written by others . . . L. Ron Hubbard received royalty payments on the sale of all of these publications.

During the 1960s, Scientology organizations around the world were required to pay directly to L. Ron Hubbard, ten percent of their income. These payments were termed "debt repayments" because they were designed to compensate Hubbard for his work in originating the Scientology religion. The Tax Court concluded that during 1971–1972 the Church continued to make debt repayments to Hubbard.

In 1968, L. Ron Hubbard, Mary Sue Hubbard, and Leon Steinberg incorporated a Panamanian corporation called Operation Transport Corp., Ltd. (OTC). OTC was a for-profit corporation. Shortly after the corporation's formation, Hubbard, Mary Sue Hubbard and Steinberg resigned and were replaced by three Flag employees. During the years in question, the new directors performed only one function. In the summer of 1972, they approved L. Ron Hubbard's decision to transfer approximately two million dollars from an OTC bank account in Switzerland to the *Apollo*. The money was stored in a locked file cabinet to which Mary Sue Hubbard had the only set of keys.

Between 1971 and 1972, the Church made payments in excess of three and a half million dollars to OTC. During these years, the Church also made payments totaling nearly $175,000 to the Central Defense and Dissemination Fund. According to the Church, these payments were placed in the United States Church of Scientology Trust of which L. Ron Hubbard was the sole trustee. The trust funds were deposited in several Swiss bank accounts. L. Ron Hubbard and Mary Sue Hubbard were signatories of the accounts, and L. Ron Hubbard kept the trust checkbooks.

Internal Revenue Code §501 exempts certain organizations from taxation. Section 501(c)(3) exempts: corporations and any community chest, fund, or foundation, organized and operated exclusively for religious ... purposes, ... no part of the net earnings of which inures to the benefit of any private shareholder or individual.... To qualify for exemption, a church must show that it is (1) organized, and (2) operated, exclusively for religious or charitable purposes....

The Church strenuously argues that the trial court failed to recognize it as a bona fide religion. This argument goes to whether the Church meets the organizational test. Neither the Commissioner, nor the Tax Court, nor this court questions that the Church of Scientology of California was organized for a bona fide religious purpose. The only question before the court is whether the Church met the second requirement for tax exempt status, the operational test.

Four elements compose the operational test. First, the organization must engage primarily in activities which accomplish one or more of the exempt purposes specified in §501(c)(3). Second, the organization's net earnings may not inure to the benefit of private shareholders or individuals. Third, the organization must not expend a substantial part of its resources attempting to influence legislation or political campaigns.

Courts have imposed a fourth element. Organizations seeking exemption from taxes must serve a valid public purpose and confer a public benefit. *Bob Jones University v. United States*, 461 U.S. 574, 585-92 (1983). If an organization fails to comply with any one of these four elements, it will fail the operational test and lose its eligibility for tax exempt status. *Harding Hospital, Inc. v. United States*, 505 F.2d 1068, 1072 (6th Cir. 1974).

We conclude that the Church failed to establish that "no part of the net earnings ... inures to the benefit of any private shareholder or individual...." 26 U.S.C. §501(c)(3). Because we may affirm the Tax Court on this ground, we do not reach the questions of whether the Church operated for a substantial commercial purpose or whether it violated public policy.

Congress conferred tax exemption on churches and other organizations in recognition of the benefit society derives from the activities of these organizations.... The government leaves funds in the hands of charitable organizations rather than taxing them and spending the funds on public projects. Implicit in this purpose is that charities must promote the public good to qualify for tax exemption. *Presbyterian and Reformed Publishing Co. v. Commissioner*, 743 F.2d 148, 153 (3d Cir. 1984).

Section 501(c)(3) embodies this policy. Churches are eligible for tax exempt status only if no part of their net earnings inure to the benefit of private individuals. Each phrase of the statute has significance. The term "no part" is absolute. The organization loses tax exempt status if even a small percentage of income inures to a private individual.... The sole beneficiary of the church's activities must be the public at large....

Courts have construed broadly the term "net earnings."... "Net earnings" includes more than gross receipts minus disbursements as shown on the books of the organization.... Only those ordinary expenses necessary to the operation of the church are not included in net earnings....

The heart of §501(c)(3) tax-exempt status is the phrase "inures to the benefit." Payment of reasonable salaries to church officials does not constitute inurement.... However, payment of excessive salaries will result in a finding of inurement.... Inurement can also result from distributions other than the payment of excessive salaries.... Unaccounted for diversions of a charitable organization's resources by one who has complete and unfettered control can constitute inurement....

Finally, the regulations define "private shareholder or individual" broadly as any person "having a personal and private interest in the activities of the organization." 26 C.F.R. 1.501(a)-1(c).

While we remain solicitous of Congress' intent to confer tax-exempt status on religious organizations, this court has previously affirmed the denial of tax exemption where church income inures to private individuals. [The court described three cases in which courts found private inurement in churches.]... These cases emphasize that excessive compensation and potential for abuse, even absent a showing of actual abuse, will constitute inurement.[2]

The finding of the Tax Court that a portion of the Church's net earnings inured to the benefit of L. Ron Hubbard, his family, and OTC, a private for-profit corporation, is a factual finding.... We review this finding for clear error....

The taxpayer has the burden to demonstrate that it is entitled to tax-exempt status.... This is especially true in situations where there is a great potential for abuse created by one individual's control of the church.... The Church must come forward with candid disclosure of the facts bearing on the exemption application. Doubts will be resolved in favor of the government....

---

[2] [FN 4]We recognize that not every instance in which payments are made to private individuals will result in inurement. *See, e.g., Presbyterian and Reformed Publishing Co. v. Commissioner*, 743 F.2d 148 (3d Cir. 1984). In *Presbyterian and Reformed Publishing*, the Third Circuit reversed the Tax Court's denial of tax-exempt status because the publishing company paid nothing more than reasonable salaries to the founder's family and employees.

In finding that a portion of the Church's net earnings inured to the benefit of L. Ron Hubbard, his family and OTC, the court isolated two indicia of inurement, overt and covert. The overt indicia included salaries, living expenses, and royalties. The covert indicia included "debt repayments" and L. Ron Hubbard's unfettered control over millions of dollars of Church assets. The court concluded that these indicia, when viewed in light of the self-dealing associated with them, coupled with the Church's failure to carry its burden of proof and to disclose the facts candidly, proved conclusively that the Church was operated for the benefit of L. Ron Hubbard and his family.

The Church challenges the overt indicia of inurement on the ground that the salaries, expenses and royalties, were reasonable. It notes that the court did not find them unreasonable, considered separately. The Church questions the logic of the finding that several reasonable payments add up to inurement.

The Church paid L. Ron Hubbard and Mary Sue Hubbard combined salaries of $20,249 in 1970, $49,648 in 1971 and $115,680 in 1972. We cannot say that these salaries were excessive.

In addition to Hubbard's salary, the Church paid for all of the Hubbards' living and medical expenses aboard the cruise ship *Apollo*. These expenses amounted to about $30,000 per year. Because it is unnecessary to our decision, we express no opinion on whether supporting a Church's founder and his family aboard a yacht cruising the Mediterranean constitutes a reasonable Church expense.

The Church also paid substantial royalties to L. Ron Hubbard for his books, recordings and E-Meters. Churches, especially less established ones, rely on the distribution of church literature to propagate their beliefs. Financing church operations through the sale of religious literature does not necessarily violate the requirements for tax exemption. *See Presbyterian and Reformed Publishing Co.*, 743 F.2d at 158-59. Furthermore, a church may pay the author reasonable compensation in the form of royalties for his literary works. However, the payments in this case, cross the line between reasonable and excessive. Here, the evidence indicates that Hubbard used the Church to generate copyrighted literature and market his products. Scientology policy mandated that any book on Dianetics and Scientology be copyrighted in the name of L. Ron Hubbard. Pursuant to this policy, a number of publications copyrighted by L. Ron Hubbard were actually written by Church employees. Furthermore, the Church encouraged its staff members to market aggressively his products. We agree with the Tax Court that the royalty payments support a finding of inurement.

The Church argues that the evidence does not support the Tax Court's finding of covert inurement. However, the record reveals that L. Ron Hubbard had unfettered control over millions of dollars in Church assets. The Church transferred several million dollars to OTC during 1970-72. These payments were designated as "charter mission expenses." L. Ron Hubbard and Mary Sue Hubbard controlled OTC funds. Sometime during 1972, OTC transferred approximately two million dollars from OTC bank accounts in Switzerland to the *Apollo*. The finding that OTC was a sham corporation is sustained. During the tax years in question, OTC funneled millions of dollars of Church assets to L. Ron Hubbard....

The record also supports the Tax Court's conclusion that L. Ron Hubbard had unfettered control over Church of Scientology Trust Fund assets. The Church deducted payments of $28,930.34 in 1970, $67,892.40 in 1971, and $77,986.62 in 1972 to the Central Defense and Dissemination Fund. According to the Church, these payments were made to the United States Church of Scientology Trust. L. Ron Hubbard was the sole trustee of the Trust during the years in question. Trust funds were deposited in several Swiss bank accounts. L. Ron Hubbard and Mary Sue Hubbard were two of the three signatories on the Trust accounts. L. Ron Hubbard kept the Trust checkbooks. In 1972, over a million dollars was withdrawn from the Trust accounts in Switzerland and brought aboard the *Apollo* where it was kept in a locked file cabinet. Mary Sue Hubbard had the only keys to the cabinet.

The Church disputes that control over assets compels a finding of inurement. It argues that every Sunday morning pastors all over America collect money from parishioners and hold that money for Church uses. It asserts that OTC funds were used for expenses associated with operation of the *Apollo* and in providing banking services for Flag. Witnesses testified that the Church used Trust monies to defend Scientology against attack and to propagate the religion. Finally, the Church argues that the three million dollars brought aboard the *Apollo* from the OTC and Trust accounts remained on the *Apollo* during the years in question. It cites the testimony of a Trust accountant who counted the cash aboard the *Apollo* and testified that none of it was missing.

We find these arguments unpersuasive. Unlike the typical Saturday or Sunday when parishioners donate their money to the church, here the Church transferred millions of dollars to bank accounts controlled by a private individual who had no official responsibility for managing church assets. Although witnesses testified that the money was used for Church purposes, the Church presented little documentation to show that the majority of Trust or OTC money was actually spent on bona-fide Church activities. Finally, the self-serving testimony of a Church employee that the three million dollars remained in the *Apollo* safe proves nothing.

The fact that there were three million dollars in the safe on the day the Church accountant checked, is not inconsistent with the Tax Court's finding that L. Ron Hubbard had unfettered control over millions of dollars in money that originated with the Church. The Church failed to come forward with testimony from key individuals such as L. Ron Hubbard and Mary Sue Hubbard and failed to present the documentation necessary to trace the source and use of OTC and Trust monies. In sum, the Church failed to carry its burden of proof in a situation where "the potential for abuse created by the [founder's] control of the Church required open and candid disclosure of facts bearing on the exemption application." *Bubbling Well Church*, 670 F.2d at 105.

The Tax Court found that Church income inured to the benefit of L. Ron Hubbard in a "grand scale" in the form of "debt repayments." During the 1950's,

Hubbard was paid a portion of the gross income of Scientology congregations, franchises and organizations.... This compensation scheme was called the "proportional pay plan." During the 1960s these tithes became known as "Founding Debt Payments" (sometimes also called "LRH RR" or "LRH 10").

Although the form changed, the payments continued through the years at issue in this case. Church records indicate that between October 9, 1972 and December 28, 1972, it made debt repayments totaling $19,324.41. A policy letter dated September 7, 1972 entitled "Repayment or Due Money Collected for LRH Personally" set out a program to reimburse Hubbard for past use of Hubbard's personal income and capital; research and development of the technology of Dianetics and Scientology; and the use of Hubbard's goodwill and high credit rating. The letter establishes the post of "LRH accounts officer" to monitor collection of debt repayments.

The Church argues that the Tax Court's finding of continued debt repayments is clearly erroneous. The policy letter establishing the post of "LRH accounts officer" was canceled two days after it was promulgated. According to the Church, the only credible evidence of payments were the checks issued between October and December 1972. It contends that these payments, even though invoiced in the Church's records as "Per HCO Policy Letter 7 Sept. 72," "LRH Repayments," and "Founding Debt Payment," were actually deposited in an OTC bank account for the benefit of the Church. Finally, even if the evidence is believed, argues the Church, it accounts for only a four-month period and is insufficient to support revocation of tax exemption for all three years.

These arguments are unavailing. Even though the payments were called debt repayments, the Church produced no evidence of bona fide indebtedness. The typical indicia of a debt are a sum certain payable over a specific period of time at a stipulated rate of interest. Here, the evidence indicates a continuing obligation to make uncertain payments based on a percentage of the Church's total receipts. In enforcing federal tax laws, courts look to the substance of a transaction rather than its form.... These payments more closely resemble tithes to L. Ron Hubbard than debt repayments. It makes no difference whether the $19,000 was the tip of the iceberg, as the Tax Court concluded, or the total of all debt repayments made by the Church. *No part* of the Church's income could inure to L. Ron Hubbard if it was to maintain tax exempt status.... Even if the money went into an OTC account, it inured to the benefit of L. Ron Hubbard because he had unrestrained and unaccounted for access to that account.... The Church failed to come forward with credible proof that the funds were actually spent on behalf of the Church....

In sum, we hold that significant sums of Church money inured to the benefit of L. Ron Hubbard and his family during the tax years 1970, 1971, and 1972. Although neither the salaries nor the living expenses necessarily constituted evidence of inurement, the cumulative effect of Hubbard's use of the Church to promote royalty income, Hubbard's unfettered control over millions of dollars of church assets, and his receipt of untold thousands of dollars worth of "debt repayments" strongly demonstrate inurement. We find no clear error....

We affirm the Tax Court decision upholding the Commissioner's revocation of the Church of Scientology of California's tax exempt status on the ground that a portion of its income inured to the benefit of L. Ron Hubbard and others. We reject the Church's argument that the notice of deficiency was constitutionally and administratively defective. Finally, we uphold the Commissioner's imposition of a penalty on the Church for failure to file the proper returns.

NOTE

The IRS continues to revoke exemptions and to deny recognition of exemption on the basis of private inurement. Sometimes it even denies recognition of exemption because of a potential for private inurement. *See, e.g.,* PLR 201233017 (organization with lifetime appointments for board members who are also paid in their roles as officers is not eligible for recognition of exemption, in part because of a potential for private inurement); PLR 201533022 (religious organization's exemption revoked because its funds were used to pay for its president's personal expenses and to grant a no-interest loan to president's for-profit company); *Educational Assistance Foundtn. for the Descendants of Hungarian Immigrants in the Performing Arts, Inc. v. U.S.,* 111 F. Supp. 3d 34 (D.D.C., 2015) (organization that made scholarship grants to members of one family ruled ineligible for tax exemption on grounds of private inurement).

III. PRIVATE BENEFIT

You should remember that the determination of whether an organization obtains tax-exempt status often depends upon whether it can show that it offers a "community benefit."[3] The flip side of a community benefit is a "private benefit," and it is evident that an organization can neither obtain nor retain its exempt status if it confers private benefit on an individual or another organization. The *UCC* case reproduced above suggests that the private benefit doctrine can be applied when the private inurement doctrine is inapplicable because the person who benefited from the organization is not a "shareholder or other individual." The *UCC* case was settled before the lower court, to which the case had been remanded, determined how the private benefit doctrine applied, but the court's emphasis on this doctrine points out its importance.

Private benefit is a broader concept than that of inurement because it applies to anyone, regardless of his or her status as an insider. In another sense, however, private benefit is less broad because "incidental" private benefit is allowed. The penalty for obtaining private benefit from the organization is the same under either concept: loss of exempt status. As you read the following materials, determine how you would have decided the *UCC* case if it had been brought under the theory of private benefit instead of under the theory of inurement.

---

[3] See Chapter 4 for more detail on this concept.

TREASURY REGULATIONS §1.501(C)(3)-1(D)(1)(II)-(III)

d. Exempt purposes...

(ii) An organization is not organized or operated exclusively for one or more of the purposes specified in subdivision (i) of this subparagraph unless it serves a public rather than a private interest. Thus, to meet the requirement of this subdivision, it is necessary for an organization to establish that it is not organized or operated for the benefit of private interests such as designated individuals, the creator or his family, shareholders of the organization, or persons controlled, directly or indirectly, by such private interests.

(iii) Examples. The following examples illustrate the requirement of paragraph (d)(1)(ii) of this section that an organization serve a public rather than a private interest:

Example 1

(i) O is an educational organization the purpose of which is to study history and immigration. O's educational activities include sponsoring lectures and publishing a journal. The focus of O's historical studies is the genealogy of one family, tracing the descent of its present members. O actively solicits for membership only individuals who are members of that one family. O's research is directed toward publishing a history of that family that will document the pedigrees of family members. A major objective of O's research is to identify and locate living descendants of that family to enable those descendants to become acquainted with each other.

(ii) O's educational activities primarily serve the private interests of members of a single family rather than a public interest. Therefore, O is operated for the benefit of private interests in violation of the restriction on private benefit in paragraph (d)(1)(ii) of this section. Based on these facts and circumstances, O is not operated exclusively for exempt purposes and, therefore, is not described in section 501(c)(3).

Example 2

(i) O is an art museum. O's principal activity is exhibiting art created by a group of unknown but promising local artists. O's activity, including organized tours of its art collection, promotes the arts. O is governed by a board of trustees unrelated to the artists whose work O exhibits. All of the art exhibited is offered for sale at prices set by the artist. Each artist whose work is exhibited has a consignment arrangement with O. Under this arrangement, when art is sold, the museum retains 10 percent of the selling price to cover the costs of operating the museum and gives the artist 90 percent.

(ii) The artists in this situation directly benefit from the exhibition and sale of their art. As a result, the principal activity of O serves the private interests of these artists. Because O gives 90 percent of the proceeds from its sole activity to the individual artists, the direct benefits to the artists are substantial and O's provision of these benefits to the artists is more than incidental to its other purposes and activities. This arrangement causes O to be operated for the benefit of private interests in violation of the restriction on private benefit in paragraph (d)(1)(ii) of this section. Based on these facts and circumstances, O is not operated exclusively for exempt purposes and, therefore, is not described in section 501(c)(3).

Example 3

(i) O is an educational organization the purpose of which is to train individuals in a program developed by P, O's president. The program is of interest to academics and professionals, representatives of whom serve on an advisory panel to O. All of the rights to the program are owned by Company K, a for-profit corporation owned by P. Prior to the existence of O, the teaching of the program was conducted by Company K. O licenses, from Company K, the right to conduct seminars and lectures on the program and to use the name of the program as part of O's name, in exchange for specified royalty payments. Under the license agreement, Company K provides O with the services of trainers and with course materials on the program. O may develop and copyright new course materials on the program but all such materials must be assigned to Company K without consideration if and when the license agreement is terminated. Company K sets the tuition for the seminars and lectures on the program conducted by O. O has agreed not to become involved in any activity resembling the program or its implementation for 2 years after the termination of O's license agreement.

(ii) O's sole activity is conducting seminars and lectures on the program. This arrangement causes O to be operated for the benefit of P and Company K in violation of the restriction on private benefit in paragraph (d)(1)(ii) of this section, regardless of whether the royalty payments from O to Company K for the right to teach the program are reasonable. Based on these facts and circumstances, O is not operated exclusively for exempt purposes and, therefore, is not described in section 501(c)(3).

AMERICAN CAMPAIGN ACADEMY V. COMM'R

92 T.C. 1053 (1989)

[*Editor's Note:* Chapter 4 includes this case as part of the definition of an "educational" organization. *American Campaign Academy* is also one of the few published cases that deals with the concept of "private benefit." Recall that the school trained individuals for careers as political campaign professionals, but almost all the graduates worked for the Republican Party after graduation. The Tax Court concluded that the school was not organized and operated for exempt purposes; rather, it benefited the private interests of the Republican Party.]

Unrelated Parties and Private Interests

We begin our analysis by considering whether an organization may transgress the "public rather than a private interest" mandate of section 1.501(c)(3)-1(d)(1)(ii), Income Tax Regs., by conferring benefits on persons not having a personal and private interest in the activities of the organization. *See* sections 1.501(c)(3)-1(c)(2) and 1.501(a)-1(c), Income Tax Regs. Petitioner maintains that the prohibition against private benefit is limited to situations in which an organization's insiders are benefited. Petitioner further contends that since "Republican Party entities and candidates" cannot be construed as insiders of its organization, no transgression of the operational test exists.

In support of limiting the private benefit analysis to insiders, petitioner compares the language of section 1.501(c)(3)-1(d)(1)(ii), Income Tax Regs.... to the statutory and regulatory language prohibiting the inurement of organizational earnings to private shareholders and individuals. Section 501(c)(3) and sections 1.501(c)(3)-1(c)(2) and 1.501(a)-1(c). Petitioner asserts that the class of persons illustrated in section 1.501(c)(3)-1(d)(1)(ii) (i.e., designated individuals, the creator or his family, shareholders of the organization, or persons controlled directly or indirectly by such private interests), overlaps with the class of persons identified by section 501(c)(3) and section 1.501(a)-1(c), Income Tax Regs., as insiders in the private inurement context (i.e., persons having a personal and private interest in the activities of the organization). Petitioner believes that this overlap "clearly indicates" that both the prohibition against private inurement and the prohibition against conferral of substantial private benefits exclusively target the same class of persons.

Petitioner reasons that because this Court has explicitly excluded unrelated third parties from the ambit of the term "private shareholder or individual" in the earnings inurement context, *People of God Community v. Commissioner*, 75 T.C. 127, 133 (1980), unrelated third parties must likewise be excluded from the class of private persons whose receipt of a substantial benefit would cause the organization to be operated other than exclusively for exempt purposes. Section 1.501(c)(3)-1(d)(1)(ii), Income Tax Regs. Accordingly, petitioner concludes that since Republican entities and candidates are not interested insiders, the private benefit analysis of section 1.501(c)(3)-1(d)(1)(ii), Income Tax Regs., is inapplicable in the case at bar. We do not agree.

Petitioner misconstrues the overlapping characteristics of the private benefit and private inurement prohibitions. We have consistently recognized that while the prohibitions against private inurement and private benefits share common and often overlapping elements, ... the two are distinct requirements which must independently be satisfied. *Canada v. Commissioner* 75 T.C. 337 (1980).... Nonetheless, we have often observed that the prohibition against private inurement of net earnings appears redundant, since the inurement of earnings to an interested person or insider would constitute the conferral of a benefit inconsistent with operating exclusively for an exempt purpose.... In other words, when an organization permits its net earnings to inure to the benefit of a private shareholder or individual, it transgresses the private inurement prohibition and operates for a nonexempt private purpose.

The absence of private inurement of earnings to the benefit of a private shareholder or individual does not, however, establish that the organization is operated exclusively for exempt purposes. Therefore, while the private inurement prohibition may arguably be subsumed within the private benefit analysis of the operational test, the reverse is not true. Accordingly, when the Court concludes that no prohibited inurement of earnings exists, it cannot stop there but must inquire further and determine whether a prohibited private benefit is conferred.

Moreover, an organization's conferral of benefits on disinterested persons may cause it to serve "a private interest" within the meaning of section 1.501(c)(3)-1(d)(1)(ii).... In this connection, we use "disinterested" to distinguish persons who are not private shareholders or individuals having a personal and private interest in the activities of the organization within the meaning of section 1.501(a)-1(c), Income Tax Regs.

NOTES

1. Assume that the *United Cancer Council* case, reproduced above, was returned to the 7th Circuit with a question of whether Watson & Hughey (W & H) had received sufficient private benefit to justify revocation of UCC's tax exemption. You are the judge. What do you decide?
2. For a discussion of the private benefit doctrine and the American Campaign Academy case, see John D. Colombo, *Private Benefit: What Is It—And What Do We Want It to Be?* (2011), Annual Conference of the National Center on Philanthropy and the Law, New York, NY, 2011. Available at http://ssrn.com/abstract=2350470.

IV. INTERMEDIATE SANCTIONS AND EXCESS BENEFIT TRANSACTIONS

In the early 1990s, a series of high-profile scandals highlighted incidents in which individuals profited from the nonprofit organizations with which they were working. One of the larger scandals involved William Aramony, the chief executive officer (CEO) of the United Way of America, who eventually spent seven years in jail for fraud and embezzlement. These scandals drove home the limitations of private benefit and private inurement doctrines. The IRS, understandably, is reluctant to revoke the tax exemption of otherwise charitable organizations if someone has unlawfully benefited from the organization, especially if the organization did not participate in the actions. In addition, under the private benefit and private inurement doctrines, the penalty falls on the organization, not on the wrongdoer. In reaction to this situation, Congress enacted the intermediate sanctions provisions that are reproduced below. An article by the former director of the Exempt Organizations Division of the IRS follows, which explains the IRS's interpretation of these provisions.

INTERNAL REVENUE CODE §4958

(a) Initial taxes

(1) On the disqualified person. There is hereby imposed on each excess benefit transaction a tax equal to 25 percent of the excess benefit. The tax imposed by this paragraph shall be paid by any disqualified person referred to in subsection (f)(1) with respect to such transaction.

(2) On the management. In any case in which a tax is imposed by paragraph (1), there is hereby imposed on the participation of any organization manager in the excess benefit transaction, knowing that it is such a transaction, a tax equal to 10 percent of the excess benefit, unless such participation is not willful and is due to reasonable cause. The tax imposed by this paragraph shall be paid by any organization manager who participated in the excess benefit transaction.

(b) Additional tax on the disqualified person. In any case in which an initial tax is imposed by subsection (a)(1) on an excess benefit transaction and the excess benefit involved in such transaction is not corrected within the taxable period, there is hereby imposed a tax equal to 200 percent of the excess benefit involved. The tax imposed by this subsection shall be paid by any disqualified person referred to in subsection (f)(1) with respect to such transaction.

(c) Excess benefit transaction; excess benefit. For purposes of this section—

(1) Excess benefit transaction.

(A) In general. The term "excess benefit transaction" means any transaction in which an economic benefit is provided by an applicable tax-exempt organization directly or indirectly to or for the use of any disqualified person if the value of the economic benefit provided exceeds the value of the consideration (including the performance of services) received for providing such benefit. For purposes of the preceding sentence, an economic benefit shall not be treated as consideration for the performance of services unless such organization clearly indicated its intent to so treat such benefit.

(B) Excess benefit. The term "excess benefit" means the excess referred to in subparagraph (A)....

(4) Authority to include certain other private inurement. To the extent provided in regulations prescribed by the Secretary, the term "excess benefit transaction" includes any transaction in which the amount of any economic benefit provided to or for the use of a disqualified person is determined in whole or in part by the revenues of 1 or more activities of the organization but only if such transaction results in inurement not permitted under paragraph (3) or (4) of section 501(c), as the case may be. In the case of any such transaction, the excess benefit shall be the amount of the inurement not so permitted.

(d) Special rules. For purposes of this section—

(1) Joint and several liability. If more than 1 person is liable for any tax imposed by subsection (a) or subsection (b), all such persons shall be jointly and severally liable for such tax.

(2) Limit for management. With respect to any 1 excess benefit transaction, the maximum amount of the tax imposed by subsection (a)(2) shall not exceed $ 20,000.

(e) Applicable tax-exempt organization. For purposes of this subchapter, the term "applicable tax-exempt organization" means—

(1) any organization which (without regard to any excess benefit) would be described in paragraph (3) or (4) of section 501(c) and exempt from tax under section 501(a), and

(2) any organization which was described in paragraph (1) at any time during the 5-year period ending on the date of the transaction. Such term shall not include a private foundation (as defined in section 509(a)).

(f) Other definitions. For purposes of this section—

(1) Disqualified person. The term "disqualified person" means, with respect to any transaction—

(A) any person who was, at any time during the 5-year period ending on the date of such transaction, in a position to exercise substantial influence over the affairs of the organization,

(B) a member of the family of an individual described in subparagraph (A), and

(C) a 35-percent controlled entity....

(2) Organization manager. The term "organization manager" means, with respect to any applicable tax-exempt organization, any officer, director, or trustee of such organization (or any individual having powers or responsibilities similar to those of officers, directors, or trustees of the organization).

(3) 35-percent controlled entity.

(A) In general. The term "35-percent controlled entity" means—

(i) a corporation in which persons described in subparagraph (A) or (B) of paragraph (1) own more than 35 percent of the total combined voting power,

(ii) a partnership in which such persons own more than 35 percent of the profits interest, and

(iii) a trust or estate in which such persons own more than 35 percent of the beneficial interest.

(B) Constructive ownership rules. Rules similar to the rules of paragraph (3) and (4) of section 4946(a) shall apply for purposes of this paragraph

(4) Family members. The members of an individual's family shall be determined under section 4946(d); except that such members also shall include the brothers and sisters (whether by the whole or half blood) of the individual and their spouses.

(5) Taxable period. The term "taxable period" means, with respect to any excess benefit transaction, the period beginning with the date on which the transaction occurs and ending on the earliest of—

(A) the date of mailing a notice of deficiency under section 6212 with respect to the tax imposed by subsection (a)(1), or

(B) the date on which the tax imposed by subsection (a)(1) is assessed.

(6) Correction. The terms "correction" and "correct" mean, with respect to any excess benefit transaction, undoing the excess benefit to the extent possible, and taking any additional measures necessary to place the organization in a financial position not worse than that in which it would be if the disqualified person were dealing under the highest fiduciary standards....

STEVEN MILLER, EASIER COMPLIANCE IS GOAL OF NEW INTERMEDIATE SANCTION REGULATIONS

www.irs.gov/pub/irs-utl/m4958art.pdf (Oct. 29, 2002)

[*Editor's Note:* The following article, written by the Director of Exempt Organizations of the Internal Revenue Service in 2002, is a comprehensive summary of the intermediate sanctions legislation and regulations. The regulations have since been updated, but the changes do not affect this article, except for two instances in which the monetary amounts have changed. Those changes are noted in footnotes.]

I am providing this brief analysis [of §4958], hoping to make the Regulations easier to understand and follow. In my view, the primary purpose of the statute and the regulations is not solely to give the Service another tool in its enforcement arsenal, but to provide a roadmap by which an organization may steer clear of situations that may give rise to inurement. Needless to say, my analysis reflects my own views and does not necessarily represent the official views of the Treasury Department or the Internal Revenue Service.

1. The Regulations Only Apply to 501(c)(3) and 501(c)(4) Organizations

It is important to emphasize that the Regulations only apply to certain "applicable" section 501(c)(3) and 501(c)(4) organizations. An applicable tax-exempt organization is a section 501(c)(3) or a section 501(c)(4) organization that is tax-exempt under section 501(a), or was such an organization at any time during a five-year period ending on the day of the excess benefit transaction. An applicable tax-exempt organization does not include:

- A private foundation as defined in section 509(a).
- A governmental entity that is exempt from (or not subject to) taxation without regard to section 501(a).
- Certain foreign organizations.

An organization is not treated as a section 501(c)(3) or 501(c)(4) organization for any period covered by a final determination that the organization was not tax-exempt under section 501(a), but only if the determination was not based on private inurement or one or more excess benefit transactions.

2. Section 4958 Only Applies to Certain Influential or "Disqualified" Persons

The vast majority of section 501(c)(3) or 501(c)(4) organization employees and contractors [are] not . . . affected by the section 4958 Regulations. Only the few influential persons within these organizations are covered by the Regulations when they receive benefits, such as compensation, fringe benefits, or contract payments. The IRS calls this class of covered individuals "disqualified persons." A disqualified person, regarding any transaction, is any person who was in a position to exercise substantial influence over the affairs of the applicable tax-exempt organization at any time during a five-year period ending on the date of the transaction. Persons who hold certain powers, responsibilities, or interests are among those who are in a position to exercise substantial influence over the affairs of the organization. This would include, for example, voting members of the governing body, and persons holding the power of:

- Presidents, chief executive officers, or chief operating officers.
- Treasurers and chief financial officers.

A disqualified person also includes certain family members of a disqualified person, and 35% controlled entities of a disqualified person.

3. Persons Who Are Not Disqualified

The Regulations also clarify which persons are not considered to be in a position to exercise substantial influence over the affairs of an organization. They include:

- An employee who receives benefits that total less than the "highly compensated" amount in section 414(q)(1)(B)(i) [$120,000 in 2016][4] and who does not hold the executive or voting powers just mentioned; is not a family member of a disqualified person; and is not a substantial contributor;
- Tax-exempt organizations described in section 501(c)(3); and
- Section 501(c)(4) organizations with respect to transactions engaged in with other section 501(c)(4) organizations.

---

[4] [The original amount was $85,000 in 2001. IRS Notice 2015-75 (November 16, 2015) set forth the amount for 2016, which was unchanged from 2015.—Ed.]

4. Other Persons Are Subject to a Facts and Circumstances Test

Other persons not described in Sections 2 or 3 above can also be considered disqualified persons, depending on all the relevant facts and circumstances.

Facts and Circumstances Tending to Show Substantial Influence

- The person founded the organization.
- The person is a substantial contributor to the organization under the section 507(d)(2)(A) definition, only taking into account contributions to the organization for the past 5 years.
- The person's compensation is primarily based on revenues derived from activities of the organization that the person controls.
- The person has or shares authority to control or determine a substantial portion of the organization's capital expenditures, operating budget, or compensation for employees.
- The person manages a discrete segment or activity of the organization that represents a substantial portion of the activities, assets, income, or expenses of the organization, as compared to the organization as a whole.
- The person owns a controlling interest (measured by either vote or value) in a corporation, partnership, or trust that is a disqualified person.
- The person is a non-stock organization controlled directly or indirectly by one or more disqualified persons.

Facts and Circumstances Tending to Show No Substantial Influence

- The person is an independent contractor whose sole relationship to the organization is providing professional advice (without having decision-making authority) with respect to transactions from which the independent contractor will not economically benefit.
- The person has taken a vow of poverty.
- Any preferential treatment the person receives based on the size of the person's donation is also offered to others making comparable widely solicited donations.
- The direct supervisor of the person is not a disqualified person.
- The person does not participate in any management decisions affecting the organization as a whole or a discrete segment of the organization that represents a substantial portion of the activities, assets, income, or expenses of the organization, as compared to the organization as a whole. . . .

5. Section 4958 Only Applies to "Excess Benefit" Transactions of Disqualified Persons

Fair market value determines whether the tax exempt organization provides an excess benefit to a disqualified person. An excess benefit transaction is a transaction in which an economic benefit is provided by an applicable tax-exempt organization, directly or indirectly, to or for the use of any disqualified person, and the value of the economic benefit provided by the organization exceeds the value of the consideration (including the performance of services) received for providing such benefit. To determine whether an excess benefit transaction has occurred, all consideration and benefits exchanged between a disqualified person and the applicable tax-exempt organization, and all entities it controls, are taken into account. For purposes of determining the value of economic benefits, the value of property, including the right to use property, is the fair market value. Fair market value is the price at which property, or the right to use property, would change hands between a willing buyer and a willing seller, neither being under any compulsion to buy, sell or transfer property or the right to use property, and both having reasonable knowledge of relevant facts. An excess benefit can occur in an exchange of compensation and other compensatory benefits in return for the services of a disqualified person, or in an exchange of property between a disqualified person and the exempt organization.

6. Compensation Provided by Tax Exempts Is Not Excessive If "Reasonable"

Reasonable compensation is the value that would ordinarily be paid for like services by like enterprises under like circumstances. This is the section 162 standard that will apply in determining the reasonableness of compensation. The fact that a bonus or revenue-sharing arrangement is subject to a cap is a relevant factor in determining the reasonableness of compensation. For determining the reasonableness of compensation, all items of compensation provided by an applicable tax-exempt organization in exchange for the performance of services are taken into account in determining the value of compensation (except for certain economic benefits that are disregarded, as discussed at paragraph 8 below). Items of compensation include:

- All forms of cash and non-cash compensation, including salary, fees, bonuses, severance payments, and deferred and noncash compensation.
- The payment of liability insurance premiums for, or the payment or reimbursement by the organization of taxes or certain expenses under section 4958, unless excludable from income as a de minimis fringe benefit under section 132(a)(4). (A similar rule applies in the private foundation area.) Inclusion in compensation for purposes of determining reasonableness under section 4958 does not control inclusion in income for income tax purposes.
- All other compensatory benefits, whether or not included in gross income for income tax purposes.
- Taxable and nontaxable fringe benefits, except fringe benefits described in section 132.
- Forgone interest on loans.

7. Written Intent Required to Treat Benefits as Compensation

An economic benefit is not treated as consideration for the performance of services unless the organization providing the benefit clearly indicates its intent to treat the benefit as compensation when the benefit is paid. . . .

8. Disregarded Benefits

The following economic benefits are disregarded for purposes of section 4958:

- Nontaxable fringe benefits: An economic benefit that is excluded from income under section 132.
- Benefits to volunteer: An economic benefit provided to a volunteer for the organization if the benefit is provided to the general public in exchange for a membership fee or contribution of $75.00 or less per year.
- Benefits to members or donors: An economic benefit provided to a member of an organization due to the payment of a membership fee, or to a donor as a result of a deductible contribution, if a significant number of nondisqualified persons make similar payments or contributions and are offered a similar economic benefit.
- Benefits to a charitable beneficiary: An economic benefit provided to a person solely as a member of a charitable class that the applicable tax-exempt organization intends to benefit as part of the accomplishment of its exempt purpose.
- Benefits to a governmental unit: A transfer of an economic benefit to or for the use of a governmental unit, as defined in section 170(c)(1), if exclusively for public purposes.

9. Special Exception for Initial Contracts

Section 4958 does not apply to any "fixed payment" made to a person pursuant to an initial contract. This is a very important exception, since it would potentially apply, for example, to all initial contracts with new, previously unrelated officers and contractors. An "initial contract" is a binding written contract between an applicable tax-exempt organization and a person who was not a disqualified person immediately prior to entering into the contract.

A "fixed payment" is an amount of cash or other property specified in the contract, or determined by a fixed formula that is specified in the contract, which is to be paid or transferred in exchange for the provision of specified services or property.

A "fixed formula" may, in general, incorporate an amount that depends upon future specified events or contingencies, as long as no one has discretion when calculating the amount of a payment or deciding whether to make a payment (such as a bonus).

Treatment as New Contract

A binding written contract, providing that it may be terminated or cancelled by the applicable tax-exempt organization without the other party's consent (except as a result of substantial non-performance) and without substantial penalty, is treated as a new contract, as of the earliest date that any termination or cancellation would be effective. Also, a contract in which there is a "material change," which includes an extension or renewal of the contract (except for an extension or renewal resulting from the exercise of an option by the disqualified person), or a more than incidental change to the amount payable under the contract, is treated as a new contract as of the effective date of the material change. Treatment as a new contract may cause the contract to fall outside the initial contract exception, and it thus would be tested under the fair market value standards of section 4958.

10. Tax-Exempts Can Create a Rebuttable Presumption of Reasonableness

We understand how concerned many tax-exempt officials may be that they could be forced to reach into their pockets and come up with substantial taxes and interest because a mistake was made in determining or recording their compensation and other benefits. Congress was aware of these concerns, and thus proposed a type of safe harbor—a "rebuttable presumption"—in the legislative history. We have incorporated this presumption in the new regulations in the form of a step-by-step, "cookbook" procedure. Following this "recipe" will require some time and effort, but it should be relatively easy in most cases and will give the organization's disqualified persons substantial comfort and confidence.

Payments under a compensation arrangement are presumed to be reasonable and the transfer of property (or right to use property) is presumed to be at fair market value, if the following three conditions are met.

- The transaction is approved by an authorized body of the organization (or an entity it controls) which is composed of individuals who do not have a conflict of interest concerning the transaction.
- Prior to making its determination, the authorized body obtained and relied upon appropriate data as to comparability. There is a special safe harbor for small organizations—if the organization has gross receipts of less than $1 million, appropriate comparability data includes data on compensation paid by three comparable organizations in the same or similar communities for similar services.
- The authorized body adequately documents the basis for its determination concurrently with making that determination. The documentation should include:
- The terms of the approved transaction and the date approved;
- The members of the authorized body who were present during debate on the transaction that was approved and those who voted on it;

- The comparability data obtained and relied upon by the authorized body and how the data was obtained;
- Any actions by a member of the authorized body having a conflict of interest; and
- Documentation of the basis for the determination before the later of the next meeting of the authorized body or 60 days after the final actions of the authorized body are taken, and approval of records as reasonable, accurate and complete within a reasonable time thereafter.

11. Special Rebuttable Presumption Rule for Non-fixed Payments

As a general rule, in the case of a non-fixed payment, no rebuttable presumption arises until the exact amount of the payment is determined, or a fixed formula for calculating the payment is specified, and the three requirements creating the presumption have been satisfied. However, if the authorized body approves an employment contract with a disqualified person that includes a non-fixed payment (e.g., discretionary bonus) with a specified cap on the amount, the authorized body may establish a rebuttable presumption as to the non-fixed payment when the employment contract is entered into by, in effect, assuming that the maximum amount payable under the contract will be paid, and satisfying the requirements giving rise to the rebuttable presumption for that maximum amount.

12. The IRS Has the Burden of Overcoming the Presumption

The Internal Revenue Service may refute the presumption of reasonableness only if it develops sufficient contrary evidence to rebut the probative value of the comparability data relied upon by the authorized body. This provision gives taxpayer's added protection if they faithfully find and use *contemporaneous* persuasive comparability data when they provide the benefits.

13. Organizations Not Establishing Presumption Can Still Comply with Section 4958

In some cases, an organization may find it impossible or impracticable to fully implement each step of the rebuttable presumption process described above. In such cases, the organization should try to implement as many steps as possible, in whole or in part, in order to substantiate the reasonableness of benefits as timely and as well as possible. If an organization does not satisfy the requirements of the rebuttable presumption of reasonableness, a facts and circumstances approach will be followed, using established rules for determining reasonableness of compensation and benefit deductions in a manner similar to the established procedures for section 162 business expenses.

14. The Excess Benefit Usually Occurs on the Date the Disqualified Person Receives the Benefit

An excess benefit transaction occurs on the date the disqualified person receives the economic benefit from the organization for Federal income tax purposes. However, when a single contractual arrangement provides for a series of compensation payments or other payments to a disqualified person during the disqualified person's taxable year, any excess benefit transaction with respect to these payments occurs on the last day of the taxpayer's taxable year. In the case of the transfer of property subject to a substantial risk of forfeiture, or in the case of rights to future compensation or property, the transaction occurs on the date the property, or the rights to future compensation or property, is not subject to a substantial risk of forfeiture. Where the disqualified person elects to include an amount in gross income in the taxable year of transfer under section 83(b), the excess benefit transaction occurs on the date the disqualified person receives the economic benefit for Federal income tax purposes.

15. Excise Taxes under Section 4958

Tax on Disqualified Persons

An excise tax equal to 25% of the excess benefit is imposed on each excess benefit transaction between an applicable tax-exempt organization and a disqualified person. The disqualified person who benefited from the transaction is liable for the tax. If the 25% tax is imposed and the excess benefit transaction is not corrected within the taxable period, an additional excise tax equal to 200% of the excess benefit is imposed. If a disqualified person makes a payment of less than the full correction amount, the 200% tax is imposed only on the unpaid portion of the correction amount. If more than one disqualified person received an excess benefit from an excess benefit transaction, all such disqualified persons are jointly and severally liable for the taxes.

To avoid the imposition of the 200% tax, a disqualified person must correct the excess benefit transaction during the taxable period. The taxable period begins on the date the transaction occurs and ends on the earlier of the date the statutory notice of deficiency is issued or the section 4958 taxes are assessed. This 200% tax may be abated if the excess benefit transaction subsequently is corrected during a 90-day correction period.

Tax on Organization Managers

An excise tax equal to 10% of the excess benefit may be imposed on the participation of an organization manager in an excess benefit transaction between an applicable tax-exempt organization and a disqualified person. This tax, which may not exceed [$20,000][5] with respect to any single transaction, is only imposed

---

[5] [The dollar amount for this tax was originally $10,000 but has been increased to $20,000, and so I have modified the article at this point to make it accurate.—Ed.]

if the 25% tax is imposed on the disqualified person, the organization manager knowingly participated in the transaction, and the manager's participation was willful and not due to reasonable cause. There is also joint and several liability for this tax. A person may be liable for both the tax paid by the disqualified person and this organization manager tax in appropriate circumstances.

An organization manager is any officer, director, or trustee of an applicable tax-exempt organization, or any individual having powers or responsibilities similar to officers, directors, or trustees of the organization, regardless of title. An organization manager is not considered to have participated in an excess benefit transaction where the manager has opposed the transaction in a manner consistent with the fulfillment of the manager's responsibilities to the organization. For example, a director who votes against giving an excess benefit would ordinarily not be subject to this tax. A person participates in a transaction knowingly if the person has actual knowledge of sufficient facts so that, based solely upon such facts, the transaction would be an excess benefit transaction. Knowing does not mean having reason to know. The organization manager ordinarily will not be considered knowing if, after full disclosure of the factual situation to an appropriate professional, the organization manager relied on the professional's reasoned written opinion on matters within the professional's expertise or if the manager relied on the fact that the requirements for the rebuttable presumption of reasonableness have been satisfied. Participation by an organization manager is willful if it is voluntary, conscious and intentional. An organization manager's participation is due to reasonable cause if the manager has exercised responsibility on behalf of the organization with ordinary business care and prudence.

16. Correcting the Excess Benefit

A disqualified person corrects an excess benefit transaction by undoing the excess benefit to the extent possible, and by taking any additional measures necessary to place the organization in a financial position not worse than that in which it would be if the disqualified person were dealing under the highest fiduciary standards. The organization is not required to rescind the underlying agreement; however, the parties may need to modify an ongoing contract with respect to future payments. A disqualified person corrects an excess benefit by making a payment in cash or cash equivalents equal to the correction amount to the applicable tax-exempt organization. The correction amount equals the excess benefit plus the interest on the excess benefit; the interest rate may be no lower than the applicable Federal rate. There is an anti-abuse rule to prevent the disqualified person from effectively transferring property other than cash or cash equivalents.

Property

With the agreement of the applicable tax-exempt organization, a disqualified person may make a payment by returning the specific property previously transferred in the excess benefit transaction. The return of the property is considered a payment of cash (or cash equivalent) equal to the lesser of:

- The fair market value of the property on the date the property is returned to the organization, or
- The fair market value of the property on the date the excess benefit transaction occurred.

Insufficient Payment

If the payment resulting from the return of the property is less than the correction amount, the disqualified person must make an additional cash payment to the organization equal to the difference.

Excess Payment

If the payment resulting from the return of the property exceeds the correction amount described above, the organization may make a cash payment to the disqualified person equal to the difference. . . .

20. Section 4958 Does Not Replace Revocation of Exemption

Section 4958 does not affect the substantive standards for tax exemption under section 501(c)(3) or section 501(c)(4), including the requirements that the organization be organized and operated exclusively for exempt purposes, and that no part of its net earnings inure to the benefit of any private shareholder or individual. The legislative history indicates that in most instances, the imposition of this intermediate sanction will be in lieu of revocation. IRS has indicated that the following four factors will be considered in determining whether to revoke an applicable tax-exempt organization's exemption status where an excess benefit transaction has occurred:

- Whether the organization has been involved in repeated excess benefit transactions;
- The size and scope of the excess benefit transaction;
- Whether, after concluding that it has been party to an excess benefit transaction, the organization has implemented safeguards to prevent future recurrences; and
- Whether there was compliance with other applicable laws.

21. Conclusion

While summary in nature, I hope that the above explanation will help you understand and comply with the new Regulations. For further explanation, you should refer to the thorough "Explanation of Provisions" that precedes the text of the Regulations in the official published version. . . .

INTERNAL REVENUE SERVICE, TE/GE TECHNICAL
ADVICE MEMORANDUM 200243057 (2002)

[*Editor's Note:* A technical advice memorandum (TAM) is a memorandum that the Office of Chief Counsel prepares in response to technical or procedural questions that develop during a proceeding, such as an examination or a claim for a refund. The advice represents the IRS's position with respect to the specific issue in the case in which the advice is issued. The IRS issues TAMs only on closed transactions, and they are made public once all identifiable information about the taxpayer has been removed. They are not precedential, but they do reflect the IRS position at the time and provide one way for the IRS to communicate to taxpayers. The redaction of identifiable information can make TAMs difficult to read. The following TAM has been altered by changing the initials representing the parties into names: Ben, Charitable Car Corp, David, Excel Towing, Frank's Used Cars, Kendall, and Nigel were originally B, C, D, E, F, K, and N, respectively, in the TAM.]

Facts

… Charitable Car Corp is a tax exempt entity that is recognized as exempt under section 501(c)(3) of the Internal Revenue Code. Ben, who was a used car salesman, created Charitable Car Corp. The purpose of Charitable Car Corp is to allow individuals to donate their used vehicles for a tax deduction, and at the same time choose the nonprofit charity they wanted the proceeds to be sent to. If the donors do not designate a charity, the proceeds go into a general fund. The general funds, after expenses, are then distributed to various charities and social service organizations within the community….

Charitable Car Corp operated on the same premises as Frank's Used Cars. Frank's Used Cars is a used car lot owned by David, the son of Ben….

Charitable Car Corp's original Board of Directors consisted of: Ben, Charitable Car Corp's founder, Ben's wife, Ben's father-in-law, and a CPA. At all relevant times from incorporation until February 8, 2000, Ben was President, Executive Director and in control of Charitable Car Corp's activities. Ben stated there were four or five Board of Directors' meetings. They met in person in Charitable Car Corp's office. Directors also discussed things over the phone. According to Ben, they kept minutes which he left with Charitable Car Corp. According to the new officers of Charitable Car Corp, they do not have copies of the minutes for 1998 and 1999.

The CPA, the only non-family member director, resigned on November 11, 1998. Agent secured a copy of the CPA's resignation letter, which stated that the thirteen checks he reviewed were enough to cause loss of Charitable Car Corp's 501(c)(3) status. Even after he explained to Ben that no part of any of Charitable Car Corp's revenues may inure to any private shareholder or individual as this will cause the loss of exemption, Ben continued with the same pattern of conduct. Additionally, the CPA indicated that no board meetings were held while he served as a board member.

Approximately two months before the agent did his on site examination, Ben relinquished his position as President and Executive Director of Charitable Car Corp, and "completely and commensurately" disbanded the old Board of Directors.

The examination findings respecting Charitable Car Corp's Car Donation Program disclosed that individual donors took charitable deductions greater than the fair market value of the donors' vehicles. In 1998, 1999 and part of 2000, Charitable Car Corp provided donors with only the retail Kelley Blue Book value, in writing, along with a signed Form 8283. Charitable Car Corp did not provide the loan or trade-in value, even though some of the vehicles were not able to be driven and were sold for scrap.

The following is a list of transactions between Charitable Car Corp and Ben and Ben's family:

1. Ben claims that he loaned Charitable Car Corp $ ... at ... % interest for start-up costs.... [*Editor's Note:* The only documentation for this loan came through bank statements showing deposits to Ben, a spreadsheet with a payback schedule, and a letter to the certified public accountant (CPA) from Ben that stated:] "The fact remains that Charitable Car Corp owes me money, and from time to time as it can afford it, I will be paid back the money owed me. I am charging Charitable Car Corp no interest, and am doing this simply because I want Charitable Car Corp to be a success...."

Neither Ben nor Charitable Car Corp have provided any other documentation evidencing a loan: no promissory note or other evidence of indebtedness, no record of the rate and amount of interest, no evidence of any security or collateral, and no fixed maturity date. While there were some records of alleged repayments by Charitable Car Corp to Ben, the repayments and the records were sporadic, haphazard, and informal.

2. Charitable Car Corp paid Excel Towing Company $... in 1998 and $... in 1999. Excel is a for-profit towing company created in October 1998 by David, the son of Ben.

The new trustees state that they do not use Excel's towing services anymore because it is too expensive. David never did towing until his father began operation of Charitable Car Corp. The new trustees' towing services are approximately ...% less than Excel's towing fees. The new trustees use three different towing companies and companies put bids in for their services. Ben, as President and Executive Director of Charitable Car Corp, never requested any written bids for towing services; he just assigned the towing service to his son David.

In 1999, Excel towing services received various advances on towing, which outside towing services would not have received. In some instances, Excel charged Charitable Car Corp two towing charges—one to tow the vehicle to one Charitable Car Corp lot, then another to tow the same vehicle to Charitable Car Corp's other lot.

3. According to the new trustees, Charitable Car Corp provided a leased 1999 [car] at a cost of $... per month to Ben. There was no accountability for the use of this vehicle and the personal use of this vehicle was not reported on either a Form W-2 or 1099.

According to the new trustees, a 1991...car was donated to Charitable Car Corp, which Ben's wife drove. Ben's daughter, a Charitable Car Corp part-time employee, drove a donated 1991 [car]. Charitable Car Corp spent money to fix these vehicles that were used by family members of Ben. [*Editor's Note*: The office manager never saw evidence that the Board approved the personal use of the automobiles or any verbal or written accounting for this use.]...

[*Editor's Note*: The discussion of applicable law is omitted. The TAM described section 4958 of the Internal Revenue Code; *Founding Church of Scientology v. United States*, 412 F.2d 1197 (Ct. Cl. 1969), *cert. denied*, 397 U.S. 1009 (1970); and *John Marshall Law School v. United States*, 228 Ct. Cl. 902 (1981), in which the law school's payment for the founding family's automobiles, education, travel expenses, insurance policies, basketball and hockey tickets, membership in a private eating establishment, membership in a health spa, interest-free loans, home repairs, personal household furnishings and appliances, and golfing equipment were found to be prohibited payments of the law school's earnings to the founder and his brother.]

Analysis

Issue 1—Was Ben, Charitable Car Corp's former President, Executive Director and founder an IRC 4958 disqualified person in 1998 and years forward?

Section 4958(f)(1) of the Code defines "disqualified person" as including any person who was, at any time during the five-year period ending on the date of a transaction, in a position to exercise substantial influence over the affairs of the organization.

Section 53.4958-3(c) of the regulations further provides that voting members of the governing body, presidents, chief executive officers, or chief operating officers are persons who are in a position to exercise substantial influence over the affairs of the organization.

Ben was the founder of Charitable Car Corp, having incorporated Charitable Car Corp on May 6, 1998. Ben served as a member of the board of Directors, President, and Executive Director of Charitable Car Corp. At all times until he relinquished control of Charitable Car Corp on February 8, 2000, he was in a position to exercise substantial influence over the affairs of Charitable Car Corp. Therefore, Ben was a disqualified person within the meaning of section 4958(f)(1) of the Code.

Issue 2—Was Ben an IRC 4958 organization manager with respect to Charitable Car Corp in 1998 and years forward?

Section 4958(f)(2) of the Code defines "organization manager" as any officer, director, or trustee of an exempt organization or any individual having powers or responsibilities similar to those of an officer, director, or trustee. Ben was the founder of Charitable Car Corp, having incorporated Charitable Car Corps on May 6. 1998. Ben served as a member of the board of Directors, President, and Executive Director of Charitable Car Corp. Therefore Ben was an organization manager within the meaning of section 4958(f)(2) of the Code.

Issue 3—Is any part of the ... salary paid to Ben in 1999 an IRC 4958 excess benefit to Ben?

Charitable Car Corp paid Ben $... in "salary" in 1999. Neither Charitable Car Corp nor Ben has provided any evidence of the number of hours Ben worked. He has not documented or described the services that he provided. He has provided no evidence of comparable salaries for similar services. There were no Board minutes authorizing the payment of his salary.

Moreover, the record indicates that it was the custom and practice of Charitable Car Corp and Ben to provide each donor, in writing, with only the retail Kelley Blue Book value of the donated vehicle, together with an IRS Form 8283. This was done for all vehicles, regardless of the condition of the vehicle. In many cases the vehicles were inoperable and had to be resold by Charitable Car Corp as salvage or scrap. In issue 16 below, we have concluded the Ben, through Charitable Car Corp, aided and abetted understatement of the tax liabilities of donors to Charitable Car Corp.

Given these circumstances—the failure of Ben to carry his burden of proving what if any salary was reasonable, and his activities to aid and abet understatement of tax liabilities—we conclude that all of the $... must presumptively be treated as a section 4958 excess benefit to Ben.

If credible, probative evidence can be provided of any time in 1999 Ben spent ... administering a charitable program of Charitable Car Corp, and of the value of such services, then it is possible that such value might be used to reduce the $...excess benefit....

Issue 5—Were Charitable Car Corp's repayments of undocumented loans by Ben an IRC 4958 excess benefit to Ben?

The clearest evidence of the existence of a loan is a written agreement between the parties. Neither Charitable Car Corp nor Ben provided a loan agreement evidencing any loan between Charitable Car Corp and Ben. Without an agreement we are left to determine its existence based upon the facts and circumstances. The burden of proof is on Ben to show enough facts and circumstances to determine the existence of a loan....

The best that can be said based upon the evidence is that Ben disregarded (1) any sort of requirement to properly maintain Charitable Car Corp's accounts and (2) proper form in the operation of Charitable Car Corp and Ben's other for-profit entities. When Charitable Car Corp needed money, he transferred money from one of his for-profit entities. When he needed money, as in the case of the downpayment [sic] for property in Kendall, he wrote a check from Charitable Car Corp and labeled it "Loan Payable." Charitable Car Corp has written checks to cash, Ben, ... , Frank's Used Cars, and [others] and has labeled them "Loan

Payable" for loans of which Charitable Car Corp has no documentation. There is no explanation why the alleged loan repayments were so sporadic or why no payment was made for almost a year.

Repayments of alleged loans to an organization's founder constitute a classic form of prohibited inurement, *e.g., Founding Church of Scientology v. United States, supra.* This same type of transaction also constitutes an excess benefit transaction. The burden of proving the existence of a loan rests on Charitable Car Corp and Ben. *Vinikoor v. Commissioner, supra.* The burden has not been met, and the alleged repayments to Ben thus constitute section 4958 excess benefits.

If credible, probative evidence can be provided by Ben to explain the many inconsistencies in the current information, then it is possible that such evidence might be used to determine, based upon the facts and circumstances, that a loan existed between Charitable Car Corp and Ben. The examination agent has the discretion to adjust all or part of the excess benefit transaction based upon such evidence.

Issue 6—Were payments to Excel towing company in excess of the fair market value an IRC 4958 excess benefit to Ben, David, and Excel?

In October 1998, Charitable Car Corp made Excel its exclusive tow company for picking up and transferring donated vehicles. Charitable Car Corp made payments to Excel for these services rendered....

The relationship between Charitable Car Corp and Excel towing company provided a section 4958 excess benefit to Excel and David for several reasons. David is the son of Ben and was the exclusive towing service provider of Charitable Car Corp. The fees charges by Excel were greater than fees normally charged by tow service providers in the area....

David created Excel in October 1998, several months after his father created Charitable Car Corp. Excel immediately became the sole provider of towing services to Charitable Car Corp. However, Charitable Car Corp is not in possession of any service agreement between Charitable Car Corp and Excel. Charitable Car Corp has no board meeting minutes to indicate that discussions concerning towing companies were being evaluated or that a bidding process was used. Charitable Car Corp has no notes or other writing to help determine why its previous tow company was replaced by Excel. It is unknown what the terms and conditions of this relationship was [sic], who negotiated it, reviewed it, or signed off on it.

Nigel (Charitable Car Corp's Director) indicated that Excel was created for the sole purpose of towing for Charitable Car Corp. Prior to Excel's creation, Charitable Car Corp used an unrelated towing company at a fee which was less than that charged by Excel. After Ben relinquished control of Charitable Car Corp, Excel ceased providing towing services to Charitable Car Corp. It appears that Excel sold its tow trucks to Charitable Car Corp and got out of the business.

The amounts paid to Excel varied but evidence indicates that they were in excess of the fair market value. After Excel ceased providing towing services, Charitable Car Corp used three different towing services, each charging substantially less than what Excel charged.... Charitable Car Corp's payments to Excel resulted in a section 4958 excess benefit transaction to Excel and David. To the extent Charitable Car Corp's payments to Excel and David were in excess to the fair market value or reasonable compensation, they also constitute section 4958 excess benefits to Ben. Excel received these excessive payments from Charitable Car Corp solely by reason of the fact that it was the wholly owned company of the son of the president of Charitable Car Corp. If Ben had used his authority as president of Charitable Car Corp to take cash in the amount of the excess payments, place it in his personal bank account, and then transfer the funds to his son, the payments would obviously be excess benefits to Ben. The fact that the father, Ben, caused Charitable Car Corp to directly transfer the funds to the company of his son—the natural object of his bounty—cannot eliminate the father's excess benefit liability. See *John Marshall Law School v. United States*. 228 CL 902 (1981). Father and son have joint and several liability for the section 4958 excise taxes on these excess benefits. The examiner should determine the exact amount of the excess benefit, based on the extent to which the payments exceed the fair market value of the services rendered or property transferred....

Issue 8—Was the value of autos furnished to Ben's wife, Ben's daughter, and David an IRC 4958 excess benefit to Ben?

The value of the autos furnished to Ben's wife, Ben's daughter, and Ben's son constitutes section 4958 excess benefit transactions. These individuals received an economic benefit from personal use of these vehicles that were donated to Charitable Car Corp.

Charitable Car Corp does not have written documentation to show that the Board of Directors actually approved Ben's wife's, Ben's daughter's, or Ben's son's use of Charitable Car Corp vehicles either for Charitable Car Corp purposes or for their personal use. Charitable Car Corp has not adopted any policy concerning the use of Charitable Car Corp vehicles or procedures for tracking their use. There is no accountability for the use of this [sic] vehicles through the use of logbooks or other forms of documentation. Additionally, personal use of the vehicles was not reported as income on either Form W-2 or 1099 to the individuals.

Use of Charitable Car Corp's cars must be documented to show that their use is in furtherance of Charitable Car Corp's exempt purpose. Without documentation, it is impossible to show that a vehicle's use furthers an organization's exempt purpose. The value of these benefits was not substantiated as compensation, and thus constituted an excess benefit in their entirety.

The wife, daughter, and son of Ben are disqualified persons under section 4958(f)(1)(B). As explained under Issue 6 above, Ben was responsible for improperly transferring assets from Charitable Car Corp and giving them to the natural objects of his bounty. Accordingly, Ben is jointly and severally liable for section 4958 sanctions on these excess benefits. See *John Marshall Law School v. United States, supra.*

The examiner should determine the fair market value of the use of these vehicles by the wife, daughter, and son. That value constitutes a section 4958 excess benefit....

Issue 14—Is Ben subject to the organization manager tax under IRC 4958?

Section 4958(a)(2) imposes a tax on the participation of an organization manager in an excess benefit transaction. As discussed in Issue 2, Ben was an organization manager within the meaning of section 4958(f)(2) of the Code. Ben's participation in these excess benefit transactions was willful and was not due to reasonable cause, within the meaning of section 4958(a)(2). Ben continued to participate in excess benefit transactions even after CPA, a former director of Charitable Car Corp, warned him of the ramifications of excess benefit transactions. After the CPA's warning and resignation from Charitable Car Corp's Board of Directors, Ben continued to knowingly participate in excess benefit transactions.

V. RELATIONSHIP BETWEEN INUREMENT AND INTERMEDIATE SANCTIONS

TREASURY REGULATIONS §1.501(C)(3)-1(F)(2)

(f) Interaction with section 4958—

(2) Substantive requirements for exemption still apply to applicable tax-exempt organizations described in section 501(c)(3)—

(i) In general.

Regardless of whether a particular transaction is subject to excise taxes under section 4958, the substantive requirements for tax exemption under section 501(c)(3) still apply to an applicable tax-exempt organization (as defined in section 4958(e) and §53.4958–2) described in section 501(c)(3) whose disqualified persons or organization managers are subject to excise taxes under section 4958....

(ii) Determination of whether revocation of tax-exempt status is appropriate when section 4958 excise taxes also apply.

In determining whether to continue to recognize the tax-exempt status of an applicable tax-exempt organization (as defined in section 4958(e) and §53.4958–2) described in section 501(c)(3) that engages in one or more excess benefit transactions (as defined in section 4958(c) and §53.4958–4) that violate the prohibition on inurement under section 501(c)(3), the Commissioner will consider all relevant facts and circumstances, including, but not limited to, the following—

(A) The size and scope of the organization's regular and ongoing activities that further exempt purposes before and after the excess benefit transaction or transactions occurred;

(B) The size and scope of the excess benefit transaction or transactions (collectively, if more than one) in relation to the size and scope of the organization's regular and ongoing activities that further exempt purposes;

(C) Whether the organization has been involved in multiple excess benefit transactions with one or more persons;

(D) Whether the organization has implemented safeguards that are reasonably calculated to prevent excess benefit transactions; and

(E) Whether the excess benefit transaction has been corrected (within the meaning of section 4958(f)(6) and § 53.4958-7), or the organization has made good faith efforts to seek correction from the disqualified person(s) who benefited from the excess benefit transaction.

(iii) All factors will be considered in combination with each other. Depending on the particular situation, the Commissioner may assign greater or lesser weight to some factors than to others. The factors listed in paragraphs (f)(2)(ii)(D) and (E) of this section will weigh more heavily in favor of continuing to recognize exemption where the organization discovers the excess benefit transaction or transactions and takes action before the Commissioner discovers the excess benefit transaction or transactions. Further, with respect to the factor listed in paragraph (f)(2)(ii)(E) of this section, correction after the excess benefit transaction or transactions are discovered by the Commissioner, by itself, is never a sufficient basis for continuing to recognize exemption.

NOTES AND QUESTIONS

1. Now that you understand the relationship between intermediate sanctions and §501(c)(3), do you believe that Charitable Car Corp., the charity described in TE/GE Technical Advice Memorandum 200243047, reproduced above, should also lose its §501(c)(3) tax exemption? What factors are important, and why?

2. In *Caracci v. Comm'r*, 456 F.3d 444 (5th Cir. 2006) the IRS had questioned a transaction in which a nonprofit health care organization converted to a for-profit. The Caracci family had purchased the for-profit organization by acquiring the debt of the old organization, which they maintained was its fair market value. The IRS alleged that the organization was worth far more than that and assessed intermediate sanctions of more than $250 million. The Carracis lost at the trial court level because they could not prove that the price was reasonable, and they also had not followed the procedures that would allow them to use the rebuttable presumption that the transaction was fair. The court imposed sanctions of more than $5 million. *Caracci v. Comm'r*, 118 T.C. 379 (2002). The Fifth Circuit reversed, finding that the

valuation process that the Carracis used was valid. *Caracci v. Comm'r*, 456 F. 3d 444 (5th Cir. 2006). For further discussion, see Chapter 13.

3. The Pension Protection Act of 2006 (P.L. No. 109-280) revised the intermediate sanctions rules to specify that certain transactions are automatically excess benefit provisions. Any grant, loan, compensation, or other similar payment from a donor-advised fund to a person who is a donor, donor adviser, or a related person to that fund is an excess benefit transaction. Similarly, a grant, loan, or compensation from a Type III supporting organization to a substantial contributor or a related person constitutes an excess benefit transaction. Both the donor and the organization manager are penalized, and the entire payment is considered an excess benefit. See Chapter 7, section VI, for more information.

4. The facts that lead to concerns about private inurement, private benefit, and excess benefit transactions at the federal level are also state law issues, and state charity officials can be quite aggressive in pursuing claims on state law grounds. In recent years, California has sued the officers and directors of two car donation charities and a veteran's organization for excessive compensation packages, among other claims. As this book went to press, California had obtained a $2 million settlement from the former directors of the veteran's organization, and the car donation suits were ongoing.[6] New York regularly publicizes its actions against nonprofit leaders who are pocketing the organization's funds. In recent years, former officers and directors have agreed to pay back millions of dollars, and some have even gone to jail.[7] Massachusetts has also pursued claims against presidents of colleges, among others. The president of one college with 200 students allegedly pocketed a $730,000 salary, awarded himself a $150,000 bonus without board approval, and purchased a $4.5 million oceanfront property for a personal residence at a time when the college had assets of only $3.5 million. The property was later sold at a significant loss. Another college president took himself and his family on personal trips overseas, purchased electronic equipment for personal use, and lied about these transactions.[8]

---

[6] *Attorney General Kamala D. Harris Files Lawsuits Against Two Car Donation Charities for Misrepresenting Charitable Programs and Misdirecting Donations*, Dec. 1, 2015, https://oag.ca.gov/news/press-releases/attorney-general-kamala-d-harris-files-lawsuits-against-two-car-donation, accessed April 13, 2016; *Attorney General Kamala D. Harris Announces New Leadership, Restitution for Help Hospitalized Veterans Charity*, Sept. 2013, https://oag.ca.gov/news/press-releases/attorney-general-kamala-d-harris-announces-new-leadership-restitution-help, accessed April 8, 2016.

[7] CharitiesNYS.com, https://www.charitiesnys.com/home.jsp, accessed April 13, 2016.

[8] Walter V. Robinson, *Coakley Lawsuit Wants College's Ex-Chief to Repay Millions*, BOSTON GLOBE (April 23, 2014); Office of the Inspector General, Commonwealth of Massachusetts, Review of Spending Practices by Former Westfield State University President, Evan S. Dobrelle (July 31, 2014).

VI. ISSUES REGARDING NONPROFIT COMPENSATION

Even though the legal doctrines of private inurement, private benefit, and excess benefit transactions are broad enough to encompass especially high compensation packages,[9] public policy issues about compensation in the nonprofit sector remain. At base, we are still debating whether nonprofit compensation packages are, or should be, equivalent to those in the for-profit sector. The following discussion considers (1) what the compensation levels in the nonprofit sector actually are, (2) whether and how nonprofit organizations ensure that compensation agreements meet the requirements of the rebuttable presumption suggesting that the compensation is reasonable, (3) whether states should follow the same standards as the IRS, and (4) whether high compensation is necessary to attract top talent or is a wasteful use of charitable resources.

1. How much compensation do employees in the nonprofit sector actually receive?

Despite the widespread conception that pay in the nonprofit sector tends to be lower than that in the for-profit sector, recent research suggests that this conception is misleading. According to the Bureau of Labor Statistics:

> If we use total compensation costs rather than wages as our pay measure, . . . there is no statistical compensation gap between nonprofit and for-profit businesses for management, professional, and related workers and for sales and office workers, but there is a compensation premium for service workers at nonprofits. These results highlight the importance of a pay measure that includes benefits: across both occupations and levels, workers at nonprofits receive more costly benefits. Thus, ignoring this component of pay can lead to incorrect inferences regarding the pay gap.[10]

Despite this finding, service workers generally are on the low end of the compensation scale, and one of the policy issues surrounding nonprofit pay concerns this low pay. At the Downtown Emergency Service Center in Seattle, for example, many of the employees qualify for the same benefits as the homeless people that they serve, and the executive director of that organization is frank in explaining that an increase in the minimum wage will likely lead to a reduction of services. Paul Tipps and Jesse Inman, *How Nonprofit Workers Get Squeezed When Minimum Wages Increase*, PBS NEWS HOUR (April 25, 2014). A second policy issue concerns the persistent gender gap in compensation in the nonprofit sector. Eden Stiffman, *Women Nonprofit Leaders Still Make Less Than Men, Study Finds*, CHRONICLE OF PHILANTHROPY (Sept. 15, 2015). A third

---

[9] Private foundations are governed by the self-dealing rules (§4945) that were covered in Chapter 7. State laws dealing with this issue were covered in Chapters 1–3 of this book.

[10] Bureau of Labor Statistics, *Nonprofit Pay and Benefits: Estimates from the National Compensation Survey*, MONTHLY LABOR REVIEW (Jan. 2016), http://www.bls.gov/opub/mlr /2016/article/nonprofit-pay-and-benefits.htm, accessed April 6, 2016.

question is whether the low wages in parts of the nonprofit sector are a result of economic bullying. *See* John Tropman and Emily Nicklett, *Balancing the Budget Through Social Exploitation: Why Hard Times Are Even Harder for Some*, ADVANCES IN APPLIED SOCIOLOGY (2012), available online at http://file.scirp.org/pdf/AASoci20120200003_44746157.pdf.

On the other end of the economic spectrum, some salaries in the education, health, and museum sectors are quite high. These are the salaries that get the attention of journalists, charity regulators, legislators, and the IRS. In 2012, presidents of 36 private colleges and 2 public universities received compensation in excess of $1 million. Colin Campbell, *36 Private-College Presidents Make More Than $1 Million*, BALTIMORE SUN, Dec. 7, 2014). Increasingly, college presidents' retirement packages and bonuses are also in the millions. Yale president Richard Levin, for example, received $1.1 million in base pay and $8.5 million in a retirement package in 2013. Michael McDonald, *Ivy League Presidents Are Beginning to Get Paid Like Corporate Executives*, BLOOMBERG NEWS, May 2014.

In 2008, the IRS began a study of colleges and universities by sending letters to a random selection of 400 colleges and universities. That study found that the average salary of the six highest-paid officers, directors, trustees, and key employees at large colleges and universities was almost $800,000, and the median was $352,000. At small colleges and universities, however, the average compensation was $145,000 and the median $98,000. The highest-paid employee was a sports coach at 43% of organizations and a faculty member at 34% of organizations. Internal Revenue Service, *Exempt Organizations Colleges and Universities Interim Compliance Report*, May 2010.

In the healthcare sector, high salaries also abound, and CEOs at nonprofit hospitals often make seven-figure salaries. The average CEO compensation in 2012 of the 147 nonprofit hospitals that Modern Health examined was $2.2 million. The salaries in that study ranged from $178,819 for the CEO of a mental health and substance abuse hospital to $10.7 million for the president of Atlantic Health System in Morristown, New Jersey. (You may remember from Chapter 4 that the Morristown hospital lost its property tax exemption in 2015 because of its commercial activity, which included hefty compensation packages for doctors and administrators.) The CEOs averaged a 24.5% pay raise between 2011 and 2012, compared to a 2% raise for low-level hospital workers. The boards and consultants advising those boards stated that these executive compensation increases were necessary to attract the best talent. Rachel Landen, *Another Year of Pay Hikes for Non-Profit Hospital CEOs*, MODERN HEALTHCARE (Aug. 9, 2014). They may well be right. Another study found a positive correlation between higher pay for nonprofit health care executives and better quality of care. David Koepke, David Foster, Deborah Bilak, Stephen S. Pollack, Jean Chenoweth, Thomas P. Flannery, and Anne Seaman, *CEO Compensation at Nonprofit Hospitals: Associations with Performance Measures*, MERCER TRUVEN ANALYTICS (2016).

2. Meeting the rebuttable presumption under §4958

Legally, these salaries are probably acceptable, at least in terms of federal tax law, if the §501(c)(3) has followed the three-step rebuttable presumption process. This is because at that point, the burden shifts to the IRS to prove that the compensation is unreasonable. The IRS has conducted three compliance projects, designed in part to determine the extent to which §501(c)(3)s engage in this process. All three projects determined that most §501(c)(3)s attempt to follow this rebuttable presumption process and are generally compliant. The Executive Compensation Compliance Project found some errors and omissions, particularly in the area of loans to officers, and the Colleges and Universities Compliance Report determined that approximately 20% of the audited organizations either failed to use total compensation instead of salaries, used inappropriate comparability data, or failed to specify why the data was comparable.[11]

Data are also available at the individual charity level about whether charities follow the rebuttable presumption process. Form 990, the tax information form that §501(c)(3)s file with the IRS on an annual basis, asks how the filing organization has determined the compensation of its top management officials, directors, and key employees. This compensation question specifically asks whether the organization has followed all three steps that would provide it with the rebuttable presumption of §4958. Although the form does not require organizations to follow these steps, a negative answer to this question will at least announce to the IRS, state charity officials, and the public that the filing organization does not follow "best practices."

3. State law considerations when preparing compensation packages

Compensation agreements must also meet the requirements of state laws. California has a special provision requiring the board or a compensation committee of a public charity to review and approve "just and reasonable" compensation packages for their executives,[12] and all states' nonprofit corporation acts codify both the nondistribution constraint and the fiduciary duty requirements. How do those requirements relate to §4958 of the Internal Revenue Code? The states are not bound by this provision, but they may be influenced by it because it provides a road map for determining whether transactions between the organization and its officers and directors are fair.

In 2009, Massachusetts Attorney General Martha Coakley sent a memo to several hospital and health insurance systems, noting that her office was increasing its oversight of compensation agreements. The memo recognized analogies between §4958 and several provisions of Massachusetts state law and

---

[11] Internal Revenue Service, *Report on Exempt Organizations Executive Compensation Compliance Project—Parts I and II* (2007); Internal Revenue Service, *IRS Exempt Organizations (TE/GE) Hospital Compliance Project Final Report* (2009); Internal Revenue Service, *Colleges and Universities Compliance Project Final Report* (2013).

[12] California Nonprofit Integrity Act of 20004, S.B. 1262, 2004 Cal. Legis. Serv. ch. 919; Gov. Code §12586(e)(1)

stated that an organization's compliance with §4958 would be a material factor in its analysis of a compensation package. It also noted that it was not bound by §4958, particularly the rebuttable presumption process that permits organizations to examine the data of comparable organizations. It cited a Maryland case that held that a compensation package that is "comparable" under §4958 is not necessarily "reasonable" under state law. The memo also noted that the use of compensation consultants tended to cause compensation to rise and worried that §4958 "intended only to establish a ceiling, may instead have created a floor."[13] Thus, charities entering into compensation packages with officers, directors, and other key employees may need to do more than follow the rebuttable presumption process as they consider the package.[14]

4. Are high salaries necessary or excessive, and should there be a limit?

Whatever the legal concerns, charities can also face a public relations backlash when compensation packages are high. The concern is that executives are siphoning off money that should be going to the charitable mission, and charities that pay their executives high salaries risk losing donations once that information becomes public. Donor anger can be so great that charities with similar missions fear losing donations as well.

High salaries can also earn the ire of elected officials. Congress held hearings in 2010 after learning that the CEO of the Boys & Girls Clubs earned $1 million in 2008,[15] and it questioned the head of Planned Parenthood in 2016 over her $529,000 salary.[16] At the state level, New York governor Governor Andrew Cuomo has gone so far as to limit the amount of state-authorized funds that may be used toward a nonprofit's administrative costs and executive compensation.[17]

And yet, large public charities are complex businesses that demand talent who can deal with such complexity. The CEO of the Boys & Girls Club who earned $1 million was responsible for 4,000 chapters, with a total of $1.4 billion in revenue. She resigned because the negative publicity was hurting the organization, but she would likely have made the equivalent in a for-profit

---

[13] Commonwealth of Massachusetts, Office of Attorney General, Memo re: Examination of Executive and Director Compensation; Increased Oversight (Sept. 2, 2009), http://www.mass.gov /ago/docs/nonprofit/findings-and-recommendations/bcbs-memo-090209.pdf, accessed April 13, 2016.

[14] *See* Martha White, *Vet Groups Worried About Donations After Wounded Warrior Firings*, NBC NEWS (March 11, 2016).

[15] *Jack Siegel, Senators Tom Coburn and Charles Grassley Shouldn't Be Criticizing Anybody over Financial Management,* NONPROFIT GOVERNANCE BLOG (Aug. 9. 2010), http://www.charitygovernance.com/charity_governance/2010/08/senators-tom-coburn-and-charles-grassley-shouldnt-be-criticizing-anybody-over-financial-management.html, accessed April 18, 2016.

[16] Margot Sanger-Katz and Claire Cain Miller, *Is Planned Parenthood's President Overpaid?* The Upshot, NY TIMES (Sept. 30, 2015), http://www.nytimes.com/2015/10/01/upshot/is-planned-parenthoods-president-overpaid.html?_r=1,

[17] New York State, Executive Order 38, http://executiveorder38.ny.gov, accessed April 13, 2016.

organization.[18] Likewise, the $529,000 salary of the CEO of Planned Parenthood placed her in the 53rd percentile of CEOs running nonprofit healthcare organizations of a similar size.[19] These salaries were obviously reasonable in some contexts and not in others. As future board members and possibly legislators, do you believe that nonprofit-sector salaries should have a limit? If so, how should that limit be determined?

PROBLEM: APPLYING INUREMENT, PRIVATE BENEFIT, AND EXCESS BENEFIT CONCEPTS

You are an IRS examiner. You are auditing Land Conservation, Inc. (LCI), a nonprofit that preserves land from development by buying and reselling it with easements that prohibit future development of the land except for a single-family house. Larry Luck, the executive director and chairman of the board, recently purchased one of those lots. LCI bought the land for $1 million, placed the easement on it, and then said it was worth only $500,000 because of the restriction. Luck bought it for $500,000, which was financed entirely with a no-interest loan from LCI. The board of directors approved this transaction in its last meeting. LCI's lawyer, Luck's wife, prepared an appraisal of the land before they voted and presented the appraisal to the board. She didn't compare the land to any other land; she simply said that the value of the land "must have been reduced substantially due to the restrictions." Nor did she mention that the local banks were requiring 20% down and 5% interest on all loans.

Are there grounds for imposing intermediate sanctions? If so, what transaction or transactions concern you? Who should be sanctioned? What should the penalty be? Do you think that the tax exemption should be revoked? Why or why not? Assume that you are also working with state charity officials. What state law principles, which were covered in Chapters 2 and 3, may have been broken?

---

[18] Siegel, *supra* note 15.

[19] Art Golab, *Think a $500K Salary for Planned Parenthood's CEO is a Ton of Dough? Think Again,* VITAL HEALTH BLOG (Sept. 30, 2015), http://www.modernhealthcare.com/article/20150930/BLOG/150939985.

CHAPTER 10

COMPLEX COMMERCIAL TRANSACTIONS

Purposes of this chapter:

- Consider the circumstances under which §501(c)(3) tax-exempt organizations would choose to create subsidiaries or enter into joint ventures with other organizations
- Explore the ways that such commercial ventures could subvert the principles behind tax exemption
- Examine whether the policy issues are different if the subsidiary or joint-venture partner is for profit or nonprofit
- Understand the ways that Congress, the Internal Revenue Service (IRS), and the courts have chosen to address the issues raised by complex commercial ventures
- Determine whether better ways to approach these issues exist

To think about as you read:

If you have created a virtual nonprofit for this course, assume that it has progressed to the point that it intends to create a subsidiary or enter into a joint venture. Otherwise, imagine that you represent a local art museum that wants to use television and the Internet to tell the story of its collection and of art in general. Should the art museum develop its own television and Internet expertise so that it can handle these activities within the art museum? Should it instead partner with another organization? If so, should the relationship be that of a subsidiary or a joint venture? How do you decide which structure would best serve the organization? What legal issues will you try to avoid as you structure this deal?

I. INTRODUCTION

Increasingly, nonprofit organizations find themselves involved in complex business transactions, involving subsidiaries, joint ventures, or both. *Subsidiaries* are business organizations that another organization (the "parent") owns or controls. This book discussed a parent-subsidiary situation in Chapter 7, when it covered Type I supporting organizations (SOs). To review, a Type I SO is able to piggyback onto the tax exemption of the supported organization because the supported organization elects the board of the SO. The right to elect the board gives the supported organization control over the SO and creates a subsidiary relationship. (Why is it incorrect to say the supported organization "owns" the subsidiary in this situation?) *Joint ventures* are business relationships between two or more entities that are created to pursue a common activity. They can bring a much-needed cash infusion into an organization's programs, but if they are not structured carefully, they can also bring tax problems. Joint ventures can be formed as contractual arrangements or partnerships. Sometimes, as we will see, two organizations form a partnership to create a separate corporation.

However complex the transactions, the legal issues should be familiar. One concern is whether a §501(c)(3) organization that enters into one of these complex business dealings now has too large a commercial purpose to retain its tax exemption. A second concern is whether transactions between the parties create unrelated business taxable income. A third concern is whether the for-profit organization benefits from the nonprofit in a way that raises private inurement, private benefit, or intermediate sanctions issues. In fact, virtually any issue that arises with tax-exempt organizations can also arise once the organization creates a subsidiary or enters into a joint venture.

This chapter begins with a discussion of the reasons why nonprofits decide to conduct exempt activities through subsidiaries. It follows with a discussion of some of the issues that can arise with subsidiaries. The next section of the chapter discusses issues that surround joint ventures between §501(c)(3) organizations and for-profit organizations. The final section brings back the topic of social enterprises, which was introduced in Chapter 2. The most common way to organize a "hybrid" business—one with both for-profit and nonprofit goals—is to utilize one of these complex structures, and this section allows us to consider some of the public policy issues raised by these structures.

II. SUBSIDIARIES OF §501(c)(3) TAX-EXEMPT ORGANIZATIONS

A tax-exempt §501(c)(3) organization can decide to create a subsidiary for any number of reasons. Following is an article by a Michigan law firm with a nonprofit and tax-exempt practice that explains some of these reasons, discusses the relationship between parent organizations and their subsidiaries, and outlines legal issues relating to the separate corporate existence of the organizations. After that article, four other issues relating to subsidiaries of tax-exempt organizations are covered: (1) the choice of entity for the subsidiary, (2) whether the subsidiary is truly a separate entity, (3) whether the subsidiary jeopardizes the parent's exempt status, and (4) whether unrelated business income issues exist.

A. WHY SUBSIDIARIES EXIST AND HOW THEY WORK

THOMPSON AND THOMPSON, PC, SUBSIDIARIES OF
TAX-EXEMPT ORGANIZATIONS

www.t-tlaw.com/bus-04.htm

As tax-exempt organizations have grown in size and complexity, it is not uncommon to find such organizations owning and/or controlling one or more subsidiary corporations. These subsidiary corporations may be nonprofit tax-exempt subsidiaries, or they may be for-profit subsidiaries. In either case, a tax-exempt organization may own and/or control a subsidiary corporation, whether nonprofit or for-profit, without jeopardizing its tax-exempt status.

The For-Profit Subsidiary

There are many reasons why a tax-exempt organization may establish a subsidiary corporation. In the case of a nonprofit organization having a for-profit subsidiary, the usual reasons for its organization are: (1) that the tax-exempt organization desires to engage in business activities unrelated to its exempt purpose; (2) that the existing or projected revenues from the unrelated business activity are substantial; (3) that the tax-exempt organization prefers not to engage in any unrelated business, income-producing activities because the income may be reportable on IRS Form 990T; or (4) that the unrelated business income-producing activities are so substantial that the income may exceed revenues received by the tax-exempt organization, thus risking the organization's exempt status; (5) that the business activities may carry risks of liability unacceptable to the organization; (6) that the organization desires to own an asset of increasing value; (7) that the organization desires to reward certain employees with increasing compensation, etc.

The Nonprofit Subsidiary

When it comes to establishing a nonprofit subsidiary of a tax-exempt organization, the usual reasons for its organization are: (1) that certain activities are distinct from and perhaps incompatible with the exempt purposes of the parent organization and are better pursued in an independent, but controlled subsidiary; (2) that the prospect of obtaining government grants is enhanced if certain activities are separated into an independent subsidiary corporation; (3)

that substantial revenues will be generated by business activities related to the subsidiary's purposes which may be unrelated to the parent organization's exempt purposes.

The Parent/Subsidiary Relationship

It is common to use the term "parent/subsidiary" when describing the relationship between a nonprofit organization and its subsidiary. This is true whether the subsidiary is a for-profit or a nonprofit subsidiary. But, a caveat is in order here. The term "parent/subsidiary" is not equivalent to the term "parent/child." This is an important point. While the parent nonprofit organization may incorporate its subsidiary corporation, name its board of directors and officers, enunciate the subsidiary's business purpose or tax-exempt mission, adopt bylaw provisions preserving the parent's control of its subsidiary, etc., it is important that the subsidiary be established and recognized by the parent, as well as third parties, as an independent corporation managed by a board of directors.

Subsidiary Independence: A Stumbling Block?

The matter of subsidiary independence is oftentimes a stumbling block to the parent nonprofit organization which may view an independent subsidiary as an uncontrolled subsidiary. But recognizing a subsidiary as an "independent" corporation is not the equivalent of regarding the subsidiary as "uncontrolled." At all times, provided that appropriate bylaw provisions are adopted and maintained, the parent has the legal authority to hold the subsidiary accountable to meet "bottom line" financial objectives, to pursue acceptable policy mandates, to fulfill its charitable mission (if a nonprofit subsidiary) and to otherwise conduct its affairs in a manner pleasing to the parent.

How Does the Parent Control an Independent Subsidiary?

Upon reaching a decision to organize or acquire a subsidiary corporation, the nonprofit organization parent controls its nonprofit subsidiary by being its sole voting member, or in states permitting "stock" nonprofits, such as Delaware and Michigan, the parent simply holds all of the subsidiary's issued and outstanding voting stock. In the case of a for-profit subsidiary, the parent simply holds stock. By holding, i.e., by owning all of the subsidiary's voting stock, or by being the sole voting member of a nonprofit subsidiary in states not permitting "stock" nonprofits, the parent has the power to elect and remove the entire board of directors.

To maintain control of a subsidiary and at the same time allow the subsidiary to operate as an independent entity under the direction of its board of directors, a parent nonprofit organization should: (1) be the sole shareholder or sole voting member of the subsidiary; (2) include voting control provisions in the subsidiary's articles of incorporation along with provisions that prohibit amendment of the articles without the approval of the sole shareholder or sole voting member; (3) prepare comprehensive bylaws defining the designation and authority of officers, their term of office, their removal (for cause, or for any or no reason); (4) include in the bylaws the procedure whereby the parent elects and removes directors; and (5) prohibit bylaw amendments without the sole shareholder's or sole voting member's approval, etc.

The board of directors of the subsidiary are [sic—*Ed.*] responsible to manage the business and affairs of the subsidiary. The board selects officers and the officers are responsible to execute the policies of the board. The officers of the subsidiary do not "report" to the officers or board of the parent nor are they responsible to the officers or board of the parent corporation. This does not mean, however, that there is no communication between the subsidiary's CEO and the parent. After all, the parent owns the subsidiary (if a for-profit subsidiary, or controls the subsidiary if nonprofit) and by virtue of its ownership or control is entitled to examine the subsidiary's financial reports and business plan, and to otherwise hold the subsidiary and its management accountable for the performance expectations of the parent.

What Legal Risks Are Likely in The Parent/Subsidiary Relationship?

A parent corporation may hold its subsidiary (whether profit or nonprofit) accountable for the expectations of its board of directors. And, this is the purpose of the parent's control of its subsidiary: to hold it accountable for performance. As long as the parent permits the subsidiary to act independently under the direction of its board, there is little risk to the parent of being found liable for the negligence or wrong-doing of the subsidiary. After all, the parent in a parent/subsidiary relationship is merely a stockholder, or a voting member, and the law is clear that a stockholder, or voting member, is not liable for the actions, debts, or obligations of the corporation.

However, if the parent exercises excessive control over the subsidiary by, e.g., commingling funds, interchanging employees, having its board serve as the board of the subsidiary, sharing office facilities, using a common letterhead, and otherwise blurring the distinctions between the parent and the subsidiary as separate independent corporations, then each corporation is at risk for the unfunded liabilities of the other under the legal doctrine of "alter ego." Under this doctrine, a litigant may "pierce the corporate veil" of the subsidiary corporation and reach the assets of the parent corporation under the theory that the two corporations, for legal liability purposes, are not two independent corporations, but are but one corporation in fact. In this way, the litigant may seek payment of an unfunded liability of one corporation from another corporation. It must be noted, however, that a litigant pursuing an alter ego theory of liability has an uphill fight. Courts are not likely to permit a litigant to "pierce the corporate veil" of a corporation and reach the assets of its shareholder, or member, that is the parent, unless it is abundantly clear that the two corporations were indistinguishable as separate corporate entities and are operating as one corporation.

How Should the Parent/Subsidiary Relationship Be Managed?

The parent corporation, by virtue of its voting control of the subsidiary, has the power to hold the subsidiary accountable for its performance. Since the parent retains voting control, it has the authority to select the subsidiary's directors. This is a most important aspect of the parent's control of its subsidiary. By selecting qualified, and to some extent indoctrinated, directors, the parent puts into place the subsidiary's board of directors. This board manages the business and affairs of the subsidiary, makes policy, selects its officers, provides oversight of the subsidiary's activities, and functions as the subsidiary's governing body.

The parent's selection of the subsidiary's directors is a critical exercise of authority. A wrong-headed decision here risks mismanagement of the subsidiary. Thus, not only should the subsidiary's directors be selected with care, they should be "schooled" in a formal board training program which teaches individuals what they should know about being a director of a nonprofit or a for-profit corporation, as the case may be. Not everyone is suited for being a director of a corporation. Today, nonprofit and for-profit organizations alike confront challenges which tax the ability of the most gifted board members. While it would be a stretch to impute liability to a parent corporation for its "negligent" selection of subsidiary directors, nevertheless prudent selections should be made, and individuals selected as directors should undertake a board training experience.

B. CHOICE OF ENTITY FOR THE SUBSIDIARY

As noted above, the subsidiary is a separate business entity that can be organized under any of the business entity choices discussed in Chapter 2. For the most part, this decision is no different from the one discussed in that chapter. Those who are founding the subsidiary will determine whether they need the tax-deductible contributions and the halo effect that they could achieve with a nonprofit, or whether they can better capitalize as a for-profit and perhaps provide better financial incentives to employees and investors. If they choose a nonprofit form, they will ordinarily create a §501(c)(3), which will be governed by the laws and regulations discussed in this book. Although the parent might own some of or all the assets of the new organization, it will not own the nonprofit. Instead, it will elect the board and have control over the §501(c)(3) in that respect.

If, instead, the founding organization chooses a for-profit form for the subsidiary, it will choose one of the forms outlined in Chapter 2. Then, except in unusual circumstances, the subsidiary, which will be a separate for-profit entity, will be taxed in the same way that other for-profit entities of its type are taxed.[1]

---

[1] See Chapter 2, Part III. A.

Remember that for-profit subsidiaries were not always required to pay their own income taxes. Prior to 1950 and the passage of the unrelated business income tax law, the destination-of-income doctrine allowed the income generated by activities of the subsidiaries of §501(c)(3)s to remain exempt, even if those activities were unrelated to the charity's exempt purpose, so long as the subsidiary's income "fed" its profits to the charity. Such subsidiaries are called *feeder organizations.* In 1950, §502 of the Internal Revenue Code overruled this destination of income rule, stating in relevant part: "An organization operated for the primary purpose of carrying on a trade or business for profit shall not be exempt from taxation under section 501 on the ground that all of its profits are payable to one or more organizations exempt from taxation under section 501." Section 502 thus ensures that wholly owned subsidiaries will pay taxes unless they are themselves tax-exempt.

Occasionally, however, subsidiaries that are organized as for-profit entities can utilize the tax-exempt status of their parents to avoid paying taxes. For example, the "integral part" doctrine, discussed below, is a carefully crafted exception to the feeder organization rule. And if the subsidiary is a limited liability company (LLC), it can be a disregarded entity for tax purposes under certain circumstances that are also discussed below.

1. The Integral-Part Doctrine

The "integral part" doctrine recognizes that, in some rare situations, the subsidiary is so closely related to the parent's exempt purpose that the parent's tax exemption should be attributed to the subsidiary. Treas. Reg. § 1.502-1(b) (26 C.F.R. § 1.502-1) states in part:

> If a subsidiary organization of a tax-exempt organization would itself be exempt on the ground that its activities are an integral part of the exempt activities of the parent organization, its exemption will not be lost because, as a matter of accounting between the two organizations, the subsidiary derives a profit from its dealings with the parent organization. . . .

This regulation recognizes that an organization can be an integral part of the parent organization only if the parent is its only customer. The following case illustrates this doctrine.

IHC HEALTH PLANS, INC. V. COMM'R

---

325 F.3d 1188 (10th Cir. 2003)

[*Editor's Note:* This case appeared in Chapter 4 in the discussion about exemption requirements for health care organizations. Recall that the court concluded that the health maintenance organizations (HMOs) in question did not operate with sufficient community benefit to qualify for §501(c)(3) tax exemptions as a health care organization. We did not pay particular attention to the corporate structure at that time, but the second issue in the case is whether the subsidiaries are so closely related to the parent that the parent's tax exemption should be attributed to the subsidiaries. Thus, the corporate structure is important to this second issue.

To review: At the time of this lawsuit, IHC Health Plans (IHC), the petitioner in this case, was the §501(c)(3) tax-exempt parent organization of two medical enterprises: Health Services, which operated 22 hospitals in its network, and Health Plans, a state-licensed HMO and preferred provider organization (PPO). Health Plans, in turn, had two subsidiaries that offered qualified health plans that federal law prohibited Health Plans from operating directly—Care and Group. In 1999, the IRS revoked Health Plans's §501(c)(3) tax exemption and issued a final adverse determination letter for Care and Group, arguing that none of the three should be recognized as tax exempt under §501(c)(3).

If one were to draw a diagram of this corporate arrangement, it would look like this:

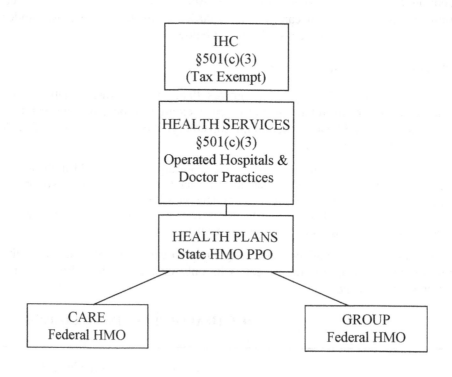

The Tenth Circuit held that Health Plans, Care, and Group did not provide the community benefits required for an exempt health care provider under IRC §501(c)(3). (See Chapter 4 for the presentation of that issue in this case.) A second issue was whether the petitioners qualified for tax-exempt status as an "integral part" of Health Services. That discussion is reproduced below.]

Petitioners contend that even if they do not qualify for tax exemption standing alone, they qualify based on the fact that their activities are an "integral part" of Health Services, essential to Health Services in accomplishing its tax-exempt purpose. We disagree.

In general, "separately incorporated entities must qualify for tax exemption on their own merits." *Geisinger Health Plan v. C.I.R.*, 30 F.3d 494, 498 (3d Cir. 1994).... Several circuits, however, have recognized a so-called "exception" to this general rule, commonly called the integral-part doctrine.... Under the integral-part doctrine, where an organization's sole activity is an "integral part" of an exempt affiliate's activities, the organization may derive its exemption from that of its affiliate. . . .

To the extent [that] the integral-part doctrine rests on a derivative theory of exemption, it runs contrary to two fundamental tenets of tax law: (1) the "doctrine of corporate entity," under which a corporation is a separate and distinct taxable entity; and (2) the canon of statutory interpretation requiring strict construction of exemptions from taxation.[2] IHC separately incorporated Health Services, Health Plans, Care, and Group. "It cannot now escape the tax consequences of that choice, no matter how bona fide its motives or longstanding its arrangements." *Nat'l Carbide Corp. v. C.I.R.*, 336 U.S. 422, 439, 69 S. Ct. 726, 93 L. Ed. 779 (1949). Further, we reject petitioners' contention that the integral-part doctrine constitutes a "less rigorous" road to tax exemption. The rigor of the charitable-purpose requirement remains constant, regardless of the theory upon which the taxpayer bases its entitlement to tax exemption under section 501(c)(3).

Nevertheless, to the extent the integral-part doctrine recognizes that we should consider the totality of the circumstances in determining an organization's purpose, the doctrine is in accord with our section 501(c)(3) jurisprudence. . . .

Using the example cited in Treasury Regulation 1.502-1(b) [of a subsidiary whose sole purpose is furnishing electrical power to a tax-exempt educational institution], if we were to consider the nature of the subsidiary's activity in isolation—furnishing electricity—we would have no indication that the subsidiary serves an exempt purpose. On the other hand, when we look at the totality of the circumstances, it becomes clear that the subsidiary's activity furthers the exempt purpose of education: the product provided is essential; the subsidiary furnishes its product solely to the tax-exempt affiliate; and the tax-exempt parent exercises control over the subsidiary. These facts, considered in conjunction with the exempt purpose for which the tax-exempt parent operates, support a strong inference that the subsidiary operates for the same exempt purpose as does the parent.

---

[2] [FN 31] As the Third Circuit noted in *Geisinger II*, the "integral-part doctrine" is not codified. 30 F.3d at 499. Although it finds support in 26 C.F.R. §1.502-1(b), it must ultimately be justified under section 501(c)(3) and its charitable-purpose requirement.

In this case, we need not decide whether petitioners provide a service necessary to Health Services in conducting its exempt activities. The required nexus between the activities of petitioners and Health Services is lacking. As the Tax Court noted,

> petitioner[s]' enrollees received approximately 20 percent of their physician services from physicians employed by or contracting with Health Services, while petitioner contracted for the remaining 80 percent of such physician services directly with independent physicians." *Health Plans*, 82 T.C.M. at 606. Thus, unlike the subsidiary furnishing electricity in Treasury Regulation §1.502-1(b), petitioners do not function solely to further Health Services' performance of its exempt activities. Rather, a substantial portion (eighty percent) of petitioners' enrollees received physician services from "physicians with no direct link to [Health Services]." *Health Plans*, 82 T.C.M. at 606. Thus, our consideration of petitioners' "connectedness" to Health Services in no way detracts from our earlier conclusion that petitioners do not qualify for a charitable tax exemption under section 501(c)(3).

Based on the foregoing, we AFFIRM the Tax Court's decision denying petitioners tax-exempt status under 26 U.S.C. §501(c)(3).

2. LLCs

LLCs are unincorporated associations that receive protection against liability, much as corporations do, but they can choose whether to be taxed as a separate corporation or whether their net taxable income should be included as part of the owner's taxable income. An LLC that chooses the latter option is called a "disregarded entity." If the LLC is a disregarded entity, the member (owner) in a single-member LLC is taxed as a sole proprietor, and multiple members are treated for tax purposes as if they were in a partnership.

Assume that a §501(c)(3) homeless shelter creates an affiliated LLC to run a food pantry and is its only member. Assume, too, that the food is offered on a sliding-scale basis, but is not offered for free. What are the tax consequences? If the LLC is a disregarded entity, its activities are treated as the activities of its owner. So long as its activities are related to the homeless shelter's exempt purpose, the proceeds from those activities will not be taxed because the income from the food pantry is related to the parent's exempt purpose. But if the food pantry's activities are contrary to the homeless shelter's tax-exempt purposes, it could either adversely affect the shelter's tax-exempt status or create unrelated business taxable income (UBTI) for the shelter.

The analysis to determine whether the food pantry's proceeds should be taxable to the homeless shelter or remain tax exempt is the same analysis explained in Chapter 8. If the activities are geared toward helping the homeless and other low-income people who may be in danger of losing their homes, they will be related to the homeless shelter's exempt purpose. Providing food on a sliding-scale basis could satisfy these requirements, but if the organizational documents or the activities begin to look too much like a grocery store and become unrelated to the exempt purpose, the proceeds will be taxable to the owner of the LLC (in this case, the homeless shelter). So long as the unrelated commercial activity is not so great as to jeopardize the tax exemption, the shelter would simply pay unrelated business income tax (UBIT) on the proceeds. If, however, the pantry/grocery store became very successful, it could jeopardize the tax exemption of the shelter.

The above example assumes the shelter is the only member of the LLC. If, instead, the LLC is one of two or more owners of a disregarded LLC, the LLC will be treated as a partnership. So long as the LLC has the same exempt purpose as the shelter, the proceeds will not be taxable to the shelter. A second owner may have to pay taxes on those proceeds, however.

Should the LLC choose to be treated as a corporation, it could then be a for-profit LLC, taxed as an ordinary corporation, or it could seek tax-exempt status if it is chartered in a state that recognizes nonprofit LLCs. The IRS has set forth 12 conditions that must be met for the LLC to be recognized as a §501(c)(3) exempt organization. They parallel the requirements for a nonprofit corporation to meet exemption requirements. Whether the LLC is recognized as a §501(c)(3) organization or not, so long as it is not a disregarded entity, the legal issues between the §501(c)(3) and the LLC member would be the same as the issues between a §501(c)(3) and a nonprofit or for-profit subsidiary.[3]

C. IS THE SUBSIDIARY A SEPARATE ORGANIZATION?

The alter ego doctrine discussed in the Thompson article above allows a court to "pierce the corporate veil" if the activities of the two organizations are not independent enough. As the article pointed out, the parent can control the subsidiary by maintaining voting control on the board of the subsidiary, but it cannot be so involved that the organizations are, in effect, two organizations. It is very rare for a court to pierce a corporate veil, but it does happen occasionally. An example follows.

NETWORK FOR GOOD V. UNITED WAY OF THE BAY AREA, FINDINGS OF FACT AND CONCLUSIONS OF LAW

California Superior Court, San Francisco County,
Case No. 436186, pp. 66-72 (Oct. 19, 2007)

[*Editor's Note:* During the 1990s, United Way chapters throughout the United States began offering donors the opportunity to direct their donations to

---

[3] *See* Richard A. McCray & Ward L. Thomas, *Limited Liability Companies as Exempt Organizations—Update*, Exempt Organizations Technical Instruction Program for FY 2001, 27-33, www.irs.gov/pub/irs-tege/eotopicb01.pdf. This article has additional information on issues that arise when a member of an LLC is a tax-exempt organization.

various charities. Several of those chapters contracted with the United Way of the Bay Area (UWBA) to handle the "back office" functions—keeping account of the gifts, ensuring that the money is transferred to the designated charities, and generating receipts and acknowledgments. Helping.org, the precursor to Network for Good (NFG), also contracted with UWBA for back office services for its website, which offered (and still offers) donors the opportunity to make a gift to any charitable organization in the United States. To see how this works, go to www.networkforgood.org.

In 2000, UWBA spun off a nonprofit subsidiary, PipeVine, to handle these transactions. PipeVine provided finance, accounting, pledge processing, and fundraising campaign management for UWBA, NFG, and several other corporations. In June 2003, PipeVine suddenly shut its doors and ceased operations. The receiver appointed at the request of the California attorney general found that at the time it closed, PipeVine had received $17.7 million in donations that had not been distributed. Almost $3 million of those funds was owed to charities that had been designated by donors through the NFG site. In August 2003, NFG paid $2.36 million to 2,300 charities and then brought this lawsuit for recovery of damages.

The trial court agreed with NFG that PipeVine was too closely related to UWBA to avoid alter ego liability. Among its factual findings was that UWBA started PipeVine with several million in liabilities on its books, without providing sufficient capital to pay off these debts. Thus, from its first day of existence, PipeVine was using money earmarked to specific charities to pay off older debts to other charities. The court also noted that the UWBA board had not spent enough time considering whether PipeVine had sufficient capitalization, that UWBA and PipeVine changed their accounting to make it more difficult to recognize this undercapitalization, and that the two organizations did not do enough to separate their books, offices, board members, and personnel.

As you read the following opinion, think about the reasons why UWBA may have wanted to create a subsidiary. What could or should UWBA have done to avoid this result? Would the court's decision have been different if the case involved a for-profit corporation and its wholly owned subsidiary? Do any of the issues that we have already discussed in this book come into play in this situation?]

UWBA Is the Alter Ego of PipeVine and Therefore Liable for All Damages Suffered by Network for Good

Any discussion of the alter ego doctrine in the context of charitable giving and nonprofits like NFG and UWBA needs to include §17510.8 of the California Business and Professions Code. "Notwithstanding any other provision of this article, there exists a fiduciary relationship between a charity and any person soliciting on behalf of a charity, and the person for whom a charitable contribution is being solicited. The acceptance of charitable contributions by a charity or any person soliciting on behalf of a charity *establishes* a *charitable trust* and a *duty* on the part of the charity and person soliciting on behalf of the charity to use those *charitable* contributions for the *declared charitable purposes* for which they are sought...."

This directive by the Legislature reflects a public policy that caretakers of charitable donations need to be especially focused and, indeed, vigilant, in the distributions of such funds. The integrity of the public giving process is at stake. When NFG contracted with Defendant to distribute donations through PipeVine, a spinoff of UWBA, it was expecting UWBA would observe the import of this legislative policy. Arguably, NFG decided to cover outstanding donations after the collapse of PipeVine with the alacrity it did using its own resources because of NFG's cognizance of charitable trust obligations. Significantly, the evidence developed in the Findings of Fact provides a legal basis for the Court's conclusion UWBA failed to adequately implement its "duty" as caretaker of NFG donations "to use those charitable contributions for the declared charitable purposes." The charitable trust was breached.

Because of §17510.8, UWBA had greater responsibility than simply create a spinoff called PipeVine to disseminate on-line charitable donations. It had a statutory duty to see that operations were in place to properly distribute donations from the time of PipeVine's inception. The charitable contributions that filtered through PipeVine needed to go to charities, not other business costs that should have been better understood by UWBA before and during PipeVine's three year existence.

This is not your garden variety breach of contract between two entities seeking implementation of alter ego liability. To this Court, the public policy articulated in §17510.8 triggers a higher level of accountability on the part of UWBA and its development of PipeVine. Acknowledged as a feature of Defendant's oversight, the statute assists the Court in exercising its judicial assessment of the events in the lawsuit.

The two general requirements for application of the alter ego doctrine are (1) that there is such unity of interest and ownership that the separate personalities of the two entities no longer exist and (2) that, if the acts are treated as those of the subsidiary alone, an inequitable result will follow. *Automo[t]riz, supra*, 47 Cal. 2d at 796.... These requirements similarly apply whether the entity sought to be held liable is a[n] individual or another corporation like a parent. ...

[S]everal factors . . . identify unity of interest and the inequitable result or fraud and injustice prongs of that case. . . . Review of these . . . factors to the facts in this case at least supports the conclusion that commingling of assets and improper asset diversion; use of a common business location; employment of the same officers, and legal and accounting services; failure to adequately capitalize the spin-off PipeVine at inception; the continued undercapitalization of PipeVine during its existence; the lack of arm's length dealing between UWBA and PipeVine; and the diversion of employees and assets from one entity to the other at critical times in the PipeVine operation, are several enumerated factors allowing this Court to adopt the alter ego theory of liability regarding UWBA. These factors are already detailed in the Findings of Fact portion of this opinion.

This Court does seek to comment on the particular factor of undercapitalization in this case from a legal perspective. As the Findings of Fact support, the spin-off of PipeVine from Defendant UWBA was improperly funded at the outset. Inadequate capital support also plagued PipeVine until it went into receivership less than three years after creation. The legal complicity of UWBA in this scenario is most supportive of the Court's decision to apply alter ego principles to the case . . . . Failure to recognize responsibility of the alter ego where there is an inadequate capital at the outset would tolerate an abuse of the corporate privilege.... [T]he degree of undercapitalization in PipeVine tolerated by UWBA is viewed as flagrant and critical to the legal issues of the case.

Network for Good need not demonstrate that UWBA was PipeVine's alter ego for all purposes; it must demonstrate only that under the particular facts of this case, justice and equity can best be accomplished by disregarding the distinct entity of the corporate form.

It is not necessary to show the existence of fraud or bad faith for the alter ego doctrine to apply. Rather, "[i]t is enough if the recognition of the two entities as separate would result in an injustice."...

Network for Good has shown, by a preponderance of the evidence, a unity of interest and ownership between UWBA and PipeVine in the context of this case. The evidence demonstrates that UWBA did not consider the issues of PipeVine's capitalization or liquidity prior to its separation from UWBA; that PipeVine was significantly undercapitalized when it was "spun off" from UWBA; that PipeVine upon its separation from UWBA had insufficient assets to pay its obligations when they came due and had to use new donor contributions to do so; that UWBA manipulated its own and PipeVine's accounting records and financial statements to conceal PipeVine's undercapitalization and lack of liquidity; that, after separation, UWBA and PipeVine operated as if they were a single entity; that UWBA exerted control over PipeVine after it was "spun off" from UWBA; and that the two entities had overlapping officers, directors, counsel and auditor and commingled their assets, accounts and books and records.

Network for Good has shown, by a preponderance of the evidence, that inequity would result if PipeVine's acts are treated as separate from those of UWBA. Because the operations, finances, and personnel of UWBA and PipeVine were so intertwined, UWBA became privy early on to the growing financial calamity at PipeVine and was able to take action that Network for Good and PipeVine's other customers were not.

Moreover, inequity would result not only in light of the relationship between the parties to this case, but in light of the broader non-profit sector in which the parties and PipeVine operated. UWBA ostensibly spun off PipeVine to provide services to charitable organizations, and UWBA's CEO, Anne Wilson, among others, admitted that PipeVine's collapse harmed the non-profit community.

Because the evidence demonstrates UWBA's significant role in the events leading up to that collapse, it would be inequitable to allow UWBA to escape responsibility for such conduct.

Accordingly, the Court concludes that UWBA is liable to Network for Good for any injuries Network for Good suffered due to misconduct by PipeVine.

D. POTENTIAL INUREMENT ISSUES

TECHNICAL ADVICE MEMORANDUM 200437040

[*Editor's Note:* As we saw in Chapter 9, a TAM is the IRS's response to technical or procedural questions that develop during an IRS proceeding. The TAM applies to a single, already closed proceeding and has no precedential value, but it does signal the IRS's thoughts about specific issues. In this case, the IRS did not revoke the organization's exemption, but it did point out the possibility that a subsidiary could be used to funnel a charity's funds to a founder and his or her family.

TAMs never include information that could identify the taxpayer; however, CCH has identified the taxpayer in this TAM as the Foundation of Human Understanding, the plaintiff in *Foundation of Human Understanding v. Comm'r*, which was included in Chapter 4.[4] If that is the case, the founder would be Roy Masters, and you can substitute Masters's name for "A" and the Foundation's for "X" as you read the TAM. This conclusion is logical because the facts of the TAM are the same as those in the *Foundation of Human Understanding* case, and one of the TAM's issues that is not reproduced below is whether the taxpayer should lose its status as a church but remain a §501(c)(3) religious organization.]

Issue

Did X, an organization recognized under section 501(c)(3) of the Internal Revenue Code, have a substantial nonexempt purpose during the years..., and, if so, should X's exempt status be revoked?...

Facts: Background

X was incorporated by A for charitable and religious purposes in ... and was recognized by the Service as exempt from federal income tax under section 501(a) of the Code as an organization described in section 501(c)(3) in a letter dated December 20, ...

---

[4] CCH Tax News Headlines, *Nonprofit Organization Not a Church; Associational Aspects Lacking* (Foundation of Human Understanding, CA-FC) (Aug. 30, 2010), http://tax.cchgroup.com /news/headlines/2010/nws083010.htm.

In ... X amended its articles of incorporation to state that it was a church. It was subsequently ruled that X qualified as an organization described in IRC section 170(b)(1)(A)(i), as a church. At that time, X . . . conduct[ed] regular religious services three or four times a week . . . for congregations consisting of 50 to 350 persons. . . .

[*Editor's Note:* In the years in question, X no longer conducted regular religious services. It did conduct counseling sessions, for which it charged a fee, and it sold books and tapes. The board consisted of A, his wife, and members of his immediate family. X's bylaws were written so that A remained in control for life, to be replaced by his wife for life, and then by her five children upon her death.

X's assets included real estate and a for-profit subsidiary. The subsidiary's directors included A, his wife, their two sons, and D, who was responsible for the subsidiary's daily operations but appeared not to be related to A's family]

In an effort to cover X's operating deficits and expand its exempt activities, it invested . . . over a period of several years, in a for-profit subsidiary that carried on a wholly secular activity. In the years in issue, and apparently for some years thereafter, this subsidiary suffered net operating losses. At the same time, the subsidiary grew rapidly, and is claimed to have a value that is several times the amount invested. The subsidiary provided some services to X's exempt activities, for which the subsidiary was paid a monthly fee. However, most of the subsidiary's activities have been solely secular and commercial.

[*Editor's note:* The IRS first discussed whether X's accumulation of assets, including large amounts of real estate and a loan to the subsidiary, constituted a substantial nonexempt purpose. Citing *Better Business Bureau v. United States,* 326 U.S. 279, 283 (1945), *In Presbyterian and Reformed Publishing Co. v. Commissioner,* 743 F.2d 148 (3d Cir. 1984), and *Church of Scientology v. Commissioner,* 83 T.C. 381, 489 and fn. 8 (1984), aff'd, 823 F.2d 1310 (9th Cir. 1987), the IRS determined that "X has provided sufficient information as to its needs and reasonably anticipated needs for its accumulations—at least during the three years (...) in issue. For several years, X operated its tax-exempt programs at substantial deficits, and the income from the investment real estate was available to cover the deficits." Its discussion of X's relationship with its subsidiary follows.]

In post-audit years, it appears that the subsidiary grew rapidly—perhaps beyond X's expectations. It is now worth several times X's investment in the subsidiary, although it apparently had not earned an operating profit through [a certain date]. This growth presents a continuing obligation on X to translate this valuable asset into funds, and use those funds for the expansion of its charitable religious activities. For example, X may have to give consideration to selling some of the subsidiary's assets, or selling a portion of the stock of the subsidiary, to an unrelated party. The proceeds of such transactions must be used to fund or expand X's charitable or religious activities. The subsidiary should give highest priority to repaying X's investment loans once it begins generating cash flow or earnings and profits, so that these funds can be used for X's charitable or religious activities. X cannot be allowed to focus its energies on expanding its subsidiary's commercial business and assets, and neglect to translate that financial success into specific, definite, and feasible plans for the expansion of its charitable religious activities. Moreover, plans for such expansion are not sufficient. In the near future, X will have to demonstrate that at least some of its plans have been implemented.... A church has a substantial nonexempt purpose where the majority of its funds are devoted to investment or commercial activities without any feasible plan for using the gains from such investments for charitable or religious purposes....

The fact that the assets are being accumulated in a for-profit company under the formal legal control of X does not excuse X from using such assets for charitable religious purposes. Excess accumulations maintained in a subsidiary entity under legal control of the exempt organization, but under the de facto control of the founder, are deemed to be for the founder's personal purposes if no exempt purpose is documented or implemented. *Airlie Foundation v. United States*, 826 F. Supp. 537, 551 (D.D.C. 1993), 55 F.3d 684 (D.C. Cir. 1995). If the founder's control is complete and there is no exempt purpose, it matters not whether the funds are kept in an entity legally controlled by the organization but de facto controlled by the founder (*Airlie Foundation v. United States, supra*; *Church of Scientology v. Commissioner, supra*), or a safe under the founder's control (*Church of Scientology v. Commissioner, supra*); or in other nonprofits controlled by the founder (*Easter House v. United States*, 12 Cl. Ct. 476, 488 (Cl. Ct. 1987), *aff'd*, 846 F.2d 78 (Fed. Cir. 1987) (founder used organization's funds to loan to other nonprofits de facto controlled by himself).

Small, closely controlled exempt organizations—and especially those that are closely controlled by members of one family—with related business entities require thorough examination to insure that the arrangements serve charitable purposes rather than private interests. Qualifying for exemption is a facts and circumstances test. There is nothing that precludes an organization that is closely controlled or has related for-profit organizations from qualifying, or continuing to qualify, for exemption. However, the lack of institutional protections, that is, a board of directors comprised of active, disinterested persons, and the potential for such organizations to be abused requires IRS to closely examine actual operations to analyze whether they continue to serve exclusively charitable purposes. Further, the fact that IRS has concluded that a closely held organization has operated so as to continue to qualify for exemption does not guarantee that it will continue to do so in the future.

Accordingly, counsel to closely held organizations should take care to ensure that for-profit subsidiaries are not being used to divert exempt organization financial assets, resources, and income to the founding families and other insiders. IRS may examine ongoing activities to verify that there is a plan for using income and assets generated by subsidiaries for the organization's underlying exempt purposes. De minimis levels of exempt activities, millions of dollars in unsecured loans to closely controlled affiliates, with or without formal repayment arrangements, and/or failures to create and implement documented plans for asset accumulations to be used for exempt purposes are likely to be subject to further—and detailed—IRS scrutiny.

E. UNRELATED BUSINESS INCOME ISSUES

1. Typical UBIT Issues with Subsidiaries

PRIV. LTR. RUL. 201503018[5]

Dear * * *:

We have considered your ruling request dated September 5, 2014. You have requested rulings relating to the tax consequences under section 501(c)(3) and 512 of the Internal Revenue Code stemming from your formation of B a wholly-owned for-profit subsidiary.

FACTS

You are a not-for-profit corporation organized under the laws of State X as of Year x1. You are recognized as an organization exempt under section 501(c)(3) of the Code as an educational institution. You were formed in Year x2 as an accounting and secretarial school, and you have now evolved into a multi-disciplinary institution.

You offer degrees at the associate's, bachelor's, masters', and doctoral levels. You have graduate and undergraduate programs in business, education, hospitality, community economic development, and liberal arts. There are approximately x1 full- and part-time students currently enrolled in various courses offered by you directly or through one of your divisions. Students can participate in traditional campus daytime programs or evening and weekend part-time and hybrid courses at your regional centers. You also offer all of your continuing education programs online.

You launched Program A as a division of you and not a separate entity to improve educational opportunities to working adults. Your financial activities are combined with that of Program A and are reported in your annual Form 990 information returns.

---

[5] [The IRS defines a letter ruling as: "a written determination issued to a taxpayer by an Associate office in response to the taxpayer's written inquiry, filed prior to the filing of returns or reports that are required by the tax laws, about its status for tax purposes or the tax effects of its acts or transactions. A letter ruling interprets the tax laws and applies them to the taxpayer's specific set of facts. A letter ruling is issued when appropriate in the interest of sound tax administration." Rev. Proc. 2016-1, 2016-1 IRB—*Ed.*]

Rev. Proc. 2010-4, 2010-2 I.R.B. 234.

Program A is an online educational program that allows students to enroll in educational courses through a self-paced and self-directed model. This program differs from the traditional class setting where students are required to take a pre-defined number of courses to graduate. Before students can advance in Program A and obtain degrees they have to prove mastery in certain core competencies related to the degree. At the time of implementing Program A, there were no other universities offering degree programs based on this structure of competency-based learning. Since this competency-based learning program was unique to Program A, there was no existing computer architecture to run and track the program. Consequently, you developed Software X as your own proprietary software.

There have been other unaffiliated educational institutions also interested in offering competency-based programs that have inquired about licensing Software X from you. You are in the process of determining whether the licensing of Software X to other entities could be a viable commercial business. You formed B and it was incorporated in State Y on Date x to further develop Software X and license it to other educational institutions and commercial businesses. B currently does not have any employees or any activities.

You propose to contribute Software X to B while retaining a royalty-free license for use in your own operations. B would determine and charge a fair market value for the license of Software X to other unaffiliated organizations for use in creating their educational programs.

You will own 100% of the stock in B and will appoint all of its directors. The initial Board of Directors of B will consist of three members of your Board of Directors. You plan to expand the Board of Directors of B to include seven persons within six months of formation and prior to the commencement of any substantial activities. Pursuant to B's Bylaws, a majority of the directors shall not be employed by you nor be on your Board of Directors or related to a person employed by, or on your Board. The president of B will not be either a person who is on your Board nor one of your employees.

All compensation that B pays to its directors, officers, employees, and agents for services rendered will be reasonable. Having a for-profit subsidiary such as B, you believe, will allow it to attract and retain key employees with an equity-based compensation system. Thus, any equity-based compensation system for B's directors and employees will conform to those offered by comparable entities.

You will not actively participate in the day-to-day operations of B. B will also maintain separate facilities, addresses, telephone numbers, telephone listings, and bank accounts and other financial records. In the event that B does lease office space from you or receives administrative services from you, then B, as required by its Bylaws, will reimburse you for fair market value of such use. The dividends that you expect to receive from B will be an insignificant percentage of your total support.

RULINGS REQUESTED

2) The gross income realized by <u>B</u> will not be treated as unrelated business taxable income to you under <u>section 512(a)(1)</u>.

3) The dividends that you may receive from <u>B</u> will be excluded under <u>section 512(b)(1)</u> from the computation of unrelated business taxable income under section 512(a)(1).

LAW

[The IRS summarized §501(c)(3) and its regulations as well as §§511-513 and some relevant case law.]

ANALYSIS

[The IRS found that the tax-exempt organization had set up its subsidiary successfully.] Based on the facts and representations stated above, <u>B</u> should be treated as a separate entity for tax purposes. Thus, <u>B</u>'s activities and income should not be attributed to you as the parent to adversely affect your tax-exempt status under <u>section 501(c)(3)</u>. Likewise, none of <u>B</u>'s gross income should result in any unrelated business taxable income to you under <u>section 512(a)(1)</u>. <u>B</u>'s activities and operations are conducted solely by <u>B</u> and are not attributed to you and therefore are not considered to be a trade or business that is "regularly carried on" by you. See Section 1.513-1(a); see also Section 1.513-1(c)(1).

Whether the dividends you may receive from <u>B</u> should be excluded from the computation of unrelated business taxable income under <u>section 512(a)(1)</u> would depend on if the dividends are an allowable modification permitted in subsection (b) and not a specified payment within the meaning of subsection (c). . . [D]vidend income is not a specified payment. Inasmuch as <u>B</u> is a separate tax entity, any dividends you receive from <u>B</u> would be a modification under <u>section 512(b)(2)</u>. Accordingly, any dividend income that you may receive from <u>B</u> will not be subject to the unrelated business income tax.

RULINGS

1) Your ownership of <u>B</u> will not have an adverse effect on your tax-exempt status under <u>section 501(c)(3)</u>.

2) The gross income realized by <u>B</u> will not be treated as unrelated business taxable income to you under <u>section 512(a)(1)</u>.

3) Any dividends you may receive from <u>B</u> will be excluded under <u>section 512(b)(1)</u> from the computation of unrelated business taxable income under section 512(a)(1).

2. Special Circumstances with Controlled Organizations: §512(b)(13)

We learned in Chapter 9 that passive income payments are not taxable as UBTI. Section 512(b)(13) provides an exception to this rule when the exempt organization receives interest, annuities, rents, or royalties from a "controlled entity," to the extent that those payments exceed fair market value.[6] A controlled entity is an organization that is more than 50% owned or otherwise controlled by the parent organization.

The purpose of this provision is to prevent an exempt organization from using a separate but controlled organization to avoid UBTI. For example, assume that a §501(c)(3) food pantry with the purpose of addressing food insecurity decides that it can make money selling baseball hats. If it sells the hats itself on a regular basis, the income from these sales would be unrelated business income because the sales of hats do not help feed the hungry except to the extent that they bring income to the organization. If, instead, a third party sells the hats and the food pantry licenses the logo to that third party as a royalty payment, the unrelated business income provisions allow the income from the use of that logo to be excluded from the calculation of unrelated business income [IRC §512 (b)(2)]. What if, instead of licensing the logo to a third party, the §501(c)(3) organization created a subsidiary to sell the hats? If §512 (b)(13) were not in place, the food pantry could price the royalty at a sufficiently high price to equal the profit from the sale of the hats, which we'll assume is a higher price than the licensing fee would be if it negotiated with a third party. The subsidiary would deduct the royalty payments as a business expense, and the parent would use the royalty exception to the UBIT rules to avoid UBIT.

In the past, the law disallowed the passive income exception to *all* tax-exempt organizations that received interest, annuities, royalties, and rent from a "controlled entity" because Congress saw the creation of a subsidiary as a ruse to avoid UBIT. Thus, in the example above, the royalty income that the §501(c)(3) food pantry received from its wholly owned subsidiary would have been characterized as unrelated business income, just as if the organization were selling the hats itself, no matter what the price of the licensing agreement was.

That restriction came under fire by tax-exempt organizations, however, because royalties, interest, annuities, and rent from subsidiaries created taxable income, but royalties from third parties did not—even if the price for the royalty was identical. They maintained that if the parent and the subsidiary were dealing with each other at arm's length, there would be no abuse.

Congress responded to this reasoning by allowing the passive income exception to interest, annuities, royalty, and rent that a tax-exempt organization receives from a controlled entity, so long as the price is at fair market value. Between 2006 and 2015, this provision expired every December 31 and was

---

[6] Note that dividends are not included in this list; therefore, the educational institution in the Private Letter Ruling was not affected by this doctrine.

renewed sometime during the following year, which created uncertainty with regard to this rule. Congress made this provision permanent in 2015 [Consolidated Appropriations Act, 2016 (PL 114-113)].

NOTES AND QUESTIONS

1. The business relationship between a tax-exempt parent and its subsidiary can be quite complex. The parent could charge rent to the subsidiary, license its logo, purchase goods and services from the nonprofit, and even loan money to the subsidiary. All these transactions must be arms-length transactions in order to avoid private benefit issues. In fact, virtually every issue seen so far in this book could arise in the context of a subsidiary relationship with a §501(c)((3). Did the board invest wisely when it chose to use the charitable assets for a subsidiary, or did it do so in dereliction of its fiduciary duties? Are the payments from the subsidiary to the parent charitable contributions or payments for goods and services? Have the payments from the subsidiary to the parent become such a large part of the §501(c)(3)'s budget that its public charity status is in jeopardy?

2. For further reading, see David A. Levitt, Steven R. Chiodini, *Taking Care of Business: Use of a For-Profit Subsidiary by a Nonprofit Organization,* BUSINESS LAW TODAY (June 6, 2014); David S. Walker, *A Consideration of an LLC for a 501(c)(3) Nonprofit Organization,* 38 WM. MITCHELL L. REV. 627 (2012); Cassady V. Brewer, *Nonprofit and Charitable Uses of LLC,* in Robert Hillman & Mark Loewenstein (eds.), *Research Handbook on Partnerships, LLCs and Alternative Forms of Business Organizations* (Edward Elgar, Ltd., 2015); Henry Gutman, *Taxing Transactions Between Exempt Parents and Their Affiliates,* 26 EXEMPT ORG. TAX REV. 45 (1999).

III. JOINT VENTURES

A. BACKGROUND

In addition to subsidiaries (and often in conjunction with them), §501(c)(3) organizations can enter into partnerships and other forms of joint ventures with for-profit organizations. Following are some definitions that should help clarify the materials in the rest of this chapter:

- *Partnership.* An association of two or more persons or entities to carry on a for-profit business as co-owners. For tax purposes, a partnership is treated as a pass-through entity and is, therefore, not subject to taxation. The partners are liable for income tax in their individual capacities. The various items of partnership income, loss, deduction, and credit flow through to the individual partners and are reported on their personal income tax returns.

- *Joint venture.* A limited association of two or more persons or entities in a business undertaking. The parties are not co-owners and have no continuing relationship beyond this joint venture. The joint venture is treated as a partnership for federal income tax purposes.
- *Whole hospital joint venture.* A partnership of a §501(c)(3) hospital with a for-profit organization, in which the hospital contributes substantially all its operating assets to the partnership. The for-profit organization usually assumes control over the assets and manages the day-to-day operations of the venture, and the health care organization no longer engages in health care activities.
- *Ancillary joint venture.* In the whole hospital joint venture, the exempt organization transfers all its assets to the joint venture. The ancillary joint venture, on the other hand, leaves some of the nonprofit functions in the tax-exempt organization while it engages in a partnership with a for-profit business entity.

A §501(c)(3) organization might enter into a joint venture with a for-profit organization that has expertise or that funds the §501(c)(3) organization's needs for the project. The examples below involve hospitals, but a museum could partner with a television network, or a food pantry with a chain of restaurants. Many of the early cases involved the financing of theater productions. Any number of combinations is possible.

A joint venture does not involve a contribution. An organization with the expertise or funds that the §501(c)(3) needs could, of course, donate the goods, services, or money,[7] but if it expects a return on investment, the situation is more complicated. The for-profit cannot simply purchase stock in the nonprofit because no one owns the nonprofit. It can provide a loan or structure the arrangement as a joint venture, however.

The joint venture can be structured in several different ways. The two organizations can enter into a partnership agreement, become members of an LLC, or create a separate corporation to conduct the activities of the joint venture. Both parties invest in the joint venture. Usually the for-profit is investing cash and the nonprofit some of or all its charitable assets. Perhaps you can begin to see the legal issues that can arise, apart from the business creation ones, if the state is to protect the charitable assets. Among those issues are the following: (1) Does participation in these ventures alter the primary purpose of the nonprofit organization, such that it is no longer primarily organized and operated for charitable purposes? (2) Is there any inurement or private benefit to the for-profit entity? (3) Should there be any intermediate sanctions penalties? (4) Is income from the venture unrelated business income to the exempt organization? (5) Is the unrelated income so significant that the exempt organization should lose its

---

[7] In this type of gift situation, if the funder wanted recognition, the two organizations might want to enter into a sponsorship agreement, as discussed in Chapter 8.

exemption? (6) Is the investment a prudent one, in which the board has exercised its fiduciary duties faithfully?

Originally, the IRS revoked the tax exemption of any §501(c)(3) that entered into a joint venture with a for-profit organization, on the grounds that the §501(c)(3) was no longer operating "exclusively" for charitable purposes. That policy changed after *Plumstead Theatre Society v. Commissioner*, 675 F.2d 244 (9th Cir. 1982), *aff'g* 74 T.C. 1324 (1980), in which a theater company, which was organized to foster the performing arts, entered into a limited partnership with three for-profit investors to raise the revenue needed to produce a stage play. The Ninth Circuit reasoned that the limited partnership agreement insulated Plumstead from potential conflicts with its exempt purpose and held that Plumstead was therefore operated exclusively for charitable and educational purposes and entitled to exemption.

Since *Plumstead*, the IRS and the courts have struggled to find a way to articulate a rule that will allow joint ventures without permitting the for-profit partners to benefit from the charitable assets at the expense of the charity. In 1998, the IRS published Rev. Rul. 98-15 to provide some guidance. It set forth two situations—the first, with facts that would allow the tax-exempt partner to maintain its exemption, and the second, which would lead to the revocation of exemption. In both situations, the tax-exempt organization that operates and maintains an acute-care hospital enters into a joint venture with a for-profit partner. The tax-exempt partner contributes all its operating assets, including the hospital, to an LLC. The for-profit also contributes assets, and they each receive ownership interests in the LLC in proportion to their respective contributions. The following diagram illustrates this transaction.

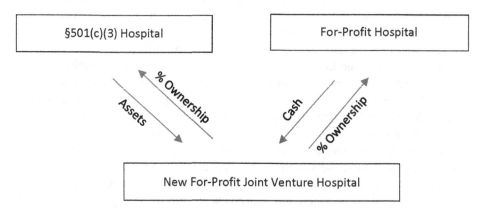

In the first situation, the LLC's governing documents state that it will be operated in such a way as to further the exempt partner's charitable purpose, and if a conflict should arise between the charitable purpose and the financial benefit of the owners, the board has a fiduciary duty to further the charitable purpose. The governing documents also provide for the tax-exempt partner to choose the majority of the directors, and for a majority of directors to approve certain major decisions. Finally, they require that all returns of capital and distributions of earnings be proportional to the partners' ownership interests in the LLC. Additional relevant facts include that the LLC is entering into a reasonably priced five-year renewable management agreement with an organization that has no relation to either partner. In addition, none of the tax-exempt's officers or directors have been offered employment or have any financial interest in the LLC. Finally, the tax-exempt partner will use its distributions from the LLC to fund grants that would promote community health, and that grant-making activity would be its only activity.

In the second situation, the LLC's governing documents state that the LLC's purpose is to further health care and to engage in other health-related activities. Each partner will appoint three board members, and all distributions will be proportionate to the partners' contributions. The LLC had entered into a reasonably priced five-year management contract with a subsidiary of the for-profit partner, and the contract would be renewable at the sole discretion of this subsidiary. The LLC's chief executive officer (CEO) and chief financial officer (CFO) had both previously worked for the for-profit partner, and they would receive fair compensation that was commensurate with their experience in their roles at the LLC. As in the first situation, the exempt partner planned to use any distributions that it received to provide grants that promote health and help the indigent receive health care, and grant making would be its only activity.

Once the joint venture is established, both exempt partners will provide grants to promote health and help the indigent receive health care, but only the exempt partner in the first situation will continue to operate exclusively for a charitable purpose. The second situation simply leaves too much to the control of the nonexempt partner for the IRS to be able to conclude that the exempt partner in that situation continues to further its exempt purpose.

Four factual differences explain this different conclusion. First, in the second situation, the governing documents fail to stress the priority of the charitable purpose, so the LLC would be free to deny health care to entire segments of the community, such as the indigent. Second, in that second situation, the exempt partner does not appoint a majority of the board, which would prevent the exempt partner from instituting a major change that could protect the charitable purpose without the agreement of at least one board member appointed by the for-profit partner. Third, the executives, who will provide the board with most of its information, are former employees of the for-profit partner. Finally, the management company, which has broad discretion over most decisions of the LLC, is run by a subsidiary of the for-profit and can unilaterally renew the management agreement. These facts combine to suggest that the exempt organization is no longer operating exclusively for charitable purposes and that the for-profit partner is receiving a private benefit that is more than incidental to the furtherance of an exempt purpose.

Revenue Ruling 98-15 provides guidance for exempt organizations interested in a joint venture, but very few are structured exactly like one or the other described in that ruling. As a result, questions continued to be raised. The next section includes a case about a whole hospital joint venture with slightly different facts, as well as Revenue Ruling 2004-51, which sets forth IRS thinking on ancillary joint ventures.

B. WHOLE HOSPITAL JOINT VENTURES

ST. DAVID'S HEALTH CARE SYSTEM V. UNITED STATES OF AMERICA

349 F.3d 232 (5th Cir. 2003)

EMILIO M. GARZA, Circuit Judge:

St. David's Health Care System, Inc. ("St. David's") brought suit in federal court to recover taxes that it paid under protest. St. David's argued that it was a charitable hospital, and therefore tax-exempt under 26 U.S.C. §501(c)(3). The Government responded that St. David's was not entitled to a tax exemption because it had formed a partnership with a for-profit company and ceded control over its operations to the for-profit entity....

For many years, St. David's owned and operated a hospital and other health care facilities in Austin, Texas. For most of its existence, St. David's was recognized as a charitable organization entitled to tax-exempt status under §501(c)(3).

In the 1990s, due to financial difficulties in the health care industry, St. David's concluded that it should consolidate with another health care organization. Ultimately, in 1996, St. David's decided to form a partnership with Columbia/HCA Healthcare Corporation ("HCA"), a for-profit company that operates 180 hospitals nationwide. HCA already owned several facilities in the suburbs of Austin, and was interested in entering the central Austin market. A partnership with St. David's would allow HCA to expand into that urban market.

St. David's contributed all of its hospital facilities to the partnership. HCA, in turn, contributed its Austin-area facilities. The partnership hired Galen Health Care, Inc. ("Galen"), a subsidiary of HCA, to manage the day-to-day operations of the partnership medical facilities.

In 1998, the IRS audited St. David's and concluded that, due to its partnership with HCA, St. David's no longer qualified as a charitable (and, thus, tax-exempt) hospital. The IRS ordered St. David's to pay taxes. St. David's paid the requisite amount under protest, and subsequently filed the instant action, requesting a refund.

The parties filed cross-motions for summary judgment. The district court granted the motion filed by St. David's and ordered the Government to refund the taxes paid by the hospital for the 1996 tax year.... The Government filed this appeal.

II

... The Government claims that the district court erred in concluding that St. David's was entitled to §501(c)(3) tax-exempt status. The burden was on St. David's to prove that it qualified for a tax exemption. *See Nationalist Movement v. Commissioner, 37 F.3d 216, 219 (5th Cir. 1994)*; *Senior Citizens Stores, Inc. v. United States*, 602 F.2d 711, 713 (5th Cir. 1979) ("It is the burden of the party claiming the exemption ... to prove entitlement to it.").

In order to qualify for tax-exempt status, St. David's was required to show that it was "organized and operated exclusively" for a charitable purpose. 26 C.F.R. §1.501(c)(3)-1(a). The "organizational test" required St. David's to demonstrate that its founding documents: (1) limit its purpose to "one or more exempt purposes"; and (2) do not expressly empower St. David's to engage more than "an insubstantial part of its activities" in conduct that fails to further its charitable goals. *Id.* §1.501(c)(3)-1(b). The parties agree that St. David's articles of incorporation satisfy the organizational test.

To pass the "operational test," St. David's was required to show: (1) that it "engages primarily in activities which accomplish" its exempt purpose; (2) that its net earnings do not "inure to the benefit of private shareholders or individuals"; (3) that it does "not expend a substantial part of its resources attempting to influence legislation or political campaigns"; and (4) that it "serves a valid purpose and confers a public benefit." *Nationalist Movement*, 37 F.3d at 219-20. The parties appear to agree that, because St. David's contributed all of its medical facilities to the partnership, we must look to the activities of the partnership to determine if St. David's satisfies the operational test.

The Government argues that St. David's cannot demonstrate the first element of the operational test. The Government asserts that, because of its partnership with HCA, St. David's cannot show that it engages "primarily" in activities that accomplish its charitable purpose. The Government does not contend that a non-profit organization should automatically lose its tax-exempt status when it forms a partnership with a for-profit entity. Instead, the Government argues that a non-profit organization must sacrifice its tax exemption if it cedes control over the partnership to the for-profit entity. The Government asserts that, when a non-profit cedes control, it can no longer ensure that its activities via the partnership primarily further its charitable purpose. In this case, the Government contends that St. David's forfeited its exemption because it ceded control over its operations to HCA.

St. David's responds in part that the central issue in determining its tax-exempt status is not which entity *controls* the partnership. Instead, St. David's appears to assert, the pivotal question is one of *function*: whether the partnership engages in activities that further its exempt purpose. St. David's argues that it passes the "operational test" because its activities via the partnership further its charitable purpose of providing health care to all persons.

St. David's relies in particular on a revenue ruling issued by the IRS, which provides guidelines for hospitals seeking a §501(c)(3) exemption. Revenue Ruling 69-545 sets forth what has come to be known as the "community benefit standard." *See IHC Health Plans, Inc. v. Commissioner, 325 F.3d 1188, 1197 (10th Cir. 2003)....*

Under the "community benefit standard," a non-profit hospital can qualify for a tax exemption if it: (1) provides an emergency room open to all persons, regardless of their ability to pay; (2) is willing to hire any qualified physician; (3) is run by an independent board of trustees composed of representatives of the community ("community board"); and (4) uses all excess revenues to improve facilities, provide educational services, and/or conduct medical research. A hospital need not demonstrate all of these factors in order to qualify for §501(c)(3) tax-exempt status....

St. David's contends that its activities via the partnership more than satisfy the community benefit standard. St. David's notes that the partnership hospitals perform a number of charitable functions in the Austin community. According to St. David's, the partnership not only provides free emergency room care, but also has opened the rest of its facilities to all persons, regardless of their ability to pay.[8] In addition, St. David's asserts, the partnership hospitals maintain open medical staffs. Finally, St. David's states that it uses the profits that it receives from the partnership revenues to fund research grants and other health-related initiatives.[9]

We have no doubt that St. David's via the partnership provides important medical services to the Austin community. Indeed, if the issue in this case were whether the partnership performed any charitable functions, we would be inclined to affirm the district court's grant of summary judgment in favor of St. David's.

---

[8] [FN 3] The Government suggests that there is a factual dispute regarding whether the partnership provides free care, because the partnership hospitals seek to collect payment from all patients. However, as the Government concedes in its original brief, "collection efforts do not definitively indicate that...care [is] not charitable."...

[9] [FN 4] The Government contends that the partnership hospitals do not satisfy the community benefit standard, because the partnership lacks a community board. The Government notes that half of the members of the partnership's Board of Governors are appointed by HCA, and that two of the members appointed by St. David's are physicians at partnership hospitals. The Government contends that these individuals have a financial interest in the partnership hospitals, and therefore cannot be deemed "independent" representatives of the community who are likely to give a high priority to charitable concerns.... The Government may be correct in asserting that the partnership does not have a community board. However, this fact does not suggest that the partnership hospitals fail to meet the community benefit standard. As we have just explained, a hospital need not demonstrate every factor set forth in Revenue Ruling 69-545 in order to qualify for a tax exemption. The partnership hospitals can therefore satisfy the community benefit standard, whether or not they are run by an independent community board.

However, we cannot agree with St. David's suggestion that the central issue in this case is whether the partnership provides some (or even an extensive amount of) charitable services. It is important to keep in mind that §501(c)(3) confers tax-exempt status only on those organizations that operate *exclusively* in furtherance of exempt purposes. 26 C.F.R. §1.501(c)(3)-1(a). As a result, in determining whether an organization satisfies the operational test, we do not simply consider whether the organization's activities further its charitable purposes. We must also ensure that those activities do *not* substantially further other (non-charitable) purposes. If more than an "insubstantial" amount of the partnership's activities further non-charitable interests, then St. David's can no longer be deemed to operate *exclusively* for charitable purposes. *See Nationalist Movement, 37 F.3d at 220* ("'An organization will not be ... regarded [as operated exclusively for an exempt purpose] if more than an insubstantial part of its activities is not in furtherance of an exempt purpose.'") (quoting 26 C.F.R. §1.501(c)(3)-1(c)(1)).

In order to ascertain whether an organization furthers non-charitable interests, we can examine the structure and management of the organization. In other words, we look to which individuals or entities *control* the organization. If private individuals or for-profit entities have either formal or effective control, we presume that the organization furthers the profit-seeking motivations of those private individuals or entities. That is true, even when the organization is a partnership[10] between a non-profit and a for-profit entity. When the non-profit organization cedes control over the partnership to the for-profit entity, we assume that the partnership's activities substantially further the for-profit's interests. As a result, we conclude that the non-profit's activities via the partnership are not exclusively or primarily in furtherance of its charitable purposes. Thus, the non-profit is not entitled to a tax exemption. *See* Rev. Rul. 98-15, 1998-1 C.B. 718 (1998) ("If a private party is allowed to control or use the non-profit organization's activities or assets for the benefit of the private party, and the benefit is not incidental to the accomplishment of exempt purposes, the organization will fail to be organized and operated exclusively for exempt purposes.");...

Conversely, if the non-profit organization enters into a partnership agreement with a for-profit entity, and retains control, we presume that the non-profit's activities via the partnership primarily further exempt purposes. Therefore, we can conclude that the non-profit organization should retain its tax-exempt status....

The present case illustrates why, when a non-profit organization forms a partnership with a for-profit entity, courts should be concerned about the relinquishment of control. St. David's, by its own account, entered the partnership with HCA out of financial *necessity* (to obtain the revenues needed

---

[10] [FN 7] For purposes of simplicity, we use the term "partnership" to refer to a number of similar combinations between non-profit organizations and for-profit entities, including limited partnerships and limited liability companies.

for it to stay afloat). HCA, by contrast, entered the partnership for reasons of financial *convenience* (to enter a new market). The starkly different financial positions of these two parties at the beginning of their partnership negotiations undoubtedly affected their relative bargaining strength. Because St. David's "needed" this partnership more than HCA, St. David's may have been willing to acquiesce to many (if not most) of HCA's demands for the final Partnership Agreement. In the process, of course, St. David's may not have been able to give a high priority to its charitable objectives. As a result, St. David's may not have been able to ensure that its partnership with HCA would continually provide a "public benefit" as opposed to a private benefit for HCA. *Cf. IHC Health Plans, 325 F.3d at 1195* (noting that tax exemptions under §501(c)(3) constitute a kind of "*quid pro quo*" and " 'are justified on the basis that the exempt entity confers a *public benefit*—a benefit which the society or the community may not itself choose or be able to provide, or which supplements and advances the work of public institutions already supported by tax revenues' ") (quoting *Bob Jones Univ. v. United States*, 461 U.S. 574, 591, 76 L. Ed. 2d 157, 103 S. Ct. 2017 (1983)) (emphasis in original).

These precedents and policy concerns indicate that, when a non-profit organization forms a partnership with a for-profit entity, the non-profit should lose its tax-exempt status if it cedes control to the for-profit entity. Therefore, in our review of the district court's summary judgment ruling, we examine whether St. David's has shown that there is no genuine issue of material fact regarding whether St. David's ceded control to HCA.

A recent IRS revenue ruling provides a starting point for our analysis. In Revenue Ruling 98-15, the IRS indicated how a non-profit organization that forms a partnership with a for-profit entity can establish that it has retained control over the partnership's activities. *See* Rev. Rul. 98-15, 1998-1 C.B. 718 (1998). The revenue ruling states that a non-profit can demonstrate control by showing some or all of the following: (1) that the founding documents of the partnership expressly state that it has a charitable purpose and that the charitable purpose will take priority over all other concerns; (2) that the partnership agreement gives the non-profit organization a majority vote in the partnership's board of directors; and (3) that the partnership is managed by an independent company (an organization that is not affiliated with the for-profit entity).

The partnership documents in the present case, examined in light of the above factors, leave us uncertain as to whether St. David's has ceded control to HCA. St. David's did manage to secure some protections for its charitable mission. First of all, Section 3.2[11] of the Partnership Agreement expressly states

---

[11] [FN 11] The Government contends that Section 3.2 of the Partnership Agreement does not meet the standard established by Revenue Ruling 98-15. The Government argues that it is not sufficient for a partnership agreement to state that a manager "shall" abide by the community benefit standard; the agreement must also *expressly* require the manager to place charitable concerns above other goals. We are not persuaded by the Government's narrow interpretation of Revenue Ruling 98-15. The term "shall" clearly indicates that the manager of this partnership is

that the manager of the partnership "shall" operate the partnership facilities in a manner that complies with the community benefit standard. This provision appears to comport with the first factor in Revenue Ruling 98-15, which indicates that the partnership's founding documents should contain a statement of the partnership's charitable purpose. . . . St. David's asserts that if Galen, the manager of the partnership facilities, fails to adhere to this requirement, St. David's can sue in Texas state court for specific performance of the Partnership Agreement.

The Management Services Agreement between Galen and the Partnership further provides that, if Galen takes any action with a "material probability of adversely affecting" St. David's tax-exempt status, that action will be considered an "event of default." Management Services Agreement, section 7(d). The Management Services Agreement authorizes St. David's to unilaterally terminate the contract with Galen if it commits such a "default." *See* Management Services Agreement, section 7 ("If any Event of Default shall occur and be continuing, the non-defaulting party may terminate this Agreement ... Any action to be taken by the Partnership under this paragraph may be taken by the [St. David's] representatives on the Governing Board[.]").

In addition, St. David's can exercise a certain degree of control over the partnership via its membership on the partnership's Board of Governors. St. David's and HCA each appoint half of the Board. No measure can pass the Board without the support of a majority of the representatives of *both* St. David's and HCA. *See* Partnership Agreement, section 1.8 (noting that Board approval "means approval of not less than a majority of a quorum of [HCA] Governors and not less than a majority of a quorum of [St. David's] Governors"). Thus, through its voting power, St. David's can effectively veto any proposed action of the Board of Governors.

St. David's also contends that the Partnership Agreement gives it authority over the partnership's Chief Executive Officer ("CEO"). The agreement permitted St. David's to appoint the initial CEO, subject to the approval of the HCA members of the Board of Governors. *See* Partnership Agreement, section 8.2. The agreement further provides that either HCA or St. David's can unilaterally remove the CEO. *See id.* St. David's suggests that this termination power enables it to ensure that the CEO will promote charitable objectives.

Finally, St. David's argues that its power to dissolve the partnership provides it with a significant amount of control over partnership operations. The Partnership Agreement states that, if St. David's receives legal advice (from an attorney that has been deemed acceptable by both HCA and St. David's) that its participation in the partnership will hinder its tax-exempt status, St. David's can request dissolution. *See* Partnership Agreement, section 15.1(f). St. David's asserts that it can use the threat of dissolution to force the partnership to give priority to charitable concerns.

---

required to abide by the community benefit standard...., [A]s a purely textual matter, the purpose statement in Section 3.2 appears to comply with the first factor listed in Revenue Ruling 98-15.

According to St. David's, the above protections in the partnership documents (the purpose statement in the Partnership Agreement; St. David's power to terminate the Management Services Agreement and the CEO; its ability to block proposed action of the Board of Governors; and its power of dissolution) provide it with a large measure of control over partnership operations.

However, as the Government argues, there are reasons to doubt that the partnership documents provide St. David's with sufficient control. First of all, St. David's authority within the Board of Governors is limited. St. David's does not control a majority of the Board. *See* Rev. Rul. 98-15, 1998-1 C.B. 718 (1998) (indicating that a non-profit can retain control over a partnership with a for-profit if it selects a majority of the partnership's board of directors, but will have difficulty controlling the partnership if it has only an equal share of the board). As a result, although St. David's can veto board actions, it does not appear that it can initiate action without the support of HCA. Thus, at best, St. David's can prevent the partnership from taking action that might undermine its charitable goals; St. David's cannot necessarily ensure that the partnership will take new action that furthers its charitable purposes. . . .

Second, Galen, which manages the operations of the partnership on a day-to-day basis, is a for-profit subsidiary of HCA. As a result, it is not apparent that Galen would be inclined to serve charitable interests. It seems more likely that Galen would prioritize the (presumably non-charitable) interests of its parent organization, HCA. *See* Rev. Rul. 98-15, 1998-1 C.B. 718 (1998) (indicating that a charitable hospital is unlikely to be in control of a partnership with a for-profit entity when the partnership manager is a subsidiary of the for-profit entity); *see also Redlands, 113 T.C. at 83-84* ("This long-term management contract with an affiliate of [the for-profit entity] is a salient indicator of [the non-profit's] surrender of effective control over the [partnership's] operations.").[12]

Galen's apparent conflict of interest is only partly mitigated by the fact that Section 3.2 of the Partnership Agreement requires the manager to abide by the community benefit standard. As the Government points out, that requirement is useful only to the extent that the governing documents of the partnership empower St. David's to enforce the provision. St. David's appears to assert that the primary means through which it can force Galen to comply with Section 3.2 is by taking legal action. Given the time and expense of judicial proceedings, we doubt that St. David's will resort to litigation every time Galen makes a single decision that appears to conflict with the community benefit standard.

---

[12] [FN 13] Our concerns about Galen's affiliation with HCA are magnified by the fact that the partnership's contract with Galen appoints the manager for an extraordinarily long term. The Management Services Agreement states that Galen will remain the manager until 2050, as long as an HCA affiliate continues to be a general partner of the partnership. *See* Management Services Agreement, section 6. Such "job security" could make Galen less responsive to any allegations by St. David's that Galen was not managing the partnership in accordance with the community benefit standard. . . .

St. David's also asserts that it can control the management of the partnership via its position on the Board of Governors. However, the power of the Board is limited in scope. The Board of Governors is empowered to deal with only major decisions, not the day-to-day operation of the partnership hospitals. Thus, St. David's could not, via its position on the Board, overrule a management decision that fell outside the range of the Board's authority.

The Management Services Agreement does appear to provide St. David's with a certain degree of control over Galen. The agreement permits St. David's to unilaterally cancel the contract with Galen if the manager takes action that has a "material probability" of undermining St. David's tax-exempt status. It is not entirely clear whether St. David's would be willing to exercise this termination option without the consent of HCA. Nor is it clear whether St. David's could ensure that Galen was replaced by a manager that would prioritize charitable purposes. Nonetheless, the Management Services Agreement does appear to give St. David's some authority over Galen, and therefore seems to provide St. David's with a degree of control over partnership operations.

We are also uncertain about the amount of control that St. David's exercises over the partnership's CEO. St. David's appears to assert that its authority to appoint the initial CEO, and its power to terminate the officer, demonstrate its control within the partnership. The Government has created a general issue of material fact, however, regarding St. David's by pointing to instances in which the CEO failed to comply with the Partnership Agreement. Although the Partnership Agreement states that the CEO "shall" provide the Board of Governors with annual reports of the amount of charity care, *see* Partnership Agreement, section 8.4(f), it seems that no such report was prepared for 1996 (the first year of the partnership and the tax year at issue in this case). Indeed, it does not appear that any annual report on charity care was prepared until after the IRS began auditing the partnership. Despite St. David's assertions about its power over the CEO, the non-profit does not claim to have taken *any* punitive action against the CEO for failing to prepare these reports. If St. David's was in fact unable to enforce a provision of the Partnership Agreement dealing specifically with charity care, that raises serious doubts about St. David's capacity to ensure that the partnership's operations further charitable purposes.

Finally, we question the degree to which St. David's has the power to control the partnership by threatening dissolution. First of all, the Partnership Agreement appears to permit St. David's to request dissolution only when there is a change in the law, not simply when the partnership fails to perform a few charitable functions. *See* Partnership Agreement, section 15.1(f) (indicating that the partnership "shall" be dissolved upon "the request of [St. David's] for dissolution ... in the event [St. David's] receives an opinion of counsel, from counsel reasonably acceptable to [St. David's] and the [HCA] Governors, that as a result of a rule, regulation, statute, Internal Revenue Service government pronouncement, or court decision ... enacted or issued subsequent to the date hereof which would cause the participation of [St. David's] or the [St. David's]

Affiliates in the Partnership to be inconsistent with [their] Status ... as organizations described in Section 501(c)(3) of the Code"). Second, HCA may not take seriously any threat of dissolution made by St. David's. HCA must be aware that St. David's has a strong incentive not to exercise its power to dissolve the corporation. The partnership documents include a non-compete clause, which provides that, in the event of dissolution, neither partner can compete in the Austin area for two years. *See* Contribution Agreement, section 11.1. That result might be slightly unpleasant for HCA, but would not destroy the entity; HCA would still have its nationwide health care business. For St. David's, by contrast, dissolution would be disastrous. St. David's serves only the Austin community. If it were forbidden from competing in that area, St. David's would (in effect) cease to exist. In light of the realities of the situation, it seems unlikely that St. David's would exercise its option to dissolve the partnership even if the partnership strayed from St. David's charitable mission.

The evidence presented by the parties demonstrates that there remain genuine issues of material fact regarding whether St. David's ceded control to HCA. Therefore, we vacate the district court's grant of summary judgment in favor of St. David's.

C. ANCILLARY JOINT VENTURES

REVENUE RULING 2004-51, 2004-22 I.R.B.

Joint ventures. This ruling illustrates the tax consequences for a section 501(c)(3) organization that enters into a joint venture with a for-profit organization as an insubstantial part of its activities.

Issues

1. Whether, under the facts described below, an organization continues to qualify for exemption from federal income tax as an organization described in §501(c)(3) of the Internal Revenue Code when it contributes a portion of its assets to and conducts a portion of its activities through a limited liability company (LLC) formed with a for-profit corporation.

2. Whether, under the same facts, the organization is subject to unrelated business income tax under §511 on its distributive share of the LLC's income.

Facts

M is a university that has been recognized as exempt from federal income tax under §501(a) as an organization described in §501(c)(3). As a part of its educational programs, *M* offers summer seminars to enhance the skill level of elementary and secondary school teachers.

To expand the reach of its teacher training seminars, M forms a domestic LLC, L, with O, a company that specializes in conducting interactive video training programs. L's Articles of Organization and Operating Agreement ("governing documents") provide that the sole purpose of L is to offer teacher training seminars at off-campus locations using interactive video technology. M and O each hold a 50 percent ownership interest in L, which is proportionate to the value of their respective capital contributions to L. The governing documents provide that all returns of capital, allocations and distributions shall be made in proportion to the members' respective ownership interests.

The governing documents provide that L will be managed by a governing board comprised of three directors chosen by M and three directors chosen by O. Under the governing documents, L will arrange and conduct all aspects of the video teacher training seminars, including advertising, enrolling participants, arranging for the necessary facilities, distributing the course materials and broadcasting the seminars to various locations. L's teacher training seminars will cover the same content covered in the seminars M conducts on M's campus. However, school teachers will participate through an interactive video link at various locations rather than in person. The governing documents grant M the exclusive right to approve the curriculum, training materials, and instructors, and to determine the standards for successful completion of the seminars. The governing documents grant O the exclusive right to select the locations where participants can receive a video link to the seminars and to approve other personnel (such as camera operators) necessary to conduct the video teacher training seminars. All other actions require the mutual consent of M and O.

The governing documents require that the terms of all contracts and transactions entered into by L with M, O and any other parties be at arm's length and that all contract and transaction prices be at fair market value determined by reference to the prices for comparable goods or services. The governing documents limit L's activities to conducting the teacher training seminars and also require that L not engage in any activities that would jeopardize M's exemption under §501(c)(3). L does in fact operate in accordance with the governing documents in all respects.

M's participation in L will be an insubstantial part of M's activities within the meaning of §501(c)(3) and §1.501(c)(3)-1(c)(1) of the Income Tax Regulations. Because L does not elect under §301.7701-3(c) of the Procedure and Administration Regulations to be classified as an association, L is classified as a partnership for federal tax purposes pursuant to §301.7701-3(b).

Law

Exemption Under §501(c)(3)

Section 501(c)(3) provides, in part, for the exemption from federal income tax of corporations organized and operated exclusively for charitable, scientific, or educational purposes, provided no part of the organization's net earnings inures to the benefit of any private shareholder or individual.

Section 1.501(c)(3)-1(c)(1) provides that an organization will be regarded as operated exclusively for one or more exempt purposes only if it engages primarily in activities that accomplish one or more of the exempt purposes specified in §501(c)(3). Activities that do not further exempt purposes must be an insubstantial part of the organization's activities. In Better Business Bureau of Washington, D.C. v. United States, 326 U.S. 279, 283 (1945), the Supreme Court held that "the presence of a single ... [non-exempt] purpose, if substantial in nature, will destroy the exemption regardless of the number or importance of truly ... [exempt] purposes."

Section 1.501(c)(3)-1(d)(1)(ii) provides that an organization is not organized or operated exclusively for exempt purposes unless it serves a public rather than a private interest. To meet this requirement, an organization must "establish that it is not organized or operated for the benefit of private interests...."

Section 1.501(c)(3)-1(d)(2) defines the term "charitable" as used in §501(c)(3) as including the advancement of education.

Section 1.501(c)(3)-1(d)(3)(i) provides, in part, that the term "educational" as used in §501(c)(3) relates to the instruction or training of the individual for the purpose of improving or developing his capabilities.

Section 1.501(c)(3)-1(d)(3)(ii) provides examples of educational organizations including a college that has a regularly scheduled curriculum, a regular faculty, and a regularly enrolled body of students in attendance at a place where the educational activities are regularly carried on and an organization that presents a course of instruction by means of correspondence or through the utilization of television or radio.

Joint Ventures

Rev. Rul. 98-15, 1998-1 C.B. 718, provides that for purposes of determining exemption under §501(c)(3), the activities of a partnership, including an LLC treated as a partnership for federal tax purposes, are considered to be the activities of the partners. A §501(c)(3) organization may form and participate in a partnership and meet the operational test if 1) participation in the partnership furthers a charitable purpose, and 2) the partnership arrangement permits the exempt organization to act exclusively in furtherance of its exempt purpose and only incidentally for the benefit of the for-profit partners.

Redlands Surgical Services, 113 T.C. 47, 92-93 (1999), aff'd 242 F.3d 904 (9th Cir. 2001), provides that a nonprofit organization may form partnerships, or enter into contracts, with private parties to further its charitable purposes on mutually beneficial terms, "so long as the nonprofit organization does not thereby impermissibly serve private interests." The Tax Court held that the operational standard is not satisfied merely by establishing "whatever charitable benefits [the partnership] may produce," finding that the nonprofit partner lacked "formal or informal control sufficient to ensure furtherance of charitable purposes."

Affirming the Tax Court, the Ninth Circuit held that ceding "effective control" of partnership activities impermissibly serves private interests. 242 F.3d at 904.

St. David's Health Care System v. United States, 349 F.3d 232, 236-237 (5th Cir. 2003), held that the determination of whether a nonprofit organization that enters into a partnership operates exclusively for exempt purposes is not limited to "whether the partnership provides some (or even an extensive amount of) charitable services." The nonprofit partner also must have the "capacity to ensure that the partnership's operations further charitable purposes." *Id.* at 243. "[T]he non-profit should lose its tax-exempt status if it cedes control to the for-profit entity." *Id.* at 239.

Tax on Unrelated Business Income

Section 511(a), in part, provides for the imposition of tax on the unrelated business taxable income (as defined in §512) of organizations described in §501(c)(3).

Section 512(a)(1) defines "unrelated business taxable income" as the gross income derived by any organization from any unrelated trade or business (as defined in §513) regularly carried on by it less the deductions allowed, both computed with the modifications provided in §512(b).

Section 512(c) provides that, if a trade or business regularly carried on by a partnership of which an organization is a member is an unrelated trade or business with respect to the organization, in computing its unrelated business taxable income, the organization shall, subject to the exceptions, additions, and limitations contained in §512(b), include its share (whether or not distributed) of the gross income of the partnership from the unrelated trade or business and its share of the partnership deductions directly connected with the gross income.

Section 513(a) defines the term "unrelated trade or business" as any trade or business the conduct of which is not substantially related (aside from the need of the organization for income or funds or the use it makes of the profits derived) to the exercise or performance by the organization of its charitable, educational, or other purpose or function constituting the basis for its exemption under §501.

Section 1.513-1(d)(2) provides that a trade or business is "related" to an organization's exempt purposes only if the conduct of the business activities has a causal relationship to the achievement of exempt purposes (other than through the production of income). A trade or business is "substantially related" for purposes of §513, only if the causal relationship is a substantial one. Thus, to be substantially related, the activity "must contribute importantly to the accomplishment of [exempt] purposes." Section 1.513-1(d)(2). Section 513, therefore, focuses on "the manner in which the exempt organization operates its business" to determine whether it contributes importantly to the organization's charitable or educational function. United States v. American College of Physicians, 475 U.S. 834, 849 (1986).

Analysis

L is a partnership for federal tax purposes. Therefore, *L*'s activities are attributed to *M* for purposes of determining both whether *M* operates exclusively for educational purposes and therefore continues to qualify for exemption under §501(c)(3) and whether *M* has engaged in an unrelated trade or business and therefore may be subject to the unrelated business income tax on its distributive share of *L*'s income.

The activities *M* is treated as conducting through *L* are not a substantial part of *M*'s activities within the meaning of §501(c)(3) and §1.501(c)(3)-1(c)(1). Therefore, based on all the facts and circumstances, *M*'s participation in *L*, taken alone, will not affect *M*'s continued qualification for exemption as an organization described in §501(c)(3).

Although *M* continues to qualify as an exempt organization described in §501(c)(3), *M* may be subject to unrelated business income tax under §511 if *L* conducts a trade or business that is not substantially related to the exercise or performance of *M*'s exempt purposes or functions.

The facts establish that *M*'s activities conducted through *L* constitute a trade or business that is substantially related to the exercise and performance of *M*'s exempt purposes and functions. Even though *L* arranges and conducts all aspects of the teacher training seminars, *M* alone approves the curriculum, training materials and instructors, and determines the standards for successfully completing the seminars. All contracts and transactions entered into by *L* are at arm's length and for fair market value, *M*'s and *O*'s ownership interests in *L* are proportional to their respective capital contributions, and all returns of capital, allocations and distributions by *L* are proportional to *M*'s and *O*'s ownership interests. The fact that *O* selects the locations and approves the other personnel necessary to conduct the seminars does not affect whether the seminars are substantially related to *M*'s educational purposes. Moreover, the teacher training seminars *L* conducts using interactive video technology cover the same content as the seminars *M* conducts on *M*'s campus. Finally, *L*'s activities have expanded the reach of *M*'s teacher training seminars, for example, to individuals who otherwise could not be accommodated at, or conveniently travel to, *M*'s campus. Therefore, the manner in which *L* conducts the teacher training seminars contributes importantly to the accomplishment of *M*'s educational purposes, and the activities of *L* are substantially related to *M*'s educational purposes. Section 1.513-1(d)(2). Accordingly, based on all the facts and circumstances, *M* is not subject to unrelated business income tax under §511 on its distributive share of *L*'s income.

Holdings

1. *M* continues to qualify for exemption under §501(c)(3) when it contributes a portion of its assets to and conducts a portion of its activities through *L*.

2. *M* is not subject to unrelated business income tax under §511 on its distributive share of *L*'s income.

NOTES AND QUESTIONS

1. Upon remand of the *St. David's* case, a jury allowed St. David's to retain its tax exemption. Darryll Jones, a critic of the IRS's view of joint ventures, commented: "The greatest irony is that the Fifth Circuit remanded the case for trial and a jury later found that St. David's should retain its tax exemption even though the partnership agreement did not comply with Rev. Rul. 98-15. We might speculate that laypersons take a more pragmatic view of profit and charity than those of us who reside more often in theoretical realms. In any event, the parties settled before a second appeal." Darryll Jones, *The Greedy and the Good in Nonprofit/For-Profit Partnerships*, 53 EXEMPT ORG. TAX REV. 69 (2006). For a contrary view, see Paul Streckfus, *Letter to the Editor*, 53 EXEMPT ORG. TAX REV. 243 (2006).

2. Revenue Ruling 2004-51 applies when an insubstantial part of the tax-exempt organization's assets is moved to the new organization. Neither the code nor the regulations define *insubstantial*, however. Should the definition be defined in monetary terms, such that a certain percentage is "substantial" and a lesser percentage is not? Or should the definition be more nuanced, depending on the type of assets being contributed to the new venture? One can imagine a nonprofit sitting on very valuable land contributing the heart of its programming to a new venture, but retaining the valuable land. If it contributed the main program, but not the land, to the new joint venture, would this be an ancillary joint venture or a complete one? Or something in between?

3. In 2015, the National Geographic Society entered into a second joint venture agreement with 21st Century Fox. The first joint venture began in 1997, when both parties invested in the for-profit National Geographic Channels. In this second transaction, the parties created National Geographic Partners. The National Geographic Society contributed its consumer-oriented assets to the new venture, which included its flagship magazine, its books and maps, its travel business, and all other consumer-oriented businesses. National Geographic Channels also became part of the new venture. 21st Century Fox contributed $725 million to the joint venture. According to the terms of the joint venture that became public, 21st Century Fox owned 73% of the venture and National Geographic 27%. The partners had equal representation on the board of directors, and the bylaws stated that the board chair will alternate annually, with the National Geographic Society's president and CEO chairing the first term. As a result of this transaction, the §501(c)(3) National Geographic Society now has an endowment of $1 billion. How does this agreement seem similar to or different from Rev. Rul. 98-15? Does the agreement appear to protect the National Geographic Society's §501(c)(3) exemption? Press Release, *National Geographic Society and 21st Century*

Fox Agree to Expand Partnership (Sept. 9, 2015), http://press. nationalgeographic.com/2015/09/09/national-geographic-society-21st-century-fox-agree-to-expand-partnership/. An article with an infographic explaining this joint venture is R. Breil, *21st Century Fox Expands National Geographic Brand Activities*, Broadband TV News (Sept. 9. 2015).

4. In 2013, an independent nonprofit business school, the Thunderbird School of Global Management, attempted to enter into a joint venture with a for-profit educational organization, Laureate Education, Inc. Laureate would have bought the property and leased it back to Thunderbird. The two entities also would have entered into a joint venture in which Laureate produced the cash and Thunderbird the educational component. Laureate would have had fewer than half the board seats, and there was an exit clause. The deal fell through, and Thunderbird is now part of Arizona State University. Media reports do not indicate why this change in plans occurred, and undoubtedly the reasons were mainly financial and political. Looking at the rules surrounding joint ventures, however, can you come up with reasons why these deals would be difficult to pull together? Melissa Korn, *Struggling Thunderbird Business School Finds a For-Profit Lifeline*, WALL ST. J. (July 8, 2013); Corina Vanek, *ASU Finalizes Merge with Thunderbird School of Global Management*, THE STATE PRESS (Jan. 12, 2015).

5. For further reading on joint ventures, see Michael I. Sanders, *Update on Joint Ventures*, PAUL STRECKFUS' EO TAX J. 43 (2006); John D. Colombo, *In Search of Private Benefit*, 58 FLA. L. REV. 1063 (2006); Janet James Mahon, *Joint Ventures Between Non-profit and For-Profit Organization; St. David's Case—Worthy Destination, but Road Under Construction*, 56 TAX LAW. 845 (2003); Phil Royalty & Donna Steel Flynn, *Not-For-Profit/For-Profit Joint Ventures: A White Paper*, 25 EXEMPT ORG. TAX REV. 37 (1999).

IV. SOCIAL ENTERPRISE REVISITED

Chapter 2 introduced the concept of the "social enterprise," defined as an enterprise that generates earned income in support of social purposes. In that chapter, a for-profit social enterprise was seen as an alternative business form for a founder to consider when making the decision on the best business form for a new enterprise. As we have seen in this chapter, however, nonprofits can begin working with for-profits at any point during the life cycle of the organization. Using the definition set forth in this book, nonprofits that establish for-profit subsidiaries and engage with for-profits in joint ventures are also creating social enterprises because they are generating revenue in the pursuit of a social mission. Much of this chapter has discussed the steps that §501(c)(3)s need to take in order to protect that social mission and retain their tax exemption once they become involved with that for-profit entity.

Many definitions of "social enterprise" are narrower than the one used in this book. Some definitions require that the business be innovative enough to tackle a seemingly intractable problem at its roots and have a maximum impact. Under such a definition, the Internet is a major social enterprise, connecting people all over the world at a price that is close to being free. Others insist a social enterprise exists only when the potential solution to an intractable problem is "baked into" the business model. Seventh Generation, which is helping to improve the environment through its cleaning products, fits this definition. If it begins producing products that are harmful to the environment, it not only betrays its mission, but it also betrays its name, which suggests that every decision must take the interests of future generations into account. Still other definitions require that the enterprise pay attention to environmental goals as well as to social and financial goals.

Under these narrower definitions, some of the organizations in this chapter do not qualify as social enterprises. Hospitals, for example, help make people well, but they rarely work to eradicate the root problem that creates poor health. Even using narrow definitions, however, a common way to create a social enterprise is to combine a nonprofit and a for-profit form, either by creating a subsidiary or entering into a joint venture.

Before 2008, combining a for-profit and a nonprofit venture was basically the only way to create a social enterprise. A single §501(c)(3) could engage in revenue-producing activities, of course, but that option could create unrelated business income concerns, and the §501(c)(3) could never issue stock in order to incentivize employees, investors, or both. Since 2008, however, it has been possible to combine financial and social goals within a single entity by using the L^3C (low-profit limited liability company), the benefit corporation, or another business form that resembles one or the other of these two entities,[13] A review of those choices can help determine when and if one of those entities would be preferable to setting up a subsidiary or a joint venture. Although the decision will depend, to a large extent, on the circumstances of the business and the client's willingness to take risks, a comparison of the approach that each of these entities takes to the mission, the distribution of revenues, taxes, and transparency can also aid in that choice.

As we have seen in this chapter and throughout the book, the §501(c)(3) business entity has multiple ways to protect the charitable mission. The IRS determines whether the mission is suitably charitable and whether the activities of the §501(c)(3) further that charitable purpose. Although §501(c)(3)s can engage in some unrelated business activity, too much of such activity jeopardizes the exemption, as does too much lobbying. Further, profits can never be distributed to an individual, and political campaign activity is forbidden. In return for abiding by these restrictions, §501(c)(3)s receive favored tax status. They do not pay a federal income tax themselves, and contributions to these entities are

---

[13] Other options include the public benefit corporation, the social purpose corporation, and the benefit LLC. The public benefit corporation is probably the most important of these options, because it is recognized in Delaware, the favored state for business creation in the United States.

tax deductible. Should a §501(c)(3) run afoul of these rules, it will lose its tax exemption and the ability to collect tax-deductible contributions.

Section 501(c)(3)s can and do enter into subsidiary relationships and joint ventures with for-profit entities. If structured correctly, the for-profit subsidiary or partner may distribute its net earnings to its owners and the net profits are taxable, while the nonprofit parent continues to follow the rules described above and remains tax exempt. If structured incorrectly, however, the §501(c)(3) can lose its exemption. In both subsidiary and joint venture situations, care must be taken to ensure that the for-profit does not benefit unfairly from the nonprofit's charitable status. With joint ventures, the requirement that the nonprofit remain in control should ensure there is not even a potential for private benefit.

Funders, customers, and employees all have access to financial information about the §501(c)(3)s and their related organizations because all tax-exempt organizations must file Form 990 on an annual basis, under penalty of perjury. Forms 990 are made available to the public, and failure to file them can lead to penalties and loss of exemption.

L^3Cs and benefit corporations start with different premises from §501(c)(3)s. They are for-profit organizations. Their income is taxable and they can distribute their profits to their owners

L^3Cs are designed to retain the flexibility of an LLC at the same time as they keep the achievement of a charitable goal as their primary motivation. They are not actually required to keep their profits low, so long as the charitable purpose remains paramount. In this sense, the name L^3C is something of a misnomer. L^3Cs were designed to facilitate social investing from private foundations through program-related investments (PRIs), which are investments that private foundations can make in social enterprises without jeopardizing their tax-exempt status.[14] As such, L^3Cs must meet the same three requirements that foundations must follow when they invest in a PRI—they must have a charitable purpose, ensure that making a profit is not the primary purpose, and refrain from lobbying and political campaign intervention. L^3Cs that fail to maintain any of these three provisions become LLCs. L^3Cs are taxed in the same way that LLCs are. Their owners can choose whether to be taxed as a partnership (the "pass-through option," because the entity itself will not be taxed) or as a corporation. Given that this pass-through option usually generates a smaller tax, most LLCs and L^3Cs make that choice. There is no public reporting requirement. In 2016, the L^3C was recognized in eight states and three Indian nations, and approximately 1,300 companies had registered as L^3Cs.[15]

---

[14] IRC §4944(c). Chapter 7 covered this rule briefly.

[15] Intersetor L^3C Tally, http://www.intersectorl3c.com/l3c_tally.html, last accessed May 16, 2016. A list of the states that have adopted legislation recognizing L^3Cs and benefit corporations can be found in Carter Bishop, Fifty State Series: L^3C & B Corporation Legislation Table (Suffolk U. L. Sch. Legal Studies Research Paper Series, Research Paper No. 10-11, 2014), http://ssrn.com/abstract=1561783.

Like nonprofit corporations, L^{3}Cs can cover a wide variety of businesses. The early adopters of this business form in Vermont had purposes that included motorcycle safety, brain imaging research, better timbering practices, and improved medical access for the poor. The L^{3}C has been touted as a business solution for the newspaper industry and as a way to save jobs in economically depressed areas. In those cases, the hope is that foundations, which expect a high social return and a low monetary return, would provide a large enough investment in the L^{3}C that the economic risk to investors that seek a higher return would be less daunting. An L^{3}C with sufficient funding in an economically depressed area could buy factories, modernize them, and then lease them back to manufacturers at a low rate—steps that could help the manufacturers become more competitive and save jobs.[16]

Benefit corporations must serve a general public benefit and have a material positive impact overall. They also have the option of requiring a specific public benefit in their governing documents. The members of their boards of directors must take social and environmental considerations into account when making corporate decisions, and most states require benefit corporations to file and make available to the public an annual benefit report. Benefit corporations are corporate entities, which means that their earnings are taxed at both the corporate level and at the individual level, assuming that the benefit corporation makes a distribution of its profits to its shareholders. The corporation itself, its directors, and shareholders with a 2% interest in the benefit corporation can bring a benefit enforcement proceeding to require the corporation, its directors, and officers to pursue a general public benefit. The proceeding can also require the pursuit of a specific benefit if the articles of incorporation include a specific benefit. A benefit enforcement proceeding also can require the corporation to create and publish the benefit report, and it can be used to require the directors and officers to pursue a standard of conduct outlined in the statute. Unless the bylaws state otherwise, however, neither the board members nor the corporation will be liable for monetary damages for failure to carry out these requirements of the benefit corporation statute. As of 2016, 31 states recognized the benefit corporation, and almost 4,000 benefit corporations were identified on the Benefitcorp website.[17]

---

[16] *See* Elizabeth Schmidt, *Vermont's Social Hybrid Pioneers: Early Observations and Questions to Ponder*, 35 VT L. REV. 163 (2010). The L^{3}C legislation that the North Carolina legislature passed in July 2010 was originally titled "The Endangered Manufacturing and Jobs Act." It was later repealed—possibly because it promised too much.

[17] Find a Benefit Corporation, Benefit Corporation, http://benefitcorp.org/businesses/find-a-benefit-corp, accessed May 16, 2016.

	Mission	Distribution of Profits	Taxes	Reports	Remedies if Social Purpose lost
Joint venture	501(c)(3) partner must maintain control in order to protect mission	For-profit partner may distribute profits; nonprofit partner may not	For-profit partner taxed; NP partner tax exempt	Form 990 of nonprofit discloses related parties	Revocation of exemption
For-profit subsidiary of a nonprofit	Careful structure of relations between for-profit and nonprofit to protect nonprofit mission	For-profit subsidiary may distribute profits; nonprofit parent may not	For-profit subsidiary taxed; nonprofit parent tax exempt	Form 990 of nonprofit discloses related parties	Revocation of exemption
L³C	Charitable purpose	Can distribute profits, but pursuit of profits not primary purpose	Taxed as an LLC	None required	Becomes an LLC
Benefit corporation	General public purpose; materially positive impact	Distribution of profits to owners	Taxed as a corporation	Benefit report in most states	No legal remedy in most states

Much has been written about these new hybrid business forms, but they represent a small portion of the social enterprises in the United States. They are still quite new, and many people, including lawyers, are unaware of the possibilities. Even those who are well aware of these options, however, recognize that each option has its own strengths and weaknesses. Depending on which form is used, the definition of a social purpose differs, as does the ability of the organization to distribute profits to shareholders, the transparency requirements, and the consequences for not following the rules set forth in the governing statutes.

The social enterprise concept raises a number of questions that are as yet unanswered. Among them are the following: Are these new business organizational necessary for those who want to pursue social enterprise? Certainly, nonprofits and for-profits can already work together, as we have seen in this chapter. Assuming that these new business forms are here to stay, what kind of regulation is necessary to protect the social mission? Does either the L^{3}C or the benefit corporation provide sufficient protection for the social purpose? Are they instead creating loopholes for those who want to become rich while pretending to be socially beneficial? Should charitable solicitation laws apply? What kind of governance structure can best help protect the social mission? Should special tax benefits apply?

Even assuming that the policy questions surrounding these forms can be answered, those of us in the nonprofit sector should question whether this new movement is a threat to the nonprofit sector. If it is a threat, how much of a threat is it, and what should we do about that? Further, does this movement shed light on aspects of the nonprofit sector's regulations that policymakers should address? Not a single entrepreneur who responded to a survey about reasons for adopting the L^{3}C in its first 18 months of existence considered starting a §501(c)(3) organization, usually because the rules and regulations were too complicated.[18] As students trying to understand this material, you might agree. If so, which provisions do you think could be made simpler?

NOTES AND QUESTIONS

1. For further reading on the new hybrid forms, see Benjamin Leff, *Preventing Private Inurement in Tranched Social Enterprises*, 45 SETON HALL L. REV. 1 (2015); Alicia Plerhoples, *Social Enterprise as Commitment: A Roadmap*, 48 WASH. U. J.L. & POL'Y 89 (2015); John E. Tyler III, Evan Absher, Kathleen Garman, and Anthony J. Luppino, *Producing Better Mileage: Advancing the Design and Usefulness of Hybrid Vehicles for Social Business Ventures* 33 QUINNIPIAC L. REV. 235 (2015); Lloyd Hitoshi Mayer, *Taxing Social Enterprise*, 66 Stan. L. Rev. 387 (2014); J. Haskell Murray, *Choose Your Own Master: Social Enterprise, Certifications, and Benefit Corporation Statutes*, 2 AMERICAN U. BUS. LAW REV. 1 (2012); Dana Brakman Reiser, *Blended Enterprise and the Dual Mission Dilemma*, 35 VT. L. REV. 105 (2010).

2. An article that discusses nonprofits' use of subsidiaries to create social enterprises is Philip Roundy, *Becoming a Hybrid Organization: When Nonprofits Found Small Businesses* (2015), available at http://ssrn.com/abstract=2633729. *See also* Daniel E. Lichtig, *Joint Ventures and New-Age Business*, 26 TAX'N EXEMPTS 31(2015).

---

[18] Schmidt, *supra* note 16.

3. As mentioned in Chapter 2, businesses can also receive a social enterprise credential by becoming certified B corporations. Any for-profit enterprise can become a certified B corporation if it meets certain social and environmental standards. In other words, traditional corporations, LLCs, L3Cs, and benefit corporations can all receive this certification. As of 2016, 1,674 enterprises in 41 countries had attained the certified B corporation status. Certified B Corporations, http://bcorporation.net, accessed May 16, 2016.

PROBLEMS

1. Alfalfa Animal Shelter (Alfalfa) is a §501(c)(3) tax-exempt organization dedicated to the prevention of cruelty to animals. Since 2008, it has owned all or part of three independent for-profit entities. Alfalfa owns 100% of Better Animal Behavior, Inc. (Better), an animal training school incorporated as a C corporation, and 25% of Cats-R-Us (Cats), a retail store that sells cat supplies and novelties and that is also a C corporation. Alfalfa has also entered into a joint venture with Major Brand Dog Food, another C corporation. Together, they created Doggie Delight (Doggie), an LLC that manufactures and distributes gourmet dog food. They each own 50% of Doggie. This year, Better, Cats, and Doggie have all been profitable. Better and Cats will provide $1,000 each in dividends to Alfalfa. Alfalfa will also receive $100 in interest on each of the loans that it made to Better, Cats, and Doggie. In addition, Better, Cats, and Doggie will each pay $10,000 in royalty payments to Alfalfa in exchange for a license to use its trademark and logo on their products. Finally, Better, Cats, and Doggie each will pay $10,000 a year in rent for the office space that Alfalfa leases to them. Assume that Alfalfa owns the office space debt free and simply rents the space, without offering any services or furnishings. Also, assume that all transactions have been fair to all the parties.

   a. Who pays taxes on the profits that Better, Cats, and Doggie make?
   b. Does Alfalfa pay taxes on the dividends that it receives from Better and Cats? Why doesn't it receive dividends from Doggie?
   c. Does Alfalfa pay taxes on the interest that it receives from Better, Cats, and Dogs?
   d. Are the royalty payments taxable to Alfalfa?
   e. Are the rental payments taxable to Alfalfa? Why is it important that Alfalfa not hold debt on the office space or provide services with the rent, at least to one of the businesses?
   f. If you were advising Alfalfa, what would you suggest that it put into its agreement with Major Brand Dog Food to ensure that the joint venture does not endanger Alfalfa's tax-exempt status?

2. Some law schools have begun to discuss the possibility of running law firms as a way to provide more practical experience to law students and young

lawyers. Assume that a §501(c)(3) law school is considering three options for setting up this practice: (1) as a program within the school, (2) as a subsidiary, or (3) as part of a joint venture with a local law practice. What advice would you give the administration with regard to tax-exempt issues? If it decides to set up a subsidiary, should that subsidiary be a §501(c)(3), a traditional for-profit organization, an L^{3}C, or a benefit corporation? Explain your decisions.

CHAPTER 11

LOBBYING AND POLITICAL CAMPAIGN ACTIVITIES

Purposes of this chapter:

- Understand law and policies behind lobbying and political campaign restrictions
- Determine the best strategies to maximize what is permissible
- Explore the loopholes that Congress, the Internal Revenue Service (IRS), and the courts may want to close
- Discuss whether religious institutions should have different rules
- Introduce affiliations between §501(c)(3)s and other tax-exempt organizations that can engage in more types of political activity than can §501(c)(3)s
- Explore the use of other tax-exempt organizations for political purpose and the current and potential effects that such activity could have on §501(c)(3)s

To think about as you read:

Assume that you are the executive director of your local art museum. School group visits bring in half your revenue for the year. In recent years, the local school board has been making severe budget cuts and you are worried that field trips—especially ones with a fee involved—will be cut from the budget. You are convinced that you will not be able to continue pursuing the art museum's mission of educating the public about art if you lose this audience. Therefore, you plan to do everything in your power, short of losing your organization's tax exemption or incurring an excise tax, to enter the political arena and avoid this fate. What can you do? What should you do to protect yourself and the organization? If you have created your own virtual organization for this course, think of a political situation that you believe could endanger your mission and think about actions that could help the situation without endangering your organization's tax exemption or incurring excise taxes. Also consider whether it might be worth incurring excise taxes in some situations.

I. INTRODUCTION

The final two clauses of §501(c)(3) deal with advocacy activities. The first permits §501(c)(3) organizations to engage in an unspecified amount of lobbying (influencing legislation), and the second prohibits all participation in any political campaign. Treasury regulations identify organizations that fail to qualify as §501(c)(3) organizations because of their political activity as "action organizations." We touched on this concept in Chapter 4, when we examined whether an advocacy organization had an "educational" purpose or was instead an "action" organization. This chapter looks at the flip side of the equation—when is the advocacy activity in violation of one or both of these final two clauses of §501(c)(3)?

As with other clauses in §501(c)(3), the statute and its regulations are not always the most effective way to regulate activities. With respect to the lobbying restrictions, for example, the §501(c)(3) language provides that an organization can qualify for exemption under this section only if "no substantial part of the activities ... is carrying on propaganda, or otherwise attempting, to influence legislation." As we will see shortly, the definition of "substantial" depends on a facts and circumstances test that provides little guidance to the organization that is attempting to influence legislation.[1] In 1976, Congress passed §501(h), which provides a mathematical formula for determining how much lobbying is permissible. Organizations that are concerned about the inherent ambiguity of §501(c)(3) can elect to use the §501(h) test by filing Form 5768 with the IRS.

The political campaign prohibition is absolute. It disallows *all* participation in a political campaign. Determining who is a candidate for office, what a political campaign is, and what constitutes participation or intervention, nevertheless, can be difficult. An additional problem with both the insubstantial lobbying and the campaign prohibition clauses of §501(c)(3) is that the violation does not always seem egregious enough to warrant the loss of tax exemption, which is the penalty for violating these two clauses. Several excise tax measures—§4911, §4912, and §4955—attempt to deal with that difficulty by imposing sanctions that are less severe than revocation. In some cases, they can also provide an additional tax once exemption has been revoked.

The relationship between §501(c)(3) organizations and other tax-exempt organizations that engage in political campaigns is also important, as many §501(c)(3)s are affiliated with one or more of these organizations. Section 501(c)(4) social welfare organizations, for example, can engage in lobbying and in political campaign intervention, so long as those are not their primary activities. Social welfare organizations have become an increasingly significant force in political campaigns—a situation that can lead to some thorny public policy issues for the nonprofit sector as a whole, even for §501(c)(3) organizations.

---

[1] Note that private foundations are governed by stricter rules that forbid any legislative activity [IRC §4945(d)(1)], and thus are not covered by either the "substantial activity" or the "501(h) expenditure" test.

Following are articles, cases, statutes, tax rulings, and notes that expand on these topics. As you read these materials, consider why the political activity limitations are in place and whether the statutes and regulations are an effective means of reaching those policy goals. Do the statutes and regulations provide so many loopholes that they are ineffective? Would more regulation help? Better enforcement? Or should we allow more lobbying and political activity for §501(c)(3) organizations than we currently do?

II. LOBBYING

JEFFREY BERRY, THE LOBBYING LAW IS MORE CHARITABLE THAN THEY THINK

Wash. Post (Nov. 30, 2003), p. B-01.

The leaders of the nation's nonprofits do many things well, but representing their clients' interests before government is not one of them. In the course of a major research study that included interviews with the chief executives of tax-deductible nonprofits, I found them remarkably ill-informed about the primary law that governs their operations. When it comes to their rights to lobby, many believe they have no rights at all. "I have to wait until a legislator contacts us," said one executive director. Another stated unequivocally, "We're not allowed to lobby. We're not allowed to influence public policy."

Such views are not merely wrong, they're harmful. Not only can charitable nonprofits engage in more lobbying than is commonly accepted, they can lobby extensively if they take advantage of a 1976 law that the Internal Revenue Service seems to have no interest in publicizing.

Nonprofits that can offer donors a tax deduction for their contributions play a special role in American society, and that role is growing. . . .Among those large enough to file a tax return . . . roughly half are either health care or social service providers. They are the foot soldiers in a largely private system that delivers critical services to the disadvantaged. They are often closer to the problems—and the solutions—than the policymakers in city halls, state capitals and Washington. Yet the fear of an IRS audit, no matter how unlikely, has deprived many nonprofits of their voice and has hurt the very constituencies that they intend to serve.

To gather systematic evidence on the role of nonprofits in the public policymaking process, my research team and I surveyed more than 1,700 tax-deductible nonprofits drawn randomly from IRS records. . . .

We found that the typical executive director of a 501(c)(3) has little understanding of what the law actually says. Almost half of those surveyed are so ignorant of the law that they don't even believe their organization has the right to take a public stand on federal legislation (perfectly permissible), while 45percent believe they are not allowed to sponsor a debate featuring candidates running for public office (they can't support a candidate, but a candidate forum is just fine).

There's good reason why many nonprofit leaders have trouble understanding what they can and cannot do in the public policymaking process. The law is a patchwork of confusing, contradictory and unworkable provisions. The heart of the problem is that 501(c)(3) says that nonprofits may lobby but not to any "substantial" degree. Despite repeated requests over the years, the IRS resolutely refuses to define what qualifies as "substantial." Nonprofits are left to guess.

Yet, nonprofits are allowed to educate legislators and staffers without constraint. So leaders of nonprofits believe they can "educate" substantially, but not "lobby" substantially. For political scientists, this is a preposterous distinction. To educate policymakers is to lobby.

The inconsistencies and contradictions under 501(c)(3) are breathtaking—they're a logician's nightmare. Nevertheless, it is difficult to simply get rid of this regulatory framework. A nonprofit that receives a tax-deductible donation is getting an indirect government subsidy. The dollars that the Treasury loses to nonprofits must be made up through higher taxes on all of us. No one would argue that nonprofits should be able to do whatever they want with charitable donations.

Although regulation is necessary, this particular set of restrictions is strikingly discriminatory. No other sector of the interest group universe is as constrained in its advocacy as are 501(c)(3)s. This creates a huge imbalance. The so-called Gucci crowd on K Street can lobby as much as it wants and spend as much as it wants in representing trade associations or corporations before government. Yet, legally speaking, disability groups, hospices, community health centers and other 501(c)(3)s are regarded as something of a threat to the integrity of our political process. This is too large a price to pay for tax deductibility. . . .

Many of our interviewees told us they believed that the IRS was vigilantly monitoring their political activity. On a number of occasions we heard the story of how the IRS busted the Sierra Club for its lobbying. The venerable environmental group infuriated a powerful member of Congress, Democratic Rep. Wayne Aspinall of Colorado, by taking out newspaper ads ridiculing a proposal to flood part of the Grand Canyon. The day after the ads ran, the IRS revoked the Sierra Club's tax-deductible status. Our respondents spoke knowingly of this episode, as if it happened recently.

It took place in 1966.

That the Sierra Club case still reverberates today is testament to how scared nonprofits are of the IRS. This is ironic because the modest, cobwebby Tax Exempt Office at the IRS hardly has the resources to engage in anything more than symbolic oversight of nonprofits. . . .

If the IRS has a coherent strategy, it seems to be selective enforcement. Agency officials know that audits of a small number of nonprofits send shock waves throughout their larger communities. Most worrisome is that the office will undertake a review based on the complaints of an organization's rivals.

Compounding the problem of an ambiguous law and erratic enforcement is the passivity of nonprofit CEOs. By failing to learn the law, they are willing accomplices. Too often, when they do lobby, they pretend otherwise. One executive director told me that "We harass our state legislator all the time," while insisting that her organization did not belong in our study because "we are not involved in public affairs."

The irony in all of this is that there is a solution already in place that allows nonprofits to lobby without having to worry. In 1976 Congress passed a tax bill that included a specific accounting mechanism so that nonprofits no longer would have to guess what divides substantial from insubstantial lobbying. This much-needed alternative method was then, unfortunately, turned over to the IRS's Tax Exempt Office to implement. To call its pace in writing the regulations snail-like would be unfair to snails. It took 14 years before the office issued regulations.

The 1976 alternative, known as the "H election," is crystal clear in specifying the amounts that a nonprofit can expend on lobbying. Based on a sliding scale keyed to annual income, a nonprofit can spend up to as much as 20 percent of its revenues on lobbying. And because the regulations for the H election define lobbying rather narrowly, very little of what a nonprofit H elector does in its advocacy efforts counts as a lobbying expenditure. In short, it's difficult for a typical nonprofit to ever reach the H expenditure ceilings.

The H election is something of a stealth policy. Only about 2 percent of all 501(c)(3)s have chosen this option. When we asked the head of one statewide nonprofit association if he knew of the H election, his response was a common one. "I'm completely ignorant of it," he confessed.

So what's the catch? There isn't one, really—only that the H election requires nonprofits to keep a record of their spending so they can prove they haven't exceeded the established limits.

The good news is that taking the H election could not be easier. Form 5768, which can be downloaded from the tax forms box at www.irs.gov, only asks for an organization's name, address and a signature. It takes no more than 60 seconds to fill out. The IRS has also issued formal guidelines indicating that the H election is not a red flag for an audit and it appears to have kept its word.

Nonprofits are a lifeline for millions—for battered women, immigrants, homebound senior citizens, AIDS patients, . . . and countless other constituencies who all too often fall through this nation's safety net. As government itself grows leaner, it is relying ever more heavily on nonprofits to do its work. From a standpoint of good government, the best policy would promote communication between government and its vendors.

Although it is legal for nonprofits to lobby under the "substantial" standard, it's clear that most are inhibited by it. By taking the H election, 501(c)(3)s can maintain their tax deductibility while becoming more aggressive on behalf of the disadvantaged segments of American society who come to them for social services and health care. It's unlikely, however, that the H election will ever become widely adopted without a firm push from the IRS. As a result, those most in need of a powerful voice in the political system will continue to receive the least representation. The obstacles created by Section 501(c)(3) aren't just bad public policy. They're unjust.

A. CONSTITUTIONALITY OF LOBBYING RESTRICTIONS

CHRISTIAN ECHOES NATIONAL MINISTRY, INC. V. UNITED STATES

---

470 F.2d 849 (10th Cir. 1972), *cert. denied*, 414 U.S. 864 (1973)

BARRETT, Circuit Judge.

Christian Echoes is a nonprofit religious corporation organized in 1951 under the laws of Oklahoma by Dr. Billy James Hargis, its president, chief spokesman and an ordained minister. The Articles of Incorporation state in part that the corporation is founded "to establish and maintain weekly religious, radio and television broadcasts, to establish and maintain a national religious magazine and other religious publications, to establish and maintain religious educational institutions...." Article III of the Articles of Faith in the corporate bylaws reads as follows:

> We believe in God, Supreme and Eternal, and in Jesus Christ as His Son, perfect Deity, and in the Holy Comforter and Challenger of this age, The Holy Ghost, and in the Bible as the inspired Word of God.
>
> We believe that the solution of the World's problems, economic, political and spiritual, is found by the application of Christian Teachings in the lives of men and nations rather than in political ideologies of any kind....
>
> We realize atheistic world forces seek the destruction and overthrow of all the religions of the World, including particularly that founded upon the teachings of Jesus Christ. The same forces seek also the destruction of all free governments, in which the lives and property of the people are protected by civil, moral and spiritual law....
>
> We believe in the fundamentals of New Testament Christianity, and we propose to promulgate the eternal truths thereof at all costs.

The activities of the organization have been addressed to that theology ever since the date of incorporation.

Christian Echoes maintains religious radio and television broadcasts, authors publications, and engages in evangelistic campaigns and meetings for the promotion of the social and spiritual welfare of the community, state and nation. Dr. Hargis has stated that its mission is a battle against Communism, socialism and political liberalism, all of which are considered arch enemies of the Christian faith. Dr. Hargis testified that Christian Echoes supports "Christian conservative statesmen..." without regard to party political labels. The organization publishes a monthly anti-Communist magazine, Christian Crusade, a weekly "intelligence report," Weekly Crusader, and a newspaper column, "For and Against." It also distributes pamphlets, leaflets and broadcast reprints on aspects of anti-

Communist activity; it distributes tapes and records of selected broadcasts; and it conducts an annual anti-Communist leadership school whose goal is to answer the question, "What can my community do to stem the forces of liberalism and thus stop the growth of socialism and communism?" In 1962 it established a Summer Anti-Communist University and formed youth groups, Torchbearer Chapters, to educate the public on the threat of Communism. In 1964 Christian Echoes encouraged adults to organize local Christian Crusade chapters. Christian Echoes appealed for contributions from the public to carry on its campaign. It earned money from the sale of its publications, tapes, films and admission fees at rallies. From 1961 through 1966 its gross receipts ranged from about $677,000 to $1,000,000 per year. It spent 52% of this income on radio, television, publications and postage.

On March 12, 1953 the Internal Revenue Service ruled that Christian Echoes qualified as a tax-exempt religious and educational organization under Section 501(c)(3) of the 1954 Code, formerly Section 101(6) of the 1939 Code. Section 501(c)(3) states as follows:

> Corporations, and any community chest, fund, or foundation, organized and operated exclusively for religious, charitable, scientific, testing for public safety, literary, or educational purposes ... which does not participate in, or intervene in (including the publishing or distributing of statements), any political campaign on behalf of any candidate for public office....

[*Editor's Note:* The IRS reviewed Christian Echoes' activities and financial affairs several times between 1962 and 1966.] The District Director notified Christian Echoes on September 22, 1966 that its exempt status was being revoked for three reasons: (1) it was not operated exclusively for charitable, educational or religious purposes; (2) it had engaged in substantial activity aimed at influencing legislation; and (3) it had directly and indirectly intervened in political campaigns on behalf of candidates for public office. Christian Echoes filed further protests without avail. It paid the taxes as assessed. Christian Echoes then filed this refund suit, claiming its right to exemption.

The District Court held that the taxpayer was entitled to tax-exempt status under Section 501(c)(3). The Court ruled that Christian Echoes qualified in that no substantial part of its activities had been devoted to attempts to influence legislation or intervene in political campaigns. The Court found that the only activity of Christian Echoes relating to an attempt to influence legislation was in support of the Becker Amendment urging support of restoration of prayers in the public schools. . . .

It also held that all of its activities were motivated by sincere religious convictions; that the First Amendment prohibits the Government and courts from determining whether the activities are religious or political; and that the IRS had revoked Christian Echoes' exempt status without evidence to support its action and without constitutionally justifiable cause in violation of the First Amendment. It found that the taxpayer had been denied its right to due process under the Fifth Amendment because the Government had arbitrarily selected it from organizations engaged in similar activities and had violated its published administrative procedures in the steps leading to the revocation.

The Government appealed directly to the United States Supreme Court which dismissed the appeal for lack of jurisdiction, vacated the District Court's judgment and remanded for entry of a new decree. The IRS appeals from the District Court's holding in favor of Christian Echoes following remand.

The Government contends that: (1) the taxpayer failed to qualify as tax-exempt under Section 501(c)(3); (2) its interpretation and application of Section 501(c)(3) did not violate the taxpayer's rights under the First Amendment; (3) its revocation of tax-exempt status to the taxpayer under Section 501(c)(3) did not violate the taxpayer's rights of due process under the Fifth Amendment; and (4) the Commissioner did not abuse his discretion in revoking the exemption with retroactive effect.

[*Editor's Note:* Part I of this case, which is reproduced later in this chapter, applied the "no substantial part" test to determine whether Christian Echoes engaged in so much lobbying that it should lose its §501(c)(3) status. Parts II and III, next, discuss the constitutional issues relating to the lobbying restrictions.]

II

The Government contends that its application of Section 501(c)(3) does not violate the free exercise clause in the First Amendment. Christian Echoes argues strenuously that denial of its tax-exempt status is a direct infringement upon its First Amendment right of free exercise of religion, and discrimination against the religion of its followers. The District Court agreed. . . . We hold that the Court erred.

If we were to adopt the District Court's findings and the arguments advanced by Christian Echoes, we would be compelled to hold that Congress is constitutionally restrained from withholding the privilege of tax exemption whenever it enacts legislation relating to a nonprofit religious organization. This is fully evidenced by the trial court's Conclusion of Law No. 4 which . . . concluded in part:

> The Court having found as fact that plaintiff through its followers believes in the religious nature of its activities, neither defendant nor this Court may inquire into such activities and work product of plaintiff for the purpose of determining whether those activities claimed by plaintiff to be religious are religious or political and, if political, whether substantial, for the purpose of denying tax exempt status to plaintiff. . . . To do so would require an interpretation of the meaning of the church doctrine espoused by plaintiff and a determination of the relative significance of the religion of plaintiff to its activities.

We know of no legal authority supporting the conclusion set forth above. Such conclusion is tantamount to the proposition that the First Amendment right of free exercise of religion, ipso facto, assures no restraints, no limitations and, in effect, protects those exercising the right to do so unfettered. We hold that the limitations imposed by Congress in Section 501(c)(3) are constitutionally valid.

The free exercise clause of the First Amendment is restrained only to the extent of denying tax exempt status and then only in keeping with an overwhelming and compelling Governmental interest: That of guarantying that the wall separating church and state remains high and firm. We reject both the District Court's findings and conclusions on the First Amendment constitutional issue just as the United States Supreme Court put down attacks against the enforcement of the provisions of the "Hatch Act" predicated on First Amendment free speech and assembly rights, restraining political activities by certain federal officers and employees in United Public Workers of America (C.I.O.) v. Mitchell, 330 U.S. 75, 67 S. Ct. 556, 91 L. Ed. 754 (1947), and Oklahoma v. United States Civil Service Commission, 330 U.S. 127, 67 S. Ct. 544, 91 L. Ed. 794 (1947). In these decisions the courts held that the First Amendment rights are not absolutes and that courts must balance First Amendment freedoms against the congressional enactment in order to protect society against political partisanship by Government employees.

In light of the fact that tax exemption is a privilege, a matter of grace rather than right, we hold that the limitations contained in Section 501(c)(3) withholding exemption from nonprofit corporations do not deprive Christian Echoes of its constitutionally guaranteed right of free speech. The taxpayer may engage in all such activities without restraint, subject, however, to withholding of the exemption or, in the alternative, the taxpayer may refrain from such activities and obtain the privilege of exemption. The parallel to the "Hatch Act" prohibitions relating to political activities on the part of certain federal and state employees is clear: The taxpayer may opt to enter an area of federal employment subject to the restraints and limitations upon his First Amendment rights. Conversely, he may opt not to receive employment funds at the public trough in the areas covered by the restraints and thus exercise his First Amendment rights unfettered. The Congressional purposes evidenced by the 1934 and 1954 amendments are clearly constitutionally justified in keeping with the separation and neutrality principles particularly applicable in this case and, more succinctly, the principle that government shall not subsidize, directly or indirectly, those organizations whose substantial activities are directed toward the accomplishment of legislative goals or the election or defeat of particular candidates. From a review of the entire record we hold that the trial court's findings of fact and conclusions of law in this area are clearly erroneous.

III

The Government also contends that its application of Section 501(c)(3) did not arbitrarily discriminate against Christian Echoes in violation of the Fifth Amendment due process clause as found by the District Court. The Court found that the Government had arbitrarily selected Christian Echoes in violation of the due process clause. The Fifth Amendment provides that no person shall be deprived of life, liberty or property without due process of law. An organization is being discriminated against in violation of the due process clause only when there is no reasonable relationship to a proper governmental objective. In order to establish discrimination violating the due process clause, the taxpayer must show discrimination based on differences of religion, race, politics or an unacceptable classification. No discrimination is apparent in the record. The fact that the Commissioner has not proceeded against other organizations similar to Christian Echoes does not amount to a denial of due process.

The District Court also erred in its holding that the IRS's departure from its administrative procedures constituted a denial of due process. The taxpayer has not shown any prejudice by deviations from normal procedures....
Reversed.

REGAN V. TAXATION WITH REPRESENTATION OF WASHINGTON

461 U.S. 540 (1983)

Justice REHNQUIST delivered the opinion of the Court

Appellee Taxation With Representation of Washington (TWR) is a nonprofit corporation organized to promote what it conceives to be the "public interest" in the area of federal taxation. It proposes to advocate its point of view before Congress, the Executive Branch, and the Judiciary. This case began when TWR applied for tax-exempt status under §501(c)(3) of the Internal Revenue Code, 26 U.S.C. §501(c)(3). The Internal Revenue Service denied the application because it appeared that a substantial part of TWR's activities would consist of attempting to influence legislation, which is not permitted by §501(c)(3).

TWR then brought this suit in District Court against the appellants, the Commissioner of Internal Revenue, the Secretary of the Treasury, and the United States, seeking a declaratory judgment that it qualifies for the exemption granted by §501(c)(3). It claimed the prohibition against substantial lobbying is unconstitutional under the First Amendment and the equal protection component of the Fifth Amendment's Due Process Clause....

TWR was formed to take over the operations of two other nonprofit corporations. One, Taxation With Representation Fund, was organized to promote TWR's goals by publishing a journal and engaging in litigation; it had tax-exempt status under §501(c)(3). The other, Taxation With Representation, attempted to promote the same goals by influencing legislation; it had tax-exempt status under §501(c)(4). Neither predecessor organization was required to pay federal income taxes. For purposes of our analysis, there are two principal differences between §501(c)(3) organizations and §501(c)(4) organizations. Taxpayers who contribute to §501(c)(3) organizations, are permitted by §170(c)(2) to deduct the amount of their contributions on their federal income tax returns, while contributions to §501(c)(4) organizations are not deductible. Section 501(c)(4) organizations, but not §501(c)(3) organizations, are permitted to engage in substantial lobbying to advance their exempt purposes.

In [this case], TWR is attacking the prohibition against substantial lobbying in §501(c)(3) because it wants to use tax-deductible contributions to support substantial lobbying activities. To evaluate TWR's claims, it is necessary to understand the effect of the tax-exemption system enacted by Congress.

Both tax exemptions and tax deductibility are a form of subsidy that is administered through the tax system. A tax exemption has much the same effect as a cash grant to the organization of the amount of tax it would have to pay on its income. Deductible contributions are similar to cash grants of the amount of a portion of the individual's contributions.[2] The system Congress has enacted provides this kind of subsidy to nonprofit civic welfare organizations generally, and an additional subsidy to those charitable organizations that do not engage in substantial lobbying. In short, Congress chose not to subsidize lobbying as extensively as it chose to subsidize other activities that nonprofit organizations undertake to promote the public welfare.

It appears that TWR could still qualify for a tax exemption under §501(c)(4). It also appears that TWR can obtain tax-deductible contributions for its nonlobbying activity by returning to the dual structure it used in the past, with a §501(c)(3) organization for nonlobbying activities and a §501(c)(4) organization for lobbying. TWR would, of course, have to ensure that the §501(c)(3) organization did not subsidize the §501(c)(4) organization; otherwise, public funds might be spent on an activity Congress chose not to subsidize.[3]

TWR contends that Congress' decision not to subsidize its lobbying violates the First Amendment. It claims, relying on Speiser v. Randall, 357 U.S. 513 (1958), that the prohibition against substantial lobbying by §501(c)(3) organizations imposes an "unconstitutional condition" on the receipt of tax-deductible contributions. In Speiser, California established a rule requiring anyone who sought to take advantage of a property tax exemption to sign a declaration stating that he did not advocate the forcible overthrow of the Government of the United States. This Court stated that "[to] deny an exemption to claimants who engage in certain forms of speech is in effect to penalize them for such speech." Id. at 518.

TWR is certainly correct when it states that we have held that the government may not deny a benefit to a person because he exercises a constitutional right. See Perry v. Sindermann, 408 U.S. 593, 597 (1972). But

---

[2] [FN 5] In stating that exemptions and deductions, on the one hand, are like cash subsidies, on the other, we of course do not mean to assert that they are in all respects identical. See, e.g., Walz v. Tax Comm'n, 397 U.S. 664, 674-676 (1970); id., at 690-691 (Brennan, J., concurring); id. at 699 (opinion of Harlan, J.).

[3] [FN 6] TWR and some amici are concerned that the IRS may impose stringent requirements that are unrelated to the congressional purpose of ensuring that no tax-deductible contributions are used to pay for substantial lobbying, and effectively make it impossible for a §501(c)(3) organization to establish a §501(c)(4) lobbying affiliate. No such requirement in the Code or regulations has been called to our attention, nor have we been able to discover one. The IRS apparently requires only that the two groups be separately incorporated and keep records adequate to show that tax-deductible contributions are not used to pay for lobbying. This is not unduly burdensome. We also note that TWR did not bring this suit because it was unable to operate with the dual structure and seeks a less stringent set of bookkeeping requirements. Rather, TWR seeks to force Congress to subsidize its lobbying activity.

TWR is just as certainly incorrect when it claims that this case fits the Speiser-Perry model. The Code does not deny TWR the right to receive deductible contributions to support its nonlobbying activity, nor does it deny TWR any independent benefit on account of its intention to lobby. Congress has merely refused to pay for the lobbying out of public moneys. This Court has never held that Congress must grant a benefit such as TWR claims here to a person who wishes to exercise a constitutional right.

This aspect of these cases is controlled by Cammarano v. United States, 358 U.S. 498 (1959), in which we upheld a Treasury Regulation that denied business expense deductions for lobbying activities. We held that Congress is not required by the First Amendment to subsidize lobbying. Id. at 513. In these cases, as in Cammarano, Congress has not infringed any First Amendment rights or regulated any First Amendment activity. Congress has simply chosen not to pay for TWR's lobbying. We again reject the "notion that First Amendment rights are somehow not fully realized unless they are subsidized by the State." Id. at 515 (Douglas, J., concurring).

TWR also contends that the equal protection component of the Fifth Amendment renders the prohibition against substantial lobbying invalid. TWR points out that §170(c)(3) permits taxpayers to deduct contributions to veterans' organizations that qualify for tax exemption under §501(c)(19). Qualifying veterans' organizations are permitted to lobby as much as they want in furtherance of their exempt purposes.[4] TWR argues that because Congress has chosen to subsidize the substantial lobbying activities of veterans' organizations, it must also subsidize the lobbying of §501(c)(3) organizations.

Generally, statutory classifications are valid if they bear a rational relation to a legitimate governmental purpose. Statutes are subjected to a higher level of scrutiny if they interfere with the exercise of a fundamental right, such as freedom of speech, or employ a suspect classification, such as race.... Legislatures have especially broad latitude in creating classifications and distinctions in tax statutes. More than 40 years ago we addressed these comments to an equal protection challenge to tax legislation:

> ... Traditionally classification has been a device for fitting tax programs to local needs and usages in order to achieve an equitable distribution of the tax burden. It has, because of this, been pointed out that in taxation, even more than in other fields, legislatures possess the greatest freedom in classification. Since the members of a legislature necessarily enjoy a familiarity with local conditions which this Court cannot have, the presumption of constitutionality can be

---

[4] [FN 8] The rules governing deductibility of contributions to veterans' organizations are not the same as the analogous rules for §501(c)(3) organizations. For example, an individual may generally deduct up to 50% of his adjusted gross income in contributions to §501(c)(3) organizations, but only 20% in contributions to veterans' organizations. Compare §170(b)(1)(A) with §170(b)(1)(B). Taxpayers are permitted to carry over excess contributions to §501(c)(3) organizations, but not veterans' organizations, to the next year. §170(d). There are other differences. If it were entitled to equal treatment with veterans' organizations, TWR would, of course, be entitled only to the benefits they receive, not to more.

overcome only by the most explicit demonstration that a classification is a hostile and oppressive discrimination against particular persons and classes. . . .

We have already explained why we conclude that Congress has not violated TWR's First Amendment rights by declining to subsidize its First Amendment activities. The case would be different if Congress were to discriminate invidiously in its subsidies in such a way as to " '[aim] at the suppression of dangerous ideas.' " Cammarano, supra, at 513, quoting Speiser, 357 U.S., at 519. But the veterans' organizations that qualify under §501(c)(19) are entitled to receive tax-deductible contributions regardless of the content of any speech they may use, including lobbying. We find no indication that the statute was intended to suppress any ideas or any demonstration that it has had that effect. The sections of the Internal Revenue Code here at issue do not employ any suspect classification. The distinction between veterans' organizations and other charitable organizations is not at all like distinctions based on race or national origin.

The Court of Appeals nonetheless held that "strict scrutiny" is required because the statute "[affects] First Amendment rights on a discriminatory basis." 219 U.S. App. D.C., at 130, 676 F.2d, at 728 (emphasis supplied). Its opinion suggests that strict scrutiny applies whenever Congress subsidizes some speech, but not all speech. This is not the law. Congress could, for example, grant funds to an organization dedicated to combating teenage drug abuse, but condition the grant by providing that none of the money received from Congress should be used to lobby state legislatures. Under Cammarano, such a statute would be valid. Congress might also enact a statute providing public money for an organization dedicated to combating teenage alcohol abuse, and impose no condition against using funds obtained from Congress for lobbying. The existence of the second statute would not make the first statute subject to strict scrutiny.

Congressional selection of particular entities or persons for entitlement to this sort of largesse "is obviously a matter of policy and discretion not open to judicial review unless in circumstances which here we are not able to find.... For the purposes of these cases appropriations are comparable to tax exemptions and deductions, which are also "a matter of grace [that] Congress can, of course, disallow ... as it chooses." Commissioner v. Sullivan, 356 U.S. 27, 28 (1958).

These are scarcely novel principles. We have held in several contexts that a legislature's decision not to subsidize the exercise of a fundamental right does not infringe the right, and thus is not subject to strict scrutiny. Buckley v. Valeo, 424 U.S. 1 (1976), upheld a statute that provides federal funds for candidates for public office who enter primary campaigns, but does not provide funds for candidates who do not run in party primaries. We rejected First Amendment and equal protection challenges to this provision without applying strict scrutiny. Id. at 93-108. Harris v. McRae, supra, and Maher v. Roe, 432 U.S. 464 (1977), considered legislative decisions not to subsidize abortions, even though other medical procedures were subsidized. We declined to apply strict scrutiny and rejected equal protection challenges to the statutes.

The reasoning of these decisions is simple: "although government may not place obstacles in the path of a [person's] exercise of ... freedom of [speech], it need not remove those not of its own creation." Harris, 448 U.S., at 316. Although TWR does not have as much money as it wants, and thus cannot exercise its freedom of speech as much as it would like, the Constitution "does not confer an entitlement to such funds as may be necessary to realize all the advantages of that freedom." Id. at 318. As we said in Maher, "[constitutional] concerns are greatest when the State attempts to impose its will by force of law...." 432 U.S., at 476. Where governmental provision of subsidies is not " 'aimed at the suppression of dangerous ideas,' " Cammarano, 358 U.S., at 513, its "power to encourage actions deemed to be in the public interest is necessarily far broader." Maher, supra, at 476.

We have no doubt but that this statute is within Congress' broad power in this area. TWR contends that §501(c)(3) organizations could better advance their charitable purposes if they were permitted to engage in substantial lobbying. This may well be true. But Congress—not TWR or this Court—has the authority to determine whether the advantage the public would receive from additional lobbying by charities is worth the money the public would pay to subsidize that lobbying, and other disadvantages that might accompany that lobbying. It appears that Congress was concerned that exempt organizations might use tax-deductible contributions to lobby to promote the private interests of their members. See 78 Cong. Rec. 5861 (1934) (remarks of Sen. Reed); id., at 5959 (remarks of Sen. La Follette). It is not irrational for Congress to decide that tax-exempt charities such as TWR should not further benefit at the expense of taxpayers at large by obtaining a further subsidy for lobbying.

It is also not irrational for Congress to decide that, even though it will not subsidize substantial lobbying by charities generally, it will subsidize lobbying by veterans' organizations. Veterans have "been obliged to drop their own affairs to take up the burdens of the nation," Boone v. Lightner, 319 U.S. 561, 575 (1943), " 'subjecting themselves to the mental and physical hazards as well as the economic and family detriments which are peculiar to military service and which do not exist in normal civil life.' " Johnson v. Robison, 415 U.S. 361, 380 (1974) (emphasis deleted). Our country has a longstanding policy of compensating veterans for their past contributions by providing them with numerous advantages. This policy has "always been deemed to be legitimate." Personnel Administrator v. Feeney, 442 U.S. 256, 279, n. 25 (1979).

The issue in these cases is not whether TWR must be permitted to lobby, but whether Congress is required to provide it with public money with which to lobby. For the reasons stated above, we hold that it is not. Accordingly, the judgment of the Court of Appeals is Reversed.

Justice BLACKMUN, with whom Justice BRENNAN and Justice MARSHALL join, concurring.

I join the Court's opinion. Because 26 U.S.C. §501s discrimination between veterans' organizations and charitable organizations is not based on the content of their speech, ante, at 548, I agree with the Court that §501 does not deny charitable organizations equal protection of the law. The benefit provided to veterans' organizations is rationally based on the Nation's time-honored policy of "compensating veterans for their past contributions."... As the Court says, ... a statute designed to discourage the expression of particular views would present a very different question.

I also agree that the First Amendment does not require the Government to subsidize protected activity, ... and that this principle controls disposition of TWR's First Amendment claim. I write separately to make clear that in my view the result under the First Amendment depends entirely upon the Court's necessary assumption—which I share—about the manner in which the Internal Revenue Service administers §501.

If viewed in isolation, the lobbying restriction contained in §501(c)(3) violates the principle, reaffirmed today, ... "that the government may not deny a benefit to a person because he exercises a constitutional right." Section 501(c)(3) does not merely deny a subsidy for lobbying activities, see Cammarano v. United States, 358 U.S. 498 (1959); it deprives an otherwise eligible organization of its tax-exempt status and its eligibility to receive tax-deductible contributions for all its activities, whenever one of those activities is "substantial lobbying." Because lobbying is protected by the First Amendment, ... §501(c)(3) therefore denies a significant benefit to organizations choosing to exercise their constitutional rights.

The constitutional defect that would inhere in §501(c)(3) alone is avoided by §501(c)(4). As the Court notes, ... TWR may use its present §501(c)(3) organization for its nonlobbying activities and may create a §501(c)(4) affiliate to pursue its charitable goals through lobbying. The §501(c)(4) affiliate would not be eligible to receive tax-deductible contributions.

Given this relationship between §501(c)(3) and §501(c)(4), the Court finds that Congress' purpose in imposing the lobbying restriction was merely to ensure that "no tax-deductible contributions are used to pay for substantial lobbying." Consistent with that purpose, "[the] IRS apparently requires only that the two groups be separately incorporated and keep records adequate to show that tax-deductible contributions are not used to pay for lobbying." As long as the IRS goes no further than this, we perhaps can safely say that "[the] Code does not deny TWR the right to receive deductible contributions to support its nonlobbying activity, nor does it deny TWR any independent benefit on account of its intention to lobby."... A §501(c)(3) organization's right to speak is not infringed, because it is free to make known its views on legislation through its §501(c)(4) affiliate without losing tax benefits for its nonlobbying activities.

Any significant restriction on this channel of communication, however, would negate the saving effect of §501(c)(4). It must be remembered that §501(c)(3) organizations retain their constitutional right to speak and to petition the Government. Should the IRS attempt to limit the control these organizations exercise over the lobbying of their §501(c)(4) affiliates, the First Amendment problems would be insurmountable. It hardly answers one person's objection to a restriction on his speech that another person, outside his control, may speak for him. Similarly, an attempt to prevent §501(c)(4) organizations from lobbying explicitly on behalf of their §501(c)(3) affiliates would perpetuate §501(c)(3) organizations' inability to make known their views on legislation without incurring the unconstitutional penalty. Such restrictions would extend far beyond Congress' mere refusal to subsidize lobbying.... In my view, any such restriction would render the statutory scheme unconstitutional.

I must assume that the IRS will continue to administer §§501(c)(3) and 501(c)(4) in keeping with Congress' limited purpose and with the IRS's duty to respect and uphold the Constitution. I therefore agree with the Court that the First Amendment questions in these cases are controlled by Cammarano v. United States, 358 U.S. 498, 513 (1959), rather than by Speiser v. Randall, 357 U.S. 513, 518-519 (1958), and Perry v. Sindermann, 408 U.S. 593, 597 (1972).

NOTES AND QUESTIONS

1. How does the reasoning in the majority opinion in *Regan v. Taxation with Representation* differ from the reasoning in the concurrence? If you had been a Supreme Court justice in 1983, would you have joined the majority or the concurrence? Why? Would you have dissented instead? On what grounds?

2. The last two clauses of §501(c)(3) together are considered the "advocacy" clauses, but they are distinctly different. The first covers attempts to influence legislation, which is commonly called "lobbying." The second covers intervention in political campaigns. What policy reasons exist for restricting §501(c)(3)s from foraying into the political realm? Why is intervention in a political campaign more restricted than lobbying?

B. NO SUBSTANTIAL PART TEST

IRC §501(C)(3)

(3) Corporations, and any community chest, fund, or foundation, organized and operated exclusively for religious, charitable, scientific, testing for public safety, literary, or educational purposes, or to foster national or international amateur sports competition (but only if no part of its activities involve the provision of athletic facilities or equipment), or for the prevention of cruelty to children or animals, no part of the net earnings of which inures to the benefit of any private shareholder or individual, *no substantial part of the activities of which is carrying on propaganda, or otherwise attempting, to influence legislation* (except as otherwise provided in subsection (h)), and which does not participate in, or intervene in (including the publishing or distributing of statements), any political campaign on behalf of (or in opposition to) any candidate for public office. (Emphasis added.)

TREASURY REGULATIONS §1.501(C)(3)-1(C)(3)

(3) Action organizations.

(i) An organization is not operated exclusively for one or more exempt purposes if it is an action organization as defined in subdivisions (ii), (iii), or (iv) of this subparagraph.

(ii) An organization is an action organization if a substantial part of its activities is attempting to influence legislation by propaganda or otherwise. For this purpose, an organization will be regarded as attempting to influence legislation if the organization:

(a) Contacts, or urges the public to contact, members of a legislative body for the purpose of proposing, supporting, or opposing legislation; or

(b) Advocates the adoption or rejection of legislation.

The term legislation, as used in this subdivision, includes action by the Congress, by any State legislature, by any local council or similar governing body, or by the public in a referendum, initiative, constitutional amendment, or similar procedure. An organization will not fail to meet the operational test merely because it advocates, as an insubstantial part of its activities, the adoption or rejection of legislation. An organization for which the expenditure test election of section 501(h) is in effect for a taxable year will not be considered an action organization by reason of this paragraph (c)(3)(ii) for that year if it is not denied exemption from taxation under section 501(a) by reason of section 501(h).

IRC §504. STATUS AFTER ORGANIZATION CEASES TO QUALIFY FOR EXEMPTION UNDER SECTION 501(C)(3) [26 USCS §501(C)(3)] BECAUSE OF SUBSTANTIAL LOBBYING OR BECAUSE OF POLITICAL ACTIVITIES

(a) General rule. An organization which—

(1) was exempt (or was determined by the Secretary to be exempt) from taxation under section 501(a) [26 USCS §501(a)] by reason of being an organization described in section 501(c)(3) [26 USCS §501(c)(3)], and

(2) is not an organization described in section 501(c)(3) [26 USCS §501(c)(3)]—

(A) by reason of carrying on propaganda, or otherwise attempting, to influence legislation, or

(B) by reason of participating in, or intervening in, any political campaign on behalf of (or in opposition to) any candidate for public office, shall not at any time thereafter be treated as an organization described in section 501(c)(4) [26 USCS §501(c)(4)]

IRC §4912. TAX ON DISQUALIFYING LOBBYING EXPENDITURES OF CERTAIN ORGANIZATIONS

(a) Tax on organization: If an organization to which this section applies is not described in section 501(c)(3) for any taxable year by reason of making lobbying expenditures, there is hereby imposed a tax on the lobbying expenditures of such organization for such taxable year equal to 5 percent of the amount of such expenditures. The tax imposed by this subsection shall be paid by the organization.

(b) On management: If tax is imposed under subsection (a) on the lobbying expenditures of any organization, there is hereby imposed on the agreement of any organization manager to the making of any such expenditures, knowing that such expenditures are likely to result in the organization not being described in section 501(c)(3), a tax equal to 5 percent of the amount of such expenditures, unless such agreement is not willful and is due to reasonable cause. The tax imposed by this subsection shall be paid by any manager who agreed to the making of the expenditures.

(c) Organizations to which section applies.

(i)_ In general. Except as provided in paragraph (2), this section shall apply to any organization which was exempt (or was determined by the Secretary to be exempt) from taxation under section 501(a) by reason of being an organization described in section 501(c)(3).

(ii) Exceptions. This section shall not apply to any organization—

A. to which an election under section 501(h) applies,

B. which is a disqualified organization (within the meaning of section 501(h)(5)), or

C. which is a private foundation.

(d) Definitions

(i) Lobbying expenditures: The term "lobbying expenditure" means any amount paid or incurred by the organization in carrying on propaganda, or otherwise attempting to influence legislation.

(ii) Organization manager: The term "organization manager" has the meaning given to such term by section 4955(f)(2).

(iii) Joint and several liability: If more than 1 person is liable under subsection (b), all such persons shall be jointly and severally liable under such subsection.

CHRISTIAN ECHOES NATIONAL MINISTRY, INC. V. UNITED STATES

470 F.2d 849 (10th Cir. 1972), *cert. denied,* 414 U.S. 864 (1973)

[*Editor's Note:* In addition to the constitutional questions discussed above, the *Christian Echoes* court applied the "no substantial part" test to that case. That part of the *Christian Echoes* case is reproduced below.]

The Government contends that Christian Echoes failed to qualify as tax-exempt under Section 501(c)(3) because: (1) a substantial part of its activities consisted of carrying on propaganda, or otherwise attempting to influence legislation; and (2) it participated or intervened in political campaigns on behalf of candidates for public office. The issue raises the interpretation and application of Section 501(c)(3).

Almost since the earliest days of the federal income tax, Congress has exempted certain corporations from taxation. The exemption to corporations organized and operated exclusively for charitable, religious, educational or other purposes carried on for charity is granted because of the benefit the public obtains from their activities and is based on the theory that

> ... the Government is compensated for the loss of revenue by its relief from financial burden which would otherwise have to be met by appropriations from public funds, and by the benefits resulting from the promotion of the general welfare." H.R. Rep. No. 1860, 75th Cong., 3d Sess. 19 (1939).

Tax exemptions are matters of legislative grace and taxpayers have the burden of establishing their entitlement to exemptions.... The limitations in Section 501(c)(3) stem from the Congressional policy that the United States Treasury should be neutral in political affairs and that substantial activities directed to attempts to influence legislation or affect a political campaign should not be subsidized.

The limitation in Section 501(c)(3) originated in the Revenue Act of 1934, allowing tax exempt status to organizations, if "no substantial part of the activities of which is carrying on propaganda, or otherwise attempting, to influence legislation." The case which led to the 1934 legislation was Slee v. Commissioner of Internal Revenue, 42 F.2d 184 (2d Cir. 1930). There the Court held that the American Birth Control League was not entitled to a charitable exemption because it disseminated propaganda to legislators and the public aimed at the repeal of laws preventing birth control. The IRS denied tax exempt status because the Birth Control League's purposes were not exclusively charitable, educational or scientific. In 1954 Congress attached a further condition to exempt status by adding the bar against participation or intervention in political campaigns on behalf of candidates for public office.

A religious organization that engages in substantial activity aimed at influencing legislation is disqualified from tax exemption, whatever the motivation. The Government has at all times recognized Christian Echoes as a religious organization. Indeed, the Government acknowledges that in all of its activities, Christian Echoes has been religiously motivated.

The critical issue is whether the limitation on attempts to influence legislation should be given the narrow interpretation applied by the District Court or a broader construction. The District Court held that the only attempt to influence legislation by Christian Echoes was in its support of the Becker Amendment relating to restoration of prayers in the public schools. By this construction, there must be specific legislation before Congress in order for the "attempt to influence legislation" prohibition to come into play. We disagree. We hold that the Trial Court was clearly erroneous in this interpretation of law.

Treasury Regulation 1.501(c)(3)-1(c)(3)(ii) states that an organization will be regarded as attempting to influence legislation if the organization:

> (a) Contacts, or urges the public to contact, members of a legislative body for the purpose of proposing, supporting, or opposing legislation; or
>
> (b) Advocates the adoption or rejection of legislation."
>
> Legislation is defined in the regulations as: "... action by the Congress, by any State legislature, by any local council or similar governing body, or by the public in a referendum, initiative, constitutional amendment, or similar procedure." Treas. Reg. 1.501(c)(3)-1(c)(3)(ii)(b).

The Regulation goes well beyond the District Court's interpretation of Section 501(c)(3). It includes direct and indirect appeals to legislators and the public in general. We hold that the Regulation properly interprets the intent of Congress. A capsule review of the "substantial" activities of Christian Echoes will adequately demonstrate, we believe, that Congress intended that the limitations be given a broad or liberal interpretation.

Christian Echoes' publications, such as the *Christian Crusade*, contained numerous articles attempting to influence legislation by appeals to the public to react to certain issues. These articles were either authored by Dr. Hargis, members of his organization, solicited contributors, or unsolicited authors—but all such articles had the stamp of approval of Dr. Hargis before acceptance for publication. The fact that specific legislation was not mentioned does not mean that these attempts to influence public opinion were not attempts to influence legislation. For example, Christian Echoes appealed to its readers to: (1) write their Congressmen in order to influence the political decisions in Washington; (2) work in politics at the precinct level; (3) support the Becker Amendment by writing their Congressmen; (4) maintain the McCarran-Walter Immigration law; (5) contact their Congressmen in opposition to the increasing interference with freedom of speech in the United States; (6) purge the American press of its responsibility for grossly misleading its readers on vital issues; (7) inform their Congressmen that the House Committee on UnAmerican Activities must be retained; (8) oppose an Air Force Contract to disarm the United States; (9) dispel the mutual mistrust between North and South America; (10) demand a congressional investigation of the biased reporting of major television networks; (11) support the Dirksen Amendment; (12) demand that Congress limit foreign aid spending; (13) discourage support for the World Court; (14) support the Connally Reservation; (15) cut off diplomatic relations with communist countries; (16) reduce the federal payroll by discharging needless jobholders, stop waste of public funds and balance the budget; (17) stop federal aid to education, socialized medicine and public housing; (18) abolish the federal income tax; (19) end American diplomatic recognition of Russia; (20) withdraw from the United Nations; (21) outlaw the Communist Party in the United States; and (22) to restore our immigration laws.

The taxpayer also attempted to mold public opinion in civil rights legislation, Medicare, the Postage Revision Act of 1967, the Honest Election Law of 1967, the Nuclear Test Ban Treaty, the Panama Canal Treaty, firearms control legislation, and the Outer Space Treaty. These appeals urging the readers to action all appeared in Christian Echoes' publications between 1961 and 1968. They were all attempts to influence legislation through an indirect campaign to mold public opinion. This was directly evidenced by Dr. Hargis' keynote address delivered at the Anti-Communist Leadership School on February 11, 1963, entitled "Counter Strategy for Counter Attack." After setting forth a 10-point program, he stated that "Your opinion isn't worth a nickel without your action to back it up."

The political activities of an organization must be balanced in the context of the objectives and circumstances of the organization to determine whether a substantial part of its activities was to influence or attempt to influence legislation.... A percentage test to determine whether the activities were substantial obscures the complexity of balancing the organization's activities in relation to its objectives and circumstances.... An essential part of the program of Christian Echoes was to promote desirable governmental policies consistent with its objectives through legislation. Kuper v. Commissioner of Internal Revenue, 332 F.2d 562 (3d Cir. 1964), cert. denied 379 U.S. 920, 85 S. Ct. 276, 13 L. Ed. 2d 335 (1964). The activities of Christian Echoes in influencing or attempting to influence legislation were not incidental, but were substantial and continuous. The hundreds of exhibits demonstrate this. These are the activities which Congress intended should not be carried on by exempt organizations.

In addition to influencing legislation, Christian Echoes intervened in political campaigns. Generally it did not formally endorse specific candidates for office but used its publications and broadcasts to attack candidates and incumbents who were considered too liberal. It attacked President Kennedy in 1961 and urged its followers to elect conservatives like Senator Strom Thurmond and Congressmen Bruce Alger and Page Belcher. It urged followers to defeat Senator Fulbright and attacked President Johnson and Senator Hubert Humphrey. The annual convention endorsed Senator Barry Goldwater. These attempts to elect or defeat certain political leaders reflected Christian Echoes' objective to change the composition of the federal government.

NOTE: THOUGHTS ON THE "SUBSTANTIAL PART" TEST

Despite the language in §501(c)(3) that suggests all §501(c)(3) organizations are covered by the restriction on influencing legislation, the language actually only covers public charities. Private foundations, as you may remember, cannot engage in any lobbying, because IRC §4945(d)(1) classifies all funds spent on propaganda or on attempting to influence legislation as taxable expenditures. No matter how insubstantial the lobbying, a private foundation must pay an excise tax on these expenditures. Thus, the two tests explored in this part of the chapter, the "no substantial part test," and the "501(h) expenditure test," apply only to public charities. Furthermore, the "substantial part" test that we are exploring in this part of the chapter does not apply to those organizations that have elected to be judged by the 501(h) expenditure test.

Unfortunately, the materials reproduced above provide almost all the guidance that exists to help nonprofit organizations meet the "no substantial part test." The term "legislation" is defined in the Treasury Regulations described above, but "substantial" is not. In addition to the list of legislative activities in the regulations, the IRS would include an attempt to influence the Senate confirmation of a judicial nominee. It would not, however, automatically attribute the legislative activities of students and faculty to the school unless they were official acts of those institutions. The IRS also recognizes that an organization does not engage in legislative activities if it presents issues in a nonpartisan manner for the purpose of educating the public or if it responds to a request from a legislative committee to testify.[5]

Determining what is "substantial" under this test is entirely a question of facts and circumstances, without a definitive list of the factors to be included in the calculation. *Christian Echoes* explicitly rejected an objective test based solely on the percentage of the organization's funds spent on lobbying. Instead, the court listed the factors that it found important to that particular case. Thus, it appears that "substantial" activities can include the percentage of funds spent on legislative activities, as well as the time and effort spent lobbying; the importance the organization attaches to its lobbying activities; the frequency of its legislative activities; and its success in actually influencing legislation. The questions the IRS currently asks organizations that lobby under the substantial part test to complete on their Forms 990 are reproduced in the illustration below.

Part II-B Complete if the organization is exempt under section 501(c)(3) and has NOT filed Form 5768 (election under section 501(h)).			
	(a)		(b)
For each "Yes," response on lines 1a through 1i below, provide in Part IV a detailed description of the lobbying activity.	Yes	No	Amount
1 During the year, did the filing organization attempt to influence foreign, national, state or local legislation, including any attempt to influence public opinion on a legislative matter or referendum, through the use of:			
a Volunteers?			
b Paid staff or management (include compensation in expenses reported on lines 1c through 1i)?			
c Media advertisements?			
d Mailings to members, legislators, or the public?			
e Publications, or published or broadcast statements?			
f Grants to other organizations for lobbying purposes?			
g Direct contact with legislators, their staffs, government officials, or a legislative body?			
h Rallies, demonstrations, seminars, conventions, speeches, lectures, or any similar means? . .			
i Other activities?			
j Total. Add lines 1c through 1i			
2a Did the activities in line 1 cause the organization to be not described in section 501(c)(3)? . .			
b If "Yes," enter the amount of any tax incurred under section 4912			
c If "Yes," enter the amount of any tax incurred by organization managers under section 4912 .			
d If the filing organization incurred a section 4912 tax, did it file Form 4720 for this year? . . .			

---

[5] Notice 88-76, 1988-2 C.B. 392 is the IRS statement with respect to judicial nominees. Rev. Rul. 72-513, 1972-2 C.B. 246 recognized that the legislative activities of a student newspaper were not attributable to the university. Reg. §1.501(c)(3)-1(c)(3)(iv) provides the exception for nonpartisan analysis, and Rev. Rul. 70-449, 1970-2 C.B. 111 recognizes the exception for a charitable organization's responding to a request that it testify.

Revocation of an organization's tax exemption is not the only penalty for engaging in substantial lobbying. The organization and the organization manager could also be required to pay an excise tax under §4912. Additionally, an organization that has had its §501(c)(3) status revoked because of substantial lobbying cannot revert to §501(c)(4) status. These are quite hefty penalties for organizations that have no safe harbor to tell them how much lobbying is "substantial."

C. §501(h) EXPENDITURE TEST

1. The Elements of the Test

In response to the uncertainty of the "no substantial part test," Congress enacted §501(h) in 1976. This provision allows public charities[6] to use a mathematical formula to determine how much of their exempt-purpose budgets can be spent on lobbying without incurring a penalty. Those organizations that file a Form 5768 with the IRS have "elected" to be covered under this "expenditure" test. Organizations that do not file this form remain subject to the substantial part test.

Section 501(h) requires an understanding of several concepts, which you should be able to understand after reading the statutes and regulations below. Among those concepts are the definitions of direct lobbying and grassroots lobbying. For lobbying to occur under §501(h), the communication must address specific legislation. "Legislation" includes bills, resolutions, repeal proposals, and referenda at the federal, state, and local levels. It even includes specific proposals that have not yet been introduced in a legislative body. Direct lobbying includes communication that is directed to a legislator or employee of a legislative body, refers to specific legislation, and reflects a view on that legislation. Grassroots lobbying, on the other hand, is directed to the general public. It refers to specific legislation and expresses an opinion on that legislation, but it encourages the public to take action with respect to the legislation.

These concepts inform the calculation of the lobbying nontaxable amount (LNTA)—the amount an organization can spend without facing a penalty. This amount equals 20% of the first $500,000 of a charity's exempt-purpose expenditures and follows a sliding-scale formula as the exempt-purpose expenditures rise, reaching a maximum of $1 million per year. Additionally, only 25% of this amount may be devoted to grassroots lobbying without incurring an excise tax. Table 11-1 illustrates this rule.

---

[6] Private foundations, churches, and their auxiliaries are ineligible for §501(h) treatment.

Table 11-1

EXEMPT-PURPOSE EXPENDITURES	LNTA	GRASSROOTS NONTAXABLE AMOUNT
Not over $500,000	20% of exempt-purpose expenditures (up to $100,000)	5% of exempt-purpose expenditures (or 25% of lobbying nontaxable amount) (up to $25,000)
$500,000-$1,000,000	$100,000 + 15% of excess over $500,000	$25,000 + 3.75% of excess over $500,000
$1,000,000-$1,500,000	$175,000 + 10% of excess over $1 million	$43,750 + 2.5% of excess over $1 million
$1,500,000 to $17,000,000	$225,000 + 5% of excess over $1,500,000	$56,250 + 1.25% of excess over $1,500,000
Over $17 million	$1 million	$250,000

If an organization that has elected to be subject to §501(h) exceeds either the overall LNTA or the grassroots nontaxable amount during any tax year, the organization is subject to a penalty tax equal to 25% of the excess. These excess lobbying expenditures, however, will not result in revocation of the public charity's tax-exempt status unless the organization normally makes expenditures that exceed either the lobbying ceiling amount or the grassroots ceiling amount. An organization "normally" exceeds these limits if it does so over a four-year period. Thus, a §501(c)(3) organization will not lose its tax exemption unless and until it exceeds the lobbying limits by more than 150% over a four-year period. The relevant statutory and regulatory language is reproduced below.

IRC §501(h). EXPENDITURES BY PUBLIC CHARITIES TO INFLUENCE LEGISLATION

(1) *General rule.* In the case of an organization to which this subsection applies, exemption from taxation under subsection (a) shall be denied because a substantial part of the activities of such organization consists of carrying on

propaganda, or otherwise attempting, to influence legislation, but only if such organization normally

(A) makes lobbying expenditures in excess of the lobbying ceiling amount for such organization for each taxable year, or

(B) makes grass roots expenditures in excess of the grass roots ceiling amount for such organization for each taxable year.

(2) *Definitions.* For purposes of this subsection—

(A) *Lobbying expenditures.* The term "lobbying expenditures" means expenditures for the purpose of influencing legislation (as defined in section 4911(d)).

(B) *Lobbying ceiling amount.* The lobbying ceiling amount for any organization for any taxable year is 150 percent of the lobbying nontaxable amount for such organization for such taxable year, determined under section 4911.

(C) *Grass roots expenditures.* The term "grass roots expenditures" means expenditures for the purpose of influencing legislation (as defined in section 4911(d) without regard to paragraph (1)(B) thereof).

(D) *Grass roots ceiling amount.* The grass roots ceiling amount for any organization for any taxable year is 150 percent of the grass roots nontaxable amount for such organization for such taxable year, determined under section 4911.

(3) *Organizations to which this subsection applies.* This subsection shall apply to any organization which has elected (in such manner and at such time as the Secretary may prescribe) to have the provisions of this subsection apply to such organization and which, for the taxable year which includes the date the election is made,

(A) is described in subsection (c)(3) and—

(B) is described in paragraph (4), and is not a disqualified organization under paragraph (5).

(4) *Organizations permitted to elect to have this subsection apply.* An organization is described in this paragraph if it is described in—

(A) section 170(b)(1)(A)(ii) (relating to educational institutions),

(B) section 170(b)(1)(A)(iii) (relating to hospitals and medical research organizations),

(C) section 170(b)(1)(A)(iv) (relating to organizations supporting government schools),

(D) section 170(b)(1)(A)(vi) (relating to organizations publicly supported by charitable contributions),

(E) section 509(a)(2) (relating to organizations publicly supported by admissions, sales, etc.), or

(F) section 509(a)(3) (relating to organizations supporting certain types of public charities) except that for purposes of this subparagraph, section 509(a)(3) shall be applied without regard to the last sentence of section 509(a).

(5) *Disqualified organizations.* For purposes of paragraph (3) an organization is a disqualified organization if it is—

(A) described in section 170(b)(1)(A)(i) (relating to churches),

(B) an integrated auxiliary of a church or of a convention or association of churches, or

(C) a member of an affiliated group of organizations (within the meaning of section 4911(f)(2)) if one or more members of such group is described in subparagraph (A) or (B).

(6) *Years for which election is effective.* An election by an organization under this subsection shall be effective for all taxable years of such organization which—

(A) end after the date the election is made, and

(B) begin before the date the election is revoked by such organization (under regulations prescribed by the Secretary).

(7) *No effect on certain organizations.* With respect to any organization for a taxable year for which—

(A) such organization is a disqualified organization (within the meaning of paragraph (5)), or

(B) an election under this subsection is not in effect for such organization, nothing in this subsection or in section 4911 shall be construed to affect the interpretation of the phrase, "no substantial part of the activities of which is carrying on propaganda, or otherwise attempting, to influence legislation," under subsection (c)(3).

(8) *Affiliated organizations.* For rules regarding affiliated organizations, see section 4911(f).

IRC §4911. TAX ON EXCESS EXPENDITURES TO INFLUENCE LEGISLATION

(a) *Tax imposed*

(1) *In general.* There is hereby imposed on the excess lobbying expenditures of any organization to which this section applies a tax equal to 25 percent of the amount of the excess lobbying expenditures for the taxable year.

(2) *Organizations to which this section applies.* This section applies to any organization with respect to which an election under section 501(h) (relating to lobbying expenditures by public charities) is in effect for the taxable year.

(b) *Excess lobbying expenditures.* For purposes of this section, the term "excess lobbying expenditures" means, for a taxable year, the greater of—

(1) the amount by which the lobbying expenditures made by the organization during the taxable year exceed the lobbying nontaxable amount for such organization for such taxable year, or

(2) the amount by which the grass roots expenditures made by the organization during the taxable year exceed the grass roots nontaxable amount for such organization for such taxable year.

(c) *Definitions.* For purposes of this section—

(1) *Lobbying expenditures.* The term "lobbying expenditures" means expenditures for the purpose of influencing legislation (as defined in subsection (d)).

(2) *Lobbying nontaxable amount.* The lobbying nontaxable amount for any organization for any taxable year is the lesser of (A) $1,000,000 or (B) the amount determined under the following table:

IF THE EXEMPT PURPOSE EXPENDITURES ARE—	THE LOBBYING NONTAXABLE AMOUNT IS—
Not over $500,000	20% of the exempt purpose expenditures.
Over $500,000 but not over $1,000,000	$100,000 plus 15% of the excess of the exempt purpose expenditures over $500,000.
Over $1,000,000 but not over $1,500,000	$175,000 plus 10% of the excess of the exempt purpose expenditures over $1 million.
Over $1,500,000	$225,000 plus 5% of the excess of the exempt purpose expenditures over $1,500,000.

(3) *Grass roots expenditures.* The term "grass roots expenditures" means expenditures for the purpose of influencing legislation (as defined in subsection (d) without regard to paragraph (1)(B) thereof).

(4) *Grass roots nontaxable amount.* The grass roots nontaxable amount for any organization for any taxable year is 25 percent of the lobbying nontaxable amount (determined under paragraph (2)) for such organization for such taxable year.

(d) *Influencing legislation*

(1) *General rule.* Except as otherwise provided in paragraph (2), for purposes of this section, the term "influencing legislation" means—

(A) any attempt to influence any legislation through an attempt to affect the opinions of the general public or any segment thereof, and

(B) any attempt to influence any legislation through communication with any member or employee of a legislative body, or with any government official or employee who may participate in the formulation of the legislation.

(2) *Exceptions.* For purposes of this section, the term "influencing legislation," with respect to an organization, does not include—

(A) making available the results of nonpartisan analysis, study, or research;

(B) providing of technical advice or assistance (where such advice would otherwise constitute the influencing of legislation) to a governmental body or to a committee or other subdivision thereof in response to a written request by such body or subdivision, as the case may be;

(C) appearances before, or communications to, any legislative body with respect to a possible decision of such body which might affect the existence of the organization, its powers and duties, tax-exempt status, or the deduction of contributions to the organization;

(D) communications between the organization and its bona fide members with respect to legislation or proposed legislation of direct interest to the organization and such members, other than communications described in paragraph (3); and

(E) any communication with a government official or employee, other than—

(3) *Communications with members.*

(A) A communication between an organization and any bona fide member of such organization to directly encourage such member to communicate as provided in paragraph (1)(B) shall be treated as a communication described in paragraph (1)(B).

(B) A communication between an organization and any bona fide member of such organization to directly encourage such member to urge persons other than members to communicate as provided in either subparagraph (A) or subparagraph (B) of paragraph (1) shall be treated as a communication described in paragraph (1)(A).

(e) *Other definitions and special rules.*

(1) *Exempt purpose expenditures.*

(A) *In general.* The term "exempt purpose expenditures" means, with respect to any organization for any taxable year, the total of the amounts paid or incurred by such organization to accomplish purposes described in section 170(c)(2)(B) (relating to religious, charitable, educational, etc., purposes).

(B) *Certain amounts included.* The term "exempt purpose expenditures" includes—

(i) administrative expenses paid or incurred for purposes described in section 170(c)(2)(B), and

(ii) amounts paid or incurred for the purpose of influencing legislation (whether or not for purposes described in section 170(c)(2)(B)).

(C) *Certain amounts excluded.* The term "exempt purpose expenditures" does not include amounts paid or incurred to or for—

(i) a separate fundraising unit of such organization, or

(ii) one or more other organizations, if such amounts are paid or incurred primarily for fundraising.

(2) *Legislation.* The term "legislation" includes action with respect to Acts, bills, resolutions, or similar items by the Congress, any State legislature, any local council, or similar governing body, or by the public in a referendum, initiative, constitutional amendment, or similar procedure.

(3) *Action.* The term "action" is limited to the introduction, amendment, enactment, defeat, or repeal of Acts, bills, resolutions, or similar items.

TREASURY REGULATIONS §1.501(h)-3(b)

(b) Loss of exemption—

(1) In general. Under section 501(h)(1), an organization that has elected the expenditure test shall be denied exemption from taxation under section 501(a) as an organization described in section 501(c)(3) for the taxable year following a determination year if—

(i) The sum of the organization's lobbying expenditures for the base years exceeds 150 percent of the sum of its lobbying nontaxable amounts for the base years, or

(ii) (ii) The sum of the organization's grass roots expenditures for its base years exceeds 150 percent of the sum of its grass roots nontaxable amounts for the base years.

The organization thereafter shall not be exempt from tax under section 501(a) as an organization described in section 501(c)(3) unless, pursuant to paragraph (d) of this section, the organization reapplies for recognition of exemption and is recognized as exempt.

2. Example: How to Calculate Excess Lobbying Under §501(h)

Editor's Note: This example is borrowed from Example 2 in 26 CFR §1.501(h)-3(e). The explanation has been revised to be more user friendly.

Example

Organization W, whose taxable year is the calendar year, made the expenditure test election under §501(h) effective for taxable years beginning with 1979 and has not revoked the election. W has been treated as an organization described in §501(c)(3) for each of its taxable years beginning within its taxable year 1974. Should W pay excise taxes and/or lose its exemption due to its activities influencing legislation in years 2012-2015?

YEAR	EXEMPT PURPOSE EXPENDITURES	LOBBYING EXPENDITURES	GRASSROOTS EXPENDITURES
2012	$700,000	$120,000	$30,000
2013	$800,000	$100,000	$60,000
2014	$800,000	$100,000	$65,000
2015	$900,000	$150,000	$65,000
Total	$3,200,000	$470,000	$220,000

Approach to the Example

1. Determine the LNTA that W was allowed each year. Also, determine whether W spent in excess of the LNTA in each of those years, and, if so, by how much.

YEAR	EXEMPT PURPOSE EXPENDITURES	LOBBYING EXPENDITURES	CALCULATION	LNTA
2012	$700,000	$120,000	20% of $500,000 + 15% of $200,000	$130,000
2013	$800,000	$100,000	20% of $500,000 + 15% of $300,000	$145,000
2014	$800,000	$100,000	20% of $500,000 + 15% of $300,000	$145,000
2015	$900,000	$150,000	20% of $500,000 + 15% of $400,000	$160,000
Total	$3,200,000	$470,000		$580,000

2. Determine the tax for excess lobbying expenditures that is owed for each year. In this case, no lobbying expenditures have exceeded the LNTA.
3. Determine the grassroots nontaxable amount and whether there are excess grassroots lobbying expenditures. There were excess grassroots lobbying expenditures in 2013, 2014, and 2015.

YEAR	EXEMPT PURPOSE EXPENDITURES	GRASS ROOTS EXPENDITURES	CALCULATION (25% of LNTA)	GRASSROOTS NONTAXABLE AMOUNT
2012	$700,000	$30,000	25% of $130,000	$32,500
2013	$800,000	$60,000	25% of $145,000	$36,250
2014	$800,000	$65,000	25% of $145,000	$36,250
2015	$900,000	$65,000	25% of $160,000	$40,000
Total	$3,200,000	$220,000		$145,000

4. The next step is to determine how much tax Organization W must pay for each of the years that it had excess grassroots lobbying expenditures.

   a. 2012: No excess grassroots lobbying expenditure
   b. 2013: 25% of ($60,000 − $32,500) = $6,875.00
   c. 2014: 25% of ($65,000 − $36,250) = $7,187.50
   d. 2015: 25% of ($65.000 − $40,000) = $6,250.00

5. Determine whether the organization loses its tax exemption because it has "normally" made lobbying expenditures in excess of the lobbying ceiling amount over the past four years.

   a. The organization has no problem with the LNTA. It could have spent 150% of $580,000, or $870,000, before losing its tax exemption. The organization spent $470,000, significantly less than the 150% allowed.
   b. The organization spent a total of $220,000 over the four years on grassroots lobbying. The total grassroots LNTA for those four years was $145,000, and 150% of $145,000 is $217,500. Thus, W loses its exemption for 2010.

PROBLEMS

1. Rochester Unleaded is a nonprofit dedicated to removing lead-based paint from inner-city homes in Rochester, New York. It has a large volunteer labor force. More than three-fourths of the time and effort that the organization spends trying to reach its mission goes toward lobbying the Rochester City Council to improve the laws regarding lead cleanup and health care for lead poisoning. Only one-tenth of its actual budget is spent on lobbying, however, because the volunteers pick up so much of the slack. Should it lose its §501(c)(3) status due to substantial lobbying? [It has not made the §501(h) election.]

2. Why might an organization whose purpose is to reform, repeal, and decriminalize laws that discriminate against gay, lesbian, transgender, and bisexual individuals have difficulty attaining recognition as a §501(c)(3) tax-exempt organization?

3. In 2008, the California ballot included Proposition 8, which outlawed same-sex marriage in that state. According to the *Los Angeles Times*, the Church of Latter-Day Saints contributed $180,000 in in-kind donations to help pass the proposition, and the *Wall Street Journal* reported that individual Mormons donated several million dollars, mostly in response to exhortations from church leaders.[7] These revelations led some to argue that the church engaged in too much lobbying to retain its §501(c)(3) status. Assuming that the newspaper articles were correct, why would it be unlikely that the church had engaged in substantial legislative activities?

4. The Hampton Roads Resettlement Project has a budget of $100,000. For each of the past four years it has spent $20,000 of its $100,000 annual budget educating the public about refugee resettlement laws that need changing and another $10,000 educating legislators about specific ways to change those laws. Is this allowed, assuming that it made the §501(h) election?

5. Equal Rights Advocates, a civil rights organization that engages in community organizing, decided a few years ago that it would be more effective if it engaged in some lobbying. It made the §501(h) election and began spending 25% of its budget on lobbying each year. A considerable amount of that lobbying could be considered grassroots lobbying, which represented 10% of its budget each year. Table 11-2 outlines its expenditures. Is it liable for excise taxes under §4911 for any of these years? Will it lose its tax exemption for excess lobbying under §501(h)?

Table 11-2

YEAR	EXEMPT-PURPOSE EXPENDITURES	TOTAL LOBBYING EXPENDITURES	GRASSROOTS EXPENDITURES
2010	$400,000	$100,000	$40,000
2011	$500,000	$125,000	$50,000
2012	$500,000	$125,000	$50,000
2013	$1,000,000	$250,000	$100,000
Total	$2,400,000	$600,000	$240,000

---

[7] *Mormon Church Reports Spending $180,000 on Proposition 8*, L.A. Now (Jan. 30, 2009), http://latimesblogs.latimes.com/lanow/2009/01/top-officials-w.html; Mark Schoofs, *Mormons Boost Antigay Marriage Effort*, WALL ST. J., Sept. 20, 2008, http://online.wsj.com/article /SB122186063716658279.html.

III. POLITICAL CAMPAIGN ACTIVITY

IRC §501(c)(3)

Corporations, and any community chest, fund, or foundation organized and operated exclusively for religious, charitable, scientific, testing for public safety, literary, or educational purposes, or to foster national or international amateur sports competition (but only if no part of its activities involve the provision of athletic facilities or equipment), or for the prevention of cruelty to children or animals, no part of the net earnings of which inures to the benefit of any private shareholder or individual, no substantial part of the activities of which is carrying on propaganda, or otherwise attempting, to influence legislation (except as otherwise provided in subsection (h)), *and which does not participate in, or intervene in (including the publishing or distributing of statements), any political campaign on behalf of (or in opposition to) any candidate for public office.* (emphasis added).

TREASURY REGULATION §1.501(c)(3)-1(c)(3)(iii)

(iii) An organization is an action organization if it participates or intervenes, directly or indirectly, in any political campaign on behalf of or in opposition to any candidate for public office. The term *candidate for public office* means an individual who offers himself, or is proposed by others, as a contestant for an elective public office, whether such office be national, State, or local. Activities which constitute participation or intervention in a political campaign on behalf of or in opposition to a candidate include, but are not limited to, the publication or distribution of written or printed statements or the making of oral statements on behalf of or in opposition to such a candidate.

IRC §4955. TAXES ON POLITICAL EXPENDITURES OF SECTION 501(c)(3) ORGANIZATIONS

(a) *Initial taxes.*

(1) *On the organization.* There is hereby imposed on each political expenditure by a section 501(c)(3) organization a tax equal to 10 percent of the amount thereof. The tax imposed by this paragraph shall be paid by the organization.

(2) *On the management.* There is hereby imposed on the agreement of any organization manager to the making of any expenditure, knowing that it is a political expenditure, a tax equal to 2½ percent of the amount thereof, unless such agreement is not willful and is due to reasonable cause. The tax

imposed by this paragraph shall be paid by any organization manager who agreed to the making of the expenditure.

(b) *Additional taxes.*

(1) *On the organization.* In any case in which an initial tax is imposed by subsection (a)(1) on a political expenditure and such expenditure is not corrected within the taxable period, there is hereby imposed a tax equal to 100 percent of the amount of the expenditure. The tax imposed by this paragraph shall be paid by the organization.

(2) *On the management.* In any case in which an additional tax is imposed by paragraph (1), if an organization manager refused to agree to part or all of the correction, there is hereby imposed a tax equal to 50 percent of the amount of the political expenditure. The tax imposed by this paragraph shall be paid by any organization manager who refused to agree to part or all of the correction.

(c) *Special rules.* For purposes of subsections (a) and (b)—

(1) *Joint and several liability.* If more than 1 person is liable under subsection (a)(2) or (b)(2) with respect to the making of a political expenditure, all such persons shall be jointly and severally liable under such subsection with respect to such expenditure.

(2) *Limit for management.* With respect to any 1 political expenditure, the maximum amount of the tax imposed by subsection (a)(2) shall not exceed $5,000, and the maximum amount of the tax imposed by subsection (b)(2) shall not exceed $10,000.

(d) *Political expenditure.* For purposes of this section—

(1) *In general.* The term "political expenditure" means any amount paid or incurred by a section 501(c)(3) organization in any participation in, or intervention in (including the publication or distribution of statements), any political campaign on behalf of (or in opposition to) any candidate for public office.

(2) *Certain other expenditures included.* In the case of an organization which is formed primarily for purposes of promoting the candidacy (or prospective candidacy) of an individual for public office (or which is effectively controlled by a candidate or prospective candidate and which is availed of primarily for such purposes), the term "political expenditure" includes any of the following amounts paid or incurred by the organization:

(A) Amounts paid or incurred to such individual for speeches or other services.

(B) Travel expenses of such individual.

(C) Expenses of conducting polls, surveys, or other studies, or preparing papers or other materials, for use by such individual.

(D) Expenses of advertising, publicity, and fundraising for such individual.

(E) Any other expense which has the primary effect of promoting public recognition, or otherwise primarily accruing to the benefit, of such individual.

(e) *Coordination with sections 4945 and 4958.*

If tax is imposed under this section with respect to any political expenditure, such expenditure shall not be treated as a taxable expenditure for purposes of section 4945 [26 USCS §4945] or an excess benefit for purposes of section 4958 [26 USCS §4958].

REVENUE RULING 2007-41. EXEMPT ORGANIZATIONS; POLITICAL CAMPAIGNS

Issue

In each of the … situations described below, has the organization participated or intervened in a political campaign on behalf of (or in opposition to) any candidate for public office within the meaning of section 501(c)(3)?

Law

Section 501(c)(3) provides for the exemption from federal income tax of organizations organized and operated exclusively for charitable or educational purposes, no substantial part of the activities of which is carrying on propaganda, or otherwise attempting to influence legislation (except as otherwise provided in section 501(h)), and which does not participate in, or intervene in (including the publishing or distributing of statements), any political campaign on behalf of (or in opposition to) any candidate for public office.

Section 1.501(c)(3)-1(c)(3)(i) of the Income Tax Regulations states that an organization is not operated exclusively for one or more exempt purposes if it is an "action" organization.

Section 1.501(c)(3)-1(c)(3)(iii) of the regulations defines an "action" organization as an organization that participates or intervenes, directly or indirectly, in any political campaign on behalf of or in opposition to any candidate for public office. The term "candidate for public office" is defined as an individual who offers himself, or is proposed by others, as a contestant for an elective public office, whether such office be national, State, or local. The regulations further provide that activities that constitute participation or intervention in a political campaign on behalf of or in opposition to a candidate include, but are not limited to, the publication or distribution of written statements or the making of oral statements on behalf of or in opposition to such a candidate.

Whether an organization is participating or intervening, directly or indirectly, in any political campaign on behalf of or in opposition to any candidate for public office depends upon all of the facts and circumstances of each case....

Analysis of Factual Situations

...

Voter Education, Voter Registration and Get Out the Vote Drives

Section 501(c)(3) organizations are permitted to conduct certain voter education activities (including the presentation of public forums and the publication of voter education guides) if they are carried out in a non-partisan manner. In addition, section 501(c)(3) organizations may encourage people to participate in the electoral process through voter registration and get-out-the-vote drives, conducted in a non-partisan manner. On the other hand, voter education or registration activities conducted in a biased manner that favors (or opposes) one or more candidates is prohibited.

Situation 1: B, a section 501(c)(3) organization that promotes community involvement, sets up a booth at the state fair where citizens can register to vote. The signs and banners in and around the booth give only the name of the organization, the date of the next upcoming statewide election, and notice of the opportunity to register. No reference to any candidate or political party is made by the volunteers staffing the booth or in the materials available at the booth, other than the official voter registration forms which allow registrants to select a party affiliation. B is not engaged in political campaign intervention when it operates this voter registration booth.

Situation 2: C is a section 501(c)(3) organization that educates the public on environmental issues. Candidate G is running for the state legislature and an important element of her platform is challenging the environmental policies of the incumbent. Shortly before the election, C sets up a telephone bank to call registered voters in the district in which Candidate G is seeking election. In the phone conversations, C's representative tells the voter about the importance of environmental issues and asks questions about the voter's views on these issues. If the voter appears to agree with the incumbent's position, C's representative thanks the voter and ends the call. If the voter appears to agree with Candidate G's position, C's representative reminds the voter about the upcoming election, stresses the importance of voting in the election and offers to provide transportation to the polls. C is engaged in political campaign intervention when it conducts this get-out-the-vote drive.

Individual Activity by Organization Leaders

The political campaign intervention prohibition is not intended to restrict free expression on political matters by leaders of organizations speaking for themselves as individuals. Nor are leaders prohibited from speaking about important issues of public policy. However, for their organizations to remain tax exempt under section 501(c)(3), leaders cannot make partisan comments in official organization publications or at official functions of the organization. To avoid potential attribution of their comments outside of organization functions and publications, organization leaders who speak or write in their individual capacity are encouraged to clearly indicate that their comments are personal and not intended to represent the views of the organization.

Situation 3: President A is the Chief Executive Officer of Hospital J, a section 501(c)(3) organization, and is well known in the community. With the permission of five prominent healthcare industry leaders, including President A, who have personally endorsed Candidate T, Candidate T publishes a full page ad in the local newspaper listing the names of the five leaders. President A is identified in the ad as the CEO of Hospital J. The ad states, "Titles and affiliations of each individual are provided for identification purposes only." The ad is paid for by Candidate T's campaign committee. Because the ad was not paid for by Hospital J, the ad is not otherwise in an official publication of Hospital J, and the endorsement is made by President A in a personal capacity, the ad does not constitute campaign intervention by Hospital J.

Situation 4: President B is the president of University K, a section 501(c)(3) organization. University K publishes a monthly alumni newsletter that is distributed to all alumni of the university. In each issue, President B has a column titled "My Views." The month before the election, President B states in the "My Views" column, "It is my personal opinion that Candidate U should be reelected." For that one issue, President B pays from his personal funds the portion of the cost of the newsletter attributable to the "My Views" column. Even though he paid part of the cost of the newsletter, the newsletter is an official publication of the university. Because the endorsement appeared in an official publication of University K, it constitutes campaign intervention by University K.

Situation 5: Minister C is the minister of Church L, a section 501(c)(3) organization and Minister C is well known in the community. Three weeks before the election, he attends a press conference at Candidate V's campaign headquarters and states that Candidate V should be reelected. Minister C does not say he is speaking on behalf of Church L. His endorsement is reported on the front page of the local newspaper and he is identified in the article as the minister of Church L. Because Minister C did not make the endorsement at an official church function, in an official church publication or otherwise use the church's assets, and did not state that he was speaking as a representative of Church L, his actions do not constitute campaign intervention by Church L....

Candidate Appearances

Depending on the facts and circumstances, an organization may invite political candidates to speak at its events without jeopardizing its tax-exempt status. Political candidates may be invited in their capacity as candidates, or in their individual capacity (not as a candidate). Candidates may also appear without an invitation at organization events that are open to the public.

When a candidate is invited to speak at an organization event in his or her capacity as a political candidate, factors in determining whether the organization participated or intervened in a political campaign include the following:

- Whether the organization provides an equal opportunity to participate to political candidates seeking the same office;
- Whether the organization indicates any support for or opposition to the candidate (including candidate introductions and communications concerning the candidate's attendance); and
- Whether any political fundraising occurs.

In determining whether candidates are given an equal opportunity to participate, the nature of the event to which each candidate is invited will be considered, in addition to the manner of presentation. For example, an organization that invites one candidate to speak at its well attended annual banquet, but invites the opposing candidate to speak at a sparsely attended general meeting, will likely have violated the political campaign prohibition, even if the manner of presentation for both speakers is otherwise neutral.

When an organization invites several candidates for the same office to speak at a forum, factors in determining whether the forum results in political campaign intervention include the following:

- Whether questions for the candidate are prepared and presented by an independent nonpartisan panel,
- Whether the topics discussed by the candidates cover a broad range of issues that the candidates would address if elected to the office sought and are of interest to the public,
- Whether each candidate is given an equal opportunity to present his or her view on the issues discussed,
- Whether the candidates are asked to agree or disagree with positions, agendas, platforms or statements of the organization, and
- Whether a moderator comments on the questions or otherwise implies approval or disapproval of the candidates.

Situation 7: President E is the president of Society N, a historical society that is a section 501(c)(3) organization. In the month prior to the election, President E invites the three Congressional candidates for the district in which Society N is located to address the members, one each at a regular meeting held on three successive weeks. Each candidate is given an equal opportunity to address and field questions on a wide variety of topics from the members. Society N's publicity announcing the dates for each of the candidate's speeches and President E's introduction of each candidate include no comments on their qualifications or any indication of a preference for any candidate. Society N's actions do not constitute political campaign intervention.

Situation 8: The facts are the same as in Example 7 except that there are four candidates in the race rather than three, and one of the candidates declines the invitation to speak. In the publicity announcing the dates for each of the candidate's speeches, Society N includes a statement that the order of the speakers was determined at random and the fourth candidate declined the Society's invitation to speak. President E makes the same statement in his opening remarks at each of the meetings where one of the candidates is speaking. Society N's actions do not constitute political campaign intervention....

Candidate Appearances Where Speaking or Participating as a Non-Candidate

Candidates may also appear or speak at organization events in a non-candidate capacity. For instance, a political candidate may be a public figure who is invited to speak because he or she: (a) currently holds, or formerly held, public office; (b) is considered an expert in a non political field; or (c) is a celebrity or has led a distinguished military, legal, or public service career. A candidate may choose to attend an event that is open to the public, such as a lecture, concert or worship service. The candidate's presence at an organization-sponsored event does not, by itself, cause the organization to be engaged in political campaign intervention. However, if the candidate is publicly recognized by the organization, or if the candidate is invited to speak, factors in determining whether the candidate's appearance results in political campaign intervention include the following:

- Whether the individual is chosen to speak solely for reasons other than candidacy for public office;
- Whether the individual speaks only in a non-candidate capacity;
- Whether either the individual or any representative of the organization makes any mention of his or her candidacy or the election;
- Whether any campaign activity occurs in connection with the candidate's attendance.
- Whether the organization maintains a nonpartisan atmosphere on the premises or at the event where the candidate is present; and
- Whether the organization clearly indicates the capacity in which the candidate is appearing and should not mention the individual's political candidacy or the upcoming election in the communications announcing the candidate's attendance at the event.

Situation 10: Historical society P is a section 501(c)(3) organization. Society P is located in the state capital. President G is the president of Society P and customarily acknowledges the presence of any public officials present during meetings. During the state gubernatorial race, Lieutenant Governor Y, a candidate, attends a meeting of the historical society. President G acknowledges the Lieutenant Governor's presence in his customary manner, saying, "We are happy to have joining us this evening Lieutenant Governor Y." President G makes no reference in his welcome to the Lieutenant Governor's candidacy or the election. Society P has not engaged in political campaign intervention as a result of President G's actions....

Situation 13: Mayor G attends a concert performed by Symphony S, a section 501(c)(3) organization, in City Park. The concert is free and open to the public. Mayor G is a candidate for reelection, and the concert takes place after the primary and before the general election. During the concert, the chairman of S's board addresses the crowd and says, "I am pleased to see Mayor G here tonight.

Without his support, these free concerts in City Park would not be possible. We will need his help if we want these concerts to continue next year so please support Mayor G in November as he has supported us." As a result of these remarks, Symphony S has engaged in political campaign intervention.

Issue Advocacy vs. Political Campaign Intervention

Section 501(c)(3) organizations may take positions on public policy issues, including issues that divide candidates in an election for public office. However, section 501(c)(3) organizations must avoid any issue advocacy that functions as political campaign intervention. Even if a statement does not expressly tell an audience to vote for or against a specific candidate, an organization delivering the statement is at risk of violating the political campaign intervention prohibition if there is any message favoring or opposing a candidate. A statement can identify a candidate not only by stating the candidate's name but also by other means such as showing a picture of the candidate, referring to political party affiliations, or other distinctive features of a candidate's platform or biography. All the facts and circumstances need to be considered to determine if the advocacy is political campaign intervention.

Key factors in determining whether a communication results in political campaign intervention include the following:

- Whether the statement identifies one or more candidates for a given public office;
- Whether the statement expresses approval or disapproval for one or more candidates' positions and/or actions;
- Whether the statement is delivered close in time to the election;
- Whether the statement makes reference to voting or an election;
- Whether the issue addressed in the communication has been raised as an issue distinguishing candidates for a given office;
- Whether the communication is part of an ongoing series of communications by the organization on the same issue that are made independent of the timing of any election; and
- Whether the timing of the communication and identification of the candidate are related to a non-electoral event such as a scheduled vote on specific legislation by an officeholder who also happens to be a candidate for public office.

A communication is particularly at risk of political campaign intervention when it makes reference to candidates or voting in a specific upcoming election. Nevertheless, the communication must still be considered in context before arriving at any conclusions....

Situation 15: Organization R, a section 501(c)(3) organization that educates the public about the need for improved public education, prepares and finances a radio advertisement urging an increase in state funding for public education in State X, which requires a legislative appropriation. Governor E is the governor of State X. The radio advertisement is first broadcast on several radio stations in

State X beginning shortly before an election in which Governor E is a candidate for reelection. The advertisement is not part of an ongoing series of substantially similar advocacy communications by Organization R on the same issue. The advertisement cites numerous statistics indicating that public education in State X is underfunded. While the advertisement does not say anything about Governor E's position on funding for public education, it ends with "Tell Governor E what you think about our under-funded schools." In public appearances and campaign literature, Governor E's opponent has made funding of public education an issue in the campaign by focusing on Governor E's veto of an income tax increase the previous year to increase funding of public education. At the time the advertisement is broadcast, no legislative vote or other major legislative activity is scheduled in the State X legislature on state funding of public education. Organization R has violated the political campaign prohibition because the advertisement identifies Governor E, appears shortly before an election in which Governor E is a candidate, is not part of an ongoing series of substantially similar advocacy communications by Organization R on the same issue, is not timed to coincide with a non election event such as a legislative vote or other major legislative action on that issue, and takes a position on an issue that the opponent has used to distinguish himself from Governor E....

Business Activity

The question of whether an activity constitutes participation or intervention in a political campaign may also arise in the context of a business activity of the organization, such as selling or renting of mailing lists, the leasing of office space, or the acceptance of paid political advertising. In this context, some of the factors to be considered in determining whether the organization has engaged in political campaign intervention include the following:

- Whether the good, service or facility is available to candidates in the same election on an equal basis,
- Whether the good, service, or facility is available only to candidates and not to the general public,
- Whether the fees charged to candidates are at the organization's customary and usual rates, and
- Whether the activity is an ongoing activity of the organization or whether it is conducted only for a particular candidate.

Situation 17: Museum K is a section 501(c)(3) organization. It owns an historic building that has a large hall suitable for hosting dinners and receptions. For several years, Museum K has made the hall available for rent to members of the public. Standard fees are set for renting the hall based on the number of people in attendance, and a number of different organizations have rented the hall. Museum K rents the hall on a first come, first served basis. Candidate P rents Museum K's social hall for a fundraising dinner. Candidate P's campaign pays the standard fee for the dinner. Museum K is not involved in political campaign intervention as a result of renting the hall to Candidate P for use as the site of a campaign fundraising dinner.

Situation 18: Theater L is a section 501(c)(3) organization. It maintains a mailing list of all of its subscribers and contributors. Theater L has never rented its mailing list to a third party. Theater L is approached by the campaign committee of Candidate Q, who supports increased funding for the arts. Candidate Q's campaign committee offers to rent Theater L's mailing list for a fee that is comparable to fees charged by other similar organizations. Theater L rents its mailing list to Candidate Q's campaign committee. Theater L declines similar requests from campaign committees of other candidates. Theater L has intervened in a political campaign.

Web Sites

The Internet has become a widely used communications tool. Section 501(c)(3) organizations use their own web sites to disseminate statements and information. They also routinely link their web sites to web sites maintained by other organizations as a way of providing additional information that the organizations believe is useful or relevant to the public.

A web site is a form of communication. If an organization posts something on its web site that favors or opposes a candidate for public office, the organization will be treated the same as if it distributed printed material, oral statements or broadcasts that favored or opposed a candidate.

An organization has control over whether it establishes a link to another site. When an organization establishes a link to another web site, the organization is responsible for the consequences of establishing and maintaining that link, even if the organization does not have control over the content of the linked site. Because the linked content may change over time, an organization may reduce the risk of political campaign intervention by monitoring the linked content and adjusting the links accordingly.

Links to candidate-related material, by themselves, do not necessarily constitute political campaign intervention. The IRS will take all the facts and circumstances into account when assessing whether a link produces that result. The facts and circumstances to be considered include, but are not limited to, the context for the link on the organization's web site, whether all candidates are represented, any exempt purpose served by offering the link, and the directness of the links between the organization's web site and the web page that contains material favoring or opposing a candidate for public office.

Situation 19: M, a section 501(c)(3) organization, maintains a web site and posts an unbiased, nonpartisan voter guide that is prepared consistent with the principles discussed in the voter guide section above. For each candidate covered in the voter guide, M includes a link to that candidate's official campaign web site. The links to the candidate web sites are presented on a consistent neutral basis for each candidate, with text saying "For more information on Candidate X, you may consult [URL]." M has not intervened in a political campaign because the links are provided for the exempt purpose of educating voters and are presented in a neutral, unbiased manner that includes all candidates for a particular office....

BRANCH MINISTRIES, INC. V. ROSSOTTI

211 F.3d 137 (D.C. Cir. 2000)

BUCKLEY, Senior Judge: Four days before the 1992 presidential election, Branch Ministries, a tax-exempt church, placed full-page advertisements in two newspapers in which it urged Christians not to vote for then-presidential candidate Bill Clinton because of his positions on certain moral issues. The Internal Revenue Service concluded that the placement of the advertisements violated the statutory restrictions on organizations exempt from taxation and, for the first time in its history, it revoked a bona fide church's tax-exempt status because of its involvement in politics. Branch Ministries and its pastor, Dan Little, challenge the revocation on the grounds that (1) the Service acted beyond its statutory authority, (2) the revocation violated its right to the free exercise of religion guaranteed by the First Amendment and the Religious Freedom Restoration Act, and (3) it was the victim of selective prosecution in violation of the Fifth Amendment. Because these objections are without merit, we affirm the district court's grant of summary judgment to the Service.

I. Background

A. Taxation of Churches

The Internal Revenue Code ("Code") exempts certain organizations from taxation, including those organized and operated for religious purposes, provided that they do not engage in certain activities, including involvement in "any political campaign on behalf of (or in opposition to) any candidate for public office." 26 U.S.C. §501(a), (c)(3) (1994). Contributions to such organizations are also deductible from the donating taxpayer's taxable income. Id. §170(a). Although most organizations seeking tax-exempt status are required to apply to the Internal Revenue Service ("IRS" or "Service") for an advance determination that they meet the requirements of section 501(c)(3), id. §508(a), a church may simply hold itself out as tax exempt and receive the benefits of that status without applying for advance recognition from the IRS. Id. §508(c)(1)(A).

The IRS maintains a periodically updated "Publication No. 78," in which it lists all organizations that have received a ruling or determination letter confirming the deductibility of contributions made to them.... Thus, a listing in that publication will provide donors with advance assurance that their contributions will be deductible under section 170(a). If a listed organization has subsequently had its tax-exempt status revoked, contributions that are made to it by a donor who is unaware of the change in status will generally be treated as deductible if made on or before the date that the revocation is publicly announced.... Donors to a church that has not received an advance determination of its tax-exempt status may also deduct their contributions; but in the event of an audit, the taxpayer will bear the burden of establishing that the church meets the requirements of section 501(c)(3)....

The unique treatment churches receive in the Internal Revenue Code is further reflected in special restrictions on the IRS's ability to investigate the tax status of a church. The Church Audit Procedures Act ("CAPA") sets out the circumstances under which the IRS may initiate an investigation of a church and the procedures it is required to follow in such an investigation. 26 U.S.C. §7611. Upon a "reasonable belief" by a high-level Treasury official that a church may not be exempt from taxation under section 501, the IRS may begin a "church tax inquiry."... A church tax inquiry is defined, rather circularly, as any inquiry to a church (other than an examination) to serve as a basis for determining whether a church—

(A) is exempt from tax under section 501(a) by reason of its status as a church, or

(B) is ... engaged in activities which may be subject to taxation....

If the IRS is not able to resolve its concerns through a church tax inquiry, it may proceed to the second level of investigation: a "church tax examination." In such an examination, the IRS may obtain and review the church's records or examine its activities "to determine whether [the] organization claiming to be a church is a church for any period." Id. §7611(b)(1)(A), (B).

B. Factual and Procedural History

Branch Ministries, Inc. operates the Church at Pierce Creek ("Church"), a Christian church located in Binghamton, New York. In 1983, the Church requested and received a letter from the IRS recognizing its tax-exempt status. On October 30, 1992, four days before the presidential election, the Church placed full-page advertisements in USA Today and the Washington Times. Each bore the headline "Christians Beware" and asserted that then-Governor Clinton's positions concerning abortion, homosexuality, and the distribution of condoms to teenagers in schools violated Biblical precepts. The following appeared at the bottom of each advertisement:

> This advertisement was co-sponsored by the Church at Pierce Creek, Daniel J. Little, Senior Pastor, and by churches and concerned Christians nationwide. Tax-deductible donations for this advertisement gladly accepted. Make donations to: The Church at Pierce Creek [mailing address].

The advertisements did not go unnoticed. They produced hundreds of contributions to the Church from across the country and were mentioned in a New York Times article and an Anthony Lewis column which stated that the sponsors of the advertisement had almost certainly violated the Internal Revenue Code. Peter Applebome, Religious Right Intensifies Campaign for Bush, N.Y. Times, Oct. 31, 1992, at A1; Anthony Lewis, Tax Exempt Politics?, N.Y. Times, Dec. 1, 1992, at A15.

The advertisements also came to the attention of the Regional Commissioner of the IRS, who notified the Church on November 20, 1992 that he had authorized a church tax inquiry based on "a reasonable belief ... that you may not be tax-exempt or that you may be liable for tax" due to political activities and expenditures. Letter from Cornelius J. Coleman, IRS Regional Commissioner, to The Church at Pierce Creek (Nov. 20, 1992). The Church denied that it had engaged in any prohibited political activity and declined to provide the IRS with certain information the Service had requested. On February 11, 1993, the IRS informed the Church that it was beginning a church tax examination. Following two unproductive meetings between the parties, the IRS revoked the Church's section 501(c)(3) tax-exempt status on January 19, 1995, citing the newspaper advertisements as prohibited intervention in a political campaign.

The Church and Pastor Little (collectively, "Church") commenced this lawsuit soon thereafter. This had the effect of suspending the revocation of the Church's tax exemption until the district court entered its judgment in this case. See 26 U.S.C. §7428(c). The Church challenged the revocation of its tax-exempt status, alleging that the IRS had no authority to revoke its tax exemption, that the revocation violated its right to free speech and to freely exercise its religion under the First Amendment and the Religious Freedom Restoration Act of 1993, 42 U.S.C. §2000bb (1994) ("RFRA"), and that the IRS engaged in selective prosecution in violation of the Equal Protection Clause of the Fifth Amendment. After allowing discovery on the Church's selective prosecution claim, Branch Ministries, Inc. v. Richardson, 970 F. Supp. 11 (D.D.C. 1997), the district court granted summary judgment in favor of the IRS. Branch Ministries, Inc. v. Rossotti, 40 F. Supp. 2d 15 (D.D.C. 1999)....

II. Analysis

The Church advances a number of arguments in support of its challenges to the revocation. We examine only those that warrant analysis.

A. The Statutory Authority of the IRS

The Church argues that, under the Internal Revenue Code, the IRS does not have the statutory authority to revoke the tax-exempt status of a bona fide church. It reasons as follows: section 501(c)(3) refers to tax-exempt status for religious organizations, not churches; section 508, on the other hand, specifically exempts "churches" from the requirement of applying for advance recognition of tax-exempt status, id. §508(c)(1)(A); therefore, according to the Church, its tax-exempt status is derived not from section 501(c)(3), but from the lack of any provision in the Code for the taxation of churches. The Church concludes from this that it is not subject to taxation and that the IRS is therefore powerless to place conditions upon or to remove its tax-exempt status as a church.

We find this argument more creative than persuasive. The simple answer, of course, is that whereas not every religious organization is a church, every church is a religious organization. More to the point, irrespective of whether it was required to do so, the Church applied to the IRS for an advance determination of its tax-exempt status. The IRS granted that recognition and now seeks to withdraw it.... The Code, in short, specifically states that organizations that fail to comply with the restrictions set forth in section 501(c) are not qualified to receive the tax exemption that it provides. Having satisfied ourselves that the IRS had the statutory authority to revoke the Church's tax-exempt status, we now turn to the free exercise challenges.

B. First Amendment Claims and the RFRA[8]

The Church claims that the revocation of its exemption violated its right to freely exercise its religion under both the First Amendment and the RFRA. To sustain its claim under either the Constitution or the statute, the Church must first establish that its free exercise right has been substantially burdened.... We conclude that the Church has failed to meet this test.

The Church asserts, first, that a revocation would threaten its existence. The Church maintains that a loss of its tax-exempt status will not only make its members reluctant to contribute the funds essential to its survival, but may obligate the Church itself to pay taxes.

The Church appears to assume that the withdrawal of a conditional privilege for failure to meet the condition is in itself an unconstitutional burden on its free exercise right. This is true, however, only if the receipt of the privilege (in this case the tax exemption) is conditioned upon conduct proscribed by a religious faith, or...denied...because of conduct mandated by religious belief, thereby putting substantial pressure on an adherent to modify his behavior and to violate his beliefs.... Although its advertisements reflected its religious convictions on certain questions of morality, the Church does not maintain that a withdrawal from electoral politics would violate its beliefs. The sole effect of the loss of the tax exemption will be to decrease the amount of money available to the Church for its religious practices. The Supreme Court has declared, however, that such a burden "is not constitutionally significant."...

In actual fact, even this burden is overstated. Because of the unique treatment churches receive under the Internal Revenue Code, the impact of the revocation is likely to be more symbolic than substantial. As the IRS confirmed at oral argument, if the Church does not intervene in future political campaigns, it may hold itself out as a 501(c)(3) organization and receive all the benefits of that status. All that will have been lost, in that event, is the advance assurance of deductibility in the event a donor should be audited.... Contributions will remain tax deductible as long as donors are able to establish that the Church meets the requirements of section 501(c)(3).

Nor does the revocation necessarily make the Church liable for the payment of taxes. As the IRS explicitly represented in its brief and reiterated at oral argument, the revocation of the exemption does not convert bona fide donations into income taxable to the Church. See 26 U.S.C. §102 ("Gross income does not include the value of property acquired by gift...."). Furthermore, we know of no

---

[8] [RFRA stands for Religious Freedom Restoration Act, and is defined earlier in a part of the case that has been edited from this excerpt.—*Ed.*]

authority, and counsel provided none, to prevent the Church from reapplying for a prospective determination of its tax-exempt status and regaining the advance assurance of deductibility—provided, of course, that it renounces future involvement in political campaigns.

We also reject the Church's argument that it is substantially burdened because it has no alternate means by which to communicate its sentiments about candidates for public office.... As was the case with TWR [Regan v. Taxation With Representation, 461 U.S. 540 (1983)], the Church may form a related organization under section 501(c)(4) of the Code.... Although a section 501(c)(4) organization is also subject to the ban on intervening in political campaigns,[9] ... it may form a political action committee ("PAC") that would be free to participate in political campaigns....

At oral argument, counsel for the Church doggedly maintained that there can be no "Church at Pierce Creek PAC." True, it may not itself create a PAC; but as we have pointed out, the Church can initiate a series of steps that will provide an alternate means of political communication that will satisfy the standards set by the concurring justices in Regan. Should the Church proceed to do so, however, it must understand that the related 501(c)(4) organization must be separately incorporated; and it must maintain records that will demonstrate that tax-deductible contributions to the Church have not been used to support the political activities conducted by the 501(c)(4) organization's political action arm....

That the Church cannot use its tax-free dollars to fund such a PAC unquestionably passes constitutional muster. The Supreme Court has consistently held that, absent invidious discrimination, "Congress has not violated [an organization's] First Amendment rights by declining to subsidize its First Amendment activities." Regan, 461 U.S. at 548....

Because the Church has failed to demonstrate that its free exercise rights have been substantially burdened, we do not reach its arguments that section 501(c)(3) does not serve a compelling government interest or, if it is indeed compelling, that revocation of its tax exemption was not the least restrictive means of furthering that interest.

Nor does the Church succeed in its claim that the IRS has violated its First Amendment free speech rights by engaging in viewpoint discrimination. The restrictions imposed by section 501(c)(3) are viewpoint neutral; they prohibit intervention in favor of all candidates for public office by all tax-exempt organizations, regardless of candidate, party, or viewpoint....

C. Selective Prosecution (Fifth Amendment)

The Church alleges that the IRS violated the Equal Protection Clause of the Fifth Amendment by engaging in selective prosecution. In support of its claim, the Church has submitted several hundred pages of newspaper excerpts reporting

---

[9] [This statement is incorrect. As will be explained later in this chapter, a §501(c)(4) organization is permitted to participate in political campaigns, so long as that is not its primary activity.—Ed.]

political campaign activities in, or by the pastors of, other churches that have retained their tax-exempt status....

To establish selective prosecution, the Church must "prove that (1) [it] was singled out for prosecution from among others similarly situated and (2) that [the] prosecution was improperly motivated, i.e., based on race, religion or another arbitrary classification."... This burden is a demanding one because "in the absence of clear evidence to the contrary, courts presume that [government prosecutors] have properly discharged their official duties."...

[T]he Church has failed to establish selective prosecution because it has failed to demonstrate that it was similarly situated to any of those other churches. None of the reported activities involved the placement of advertisements in newspapers with nationwide circulations opposing a candidate and soliciting tax deductible contributions to defray their cost. . . .

Because the Church has failed to establish that it was singled out for prosecution from among others who were similarly situated, we need not examine whether the IRS was improperly motivated in undertaking this prosecution.

III. Conclusion

For the foregoing reasons, we find that the revocation of the Church's tax-exempt status neither violated the Constitution nor exceeded the IRS's statutory authority. The judgment of the district court is therefore Affirmed.

NOTES AND QUESTIONS

1. What public policies does the ban on political intervention serve? Do those policies apply equally when churches are involved? Is the IRS able to enforce this ban? The Congressional Research Services prepared a paper explaining the tax and Federal Election Commission (FEC) rules for §501(c)(3)s. Erika Lunden and L. Paige Whitaker, *501(c)(3)s and Campaign Activity: Analysis Under Tax and Campaign Finance Laws*, CONGRESSIONAL RESEARCH SERVICE (2013).

2. In 2005, Catholic Answers, a §501(c)(3) religious corporation, posted an e-letter from its founder on its website, which stated, in part, that the Democratic nominee, Senator John Kerry, "is nominally Catholic, and is vociferously pro-abortion. So far as I can tell, he flunks the test given in Catholic Answers' 'Voter's Guide for Serious Catholics.' He is wrong on all five 'non-negotiable' issues listed there." The IRS determined in 2008 that the e-letter constituted a political expenditure and assessed excise taxes pursuant to §4945. It also required Catholic Answers to pay a "correction amount" equal to the amount that it had spent on the e-letter. Catholic Answers brought suit in 2009, claiming that §4955 and its regulations are unconstitutionally vague. The case was dismissed as moot because the IRS abated the excise taxes and issued a refund. *Catholic Answers, Inc. v. United States*, 2009 U.S. Dist. LEXIS 70940, *affirmed* 438 Fed. Appx. 640, (9th Cir.

2011), *cert. denied* 80 U.S.L.W. 3440 (2012). Do you think these provisions are susceptible to a "void for vagueness" claim? Why or why not?

3. For the past several years, the Alliance Defending Freedom has encouraged pastors to endorse political candidates from the pulpit, in an effort to challenge the §501(c)(3) proscription against political campaign intervention. It organized Pulpit Freedom Sunday, a day in October in each election year when pastors would preach sermons defying the political intervention prescription. More than 1,400 pastors did so in 2014. Its website states: "Why should the IRS have control of your pulpit? . . . A pastor's pulpit should be accountable to God alone, and the future of religious freedom in America depends on it. It's time to put an end to the Johnson Amendment." http://www.adflegal.org/issues/religious-freedom/church/key-issues/pulpit-freedom-sunday, accessed May 26, 2016. Do you agree? Why or why not? *See* Jonathan Backer, *Thou Shalt Not Electioneer: Religious Nonprofit Political Activity and the Threat "God PACs" Pose to Democracy and Religion*, 114 MICH. L. REV. 619 (2016); Samuel D. Brunson, *Dear IRS, It Is Time to Enforce the Campaigning Prohibition. Even Against Churches,"* 87 U. COLO. L. REV. 143 (2015); E.W. Stanley, *LBJ, the IRS, and Churches: The Unconstitutionality of the Johnson Amendment in Light of Recent Supreme Court Precedent*, 24 REGENT U. L. REV. 237 (2012); Donald Toobin, *Political Campaigning by Churches and Charities: Hazardous for 501(c)(3), Dangerous for Democracy*, 95 GEORGETOWN L. REV. 1313 (2007); Johnny Rex Buckles, *Is the Ban on Participation in Political Campaigns by Charities Essential to Their Vitality and Democracy? A Reply to Professor Tobin*, 42 U. RICH. L. REV. 1057 (2008).

4. Another potential "political" problem for charities can occur when politicians are closely related to a charity. Donations can appear to be a roundabout way to curry political favor with the politician, and sometimes the politician funnels government money to "friends" (or himself or herself) within the nonprofit.

Are any or all of the examples below abuses of existing statutes? If so, which ones, and why? If not, and you have issues with these situations, should the law be changed? How? Or are these examples of perfectly acceptable speech? If you come to a different conclusion about one or more of the examples, which facts influenced your decision and why?

- The Clinton Foundation, established by former President Bill Clinton, is a §501(c)(3) that raises money from outsiders, including large banks and foreign governments. As a public charity, it does not need to release the names of its donors, but it agreed to do so when Hillary Clinton ran for president in 2008. Apparently, multimillion dollar gifts came from foreign governments during the time Hillary Clinton was secretary of state, and equally large gifts came from large banks that were under investigation by the federal government. Were these governments and banks buying access? If so, is that legally forbidden? Is it cynical to suggest that individuals and corporations are unable to separate their political preferences from their philanthropic giving? Does the Clinton Foundation's transparency absolve it of these types of accusations? After all, if it had not voluntarily agreed to make its donors public, none of this would be known. For information on this foundation and this issue, *see* David Graham, *Hillary's Campaign Is Built on a Shaky Foundation*, THE ATLANTIC (March 20, 2015); Peter Schweitzer, CLINTON CASH: THE UNTOLD STORY OF HOW AND WHY FOREIGN GOVERNMENTS AND BUSINESSES HELPED MAKE BILL AND HILLARY CLINTON RICH (Harper, 2015). In 2015, the Clinton Foundation amended several years of its Form 990 submissions when it became clear that it had failed to report the donations from foreign governments, as required in part XIII of that form. Paul Barton, *Tax Observers Scratching Heads over Clinton Foundation.*, 75 EXEMPT ORG. TAX REV. 669 (2015).

A second criticism has been lodged indirectly at the Clinton Foundation. Although Hillary Clinton evidently turns her speaking fees over to the Clinton Foundation, she charges more than $200,000 a speech, even when speaking to §501(c)(3) colleges and universities. These facts raise questions of whether she is "repurposing" charitable donations that were made for the purpose of education into gifts to the Clinton Foundation (and potentially to her own political benefit as well). These facts also raise questions about the message that she is sending to students and parents who are saddled with debt. Is this practice illegal or unethical? *See* Rick Cohen, *The Philanthropic Problem with Hilary Clinton's Huge Speaking Fees*, NONPROFIT QUARTERLY (July 11, 2014). Does it change your mind to learn that Donald Trump was paid $1.5 million to give a speech, even though the customer was not a nonprofit? Louis Hau, *The Most Expensive Speech*, FORBES (March 18, 2008).

- The Donald J. Trump Foundation also raised eyebrows in the following situations as Donald Trump was running for president in 2016:

i) In 2013, the Donald J. Trump Foundation donated $25,000 to a political committee backing Florida Attorney General Pamela Bondi, who, at that time, was both examining New York State's lawsuit against Trump University and running for reelection. Instead of including the correct name for the group on its Form 990, the Trump Foundation included a pro-abortion group from Kansas with a similar name. When investigative journalists discovered this gift in 2016, the Trump Foundation said that a low-level clerk had made a mistake, thinking that the gift was going to a charity. Should this action endanger the Trump Foundation's tax-exempt status? Do you think it is relevant that Bondi decided not to investigate Trump University and that she eventually endorsed Trump for president? David Fahrenhold and Rosalind Helderman, *Trump Camp Says $25,000 Charity Contribution to Florida AG Was a Mistake*, WASH. POST (March 22, 2016). Does it make a difference that the Trump

Foundation defended the gift in 2013 when the Tampa Bay Times questioned its ethics? Michael Van Sickler, *Trump Contribution to Pam Bondi's Re-Election Draws More Scrutiny to Her Fundraising*, TAMPA BAY TIMES (Oct. 17, 2013).

ii) Shortly before the Iowa caucuses in 2016, the Trump campaign held a rally at the Drake Hotel in Iowa and solicited donations to the Trump Foundation, stating that the donations would then be turned over to veterans' organizations. The candidate did not make any disclaimers that the campaign and foundation were separate entities. We can assume that the campaign paid all the necessary expenses. Was this a violation of the rules that you have just learned? David Cay Johnston, *News Analysis: Was Involvement of Private Foundation in Trump Event Illegal?* 77 EXEMPT ORG. TAX REV. 179 (2016).

iii) Shortly before the New Hampshire primary in 2016, the executive director of Liberty House, a small New Hampshire veterans' charity, received a call from the Trump campaign offering to deliver a $100,000 check from the Trump Foundation at a campaign rally in Londonderry, New Hampshire. The executive director refused to go to the rally, but he said he would happily accept the check in the mail. Instead, Rep. Al Baldasaro (R-NH) agreed to pick up the check for Liberty House at the rally. Does this cause a problem either for Liberty House or the Trump Foundation? Would it have made a difference if the executive director had appeared at the rally? Tim Mak, *Exclusive: Trump Tried to Pay Vets to Be Props*, THE DAILY BEAST (Feb. 6, 2016)

- In a 2010 *New York Times* article,[10] Eric Lipton revealed that at least two dozen charities with close connections to lawmakers also accepted donations from businesses seeking to influence those lawmakers. Among the charities that received such largesse were ones run by Republican John Boehner, then the Speaker of the House, and Democrat Jim Clyburn, the Assistant Minority Leader. Was this illegal?

- A 2013 article by the Center for Public Integrity found an "unsavory pattern of 'quid pro quo' links between lawmakers and 'charities." At least eight state legislators in New York had used legislative tools to steer significant amounts of government money to nonprofit groups with whom they were closely affiliated. For example, New York Senator Shirley Huntley had sent state grants to a nonprofit that she founded before pocketing some of the money, and she helped her niece and a former aide steal funds that she directed to another nonprofit that she had funded. In another case, Assemblyman Vito Lopez channeled state

---

[10] Eric Lipton, *Congressional Charities Are Pulling in Corporate Cash*, N.Y. TIMES (Sept. 5, 2010). *See also* Lipton, *Corporate Money Aids Centers Linked to Lawmakers*, Aug. 5, 2010; Jack Siegel, *The Wild, the Innocent, and the K Street Shuffle*, 54 EXEMPT ORG. TAX REV. 117 (2006).

money to Ridgewood Bushwick Senior Citizens Council, where his girlfriend was the housing director and his campaign finance director was also the executive director, with a salary of $782,000. The article noted that similar scandals had recently been uncovered in Florida, Pennsylvania, Illinois, Ohio, and South Carolina. *State Legislators' Ties to Nonprofit Groups Prove Fertile Ground for Corruption*, CENTER FOR PUBLIC INTEGRITY (June 12, 2013). What are the nonprofit law consequences of these actions?

- Shortly after Barack Obama was elected to the Senate from Illinois in 2004, his wife received a promotion from her employer, the University of Chicago Hospitals, which increased her salary from $121,910 to $316,962. The hospitals justified the promotion on the basis of her qualifications, supervisory duties, and performance, and her pay appeared to be in line with other vice presidents working for the University of Chicago Hospital. Do you see any problems with this raise?

5. For further reading, *see* Miriam Galston, *When Statutory Regimes Collide: Will* Citizens United *and* Wisconsin Right to Life *Make Federal Tax Regulation of Campaign Activity Unconstitutional?* 13 U. PENN. J. CONST'L LAW 867 (2011); Benjamin Leff, *Sit Down and Count the Cost: A Framework for Constitutionally Enforcing the 501(c)(3) Campaign Intervention Ban*, 28 VA. TAX REV. 673 (2009); Lloyd Hitoshi Mayer, *Politics at the Pulpit: Tax Benefits, Substantial Burdens, and Institutional Free Exercise*, 89 BOSTON UNIV. L. REV. 1137 (2009*)*; Laura Chisolm, *Exempt Organization Advocacy: Matching the Rules to the Rationales*, 63 IND. L.J. 201 (1987).

PROBLEMS

1. As soon as the 2012 election was completed (and perhaps before), speculation began that Hillary Clinton would run for president in the next election. She finally announced that she would do so on April 16, 2015. Assume that the Arkansas Advocates for Children and Families, a nonprofit that she cofounded in 1977, wanted to recognize her as the cofounder in March 2015. Could it have done so without violating the rule against political campaign intervention? What if the date were March 2016? Does the date make a difference?

2. A 2004 sermon at All Saints Episcopal Church of Pasadena, California, was entitled "If Jesus Debated Senator Kerry and President Bush." The sermon criticized the war in Iraq, which had begun under President George W. Bush's term, as a "failed doctrine" and derided the "dismantling of social programs that provide a decent life for children once they enter this world" as heartbreaking to God. The sermon ended with, "When you go into the voting booth on Tuesday, take with you all that you know about Jesus, the peacemaker. Take all that Jesus means to you. Then vote your deepest

values." Should the church have had its §501(c)(3) status revoked for that sermon?

IV. OTHER TAX-EXEMPT ORGANIZATIONS THAT ENGAGE IN POLITICAL ACTIVITY

Although this book concentrates on §501(c)(3) organizations, activities and controversies surrounding political campaign activity in other types of tax-exempt organizations have increased so much in the last few years that it is worth taking a detour to consider those issues. These issues are significant in their own right, and they have become so important and controversial that they have already had an effect on §501(c)(3)s and may have an even larger effect in the future.

Before starting this discussion, it might be helpful to summarize the types of policy, advocacy, and partisan activities that tax-exempt organizations can engage in: (1) issue advocacy, (2) lobbying, and (3) partisan political activity.

Remember that §501(c)(3)'s charitable and educational activities can have a political point of view. For example, even though §501(c)(3) think tanks are officially nonpartisan, they can usually be characterized as either conservative- or liberal-leaning. Voter registration drives, issue analysis, and other charitable and educational activities that educate the public about political issues are allowed. Only if the §501(c)(3)'s activities turn to lobbying or political campaign involvement is there a concern. Public charities can engage in lobbying as long as the lobbying does not become "substantial." Private foundations are not allowed to engage in lobbying, and neither public charities nor private foundations can engage in partisan political activity.

Other tax-exempt organizations have fewer restrictions on political activity, and Part A here will give a short description of these differences. When it comes to political campaign activity, these organizations can be regulated by both the Internal Revenue Code (IRC) and the Federal Election Campaign Act (FECA), depending upon which political campaign activities they pursue. Unfortunately, the statutory regimes are not entirely symmetrical, and an organization that is attempting to engage in partisan political activity will need to be aware of the requirements of both statutes.

Since 2010, §501(c) corporations (other than §501(c)s) have become a favored tool for partisan politics. Although donations to such organizations are not tax-deductible, the IRC allows them to participate in political campaign activities, so long as those activities are not their primary purpose. The IRC also protects the anonymity of donors to a §501(c) organization. FECA, on the other hand, requires the disclosure of donors under certain circumstances. As will be shown below, donors who wish to remain anonymous can find ways to make their points without triggering the FECA disclosure rules.

Following is a brief description of the tax-exempt organizations that can engage in political campaign activity, as well as the relevant IRC and FECA rules. Once those options are laid out, the rest of this chapter sets forth some of the tax and public policy issues that these choices raise: (1) How does one determine whether a §501(c) organization's primary purpose has become political? (2) Do large amounts of "dark money" allow secretive donors to buy elections? (3) Should large donors to §501(c) organizations pay a gift tax? and (4) Can and should the IRS enforce election laws? This part of the chapter ends with discussions of the recent IRS scandal and enforcement issues, the state law response to the public policy issues raised in this section, and the effect of these changes and this confusion on §501(c)(3) organizations.

A. NONCHARITABLE TAX-EXEMPT ORGANIZATIONS THAT CAN ENGAGE IN POLITICAL ACTIVITY

1. Section 501(c) Organizations, Particularly §501(c)(4)

The concurrence in *Regan v. Taxation With Representation of Washington,* 461 U.S. 540 (1983), presented above, would have upheld §501(c)(3)'s restrictions on legislative activity in part because a §501(c)(3) can establish an affiliation with another organization that has more flexibility to operate in the political arena. Among the better-known §501(c)(3) organizations with such affiliations are the Sierra Club, Planned Parenthood, and the National Rifle Association. Most often, these affiliates are §501(c)(4) social welfare organizations.

Section 501(c)(4) social welfare organizations must be organized and operated for the primary purpose of promoting social welfare. Social welfare involves "promoting the common good" and "bringing about civic betterments" and "social improvement" [Treas. Reg. §1.501(c)(4)-1(a)(2)(i)]. Intervention in a political campaign is not a social welfare activity, but some political activity is allowed, so long as the primary purpose remains promoting social welfare.

Most §501(c)(4) organizations are advocacy organizations. In §501(c)(3) parlance, they are "action organizations" and can engage in unlimited legislative activities, so long as these activities are geared toward achieving the organization's exempt purpose. For example, a §501(c)(4) organization organized to improve dogs' lives by adopting legislation that regulates the operation of kennels could engage in unlimited lobbying on this topic because that activity would be in furtherance of its exempt purpose. In contrast, a §501(c)(3) dedicated to improving dogs' lives by providing a shelter could engage in lobbying so long as that activity did not become "substantial." The two organizations could be affiliated, however.

Assuming that a §501(c)(3) organization has an affiliation with a §501(c)(4) organization, it must keep very careful account of the funds. Both organizations are tax exempt, but donations to a §501(c)(3) organization are deductible to the donor, and donations to a §501(c)(4) organization are not. Those working with both organizations must ensure that the tax-deductible donations to the §501(c)(3) organization do not find their way into the coffers of the §501(c)(4) organization.[11] Careful records, notices on fundraising appeals, and precise wording of the organizations' articles of incorporation and bylaws are mandatory for organizations trying to maintain this distinction. If one organization is controlled by the other, care must be taken to keep them separate enough that a court will not be tempted to "pierce the corporate veil," as the court did in the *Network for Good* case, reproduced in Chapter 10.[12] These steps are absolutely crucial for the §501(c)(3) organization because it will not be able to convert to a §501(c)(4) organization if it loses its §501(c)(3) tax exemption. *See* IRC §504.

Increasingly, §501(c)(4)s are also being used for political campaign intervention purposes. As mentioned above, political campaign intervention is not in furtherance of a §501(c)(4)'s exempt purpose [Treas. Reg. §1.301(c)(4)-1(a)], but it is allowed, so long as the organization remains "primarily engaged" in promoting social welfare [Treas. Reg. 1.501(c)(4)-1(a)(2)(i)]. By contrast, a §501(c)(3) organization is strictly prohibited from engaging in political campaign activity.

The IRS uses a "facts and circumstances" test to determine whether a §501(c)(4) is primarily engaged in social welfare. Relevant factors include the amount of resources, including both cash and noncash items (such as buildings and equipment), that are devoted to the organization's various activities; the time devoted to these activities by volunteers and employees; the manner in which the organization's activities are conducted; and the purposes furthered by the organization's activities.[13] Most practitioners assume that tax-exempt organizations can spend 49% of their expenses on partisan political activity, so long as at least 51% is devoted to their primary purpose. There are no official IRS regulations or statements to this effect, however, and many campaign finance groups and scholars disagree with this interpretation.[14]

The use of §501(c) organizations for political purposes mushroomed after the 2010 *Citizens United* decision, which held that corporations could spend treasury funds to support or oppose a candidate [*Citizens United v. FEC,* 558 U.S. 310 (2010)]. That case allowed all corporations, including §501(c)(4)s, to pay for political campaign communications that encourage the public to support or oppose federal and state candidates, so long as those communications are made

---

[11] As Justice Rehnquist said in *Regan v. Taxation With Representation of Washington,* 461 U.S. 540 (1983), "The IRS apparently requires only that the two groups be separately incorporated and keep records adequate to show that tax-deductible contributions are not used to pay for lobbying. This is not unduly burdensome." *Id.* at n. 6.

[12] *Network for Good v. United Way of the Bay Area,* California Superior Court, San Francisco County, Case No. 436186, pp. 66-72 (Oct. 19, 2007).

[13] Raymond Chick and Amy Henchey, Political Organizations and IRC 501(c)(4), 1995 EO CPE Text; available at https://www.irs.gov/pub/irs-tege/eotopicm95.pdf.

[14] For a discussion of public policy concerns surrounding this issue, as well as of ways in which this line could be drawn, given the language of the statutes and regulations, *see* Miriam Galston, Vision Service Plan v. U.S.: *Implications for Campaign Activities of 501(c)(4)s,* 53 EXEMPT ORG. TAX REV. 165 (2006). In 2015, the IRS commissioner gave credence to the 49%–51% interpretation, but his statement was not an official one. *See* Paul Barton, *Koskinen's Comments on Political Spending of Nonprofits Disputed,* 75 EXEMPT ORG. TAX REV. 558 (2015).

without coordinating or consulting with the candidate. Federal election law still prohibits corporations, including §501(c)(4)s, from making direct contributions to or coordinating activities with candidates.

By and large, the corporate funds to support or oppose a particular candidate have not come from major publicly traded corporations. Instead, §501(c)(4) advocacy groups have led the charge.[15] These advocacy groups are attractive political vehicles for two reasons. First, a publicly traded corporation may prefer to fund an advocacy group that promotes its position over openly supporting a political position that could offend shareholders or customers. Second, §501(c)(4) organizations need not file with the FEC unless they use specific words to support or oppose a specific candidate (i.e., engage in "express advocacy"), or if they run issue ads close to the date of an election and name a candidate.[16] Even then, under FECA express advocacy rules, they need to disclose their donors only if the money was contributed for the purpose of making an "independent expenditure." (An *independent expenditure* is a communication from an organization that expressly advocates the election or defeat of a clearly identified candidate and that is not made in cooperation or consultation with a candidate, committee, or political party). As a result, donors who wish to make a political point and remain anonymous can achieve these results by working around these rules.

2. §527 Organizations

Other political advocacy groups *do* need to disclose their donors. For example, §527 organizations are pure political organizations that must disclose their contributions pursuant to the IRC, FECA, or both. Candidate campaign committees, political party committees, PACs, and super PACs are all organized under §527 of the IRC. They are exempt from federal income tax, so long as they engage in activity designed to influence the selection, nomination, election, or appointment of a person to federal, state, or local public office, to an office in a political organization, or as an elector for president or vice president. 26 USC §527(e)(2). Contributions to §527 organizations are not tax deductible. The organizations must register with the IRS and file periodic reports of contributions and expenditures. They must disclose their donors using the criteria that the IRS has established.

---

[15] Section 501(c)(5) labor unions and §501(c)(6) business leagues have also engaged in political campaign activity, but they have spent less money and garnered less attention. When they engage in political activity, §501(c)(5) labor unions tend to support Democrats, and trade associations like the Chamber of Commerce tend to support Republicans. The rest of this chapter will discuss §501(c)(4)s because they are more prevalent, but the rules that apply to them apply equally to 501(c)(5)s and§501(c)(6)s, except for the tax-exempt purposes and filing requirements for §501(c)(4)s.

[16] Alliance for Justice Action Campaign, 501(C)(4) REPORTING: WHEN ARE DONORS DISCLOSED? Available at http://afjactioncampaign.org/wp-content/uploads/2012/08/501c4-Reporting.pdf, accessed May 26, 2016.

Section 527s that do not engage in express advocacy are subject to the IRC but *not* to the FECA. They can raise unlimited amounts of "soft money" (i.e., money that is not directed to a particular candidate), which they then use for voter mobilization and issue advocacy. Section 527 committees that avoided express advocacy, such as Swift Boat Veterans for Truth and Moveon.org, played prominent roles in the 2004 presidential election. After *Citizens United*, §527 organizations of this type have become less visible, but they continue to be active. In 2014, §527s spent $728 million—$110 million more than they spent in 2004.[17]

3. PACs and Super PACs

FECA does govern §527 organizations that do engage in express advocacy. PACs, for example, pool campaign contributions from members and then give the money directly to elect or defeat a candidate. They remain the vehicle for providing "hard money" to candidates.[18] Political action committees (PACs) raise money from a limited group of specified categories of individuals, such as the managers and shareholders of for-profit corporations and from the members of advocacy groups, unions, or business leagues. They then distribute the money to candidates, political parties, and even other PACs. PACs must register with the FEC and comply with all financial reporting requirements, including disclosing their donors.

Until 2010, contributions by individuals, PACS, and party committees to federal PACs were limited to $5,000 a year, but the decision of *SpeechNow.org v. Federal Election Commission*, 599 F.3d 686 (D.C. Cir. 2010), *cert. denied sub nom Keating v. FEC*, 2010 U.S. LEXIS 8531 (U.S., Nov. 1, 2010), invalidated this limit with regard to contributions made to PACS that make only independent expenditures.[19] This change led to the creation of super PACs, which can accept unlimited contributions from corporations and others, so long as their expenditures are independent of candidates' campaigns. Thus, a super PAC is a special kind of PAC that raises and spends money in support of or opposition to a specific candidate while remaining independent of the candidate's campaign. Super PACs are not allowed to make a contribution directly to a candidate, a political party, or to a politcal committee that gives money diretly to a candidate.

Super PACS have two distinct advantages over regular PACs. They are exempt from the fundraising and spending limits that restrict ordinary PACS,

---

[17] Center for Responsive Politics, thtp://www.opensecrets.org/527s/index.php?filter2=A#summ (April 2015), accessed May 26, 2016.

[18] *Citizens United* did not address the issue of direct contributions to candidates. As a result, FECA still prohibits corporations, including §501(c)(4)s, from using general treasury funds to make a direct contribution to a candidate. However, they can contribute to super PACs. Holly Schadler, "The Connection: Strategies for Creating and Operating 501(c)(3)s, 501(c)(4)s, and Political Organizations," *Alliance for Justice*, 3rd ed. (2012).

[19] As explained above, an independent expenditure is a political campaign communication expressly advocating the election or defeat of a political candidate that is independent of the candidate.

and they can accept contributions from the general treasuries of corporations. Super PACs must identify their donors to the FEC, so, in theory, they are quite transparent. If the donor is a shell corporation or a nonprofit that does not disclose its donors, however, the transparency can be lost. Super PACS played a large part of the 2012 presidential election, spending $609.4 million on independent expenditures in that campaign. As this book went to press, they were also active in the presidential primaries of 2016, and they are likely to be active in the general election as well.[20]

Table 11-3 outlines the differences among these tax-exempt alternatives for political activity.

Table 11-3

TYPE OF EXEMPT ORGANIZATION	RUN ADS IN SUPPORT OF OR OPPOSITION TO CANDIDATE?	PROVIDE DIRECT CONTRIBUTIONS TO CANDIDATES?	LIMITS ON FUNDS RAISED FOR POLITICAL CAMPAIGN PURPOSES?	DONORS MUST BE DISCLOSED?
§501(c)(3)	No	No	Yes [21]	No
§§501(c)(4), 501(c)(5), or 501(c)(6)[22]	Yes	No	No	No
PAC Super PAC	Yes Yes	Yes No.	Yes No	Yes Yes
Non-PAC §527	Yes	No	No	Yes[23]

This table shows the appeal of using a §501(c)(4) or other tax-exempt corporation to engage in partisan politics or participate in political campaigns, and it helps explain why §501(c)(4)s have become such a large part of the

---

[20] As of March 24, 2016, super PACS accounted for nearly 40% of the funds raised toward the presidential election, up from 22% by that date in 2012. The total raised as of that date by presidential candidates and PACs had just surpassed the $1 billion mark, up from $402.7 million by that time in 2012. Fredreka Schouten, *Presidential Race Surges Past $1 Billion Mark*, USA TODAY (March 24, 2016).

[21] The limit is set at $0. As noted earlier in this chapter, § 501(c)(3) organizations cannot engage in any political campaign activity.

[22] There is no disclosure per the IRC. Occasionally, as noted above, FECA requires disclosure.

[23] Disclosure is required by the IRS disclosure rules. FECA is not applicable to non-PAC §527 organizations. The FECA and IRC disclosure rules are similar, but not identical.

election scene. Once corporations were allowed to engage in political activity using general treasury funds, §501(c)(4) advocacy groups could replicate most of the advantages of the other political vehicles without the registration and disclosure requirements. In 2012, §501(c)(4) organizations reported spending $257 million on express advocacy to the FEC (up from $96 million in 2010). This rapid rise in the use of §501(c) organizations for political purposes has led to considerable discussion and controversy.

B. TAX AND POLICY ISSUES

1. Determining the Primary Purpose of a §501(c)(4)[24]

One of the controversies concerns whether these organizations truly have a primary tax-exempt purpose or whether their primary purpose is political. In 2015, Gregory Colvin, chair of the Drafting Committee of the Bright Lines Project[25] and an eminent advisor to tax-exempt groups, testified to Congress as to the difficulty of making this determination and suggested a solution. Portions of his testimony are reproduced below.

GREGORY COLVIN, TREASURY/IRS REGULATIONS ON POLITICAL ACTIVITY: A MUCH-NEEDED AND CONSTRUCTIVE PROCESS, TESTIMONY TO SENATE JUDICIARY SUBCOMMITTEE ON OVERSIGHT, AGENCY ACTION, FEDERAL RIGHTS AND FEDERAL COURTS

July 29, 2015

The fundamental problem affecting enforcement of the political tax rules on 501(c) tax exempts is this: they are vague, unpredictable, and difficult to interpret.

What is political intervention? Without comprehensive new regulations, the IRS interpretation must be gleaned from a few old cases and rulings, internal training materials, and a few bursts of guidance from the last decade. The current Treasury regulation defining political intervention has only 113 words; it is totally inadequate. The IRS has insisted on an open-ended "facts and circumstances" approach rather than drawing bright lines between partisan politics and truly nonpartisan forms of voter education and engagement. Political intervention under tax law is more than express advocacy under election law, the IRS has said, but it has never clearly drawn that line. . . .

---

[24] Also, §501(c)(5) unions and §501(c)(6) trade associations will lose their tax exemptions if their primary purpose is political. IRS Gen. Couns. Mem. 34233 (December 3, 1969).

[25] The Bright Lines Project has created a proposal to encourage the IRS to modify and clarify its regulations governing tax-exempt organizations' political campaign activities. It seeks to create a precise approach to defining political intervention that includes safe harbor exceptions so groups know which activities are permissible and which might jeopardize an organization's tax exemption.

Let's consider what is perhaps the toughest political tax law enforcement problem and the one that involves the largest monetary expense: the difference between political campaign advertising and so-called "issue ads" that name a candidate, say something good or bad about them, and tell the viewer to contact the candidate about the issue. [The IRS has issued contradictory rulings and has been unwilling to reconcile this contradiction]. . . .

This kind of ambiguity and uncertainty in political tax law has made advising clients and resolving cases difficult, time-consuming, and costly. Eventually, I have found, the IRS decides the vast majority of close cases in favor of the organization and its freedom to speak, but justice delayed often feels like justice denied.. . . .

In testimony I gave to another Senate Judiciary subcommittee in April 2013, I recommended that the IRS and Treasury undertake an intensive regulatory project to establish bright lines defining political intervention—that wouldn't tolerate the disguise of targeted "issue ads" that refer to and reflect a view on candidates, and that would provide safe harbors for genuine lobbying and genuine voter education. As we all know, the crisis within the IRS that came to a head the next month, May, 2013, revealed the collapse of its ability to efficiently and consistently rule on 501(c) exemption applications. This created the historic opportunity for Treasury and the IRS to commence exactly the kind of regulations project that we have needed for decades. . . .

In the effort to remedy the problems that were uncovered in the spring of 2013 regarding the IRS treatment of tax-exempt political issues, Treasury and the IRS began a rulemaking process to define candidate-related political activity for 501(c)(4) organizations, a corrective recommended by the Inspector General (TIGTA). The proposed regulations released in November, 2013, came sooner than many of us expected and were roundly criticized as a threat to Americans' free speech, drawing clumsy lines that went too far in many respects and not far enough in others. . . .

There was a record number of public comments—more than 146,000—reflecting the intensity of frustration in the nonprofit sector with the ambiguity and administration of the political intervention rules. Conservative, moderate and progressive nonprofit organizations alike opposed various elements of the proposed rules, but at the same time expressed support for addressing the current lack of clear standards. . . .

The American public is anxious for clarity in the tax rules on political intervention, too. A September 2014 survey commissioned by two polling firms, one Democratic and the other Republican, showed widespread support for a bright-lines standard:[26] . . . 87 percent of Democrats, 84 percent of Independents, and 88 percent of Republicans agree that clear rules are important. In addition, voters are very concerned about some of the consequences of unclear rules. 80 percent say political operatives, wealthy donors, and organizations abusing and

---

[26] [FN 15] Lake Research Partners, Recent Research on IRS Political Rulemaking (September 30, 2014).

taking advantage of such vague rules is a problem. 72 percent of Republicans surveyed agree. Among voters who had an opinion, a majority favored changing the way nonprofit activities are regulated to establish clearer and fairer rules for what counts as political.

I have confidence that the IRS and Treasury can guide this process to a successful conclusion. . . . I have seen firsthand the IRS and Treasury produce bright-line regulations in the political realm that have been well-crafted to guide tax-exempt organizations and achieve self-enforcement in the vast majority of situations. Between 1986 and 1990, with heavy input from the nonprofit sector, the Service developed lobbying regulations for public charities and private foundations with clear definitions and clear safe harbor exceptions. Like the current political regulations, the first draft was a rocky start, but the final result turned out quite well, . . . and for the last 23 years there have been virtually no law enforcement problems due to lack of clarity, no complaints of oppressive IRS prosecution. . . .

The Bright Lines Project has submitted detailed suggestions for IRS and Treasury consideration. . . . We define nine forms of per se political intervention and eleven safe harbors to protect grassroots lobbying, voter engagement, other types of nonpartisan speech, and the proper use and transfer of organizational resources to others. We include a glossary of 28 specific definitions for terms such as candidate, election, targeting, self-defense, and comparative voter education. We would drastically reduce the discretion the IRS could exercise, so that it could only use the "facts and circumstances" approach in situations that don't fit into predictable patterns of partisan and nonpartisan involvement in elections. . . .

I want to conclude by identifying eight decisions that Treasury and the IRS must make to achieve public acceptance of the regulations and a workable political tax law system:

1) Draw the right line dividing partisan and nonpartisan speech—we suggest it be "reflect a view" on a candidate, the standard successfully used in the IRS lobbying regulations.

2) Differentiate among forms of communication—we suggest tougher rules for paid mass media ads.

3) Distinguish communications by their target audiences—we suggest messages directed toward close contests be viewed as partisan and those directed toward underrepresented voters or an organization's natural constituency be viewed as nonpartisan.

4) Identify time periods in which rules could be more relaxed—we recommend that line be drawn at one year before the election.

5) Create and preserve safe harbors for nonpartisan speech—we suggest that grassroots lobbying, even-handed voter education, registration and GOTV, self-defense, and personal remarks not made on behalf of an organization be protected.

6) Greatly reduce, but don't eliminate, the role of "facts and circumstances"—we believe some flexibility is needed to judge new or complex situations, but the review should be structured in an orderly way.

7) Revisit the question of "how much" is too much political intervention to be exempt under Sections 501(c)(4), (5), or (6)—we recommend that a clear annual expenditure percentage limit be drawn, mindful that this will impact donor disclosure and the choice of 501(c) or 527 vehicles for election spending.

8) Issue regulations defining political intervention that go beyond 501(c)(4) organizations—we strongly feel they must apply universally and consistently across the Internal Revenue Code, for 501(c)(3) charities, all tax-exempts, tax-paying businesses, and political organizations.

These reforms would go a long way toward restoring public confidence in the tax-exempt universe, toward preventing the corruption of hidden financial leverage in our elections, and toward liberating the speech of citizen groups who have who have too long been intimidated by the fear of losing tax-exemption due to the unpredictable specter of IRS enforcement.

2. Do Large Amounts of "Dark Money" Allow Secretive Donors to Buy Elections?

A second question is whether large amounts of anonymous money pouring into electoral campaigns are actually dangerous for our democracy. This anonymous money has been called "dark money" because the IRS does not require disclosure of donors to a §501(c) tax-exempt organization, and the FEC requires disclosure only in two situations: (1) if the organization is making an independent expenditure and the donor expressly contributed the money for the purpose of making an independent expenditure; or (2) if the organization spends more than $10,000 in a calendar year on electioneering communications and the donors have donated more than $1,000 for the purpose of electioneering communications.[27] Donors who wish to remain anonymous are sophisticated enough to avoid these disclosures.

Section 501(c)(4) organizations can make their own contributions to other §501(c)(4) organizations and to super PACs. Super PACs must reveal that the §501(c)(4) made a contribution, but the donors to the §501(c)(4) are still not revealed. The Center for Responsive Politics reports that $309 million was spent by "nondisclosing groups"[28] in the 2012 election, up from $69 million in the

---

[27] Alliance for Justice Action Campaign, 501(C)(4) REPORTING: WHEN ARE DONORS DISCLOSED? available at http://afjactioncampaign.org/wp-content/uploads/2012/08/501c4-Reporting.pdf, accessed May 23, 2016. Note that lobbying activity and state laws also can lead to situations in which donors must be disclosed. *Id.* A 2016 appellate opinion affirmed the second rule cited here. *Van Hollen v. FEC,* 811 F.3d 486 (D.C. Cir. 2016). *See also* Paul Barton, *Donors to Tax-Exempts Often Give Supersized Amounts,* 75 EXEMPT ORG. TAX. REV. 561 (2015); Jasper Cummings, Citizens United *Spurs Social Welfare,* 75 EXEMPT ORG. TAX. REV. 483 (2015).

[28] The Center for Responsive Politics, a nonpartisan organization, uses this term instead of "dark money."

2008 election. As of March 2016, nondisclosing groups had spent $16 million towards the 2016 elections, which was up from $3.37 million at the same point in the election cycle in 2008.[29]

The Center for Responsive Politics attempts to shed light on the anonymous money flowing into the political system by keeping a running tally of the amounts reported to the FEC. Its website, http://www.opensecrets.org, classifies candidates' finances according to money raised by the candidates themselves and money raised by outside sources. Because the §501(c)(4) IRS forms are filed well after the money is raised and spent, the center's information about §501(c)(4)s is not current. Nevertheless, it has been able to document the rise in spending by §501(c)(4) organizations. https://www.opensecrets.org/outsidespending/nonprof_summ.php.

The Center for Responsive Politics and others advocating campaign finance reform are quite worried about the influx of anonymous money into the political system. One concern is the ability to thwart the spirit, if not the letter, of the law that is designed to create transparency in our elections. Robert McGuire, the political nonprofits investigator at the Center for Responsive Politics, wrote an op-ed in the *New York Times* that illustrated this concern. He wrote about Carolina Rising, a §501(c)(4) that spent $4.7 million over a three-month period in the fall of 2014 on ads that touted the legislative accomplishments of North Carolina's speaker of the House, Republican Thom Tillis. Tillis was at the time involved in what ultimately was a successful campaign to unseat Democratic senator Kay Hagan. When Carolina Rising filed its tax information form in August 2015, it said that it had not engaged in "direct or indirect political campaign activities on behalf of or in opposition to candidates for public office." The Republican consultant who was running Carolina Rising at the time, Dallas Woodhouse, said that the ads were not political in nature but were instead highlighting the issues that Tillis dealt with as a state legislator. Carolina Rising reported $4.88 million in contributions in 2014. In addition, $4.82 million of those gifts came from a single donor. The organization spent $4.8 million in 2014, $4.64 million of which went to Crossroads Media, which handled those ads. The identity of that donor remains, by law, unknown. Robert McGuire, *A New Low for Campaign Finance*, N.Y. TIMES (Oct. 27, 2015).[30]

A second concern is that this secret money will lead to corruption. As Fred Wertheimer, president of Democracy 21, has stated, "Secret money funding campaign spending is a surefire recipe for national scandal. . . . We have had a national consensus for 40 years that campaign donors and campaign expenditures

[29] https://www.opensecrets.org/outsidespending/disclosure.php?range=ytd. Note that this is the money that §501(c)(4)s and other organizations that did not disclose donors were required to disclose to the FEC. Observers of the election process assume that §501(c)(4) organizations spend as much as (or even more than) they report to the FEC on quasi-political activity that does not have to be reported to the FEC. *See* Peter Stone, *Fine Line Between Politics and Issues Spending by Secretive 501(c) Groups*, CENTER FOR PUBLIC INTEGRITY (Oct. 31, 2011).
[30] Carolina Rising's IRS Form 990 for FY 2014 is available online at https://assets.documentcloud.org/documents/2456438/carolina-rising-2014.pdf.

should be disclosed to the public. Even this Supreme Court, in its disastrous *Citizens United* decision, made clear that requiring the disclosure of donors who are funding independent campaign spending is constitutional and appropriate."[31] Senator John McCain and former Senator Russ Feingold have expressed similar concerns about corruption.[32] Even in the absence of corruption, however, concern has arisen that the increase of dark money creates the perception (if not the reality) that big money can buy elections and is damaging to democracy.

And yet, as this book went to press in the spring of 2016, the "dark money" was having mixed results. Bernie Sanders had raised $96 million in small donations without the help of a super PAC or a §501(c)(4). Donald Trump had leveraged his celebrity to become the Republican presumptive nominee without spending much money at all. His campaign had raised $1.9 million in outside money and $25.6 million in candidate committee money as of March 2016.[33] It was widely reported that Jeb Bush waited until he had raised a significant amount of anonymous money before declaring himself as a candidate so that he could have a war chest before he began the campaign. Yet he had such consistently low primary and caucus results that he left the campaign early. As Jack Shafer has written, "Money certainly matters—just not as much as the critics of *Citizens United* feared."[34]

Shafer has also pointed out that the Republicans were able to field a wide and diverse field in the presidential primary because so many candidates were able to find generous funders, and choice is good for democracy. Finally, he noted that the current system is better than the former system of nominating presidents— political machines that had no transparency. "I would argue that attempts to reduce campaign treasuries inevitably pushes the balance of power in the nominating process to shadowy power brokers."[35]

Other arguments favoring anonymity have been raised as well. One is that anonymous donors cannot influence candidates who do not know their identity, and a second is that some issues are so controversial that donors could justifiably wish to remain anonymous for their own safety. Reports of death threats to brothers Charles and David Koch, who are behind many of the conservative nonprofits, give some credence to these concerns. In 2016, a funder to one of these conservative organizations, Americans for Prosperity, testified that he, too, had faced death threats. And in 2014 the chief executive officer (CEO) of Mozilla was forced to resign when it became known that he had supported an

---

[31] Fred Wertheimer, *Campaign Finance Reform Behind Secret Donors?* Politico (Oct. 13, 2010), available at http://www.politico.com/arena/perm/Fred_Wertheimer_AC812C95-A953-4FA8-A1C0-E798621D44B3.html.

[32] Andy Kroll, *Follow the Dark Money*, Mother Jones (July/August 2012), http://www.motherjones.com/politics/2012/06/history-money-american-elections?page=3.

[33] These figures are from the Center for Responsive Politics, http://www.opensecrets.org/pres16, accessed May 26, 2016.

[34] Jack Shafer, *Three Cheers for* Citizens United, Politico (Aug. 25, 2015).

[35] *Id.*

anti-gay rights campaign.[36] The FEC has actually granted an exemption from its disclosure rules to the Socialist Workers Party since 1974. Perhaps this anonymity is needed to encourage political speech.

What do you think? Does the donor anonymity of a §501(c)(4) encourage political speech, or does it encourage political corruption? Would a law requiring disclosure of all contributions over a certain dollar amount pass constitutional muster?

3. Should Large Donors to §501(c)(4) Organizations Be Required to Pay a Gift Tax?

When §501(c)(4)s began receiving large amounts of money that were politically oriented in 2010, questions arose about whether those donations were subject to the federal gift tax. At that time, the IRC did not specifically exempt donors who made donations to §501(c)(4) organizations from the gift tax, even though donations to §501(c)(3)s and §527 organizations were exempt. *See* IRC §2501(a)(5). Given the multimillion dollar gifts being made to some of these organizations, the tax could get quite expensive. In 2011, the IRS sent letters to four §501(c)(4) organizations suggesting that large contributions could be subject to the tax, but the IRS never followed up on the letters, possibly because of the outcry that it heard from those who thought this action was politically motivated and raised First Amendment concerns. Congress weighed in on this debate in 2015 and explicitly exempted contributions to §501(c)(4), §(c)(5), and §(c)(6) organizations made after December 19, 2015, from the federal gift tax. Do you agree with the congressional decision? *See* Joint Committee on Taxation, Technical Explanation of the Protecting Americans From Tax Hikes Act of 2015, House Amendment #2 to the Senate Amendment to H.R. 2029, Rules Committee Print 114-40, pp. 244-246 (Dec. 15, 2015). *See also* John Lucky & Erika Lunder, *501(c)(4) and the Gift Tax: Legal Analysis,* CONGRESSIONAL RESEARCH SERVICE, R42655 (Aug. 10, 2012).

4. Can and Should the IRS Enforce Election Rules?

Another question is whether the IRS is the appropriate vehicle for enforcing these rules. The agency, which has had its budget slashed considerably in the last few years, is hardly the organization to oversee the integrity of elections. When it needs to prioritize, it will undoubtedly focus on taxpayers who will bring more money to the Treasury.

A bigger problem may be that tax regulation takes place so long after the activity that enforcement is almost impossible. Before December 19, 2015, §501(c)(4) organizations were not required to seek approval of their exempt status or notify the IRS until they filed their first tax form, which could be more

---

[36] Roy Wenzl, *Charles Koch, Employees Reveal E-Mailed Threats from Past Year,* WITCHITA EAGLE (Feb. 17, 2012); Bonnie Eslinger, *Koch Bros. Group Donor Testifies He Got Death Threats,* LAW 360 (Feb. 25, 2016); Heather Kelley, *Mozilla CEO Resigns over Same-Sex Marriage Controversy,* CNN MONEY (April 23, 2014).

than a year after they had begun their activity. For example, an organization that came into existence on January 1, 2015, would not need to contact the IRS until November 2016, assuming that it took advantage of extensions, and even then, the information on the tax form would concern only the 2015 tax year. The IRS would have to wait until November 2017 to learn what had happened the year before the election. Organizations formed after December 19, 2015,[37] do have to notify the IRS that they are operating as §501(c)(4)s, but they still do not have to seek approval, and the issues of delayed information remain. The organization could well have shut down before the IRS has enough information to know whether it was following the rules.

Some argue that the FEC is a better agency for policing political activity, and that, if Congress passes uniform donor disclosure rules, the IRS can mostly retire from its political enforcement duties. *See, e.g.,* Roger Colinvaux, *Political Activity Limits and Tax Exemption: A Gordian's Knot,* 34 VA. TAX REV. 1 (2014). Others argue against such an approach, noting that the FEC does not have jurisdiction over state and local elections and that it is often stymied by political gridlock. *See e.g.* Gregory Colvin, *Treasury/IRS Regulations on Political Activity,* Testimony to Senate Judiciary Subcommittee on Oversight, Agency Action, Federal Rights and Federal Courts (July 29, 2015), portions of which are reproduced above.

Most proponents of keeping the IRS involved in policing the boundary between tax-exempt and political purposes suggest fixing the definitional difficulties so that the IRS can do its job more effectively. The Colvin testimony reproduced above provided an important example of this view, as does the Bright Lines Project that he mentioned (http://www.brightlinesproject.org). Others have argued that the §501(c)(3) limit on political activity should be extended to all §501(c) organizations. *See, e.g.* Editorial Board, *Rewriting the Rules for 501(c)(4)s,* L.A. TIMES (March 17, 2014). A third approach would be to recognize the "inherent difficulty in trying to regulate an increasingly attractive activity that is impossible to define clearly. The solution might be simply to stop trying to impose limits on advocacy by any tax-exempt groups except charities." Suzanne Garment and Leslie Lenkowsky, *IRS Should Allow Social-Welfare Groups Unlimited Advocacy,* CHRON. OF PHIL. (May 13, 2013). And some have even argued that we should drop the limits altogether, allowing even §501(c)(3)s to engage in political activity. Darryll K. Jones, *Political Activity Regulations Will Be Rewritten Again . . . and Again,* NONPROFIT LAWPROFS BLOG, (April 16, 2014).

---

[37] As this book went to press, this requirement was suspended until 60 days after temporary regulations were in place. IRS Notice 2016-09. Note that this requirement applies only to §501(c)(4)s. It does not apply to §501(c)(5)s or §501(c)(6)s, which also can begin operations without notifying the IRS.

C. IRS SCANDAL AND ENFORCEMENT ISSUES

The number of groups applying for §501(c)(4) status more than doubled between 2010 and 2012.[38] Faced with determining whether these organizations were engaged in too much political activity to be recognized as §501(c)(4)s, the IRS began providing extra scrutiny to groups with "Tea Party" and "Patriot" in their names, a policy that had the appearance, if not the reality, of targeting groups on the basis of their political beliefs. Lois Lerner, the director of the IRS's Exempt Organizations Division in 2013, disclosed this practice shortly before the Treasury Inspector General released a report critical of this process.[39] She denied that there was any political motivation and blamed the practice on a low-level employee.

This revelation led to a series of congressional investigations and multiple governmental reports[40] that discussed whether the IRS was politically motivated. Almost immediately, two divergent answers emerged. One is that there was a deliberate conspiracy to impede conservative groups. The other is that the IRS was working with vague standards in an increasingly politicized world and that it used a clumsy way to deal with the increase in applications. For the most part, Republicans hold the first view and Democrats the second.

Both sides agree, however, that the IRS did not handle the influx in political-leaning organizations well. Although it did look at left-leaning names, such as "progressive" and "ACORN" and examined organizations affiliated with the Occupy Wall Street movement, the vast majority of organizations getting extra scrutiny were conservative. Most of them were subjected to long delays, and many were asked voluminous and inappropriate questions. As Democratic senator Ron Wyden, ranking member of the Senate Finance Committee, said, "By my count, there were seven different efforts, over more than two years, to figure out how to handle these applications, and the first six all failed. By December 2011, a total of 290 applications for 501(c)(4) status had been set aside for further review. Two of these applications had been successfully resolved. Not two hundred. Two."[41]

Eventually, but well after the scandal erupted, the IRS put in place better procedures to handle political-leaning organizations and to ease the backlog in

---

[38] Treasury Inspector Gen. For Tax Admin., *Inappropriate Criteria Were Used to Identify Tax-Exempt Applications For Review*, Reference No. 2013-10-053 (May 14, 2013) (hereinafter TIGTA Report).

[39] *Id.*

[40] In addition to the TIGTA report, *supra, see* National Taxpayer Advocate, Political Activity and the Rights of Applicants for Tax-Exempt Status (June 26, 2013); Resolution and Report of the House Oversight and Government Reform Committee, H. Rept. 113-415 (Apr. 14, 2014); Staff of the House Committee on Oversight and Government Reform, *The Internal Revenue Service's Targeting of Conservative Tax-Exempt Applicants: Report of Findings* (Dec. 23, 2014) (Oversight staff report); and Committee on Finance United States Senate, Bipartisan Investigative Report as Submitted by Chairman Hatch and Ranking Member Wyden (Aug. 5, 2015).

[41] *Wyden Floor Statement on Finance Committee Investigation of IRS Handling of Applications for Tax-Exempt Status*, U.S. Senate Committee on Finance (Aug. 5, 2015).

determining whether organizations should be recognized as tax-exempt. These backlog issues with §501(c)(4)s had spilled over into all types of tax-exempts, including §501(c)(3)s, and by August 2013, the IRS was not even assigning applications for exemption until 16 months after organizations submitted them. At one point it had a backlog of more than 60,000 applications. By 2015, the backlog had been eliminated,[42] and in 2016, the §501(c)(4) that had waited the longest to receive recognition of exemption, Grassroots GPS, was finally recognized as tax-exempt.[43]

The IRS also put into place procedures to ensure that it would not repeat its mistakes. It eliminated the use of inappropriate criteria, implemented improved and expanded training for its employees, expedited the processing of §501(c)(4) applications, and established a new process for documenting the reasons why applications are chosen for further review. It also began drafting regulations on how to measure social welfare and non–social welfare activities of §501(c)(4) organizations (the issue discussed in Part A of this chapter), but it stopped that exercise when Congress forbade it from doing so during fiscal year 2016. By 2016, the IRS had implemented all the recommendations in the TIGTA report of 2013 and the Bi-partisan Senate Report of 2015 that were under its control.[44]

The question of political bias has been less easy to resolve. The Republicans argue that it is obvious that political bias was rampant at the IRS. They point to the fact that Lois Lerner was a Democrat; that many of her emails disappeared when her computer crashed in 2011; and that the IRS misled Congress when it asked about the treatment of conservative groups. They also assert that the Department of Justice's decision not to indict Lois Lerner is evidence that the entire government is corrupt. The Democrats, on the other hand, point out that there have been no independent findings that the policy of targeting applications according to their names was politically motivated. None of the 1.5 million pages of emails and documents that the bipartisan Senate Committee reviewed indicated political motivation, and none of the more than 30 employees interviewed made such an allegation. This conclusion is consistent with the original TIGTA Report, which found no evidence of political bias in the processing of §501(c)(4) applications. Democrats also note that the IRS was targeting progressive as well as conservative groups and that many more conservative groups were organizing at that time, which explains the prevalence of conservative groups being scrutinized.

---

[42] *Prepared Remarks of John A. Koskinen Commissioner, Internal Revenue Service, Before the National Press Club* (March 31, 2015), https://www.irs.gov/uac/Newsroom/Commissioner-Koskinen-Speech-before-the-National-Press-Club, accessed May 26, 2016.

[43] Its website is http://www.crossroadsgps.org. For a description of its road to garnering §501(c)(4) status, *see* Robert McGuire, *How Crossroads GPS Beat the IRS and Became a Social Welfare Group*, CENTER FOR RESPONSIVE POLITICS (Feb. 12, 2016).

[44] *Written Testimony of John A. Koskinen Commissioner Internal Revenue Service Before the Senate Finance Committee on IRS Budget and Current Operations* (February 10, 2016), http://www.finance.senate.gov/imo/media/doc/2016%20JAK%20testimony%20SFC%20on%20FY 17%20budget%20021016x.pdf, accessed May 26, 2016.

As this book went to press, a case seeking damages from the IRS for its political bias and its practice of asking questions that were not germane to tax administration during the application process was winding its way through the courts. Early 2016 saw two procedural losses for the IRS. First, the District Court for the Southern District of Ohio allowed the suit to move forward as a class action lawsuit, *NorCal Tea Party Patriots v. IRS,* 2016 U.S. Dist. LEXIS 5889 (S.D. Ohio 2016). Then the 6th Circuit used particularly strong words to order the IRS to release its Be on the Lookout (BOLO) list, the list that targeted groups with names like "Tea Party" and "Patriot." *United States v. NorCal Tea Party Patriots (In re United States),* 2016 U.S. App. LEXIS 5213 (6th Cir. 2016). At the least, this case will keep this controversy in the public eye, and it may well shed more light on what actually happened and what else is needed to improve the system.

Those interested in the details of this controversy can read the blogs of Pepperdine law professor Paul Caron, who has published a daily commentary since the scandal erupted (http://taxprof.typepad.com/, accessed May 26, 2016). *See also* Philip Hackney, *Should the IRS Never 'Target' Taxpayers? An Examination of the IRS Tea Party Affair,* 49 VALPARAISO UNIVERSITY LAW REVIEW 453 (2015); Jasper L. Cummings, Jr., Citizens United *Spurs Welfare,* 75 EXEMPT ORG. TAX REV. 483 (2015); Lily Kahng, *The IRS Tea Party Controversy and Administrative Discretion,* 99 CORNELL L. REV. ONLINE 41 (2013).

D. THE STATE LAW RESPONSE

Several states have taken their own action in response to the rise in §501(c)(4) political activity, seeking the release of donor information from organizations that they suspected of violating state election laws with regard to campaigns in their states. Shortly before the 2012 election, for example, Idaho's secretary of state successfully sued Education Voters of Idaho (EVI), which had generously supported three Idaho ballot measures, for failure to comply with the state's so-called sunshine laws. Among the donors was New York City's mayor Michael Bloomberg and Albertson's supermarket scion Robert Scott. In California, the state's Fair Political Practices Commission forced an Arizona group to reveal the source of $11 million that it gave to two ballot initiatives. The donor was a §501(c)(4) that did not release the names of its own donors, but the commission said that it would continue to try to identify the original donor. California was also able to identify a Virginia-based group, Americans for Job Security (AJS), as the donor of an $11 million gift to oppose one tax ballot measure and to support a different measure designed to limit unions' ability to raise funds. AJS had routed the money through two other Arizona organizations before it appeared in California. In 2008, the FEC's general counsel had requested approval to investigate AJS because it appeared to fit the definition of a political organization that needed to disclose its donors, but the FEC commission deadlocked and no action was taken. As Idaho's secretary of state,

Ben Ysursa, has stated, "The fact that federal campaign laws are deficient or you've got a deadlocked Federal Election Commission—that doesn't mean the states are powerless."[45]

New York has adopted regulations requiring donor disclosure in some situations, and California has passed legislation with similar requirements. In 2012, New York's attorney general adopted regulations requiring §501(c) tax-exempt organizations that spend more than $10,000 to influence New York state and local elections to disclose the names of donors who have contributed more than $100 to this effort. New York makes these names public. Exceptions are made for contributors who specifically restrict the funds from being used for electioneering and for those who successfully request a waiver. In 2015, a state ethics commission refused to grant that waiver for the American Civil Liberties Union and Family Planning Advocates of New York, stating that they did not show that their donors faced an actual risk of reprisal that justified special treatment.[46]

California passed a law in 2014 that requires tax-exempt organizations spending more than $50,000 in one year on contributions and expenditures for California elections to disclose the names of donors who contributed $1,000 or more for such political activity within that state. Additionally, a group formed to support or oppose a state ballot measure or state candidate that raises $1 million or more for an election must disclose the top ten contributors.[47]

Both California and New York may have another tool in their arsenal, although that tool is being tested in the courts. Nonprofits registered in those states must file Schedule B of Form 990 with the state. Schedule B reports the names of all donors who contributed more than $5,000 for any reason to the nonprofit. If this requirement is upheld, these states will have the donors' names should they decide to investigate possible tax and election improprieties (or any other impropriety over which they have jurisdiction). Two California nonprofits questioned this rule, with mixed results. *See Americans for Prosperity v. Harris*, 2016 U.S. Dist. LEXIS 53679 (2016) (attorney general of California permanently enjoined from demanding AFP's Schedule B) and *Ctr. for Competitive Politics v. Harris*, 784 F.3d 1307 (9th Cir. 2015) (affirming denial of preliminary injunction

---

[45] Matea Gold and Chris Megerian, *States Crack Down on Campaigning Nonprofits*, L.A. TIMES (Nov. 26, 2012); Rick Cohen, *States Taking Political Donor Disclosure into Their Own Hands*, NONPROFIT QUARTERLY (Nov. 30, 2012).

[46] *A.G. Schneiderman Announces New Disclosure Requirements for Nonprofits That Engage in Electioneering*, http://www.ag.ny.gov/press-release/ag-schneiderman-announces-new-disclosure-requirements-nonprofits-engage-electioneering, accessed May 26, 2016; Larry Kaplan, *In NY, ACLU and Family Planning Advocates Ordered to Disclose Donors*, NONPROFIT QUARTERLY (Aug. 10, 2015).

[47] SB-27, Political Reform Act of 1974 (2013-2014), http://leginfo.legislature.ca.gov /faces/billNavClient.xhtml?bill_id=201320140SB27, accessed May 26, 2016. Utah has also passed a campaign finance bill requiring the disclosure of donors. Its requirements are being challenged in court. Paul Barton, *States Pass Washington in Policing Political Nonprofits* , 77 EXEMPT ORG. TAX REV. 106 (2016).

barring the Schedule B requirement). A New York challenge to this requirement failed. *Citizens United v. Schneiderman*, 115 F. Supp. 3d 457 (S.D. N.Y. 2015).

E. THE EFFECT OF THIS ACTIVITY ON §501(c)(3)s

This major shift of employing noncharitable §501(c) groups in electoral politics has not had a direct effect on §501(c)(3)s because they cannot engage in political campaign activity. And yet, it has already had and will continue to have an indirect effect. For example, in 2013–2015, §501(c)(3)s faced long delays in gaining recognition for exemption due to the IRS's backlog of applications for exemption for §501(c)(4) organizations that spilled over into other types of §501(c) organizations. By 2015, the IRS had reduced this backlog by having small organizations file Form 1023-EZ, which streamlines the application process considerably. Unfortunately, the process may be too streamlined, with 37 % of the approvals going to organizations that should not qualify as §501(c)(3)s.[48] Given the difficulty in revoking exemptions, it appears that the IRS may have solved one problem by creating an even more intractable one.[49]

The controversy surrounding "dark money" is also of concern for §501(c)(3)s for at least four reasons. First, if and when the IRS provides guidance as to the meaning of terms surrounding political activity, the rules are likely to apply to all §501(c) organizations. The 2013 attempt to define candidate-related political activity for §501(c)(4) organizations (described in the Colvin testimony, *supra*), would have classified nonpartisan political activity, such as voter registration drives, as campaign activity. That proposal was so controversial that it is unlikely to appear in the next set of regulations, but it underscores the importance of these issues for §501(c)(3)s. Of particular concern is whether future rules concerning donor anonymity will also apply to §501(c)(3)s. At this point, it seems implausible, but still possible, that the rules will be drawn in such a way as to eliminate donor anonymity for all 501(c) organizations, not simply the politically active ones.

Second, the controversy has led some to argue that the political campaign prohibition for §501(c)(3)s should be removed altogether. As discussed earlier in this chapter, many churches have already openly engaged in political campaign activity, with the hope that they can challenge this restriction in court. The confusion surrounding the rules and the seeming paralysis of the IRS with regard resolving it have undoubtedly also led other nonprofits to violate the campaign intervention prohibition simply because they believe they can get away with it.

The third concern is related to the second. The *Citizens United* case has led some to wonder whether that case has opened the door for reconsideration of *Regan v. Taxation With Representation of Washington*, 461 U.S. 540 (1983) and *Branch Ministries v. Rossotti*, 211 F.3d 137 (D.C. Cir. 2000), both of which appear earlier in this chapter. To recap, *TWR* upheld the §501(c)(3) "no

---

[48] National Taxpayer Advocate, *Annual Report to Congress 2015* (Jan. 6, 2016).
[49] Chapter 4, Part XII discusses Form 1023-EZ, and Chapter 13 the revocation process.

substantial part" lobbying restriction, partly because the First Amendment does not require Congress to subsidize lobbying. *Branch Ministries* upheld the §501(c)(3) prohibition on political campaign activities for a church because that prohibition did not forbid the church from engaging in political speech. Revocation of its tax exemption might lead to fewer funds with which to pursue its mission, but the Supreme Court has held that such a burden is not constitutionally significant. *Branch Ministries* at 142. *Citizens United*, on the other hand, overruled FECA provisions preventing corporations from using treasury funds to advocate for or against political candidates, on the ground that political speech does not lose its First Amendment protection simply because its source is a corporation. 558 U.S. 310, 342-343(2010).

Citizens United interpreted the First Amendment in the context of FECA, and the other two cases described above interpreted it under the IRC.[50] Thus, any discussion of whether *Citizens United* will ultimately overturn those holdings must recognize that different statutes with different policies are in play. For a discussion of this issue, *see* Miriam Galston, *When Statutory Regimes Collide: Will* Wisconsin Right to Life *and* Citizens United *Invalidate Federal Tax Regulation of Campaign Activity?* 13 U. PENN. J. CONST'L LAW 867 (2011) (concluding "the impact of the political prohibition will not be deemed a burden as a matter of constitutional law"); Lloyd Hitoshi Mayer, *Charities and Lobbying: Institutional Rights in the Wake of* Citizens United, 10 ELECTION L.J. 407, 418-419 (2011 (*Citizens United* does not undermine the lobbying limit for charities); Paul Weitzel, *Protecting Speech from the Heart: How* Citizens United *Strikes Down Political Speech Restrictions on Churches and Charities*, 16 TEX. REV. OF LAW & POL. 155 (2011) (concluding that *Citizens United* will ultimately overrule *TWR*). *See also* Ellen Aprill, *Regulating the Political Speech of Noncharitable Exempt Organizations after* Citizens United, 10 ELECTION L. J. 363 (2011).

Finally, and perhaps most important, the average person cannot tell the difference between a §501(c)(3) and another form of tax-exempt organization. Even though charities cannot engage in political campaign activity, the general public is likely to notice only that "nonprofits" are funding campaigns. Unless those nonprofits remain scrupulously honest, and perhaps even if they do, the fallout from negative publicity to the nonprofit sector in general and §501(c)(3)s in particular could be quite large.

NOTES AND QUESTIONS

1. Should §501(c) organizations be forbidden from engaging in political campaign activity? Alternatively, should they be allowed to do so, but be

---

[50] *Branch Ministries* examined the free exercise clause of the First Amendment and *TWR* the freedom of speech clause to determine whether provisions of the tax code were constitutional. *Citizens United* used a First Amendment freedom of speech analysis to determine whether a provision of FECA was constitutional.

required to report their donors? Would the test that the Bright Lines Initiative is proposing help solve the problem, or is all of this much ado about nothing?

2. Those who are concerned about the lack of clarity surrounding political campaign activity and the increase of "dark money" flowing into the political process have suggested other legal doctrines that could curb this activity. For example, in 2016, Marcus Owens, former director of the Exempt Organizations Division of the IRS, predicted that the IRS Criminal Justice Division or the Justice Department would challenge some of the misleading Forms 990 that §501(c)(4) organizations had filed. He cited a report, for instance, that suggested the National Rifle Association (NRA) had understated its political spending by millions of dollars. He also noted that many of these organizations appear to be violating the private benefit doctrine, which applies to §501(c)(4)s as well as to §501(c)(3)s. Paul Barton, *Pressure Building for Criminal Probe into Political 501(c)(4)s?* 77 EXEMPT ORG. TAX REV. 341 (2016). A third possibility is a challenge to the FEC's decision to allow groups like Crossroads GPS to choose the §501(c)(4) route. Paul Barton, *Group Portrays Case as Last Hope Against Dark Money,* 77 EXEMPT ORG. TAX REV. 339 (2016).

3. In late 2015, Congress passed the omnibus spending bill for fiscal 2016. It included a provision prohibiting the IRS from producing new regulations governing the political activities of §501(c)(4)s during 2016.[51] Why do you think Congress made this decision?

4. According to the Center for Responsive Politics, several §501(c) organizations have spent more than 50 % of their expenditures on political activity (http://www.opensecrets.org/outsidespending/nonprof_pcts.php). *See also* Will Tucker, *Two Dozen Dark Money Groups Busted 50 Percent Cap on Political Spending at Least Once,* Center for Responsive Politics (Dec. 9, 2015) (naming several of these organizations, including two that were in the 80%–90% level, and stating that only one, a liberal organization, had been denied exemption).

5. For further reading, *see* Paul C. Barton, *States Pass Washington in Policing Political Nonprofits,* 77 EXEMPT ORG. TAX REV. 106 (2016); Donald B. Tobin, *Citizens United and Taxable Entities: Will Taxable Entities Be the New Stealth Dark Money?* 49 VAL. U. L. REV. 583 (2015); Ellen P. Aprill, *The Section 527 Obstacle to Meaningful Section 501(c)(4) Regulation,* 13 PITT. TAX REV. 43 (2015); Roger Colinvaux, *Political Activity Limits and Tax Exemption: A Gordian's Knot,* 34 VA. TAX REV. 1 (2014); Alex Seitz-Wald, *Watchdog: Koch-Backed Group Bending Tax Code,* NATIONAL JOURNAL (Nov. 5, 2013) [discussing political activities of a §501(c)(6)]; Lloyd Hitoshi Mayer, *Nonprofits, Politics, and Privacy,* 62 CASE WEST. L. REV. 801 (2012).

---

[51] Paul C. Barton, *Budget Deal Will Halt IRS Nonprofit Rulemaking on Political Activities,* 77 EXEMPT ORG. TAX REV. 105 (2016)

CHAPTER 12

ACCOUNTABILITY

Purposes of this chapter:

- Define "nonprofit accountability"
- Familiarize students with state and federal laws regarding accountability
- Familiarize students with extralegal means for nonprofit accountability
- Expose students to Form 990
- Use Form 990 to review issues in the book

To think about as you read:

As you read the materials below, think about whether a satisfactory definition of "nonprofit accountability" exists. How important is it to have the rules that we have? Are there sufficient rules, or could these accountability rules actually be doing more harm than good? Are we diverting nonprofits from their mission when we ask them to complete too many reports? As the executive director of a §501(c)(3) organization, would you have a different view of these issues if you were the commissioner of the Tax-Exempt and Government Entities Division of the Internal Revenue Service (IRS)?

I. WHAT IS "NONPROFIT ACCOUNTABILITY"?

Section 501(c)(3) organizations receive their tax-exempt status because they provide a public benefit to society, and, as such, they remain accountable to the public. Their primary reporting document is Form 990, which organizations must make available to the public. This chapter discusses accountability rules, efforts made by the sector to self-police, and the IRS and state roles in enforcing these rules. It culminates with an exercise that should familiarize you with Form 990. You will be asked to examine an existing Form 990 and complete it based on hypothetical facts. This assignment will allow you to understand how the IRS gathers information about virtually every federal tax issue discussed in this book and to determine for yourself whether Form 990 is an effective accountability tool.

PETER SWORDS, NONPROFIT ACCOUNTABILITY: THE SECTOR'S RESPONSE TO GOVERNMENT REGULATION

Norman A. Sugarman Memorial Lecture, Mandel Center for Nonprofit Organizations, Case Western Reserve University, (March 16, 1999)

Before proceeding further, it will be useful to get clear on what we mean by nonprofit accountability. I like to approach this subject in terms of a continuum. At the left end of the continuum, I put improper diversions of money and assets into private hands, money and assets that would otherwise have been spent or applied to advance the exempt purposes of the organization from which the funds were improperly diverted. Included here are instances of stealing, quasi-looting, and flat out fraud as when a group sets up an entirely bogus "charity" to solicit funds all of which end up in the organizers' private hands with no charitable purpose at all being served. Also included are improper acts of self-dealing or payments of excessive compensation to key employees. I have found it useful to refer to these kinds of abuses as raising issues of negative accountability. At the other end of the continuum are issues about whether an organization is effective in doing what it sets out to do; whether what it sets out to do is worth supporting; or whether it is efficient at what it does. These issues of worthwhileness and effectiveness I refer to as positive accountability.

... I believe that when people think about nonprofit accountability what usually comes to mind is what I have been calling positive accountability. The thought goes something like this. Tens of billions of dollars are transferred each year to nonprofits and there is no market or voters to exercise discipline to assure that they are providing something of value to society. Nonprofits are accountable to no one but their boards and few boards make the effort to assure that their groups are being productive. In recognition of this problem many believe that there is a need to create effective measures so we can tell which groups merit support and which groups do not. These issues are terribly important and all the work going on to develop new measures, the experiments with outcome funding and the like, is to be applauded. But this is not my topic today.

My topic involves abuses—what I have referred to as negative accountability concerns.... There is more involved . . . than merely extirpating abuses. I believe that negative accountability issues go to the heart of what we mean by charitable. A charitable purpose is one that promotes no private gain. It is one that also promotes a public purpose but the breadth of what public purpose has come to mean under charitable trust and federal income tax law is enormously broad and nearly all of the cases where the issue of an organization's "charitableness" is raised have involved the question of whether or not there has been improper private gain. Indeed, at the heart of our definition of "charity" lies the nondistribution constraint, namely, the rule that money or assets of a charity must not be improperly transferred into private hands to advance private gain. Virtually all of negative accountability abuses instance violations of the nondistribution constraint. To the extent that our two generic regulatory agencies [the IRS and the state charities offices—*Ed.*] are enforcing negative accountability dictates, they are enforcing the nondistribution constraint and thus are assuring that charities keep charitable.

Thus, most broadly conceived, I am suggesting that the sector has an interest in assuring that its two generic regulatory agencies be strengthened to assure that the charitable sector remains charitable.

NOTES AND QUESTIONS

1. Professor Evelyn Brody has suggested one reason why nonprofit accountability is so elusive:

   Instead of searching for a "trustworthy" organizational form, we can ask the more complex question, "To whom is the nonprofit accountable?" In a business firm, "accountability" is the mechanism by which the corporate board and management (the "agents") answer to the shareholders (the "principals"). Accountability also exists in nonbusiness principal-agent relationships; for example, politicians answer to the electorate. In the nonprofit sector, however, accountability raises difficult questions because, . . . in most nonprofits there is no clear category of principals. Under law, the nonprofit firm is not the agent of a particular donor or client or beneficiary. As a result, most state nonprofit laws, perhaps without intending to, create agents without principals.

   Evelyn Brody, *Agents Without Principals: The Economic Convergence of the Nonprofit and For-Profit Organizational Forms*, 40 N.Y.L. SCH. L. REV. 457 (1996).

2. Jon Christensen identified other questions about accountability in a 2004 New York Times article: "Yet even the majority who think that NGO's[1] should be accountable do not agree on how to accomplish that goal. Should donors or recipients judge success? Should achievement be measured by those within the organization or by an independent watchdog? And what exactly should be measured? Short-term improvements or harder-to-assess long-term investments? Compiled statistics or individual interviews?" Jon Christensen, *Asking the Do-Gooders to Prove They Do Good*, N.Y. TIMES, Jan. 3, 2004, p. B-9. How would you answer Christensen's questions?

3. "Nonprofit accountability" is a major hot button in Congress and the nonprofit sector, but few people take time to define the term. A 2005 article in *Nonprofit Quarterly* suggested that accountability is "multidimensional" and its effects vary from one organization to another. Following is an excerpt from that article describing the complexity of nonprofit accountability, as well as Figure 12-1, which illustrates that complexity.

---

[1] [NGO stands for "nongovernmental organizations."—*Ed.*]

Figure 12-1
EZ Map of Nonprofit Regulatory Environment

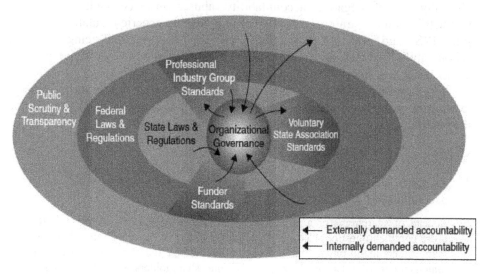

[T]he basic structure of [the regulatory] environment includes:

- A nonprofit board's own practices for ensuring that the organization is properly accountable to its stakeholders.
- The standards promulgated by a self-regulating professional group; these may be used to accredit the whole organization or various parts for a particular type of work.
- The voluntary ethics and accountability standards programs promulgated by organizations such as state associations of nonprofits, the Better Business Bureau, or the Evangelical Council for Financial Accountability.
- The various requirements (be they rigorous, modest, or whimsical) attached to grants and contracts by intermediary funding organizations, foundations, or government agencies.
- State charitable registration requirements implemented by the charities divisions of state attorneys general. Resources for monitoring and enforcement among these offices vary widely, and 12 states have no registration.
- The filing and annual reporting requirements of the IRS and the federal government.
- The increased scrutiny of the public made possible by the National Center for Charitable Statistics, GuideStar, charity watchdog organizations, and the press.... "

Ruth McCambridge, *Is Accountability the Same as Regulation? Not Exactly*, 12 NONPROFIT Q. 3-4 (2005).

4. For more on the definition of accountability, see Tracey M. Coule, *Nonprofit Governance and Accountability: Broadening the Theoretical Perspective*, 44

NONPROFIT VOLUNTARY SECTOR Q. 75 (2015).*See also* Alnoor Ebrahim, *The Many Faces of Nonprofit Accountability*, in D. Renz (ed.), THE JOSSEY-BASS HANDBOOK OF NONPROFIT LEADERSHIP AND MANAGEMENT (third edition), 110-121 (Jossey-Bass, 2010); Kenneth Anderson, *What NGO Accountability Means—and Does Not Mean*, 103 AM. J. INT'L L. 170 (2009); James A. Joseph, *Redefining Accountability*, FOUND. NEWS & COMMENT. 31 (2006).

II. FEDERAL ACCOUNTABILITY RULES

The main federal tool for ensuring that tax-exempt public charities remain accountable to the public is Form 990. All nonchurch tax-exempt entities must file some version of this form on or before the 15th day of the fifth month following the end of their fiscal year. Private foundations file Form 990-PF. The smallest public charities, those with gross receipts of $50,000 or less, file a public notice called Form 990-N. Charities with gross receipts less than $200,000 and total assets less than $500,000 file Form 990-EZ, and those above that threshold file Form 990. Any organization that fails to file a version of Form 990 for three consecutive years automatically loses its tax-exempt status.

Form 990-N is an electronic form that requires an employer identification number, the tax year, an organization's legal name and mailing address, the name and address of a principal officer, the organization's website address (if applicable), and a confirmation that the organization's gross receipts are $50,000 or less. The form must be accessed and prepared through the IRS website at www.irs.gov/charities.

Form 990-EZ core form is 4 pages long. It asks questions about an organization's finances and about activities that could jeopardize that organization's tax exemption, incur other taxes, or both. Some organizations filing Form 990-EZ will also need to complete some of the Form 990 schedules described below.

Form 990, which larger organizations file, includes an 11-page core form with 16 additional schedules. The form gathers information that will help the IRS understand an organization's operations and monitor the issues that could jeopardize its tax exemption. The core form and the schedules are outlined below. The complete form, including IRS instructions and educational material, can be found online at www.irs.gov/charities.

Once the form has been filed with the IRS, it becomes a public document, and public charities must provide copies of the form upon request. The GuideStar website publishes these forms at http://www.guidestar.org.

Form 990 was revamped extensively in 2008, and in 2015, the Advisory Committee on Tax Exempt and Government Entities (ACT) studied how well the changes were working and made suggestions for improvement. Following are (1) an excerpt from that report, (2) some IRS tips for completing the form accurately and effectively, and (3) a discussion of Part VI, the most controversial part of the form.

TAX EXEMPT AND GOVERNMENT ENTITIES, ADVISORY COMMITTEE ON TAX-EXEMPT AND GOVERNMENT ENTITIES (ACT), 2015 REPORT OF RECOMMENDATIONS (JUNE 2015)

The Revenue Act of 1943 created the first requirement for tax-exempt organizations to file an annual information return. The use of the term "information return" is not coincidental, as the information return filed by exempt organizations is much more than just a tax return, with a host of questions and schedules designed to provide the IRS and the public with information on the organization's programs, governance, officers and directors, compensation, related parties, and grant-making activities. The annual information return requirement is currently embodied in Section 6033 of the Internal Revenue Code of 1986. . . .

The forms that most tax-exempt organizations must use to comply with the annual information return requirement are the Form 990 (Return of Organization Exempt from Income Tax), Form 990-EZ (Short Form Return of Organization Exempt from Income Tax) or (more recently) Form 990-N (e-Postcard). Certain tax-exempt organizations are subject to special return filing requirements. Private foundations submit their information to the IRS on a Form 990-PF (Return of Private Foundation).

Many exempt organizations are excepted from these filing requirements, including churches, their integrated auxiliaries, conventions of associations of churches, and the exclusively religious activities of a religious order. State institutions (including state colleges and universities), instrumentalities of United States, and schools affiliated with a church or operated by a religious order are not subject to the Form 990 filing requirements. Organizations that are part of a group exemption and included on a group return filed by the central or parent organization do not have to separately file a Form 990. The IRS also has the discretion under Section 6033(a)(3)(B) to relieve additional organizations from the Form 990 filing requirements where it determines the filing is not necessary to the efficient administration of the internal revenue laws, which it has done, for example, for government units and affiliates of governmental units.

Of the 1,052,495 active Section 501(c)(3) organizations in 2013, approximately 38.1 percent filed a Form 990 or 990-EZ in 2013. . . .

The core of the Form 990 requests information on the following:

1. Basic facts about the filer
2. The types of programs the filer offers and the amounts spent on them.
3. The filer's board members, the organization's governance structure, and whether the filer changed in any significant way during the year
4. The filer's income and sources of support.
5. The filer's expenses.

6. The amount paid to the filer's top earners and salary information on these earners.

7. Information on net assets.

8. Information on transactions with insiders and information on excess benefit transactions during the year.

9. The tax-exempt status of the filer.

10. Information on the filer's lobbying activities. . . .

At the time of this report, only the very largest exempt organizations, both by asset size and number of employees, are required to electronically file the Form 990. . . . [L]arge organizations with assets of more than $10 million and which are required to file more than 250 returns during the year must e-file the Form 990. The very smallest exempt organizations are subject to an electronic filing requirement, as the Form 990-N must be filed online, although these organizations have the option of filing, either electronically or on paper, a Form 990 or Form 990-EZ. Other exempt organizations filing a Form 990 may choose, but are not required, to electronically file. . . .

Federal and state regulators, and various segments of the general public each use Form 990 for different – though complementary – purposes.

1. Government

a. Federal agencies. The primary purpose of Form 990 is enforcement of federal tax law and to meet the statutory information return requirement for tax-exempt organizations. The form generates information that the IRS may use to assess whether the filing organization continues to comply with the requirements for tax-exempt status. It provides the IRS with information that may trigger an audit or other contact with a filing organization.

The IRS Research Analysis and Statistics (RAS) Division maintains a database with images of the Forms 990 as they are received. Paper returns are scanned, while data from electronic filings are 'rendered' into images. . . . The Statistics of Income (SOI) Division of IRS, which is a part of RAS, uses data from both the paper returns and electronic filings to select, on a weekly basis, stratified data samples for published Form 990 series studies. SOI performs data analysis and develops datasets made available to the public on www.IRS.gov under TaxStats. Datasets from SOI are used for research and estimation work by the IRS, the Department of Treasury, and the Congress.

b. State Charity and Other State Officials use Form 990 data primarily for issues of governance, charitable purpose, and fundraising regulation. . . .Most states require a copy of the Form 990 only from exempt organizations that solicit funds in their state. . . .

Section 6104(c) allows the IRS to share certain information on charitable organizations with state charity regulators such as revenue agents' reports on proposed revocations of tax-exempt status and notices of deficiencies. However, state officials are subject to strict procedures to safeguard the confidentiality of taxpayer data. The lack of clarity surrounding how states can use data from the IRS to build their own cases, and the criminal penalties attached to improper disclosure of the data, have prevented most state charity regulators from incorporating IRS data in their investigations.

2. Other Users

Because the Form 990 includes questions about a tax-exempt organization's mission, exempt activities, officers' compensation, governance, finances, and investments, the data the form collects are of interest to academics, independent organizations that provide services to the sector, nonprofits themselves, the media, and the general public, including donors and potential donors. Uses of the data include identification of trends in the sector, development of products and services to help improve nonprofits, and research on particular exempt organizations by donors and potential donors.

a. Researchers and entrepreneurs. Private sector organizations use Form 990 data for both research and entrepreneurial purposes. In some cases they make data available for free, and in others they charge a fee to allow others to use the data and tools they've developed for using the data.

- GuideStar extracts Form 990 data from IRS image files and makes the digitized, searchable images available to IRS, researchers, nonprofits, and the public. Nonprofits can update their organization's profile with additional information about their activities. In conjunction with BBB Wise Giving Alliance and Independent Sector, GuideStar offers a "Charting Impact" tool that can help a nonprofit tell its story, including its goals and progress in achieving them. In addition, GuideStar also provides additional services through a range of data sets and supplemental products.

- The Foundation Center uses IRS data in developing its database of grant information on private foundations for use by grant seekers and researchers. In addition to providing information on grantors and grant recipients, it provides links to copies of multiple years of Form 990 and 990-PF. The forms are searchable through a tool called 990 Finder. The Center also conducts research on trends in grantmaking for the nonprofit sector.

- The National Center for Charitable Statistics (NCCS), a part of the National Center on Nonprofits and Philanthropy (NCNP) at the Urban Institute, cross-checks SOI data samples against published data files from IRS, fixes inconsistencies where it can, and adds classification codes. NCCS also . . . capture[s] supplemental information such as organization purposes and programs and more detail on revenues, expenses, assets and liabilities, and governance. These data are made available on the web for use by the general public through the easy to use Table Wizard/Report Builder, and to the research community through the more sophisticated DataWeb. . .

- Other websites and organizations work with Form 990 data in providing services to the sector. Examples include GiveSmart, Charity Navigator, GiveWell, Great Nonprofits, and Charity Blossom.

- Financial services firms seeking potential customers may use 990 data.
- Compensation consultants use information available on Form 990 for comparability data to determine the reasonableness of compensation of organizations' officers, key employees and independent contractors.

b. Media representatives. Reporters use Form 990 information for stories on charitable giving, nonprofit governance, and other activities of exempt organizations.

c. The general public, including donors, potential donors and grantmakers to charitable organizations, use data from the 990 to learn about the nonprofit sector and/or about particular organizations in the sector. IRS provides a search tool, Exempt Organizations Select Check, that allows users to check on an exempt Section 501(c)(3) organization's designated federal tax-exempt status. . . .

The IRS also makes information about exempt organizations available through the Exempt Organizations Business Master File Extract, which contains more detailed information about organizations, such as their 501(c) sub-section, filing requirement, and financial data based on their Form 990 filing information.

It is also possible to view a tax-exempt organization's Form 990 on GuideStar and a public charity's Form 990 may be available on the web sites of various state charity regulators. Some exempt organizations, typically for transparency reasons, choose to post their Forms 990 on their own web sites. As a result, individuals with access to the internet can view an exempt organization's Form 990 and draw their own conclusions from the information they find there.

d. Form 990 filing organizations also may use Form 990 data to compare their organization's structure, management, compensation or performance with that of other organizations. Additionally, they may use the Form 990 as a communication tool to provide information about their activities to donors, potential donors and the public. Many exempt organizations post their Form 990 on their website.

FORM 990 FILING TIPS—AUDIO WEBCAST (MAY 8, 2014)

http://www.irsvideos.gov/Form990FilingTips/

[A]s you begin preparation of your organization's Form 990, you might ask yourself, who will be reading this document? . . . Your organization's Form 990 can help tell your story and highlight your accomplishments for [a] very diverse set of audiences. Since the 2008 redesign, most organizations can no longer simply rely on their accountant or their treasurer to complete the Form 990. Instead, Form 990 prep is best approached as a group effort.

You'll save a lot of time and aggravation if you delegate preparation of sections of the Form 990 to those with specific knowledge about the organization's operations that a particular part of the form is asking about. So, you could send the governance questions, which we find in part six, to members of your board of directors or your executive committee. You could send the financial sections of the report to your CFO or your treasurer or your outside CPA. And you would probably want to send a program and activity-related questions to the organization's CEO or its program staff. . . .

Tip 1

Tip number one is to use the tools we provide in the Form 990 instructions. First off, the sequencing list in the instructions walks through what we think is the most efficient order in which to fill out the form.

An example is to complete parts one and two last, even though they are the first parts you see, because parts one and two are largely financial summaries. The order of the parts on the form is for the sake of the reader, not the preparer. The glossary defines over 100 key terms used throughout the Form 990. Whenever you see a word or a phrase in bold type in the instructions, you can check the glossary to find out what that word or phrase means. The instructions also contain 11 appendices that provide helpful explanations and background information on topics such as how to determine gross receipts, requirements for public disclosure of the Form 990-series returns, what is an excess benefit transaction, rules regarding receiving and receipting charitable contributions.

Tip 2

. . . On pages 85 and 86 of the Form 990 instructions, you'll find a list of the required schedules, forms and attachments. . . .[B]efore you file your Form 990, if you're doing this in paper, you'll want to assemble the package of forms and schedules and attachments in the following order.

Tip 3

[Y]our Form 990 team [should] pay particularly close attention to parts five and six and Schedule A. . . . Many have asked why these schedules are necessary. The IRS believes that there's a close link between good governance and tax compliance. Organizations that adopt and implement sound risk management policies greatly improve their ability to be tax compliant. Conversely, most violations of tax-exempt law that we have seen in examinations have resulted, in part, from failure to exercise good governance.

One purpose of Part V, Part VI and Schedule A serves as a self-audit and helps organizations to consider which policies and procedures can assist them with managing risk most effectively; for instance, a good record-retention policy, a conflict of interest policy, and compensation policies are tools to reduce the risk of prohibited private inurement.

Schedule A, required for 501(c)(3) organizations, and Sections 4947(a)(1), non-exempt charitable trusts, specifically addresses the organization's compliance with the public charity status and the public support test. Schedule A should also be used as a planning tool to help an organization develop policies and procedures to maintain its charity status and meet the support test in succeeding years. . . .

In general, a governing board that is proactive, informed, engaged and independent will manage an organization in a more efficient manner. The adoption of sound risk management policies and procedures will help an organization to comply with the law and achieve its mission more effectively, whether or not it is required to file a Form 990. . . .

Tip 4

The increased narrative reporting in the redesigned Form 990 gives filers an opportunity to highlight their accomplishments, for instance, part three allows an organization to describe its three largest program service accomplishments as measured by total expenses incurred.

What we suggest is that you use specific measurements to describe your organization's accomplishments, such as the number of people that you provided assistance to or the number of events you held or the number of publications you issued.

You can also describe donated services or the free use of materials in the accomplishment of these program services. You can't report these items elsewhere in the financial section, so if you get some free equipment, free service, you want to report it in part three under program service accomplishments.

Now, there may not be enough space in part three to describe all of your accomplishments, so if you want to, you can use Schedule O to tell your story. Schedule O is a blank schedule used for narrative responses to Form 990 questions. Incidentally, the Schedule O is the only one of the 16 schedules that must be filed by all Form 990 filers each year, and that's because several questions require all filers to submit a narrative answer on Schedule O. . . .

Tip 5

Tip five is compensation. . . . Even if the organization did not compensate any of its officers and governing board members, you are required to report all of them in part seven.

If the organization did not compensate any officers or directors, check the box above the Part VII compensation table that reads "Neither the organization nor any related organization compensated any current officer or director or trustee." This will save you the work of filling in the compensation columns D, E, and F with zeros, and will let the IRS know that you didn't make a mistake by leaving the Part VII table blank.

There are six categories of persons to report in Part VII, Section A, and we'll list these people in the following order: First comes individual trustees and directors. Then institutional trustees, followed by officers. Then key employees. You only report the top 20 key employees. Then the top five highest compensated employees who are not officers, directors, trustees, or key employees who received over $100,000 in compensation reported on Form W-2 or Form 1099 by the organization and/or a related organization. And then persons compensated more than $10,000 in exchange for past services provided as a director or trustee. And, finally, the top five independent contractors that received more than $100,000 in payment. . . .

[F]or each person that you list in Part VII, column A, you will list reportable compensation from the filing organization in column C. And by "reportable compensation," we mean the amounts found in Box 5 of that person's W-2 or the Box 7 of the Form 1099 miscellaneous, if that's what they received from the organization. Next in column E you'll report the person's reportable compensation from all related organizations. There is one significant exception for reporting in column E: . . . You only need to list or show reportable compensation from a related organization to a particular person if it exceeded $10,000 during the tax year.

. . . [I]n column F, your organization should estimate and report most other types of compensation, and this means compensation that doesn't appear on a Form W-2 or a 1099, and this would be both from your organization and from the related organizations. Items of other compensation includes things such as housing benefits, split dollar life insurance benefits, tuition assistance, travel and moving expenses, and sick and vacation leave that you've cashed out. However, column F has a $10,000 per item exception. . . .

An organization must complete Schedule J only if it lists in Part VII a person who received total compensation over $150,000; or if it received compensation from an individual or an unrelated organization for services that were rendered to the filing organization; or third, was reported in Part VII as a former officer, director, trustee, key employee, or highest compensated employee. Those are the categories of people that would trigger a Schedule J filing requirement.

Tip 6

E-filing, put it simply, saves time and it can also simplify your preparation process, and it reduces the IRS processing time, which would, of course, save taxpayer money. Because e-filing systems and commercial software include error detection, e-filing also reduces errors which results in more accurate and complete reporting and fewer penalties.. . . [T]here are certain large organizations that must file electronically. . . .

If an organization . . . fails to file by its due date . . ., it may incur late filing penalties. For an organization whose annual gross receipts are equal to or less than a million, the penalty is $20 per day for each day the return is late up to a maximum of $10,000 or 5 percent of the organization's gross receipts, whichever is less. For large organizations whose gross receipts exceed a million dollars annually, the penalty is $100 a day up to a maximum of $50,000. Penalties for incomplete returns, such as returns that don't include a required schedule, are identical to penalties for late filed returns. And of course, there's the ultimate penalty, which is automatic revocation for failure to file three consecutive annual returns.

ELIZABETH SCHMIDT, NONPROFIT BOARD MEMBERS—DON'T LET THE NEW FORM 990 CATCH YOU FLAT-FOOTED

Charity Channel (Sept. 17, 2008)

As a nonprofit board member, you have plenty of things to worry about, and so it's tempting to leave all aspects of the tax information form, the Form 990, to the organization's accountant. Don't.

The form has an entire . . . section, Part VI, devoted to governance, which, along with other sections, focuses on board structure and current "best practices." Although many of these practices are not legally required, the Form 990 is a public document that donors, funders, clients and other constituents of your organization can see. Most boards will therefore want to follow these best practices, if only to avoid embarrassing themselves to their constituents or drawing the attention of the IRS auditors. They are likely to end up running much stronger organizations as well.

What should the board of directors know about the . . . Form 990? I suggest you familiarize yourself with the document, examine your organization's board structure, update your policies and procedures, and then examine your practices. In other words, if your organization is already following best practices, there won't be many changes. If it isn't, the board should get to work.

1. Board Review of Form 990

The . . . Form 990 asks whether the governing body received a copy of the form before it was filed with the IRS. It also requires all organizations to describe the process, if any, the organization uses to review the Form. Organizations that can demonstrate that their boards examined and discussed the Form 990 before filing it are far more likely to have informed and engaged boards than those that answer "no" to these questions. They are also more likely to file accurate forms. Those that have not given their board the opportunity to examine the Form 990 are unlikely to convince their constituents that they are furthering their organization's mission.

2. Board Structure

The . . . form asks several questions about the board's structure. It requires a determination of the number of voting members on the board, the number of independent directors, and a list of those directors, officers or key employees who have family and business relationships with each other. The instructions to the Form 990 define these terms specifically, but the general idea is that board members who do business with the nonprofit or have family or business relationships with each other have the potential for a conflict of interest. Disclosure of such relationships is more likely to encourage decisions that are in the best interest of the organization rather than in the interests of the individuals.

The form also asks whether the organization has members who either elect the governing body or approve its decisions. It asks whether the board has delegated any management duties to a management company or other person, and the instructions ask for information about decisions the board has delegated to an executive committee. Finally, it asks questions about whether the organization has a committee that selects and oversees the work of an independent accountant that compiles, reviews, or audits its financial statements.

As the board prepares its answers to these decisions, it should discuss whether the current board composition and organization create the best situation for this particular organization. Additionally, if it uses an independent accountant, the board should ensure that a committee hires and supervises the work of that accountant. Finally, if the board makes any significant changes to its governing documents, it must notify the IRS of those changes.

3. Policies

The Form 990 asks several questions about the organization's policies and procedures. Not all these policies are appropriate for every organization, but even the smallest organizations should institute some of them. Following are the policies that are mentioned in the Form 990.

a. *Conflict of interest policy.* The Form 990 asks whether the organization has a written conflict of interest policy. If the answer is yes, the organization must answer whether officers, directors and key employees are required to disclose annually all interests that could lead to a conflict. The organization must also explain what it does to ensure the policy is monitored and enforced.

b. *Whistleblower policy and document retention and destruction policy.* Federal law protects whistleblowers and forbids document destruction in certain instances. All organizations should have policies that meet these requirements.

c. *Compensation policy.* The Form 990 requires a description of the process used to determine compensation for the organization's top management official, its other officers, and its key employees. The IRS is keenly interested in excess compensation, and an organization with paid employees should adopt such a policy. Section 4958 of the Internal Revenue Code sets forth a process that will provide the organization with a rebuttable presumption of reasonableness.

d. *Expense reimbursement policy.* Organizations that provide special treatment for employees such as first-class travel, maids, and discretionary spending accounts must state whether they have policies in place to ensure that such practices are not abused.

e. *Policy regarding joint ventures.* If the organization has been involved in a joint venture with a taxable entity during the tax year, it must state whether it adopted a written policy or procedure that ensures compliance with tax laws and safeguards the organization's exempt status. If the answer is "no," expect an audit.

f. *Disclosure policies.* The . . . Form 990 asks whether and how your organization discloses the forms that must legally be disclosed—the Form 1023, Form 990, and Form 990-T (if applicable). It also asks whether your organization makes its governing documents (articles of incorporation and bylaws), financial statements, and conflict of interest policy available to the public. Although there is no legal requirement that these later documents be made available to the public, the IRS obviously hopes that organizations will do so, and that once the documents are public, organizations will have strong incentive to follow them.

4. Practices

The IRS is not simply interested in whether tax-exempt organizations have adopted policies. Most questions are constructed so that the organization can only answer "yes" if it actually follows its policies and procedures. The questions about the procedures for board inspection of the Form 990, the compensation policy, and joint venture policies are examples of such questions. The Form 990 also asks whether there has been a contemporaneous documentation of all board and committee meetings. The threat that an organization would have to reveal that it is not following its own policies is a powerful incentive to turn these policies into practice.

The Form 990 is [not] an obscure tax information form. It is . . . a public document that asks so many governance questions that it encourages all boards to examine their structure, policies and practices. , , , [A]ll organizations should begin to determine how to put their best foot forward when they file the . . . form in the future.

NOTES AND QUESTIONS

1. Form 990 can be quite confusing for filers. In 2011, the *Chronicle of Philanthropy* found widespread underreporting of program expenses, often due to misunderstanding of the rules. Lisa Chiu, *Many Charities Don't Tell IRS How Much They Spend on Programs*, CHRONICLE OF PHILANTHROPY (May 5, 2011). The 2015 Report by the Advisory Committee on Tax Exempt and Governmental Entities (ACT), parts of which are reproduced above, recommended the development of a task force "to determine which parts and schedules of the current Form 990 and related instructions should be updated, enhanced, and/or deleted in order to allow a more clear understanding, better accuracy, [and] enhanced consistency of reporting by the various Form 990 filers." 2015 Report, *supra,* at 89. A video, a tutorial, and a book that can help explain this complicated form are Peter Swords, *How to Read the New IRS Form 990* (2011) (http://www.youtube.com/watch?v=cgrxDudlB8M); GuideStar, *Highlights of IRS Form 990* (2016), http://learn .guidestar.org/help/highlights-of-irs-form-990; and Michael Sorrells and

Andrew Lang, Completing Your IRS Form 990: A Guide for, Tax-Exempt Organizations (American Society for Association Executives, 2012).

2. The Sarbanes-Oxley Act, of 2002 was designed to bring better governance and financial controls to large for-profit organizations, as well as to make the chief executive officer (CEO) responsible for the accuracy of certain financial statements. Two Sarbanes-Oxley provisions apply to nonprofit organizations—whistleblower protection and standards regarding document destruction. There has been considerable discussion about whether Sarbanes-Oxley should be extended to nonprofit corporations. Those who oppose such an extension maintain either that Sarbanes-Oxley is so onerous that it would divert time and attention from the organizations' charitable missions or that Form 990, which must be signed by an official of the organization, already provides accountability similar to that which Sarbanes-Oxley provides in the for-profit sector. *See.* John Archer, *This SOX: Combating Public Charity Fraud with Sarbanes-Oxley* (January 20, 2016), available at http://ssrn.com/abstract=2719374; Herbert N. Watkins, *The Sarbanes-Oxley Act and Nonprofit Organizations*, 52 EXEMPT ORG. TAX REV. 267 (2006); Katherine E. David, *Non-Profit Governance in the Wake of Sarbanes-Oxley*, PRAC. TAX LAW (Winter 2007).

3. Part VI of Form 990, added in the 2008 revisions, was controversial because governance issues are traditionally state law concerns. *See e.g.* James Fishman, *Strange Silence: Attorneys General Reaction to the Internal Revenue Service's Corporate Governance Initiative*, paper delivered at Columbia University's conference on The Future of State Charities Regulation (Feb. 2013). The IRS added these questions because it assumed "[t]he absence of appropriate policies and procedures can lead to opportunities for excess benefit transactions, inurement, operation for non-exempt purposes, or other activities inconsistent with exempt status." INSTRUCTIONS TO FORM 990 (2015). A 2015 study validated this assumption. It found that §501(c)(3)s with strong governance systems were less likely to experience fraudulent activity. Erica Harris, Christine Petrovits, and Michelle Yetman, *Why Bad Things Happen to Good Organizations* (2015), available at http://ssrn.com/abstract=2604372 or http://dx.doi.org/10.2139/ssrn .2604372. These authors also published a second study that showed a positive correlation between strong governance and successful fundraising. E. Harris, C. Petrovits, and M. Yetman, *The Effect of Nonprofit Governance on Donations: Evidence from the Revised Form 990*, 90 THE ACCOUNTING REVIEW 579 (2014).

4. For further reading, see Lloyd Hitoshi Mayer and Brendan M. Wilson, *Regulating Charities in the 21st Century: An Institutional Choice Analysis*, 85 CHI-KENT L. REV. 479 (2010), John Mantague, *The Law and Financial Transparency in Churches: Reconsidering the Form 990 Exemption*, 35 CARDOZO L. REV. 203 (2013); Ronald Chester, *Improving Enforcement Mechanisms in the Charitable Sector: Can Increased Disclosure of*

Information Be Utilized Effectively? 40 NEW ENG. L. REV. 447 (2006); Ashby Jones, *With Charity for All?* CORP. COUNS. (Jan. 25, 2005);

III. STATE ACCOUNTABILITY MEASURES

At the state level, the attorney general or another state charity official is charged with overseeing the nonprofit sector and ensuring its accountability. Traditionally, state charity officials have spent the majority of their time and effort collecting information from the nonprofits in their state and trying to prevent fundraising abuses. In the last few years, however, there has been a greater emphasis on state accountability efforts. California passed the California Nonprofit Integrity Act of 2004, and New York tightened its statute in 2013. Chapter 6 covered a lawsuit that all 50 states filed against Cancer Fund of America in 2015 that was settled the following year. This chapter continues this discussion with an article on the state attorney general's role, a summary of a conversation among several charity regulators, and some notes and questions about the state's role in nonprofit accountability.

A. THE ATTORNEY GENERAL'S ROLE

MARION FREMONT-SMITH, ATTORNEY GENERAL OVERSIGHT OF CHARITIES

Hauser Center for Nonprofit Organizations, Working Paper 41 (2007)

The power of the attorney general to regulate charities has its roots in earliest English law. Its origins are to be found in the law of trusts. A trust is valid only if there are beneficiaries existing and able to ensure that the trustees fulfill their duties. An essential element of a charitable trust was, and is today, that its purposes must provide broad public benefit; as a corollary, there can be no specific identifiable beneficiaries who can monitor the trustees' actions and seek to correct abuses of trust. The dilemma was resolved by the common law courts by assigning to the attorney general, acting for the king in his role as parens patriae of the country, the duty to represent the public—as the ultimate beneficiary of all charitable trusts—in assuring that charitable trustees were fulfilling their duties. These included the duty of loyalty under which a trustee is required to act solely in the interest of the beneficiaries, refraining from any self-dealing and assuring that the purposes of the trust are carried out, and the duty of care under which a trustee is required to act prudently and not endanger the trust assets through reckless or negligent acts....

The attorney general's power is not all encompassing. Rather, it is the courts that are empowered to correct abuses, while it is the attorney general's duty to bring abuses to the attention of the court and seek correction. The courts are granted wide power to correct abuses, including removing trustees and appointing successors, ordering restitution, imposing fines, issuing injunctions to prevent continued abuses, and appointing receivers. This is not to say that an attorney general is powerless to correct abuses. In fact, the threat of suit is often as powerful a weapon as actually initiating suit, and parties are entitled to settle issues with the attorney general in order to avoid further legal action.

A concomitant of the power of the attorney general to bring suit to correct abuses by charitable fiduciaries has been a limit on the power of others to bring fiduciaries to account. With only a few exceptions, members of the general public are not permitted to sue charitable fiduciaries for breach of duties; rather this is the exclusive power of the attorney general. The rationales for this doctrine of limited standing have been that individuals will not serve as trustees if they may be subject to suits by disaffected members of the public and concern that private individuals will may [sic] use this power to advance their own ideological policy preferences. Furthermore, individuals may not bring suit to force an attorney general to sue a charity or its fiduciaries for breach of duty.

This description of early common law is also the description of current law governing the oversight powers of the attorney general in Great Britain and in every one of the United States. . . . In a number of states, these powers have been enlarged by statute as an aid to enforcement. Thus, the attorney general must be given notice of legal proceedings brought by or on behalf of a charity if the suit involves breaches of fiduciary duties or the validity of a gift for charitable purposes, a request to change charitable purposes specified by donors or alter methods of administration, or the disposition of a substantial portion of a charity's assets. In some states, notice of a petition to probate a will with charitable gifts must also be given to his office and, as more fully described below, in some states certain charities must register and file financial reports with his office.

B. CONCERNS AMONG STATE CHARITY REGULATORS

In 2005, the *Nonprofit Quarterly* published a conversation among charity regulators from New Hampshire, New York, Pennsylvania, Massachusetts, and California [Editors, *Attorneys General and Nonprofits*, NONPROFIT Q. 44 (2005)]. They spoke of their dual functions—prevention and prosecution—as well as the complexity of the sector, insufficient resources, and the need for greater transparency. Following is a summary of that conversation, and although time has passed and the people in charge of charity regulation may have changed, the issues remain.

Terry Knowles, the Registrar of Charitable Trusts with the New Hampshire Attorney General's Office, described the prevention function:

> The more board training I do the better off I am, because if these organizations are governed properly I'm not going to be looking over the shoulders of the board members.... It is often difficult for public-spirited citizens to recognize the culture of board membership has changed from the time-honored "pillar of the community' model to a new era of responsibility, public accountability, and

increased liability. At the conclusion of my training sessions invariably someone will say, "But we are only volunteers. Do we really have to do all of this?" And the answer today is, of course, "Yes."

Jamie Katz of the Massachusetts Attorney General's Office described the enforcement function:

> We clearly deal first and foremost with inappropriate governance and spending, and improper use of charitable assets, as well as the weak financial systems often found in those situations. Another set of issues revolve around fraudulent solicitation, and solicitations that involve either charities or fundraisers making misrepresentations.... On top of these more traditional problems, over the last 10 or 15 years charities have behaved differently. They have set up relationships with for-profits that were never there before. They have compensated management and trustees in ways that were not used before, and have modeled their behavior on for-profits or fundraised in ways they had not done before. Some of that is necessary and appropriate and has really helped charities perform their missions better and has strengthened their financial base ... [but w]e're seeing diversions of charitable assets and the emergence of systems and structures that do not protect charitable assets.

As Katz noted, the field is becoming more complex, which increases the duties of the state charity officials. Terry Knowles agrees with this assessment:

> There are all sorts of nuances now relating to how charities invest their money, how they carry out their board responsibilities, what level of compensation should or should not be paid to chief executive officers, what constitutes a conflict of interest, and, above all, what is the role of the Attorney General in regulating charitable activity.

But the legal issues are only part of the increased complexity. The number of charities is increasing exponentially, and both journalists and the general public have become much more interested in scrutinizing the works of nonprofit organizations in the last few years.

Unfortunately, the resources devoted to state charity enforcement have not kept up with the complexity of issues or the growth in the sector. As a result, Knowles described her approach as "triage," and Katz likened his approach to that of a traffic cop. He is hoping that charities that learn that the state is cracking down on abuses will hesitate before undertaking a similar type of abuse, just as someone who sees several cars pulled over on the interstate is likely to keep to the speed limit.

One way to deal with insufficient resources is to streamline the process. The state charity officials expressed interest in single-point filing (a single website that charities can use to register in every state in which they do business), electronic filing (which reduces the volume of paperwork and provides digital reports that are accessible to officials and the public alike), and legislation that would allow the IRS to communicate with state charity officials. These changes would help the state charity officials directly, by increasing their efficiency, and indirectly, by making the files more accessible to the public, who in turn become a secondary enforcement mechanism.

NOTES AND QUESTIONS

1. The National State Attorneys Generals Program hosts the Charities Regulation and Oversight Project at Columbia Law School. Its website (http://web.law.columbia.edu/attorneys-general/policy-areas/charities-law-project) includes a considerable amount of information about charities regulation. This program further increased its knowledge base in a 2013 conference on The Future of State Charities Regulation and Enforcement. It has posted the papers presented at that conference online.

2. In 2015, Cindy Lott and Karen Kunstler Goodman undertook a comprehensive, state-by-state analysis of the regulatory landscape of the charitable sector. They found that most state charity offices have either lost staff or stayed at the same level since 2008. Given the dramatic increase in the number of nonprofit organizations, fueled in part by the advent of Form 1023-EZ, they are concerned that these staffing levels are inadequate to prevent and punish abuse and fraud. More than half (62%) of their enforcement cases concern fundraising abuses. They also work to enforce charitable trusts (36%) and examine governance issues (36%). Which tools do they use? Three-fourths of states require charities, fund-raising professionals, or both to register with the state and file financial reports. Approximately 44% also require some form of independent audited financial statements. *See* Charities Project Updates, *Senior Counsel Cindy Lott Presents Findings of Major Research Project at NAAG/NASCO Annual Conference* (October 2015).

3. The National Association of State Charity Officials (NASCO) is an association of the state offices that oversee charitable organizations in the United States. These officials meet annually and communicate throughout the year. NASCO's website http://www.nasconet.org[2], educates nonprofits on their legal obligations and announces, actions against fraudulent and unscrupulous organizations throughout the United States. It also includes links to sites that can help improve nonprofit performance. In early 2016, its initiatives included the previously mentioned lawsuit against the American Cancer Fund and a Single Portal Initiative, both of which were discussed in Chapter 6. Chapter 6 also includes the text of the Charleston Principles and the Model Charitable Solicitations Law, both which NASCO drafted.

4. The IRS policy of complete confidentiality has prevented enforcement agencies from cooperating in the past. In 2003, William Josephson, then chief of the New York attorney general's charities division, told the *Boston Globe* about the time that an IRS agent asked him for a file on a charity that the IRS had lost. The IRS agent was not permitted to identify the charity, however, and asked Josephson to guess which file had been lost. Beth Healy et al., *Foundations' Tax Returns Left Unchecked,* BOSTON GLOBE, Dec. 29, 2003, at A-1.

---

[2] http://nasconet.org, accessed May 22, 2016. The American Cancer lawsuit was settled in March 2016, but NASCO continues to list the lawsuit as one of its initatives in May 2016.

2. The Pension Protection Act of 2006 attempted to fix this problem by allowing the IRS to share information, but it did not go far enough. In 2011, NASCO helped draft a letter, signed by 43 attorneys general, asking Congress to further ease the restrictions against sharing information. A copy of that letter may be found at http://www.nasconet.org/fedstate-information-sharing-letter/naag-info-share-letter/. As of early 2016, however, Congress had not acted.

IV. SELF-REGULATION AS A FORM OF ACCOUNTABILITY

Fortunately, given the scarce resources that state and federal governments have to enforce laws relating to the nonprofit sector, the sector has several built-in functions for self-regulation. As you read the following materials, consider whether these measures are adequate. Is self-regulation actually a better form of accountability than the reports and paperwork that one files with a charity official or the IRS? Or is the movement toward self-regulation and accountability simply a cynical way to forestall additional governmental regulation?

A. UMBRELLA GROUPS

Several groups within the nonprofit sector use education, policy proposals, and certification as ways to promote nonprofit accountability. They recognize that one bad actor can reflect poorly on the entire sector.

For example, Independent Sector, a leadership forum for charities, foundations, and corporate giving programs, has set forth 33 principles that would advance governance and self-regulation in the sector. PRINCIPLES FOR GOOD GOVERNANCE AND ETHICAL PRACTICE: A GUIDE FOR CHARITIES AND FOUNDATIONS (Panel on the Nonprofit Sector 2015). Initially adopted in 2007, the panel updated the principles in 2015 to reflect the changing circumstances in which the charitable sector functions, as well as to reflect new relationships within and between the sectors. Independent Sector also adopted the Guiding Principles for Public Policy on Charitable Giving in 2012 because it recognized the need for internal guidance in this area.

The Council on Foundations is a nonprofit membership association of grant-making foundations and corporations. It calls itself "the voice of philanthropy," providing conferences, publications, and awards that promote best practices among foundations. The Council on Foundations also has a program called the National Standards for U.S. Community Foundations. A growing number of community foundations have adopted these standards, which provide a roadmap for legal, ethical, and effective practices for community foundations. Community foundations that adopt these standards commit to operational excellence in six areas: (1) mission, structure, and governance; (2) resource development; (3) stewardship and accountability; (4) grant making and community leadership; (5)

donor relations; and (6) communications. See the Council on Foundations website, www.cof.org (last visited May 22, 2016).

The National Council of Nonprofit Associations (NCNA) is a network of state and regional nonprofit associations that works to improve nonprofit effectiveness. As with the other umbrella organizations, it holds a conference, publishes information, and promotes policy. NCNA has also released the Nonprofit Constitution, a four-point document that it asks other nonprofit organizations to sign. Signers promise dedication to the betterment of the communities that they serve and a commitment to serve others, and vow to operate with ethics and integrity and to act as a catalyst for change and innovation..NCNA also links to the principles and practices of the state nonprofit associations. *See* the National Council of Nonprofit Associations website, www.ncna.org (accessed May 22, 2016).

B. CHARITY INFORMATION WEBSITES

Another approach to accountability is to publicize certain aspects of a nonprofit's performance. GuideStar, a §501(c)(3) organization that posts Form 990s and Form 990PFs on the Internet, performs this function by providing transparency for these organizations. GuideStar does not rank charities because it assumes that donors' own values will inform their decisions about these charities. It does, however, encourage charitable organizations to provide additional information, beyond their Form 990s, so that they can paint a more complete picture of their organizations than Form 990 alone can do. *See* the Guidestar website, www.guidestar.org. Marion Fremont Smith has called GuideStar "the most important [change in charitable regulation] in terms of assisting both the regulators and the charitable universe, as well as potential donors. . . . [Its] importance . . . cannot be overstated, as . . . the IRS was not capable of providing this information in the early 2000s and . . . it has been subject to budget constraints for at least 20 years that have limited its computer capabilities." Marion Fremont Smith, *The Future of State Charity Regulations*, Columbia Law School Charities Regulation and Oversight Project Policy Conference (2013)

Charity Navigator, the American Institute of Philanthropy, and the Better Business Bureau's Wise Giving Alliance all rate charities. Charity Navigator is an independent charity evaluator that examines the financial returns of America's largest charities. It examines the organizations' financial health and accountability/transparency and then assigns stars, ranging from zero to four, for each organization. *See* www.charitynavigator.org. The American Institute of Philanthropy's Watchdog Service assigns letter grades to large national charities after examining the organizations' management practices, fundraising ratios (amounts spent to raise money), and programmatic ratios (i.e., percentages of funds spent on programs). *See* https://www.charitywatch.org/home. Finally, the Better Business Bureau's Wise Giving Alliance provides ratings on more than 1,200 charities, based on the organizations' governance, effectiveness, financial health, and their solicitation and informational materials.. The Wise Giving

Alliance also offers a charity seal for organizations that meet its standards. Organizations that earn the seal can display it online and in their solicitation materials. *See* the Better Business Bureau's site, www.give.org. These three watchdog groups differ in their methodologies, which makes direct comparison of their rankings impossible.

C. THE NONPROFIT'S OWN BOARD

Effective governance can also be an important component in an organization's positive accountability. A board that nominates and elects strong board members, adheres to its conflict of interest and other ethics policies, and upholds its fiduciary duties is more likely to use its charitable dollars wisely and less likely to engage in illegal or unethical practices.

Chapter 3 discussed the legal requirements for the board of directors of a charitable organization. Legal requirements generally set forth a minimum standard of behavior. In order to meet a positive level of accountability, would it be better to follow governance "best practices" instead of a legal minimum? Is there a difference between these concepts? If so, does the difference affect the organization's accountability? What are the implications of Form 990 on these issues?

D. IMPACT ASSESSMENT AND PERFORMANCE MEASUREMENT

Almost all grant makers require their grantees to report on the way that the grant money is spent and whether the program has been successful. Increasingly, grant makers require reports that show the impact that the grant has had on the population being served rather than a listing of how the money was spent. But measuring the impact of a grant or a nonprofit program is not easy.

The struggle here is a familiar one. Who should decide what impact is important? Will we come up with metrics that are ultimately not very helpful? How can we balance the need for accountability with the real possibility that reporting takes resources away from direct programming that carries out the charitable organization's mission? Are we simply compiling statistics that are filed away and never used to improve nonprofit performance?

Realistically, it is often the donor that determines how the impact will be measured, as the donor holds the purse strings (and hence the power). But such an emphasis on donors can fail to address the needs of the nonprofit organizations and their clients. In fact, Coralie Bryant of Columbia University has found that the nonprofit organizations that are the least dependent on donor financing are often most effective at evaluating their own work.[3]

---

[3] Jon Christensen, *Asking the Do-Gooders to Prove They Do Good*, N.Y. TIMES Jan. 3, 2004, p. B-9. The information for this section, except for the part about Charting Impact, comes from this article.

GuideStar, Independent Sector, and the Better Business Bureau have collaborated to create an assessment tool called Charting Impact, which allows nonprofits to take their own needs into account while reporting their measurement tools. Nonprofits completing Charting Impact reports answer five questions: (1) What is your organization trying to accomplish? (2) What are your strategies for making this happen? (3) What are your organization's capabilities for doing this? (4) How will your organization know if you are making progress? and (5) What have and haven't you accomplished so far? A nonprofit's Charting Impact response becomes part of its GuideStar report, which allows donors, funders, and others interested in the nonprofit to make their own judgments about the nonprofit's success. *See* htttp://www.chartingimpact.org.

Some argue that storytelling and focusing on the ultimate recipient of the grant are more effective than answering questions that the grantor has devised or looking at the nonprofit's intentions. Action Aid and the Aga Khan Rural Development Program, for example, are two international aid programs that have discovered that observations from the people who are supposed to benefit from the program are more helpful in highlighting trends and evaluating a program's effectiveness than the other statistics they collect.

Charles F. Sabel, a professor of law and social science at the Columbia Law School, proposes "learning by monitoring" as an evolving form of accountability. "Even though people can't specify what's effective and what's not, and they can't make an effective model for the right solution, they can improve enough to make it better the next round," he said. "And that is a kind of accountability." Jon Christensen, *Asking the Do-Gooders to Prove They Do Good*, N.Y. TIMES, Jan. 3, 2004.

For further reading about impact evaluation, see Susan Colby, Nan Stone, and Paul Carttar, *Zeroing in on Impact*, STANFORD SOCIAL INNOVATION REVIEW (Fall 2014); *Using Outcomes to Measure Nonprofit Success*, NONPROFIT QUARTERLY (July 2, 2013); Mark J. Epstein and Richard Larkin, *Measuring the Efficiency and Effectiveness of a Nonprofit's Performance*, STRATEGIC FINANCE (Oct. 2011); Elizabeth Schmidt and David Bonbright, *Taking Evaluation Seriously—Still a Way to Go*, ALLIANCE MAG., Dec. 1, 2007; Alnoor Ebrahim, NGOs and Organizational Change: Discourse, Reporting, and Learning (Cambridge University Press 2003).

V. IRS ENFORCEMENT

As an attorney for tax-exempt organizations, your job will be to keep your clients in compliance with the state and federal rules governing these organizations. From time to time, however, you may find your organization being examined by the IRS or disagreeing with a determination ruling. This section of the chapter explains the steps of an IRS audit and how the appeals process works if the organization wants to challenge an unfavorable determination letter or the tax findings in an examination letter. It also includes a piece that describes other, more passive ways in which the IRS enforces the provisions of the Internal Revenue Code. It concludes with notes about the audit process and information about the number and percentages of exempt organizations' returns that are examined each year.

EXAMINATION AND COMPLIANCE CHECK PROCESSES FOR EXEMPT ORGANIZATIONS

www.irs.gov/newsroom/article/0,,id=178242,00.html, FS-2008-14
(Feb. 2008)

The Internal Revenue Service has a variety of tools at its disposal to make certain that tax-exempt organizations comply with federal law designed to ensure they are entitled to any tax exemption they may claim.

Examinations vs. Compliance Checks

A review of a tax exempt organization falls into two broad categories: compliance checks and examinations.

The IRS conducts examinations, also known as audits, which are authorized under Section 7602 of the Internal Revenue Code. An examination is a review of a taxpayer's books and records to determine tax liability, and may involve the questioning of third parties. For exempt organizations, an examination also determines an organization's qualification for tax-exempt status.

EO conducts two different types of examinations: correspondence and field examinations.

A compliance check is a review to determine whether an organization is adhering to recordkeeping and information reporting requirements and is not an examination since it does not directly relate to determining a tax liability for any particular period.

Correspondence Examinations

Correspondence examinations are limited in scope and focus on only one or two items on a return. An EO specialist typically conducts the examination through letters and phone calls with the organization's officers or representatives.

If the issues become complex, or if the organization does not respond to a letter or call, EO may require the officers or representatives to bring records to an IRS office. EO may also convert a correspondence examination into a field examination.

Field Examinations

A field examination is one conducted by a revenue agent at the organization's place of business. Generally, these audits are the most comprehensive. There are two distinct types of EO field examinations—EO Team Examination Program (TEP) and EO General Program.

- EO TEP examinations are field examinations of large, complex organizations that may require a team of specialized revenue agents, as well as coordination between IRS functions and other governmental agencies. They are often conducted using coordinated team examination approaches and procedures.
- EO General Program examinations are typically performed by individual revenue agents. They usually do not require a team of specialists.

A field examination usually begins when the revenue agent notifies the organization that its return has been selected for examination. This initial contact is by telephone or by letter to schedule an initial appointment. The organization receives Publication 1, Your Rights as a Taxpayer, with the appointment letter.

In the appointment contact, the revenue agent will typically request the following documents to begin the audit:

1. Governing instruments (articles of incorporation, charter or constitution, including all amendments; and bylaws, including all amendments),
2. Pamphlets, brochures, and other printed literature describing the organization's activities,
3. Copies of the organization's Forms 990 for the years before and after the year under examination,

For the year under examination (at a minimum):

4. Minutes of meetings of the board of directors and standing committees or councils,
5. All books and records of assets, liabilities, receipts and disbursements,

   - Auditor's report, if any,
   - Copies of other federal tax returns filed and any related workpapers (Form 990-T for taxable income, Form 1120-POL for political activity, etc.),
   - Copies of employment tax returns and any related workpapers (Forms W-2, W-3, 941, 1096, 1099).

(Note: Many of these records may also be required for a correspondence examination.)

During an opening conference with the organization's officers or representatives, the revenue agent explains the audit plan and the reason the organization has been selected for examination. The revenue agent usually conducts a comprehensive interview and tours the organization's facilities to gain a basic understanding of the organization's purposes and activities.

The examination of a tax-exempt organization is multifaceted and includes a review of its operation and activities to verify the existence of an exempt purpose, as well as a review of financial records. The length of the examination will depend upon a variety of factors, such as the size of the organization, the complexity of its activities and the issues that may arise during the examination.

Some audits can be completed in just a few days; others can last for a year or more.

A field examination typically concludes with a closing conference. The revenue agent will discuss the audit with the organization's representatives, and if necessary, furnish a report explaining proposed adjustments to the organization's returns or exempt status. If the revenue agent and the organization's representatives disagree on the findings, the organization may request a meeting with the revenue agent's manager to discuss the disagreement. If the manager cannot resolve the differences, the organization may pursue its case through the IRS appeals process. For additional information on the appeals process, see Publication 892, EO Appeal Procedures for Unagreed Issues.

Compliance Checks

Exempt Organizations also maintains an active compliance check program. EO specialists conduct the checks by corresponding with or telephoning exempt organization representatives. A specialist may inquire about an item on a return, determine if specific reporting requirements have been met or whether an organization's activities are consistent with its stated tax-exempt purpose.

An officer or representative of an exempt organization may refuse to participate in a compliance check without penalty. However, EO has the option of opening a formal examination, whether or not the organization agrees to participate in a compliance check.

At the beginning of a compliance check, the specialist will inform the officer or director that the review is a compliance check and not an examination. The specialist will not ask to examine any books or records or ask questions regarding tax liabilities. The specialist may ask whether the organization understands or has questions about filing obligations for required forms. The specialist may also ask questions about the organization's activities. If, during a compliance check, the specialist decides an examination is appropriate, he or she will notify the organization that EO is commencing an examination before asking questions related to tax liability.

Because a compliance check only reviews whether an organization is adhering to record keeping and information reporting requirements or whether an organization's activities are consistent with its stated tax-exempt purpose and is not an examination, it is possible to have more than one compliance check for a tax year if facts and circumstances warrant. For more information, see Publication 4386, Compliance Checks.

Selecting Organizations for Examination or Compliance Checks

EO strives to ensure consistency and fairness in its examination and compliance check processes. In its annual Implementing Guidelines, which are available on the IRS website at www.irs.gov/eo, EO describes its proposed examination and compliance check activities for the year.

EO designs and implements comprehensive projects to address issues that carry the most non-compliance risk. To determine which organizations should be targeted, experienced specialists analyze information from Forms 990 and other sources. This analysis will usually result in the selection of a group of returns for examination or compliance check.

EO also reviews media reports and receives complaints from the general public and Congress about potential non-compliance by exempt organizations. After confirming the information, and when appropriate, these organizations may be selected for examination or to receive a compliance check. For details on how EO handles complaints about exempt organizations, see Fact Sheet 2008-13.

Regardless of the process used to select returns, EO does not presume that an organization is violating the tax laws before it begins the examination or sends a compliance check letter.

EXEMPT ORGANIZATION APPEAL PROCEDURES FOR UNAGREED ISSUES

IRS Publication 892 (Rev. 7-85)

Because people sometimes disagree on issues, the Service maintains a system of appeals.... If an organization decides not to agree with the proposed findings, it may appeal the decision as explained in Part I, Adverse Determination, Revocation, or Modification letter, or Part II, Proposed Additional Tax. If both tax and determination issues are involved, the determination issue will usually be resolved before the tax issue. In these cases, the organization's appeal should cover the requirements of both Parts I and II.

Part I—Adverse Determination, Revocation, or Modification Letter

If an organization receives from a key district office of the Internal Revenue Service a proposed adverse determination letter or a determination letter proposing revocation or modification of exempt status, the organization may, within 30 days from the date of the letter, appeal through the key district office to the Office of the Regional Director of Appeals. If no appeal is filed within the 30-day period, the proposed adverse determination, revocation, or modification letter will become final.

Key district offices must request technical advice from the National Office on any exempt organization status issue for which there is no published precedent or for which there is reason to believe that nonuniformity exists. If an organization believes that its case falls within this category, it should ask the District Director to request technical advice. If a determination letter is issued based on technical advice from the National Office, no further administrative appeal is available on the issue that was the subject of technical advice.

Regional Office Appeal

The appeal to the Office of Regional Director of Appeals should be filed with the key district office and contain the following information:

1. The organization's name, address, and employer identification number;
2. A statement that the organization wants to appeal the determination;
3. The date and symbols on the determination letter;
4. A statement of facts supporting the organization's position in any contested factual issue;
5. A statement outlining the law or other authority the organization is relying on; and
6. A statement as to whether a hearing is desired....

If a hearing is requested, it will be held at the regional office, unless the organization requests that the meeting be held at a district office convenient to both parties. If the regional office, after considering the organization's appeal as well as information presented in any hearing held, agrees with the key district office's position in whole or in part, it will notify the organization of its decision in writing, presenting a statement of the key facts, law, rationale, and conclusions for each issue contested.

The Office of Regional Director of Appeals must request technical advice from the National Office on any exempt organization status issue for which there is no published precedent or for which there is reason to believe that nonuniformity exists. If an organization believes that its case falls within this category, it should ask the Director of Appeals to request technical advice. If a determination letter is issued based on technical advice from the National Office, no further administrative appeal is available on the issue that was the subject of technical advice.

Declaratory Judgment

Final adverse determination, revocation, and modification letters concerning exemption qualification or private foundation classification are subject to court review. The letter must contain an adverse ruling on one or more of the following facts:

1. Initial or continuing qualification as an organization described in section 501(c)(3) of the Code;
2. Initial or continuing qualification as an organization described in section 170(c)(2) of the Code;
3. Initial or continuing classification of an organization as a private foundation described in section 509(a) of the Code; or
4. Initial or continuing classification of an organization as operating foundation described in section 4942(j)(3) of the Code.

An organization that has received a final adverse letter by registered or certified mail concerning any such issue may file a petition for declaratory judgment with respect to the Service decision on that issue. Within 90 days of the date the final adverse letter was mailed, the petition must be filed with the United States Tax Court, the United States Claims Court, or the United States District Court for the District of Columbia. These courts will hear declaratory judgment petitions before any amount of tax in controversy has been paid. However, processing of assessments of such taxes by the Service may continue during declaratory judgment proceedings....

Part II—Proposed Additional Tax

If, after an examination is completed, the key district office determines that the organization owes additional tax, an examination report will be issued explaining the reasons for the proposed adjustments. If the organization disagrees with the proposed adjustments, it has the right to appeal within the Service, take the case to court, or both.

The following general rules explain how to appeal a case involving proposed additional tax.

Appeal within the Service

An organization may appeal the decision of the key district office to the Office of Regional Director of Appeals. This is done by filing an appeal with the key district office within 30 days from the date of the letter transmitting the examination report.

The appeal should contain:

1. The organization's name, address, and employer identification number;
2. A statement that the organization wants to appeal the findings of the key district office to the Office of Regional Director of Appeals;
3. The date and symbols on the letter transmitting the examination report and findings that the organization is appealing;
4. The tax periods involved;
5. An itemized list of the adjustments with which the organization does not agree;
6. A statement of facts supporting the organization's position in any contested factual issue;
7. A statement outlining the law or other authority the organization is relying on; and
8. A statement as to whether a hearing is desired.

The statement of facts must be declared true under penalties of perjury....

If a hearing is requested, it will be held at the regional office, unless the organization requests that the meeting be held at a district office convenient to both parties. If the Office of Regional Director of Appeals, after considering the organization's appeal as well as information presented in any hearing held, agrees with the key district office's position in whole or in part, it will notify the organization of its decision in writing, presenting a statement of the key facts, law, rationale, and conclusions for each issue contested. A notice of deficiency will be issued at this point and to appeal further, the organization must turn to the courts....

Appeals to the Courts

If the organization and the Service disagree after appeal to the regional office, or if the organization wants to bypass the regional office appeal, it may take the case to the United States Tax Court, the United States Claims Court, or the District Court. These courts are independent judicial bodies and have no connection with the Internal Revenue Service.

Tax Court

If the case involves a disagreement over whether the organization owes additional income tax or excise tax imposed by chapters 41 through 45 of the Internal Revenue Code, the organization may go to the United States Tax Court. To do this, ask the Service to issue a notice of deficiency. The organization has 90 days from the date this notice is mailed to file a petition with the Tax Court (150 days if addressed to an organization outside the United States). If a petition is not filed within the 90-day period (or 150 days, as the case may be) the law requires that the Service assess the tax and bill the organization for the deficiency.

The Court will schedule the case for trial at a location convenient to the organization. The organization may be represented by a principal officer or trustee before the Tax Court, or it may be represented by anyone admitted to practice before that Court.

There are simplified Tax Court procedures for cases involving income tax disputes of $10,000 or less for any year or, in the case of excise taxes imposed by chapters 41 through 45, when the amount of tax in dispute is $10,000 or less for any one taxable period (or taxable event if there is no taxable period)....

District Court and Claims Court

An organization may take its case to its United States District Court or to the United States Claims Court. Generally, the District Court and the Claims Court hear tax cases only after the tax has been paid and a claim for refund has been filed. Information about procedures for filing suit in these courts can be obtained by contacting either the Clerk of the District Court, or the Clerk of the Claims Court.

MARCUS S. OWENS, FEDERAL OVERSIGHT: THE ROLE OF THE IRS

(Conference Proceedings at NYU Center on
Philanthropy and the Law, 2007)

For purposes of tax administration relating to tax-exempt organizations, the relevant Code provisions direct the IRS to ascertain which organizations should be recognized as exempt from tax, to determine the extent to which contributions should be deductible as charitable contributions, and to identify which transactions engaged in by those organizations should be subject to income or excise taxes.... In contrast, the powers over charities accruing to a state attorney general by virtue of state statute or judicial decision regarding the appropriate use of charitable funds are generally considered to be broader, at least in some respects.

That simplistic approach to defining the role of the IRS, however, is misleading because of the breadth of the specific tax administration tasks set out in the Code relating to tax-exempt organizations, as clarified by Treasury Regulations and interpreted by judicial decisions. In the name of administering tax, the IRS has been thrust into the core operations of tax-exempt organizations. For example, section 501(c)(3) asks the IRS to evaluate the operations of charities to ascertain whether private individuals are deriving some impermissible benefit from association with the organizations or whether the charities serve any other substantial nonexempt purpose. The dimensions of that directive in section 501(c)(3) of the Code are stunningly broad: the IRS clearly has been charged with reviewing the entire array of a charity's operational and financial arrangements to assay the characteristics of the benefits derived from them and to weigh the substantiality of the organization's various purposes. The scope of the IRS authority to probe and evaluate (not necessarily remedy) is thus as great, perhaps greater, than that of a state attorney general, as section 7601(a) the Code contemplates IRS review without the prerequisite of suspicious action on the part of the charity. Furthermore, while the IRS does not normally have equitable powers of the charities it regulates, its ability to discipline by imposing income and excise taxes—assessed without the need for judicial action—often allow it to coerce compliance with its directives in order to avoid harsh financial sanctions. Furthermore, the requirements of the Code apply universally to domestic charities, regardless of where their activities occur, and to foreign charities that have sought recognition of U.S. federal income tax exemption.... Nevertheless, while I would argue that IRS power, in the sense of the power to review, is omnipresent, it is not omnipotent nor is it omniscient.

The defective omniscience of the IRS is spawned by a combination of the previously noted breadth of the actual responsibilities of charity oversight under the Internal Revenue Code and the imbedding of the oversight in a tax system, dependent on tax return-based reporting and tied to concepts of numerical measurement of activities. Institutional behavior that is not easily reduced to numbers or imperfectly reflected in balance sheets and income statements is going to be incompletely reflected on a tax return. Timeliness of information is also an issue. In contrast to the reporting and disclosure demanded of publicly-traded corporations under securities laws, the annual information return, the Form 990, can be filed nearly 11 months after the close of the tax year, potentially approaching two years after the event in the case of transgressions occurring early in the tax year. The IRS thus is limited to systematically collecting historic data, data that is approaching staleness from an enforcement perspective....

Tax Administration Tools: The Bully Pulpit

To carry out its role of tax administrator, the IRS has an array of enforcement tools at its disposal, including relatively passive informational devices. Perhaps one of the most important and efficient tools for the agency takes advantage of the power of the media and the ethical obligations imposed on those professionals who practice before the IRS. By the very act of describing the minimum standards for tax compliance regarding a particular arrangement or transaction, the IRS co-opts an army of private sector attorneys and accountants to carry the message to taxpayers, including tax-exempt organizations, propelled by the ethical standards of the particular professions, backed by the powers of the IRS Director of Practice. The continuum of such tools begins with regulations, revenue rulings and revenue procedures that are vetted through several layers of personnel at the IRS and Treasury, and continues down through tax forms (with related instructions), plain language publications, news and information releases, Internal Revenue Manual ("IRM") sections, official training materials, speeches and testimony, the annual "work plan," also known as Implementing Guidelines, and, more recently, IRS website material. Closely related are the publicly-disclosed footprints of enforcement actions, such as technical advice memoranda, various counsel memoranda, and private letter rulings....

In addition to the public release of generalized informational documents, the IRS is compelled to make public certain taxpayer-specific documents pursuant to section 6110 and section 6104 of the Code. The scope of documents subject to release under either provision has steadily grown over the years.

Beginning approximately 2004, however, the Division seems to have shifted the nature and extent of the information it makes public. Training materials are no longer routinely made public, and the Continuing Professional Education Training Text that was published for 25 years appears to have been discontinued.... The number of private letter rulings has been depressed by a combination of significantly increasing user fees and by the length of time that it takes to secure such a ruling.... Even more significantly, the number of precedential guidance documents, such as revenue rulings, has declined.

Commendably, the Division has increased the production of pamphlets and documents summarizing aspects of federal tax law for a general, rather than a practitioner, audience. Additionally, the Division is making more frequent and creative use of its homepage on the IRS website, but again with an emphasis on the communication of very general discussions of the law. Information on the IRS website, however, is often undated and not assigned a document number, making it very difficult to verify whether the statements reflect current IRS views or not, and whether unapparent changes have been made to a particular discussion. The legal import of IRS website discussions is, at best, ambiguous, and should be clarified.

Tax Administration Tools: The Big Stick

In addition to the more passive Bully Pulpit tax administration tools, in the tax-exempt organizations area, the IRS retains the full arsenal of aggressive enforcement tools, as well as several that are less frequently employed by other functions of the Agency. Examples of the latter include the determination program, which allows the Service to negotiate adjustments in structure or operation before approving an exemption application, and the recently developed "compliance check" process under which a questionnaire or similar survey document is mailed to a particular category of tax-exempt organization in order to ascertain patterns of behavior in the sector. The IRS takes the position that the compliance check does not rise to the level of an examination of the organization's books and records and that there is no penalty for failure to respond. A failure to respond would, however, clearly be taken into consideration in determining whether additional action might be necessary. The compliance check tool enables the IRS to contact far more organizations in a year than traditional enforcement tools, including correspondence examinations. When focused on a discreet segment of the charitable sector, such as the recent survey of hospitals, the IRS is able to build a database of knowledge about institutional behavior in order to better inform guidance development and enforcement decisions.

Another evolutionary development in the Division's approach to examinations, and, perhaps, the polar opposite of the compliance check, has been the formation of a "Financial Investigations Unit" composed of two revenue agent groups, 18 revenue agents in total, who have received specialized forensic accounting and financial training. The FIU agents undertake examinations of more complex and sensitive matters, and provide technical tax-exempt organizations support to the IRS Criminal Investigation Division and other Agency units.

While the Division has been creative in developing efficient ways to interact with the charities, it has not been as creative in the use of the Code's enforcement provisions as it could.... For example, it has been suggested that a creative utilization of the tax shelter penalties [in §§6700 and 6701 of the Code] might be an effective way to deal with aspects of the use of charities for political campaign intervention purposes.

NOTES AND QUESTIONS

1. An organization that is audited can expect the following events to take place. The IRS examiner will contact the organization to schedule an appointment and will specify what records he or she will need at the beginning of the audit. Typically, those records will include the organization's governing documents; its Form 990s; the pamphlets, brochures, and other literature that it uses to describe its activities; the minutes of its meetings; all financial records; its employment tax returns; and any outside auditor's reports. At the first meeting, the examiner will conduct a comprehensive initial interview, tour the organization's facilities, and explain the reason for the audit. The examiner will continue to work with the organization's contact person, to request additional documents as necessary, and to examine those documents until he or she completes the audit. The examination concludes with a presentation of the findings in what is called a "closing conference." For additional reading on the IRS audit procedure, *see* Bruce Hopkins, *IRS Audits of Tax-Exempt Organizations: Policies, Practices, and Procedures* (Wiley 2008) and Ann Battle, *IRS Audits of Tax-Exempt Organizations: Understanding and Preparing for an Examination*, J. TAX PRAC. & PROC, (June–July 2004), p. 29. Marcus Owen, former director of the TE/GE division of the IRS, explains these concepts in a webinar, *The IRS and Charities Regulation* (April 7, 2015), available at http://web.law. columbia.edu/attorneys-general/policy-areas/charities-law-project/webinars /irs-and-charities-regulation-primer.

2. What is the best balance between federal and state oversight of tax-exempt organizations? Should there be a separate, independent agency that oversees charities? James Fishman has suggested that a new agency, similar to the British Charity Commission, would be an improvement over our current system. James J. Fishman, *Improving Charitable Accountability*, 62 MD. L. REV. 218, 272-287 (2003). Marcus Owens suggests an agency loosely modeled on the corporate sector's National Association of Securities Dealers. Marcus Owens, *Charity Oversight: An Alternative Approach* (Hauser Center for Nonprofit Organizations, Working Paper 33.4, 2006).

3. Would it be better to federalize the oversight, or have we, in effect, already done so? Federalization has increased to the extent that the Nonprofit and Philanthropy Law Section of the American Association of Law Schools concentrated its discussion on "The Federalization of Nonprofit and Charity Law" at its 2011 annual meeting. A modest proposal in this direction by Marion Fremont Smith is to federalize the information-gathering function in order to reduce the administrative burden on charities. *See* Marion Fremont-Smith, Attorney General Oversight of Charities, Hauser Center for Nonprofit Organizations, Working Paper 41 (2007).

4. Can there be effective enforcement without a robust IRS budget? In 2015, the IRS budget was $1.2 billion less than in 2010. As a result, it was operating with 13,000 fewer full-time employees. Prepared Remarks of John A. Koskinen, Commissioner Internal Revenue Service. Before the Urban-

Brookings Tax Policy Center, April 8, 2015. Two years earlier, the National Taxpayer Advocate had warned about this state of affairs: "The IRS has been chronically underfunded for years now, at the same time it has been required to take on more and more work, including administering benefit programs for some of the most challenging populations . . . [and] without adequate funding, the IRS will fail at its mission." National Taxpayer Advocate, *2013 Annual Report to Congress Executive Summary: Preface and Highlights*, Publication 2104C (Rev. 12-2013), Catalog Number 23655L (Washington, DC: Department of the Treasury, Internal Revenue Service, 2013).

FORM 990 EXERCISE

Congratulations! Your §501(c)(3) has been in existence for more than five years and is quite successful. Now it is time to fill in Form 990 for the last calendar year. Good luck! This task is not easy to do, but it should give you an idea of what hundreds of thousands of nonprofits face on an annual basis—many without as much financial or legal expertise as you have. This exercise should also help you determine whether Form 990 is an effective accountability tool, and it will review most of the issues discussed in this book.

Note: This exercise provides the facts, except for the name of the organization, its exempt purpose, and its programs. Do not make up your own facts or you will be hopelessly confused. If you have created your own nonprofit for the purposes of this book, use its name, mission, and programs. If not, assume this is the Acme Art Museum. The most recent version of Form 990 can be found at http://www.irs.gov/pub/irs-pdf/f990.pdf.

You will need to download the most recent core form and Schedules A and C from the website for this casebook.[4] For the purposes of this exercise, you can skip Parts X and XI of the core form, and most of the questions in Parts IV and V. Although Part IV may ask you to complete several schedules, you need to complete only Schedules A and C for this exercise.

The following instructions will substitute for the actual instructions for Form 990 and its schedules for this exercise, but if you complete a Form 990 for an actual organization, you will need to study those instructions carefully. The excerpt from the IRS webcast, Form 990 Filing Tips, which is reproduced above will also help you complete this form.

The facts are given in the order in which you should use them to complete the form, although the facts are not repeated if they are needed more than once. Occasionally, facts related to the ones being presented may seem irrelevant. If that is the case, the facts will be relevant later in the assignment.

This is not an exercise to test your math skills. Whether your numbers are accurate is not as important as your developing an understanding of the form and the issues that it is meant to address.

---

[4] Some versions of Adobe Acrobat do not allow changes to be saved. Before you complete the form, please be sure that your version accepts changes. If it does not, you may need to print out the form and complete it by hand.

Heading

Complete the heading with information of your choosing, except for G and L. Your gross receipts last year (G) were $3,500,000, and your organization was formed (L) in 2003.

Program Services (Part III)

Complete the mission statement and the narrative description of the programs that help the organization achieve its mission, using information of your own choosing.[5] This information will also be used in your answer to Part I, Question 1. At least one of the organization's programs should bring in mission-related revenue.[6] For example, a §501(c)(3) theater might have one program that produces plays for the community, another that provides acting training, and a third that produces mini-plays for nursing homes. If the theater charged for the first two programs but not the third, all three programs would incur program-related expenses, but only the first two would bring in program-related revenue. Once you have completed Parts VIII and IX, you will be able to fill in the revenues and expenses information for Part III. *Don't forget to do this.*

Revenues (Part VIII)

Note: Do not fill in any business codes.

1. *Charitable contributions and grants.* Your organization's annual campaign brought in $1,000,000 in contributions from individuals this year. All but one of these contributions were from individuals who provided gifts in the $100 to $500 range. The other gift was from a member of your board of directors, who made a $100,000 gift. No other members of the board, executives of the organization, or their family members donated any money. No one has made a pledge to make a contribution in the future or provided any noncash contributions.

You have also received several grants. Local §501(c)(3) private foundations have provided five grants of $100,000 each. The United Way (a type of federated campaign) has also provided $200,000. The government has provided a grant of $250,000. These grants are in addition to the money from individual contributions.

2. *Program service revenue.* Last year, your clients (customers) paid $1,000,000 for the program services described in Part III. None of the customers paid more than $5,000 for any of these services during the course of the year, and no member of the board purchased any of these goods or services.

---

[5] The IRS recommends completing Parts VIII and IX first, but completing the narrative of Part III first should ground you in the mission of the organization.

[6] If you find it impossible to include a program that brings in program-related revenue, imagine that you are working with another large organization that can do so, such as a theater or a museum.

3. *Fundraising event.* Your organization held a dinner dance last fall. It sold 1,000 tickets at $100 apiece. The fair market value of the dinner dance was $50. Your organization incurred $50,000 in expenses for this dinner dance.

4. *Other revenue.* Your organization received $200,000 in investment income and $50,000 from royalties. You had no income from investments of tax-exempt bonds, sales of assets other than inventory, rents, fundraising events, or gaming activities.

5. *Miscellaneous revenue.* Your organization has instituted a few other activities that have brought in revenues. These activities are not among your major programs and should be classified under "miscellaneous revenue." These activities include the following:

- The organization allows other organizations to place advertisements of any form on a billboard outside your office building, and it earns $100,000 from this advertising.
- Your organization runs a cafeteria for your employees, your clients, and people who walk in off the street and do not participate in any of the services, exhibits, or programs that your organization offers. It earned $100,000 in gross revenues from the cafeteria, of which half came from the general public and half from employees.
- The organization sells art created by the children of your employees. The money goes directly into your organization's coffers. None of it goes to the children or to their parents. The children have donated the art. None of them took a charitable contribution for their donations, because the art had no value when it was donated. The organization earned $50,000 from the sale of this art.

Expenses (Part IX)

The following figures represent total expenses, which will be reported in column A.

1. The organization does not provide grants or other assistance to governments or individuals in the United States or abroad. Nor does it pay any benefits to or for members.
2. Its directors are not supposed to be compensated, unless you have created your own charity for this book and you indicated on your Form 1023 that they are to be compensated, in which case you should include the figure that you reported.
3. The organization pays its officers and other employees the following amounts:[7]

    - The executive director (ED) and the chief financial officer (CFO) each make $300,000 a year.

---

[7] You might want to start completing Part VII here to help you determine what you need to fill in for the compensation totals in Part IX. The definitions of "key employee" and "highest-paid employee" are in the IRS tutorial reproduced earlier in this chapter.

- The development director and technology coordinator each make $200,000 a year. Assume that both are "key employees."
- The six other employees each make $50,000 a year.
- The organization has 10 volunteers.
- It contributes $25,000 a year each to the pensions of the ED and CFO, and $6,250 for each of the other employees (in other words, the other employees' pensions total $50,000).
- It spends $100,000 in health insurance and other employee benefits.
- It pays $100,000 in payroll taxes.

4. The organization raised your contributions through a telephone and direct-mail campaign targeted at its state of incorporation and three neighboring states, all of which have state charitable solicitation laws. It paid a professional fundraiser, Dollars-R-Us, $150,000 a year to run the campaign. It also paid $50,000 for advertising and promotion in conjunction with this campaign. A member of the board owns the advertising company that promotes the organization's fundraising appeals. She charged the organization only $10,000 more than she would have charged another customer. She also rents her second home to a second member of the board for $12,000 a year, but that board member pays her directly from his personal checking account.

5. Accounting costs and legal fees each totaled $150,000. The accountant is Kashem Banks of Kashem Banks, LLC, and the legal firm is Howie Dewie of Dewie, Cheatham, & Howe, LLP. The nonprofit pays the firms, not the individuals.

6. The organization also paid Karl Consult $200,000 in investment management fees. He was on the board of directors the year before last but wanted to be paid fair market value for his management advice to your organization without the appearance of a conflict, so he left the board.

7. The organization pays Laurie's Lobbying $100,000 for its advocacy of a change in the current law concerning an area related to your organization's mission. Of those funds, $70,000 is earmarked for addressing pertinent issues with legislators, and $30,000 is reserved for convincing the public to persuade their legislators. This is accomplished via personal contact, television and radio ads, rallies, speeches, and lectures. The organization has made the §501(h) election.

8. Other expenses include:

- Office expenses—$200,000
- Information technology—$100,000
- Rent/occupancy—$150,000
- Travel—$100,000
- Conferences—$50,000
- Depreciation—$50,000
- Insurance—$50,000

9. There are no other expenses.

10. These are the total expenses for column A. You need to decide which part of the total should be allocated to program services expenses, management and general expenses, and fundraising expenses, but in this example, you need to do this only for line 25. Look at the items in column A and estimate the amounts you will end up putting in line 25, columns B, C, and D. Note that the amount you put into line 25, column B, will be used in Part III, line 4e. Part III also asks you to categorize these program service expenses. You can estimate these amounts as well. In the real world, you would be able to make these allocations according to the financial records that you maintained during the year.

11. Once you have completed Parts VIII and IX, be sure to finish Part III, "Program Service Accomplishments." Note that the totals for program service revenues and program service expenses in Part III must equal the totals for Parts VIII and IX. Note, too, that the question about expenses, including grants of $X, refers to grants that the organization has made to others, not grants that it has received. In this scenario, your organization has not awarded any grants.

12. Complete Part VII, "Compensation." Do not worry about including pension benefits.

Governance (Part VI)

You can complete this part of the form using the directors that you listed on your Form 1023. In addition, the executive director is on the board, as is Howie Dewie of Dewie, Cheatham, & Howe. Mr. Dewie's wife, Milly, is also on the board. Neither Mr. Dewie nor Mrs. Dewie receives compensation for being on the board, but for the past few years, your organization has been giving them each $15,000 to cover their expenses as board members. It did not collect receipts, however, to determine whether they spent any money in their roles as board members.

Part I

Once you have completed Parts III, VII, VIII, and IX, you can complete Part I, mostly by copying information from other parts of the form. You do not need to fill in line 7b, 20, 21, or 22. The prior year's values are identical to this year's.

Part IV

Complete questions 1, 3, 4, 17, 18, 25, and 28. Read the other questions, however, to see if you understand why the IRS is asking them. What issues that have been covered in this course can you spot in this part of the form?

Part V

Answer only questions 3, 7a, and 7b, but glance at the other questions to identify issues.

Schedule A

For the purposes of Schedule A, assume that the organization brought in the same amounts of contributions and revenue, by the same means and from the same people, for each of the past five years. There were no tax revenues levied for the organization's benefit in any of those years, nor did a governmental unit provide services or facilities without charge. The net unrelated business income for each year was $50,000. (*Note:* If you have a figure for unrelated business income on the core Form 990, it will be a gross amount. This exercise does not include sufficient facts to allow you to determine the net unrelated business income, so you will have to use the number given here.) Do not forget to determine whether there have been substantial contributors (Part II, line 5, or Part III, line 7, depending on your organization).

Schedule C

For the purposes of Schedule C, also assume the organization has had the same amount in expenditures for each of the past four years.

ENDING THE ORGANIZATION

CHAPTER 13

ENDING THE ORGANIZATION: DISSOLUTION, MERGER, AND CONVERSION

Purposes of this chapter:

- Understand corporate restructuring possibilities and legal steps necessary to complete them
- Identify the pros and cons of each restructuring possibility
- Reprise: directors' liability issues; donor intent issues; nondistribution constraint
- Discuss cy pres concepts in the context of ensuring that assets remain in the charitable sector

To think about as you read:

Assume that either the virtual nonprofit you have created or the local art museum is having financial problems. The organization's concept is a good one, and under ordinary circumstances, it would be self-sustaining, but it has been run poorly, and the resulting poor publicity has led to several miserable years for fundraising. Assume that you are the outside attorney who has to explain the financial and legal options to the board—dissolution, merger, or conversion to a for-profit organization. As you read these materials, consider what you would tell the board about each of these options and how they should choose one over another. What issues should they expect to face as they try to restructure the organization? What steps would they need to take, and what would happen to the charitable assets?

I. INTRODUCTION

The final chapter in the life cycle of a §501(c)(3) organization is its dissolution and termination. Three possibilities exist for the last stage of such an organization: (1) it can actually cease existing by following the legal rules for dissolution and termination; (2) it can merge with another organization; or (3) it can convert to a for-profit organization. Whether it chooses one or another of these possibilities will depend on the situation in which the organization finds itself, such as its finances, its relative success in achieving its mission, and its ability to attract outside resources.

Once the strategic decision has been made, several legal issues arise. Despite the differences in these choices, the legal issues are quite similar. First, there are procedural issues. What process must the organization follow? Who should be notified of these changes? What steps must be taken? Second, how does the nondistribution constraint, which underlies every concept of nonprofit law, apply in each of these situations? What should happen to the organization's assets (or debts)? The third question is related to the second—are there any restricted gifts that affect the way that the organization's assets are handled? Finally, are there any special issues for the board of directors? Must the board adopt a different standard of due diligence? Are there special conflicts of interest to avoid?

This chapter begins with a discussion of cy pres and deviation, trust law concepts that have applicability to §501(c)(3) nonprofit corporations at the end of their life cycle, when a determination must be made about the fate of the charitable assets. The chapter then covers bankruptcy, which is often, but not always, a precursor to a dissolution. Next it discusses each of the three situations mentioned above—dissolution, merger, and conversion to a for-profit organization—in the context of the four issues described above.

II. CY PRES AND DEVIATION

Cy pres and deviation are trust law concepts that govern the dissolution of trusts and other instances in which the purpose of a trust is frustrated. Under cy pres, when a charity's purposes become impossible or impractical to fulfill, its assets will be used to fulfill another effort with a charitable purpose as close to the original purpose as possible. Deviation is an administrative remedy that is applied when the trust cannot function for an administrative reason. The current trend is to abolish the distinction between the two.

Although the focus of this course is on §501(c)(3) corporations, a detour into these trust law doctrines is important because nonprofit corporation law cannot parallel for-profit law in the context of dissolution or termination. A for-profit corporation distributes its assets to shareholders upon dissolution, a practice that the nondistribution constraint forbids in the nonprofit context. The question then becomes: When a nonprofit dissolves, are its assets held in trust? If so, is the doctrine of cy pres or deviation applicable? If not, does the organization actually own its assets and have the ability to dispose of them as it wishes? In other words, how much leeway does the organization have in determining what to do with those assets? The following cy pres and deviation cases provide the background for beginning to make this determination.

At common law, a court could modify the purposes of a trust if it found (1) a valid charitable trust; (2) a circumstance in which the trust's original purposes are being thwarted, such that a modification is necessary to carry out the trust's original purposes; and (3) the donor had a general charitable intent that is broader than the donor's specifically stated purposes, so it would be appropriate to apply the trust funds to another charitable purpose. Otherwise, as you will see in the *Cerio* case below, the charitable trust could fail and the funds go elsewhere.

UNITED STATES V. CERIO

831 F. Supp. 530 (E.D. Va. 1993)

ELLIS, District Judge.

I

This is a rare case. How often, after all, does the recipient of a generous bequest object to that bequest and threaten to reject it on the ground that it is too generous? Yet that is precisely what has occurred here. Indeed, this is essentially a case of looking the gift horse in the mouth and finding it too good to accept as is.

More particularly, this unique dispute concerns the validity and disposition of a retired Coast Guard Captain's testamentary gift to the United States Coast Guard Academy (the "Academy") for the purpose of establishing a trust fund, the annual income of which is to be awarded each year to the graduating cadet who attains the highest grade point average in chemistry and physics while enrolled at the Academy. So large is the gift—the trust corpus is estimated to be worth over $1 million—that the proposed cadet award would range from $65,000 to $130,000 annually. Such an annual cadet award, according to the Coast Guard, would seriously disrupt the Academy's operations and interfere with the attainment of its goals. Unless the trust is somehow modified, the Coast Guard claims it would be compelled to refuse the gift. Seeking to avoid this result, the United States brought this action on behalf of the Coast Guard seeking application of the equitable doctrine of *cy pres* to change the terms of the trust so that the Coast Guard Academy can accept the testamentary trust in a modified form. Not surprisingly, the testator's heirs-at-law, the defendants here, argue that the trust should either be performed as written or held to fail, in which event, the trust funds would pass to them under Virginia's intestate succession laws....

II. Findings of Fact

Robert T. Alexander, a resident of the Commonwealth of Virginia, died testate on April 18, 1988. A retired Coast Guard Captain, Alexander had spent his entire thirty-four year professional career with the Coast Guard.... At the time of his death in April 1988, Captain Alexander was a widower with no children. He was survived by no relatives of closer kinship than nieces and nephews or perhaps more accurately, half nieces and nephews....

Following his death, Captain Alexander's will, dated April 28, 1986, was admitted to probate in the Circuit Court of the county of Arlington, Virginia. After providing for the payment of Captain Alexander's just debts, funeral expenses, estate administration costs, and estate and inheritance taxes, the will provided for monetary bequests to eleven specified individuals, including bequests of $50,000 each to Captain Alexander's half-nieces and nephews.... He devised the remainder of his estate to the Coast Guard Academy for the purpose of establishing a scholarship fund in his name and that of his half-brother George Alexander, also an Academy graduate. . . .

Pursuant to the terms of this Residuary Clause, Daniel Cerio, the executor of Captain Alexander's estate and drafter of the Will, delivered two checks to the Coast Guard following Captain Alexander's death. . . .

Upon realizing the size of the annual award called for by the terms of the testamentary trust, the Coast Guard determined that it would not be able to accept the trust gift as written. The award of such a large cash prize, in the eyes of the Coast Guard, would disrupt the Academy's educational program and unduly interfere with its mission of preparing young men and women for a life of public service in the Coast Guard. As such, the government, on behalf of the Coast Guard, initiated this suit seeking application of the *cy pres* doctrine....

This mission [of the Coast Guard], in Admiral Versaw's view, would be jeopardized if the proposed trust were enforced as written. Specifically, he noted that an annual award of $65,000 to $130,000 to a cadet would (i) engender intense, unhealthy competition among cadets, (ii) spawn honor code offenses, (iii) distort the competition to major in the sciences at the expense of other majors, (iv) erode, if not destroy, the class and interpersonal relationships and esprit de corps so vital to the Academy's goal of instilling in cadets the value of teamwork and (v) serve to teach cadets, wrongly, that the reward for a job well done in a life of public service in the Coast Guard is cash rather than the personal satisfaction that comes from doing well one's duty as an officer. No student of human nature can seriously doubt the validity of Admiral's views in this regard. Attempts at literal enforcement of the trust would fundamentally change the Academy in ways neither contemplated, nor desired by Captain Alexander.

III. Conclusions of Law

Under Virginia law, the equitable doctrine of *cy pres* permits courts to alter a trust so as to carry out a testator's intent "as near as possible" when it is not possible to effectuate this intent in the exact manner specified by the testator. See Va. Code §55-31 (1992). For the doctrine of *cy pres* to be properly invoked, there must be: "(1) a valid charitable trust without a gift over, (2) an existing general charitable intent, and (3) the beneficiaries must be indefinite or uncertain, or (4) the purpose of the trust must be indefinite, impossible to perform, or so impracticable of performance as to characterize the fulfillment of the purpose as 'impossible.' " In this case, the Coast Guard argues that *cy pres* should be applied to save Captain Alexander's charitable bequest from failing because it cannot accept or perform the trust as written. Defendant heirs, for their part, argue that *cy pres* is inapplicable, and that the failure of the gift results in the trust funds passing to them by intestate succession. In light of the trial evidence, however, it is clear that the requirements for application of the *cy pres* doctrine are met.

First, the Residuary Clause of Captain Alexander's will unmistakably creates a valid charitable trust without a gift over. Instructive here is the Supreme Court of Virginia's expansive definition of "charity":

> A charity, in a legal sense, may be described as a gift to be applied, consistently with existing laws, for the benefit of an indefinite number of persons, either by bringing their hearts under the influence of education or religion, by relieving their bodies from disease, suffering or constraint, by assisting them to establish themselves for life, or by erecting or maintaining public buildings or works, or otherwise lessening the burdens of government. It is immaterial whether the purpose is called charitable in the gift itself, if it is so described as to show that it is charitable. Generally speaking, any gift not inconsistent with existing laws which is promotive of science or tends to the education, enlightening, benefit or amelioration of mankind or the diffusion of useful knowledge, or is for the public convenience is a charity.

Given this definition, the proposed trust created by the Residuary Clause is a valid charitable trust because (i) its purpose is to benefit an indefinite number of cadets and (ii) the proposed trust lends itself to the advancement of education by encouraging academic excellence in chemistry and physics at the Academy. . . . Moreover, no "gift over" exists in Captain Alexander's will—*i.e.*, no provision appears in the will directing an alternative disposition of the trust funds should the proposed trust fail. The absence of such a "gift over" further compels the conclusion that the proposed trust at issue here is a valid charitable trust.

The next inquiry is whether Captain Alexander possessed a general charitable intent to benefit education at the Academy, or whether he simply had a specific, charitable intent to benefit only those Academy graduates attaining the highest grade point averages in chemistry and physics. As a preliminary matter, it should be noted that courts, in construing the nature of a charitable gift, properly endeavor to find a general charitable intent whenever possible.). . . .Equally well established is that in Virginia, "charitable gifts are viewed with particular favor by the courts and every presumption consistent with the language contained in the instruments of gift will be employed in order to sustain them." *Smith v. Moore*, 225 F. Supp. 434, 441 (E.D. Va. 1963). Put another way, once the charitable nature of a trust is established, all doubts will be resolved in favor of preserving its charitable character.

Given this, the crucial question that must be answered to ascertain the nature of Captain Alexander's charitable intent is whether (i) he would have preferred that his bequest be applied to a like charitable purpose in the event that his original scheme failed, or (ii) would he instead have desired that the unused funds be removed from charitable use entirely. In light of the evidence offered at trial, it is clear that if Captain Alexander were alive today, he "probably would not direct that [the residue of his estate] be delivered to distant relatives in the event of the failure of the specific purpose set forth in his will." Instead, Captain

Alexander most likely would have preferred that the remainder of his estate be used for closely related charitable purposes if the precise terms of his original scheme could not be carried out.

Indeed, Captain Alexander's general, charitable intent is made manifest by the express language of the will itself. As noted, the Residuary Clause reads, in pertinent part:

> I hereby devise and bequeath all the remainder of my estate ... *to the UNITED STATES COAST GUARD ACADEMY* FOR THE PURPOSE OF ESTABLISHING THE GEORGE C. ALEXANDER (CLASS OF 1904) AND ROBERT T. ALEXANDER (CLASS OF 1931) SCHOLARSHIP FUND ... (emphasis added).

Significantly, the express terms of the Residuary Clause direct the remainder of Captain Alexander's estate to be given "to the United States Coast Guard Academy" for the purpose of establishing a scholarship fund to provide an annual cadet award for excellence in chemistry and physics. Fairly construed, this language makes clear that Captain Alexander intended the Academy to be the beneficiary of his largesse, and that the particular manner in which the trust was to be performed was secondary to his dominant, general charitable intent to encourage academic excellence at the Academy in chemistry and physics.

The absence of any "gift over" provision in the will further supports this conclusion. No alternative disposition for the trust corpus appears anywhere in the Residuary Clause, nor does any alternative disposition appear elsewhere in the will. It is well established that "[t]he absence of a provision for forfeiture in the case of noncompliance with a direction in a will with regard to a charitable trust is an indication that the testator did not intend that the gift should revert on failure to comply therewith while the carrying out of his general purpose is practicable." *Moore,* 225 F. Supp. At 444.

Further evidence of this intent arises from the fact that Captain Alexander made specific, testamentary bequests of $50,000 to each of the half nieces and nephews. These specific, substantial bequests, coupled with the absence of a gift over provision in the will, are convincing proof that Captain Alexander would have wanted the residue of his estate to be used to further education at the Academy, even if the precise trust terms could not be effectuated. Clearly then, one need not look beyond the four corners of the will document to discern Captain Alexander's general charitable intent.

Even assuming, *arguendo,* that such intent cannot be clearly discerned from the will itself, an examination of Captain Alexander's professional career and educational background supports a finding that he possessed a general, charitable intent to benefit the study of science, particularly of physics and chemistry, at the Academy....

But the *cy pres* analysis does not end here; a final issue must be resolved as *cy pres* applies only where a charitable trust is "indefinite, impossible to perform, or so impracticable of performance as to characterize the fulfillment of the purpose as 'impossible.'" *Moore,* 225 F. Supp. At 441. In this regard, the Coast

Guard argues that, as written, the trust is fatally indefinite and legally, as well as practically impossible to perform. . . .

Cy Pres does not require literal impossibility. That the Academy could conceivably carry out the terms of the trust does not bar application of the doctrine. It is enough that the gifts essential impracticality precludes performance.

Particularly instructive in this regard is the New Jersey supreme court decision in *Howard Sav. Institution v. Peep*, 170 A.2d 39 (N.J. 1961). In that case, the testator bequeathed money to Amherst college to be held in trust "to be used as a scholarship loan fund for deserving American born, Protestant, Gentile boys of good moral repute, not given to gambling, smoking, drinking, or similar acts." Amherst college desired to accept the gift, but only if it could do so free of the religious restrictions which, while not illegal, were contrary to the college's policies. The potential heirs-at-law argued that if Amherst did not want to perform under the trust as written, the trust failed and its funds passed to them under intestate succession.

On these facts, the Supreme Court of New Jersey held that the doctrine of *cy pres* was applicable, and permitted Amherst to accept the gift free of religious restrictions. The court based its decision on a finding that such a result was closer to the testator's intent than was the proposal to give the trust funds to the heirs. Also cited in support of the ruling were specifically, the following findings: (1) the will contained no provisions for alternative control of the trust in the event the trust was not accepted by the college; (2) the testator had attended and graduated from Amherst; and (3) the only persons who could inherit in the event of intestacy were cousins with whom the testator had not had personal relations. *Howard* and the case at bar are strikingly similar. Both cry out for the application of *cy pres*.

In this case, the award of an annual cash prize ranging from $65,000 to $130,000 to a single cadet would plainly violate Academy policy. As Admiral Versaw's persuasive testimony made pellucidly clear, an annual award of this magnitude would wreak such havoc on the Academy that the Coast Guard would be compelled to refuse the gift in the absence of any change in its terms. . . . [Thus,] the gift is "so impracticable of performance as to characterize the fulfillment of [Captain Alexander's specific] purpose as 'impossible.'"

IV

In sum then, it is clear: (i) that the proposed trust set forth in Captain Alexander's will is a valid charitable trust; (ii) that Captain Alexander possessed a general, charitable intent; and (iii) that it is "impossible" to carry out the precise terms of this proposed trust. Accordingly, application of *cy pres* doctrine is manifestly appropriate here.... Importantly, courts undertaking to alter trusts pursuant to the *cy pres* doctrine must be mindful that their discretion is not unlimited. Rather, their discretion is limited and guided by the principle that preservation of the testator's purposes is paramount and that alterations to the trust fashioned to eliminate any impossibility impracticality of performance, must, as much as possible, result in a trust that effectuates the testator's original purposes. With this guiding principle in mind, the Court concludes that the terms of the trust must be altered to provide as follows....

[*Editor's Note:* The Court then altered the terms of the trust to create the George C. Alexander and Robert T. Alexander Academic in Excellence in the Sciences Fund, to be maintained in perpetuity. The Coast Guard is the trustee and the Academy the beneficiary of the trust. The income will include small cash awards for prizes, as well as funds for senior prizes and a graduate fellowship.]

IN RE THE BARNES FOUNDATION

69 Pa. D. & C.4th 129 (2004)

[*Editor's Note:* Albert C. Barnes, who amassed a remarkable collection of Impressionist and Modernist art, founded the Barnes Foundation as a museum and school in Pennsylvania. After his death, the Barnes Foundation was governed by the Trust Indenture and Agreement that he set up to govern the foundation and continue his philosophy in perpetuity. The collection was located in Merion, a suburb of Philadelphia, near Lincoln College, a historically black college, which was to hold four of the five seats on the board. The trust instrument had several restrictions, including limiting the hours that it could be open to the public, prohibiting social functions, restricting the investment options, and forbidding the loan of the art or any type of touring exhibits. It also required that the paintings be kept in the exact same places that he put them. The Barnes Foundation fell on difficult times and went to court on several occasions to have parts of the trust instrument changed. By 2002, the Barnes Foundation announced that it would petition the court to allow it to move the collection to Philadelphia Parkway and to triple the number of trustees to 15. The judge's opinion follows.]

In this opinion, we consider the evidence presented at the second round of hearings on The Barnes Foundation's second amended petition to amend its charter and bylaws. In its pleading, the foundation sought permission, inter alia, to increase the number of trustees on its governing board and to relocate the art collection in its gallery in Merion, Pennsylvania, to a new facility in Philadelphia. After the first hearings in December of 2003, we ruled that expanding the size of the board of trustees was appropriate in today's sophisticated world of charitable fundraising. We also determined that the foundation was on the brink of financial collapse, and that the provision in Dr. Barnes' indenture mandating that the gallery be maintained in Merion was not sacrosanct, and could yield under the "doctrine of deviation," provided we were convinced the move to Philadelphia represented the least drastic modification of the indenture that would accomplish the donor's desired ends. We felt that the foundation needed to show more than the adumbration of proposed changes that was presented at the December hearings, and . . . the open areas of inquiry were distilled into three questions: (1) Can the foundation raise enough money through the sale of its non-gallery assets to keep the collection in Merion and achieve fiscal stability; and are there ethical and/or legal constraints on such a sale of assets? (2) Can the facility envisioned in Philadelphia be constructed on the proposed $100,000,000 budget? and (3) Is the foundation's three-campus model—the new facility housing the art education and public gallery functions, Merion as the site of the administrative offices and the horticulture program, and Ker-Feal, the Chester County farmhouse on 137+ acres, operating as a living museum—feasible?...

[*Editor's Note:* The case then summarizes 1,200 pages of testimony.]

Discussion

After careful consideration of this evidence, we find that the foundation met its burden of proof and the second amended petition should be granted.... [W]e find that the foundation showed clearly and convincingly the need to deviate from the terms of Dr. Barnes' indenture;[1] and we find that the three-campus model represents the least drastic modification necessary to preserve the organization. By many interested observers, permitting the gallery to move to Philadelphia will be viewed as an outrageous violation of the donor's trust. However, some of the archival materials introduced at the hearings led us to think otherwise. Contained therein were signals that Dr. Barnes expected the collection to have much greater public exposure after his death. To the court's thinking, these clues make the decision—that there is no viable alternative— easily reconcilable with the law of charitable trusts. When we add this revelation to the foundation's absolute guarantee that Dr. Barnes' primary mission—the formal education programs—will be preserved and, indeed, enhanced as a result of these changes, we can sanction this bold new venture with a clear conscience.

Our conclusion that the foundation should prevail does not mean all doubts about the viability of its plans have been allayed. Of serious concern are its fundraising goals. While Mr. Callahan was on the stand, we commented on his contagious optimism. It is clear the foundation's board will have to catch it. Mr. Callahan was only one of the many witnesses who acknowledged that the foundation is raising the bar enormously above both its own fund-raising abilities in the past and those of non-profits in general. "Ambitious" and "aggressive" were among the adjectives we heard to describe the target levels on which the Deloitte report is based. There is a real possibility that the development projections will not be realized, perhaps not in the first few years, but later on, when the interest and excitement about the new venture have faded. If that

---

[1] [FN 13] As we have cited many times in the course of the litigation involving the foundation, section 381 of the Restatement (Second) of Trusts states: A court will direct or permit the trustee of a charitable trust to deviate from a term of the trust if it appears to the court that compliance is impossible or illegal or that owing to circumstances not known to the settlor and not anticipated by him, compliance would defeat or substantially impair the accomplishment of the purposes of the trust." It is only the administrative provisions of a trust that are subject to deviation, *i.e.*, "the details of administration which the settlor has prescribed in order to secure the more important result of obtaining for the beneficiaries the advantages which the settlor stated he wished them to have." Section 561 of Bogert, *The Law of Trust and Trustees* at 27.

occurs, or the admissions do not meet expectations, or any of the other components of the Deloitte model do not reach their targets, something will have to give. We will not speculate about the nature of future petitions that might come before this court; however, we are mindful of the vehement protestations, not so long ago, that the foundation would never seek to move the gallery to Philadelphia, and, as a result, nothing could surprise us.

We make a final observation about finances and the plans now being approved. The capital cost analysis prepared by Perks Reutter Associates contemplates renovations to the Merion facility to the tune of $1,600,000. In excess of $12,000,000 was spent upgrading the gallery during the world tour of some of the foundation's works in 1993 and 1994. The irony of converting a state-of-the-art gallery into perhaps the most expensive administration building in the history of non-profits is not lost to us. Looking to the future, it is of the utmost importance that the board of trustees steer the foundation so that another such irony does not surface 10 or 15 years hence.

In light of the foregoing ... the foundation's second amended petition to amend is granted.

NOTES AND QUESTIONS

1. The Barnes Foundation collection includes paintings by Cezanne, Renoir, Braque, Matisse, Van Gogh, Modigliani, Gauguin, Monet, Seurat, and Manet. The organization has seen so much litigation and controversy that one could probably base an entire course on nonprofit law with examples from this institution. The story has spawned two books and a DVD. John Anderson, ART HELD HOSTAGE: THE BATTLE OVER THE BARNES COLLECTION (W. W. Norton 2003); THE DEVIL AND DR. BARNES: PORTRAIT OF AN AMERICAN ART COLLECTOR (Camino Books 2006); and *The Art of the Steal* (DVD, 2010). The new museum opened in Philadelphia in 2012.

2. The Corcoran Gallery of Art was the object of a cy pres proceeding in 2014. It had entered into an agreement with the National Gallery and George Washington University in early 2014, in which, if court approval were granted, the National Gallery would take over most of the art collection and George Washington University would handle the Corcoran College of Art and Design. In order to accomplish that goal, the Corcoran filed a cy pres motion in the Superior Court of the District of Columbia, requesting the court to modify the original deed of the Corcoran because the latter was no longer financially viable. The court granted the motion. *Trustees of the Corcoran Gallery of Art v. District of Columbia*, 2014 D.C. Super. LEXIS. Opponents of this change, Save the Corcoran, have preserved their arguments online at http://savethecorcoran.org/, accessed May 20, 2016.

3. The Milton Hershey Trust,[2] which was set up to create an orphanage for poor white boys, has been party to several cy pres proceedings. Over the years, the courts modified the trust to abolish race and gender restrictions and to allow the purpose of the trust to change from an orphanage to a residential school. The Hershey Trust was originally valued at $60 million, but by 1999, it had a reserve of more than $850 million. The trust initiated a cy pres proceeding, asking for permission to spend $75 million to create an institute to train teachers to educate needy children. The court denied the petition, saying, "Our discretion is not unfettered and, if exercised, must be within the limits approximating the dominant intent of Hershey." *In re Milton Hershey School and Hershey Trust Company,* Ct. Common Pleas, No. 712 (1999), quoted in Ray Madoff, *Immortality for Foundations Can Pose Big Challenges in Shifting Times,* CHRON. PHILANTHROPY (Oct. 31, 2010). By 2010, the trust's assets exceeded $2 billion, but it had no plans to serve more than 2,000 students. *Id.*

4. The Uniform Trust Code provides, in part, that "if a particular charitable purpose becomes unlawful, impracticable, impossible to achieve, or wasteful ... the court may apply cy pres to modify or terminate the trust ... in a manner consistent with the settlor's charitable purposes." Unif. Trust Code, §413(a) (amended 2005). If this provision had been adopted in Pennsylvania when the Hershey Trust cy pres petition was heard, would the result have been different? The Restatement (Third) of Trusts §67 and the ALI's Principles of the Law of Nonprofit Organizations §460(b) also add the phrase "wasteful" to the situations in which cy pres could be applied.

5. The Uniform Prudent Management of Institutional Funds Act (UPMIFA), which has been adopted in 49 states and the District of Columbia,[3] also has a cy pres provision. The preamble explains that the doctrines of cy pres and deviation apply to funds held by nonprofit corporations as well as to those held by charitable trusts. Section 6 states, "The court, upon application of an institution, may modify a restriction contained in a gift instrument regarding the management or investment of an institutional fund if the restriction has become impracticable or wasteful, if it impairs the management or investment of the fund, or if, because of circumstances not anticipated by the donor, a modification of a restriction will further the purposes of the fund." UPMIFA adds a provision that allows a charity to modify a restriction in an old (over 20 years) and small (less than $25,000)[4] fund without going to court if the restriction has become impracticable or wasteful. It must notify the state charitable regulator and wait 60 days, but if the regulator does not object, it may modify the restriction in a manner consistent with the

---

[2] Chapter 3 included two cases involving the Milton Hershey Trust, one that discussed the scope of the board of director's fiduciary duties and another that dealt with standing issues. In Chapter 7, we saw that this trust is a Type II supporting organization.

[3] For an explanation of UPMIFA, see http://upmifa.org/DesktopDefault. aspx?tabindex=5&tabid=68. Chapter 3 also discussed its provisions.

[4] Individual states may have different lengths of time or amounts in their versions of UPMIFA.

charitable purposes expressed in any documents that were part of the original gift. UPMIFA codifies and imports from trust law specific standards for the application of cy pres. Cy pres involves judicial modification of the purposes or restrictions on the use of an endowment gift if it becomes unlawful, impracticable, impossible to achieve, or wasteful. UPMIFA §§6(c) and 6(d).

III. BANKRUPTCY PROTECTION

A step that some §501(c)(3) organizations take before dissolution is to seek bankruptcy protection. Creditors cannot force a §501(c)(3) tax-exempt organization into bankruptcy, as they could with a for-profit organization, but a §501(c)(3) with significant debt could file for Chapter 11 bankruptcy as a step toward reorganization. Once a §501(c)(3) organization files for bankruptcy, the court issues an automatic stay that protects the organization and its property from creditors' actions.[5] This gives the organization time to come up with a plan of reorganization and to pay off the creditors in an orderly fashion. Sometimes the organization is able to sell a valuable asset to find the cash to keep going. Other times, the board chips in with additional funds. If the organization comes up with a plan that satisfies the creditors and the bankruptcy judge, the organization will emerge from bankruptcy with its debts discharged. If the entity cannot come up with a plan and an appointed trustee or one who is permitted by law to propose a plan cannot proffer a plan that can be confirmed, the organization will need to dissolve.

One of the difficult issues in a bankruptcy proceeding is determining which assets should be part of the bankruptcy estate. Generally, an unrestricted gift will be part of the estate, and a specifically restricted one will not. In other words, a $1 million unrestricted gift to an art museum would be part of the bankruptcy estate and could be used to pay creditors. A gift of a $1 million painting with restrictions on where and how it should be hung will not be part of the bankruptcy estate. It cannot be used to pay creditors, but it could be subject to a cy pres proceeding. As you can imagine, these proceedings can be quite complex. Three examples follow.

A. City of Detroit's Institute of Arts

When the city of Detroit filed for bankruptcy in 2013, questions arose as to whether the collection at the city-owned Detroit Institute of Arts (DIA) would be sold to help pay creditors. The attorney general of Michigan issued an opinion that "the art collection of the Detroit Institute of Arts is held by the City of Detroit in charitable trust for the people of Michigan, and no piece in the collection may thus be sold, conveyed, or transferred to satisfy city debts or

---

[5] Two exceptions to the automatic stay exist. If the organization is under investigation, that proceeding will probably not be stayed, and the stay does not prevent an educational institution from losing its accreditation.

obligations." But the creditors, which included retirees whose pensions would be cut if the debts were not repaid, did not agree, and the case was scheduled for trial in the summer of 2014. Fortunately, a group of foundations and the state of Michigan agreed to raise approximately $816 million (the value of the artwork that the city purchased) to be used to pay off creditors over a period of 20 years, a solution that has been called the "Grand Bargain." The state of Michigan and the DIA agreed to raise funds for this bargain. The bankruptcy judge approved this plan in November 2014. The foundations immediately paid $100 million into a fund that would support the city's pensions, and the city exited bankruptcy a few weeks later. Nathan Bomey, John Gallagher, and Mark Stryker, *Detroit Rising: How Detroit Was Reborn: The Inside Story of Detroit's Historic Bankruptcy Case*, DETROIT FREE PRESS (Nov. 9, 2014).

B. Bankruptcy Protection for Catholic Dioceses

Between 2004 and 2015, a dozen Catholic dioceses filed for Chapter 11 bankruptcy protection. The diocese of Portland, Oregon, was the first to file in 2004, and it emerged from bankruptcy in 2007 when a federal bankruptcy judge approved a $75 million settlement of clergy sexual abuse claims and a financial reorganization plan.[6] The most recent filing was the diocese of Minneapolis and St. Paul in 2015.

Almost all, if not all, of the filings came on the eve of lawsuits alleging sexual abuse by Catholic priests. Bankruptcy protection freezes all legal proceedings while the organization restructures its debts. It can give the bankrupt organization time to manage complex litigation and ensure that all the victims get paid, not just those who file their cases early. The archdiocese of San Diego, for example, paid 144 victims a total of $198 million when it emerged from bankruptcy. Critics of the bankruptcies, however, claim that this decision is simply one that protects the church from further embarrassment and prevents the victims from being able to tell their stories. Amy Julia Harris, *Catholic Dioceses Declare Bankruptcy on Eve of Sexual Abuse Trials*, (Center for Investigative Reporting, Feb. 2, 2015).

The diocese of Milwaukee emerged from bankruptcy protection in late 2015. It had filed for protection in 2011 and proposed a settlement in August 2015 that would pay $21 million to 330 abuse survivors (of the 575 who filed suit). That amounted to $44,000 per victim once the $7 million was subtracted for attorney fees—considerably less than victims have received in other cases.

One of the issues that kept a settlement from occurring earlier was a dispute over whether the plaintiffs could be paid with money held by a cemetery trust. Victim advocates claimed that the archdiocese deliberately moved millions of dollars into this trust when it declared bankruptcy. The archdiocese countered

---

[6] According to the Catholic News Service, 89 attorneys were involved in these bankruptcy proceedings. Ed Langlois and Robert Pfohman, *1st Catholic U.S. Bankruptcy Ends with $75 Million Settlement* (CATHOLIC NEWS SERVICE, April 29. 2007).

that burial rights are an integral part of the Catholic religion and that a court decision forcing it to tap into the cemetery funds would violate its First Amendment rights and the Religious Freedom Restoration Act. Litigation on this issue ensued, and the issue was in front of the U.S. Supreme Court in the summer of 2015 when the parties proposed a settlement that included a voluntary payment from the cemetery fund. Bruce Vielmetti, *Bankruptcy Judge Confirms Milwaukee Archdiocese Reorganization Plan*, MILWAUKEE SENTINEL JOURNAL (Nov. 9, 2015); Peter Isely, *Milwaukee Archdioces "Settles" Sex Abuse Bankruptcy, $15 Million Dollars for Hundreds of Victims; $30 Million for a Handful of Lawyers*, SNAP PRESS RELEASE (Aug. 4, 2014).

For a link to the legal documents in all 12 bankruptcies (and one in Ireland), see *Bankruptcy Protection in the Abuse Cases*, http://www.bishop-accountability.org/bankruptcy.htm.

C. August Wilson Center

Pittsburgh's August Wilson Center for African-American Culture, a cultural hub for African-American theater, art, and education, opened in 2009. Named after the Pulitzer Prize–winning playwright August Wilson, who grew up in Pittsburgh, the center faced difficulties before it even opened. The construction site had unexpected contaminants that had to be cleaned up, the price of steel tripled, and the Great Recession hit. The center opened with a huge debt, and then it attracted smaller audiences than anticipated. It filed for bankruptcy in 2013. By 2014, it was obvious that the center would have to be sold, and a sheriff's sale was set for late November. Shortly before that sale, a group of foundations agreed to purchase the center, with some help from local taxpayers. They turned it over to the Pittsburgh Cultural Trust for management. By early 2015, a new board had been formed, and the parties were entering a new phase. The hope was that new leadership, unencumbered by the debt, would develop programs that would attract audiences across racial lines, just as Wilson's plays have done. M. L. Ward, *Pittsburgh's August Wilson Center Facing Closure*, UPTOWN MAGAZINE (Feb 26, 2014); Harold Hayes, *August Wilson Center Sold*, KDKA, CBS Pittsburgh (Sept. 29, 2014); Michael B. Rose, *New Board Assumes Leadership of August Wilson Center*, PITTSBURGH COURIER (Nov. 25, 2015)

For additional reading about 501(c)(3) bankruptcies, see Reid K. Weisbord, *Charitable Insolvency and Corporate Governance in Bankruptcy Reorganization*, 10 U. C. BERKELEY BUS. L. J. 304 (2014); Dana Yankowitz Elliott and Evan C. Hallander, *Navigating a Nonprofit Corporation Through Bankruptcy*, NONPROFIT QUARTERLY (April 29. 2014); Evelyn Brody, *The Charity in Bankruptcy and Ghosts of Donor Past, Present, and Future*, 29 SETON HALL LEGIS.J. 471 (2006); Woods Bowman, *Chapter 11 for Nonprofit Organizations*, in 1999 WILEY BANKRUPTCY LAW UPDATE (Keith Shapiro & Nancy Peterman eds., John Wiley 1999), pp. 523-528.

IV. DISSOLUTION

Dissolving a §501(c)(3) corporation is mostly a matter of state law. The Internal Revenue Service (IRS) requires the organization to announce its termination on a final Form 990[7] and to follow IRS regulations about the distribution of assets on dissolution, but for the most part, the tax code concerns itself with the continuation of exemption rather than voluntary termination of tax exemption. Following are regulatory and statutory materials, as well as two cases discussing dissolution and the distribution of assets upon dissolution.

TREASURY REGULATIONS §1.501(c)(3)-1(b)(4)

Distribution of assets on dissolution.

An organization is not organized exclusively for one or more exempt purposes unless its assets are dedicated to an exempt purpose. An organization's assets will be considered dedicated to an exempt purpose, for example, if, upon dissolution, such assets would, by reason of a provision in the organization's articles or by operation of law, be distributed for one or more exempt purposes, or to the Federal government, or to a State or local government, for a public purpose, or would be distributed by a court to another organization to be used in such manner as in the judgment of the court will best accomplish the general purposes for which the dissolved organization was organized. However, an organization does not meet the organizational test if its articles or the law of the State in which it was created provide that its assets would, upon dissolution, be distributed to its members or shareholders.

MODEL NONPROFIT CORPORATION ACT, 3D ED. (2008)

Chapter 14, Dissolution

Subchapter A: Voluntary Dissolution

§14.03. Articles of Dissolution

(a) At any time after dissolution is authorized, the nonprofit corporation may dissolve by delivering to the secretary of state for filing articles of dissolution setting forth:
    (1) the name of the corporation;
    (2) the date dissolution was authorized; and
    (3) the dissolution was approved in the manner required by this Act and by the articles of incorporation and bylaws.

---

[7] *See* Schedule N, Form 990.

(b) A nonprofit corporation is dissolved upon the effective date of its articles of dissolution.

(c) For purposes of this [subchapter], "dissolved corporation" means a nonprofit corporation whose articles of dissolution have become effective and includes a successor entity to which the remaining assets of the corporation are transferred subject to its liabilities for purposes of liquidation.

§14.05. Effect of Dissolution

(a) A dissolved nonprofit corporation continues its corporate existence but may not carry on any activities except that appropriate to wind up and liquidate its affairs, including:

(1) collecting its assets;

(2) disposing of its properties that will not be distributed in kind;

(3) discharging or making provision for discharging its liabilities;

(4) distributing its remaining property as required by law and its articles of incorporation and bylaws...; and

(5) doing every other act necessary to wind up and liquidate its business and affairs.

(b) Dissolution of a nonprofit corporation does not:

(1) transfer title to the corporation's property;

(2) subject its directors or officers to standards of conduct different from those prescribed in chapter 8;

(3) change quorum or voting requirements for its board of directors or members; change provisions for selection, resignation, or removal of its directors or officers or both; or change provisions for amending its bylaws;

(4) prevent commencement of a proceeding by or against the corporation in its corporate name;

(5) abate or suspend a proceeding pending by or against the corporation on the effective date of dissolution; or

(6) terminate the authority of the registered agent of the corporation....

(c) Property held in trust or otherwise dedicated to a charitable purpose may not be diverted from its purpose by the dissolution of a nonprofit corporation unless and until the corporation obtains an order of [court] [the attorney general] to the extent required by and pursuant to the law of this state on cy pres or otherwise dealing with the nondiversion of charitable assets.

§14.09. Director Duties

(a) Directors shall cause the dissolved nonprofit corporation to discharge or make reasonable provision for the payment of claims and make distributions of assets after payment or provision for claims....

Subchapter B: Administrative Dissolution

§14.20. Grounds for Administrative Dissolution

The secretary of state may commence a proceeding under section 14.21 to administratively dissolve a nonprofit corporation if:

(1) the corporation does not pay within 120 days after they are due any taxes or penalties imposed by this [act] or other law which are collected by the secretary of state;

(2) the corporation does not deliver its annual report to the secretary of state within 120 days after it is due;

(3) the corporation is without a registered agent or registered office in this state for 120 days or more;

(4) the corporation does not notify the secretary of state within 120 days that its registered agent or registered office has been changed, that its registered agent has resigned, or that its registered office has been discontinued; or

(5) the corporation's period of duration, if any, stated in its articles of incorporation expires.

§14.21. Procedure for Administrative Dissolution

(a) If the secretary of state determines that one or more grounds exist under Section 14.20 for dissolving a nonprofit corporation, the secretary of state shall serve the corporation with notice in the form of a record of that determination under section 5.04.

(b) If the nonprofit corporation does not correct each ground for dissolution or demonstrate to the reasonable satisfaction of the secretary of state that each ground determined by the secretary of state does not exist within 60 days after service of the notice is perfected under Section 5.04, the secretary of state shall administratively dissolve the corporation by signing a certificate of dissolution that recites the ground or grounds for dissolution and its effective date. The secretary of state shall file the original of the certificate and serve a copy on the corporation under Section 5.04.

(c) The administrative dissolution of a nonprofit corporation does not terminate the authority of its registered agent....

Subchapter C: Judicial Dissolution

§14.30. Grounds for Judicial Dissolution

The [name or describe court or courts] may dissolve a nonprofit corporation:

(1) in a proceeding by the attorney general, if it is established that:

(i) the corporation obtained its articles of incorporation through fraud; or

(ii) the corporation has exceeded or abused, and is continuing to exceed or abuse the authority conferred upon it by law;

(2) except as provided in the articles of incorporation or bylaws, in a proceeding by 50 members or members holding at least 5% of the voting power, whichever is less, or by a director, if it is established that:

(i) the directors or a designated body are deadlocked in the management of the corporate affairs, the members, if any, are unable to break the deadlock, and irreparable injury to the corporation or its mission is threatened or being suffered because of the deadlock;

(ii) the directors or those in control of the corporation have acted, are acting, or will act in a manner that is illegal, oppressive, or fraudulent;

(iii) the members are deadlocked in voting power and have failed, for a period that includes at least two consecutive annual meeting dates, to elect successors to directors whose terms have, or otherwise would have, expired;

(iv) the corporate assets are being misapplied or wasted; or

(v) the corporation has insufficient assets to continue its activities and it is no longer able to assemble a quorum of directors or members;

(3) in a proceeding by a creditor, if it is established that:

(i) the creditor's claim has been reduced to judgment, the execution on the judgment returned unsatisfied, and the corporation is insolvent; or

(ii) the corporation has admitted in a record that the creditor's claim is due and owing and the corporation is insolvent; or

(4) in a proceeding by the corporation to have its voluntary dissolution continued under court supervision.

§14.31. Procedure for Judicial Dissolution

(a) Venue for a proceeding by the attorney general to dissolve a nonprofit corporation lies in [*name the county or counties*]. Venue for a proceeding brought by any other party named in section 14.30 lies in the county where a corporation's principal office (or, if none in this state, its registered office) is or was last located.

(b) It is not necessary to make directors or members parties to a proceeding to dissolve a nonprofit corporation unless relief is sought against them individually.

(c) A court in a proceeding brought to dissolve a nonprofit corporation may issue injunctions, appoint a receiver or custodian pendente lite with all powers and duties the court directs, take other action required to preserve the corporate assets wherever located, and carry on the activities of the corporation until a full hearing can be held.

SHORTER COLLEGE V. BAPTIST CONVENTION OF GEORGIA

614 S.E.2d 37 (Ga. 2005)

CARLEY, Justice.

In 1959, Shorter College (College) amended its charter to confer on the Baptist Convention of the State of Georgia (GBC) the exclusive authority to name the school's Board of Trustees (Board). As a result of the grant of this power to choose the trustees, GBC assumed the status of a "member" of the College. Over the years, GBC and the College collaborated in the trustee selection process. In 2001, however, a conflict arose as to GBC's exercise of its authority under the charter to fill two vacancies on the Board. The controversy was precipitated by the Southern Association of Colleges and Schools, which questioned the College's independence and threatened its accreditation because the power to select trustees was vested in GBC.

The dispute culminated in GBC's rejection of candidates proposed by the College and the naming of two new trustees who lacked the prior approval of the school. Contending that GBC's power to select the trustees was an encroachment on the independence of the institution which endangered its accreditation, the Board thereafter sought to amend the bylaws to allow the school some input into the process. However, GBC insisted on continued exercise of the exclusive authority granted to it by the charter, and it named several new trustees to the Board.

The College refused to recognize the new trustees selected by GBC. Instead, a majority of the "old" Board approved a plan, denominated as a "dissolution" of the College, whereby all assets of the school, including its name, would be transferred for no consideration to the Shorter College Foundation (Foundation). From the perspective of the "old" Board and its concern about accreditation, this transfer had the desired effect of divesting GBC of its authority to name the trustees, since the Foundation's directors would not be subject to approval or removal by GBC.

Thereafter, the College and Foundation filed suit to recover certain pre-dissolution funds that GBC had budgeted for the school's use. GBC answered and counterclaimed, seeking to enjoin the unilateral dissolution of the College by the "old" Board as a void transaction. The validity of the dissolution was addressed on motion for summary judgment, and the trial court granted judgment in favor of the College and Foundation. On appeal, however, the Court of Appeals reversed.... The College and Foundation (Appellants) applied for certiorari, which we granted in order to determine whether the Court of Appeals correctly held that the Board's effort to effect a "dissolution" of the College was invalid.

1. "[A] corporation is an artificial, not a natural, person." *Eckles v. Atlanta Technology Group*, 485 S.E.2d 22, 24 (Ga. 1997). As such, a corporation cannot experience a natural death, but it can undergo a "dissolution," which implies the termination of its existence and its utter extinction and obliteration as an entity or body in favor of which obligations exist or accrue or upon which liability may be imposed. Liquidation of a corporation has been defined to mean the winding up of the affairs of the corporation by reducing its assets, paying its debts, and apportioning the profit or loss. A distribution of all assets is a "winding-up of the affairs" of the corporation and is synonymous with "liquidation." This definition of a "dissolution" as the winding up and liquidation of all business affairs applies equally to both for-profit and non-profit corporations in Georgia.

The transaction at issue in this case would not constitute a "dissolution" in the context of for-profit corporations. The transfer of the assets of the College to the Foundation was not for the purpose of terminating the existence of the school and winding up its affairs, as would have occurred had the intended recipient been another educational institution already having a separate and independent existence, such as Emory, Mercer, Berry, or any number of other colleges located in this state. Indeed, the aim of this "dissolution" was the exact opposite. The Board's intent was the preservation of the assets of the College and the continuation of its existence, with the only anticipated result being the transfer of governing authority over the institution to the Foundation and the consequent termination of the power granted by the charter to GBC to select the trustees. As the Court of Appeals noted, the chair of the Board frankly acknowledged that this was the purpose of the "dissolution" in the following excerpt from a letter sent to her fellow trustees notifying them of two proposals that would be submitted for their approval at an upcoming meeting: "The first proposal seeks the Board's approval to *reorganize the College*. This *corporate reorganization* will be accomplished by dissolving the corporate entity 'Shorter College' and simultaneously ... distributing all of the College's assets and assigning all of its liabilities to (the Foundation). The Foundation, which will immediately be renamed 'Shorter College,' will *thereafter carry on all of the business and activities previously conducted by the College*." (Emphasis supplied.) *Baptist Convention*, 596 S.E.2d at 766. Such a "reorganization" fails to qualify as a valid "dissolution" of a for-profit corporation because the end result is not the extinction of any former business, but the mere transfer of the same business to another entity which thereafter will continue its operation. . . .

It appears, therefore, that resolution of this case depends upon whether there is any legal distinction to be drawn between the dissolution of a for-profit and a non-profit corporation. The current Georgia Nonprofit Corporation Code "was drawn principally from the Georgia Business Corporation Code" and reflects "the desire to conform [it] to the Business Code whenever possible and appropriate...." Comment to OCGA §14-3-101. Thus, "unless otherwise specifically noted, the fundamental rules and principles of law of profit and business corporations are equally applicable to nonprofit corporations." *Dunn v. Ceccarelli*, 489 S.E.2d 563, 565 (Ga. 1997).

With specific regard to OCGA §14-3-1406, nothing in the language of that provision indicates that the meaning of "dissolution" differs in any substantive particular from its for-profit counterpart in OCGA §14-2-1405. Indeed, the wording of the two statutes is essentially identical, and the Comment to OCGA §14-3-1406 specifies that it "is based on section 14-2-1405 of the [Georgia] Business [Corporation] Code, OCGA §§14-2-101 et seq." As statutes which are in pari materia, OCGA §§14-2-1405 and 14-3-1406 must be construed together and harmonized wherever possible. Because the "wind up and liquidate" language of OCGA §14-3-1406 was borrowed verbatim from OCGA §14-2-1405, the "dissolution" of non-profit and for-profit corporations must necessarily be analogous in that particular aspect. Therefore, the Court of Appeals correctly held that the effort to reorganize the College, which clearly would not qualify as a dissolution of a for-profit corporation, was likewise not a valid "dissolution" of a non-profit corporation within the meaning of OCGA §14-3-1406.

This is true even though, under OCGA §14-3-1402 (b), the Board had the unilateral power to approve a dissolution of the College. The mere fact that, as a procedural matter, a majority of the trustees could and did vote in favor of the "dissolution" is not dispositive. The question is whether the transaction was in fact a legally valid "dissolution," and the nomenclature used by the Board certainly is not controlling in that regard. Instead, dissolution is a "statutory procedure, [so] the statutory requirements must be complied with to accomplish an effective dissolution." Under OCGA §14-3-1406, the winding up and liquidation of the business affairs of the dissolving non-profit corporation is one of those requirements. . . . Because the transfer of the College's assets to the Foundation did not meet substantive requirements of OCGA §14-3-1406, the trustees' compliance with any of the procedures applicable to the "dissolution" of a non-profit corporation is immaterial.

Appellants urge that, because a non-profit corporation does not have financial goals, it is inequitable to require the same complete destruction of the underlying business as with the dissolution of a for-profit corporation. However, the relevant inquiry is the statutory definition of "dissolution" and, in that regard, the specific wording used by the General Assembly, not general concepts of equity, is the controlling factor. "As long as the [statutory] language is clear and does not lead to an unreasonable or absurd result, 'it is the sole evidence of the ultimate legislative intent.' " *Ray v. Barber*, 548 S.E.2d 283, 284 (2001). Under applicable statutes, the business of a corporation, regardless of whether it is operated for profit or not, cannot survive a valid "dissolution." Pursuant to OCGA §14-3-1402(b), the trustees had every right to vote to dissolve the College and to transfer its assets intact or piecemeal to other separate and independent educational institutions. Such a transfer would perpetuate the underlying beneficial purpose for which the school was created, notwithstanding its own extinction. Under OCGA §14-3-1406, however, the Board was not authorized to reorganize the school by transferring its assets to the Foundation for the purpose of maintaining the College as a functioning educational institution.

2. . . . [T]he dissent . . . concludes that "the legislature set forth different procedures for dissolving nonprofit and for-profit corporations, [so] it is wrong for this Court to mandate that they be the same." As support for this assertion, the dissent notes that, while the assets of a dissolving for-profit corporation are conveyed to its shareholders under OCGA §14-2-1405(4), OCGA §14-3-1403(b)(3) provides, in relevant part, that certain specified assets of a dissolving non-profit corporation "shall be transferred or conveyed to one or more domestic or foreign corporations, trusts, societies, or organizations engaged in activities substantially similar to those of the dissolving corporation."

Because a non-profit corporation does not have shareholders, the class of recipients authorized to receive its assets *upon dissolution* obviously cannot be the same as those who have a claim to the assets of a dissolving for-profit corporation. Because the recipients of a dissolving non-profit and for-profit corporation are different, the procedures for distribution of those assets must necessarily also differ. However, the differences in the composition of the class of those who have the ultimate claim on the assets of a dissolving corporation and in the procedures regarding the distribution of the assets to them do not have any material bearing on whether the underlying transaction upon which the distribution is based complies with the substantive requirements for accomplishing a corporate dissolution. Whether the distribution of a corporation's assets constitutes a valid dissolution is not determined by how and to whom the assets were conveyed. . . .

OCGA §14-3-1403(b)(3) provides that a dissolving non-profit corporation is authorized to distribute its assets to another corporation "engaged in activities *substantially similar* to those of the dissolving corporation." (Emphasis supplied.) Here, the Board did not comply with that statutory mandate by transferring the assets of the College to another corporation which was actually engaged in activities "substantially similar" to those of the purportedly dissolved corporation. Instead, the assets were transferred to the Foundation, which was incorporated for the express purpose of carrying on precisely the same activities formerly pursued by the corporation which the Board sought to dissolve.

That transfer was not pursuant to a valid dissolution accomplished pursuant to OCGA §14-3-1406(5). It constituted an unauthorized effort on the part of the Board to reorganize the College so as to operate the school as before, but with a new set of trustees. The dissent may be correct insofar as it suggests that the subjective intent of the trustees who approved the transfer was furtherance of the mission of the College. However, advancing the school's educational activities is simply not the legal test for determining whether the transaction satisfied the statutory requirements for a dissolution. A dissolution of the College could be accomplished only when "its" business and affairs were wound up and liquidated under OCGA §14-3-1406(5) and, pursuant to OCGA §14-3-1403(b)(3), when its assets had been transferred to another organization already engaged in "activities substantially similar" to those which it no longer was authorized to pursue.

The trustees of a non-profit corporation are charged with acting "[i]n a manner [he or she] believes in good faith to be in the best interests of the corporation. . . ." OCGA §14-3-830(1)(A). In this case, the Board fully complied with this standard of conduct, acting in the good faith belief that it was responding to a threat to the accreditation of the College. However, the underlying good faith of the trustees cannot substitute for objective compliance with applicable statutory requirements. . . . The Board did not have the power to fashion its own remedy by unilaterally transferring GBC's status and authority as a "member" of the College to the Foundation for the purpose of continuing to operate the school. Therefore, the Court of Appeals correctly reversed the grant of summary judgment in favor of Appellants and remanded the case to the trial court "with instructions to set aside the dissolution as ultra vires pursuant to OCGA §14-3-304 (c)."

Judgment affirmed. All the Justices concur, except FLETCHER, C.J., SEARS, P.J., and HUNSTEIN, J., who dissent.

FLETCHER, Chief Justice, dissenting.

The majority opinion holds that Shorter College's Board of Trustees complied with its governing documents, the Georgia Nonprofit Corporation Code, and its fiduciary duties in dissolving the College and transferring its assets to the Shorter College Foundation. Nevertheless, the majority opinion holds that because the dissolution failed to pass a fourth test—compliance with dissolution requirements applicable to for-profit corporations—it was invalid. Because this fourth test is inapposite to nonprofits and unnecessary to prevent sham dissolutions, I dissent.

The majority errs by using a definition supplied by the American Jurisprudence treatise, rather than focusing on the requirements established by the Georgia legislature. The treatise itself cautions against relying on its definition to the exclusion of state statutes: "[w]hen evaluating corporate administrative dissolution statutes that vary widely from state to state, it cannot safely be assumed that the term 'dissolution' has any strict meaning independent of the jurisdiction and precise context in which that term is applied." The majority opinion falls into this trap of ignoring context.

Because the procedure differs depending on which type of entity is being dissolved, the majority opinion is incorrect that "dissolution" means the same thing in Georgia's for-profit and nonprofit corporation codes. When a for-profit corporation is dissolved, its business ceases to exist and its remaining assets are distributed to its shareholders under OCGA §14-2-1405(4). When a nonprofit is dissolved, however, there is a different procedure: instead of distributing the nonprofit's assets to its members, they are transferred to a similar business under OCGA §14-3-1403(b)(3). Therefore, the nonprofit's business does not necessarily cease to exist, but may be carried on by a new corporation. Accordingly, the legislature made a nonprofit dissolution more closely resemble a transfer of assets or a reorganization than a for-profit dissolution.

The majority opinion compares the dissolution procedures in OCGA §14-2-1405 and OCGA §14-3-1406 and states that "the wording of the two statutes is essentially identical." But one of the ways in which it is *not* identical is that OCGA §14-3-1406, applicable to nonprofits, mandates dissolving in accordance with a "plan of dissolution." This plan of dissolution must comply with OCGA §14-3-1403, and it is that statute that contains the pertinent difference regarding the disposition of assets in nonprofit and for-profit dissolutions. Because the legislature set forth different procedures for dissolving nonprofit and for-profit corporations, it is wrong for this Court to mandate that they be the same.

I agree with the majority opinion that the Board complied with the letter of the law by dissolving the College and transferring its assets to the Foundation. It is undisputed that the College's governing documents gave only the Board, and not the Baptist Convention of the State of Georgia (GBC), the right to vote on the College's dissolution. Further, under OCGA §14-3-1402(b), the Board alone had the right to dissolve the College. Therefore, the dissolution complied with the strict letter of the law.

I also agree with the majority opinion that compliance with the letter of the law is not enough in this case. We must also ask whether the dissolution complied with the spirit of the law. The test for this is whether the dissolution violated the Board's fiduciary duties. A "sham" dissolution would violate these duties; a valid dissolution would not.

Because the College was a nonprofit, the Board owed its fiduciary duties to the College's mission, not to GBC as a member. GBC's contrary contention mistakenly equates "members" of a nonprofit corporation with "shareholders" of a for-profit corporation. In for-profit corporations, the predominant view is that the board of directors owes its fiduciary duties to the corporation's shareholders. In nonprofit corporations, however, these duties are owed not to the members, but to the nonprofit's mission.

"It is axiomatic that the board of directors [of a nonprofit] is charged with the duty to ensure that the mission of the charitable corporation is carried out. This duty has been referred to as the "duty of obedience." It requires the director of a not-for-profit corporation to "be faithful to the purposes and goals of the organization," since *"[u]nlike business corporations, whose ultimate objective is to make money, nonprofit corporations are defined by their specific objectives.... Manhattan Eye, Ear & Throat Hosp. v. Spitzer,* 715 N.Y.S.2d 575, 593 (N.Y. Sup. Ct. 1999).

Therefore, the question is whether the Board's actions furthered or hindered the College's mission. The College's mission was "to provide quality higher education ... integrat[ing] Christian values within a nurturing community...." The record shows that the College had real reason to believe that it would lose accreditation if it did not address the accreditor's concerns over GBC's influence. The loss of accreditation would have a devastating effect on any college or university, including an inability to attract the best students and faculty and a loss of essential financial aid for students. By taking the actions it did, the Board addressed the accreditor's concerns over GBC's influence, removed the barrier to reaccreditation, and thereby furthered the College's mission of "providing quality higher education."

The Foundation will also carry out the College's religious mission by continuing to promote a nurturing, Christian environment in which students will learn. Accordingly, the dissolution furthered both the College's educational and religious missions, whereas ceding to GBC's wishes would have likely cost it accreditation and severely damaged its educational mission. The Board thus fully complied with its fiduciary duties, as the majority opinion concedes.

In sum, despite the dissolution having complied with both the letter and the spirit of nonprofit law, the majority opinion also requires compliance with the procedures for dissolving a for-profit corporation. These procedures are inapposite to nonprofit dissolutions. They are also unnecessary to prevent sham dissolutions; adherence to fiduciary duties accomplishes this purpose. Because the Board complied with the College's governing documents, applicable nonprofit dissolution law, *and* its fiduciary duties, the College's dissolution was proper and must stand.

I am authorized to state that Presiding Justice Sears and Justice Hunstein join in this dissent.

IN RE MATTER OF MULTIPLE SCLEROSIS SERVICE ORGANIZATION OF NEW YORK, INC.

68 N.Y.3d 861, 496 N.E.2d 861, 505 N.Y.S.2d 841 (1986)

MEYER, Judge.

The standard governing distribution of the assets of a charitable corporation being dissolved under the Not-For-Profit Corporation Law is less restrictive and accords greater authority to the corporation's board of directors and the courts than governs the distribution of the assets held by a trustee under a will or other instrument making a disposition for charitable purposes or the assets held by the officers and trustees of a voluntary association which has received by public subscription a fund for charitable purposes from more than 1,000 contributors or than was the cy pres standard at common law.... Under the quasi cy pres standard of the Not-For-Profit Corporation Law, a Supreme Court Justice in determining whether to approve the plan of distribution proposed by the corporation's board, and if not to what other charitable organizations distribution should be made, should consider (1) the source of the funds to be distributed, whether received through public subscription or under the trust provision of a will or other instrument; (2) the purposes and powers of the corporation as enumerated in its certificate of incorporation; (3) the activities in fact carried out and services actually provided by the corporation; (4) the relationship of the activities and purposes of the proposed distributee(s) to those of the dissolving corporation; and (5) the bases for the distribution recommended by the board. The order of the Appellate Division should, therefore, be reversed, with costs to appellants, and the matter remitted to Supreme Court for a hearing in accordance herewith.

I

Petitioner, the Multiple Sclerosis Service Organization of New York, Inc. (MSSO), ... a type B corporation, ... was formed in 1965 by a group of volunteers who had been associated with the Kings County Multiple Sclerosis Society (Kings County Chapter), a chapter of the National Multiple Sclerosis Society (National Society), but who withdrew from the chapter in 1965 because they wished to focus primarily upon rehabilitation—helping MS victims to function in society to their maximum potential—while the National Society focused primarily upon research. It has neither been affiliated with nor has it had financial assistance from the National Society or any of its chapters. Its purposes, as stated in its amended certificate of incorporation, are to operate a recreational center for the use of MS victims...; to provide them with and keep in repair the specialized equipment needed by such victims...; to furnish counseling services to them relating to their conditions; to make grants to those engaged in MS research and to solicit and receive funds for the purposes mentioned and for the benefit of said victims. The petition in the instant proceeding explained MSSO's function as an attempt "to create and service a community where multiple sclerosis victims could again engage in the business of life, which had all but ended for them in the outside world."

For 17 years MSSO operated a center in Brooklyn.... In 1982, however, dwindling finances and the advancing age of its members resulted in the determination that MSSO could no longer continue its activities. According to the affidavit of its president accompanying the petition, the New York City Chapter was asked to take over the service center but declined to do so. The board then determined, after a meeting on notice to all members of the corporation, to sell the Brooklyn service center—its principal asset—pay its debts and select recognized charities to receive any assets remaining.

Sale of the center was approved by Supreme Court, its order providing that any money remaining after payment of obligations be donated to "recognized charities." A committee was then appointed to find distributees engaged in substantially similar activities. [The committee inspected likely candidates, choosing four organization with an] emphasis upon on-site care and service to clients suffering from irreversible and chronic medical conditions requiring expensive long-term treatment.... After the board adopted a resolution providing for distribution of the approximately $155,000 remaining, ... the petition in the present proceeding seeking Supreme Court approval of the proposed distribution was filed, on notice to the Attorney-General, as required by N-PCL §1002 (d).

[Editor's Note: The New York City Chapter intervened, claiming that its activities were "more akin" to those of MSSO than the selected organizations. It claimed] that funds donated to MSSO were specifically donated for aid to victims of multiple sclerosis and would be improperly diverted if distributed to other than MS-oriented charities. The Attorney-General ... stated as an affirmative defense that the proposed distributees are not engaged in activities substantially similar to those of MSSO.

... Special Term, finding that the distributees were engaged in activities substantially similar to those of MSSO "in that each renders services to permanently disabled people which enable them to function to their maximum potential," ... approved the proposed distribution.

The Appellate Division unanimously reversed. [It concluded] that despite its use of "substantially similar" the N-PCL provisions incorporated the "as nearly as possible" cy pres standard of the common law and emphasizing the presumed intent of donors to MSSO to benefit MS victims, it remitted to Special Term for a factual hearing....

From the judgment entered on that decision petitioner appeals to us pursuant to CPLR 5601 (d), bringing up for review the Appellate Division's prior nonfinal order. We conclude that in equating "substantially similar" with "as near as possible," the Appellate Division erred. We, therefore, reverse and remit to Supreme Court for a hearing.

II

The question before us is not whether principles of a cy pres nature apply to the distribution of the assets of a dissolving charitable corporation but what the governing principle is. There is no question that the common-law cy pres standard was "as near as possible," that being the literal translation of the Anglo-French from which the words were taken. There likewise is no question that the Memorandum of the Joint Legislative Committee to Study Revision of Corporation Laws referred to the provision now contained in N-PCL §1005(a)(3)(A) as "a codification of the 'cy-pres' doctrine." But in concluding that, as to the distribution by such a corporation of assets other than those received through a will or similar instrument, the common-law standard applies notwithstanding the substantially different language of N-PCL §1005(a)(3)(A), the Appellate Division failed to consider the history of cy pres in New York, its statutory development in this State generally and in relation to charitable corporations, and the very different wording of the N-PCL standard from that of related statutes and that used to express the common-law rule and thus fell into error.

A

A nonjudicial dissolution of a type B corporation, such as is here involved, is governed by N-PCL article 10. It begins with the adoption by the board of directors of a plan for dissolution and distribution of the corporation's assets. After submission to and approval by members of the corporation entitled to vote, the plan must be submitted to the Supreme Court in the judicial district in which the office of the corporation is located. The first sentence of section 1005(a)(3)(A) requires distribution, after payment of liabilities, of "[assets] received and held by the corporation for a purpose specified as Type B ... or which are legally required to be used for a particular purpose ... to one or more domestic or foreign corporations or other organizations engaged in *activities substantially similar to* those of the dissolved corporation pursuant to a plan of distribution adopted as provided in section 1001 ... or as ordered by the court to which the plan is submitted for approval under section 1002." Finally section 1008(a)(15) authorizes the Supreme Court to order distribution of assets received and held by the corporation for a type B purpose or which are "legally required to be used for a particular purpose ... to one or more domestic or foreign corporations or other organizations engaged in *activities substantially similar to* those of the dissolved corporation."

Apparent from those provisions is the Legislature's intention to require that assets given to a charitable corporation for a particular purpose be used by the corporation while it is in existence for the purpose specified by the donor, unless the restriction is released by the donor or by a court or, circumstances having so changed as to make impracticable or impossible the literal carrying out of the purpose, a court (with the consent of the donor if living) permits otherwise. But it is also apparent, for the reasons hereafter set forth, that the Legislature did not intend the stringent "as near as possible" standard of the common law to govern distribution of assets of a dissolving charitable corporation received other than through a will or other limiting instrument, but rather provided for distribution to corporations or organizations engaged in substantially similar activities and left it to the board of directors in the first instance to determine to whom distribution should be made.

B

The common-law cy pres doctrine, or "ancient doctrine of approximation" as it has been termed embodies the English concept that when a donor parts with his property for a charitable purpose it shall be forever devoted to that purpose, whether or not the particular donee continues to exist. If the donee ceases to exist, the property may be devoted to a kindred charity; one that is, "as near as may be" to the charity contemplated by the donor....

The common-law doctrine was, however, held not to prevail in New York. [*Editor's Note:* The court then cited three successive statutes that provided guidance in such a situation, culminating with the Membership Corporations Law §56(5) bylaws in 1928.] That provision authorized the court to order distribution of the property of a dissolved corporation "to such other corporation or association as shall be specified, to be administered or used in such manner as in the judgment of the court will *best accomplish the general purposes* for which the corporation so dissolved was organized or for which the property or funds are legally required to be used, *without regard to and free from any express or implied restriction, limitation or direction imposed upon such corporation*" (emphasis supplied).

It is, thus, apparent that for more than half a century the criterion governing distribution or dissolution has been not that the particular purpose of the donor be carried out "as near as possible," but that the general purpose of the donor, or for which the corporation was organized or the fund collected be "most effectively [or best] accomplished ... free from any express or implied restriction" and that the same standard has governed distribution of both the unexpended funds received for a charitable purpose by a membership corporation about to be dissolved, and the unexpended funds raised by a voluntary association through public subscription for a charitable purpose which has been accomplished.

C

The most immediately noticeable difference between N-PCL §1005(a)(3)(A) and the statutes we have so far considered is the changed standard governing distribution. The revision from "best accomplish the general purposes" to "engaged in activities substantially similar to those of the dissolved corporation" is not discussed in the legislative history of the N-PCL, but in light of the almost uniform standard of the various statutes discussed above and the provision of the Membership Corporations Law that distribution was to be "free from any express or implied restriction" imposed on the dissolving corporation, it is apparent that the "codification of the 'cy-pres' doctrine" to which the Joint Legislative Committee Memorandum referred was to the doctrine as spelled out in the Membership Corporations Law (and other statutes referred to above) rather than to the common law "as near as possible" principle. But beyond that the change to "substantially similar activities" from "best accomplishes" or "most effectively accomplishes" cannot be ignored, for, as the words are commonly understood, "substantially similar" is broader in scope and less limiting than "most effectively accomplishes."

Of importance also is the fact that whereas the common-law rule was phrased in terms of the original purpose of the testator, grantor or donor, as were all of the statutes referred to above, it is not the "purposes" but the "activities" of the dissolving corporation which under N-PCL §1005(a)(3)(A) governs the choice of recipient charities. Of course, that does not mean that a charitable corporation is not limited by the statement of purposes set forth in its charter; rather it means that to the extent that its activities have been more limited than the statement in its charter, the latter rather than the former must be taken into consideration in determining whether a proposed distributee meets the statutory test.

Nor does respondents' argument that the Joint Legislative Committee's statement that section 1005 "makes very important innovations with respect to the distribution of corporate assets upon dissolution by adopting a 'cy-pres' provision to regulate the distribution" establish the Legislature's intent to adopt the common-law standard. As noted above, that standard in modified form had been applicable to membership corporations engaged in charitable pursuits as well as to voluntary associations since 1948 or earlier. Thus the innovation was not that for the first time cy pres became applicable but that the standard to be applied to property other than particular purpose assets of a type B not-for-profit corporation was whether the recipient charities were "engaged in activities substantially similar" rather than the modified common-law standard—"best accomplish the general purposes."

It follows that, as was held in *Matter of Goehringer*, 69 Misc. 2d 145, 146-47 (N.Y. 1942), statutes under which the assets of charitable corporations are distributed upon dissolution, such as N-PCL §1005(a)(3)(A) and Education Law §220, are not quite like cy pres statutes such as EPTL 8-1.1 in that "[in] ordering distribution under the dissolution statutes, the Supreme Court is not concerned with the directions or intentions of the creator or testator but only that the funds be transferred to a charitable recipient having similar purposes to the dissolved charitable corporation." Although a cy pres concept is involved, it is not the strict standard of the common law that applies to distribution of the assets of a corporation being dissolved under the N-PCL, but a "quasi cy pres" standard.

III

The Appellate Division having used an improper standard, there must be a reversal, and because that improper standard resulted in a limited stipulation of fact rather than an evidentiary development of the factors involved in whether the plan for distribution should be approved, we remit to Supreme Court for such a hearing.

In that connection we note the further substantial change made by the N-PCL in according the board of the dissolving charitable corporation a substantial role in the selection of the corporations or organizations to which distribution is to be made. At common law, framing the scheme for application or distribution of the property was a matter for the court, which could apply cy pres and frame a scheme to which the trustees did not consent, although the court would usually give weight to the wishes of the trustees.... And under Personal Property Law §12 and Real Property Law §113, that was true not only where a trust existed but also as to property held by a charitable corporation.... But, as already noted, under N-PCL §1005(a)(3)(A), it is the board of directors which adopts the plan of distribution pursuant to which the successor corporation or organization will receive the property and the plan is not submitted to the court for approval until after it has been submitted to and approved by the members entitled to vote.

The approval of the court is not under the statute to be perfunctory, but in enacting N-PCL article 10, the Legislature "substantially revise[d] the existing law governing membership corporations," "require[d] a board resolution recommending the plan" and that "the plan of distribution ... be approved by a justice of the supreme court." It intended also that not-for-profit corporations have "a strong board of directors." Although a court, asked to approve a plan of distribution, acts in a discretionary capacity, so likewise does the board in carrying out its more formal role in devising a plan which the N-PCL has given it. Therefore, its choice of acquiring organizations and corporations should not be lightly set aside.

A further factor to be considered in assessing the propriety of the plan is how the funds, of which the moneys now in the hands of the board are the residue, were acquired. It has already been noted (n. 5 above) that there is no record evidence of any "particular purpose" gifts by will or other instrument. There are in the record letters and petitions addressed to the Attorney-General or the New York City Chapter stating the signers' belief that distribution should be to the chapter, but nothing to establish that any limitation other than the MSSO charter applied to their gifts when made. Was a public solicitation made and, if so, what was said about use of the funds by MSSO or by the donor? Absent an express or implied representation by MSSO, no "particular purpose" is established and it will be assumed that contributions made voluntarily and without restriction are general gifts for use by the charitable corporation for any of its general corporate purposes. A "particular purpose" may also be established by the donor but it will usually be the case that, as noted in *Loch v. Mayer*, 50 Misc. 442, 448 (N.Y. 1906) (dealing with a disaster relief fund solicited by a church), "[few] donations were accompanied with writings of any kind, and no such writing, so far as the evidence shows, states with any attempt at precision the terms of the trust." As to any contribution found to have been made for a restricted purpose, it will also be of importance whether it has been fully expended.

Relevant also, as already noted, will be the activities of the corporation in fact carried out under its charter, and to a lesser extent the corporate purposes stated in the charter. Specifically, in terms of the present case has the emphasis of MSSO as shown by its creation and its activities been on the *disease* or on *service*? Both are specifically mentioned in its name and both are referred to in the statement of its purposes contained in its amended certificate of incorporation.

For the foregoing reasons, the judgment appealed from and the order of the Appellate Division brought up for review should be reversed, with costs to appellants, and the matter remitted to Supreme Court, Kings County, for further proceedings in accordance with this opinion.

NOTES AND QUESTIONS

1. This book concentrates on public benefit nonprofit organizations, those that can be classified as §501(c)(3) organizations. As we saw in Chapter 2, all state laws have provisions forbidding distribution of assets at any time during the life cycle of a public benefit organization, including upon dissolution. Section 501(c)(3) and its regulations have a similar restriction. A mutual benefit corporation may be able to distribute the assets to its members, depending on the bylaws and the state laws.

2. The economic downturn of 2008–2009 forced many nonprofits to close. Human services organizations seem particularly vulnerable. "It's a triple whammy.... Donations are down. Government funding is down. Need is up." *Once Robust Charity Sector Hit with Mergers, Closings*, WALL ST. J., Feb. 2, 2010.

   There is some evidence that nonprofits are less likely than their for-profit counterparts to close, however. "[B]ecause nonprofits are not held to a 'bottom line' and 'efficiency norms,' they may be much better able to ride out the hard times. People who have an interest in literacy, health care, education, social justice and helping the needy and disadvantaged may be stymied because of the lack of funding or the departure of key personnel, but their goals are still intact and, evidently, so are their organizations." B. M. Duckles, M.A. Hager, and J. Galaskiewicz, *How Nonprofits Close*, QUALITATIVE ORGANIZATIONAL RES. 169 (2005).

3. Chapter 3 discussed the board of director's duties and actions that led to the closure of Hull House. It also mentioned Sweet Briar College, which was able to stay open after the trustees had announced plans to dissolve. You may want to revisit that chapter at this point and reconsider the facts of those situations, now that you know more about dissolution.

4. The Second Mile was a §501(c)(3) organization created to help underprivileged youth in Pennsylvania. Jerry Sandusky, an assistant football coach at Penn State, founded the nonprofit in 1977. He was convicted of child molestation in 2012, and Second Mile announced that same year that it was shutting its doors. Mindy Szkaradnik, *The Second Mile to Shut Down, Transfer Programs to Arrow Child and Family Ministries*, COLLEGIAN (May 25, 2012). It delayed transferring its assets, however, at the request of Pennsylvania's attorney general, who wanted to ensure that any claims by Sandusky's victims could be resolved before the assets were transferred. Brittany Horn, *Second Mile Delays Transfer of Assets After Request*, COLLEGIAN (Aug. 27, 2012). In 2016, a judge approved its final dissolution. Another nonprofit, Arrow Child and Family Ministries, had already been awarded some of Second Mile's assets, and the remaining assets were awarded to the Pennsylvania attorney general's office. Michaael Wyland, *PA Judge OKs Closing of Sandusky's Scandal-Plagued Second Mile Charity*, NONPROFIT QUARTERLY (March 10, 2016).

V. MERGER

Another way for a nonprofit corporation to end its existence is to merge with another nonprofit. Such arrangements can bring economies of scale and additional funding. Without proper planning, they can also bring huge headaches. Following are an excerpt from the Model Nonprofit Corporation Act, 3d ed., an article describing nonprofit mergers, and some notes.

MODEL NONPROFIT CORPORATION ACT, 3D ED.

(2008)

§11.02. Merger

(a) One or more domestic nonprofit corporations may merge with one or more domestic or foreign nonprofit corporations or eligible entities pursuant to a plan of merger, or two or more foreign nonprofit corporations or domestic or foreign eligible entities may merge into a new domestic nonprofit corporation to be created in the merger in the manner provided in this [chapter]....

(d) The plan of merger must be in the form of a record and include:

(1) the name of each domestic or foreign nonprofit corporation or eligible entity that will merge and the name of the domestic or foreign nonprofit corporation or eligible entity that will be the survivor of the merger;

(2) the terms and conditions of the merger;

(3) the manner and basis of converting the memberships of each merging domestic or foreign nonprofit membership corporation and the eligible

interests of each merging domestic or foreign eligible entity into memberships, eligible interests, securities, or obligations; rights to acquire memberships, eligible interests, securities, or obligations; cash; other property or other consideration; or any combination of the foregoing;

(4) the articles of incorporation of any corporation, or the organic documents of any eligible entity, to be created by the merger, or if a new corporation or eligible entity is not to be created by the merger, any amendments to the survivor's articles or bylaws or organic records; and

(5) any other provisions relating to the merger that the parties desire be included in the plan of merger.

§11.04. Action on a Plan of Merger

In the case of a nonprofit corporation that is a party to a merger ...

(1) The plan of merger ... must be adopted by the board of directors....

(8) If a domestic nonprofit corporation that is a party to a merger does not have any members entitled to vote thereon, a plan of merger shall be deemed adopted by the corporation when it has been adopted by the board of directors pursuant to paragraph (1).

(9) In addition to the adoption and approval of the plan of merger by the board of directors and members as required by this section, the plan of merger must also be approved in the form of a record by any person or persons whose approval is required to amend the articles of incorporation....

§11.06. Articles of Merger

(a) After a plan of merger or membership exchange has been adopted and approved as required by this [act], articles of merger or membership exchange shall be signed on behalf of each party to the merger or membership exchange by any officer or other duly authorized representative. The articles shall set forth:

(1) the names of the parties to the merger or membership exchange;

(2) if the articles of incorporation of the survivor of a merger or an exchanging nonprofit corporation are amended, or if a new corporation is created as a result of a merger, the amendments to the articles of incorporation of the survivor or exchanging corporation or the articles of incorporation of the new corporation;

(3) if the plan of merger or membership exchange required approval by the members of a domestic nonprofit corporation that was a party to the merger or membership exchange, a statement that the plan was duly approved by the members and, if voting by any separate voting group was required, by each such separate voting group, in the manner required by this /act and the articles of incorporation or bylaws;...

(c) Articles of merger or membership exchange must be delivered to the secretary of state for filing by the survivor of the merger or the acquiring corporation or eligible entity in a membership exchange and shall take effect at the effective time provided in Section 1.23. Articles of merger or membership exchange filed under this section may be combined with any filing required under the organic law of any domestic eligible entity involved in the transaction if the combined filing satisfies the requirements of both this section and the other organic law.

§11.07. Effect of Merger

(a) Subject to sections 11.01(b), (c), and (d), when a merger becomes effective:

(1) the domestic or foreign nonprofit corporation or eligible entity that is designated in the plan of merger as the survivor continues or comes into existence, as the case may be;

(2) the separate existence of every domestic or foreign nonprofit corporation or eligible entity that is merged into the survivor ceases;

(3) all property owned by, and every contract and other right possessed by, each domestic or foreign nonprofit corporation or eligible entity that merges into the survivor is vested in the survivor without reversion or impairment;

(4) all liabilities of each domestic or foreign nonprofit corporation or eligible entity that is merged into the survivor are vested in the survivor;

(5) the name of the survivor may, but need not be, substituted in any pending proceeding for the name of any party to the merger whose separate existence ceased in the merger;

(6) the articles of incorporation and bylaws or organic records of the survivor are amended to the extent provided in the plan of merger;

(7) the articles of incorporation and bylaws or organic records of a survivor that is created by the merger become effective; and

(8) the memberships of each corporation that is a party to the merger, and the eligible interests in an eligible entity that is a party to a merger, that are to be converted under the plan of merger into memberships, eligible interests, securities, or obligations; rights to acquire memberships, eligible interests, securities, or obligations; cash; other property or other consideration; or any combination of the foregoing; are converted.

DAVID LA PIANA'S FIRST MERGER

---

www.lapiana.org/resources/cases/mergers/09_1998.html (accessed November 2009)

Several years ago, there existed in Oakland, California, a small nonprofit known as PCC. PCC provided day treatment services for preschoolers who had been physically or sexually abused, as well as an outpatient counseling program for children and families. Its major sources of income were a county Medi-Cal contract for the day treatment program and fee-for-service Medi-Cal for the outpatient services. PCC also owned a building. Not unlike other small mental health agencies, PCC had deficits, staff/board conflicts, and turnover in leadership.

Ultimately, PCC's executive director resigned. We met together after he left and discussed PCC's future, which was uncertain at best. I suggested a merger between PCC and my organization as a way to preserve PCC's services. I directed the East Bay Agency for Children (EBAC) at the time, and PCC's services filled a niche in which EBAC was interested.

Through a circuitous route redolent with conspiratorial overtones, including a talk with a 3rd party intermediary on an airplane bound for LA, the subject was broached with PCC's board. Early discussions were somewhat difficult, as PCC's board was divided on its commitment to the process. The trustees also had widely varying knowledge about the issues being considered.

The hottest issue was the population served by PCC. Their county funding source (the mental health department) was limited to children with emotional disturbances. Over the years, however, PCC had evolved into an organization primarily serving children with communication and developmental disabilities. They were very skilled in this area, and did a great job with the kids they served. To PCC the difference between emotional disturbance and developmental disability was small. It was no fine point to the county, however, and I noted the discrepancy between the population and the funding guidelines to the merger negotiating team early on in the process.

The negotiating committee was made up of management and trustees from both agencies, and the reaction was quick. Before we could even properly begin "negotiations," members of the PCC board who were opposed to a merger inflamed parents of the children in the day treatment program with threats that EBAC was planning to close down their program. A mob of angry parents descended on PCC's next board meeting, and the situation deteriorated.

A subtext that emerged during this time was, unfortunately, race: PCC's board and management were all African-American. While EBAC is and was a diverse organization, the leadership was predominately white. Both EBAC and myself were accused of many things. It was unpleasant, to say the least.

The PCC Board faction's guerilla action succeeded. EBAC backed off. My board wanted to throw in the towel, and we put the matter aside. Unfortunately, however, the activist PCC trustees went a step too far. Fearing an attempt at a "hostile takeover," and not understanding legal impossibility of this maneuver in a nonprofit organization, they called their funding source (the county mental health director), and said, essentially, "Don't let EBAC take us over and make us stop serving developmentally disabled kids."

The mental health director was shocked. How could they be serving developmentally disabled kids with Mental Health funding? She responded by ordering an audit of the program.

The result of the audit was devastating. In the end, 100% of PCC's service units for the previous year were disallowed, because the children were found not eligible for the funding source. PCC was held to owe the county over $200,000.

PCC, with most of its board jumping ship, found itself unable even to assemble a quorum for its next meeting. With their situation deteriorating, they approached EBAC about the possibility of again considering a merger.

Past experience, combined with the pending doom heralded by the audit report, led me to believe that we needed to move quickly. I worked hard to persuade my board that a merger was the right way to go. It was not easy, however. In reviewing PCC's books we found that in addition to the audit disallowance, which they had no way to repay, the outpatient program was losing $60,000 a year. PCC had covered the past year's deficit by taking out an interest-only, 13% second mortgage on their building, with a balloon payment due in six months!

Now the question was, "What could be salvaged?" Our board members balked until we showed them that there was still enough equity in the PCC building to make the merger a good deal for EBAC, even if nothing beyond the building could be saved. Finally, they agreed to the merger, though only under an arrangement that, ironically, looked more like a takeover than merger. We dictated terms to PCC, and PCC's remaining board members accepted. The merger agreement was approved through a telephone poll of PCC's remaining trustees.

And thus we went ahead. EBAC paid off the second mortgage from our reserves, and negotiated with the auditors that the PCC Day Treatment program would close down in exchange for not having to repay the $200,000 audit disallowance. One relatively new trustee from the PCC board joined the EBAC board. EBAC made a commitment to try to restore the services lost in PCC's demise, and began using its building, which was acquired for half its market value, for our own overflowing programs and staff. All remaining PCC staff were laid off prior to the merger's effective date, in order to tap PCC's unemployment insurance rather than EBAC's.

Things look much brighter now. Two years after the merger, EBAC resurrected the preschool day treatment program with county funding and a new partnership with Children's Hospital Oakland. The former PCC board member who came to EBAC became the treasurer, and the PCC building is now home to EBAC's growing administrative staff.

This is not a happy story. It probably fits your idea of a merger as little as it did mine. Thus, one of the great deterrents to merger: the leap into the unknown.

Nonetheless, viewed in retrospect, this merger was pretty successful. Though PCC's program did "die" for several years, it could have been saved if we had been able to come to an agreement on the first attempt. Unfortunately PCC's board was not ready at that point. They were only interested in a merger when it became clear, after the audit, that PCC was failing—that there would be unresolved debts and even a possible board liability in a potential legal action by a former executive director. (This last factor was no small matter, but we only learned of it after the merger. Fortunately, we resolved it cheaply and quietly.)

Ultimately, however, PCC's building was kept out of the hands of its creditors, and after two years of hard work, the program was resurrected.

What did I learn from experience? Several things:

1. Never underestimate the power of group dynamics over rationality. People cannot always be counted on to act in their group's collective best interest, especially as defined by someone outside the group. I "knew" that PCC was living on borrowed time, and I knew what moves were needed to preserve the services. But this knowledge did no good. Powerful internal group dynamics can keep a dying organization from seeing its own predicament.

2. Don't threaten your partner. A threat to autonomy, identity, or other critical, deeply held values will kill a merger effort. Approach the other group respectfully, in a manner which allows its leaders to save face. The merger process must provide a way for the mission, individuality, and culture of both groups to be valued and incorporated into the new entity. Fear of change, loss of autonomy, individual egos, habit and culture all cause nonprofits to avoid mergers.

I made the mistake with PCC of assuming that once I had demonstrated in writing that PCC had no choice but to merge or dissolve, they would thank me and simply ask where to sign the document. Instead I had insulted them, questioned their deepest assumptions, and so caused them to retreat further from a consideration of the facts.

3. A minimally functioning board may not speak with one voice. While we negotiated in good faith with PCC's board, factions of this very same board were seeking the support of our mutual funders to block the merger.

4. People have assumptions about mergers that make true negotiation, worked out in good faith, difficult. Because of confusion with corporate takeovers, the "weaker" party in a merger is bound to suspect the initiator of trying to maneuver into a position of unfair advantage.

NOTES AND QUESTIONS

1. As noted in the introduction to this chapter, the legal issues surrounding mergers are generally matters of state law. The IRS does get involved, however. *See* IRS Publication 4779, *Facts about Terminating or Merging Your Exempt Organization* (2009). If either or both organizations dissolve as part of the merger, the organizations should check the termination box in the header area of Form 990; answer yes to the question in Part V asking about termination or substantial contraction; and complete Schedule N, which asks questions about the disposition of assets. It also asks whether any officer, director, trustee, or key employee of a dissolving organization is going to be involved in the successor or transferee organization by governing, controlling, or having a financial interest in the new organization. Finally, both organizations will need to attach their articles of dissolution (if applicable) and articles of merger.

2. Another case study of a nonprofit merger is described in detail in Mark Hager, *Curating Change: The Merger of Two Historic Women's Organizations*, NONPROFIT QUARTERLY (March 9, 2015). A recent survey

suggests that nonprofit organizations are increasingly considering mergers as ways to improve finances and increase their ability to serve constituents. Most often, organizations that decide not to merge with another organization cite a difference in values and mission as the reason. Michael McNee, *Nonprofit Pulse: A Leadership Survey from Marks Paneth*, http://www.markspaneth.com/publications/nonprofit-pulse-a-leadership-survey-from-marks-paneth1, accessed May 21, 2016. For further reading, see William Boyd, *Mergers, Acquisitions, and Affiliations Involving Nonprofits: Not Typical M&A Transactions*, BUSINESS LAW TODAY (June 2014).

3. Mergers between two nonprofit organizations are difficult enough. When they involve a nonprofit and an S corporation, or two nonprofits that already serve most of the market, they can raise additional antitrust and inurement issues. For further reading, see Thomas L. Greaney, *Night Landings on an Aircraft Carrier: Hospital Mergers and Antitrust Law*, 23 AM. J. L. & MED. 191 (2006); Barak D. Richman, *The Corrosive Combination of Nonprofit Monopolies and U.S.-Style Health Insurance: Implications for Antitrust and Merger Policy*, 69 LAW & CONTEMP. PROBS. 139 (2006); and Garry W. Jenkins, *The Powerful Possibilities of Nonprofit Mergers: Supporting Strategic Consolidation Through Law and Public Policy*, 74 S. CAL. L. REV. 1089 (2001). The IRS also issued a private letter ruling on the topic, LTR 200402003.

VI. CONVERSION TO FOR-PROFIT ORGANIZATIONS

A. INTRODUCTION

The third way to end a nonprofit organization is to convert it into a for-profit organization or sell its assets to a for-profit organization. Four types of for-profit conversions are possible: a merger with a for-profit organization, creation of a for-profit subsidiary, the sale of assets to a for-profit organization, and a conversion in place.

A merger with a for-profit organization ends up with the for-profit organization (or a new for-profit entity) as the surviving organization. The charitable assets, however, need to stay in the charitable stream. Most often, a private foundation is set up to address this issue. Many of the joint ventures discussed in Chapter 10 were set up this way and were, in effect, a conversion. The hospitals that put all their assets into the joint venture were, in effect, converting to for-profit status. The tax-exempt organization left behind usually became a private foundation that used the proceeds from the conversion to fund other tax-exempt health measures.

We also covered for-profit subsidiaries in Chapter 10. The charitable organization transfers its operating assets and liabilities to a subsidiary in return for stock. The parent organization, the nonprofit, retains stock in the new subsidiary and continues the charitable mission. It also chooses the subsidiary's board, thus ensuring control.

Finally, a conversion in place allows the nonprofit organization that wants to become a for-profit to amend its articles of incorporation to remove all nonprofit aspects and to add for-profit powers. Virginia is one of the few states that allow a conversion in place.

In all four situations, similar issues arise: Have the correct procedural rules been followed? Have the assets remained devoted to the public, as opposed to being a private benefit? Has the board of directors performed due diligence and refrained from conflicts of interest?

The materials that follow include the provision in the Model Nonprofit Corporation Act, 3d ed., on conversions from nonprofit to for-profit status, excerpts from and comments about cases discussed earlier in the book, suggestions for further reading, and a drafting problem.

MODEL NONPROFIT CORPORATION ACT, 3D ED.

(2008)

§9.30. For-Profit Conversion

(a) A domestic nonprofit corporation may become a domestic business corporation pursuant to a plan of for-profit conversion.

(b) A domestic nonprofit corporation may become a foreign business corporation if the for-profit conversion is permitted by the laws of the foreign jurisdiction. Regardless of whether the laws of the foreign jurisdiction require the adoption of a plan of for-profit conversion, the foreign for-profit conversion shall be approved by the adoption by the domestic nonprofit corporation of a plan of for-profit conversion in the manner provided in this [subchapter].

(c) The plan of for-profit conversion must include:

(1) the terms and conditions of the conversion;

(2) the manner and basis of:

(i) issuing at least one share in the corporation following its conversion; and

(ii) otherwise reclassifying the memberships in the corporation, if any, following its conversion into shares and other securities, obligations, rights to acquire shares or other securities, cash, other property, or any combination of the foregoing;

(3) any desired amendments to the articles of incorporation of the corporation following its conversion; and

(4) if the domestic nonprofit corporation is to be converted to a foreign business corporation, a statement of the jurisdiction in which the corporation will be incorporated after the conversion.

(d) The plan of for-profit conversion may also include a provision that the plan may be amended prior to filing articles of for-profit conversion, except that subsequent to approval of the plan by the members the plan may not be amended without the approval of members to change:

(1) the amount or kind of shares and other securities, obligations, rights to acquire shares or other securities, cash, or other property to be received by the members under the plan;

(2) the articles of incorporation as they will be in effect immediately following the conversion, except for changes permitted by section 10.05; or

(3) any of the other terms or conditions of the plan if the change would adversely affect any of the members in any material respect.

(e) Terms of a plan of for-profit conversion may be made dependent upon facts objectively ascertainable outside the plan in accordance with section 1.20(c).

(f) If any debt security, note or similar evidence of indebtedness for money borrowed, whether secured or unsecured, or a contract of any kind, issued, incurred or executed by a domestic nonprofit corporation before [*the effective date of this subchapter*] contains a provision applying to a merger of the corporation and the document does not refer to a for-profit conversion of the corporation, the provision shall be deemed to apply to a for-profit conversion of the corporation until such time as the provision is amended subsequent to that date.

§9.31. Action on a Plan of For-Profit Conversion

In the case of a conversion of a domestic nonprofit corporation to a domestic or foreign business corporation:

(1) The plan of for-profit conversion must be adopted by the board of directors.

(2) After adopting the plan of for-profit conversion, the board of directors must submit the plan to the members for their approval if there are members entitled to vote on the plan. The board of directors must also transmit to the members a recommendation that the members approve the plan, unless the board of directors makes a determination that because of conflicts of interest or other special circumstances it should not make such a recommendation, in which case the board of directors must transmit to the members the basis for that determination....

§9.32. Articles of For-Profit Conversion

(a) Articles of for-profit conversion must be signed on behalf of the converting corporation by any officer or other duly authorized representative. The articles must set forth:

(1) if the surviving corporation is a domestic business corporation, the name of the corporation immediately before the filing of the articles of for-profit conversion and if that name does not satisfy the requirements of [*the Model Business Corporation Act*], or the corporation desires to change its

name in connection with the conversion, a name that satisfies the requirements of [*the Model Business Corporation Act*];

(2) if the surviving corporation is a foreign business corporation, its name after the conversion and its jurisdiction of incorporation; and

(3) a statement that the plan of for-profit conversion was duly approved by the members in the manner required by this [act] and the articles of incorporation.

(b) If the surviving corporation is a domestic business corporation, the articles of for-profit conversion either shall contain all of the provisions that [*the Model Business Corporation Act*] requires to be set forth in articles of incorporation of a domestic business corporation and any other desired provisions permitted by [*the Model Business Corporation Act*], or shall have attached articles of incorporation that satisfy the requirements of [*the Model Business Corporation Act*]. In either case, provisions that would not be required to be included in restated articles of incorporation of a domestic business corporation may be omitted....

(c) The articles of for-profit conversion must be delivered to the secretary of state for filing, and take effect at the effective time provided in section 1.23.

§9.33. Effect of For-Profit Conversion

(a) Except as otherwise provided in section 9.03, when a conversion of a domestic nonprofit corporation to a domestic or foreign business corporation becomes effective:

(1) the title to all real and personal property, both tangible and intangible, of the corporation remains in the corporation without reversion or impairment;

(2) the liabilities of the corporation remain the liabilities of the corporation;

(3) an action or proceeding pending against the corporation continues against the corporation as if the conversion had not occurred;

(4) the articles of incorporation of the domestic or foreign business corporation become effective;

(5) the memberships of the corporation are reclassified into shares or other securities, obligations, rights to acquire shares or other securities, or into cash or other property in accordance with the plan of conversion, and the members are entitled only to the rights provided in the plan of for-profit conversion; and

(6) the corporation is deemed to:

(i) be a domestic or foreign business corporation for all purposes; and

(ii) be the same corporation without interruption as the nonprofit corporation....

B. CONSIDERING PREVIOUS CASES AS CONVERSION CASES

1. *Queen of Angels Hospital v. Younger*

Chapter 2 included *Queen of Angels Hospital v. Younger*, 136 Cal. Rptr. 36, (1977). You will remember that Queen of Angels Hospital was not allowed to lease its building to hospital entrepreneurs and use the proceeds to run clinics because the articles of incorporation required the organization to be a hospital. Had that arrangement gone through, Queen of Angels Hospital would no longer be operating a hospital; it would be running clinics. Although this transaction involved a lease, not a sale, the issues were identical to those of a sale. Its purpose was to bring a badly needed infusion of cash into the hospital. If the conversion had occurred, the hospital itself would be for-profit and the proceeds from the lease would have gone to the clinics. As with any conversion, the question of what happens to the assets was front and center. In that case, the court held that the assets could not be used for clinics, even if the clinics were charitable, because that would change the purpose of the organization.

The subsequent history of this hospital makes interesting reading and involves many of the issues that we have discussed throughout this book. Queen of Angels merged with another nonprofit hospital in 1989, but it continued to struggle financially and was placed on a conditional accreditation status in 1990 because of problems with meeting the quality of care and safety standards of its accrediting agency.

In 1997, the board of directors of the nonprofit Queen of Angels–Hollywood Presbyterian Church proposed merging with the for-profit Tenet Healthcare Corp, and the medical staff filed a lawsuit to remove the directors. Among the allegations were claims that a board member once threatened a staff member with a loaded gun and that the board overruled an internal decision to suspend a doctor who had "improperly removed a patient's breast."

Evidently, the lawsuit either failed or was settled, because in 1998, the hospital was sold to the for-profit Tenet Healthcare Corp for $86.4 million and acquisition of its debt. All proceeds from the transaction were transferred to a health care charity, Queens Care. Unlike most health care conversions, Queens Care is not a private foundation. It operates its own health care programs for Los Angeles residents. In effect, it is operating the clinics that the hospital tried to open in the 1970s, with funds gained from the sale of the hospital.

In 2004 Tenet sold the hospital again to CHA Medical Group, which agreed to continue to operate the facility as a full-service hospital with a 24-hour emergency room. Unfortunately, the hospital continued to be in the news. Now called Hollywood Presbyterian, it received a great deal of bad publicity in 2007. According to the *Los Angeles Times*,

> [a] paraplegic man wearing a soiled hospital gown and a broken colostomy bag was found crawling in a gutter in Skid Row in Los Angeles on Thursday after allegedly being dumped in the street by a Hollywood Presbyterian Medical

Center van.... The incident, witnessed by more than two dozen people, was described by police as a particularly outrageous case of "homeless dumping" that has plagued the downtown area.... Witnesses shouted at the female driver of the van, "Where's his wheelchair, where's his walker?" Gary Lett, an employee at Gladys Park, near where the incident occurred, said the woman driving the van didn't reply, but proceeded to apply makeup and perfume before driving off.

Andrew Blankstein and Richard Winton, *Paraplegic Allegedly "Dumped" on Skid Row*, L.A. TIMES, Feb. 9, 2007.

The city attorney brought suit once these allegations surfaced, and in 2008, the hospital agreed to be monitored for five years and pay a $1 million fine. In 2016, the hospital paid a ransom of 40,000 bitcoins ($17,000) after its computer system was infected by ransomware. Richard Winton, *Hollywood Hospital Pays $17,000 in Bitcoins to Hackers Who Took Control of Computers*, L.A. TIMES (Feb. 17, 2016).

The hospital building has its own history. Abandoned in 1989, when Queen of Angels merged with Hollywood Presbyterian, the building remained empty for six years, during which time it was mainly used as a backdrop in movies such as the *Patriot Games, Apollo 13, Reality Bites*, and *Naked Gun 33 1/3*. In 1996, two pastors purchased the building on behalf of the Dream Center, a Pentecostal Christian Church mission. The center provides food, clothing, job training, health care, educational programs, and residential recovery programs free of charge to anyone in need. It reaches more than 80,000 individuals and families a month. For more information, see http://www.dreamcenter.org.

2. *Caracci v. Commissioner*

Chapter 9 referred to *Caracci v. Comm'r*, 456 F.3d 444 (5th Cir. 2006). In that case, a home health care organization converted to for-profit status when the Medicare/Medicaid reimbursement policies changed in a way that made reimbursement more difficult. No money changed hands, as the purchasers of the new organization purchased the nonprofit by acquiring its debt. The IRS challenged the valuation. It assessed $46.5 million in penalty excise taxes and revoked the health care organization's tax-exempt status. The Tax Court overturned the revocation of exemption and reduced the excise taxes to $5.164 million, reflecting a different method of valuation. The Fifth Circuit then reversed the Tax Court's decision, finding that the Caraccis had followed the proper procedures for valuing the nonprofit organization and allowing the original transaction to stand. This decision prompted a series of lively letters to the editor in the *Exempt Organizations Tax Review* from the Caraccis' lawyers and an attorney who violently disagreed with the appellate court decision. Paul Streckfus, the disapproving attorney, began the salvos by stating,

> "The court somehow missed the elephant sitting in the room. The issue that went untouched was why would any rational person want to own a business that was deeply in debt and had no hope of ever making a profit.... The Fifth Circuit

never once asked why the Caraccis would willingly accept over $8 million in assets at the cost of over $13 million in liabilities . . . . Even if the Fifth Circuit does not understand what is going on, we must assume that the Caraccis are rational people. They must have believed at the time of transfer to them of the Sta-Home entities for no consideration that, at a minimum, the assets they were assuming were at least equal to the liabilities they were assuming and/or there was some future earning potential. Otherwise, they're idiots.

Paul Streckfus, *STA-Home: There's Much More to the Story*, 53 EXEMPT ORG. TAX REV. 244 (July 19, 2006).

The Caraccis' attorney, David Aughtry, responded,

As trial and appellate counsel in Sta-Home, I have long felt that someone ought to be ashamed of the way this wonderful family has been maligned. The letter I now read from the sycophant Mr. Streckfus ... adds to that list.... The terrifying but unintended point of his letter is just this: So long as someone can be punished with geometric intermediate sanctions by way of self-righteous hindsight based on concepts subject to such wild variances, no one in the exempt organization world is safe. The Fifth Circuit opinion presents the very best—if not the only—protection against that threat. It does so on the novel approach of following the record.

Response by David Aughtry, counsel of the taxpayers in the Sta-Home litigation, 53 EXEMPT ORG. TAX REV. 341 (July 25, 2006).

NOTES AND QUESTIONS

1. The amount of money involved in a conversion can be so large that it makes the concepts seem more difficult than they are. The concepts work with small amounts of money as well. For example, Lou Lou started Lou Lou's Lemonade Stand as a §501(c)(3) a few years ago in order to teach young people the value of hard work. At the time, she invested $25 of her own money into the project, for which she took a charitable deduction. Since then, the lemonade stand has taken off and is now worth $100. She realizes that she can teach young people the value of hard work, give them stock options, and make a few dollars herself, if she turns Lou Lou's Lemonade into a for-profit venture. She decides to purchase the assets of the nonprofit herself. Can she purchase the company for $75 in order to pay herself back for her investment?

    What will happen to the money that Lou Lou gives to the company in order to purchase it? She is very proud of the fact that her hard work made the lemonade stand quadruple in value. Can she keep some of it? Should she leave it in the company? Are there problems with either or both of those scenarios? If the funds do not remain in the company, where should they go?

    Who should make the decision as to the fair market value of the lemonade stand? If it is valued at $100 today and remains close to $100 for the next few years, no one will worry about the valuation, but what if lemonade suddenly becomes known for its health powers and, combined with Lou Lou's hard work and good business savvy, Lou Lou's Lemonade is worth $1,000 in five years? If she decides to sell then, should she be allowed to keep the proceeds?

2. A major issue in any conversion is the preservation of the assets for the charitable sector. When a nonprofit hospital converts to for-profit status, the sale is likely to be in the millions of dollars. In most instances, the sale proceeds are given to a new private foundation. There are now approximately 200 health care foundations in the United States. Why do you think the funds go to a private foundation rather than to a public charity? If the foundation's purpose is to promote health care in the community that the hospital serves, how should the term *health care* be defined? Should the funds be restricted to healing diseases that would normally land someone in a hospital? Can they be expanded to preventing these diseases? One of the major predictors of good health in our society is education and socioeconomic status. Can the funds be used for educational and income distribution purposes? What about the effect of the arts on someone's health?

3. During the 1990s, many hospitals, health maintenance organizations, and health insurance providers converted to for-profit status. Given the amount of money involved, legislators and charity watchdogs suspected that charitable assets were being diverted to the for-profit sector. Claims that assets were being sold for less than fair market value and that insiders were receiving huge severance packages led to legislation in 25 states designed to regulate conversion of nonprofit health facilities to for-profit status.[8] Although the trend toward conversion slowed in the first two decades of the 21st century, newspaper accounts suggest that conversions continued to occur, and in 2014, Connecticut passed its own hospital conversion law, which allowed more for-profit hospitals to do business in that state.[9] The tension between retaining the charitable purpose and finding enough money to keep the hospitals afloat has continued into these newer transactions. In 2015, for example, a New York hedge fund took over management of six nonprofit Catholic hospitals in San Francisco. California attorney general Kamala Harris approved the transaction once the hedge fund agreed to invest $280 million, maintain historic levels of charity care, and keep at least five of the safety-net facilities open for at least 10 years. More than a year earlier, Prime Healthcare Services had offered to buy the hospitals for $843 million, but it withdrew its offer several months later, claiming that the attorney general's conditions, which were similar to the ultimate conditions, were too onerous.

---

[8] Marion Fremont-Smith, *Governing Nonprofit Organizations: Federal and State Law and Regulation* 432 (Harvard College 2004).

[9] Clif LeBlanc, *Trends, Finances Drove Providence Hospital Sale*, THE STATE (July 28, 2015); Lindy Washburn, *NJ Approves Sale of St. Clare's Hospitals and Other Facilities in Morris, Sussex Counties*, NORTH JERSEY.COM (Aug. 8, 2014); Rob Weisman, *Caritas Now a For-Profit Chain*, BOSTON GLOBE (Nov. 9, 2010); *Williams Applauds Final Approval of Hospital Conversion Legislation* (June 9, 2014), http://cthousegop.com/2014/06/williams-applauds-final-approval-of-hospital-conversion-legislation/, accessed May 21, 2016.

Hedge Fund Closes Deal to Run Calif. Catholic Hospital Group, CHRON. PHIL. (Dec. 15, 2015).

For further reading about hospital conversion issues, see Karen Joynt, E. John Oray, and Ashish Jha, *Association Between Hospital Conversions to For-Profit Status and Clinical and Economic Outcomes,* 312 JAMA 1644 (2014) (finding that hospitals that convert from nonprofit to for-profit status fare better financially without sacrificing patient care); Jill R. Horwitz, *Does Nonprofit Ownership Matter?* 24 YALE J. ON REG. 139 (2007); Penina Kessler Lieber, *From Nonprofit to For-Profit: The Implications of Conversion for Charitable Organizations,* 21 PA. LAW. 48 (1999); David Hyman, *Hospital Conversions: Fact, Fantasy, and Regulatory Follies,* 23 IOWA J. CORP. L. 741 (1998); Lawrence E. Singer, *The Conversion Conundrum: The State and Federal Response to Hospitals' Changes in Charitable Status,* 23 AM. J. L. & MED. 221 (1997).

4. Other types of nonprofits also make the decision to switch to for-profit status. Although it was never a §501(c)(3), the National Football League (NFL) converted from tax-exempt to tax-paying status in early 2015. Publicity over its high salaries and questions about its tax-exempt status were "distracting," according to NFL officials. Gary Myers, *NFL No Longer Non-Profit After Giving up Tax-Exempt Status,* N.Y. DAILY NEWS (April 28, 2015); David van den Berg, *NFL Says Dropping Tax Exemption Will "Eliminate Distraction,"* 75 EXEMPT ORG. TAX REV. 666 (2015). In 2011, a §501(c)(3) that was trying to care for the medical and emotional needs of sex workers and those who work in the adult entertainment industry also converted to for-profit status in order to be "relieved from pointless harassment that came with oversight from the County Health Department" and instead be responsive to the California Medical Association. Rick Cohen, *Nonprofit Health Clinic for Sex Workers Switches to For-Profit Status,* NONPROFIT QUARTERLY (Feb. 11, 2011)

5. Conversions from for-profit to nonprofit status also take place. Once they are in operation, organizations can reconsider the decision that they made at the outset and decide that there are good reasons to be a §501(c)(3). For an example of a case study of such an institution, see Yuan Ji, *Burning Man: A Case Study of Altruism Thriving in a For-Profit Organizational Form and the Rationales for LLC-to-Nonprofit Conversion,* 9 HAST. BUS. L. J. 449 (2013).

In recent years, the IRS and the public have been skeptical of such changes. For example, several for-profit colleges and universities converted to nonprofit status after the for-profit higher education industry received bad press, and journalists immediately questioned their motives. David Halperin, *If a For-Profit College Becomes a Non-Profit, Is That Good? Not Necessarily,* HUFFINGTON POST (Feb. 11, 2013), http://www.huffingtonpost.com/davidhalperin/if-a-for-profit-college-b_b_2661788.html. The IRS was also skeptical when it received Form 1023 from an animal rescue organization and a veterinary clinic that sought §501(c)(3) status. In issuing adverse determination letters, the IRS stated that the organizations were still operating in a commercial manner and their charitable missions were insubstantial. PLR 201540016, PLR 201540019.

6. Occasionally, governmental organizations convert to §501(c)(3) status. The Detroit Institute of Arts, which played a part in the bankruptcy discussion above, was partially owned by the city of Detroit between 1919 and 2014, but became an independent nonprofit entity at the end of that year. Phillips Oppenheim, *A Brief History of the Detroit Institute of Arts*, http://www.phillipsoppenheim.com/pdf/DIA-Addendum%20-%20A-Brief-History-of-the-Detroit-Institute-of-Arts.pdf. Similarly, an Ohio hospital switched from governmental control to become a stand-alone §501(c)(3) in 2014. Cheryl Powell, *Robinson Memorial Hospital Ready to Make Switch to Nonprofit Status New Year's Day*, BEACON JOURNAL (Dec. 29, 2013). Why would organizations choose to make this change? Ironically, the Franklin Medical Center decided in 2016 to convert from a §501(c)(3) to a government-run hospital in order to avoid the regulations that the Affordable Care Act imposed on nonprofit hospitals. Michael Wyland, *Louisiana Hospital to Terminate Its Nonprofit Status*, NONPROFIT QUARTERLY (March 8. 2016).

PROBLEM

Assume that the virtual organization you created (or your local art museum) is merging with a for-profit organization. It will, in effect, dissolve, with the for-profit purchasing its assets. You live in a state that follows the Model Nonprofit Corporation Act, 3d ed. Draft the articles that you will need to effect this transaction.

TABLE OF CASES

Cases in bold are reproduced in the text.

TABLE OF STATUTES

Statutes in bold are reproduced in the text.

INDEX